History of the Great War

MILITARY OPERATIONS

TOGOLAND AND THE CAMEROONS

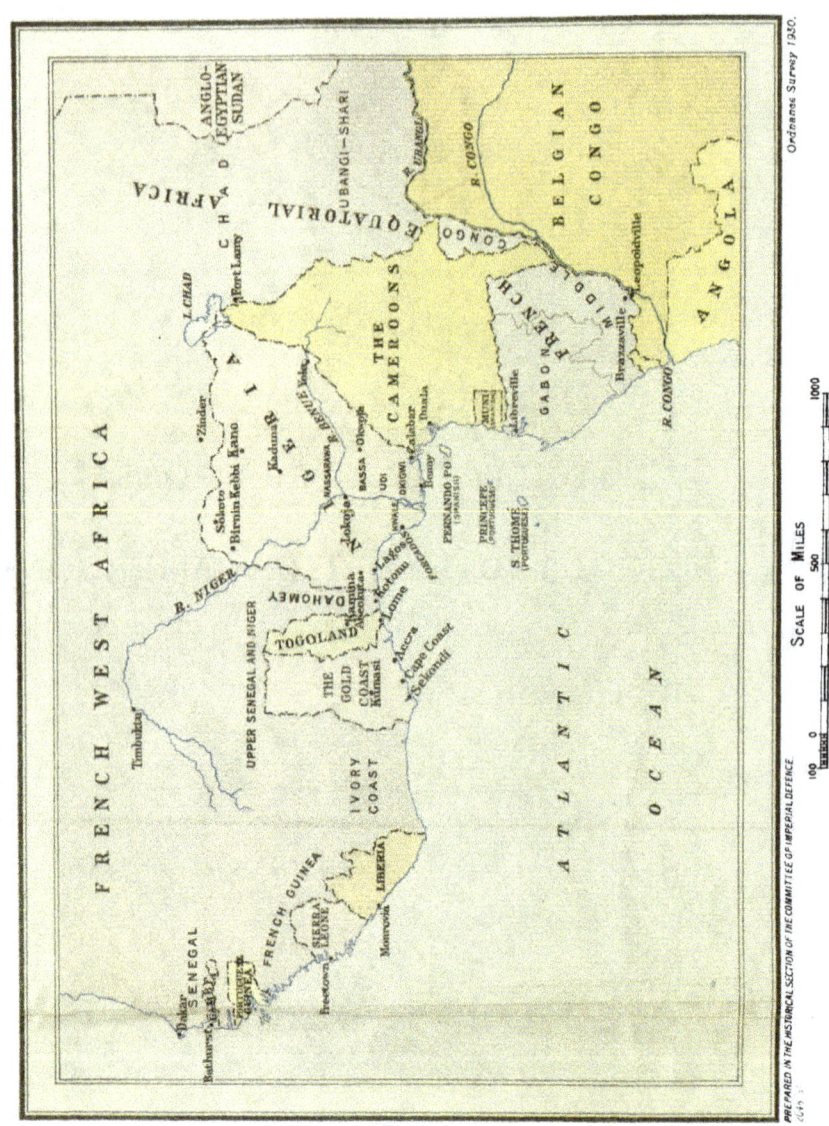

HISTORY OF THE GREAT WAR
BASED ON OFFICIAL DOCUMENTS

MILITARY OPERATIONS
TOGOLAND AND THE CAMEROONS
1914—1916

COMPILED, BY ARRANGEMENT WITH THE COLONIAL OFFICE, UNDER
THE DIRECTION OF THE HISTORICAL SECTION OF THE
COMMITTEE OF IMPERIAL DEFENCE

BY
Brig.-General F. J. MOBERLY
C.B., C.S.I., D.S.O., *p.s.c.*

The Naval & Military Press Ltd

Published by

The Naval & Military Press Ltd
Unit 5 Riverside, Brambleside
Bellbrook Industrial Estate
Uckfield, East Sussex
TN22 1QQ England

Tel: +44 (0)1825 749494

www.naval-military-press.com
www.nmarchive.com

In reprinting in facsimile from the original, any imperfections are inevitably reproduced and the quality may fall short of modern type and cartographic standards.

PREFACE

In his compilation of this history, the cost of which has been shared by the Governments of Nigeria, the Gold Coast, Sierra Leone and the Gambia, the author has received assistance from a number of people. To supplement the information contained in the official records and to secure greater accuracy of detail he has made considerable demands for information and for scrutiny and criticism of his drafts and sketch maps on the Colonial Office staff, the authorities in West Africa—especially those in Nigeria—and on a number of those who took an actual part in the operations. Many have been busy officials to whom this has meant extra work of a tedious nature, and to these and to all the others who have helped him he desires, in tendering them his grateful thanks, to express his appreciation of their cordial readiness to facilitate his task. Among them he is especially indebted to the following:—Lieutenant-General Sir C. M. Dobell, K.C.B., C.M.G., D.S.O., Admiral Sir C. T. M. Fuller, K.C.B., C.M.G., D.S.O., Mr. J. E. W. Flood and Major S. J. Cole, O.B.E., of the Colonial Office, the Chief Secretary Nigeria, the Colonial Secretaries the Gold Coast, Sierra Leone and the Gambia, The Rt. Hon. Lord Lugard, His Excellency Sir William Robertson, K.C.M.G., Mr. H. S. Newlands, Brigadier-General F. H. G. Cunliffe, C.B., C.M.G., Brigadier-General E. H. Gorges, C.B., C.B.E., D.S.O., Lieutenant-Colonel F. C. Bryant, C.M.G., C.B.E., D.S.O., Lieutenant-Colonel R. H. Rowe, D.S.O., M.C., Mr. K. V. Elphinstone, and Major D. McCallum, M.C. He is also indebted to many in the Historical Section and once again in particular to Colonel F. E. G. Talbot for his able and invaluable co-operation.

The author is further indebted to the following who have been good enough to lend him photographs for reproduction: Lieutenant-Colonels H. R. H. Crawford and C. F. S. Maclaverty, D.S.O., Major S. J. Cole, O.B.E., Mr. J. E. W. Flood, Lieutenant-Colonel F. C. Bryant, Mr. E. J. Arnett, C.M.G., Lieutenant-Colonel W. I. Webb-Bowen, the Imperial War Museum (Mr. L. A. W. Powell), Major T. D. Weir, Dr. J. H. M. Pollard,

Major A. C. L. D. Lees, Captain J. H. de Herèz Smyth, Lieutenant-Colonel J. Crookenden, D.S.O., and Captain C. G. Evans.

The spelling of place names varies somewhat from that used during the operations, but it follows the later rulings of the Permanent Committee on Geographical Names of the Royal Geographical Society.

CONTENTS

Chapter I

INCEPTION OF THE OPERATIONS AGAINST THE GERMAN POSSESSIONS IN WEST AFRICA, AND THE CAPTURE OF TOGOLAND.

	PAGE
Imperial Defence	1
Formation of a Committee to consider Operations in Foreign Territory—Possible Objective in Togoland	2
Togoland	4
The Gold Coast	6
The Gold Coast Regiment W.A.F.F.—Northern Territories Constabulary—Volunteer Corps—Police and Preventive Service—Lack of Military Administrative Services—The Gold Coast Defence Scheme	
General Dobell's Appreciation, 3rd August 1914	11
Offensive Sub-Committee, 5th August 1914	12
Action in the Gold Coast, 29th July–5th August 1914	13–16
Dobell's Appreciation of 5th August 1914	16
Operations against Togoland :	
6th August ; Summons to Lome to Surrender	17
7th August ; Occupation of Lome	19
French Action, 4th–8th August	21
8th–10th August ; Measures at Lome	22–25
Occupation of Kete Krachi	25
Captain Bryant arrives at Lome, 12th August	26
14th August ; Commencement of Advance on Kamina	27
Affair of Agbeluvoe, 15th–16th August	28
British Reinforcements	31
Events in Northern Togoland	32
Bryant halts at Agbeluvoe, 17th–18th August	33
Advance resumed, 19th August	34
Affair of Khra, 22nd August	36
German Surrender, 26th August	39
The Krachi Column	39
The German Force	40

Chapter II

PREPARATIONS TO INVADE THE CAMEROONS.

British Forces in British West Africa	42
The West African Frontier Force	42
Nigeria	43
The Cameroons	45
The Anglo-German Frontier	47

CONTENTS

Chapter II—continued

	PAGE
Coast Line	49
The Franco-German Frontier	50
Communications	50
Population—Administration	52
Military Forces	53
The Nigerian Defence Scheme	55
Dobell's Appreciation of 3rd August	57
Decision of Offensive Sub-Committee, 5th August 1914	
Action in Nigeria, 30th July–8th August	58
British Preparations and Plans, 8th–17th August	60
Dobell's Appreciation of 16th August	64
Offensive Sub-Committee, 17th August	66
Nigeria ; 13th–19th August	68
Offensive Sub-Committee, 25th August	69
Instructions to General Dobell, 29th August	71
Offensive Sub-Committee, 29th August	72

Chapter III

August–17th September 1914. The Preparations to Attack Duala and Operations Undertaken by the Allies in the North-West and South-East of the German Colony.

Duala and the Cameroon Estuary	73
British Naval Proceedings, 28th August–23rd September	74–86
Lagos, 28th–29th August	74–78
Ambas Bay, 4th–7th September	79
Off the Estuary, 7th–9th September	80
Naval Operations from Base at Suelaba, 10th–23rd September	81–86
Lagos ; 20th August 1914	86
The Maiduguri Column, 6th–29th August 1914	86–90
The Germans at Mora	87
British Reconnaissance in Force, 27th August	89
The Yola Column, 18th–31st August 1914	90–97
Affair of Tepe, 25th August	92
First Attack on Garua, 29th–30th August	93
Action at Lagos and in London, 1st–6th September	97
Colonel Cunliffe to Yola ; 6th–13th September	98
Affair at Takum, 17th September	99
The Ikom Column, 10th August–6th September	99–110
Affair of Nsanakang, 6th September	106
The Calabar Column, 3rd August–6th September	110
Calabar and Ikom Columns, 8th–16th September	111
The Maiduguri Column, 28th August–13th September	111–112
General Dobell's Progress, 31st August–17th September	112–114
Operations by the French, 31st July–September 1914	114–119
Local French Forces—French Plans—Action at Outbreak of War—Gabon—Middle Congo—Ubangi-Shari—Chad—Germans at Kuseri, 15th–25th August—Sanga and Lobaye Columns, September—Gabon, August–September.	

CONTENTS

Chapter IV

The Capture and Consolidation of Duala, and French Action Elsewhere; 17th September–17th October 1914.

PAGE

Lagos; 17th–20th September 1914	120
Organisation of the Allied Expeditionary Force	122
Operations against Duala	124–131
The Cameroon Estuary, 23rd–26th September	124
Attempted Landing at the Dibamba River	126
Surrender of Duala, 27th September 1914	129
Landing at Duala	130
Administrative Measures at Duala	131–136
Civil Administration; Naval Arrangements; Engineer and Communication Services; Supply and Transport; Ordnance; Medical.	
Consolidation of Position at Duala, September–October 1914	
Duala and the Dibamba River, 28th–30th September	136
Capture of Maka, 2nd October	139
Tiko and Misselele Plantation, 1st October	140
Attack on Yapoma Bridge, 1st–6th October	141–144
Capture of Yapoma, 6th October	143
Naval Reconnaissances	144
Instructions of H.M. Government, 30th September 1914	145
Colonel Cunliffe to control Operations from Nigeria	146
Consolidation of Position at Duala (*continued*)	146–156
First Advance on Yabasi, 6th–10th October	146–151
Unsuccessful Attack on Yabasi, 8th October	147–150
Second Advance on Yabasi, 12th–16th October	151–153
Capture of Yabasi, 14th October	152
Operations up Northern Railway, 6th–12th October	153–155
Occupation of Susa, 8th October	153
Naval Operations, 6th–16th October	155
French Operations in the South and East	156–158
Gabon, 19th–21st September; Sanga Column, 4th–17th October; Lobaye Column, 18th September–18th October; Chad Area, 2nd–21st September.	

Chapter V

October–November 1914. The Capture of Edea and Buea, and Operations in the North and South of the Cameroons.

Consolidation of Position at Duala (*continued*)	158–169
The Edea Project	158
German Attempt to Retake Susa	158
Affair at Kake, 19th October	159
Allied Estimate of Enemy Dispositions, 18th October 1914	160

CONTENTS

CHAPTER V—continued

	PAGE
Plan for Advance on Edea	161
Edea Operations, 20th–26th October	163–169
Capture of Edea, 26th October	168
Nigeria and the Northern Cameroons, October 1914	169–174
Anglo-German Frontier and Nigeria, 7th October	169
Mora, 9th–31st October	170–173
Unsuccessful Attack on Mora, 30th/31st October	172
Nigeria, 7th–31st October	173
French Operations in the South and South-East, and Arrival of a Belgian Detachment, October 1914	174
Operations Northward of Duala, 1st–9th November	175–179
Yabasi; Susa.	
Naval Coast Operations, 31st October–7th November	179–181
Naval Strength and Command, 2nd–9th November	181–183
Operations against the Cameroon Mountain and up the Northern Railway; November 1914	183–188
Occupation of Muyuka, 13th November	185
Capture of Buea, 15th November	186
Occupation of the Cameroon Mountain	186
Edea and Dibombe, 1st–17th November	188
Question of Local Naval Command	188
Franco-Belgian Operations in the South and South-East, 1st–16th November 1914	188
Northern Cameroons and Nigerian Frontier	189–194
Unsuccessful Attack on Mora, 4th/5th November	189
Marua, the Yola Column and Mora, 1st–30th November	190–193
Affair at Dukba, 16th November	192
Ibi Column, November 1914	193
Cross River Column, November 1914	194
Internal Situation, Nigeria	194

CHAPTER VI

NOVEMBER 1914 — JANUARY 1915. OCCUPATION OF THE NORTHERN RAILWAY AND DESTRUCTION OF CHANG; GERMAN COUNTER-ATTACKS IN EDEA AREA; AND FRANCO-BELGIAN ADVANCE IN THE SOUTH-EAST.

	PAGE
General Situation After the Capture of Buea	195
Proposal to make the Sanaga River the Dividing Line for Main British and French Operations	196
Operations in the Edea-Dehane-Kribi Area, November 1914	
French Reverse near Dehane, 26th November	197
Occupation of Kribi, 2nd December	198

CONTENTS

CHAPTER VI—*continued*

	PAGE
Operations up Northern Railway, December 1914	198–205
Occupation of Nkongsamba, 10th December	202
Occupation of Bare, 11th December	203
Preparations for Further Advance Northward	204
Naval Operations, December 1914	205
Kribi-Edea Area, December 1914	205–207
Unsuccessful Enemy Attacks on Kribi, 5th and 9th December	206
Northern Cameroons, November-December 1914	207–210
Action of Columns under Brisset and Webb-Bowen	207–209
Cross River Column ; Advance on Ossidinge	209–210
Ibi Column	210
Franco-Belgian Operations in the South and South-East, November–December 1914	210–212
Mvahdi Column	210
Sanga and Lobaye Columns ; Occupation of Molundu, 19th December ; Occupation of Baturi, 9th December ; Occupation of Bertua, 29th December	211–212
General Situation, December 1914	212
River Flotillas South of Duala, December 1914–January 1915	213–215
Instructions to, and Plans of, General Dobell, 19th–27th December 1914	215
Advance to, and Withdrawal from, Chang ; 25th December 1914–12th January 1915	216–222
Capture of Chang, 2nd January 1915	219
Withdrawal from Chang, 7th January	220
Arrival of Reinforcements at Duala, 27th January	222
Nigerian Frontier	222–224
Cross River Column Occupies Ossidinge, 1st January 1915	223
Ibi Column, December 1914–January 1915	223
Operations in Edea-Kribi Area, January 1915	224–227
Enemy Attacks on Kribi, 2nd and 3rd/4th January	224
Enemy Attack on Kopongo, 5th January	225
Defeat of German Attack on Edea, 5th January	225
Enemy Attack on Kribi, 8th/9th January	226
Enrolment of Levies	226
Naval Coast and River Patrols, January 1915	227
Bare and Northern Railway, January 1915	227
Casualties in Dobell's Expeditionary Force, to January 1915	228
Northern Cameroons, December 1914–January 1915	228–231
Junction of Allied Columns Opposite Garua, 14th January 1915	230
Visit of Cunliffe to Duala, 27th January	230
Franco-Belgian Operations in the South and South-East, January 1915	231–232
Commencement of Advance on Oyem ; Part of Sanga Column occupies Yukaduma, 30th January ; Lobaye Column on Line Bertua—Nyassi.	
Proposal for Allied Conference at Duala, end of January 1915	232

CONTENTS

CHAPTER VII

FEBRUARY – APRIL 1915. INDECISIVE OPERATIONS FROM NKONGSAMBA, LEADING TO ABANDONMENT OF ENEMY COUNTER-OFFENSIVE ; AND DECISIONS TO ACCELERATE CAPTURE OF GARUA AND TO CO-OPERATE FROM EDEA WITH FRENCH ADVANCE FROM SOUTH-EAST.

	PAGE
Operations about Northern Railhead, February–March 1915	233–244
Affairs near Mbureku and Harmann's Farm, 3rd February	233
Distribution of Troops at Nkongsamba and Bare, 15th February	237
Affair at Mbureku, 27th February	237
Affair of Harmann's Farm, 4th March	239–242
Events, 5th–31st March	242–244
Duala–Kribi–Edea–Yabasi Area ; February 1915	244
Evacuation of Kribi, 1st March	245
Nyong and Campo Flotillas, February 1915	245
Question of Reinforcements for General Dobell, March 1915	246
Arrival of French Mission at Duala, 12th March 1915	248
Franco-Belgian Operations in the South and South-East, February–March 1915	248–250
Occupation of Oyem, 16th February ; Mvahdi Column occupies Minkebe ; Lobaye Column Forced back to Kadei River Line at end of February.	
Nigeria and Northern Cameroons, February–March 1915	250–253
Cross River Column February–March	250
Ibi Column, February	250
Garua, February–March	251
Affair of 13th February near Garua	252
Mora, February–March	253
French Mission at Duala, March 1915	253–255
Plans agreed upon with French.	
Duala, March 1915	255
War Office assume Control of Operations, 3rd April 1915	255
Advance Eastward from Edea, April 1915	256–258
Commencement of Advance, 10th April	257
Occupation of So Dibanga, 14th April	257
Affair of Ngwe, 14th April	257
Dobell's Appreciation of the Situation, April 1915	258–264
Northern Railway, April 1915	264
Naval Operations, March–April 1915	264
Franco-Belgian Operations in the South and South-East, March–April 1915	265
Nigerian Frontier, March–April 1915	266
Ibi Column ; German Raid on Mutum Biu, 12th April	266
Cross River Column	266
Nigerian Recruiting	266
Northern Cameroons, March–April 1915	266–270
Operations at Garua ; Cunliffe, with Reinforcements, arrives on 18th April and assumes Command of Allied Force Opposite Garua.	
German Attack on Gurin repulsed, 29th April	268
Mora	270

CONTENTS

Chapter VIII

May–July 1915. The First and Unsuccessful Advance on Yaunde ; the Capture of Garua and Ngaundere ; and Franco-Belgian Progress in the South-East.

	PAGE
The First Advance on Yaunde, May–June 1915 ..	271–285
Commencement of Advance Eastward from So Dibanga and Ngwe, 1st May	271
First Affair of Wum Biagas, 3rd–4th May	272
Capture of Sende, 6th May	273
Capture of Eseka, 11th May	273
Aymerich's Co-operation Delayed	274
Concentration at Wum Biagas, 23rd May	275
Advance from Wum Biagas, 25th May	276
Affair at Ngok, 27th–30th May	276
Attack on Allied L. of C., 28th May	277
Affair at Matem, 31st May–4th June	277
Considerations leading to Dobell's Decision to Withdraw the Yaunde Column, 7th–8th June	278
Operations, 5th–13th June	279
Withdrawal to Wum Biagas, 14th June	281
Dobell at Edea and Duala, 8th–14th June	281
Enemy Attacks on So Dibanga and Wum Biagas, 15th June	282
Allied Retirement to Ngwe and Edea, 16th–18th June	282
Ngwe, 18th June–1st July	283
Retrospect	284
Question of Future Policy, 12th–23rd June 1915 ..	285–288
Northern Railway and Cameroons Coast, May–June 1915	288–290
Naval Blockade Force, June 1915	290
Distribution of Dobell's British Contingent, End of June 1915	290
Political and Civil Administration	291
Franco-Belgian Operations in the South and South-East, May–June 1915	292–294
Oyem Column checked opposite Bitam..	292
Mvahdi Column broken up, 1st June	292
Sanga Column captures Lomie, 24th June	293
Lobaye Column resumes Offensive, June	294
Northern Cameroons, May–July 1915	294–307
Garua ; the German Position	294
Cunliffe's Plans	295
Preparations to Attack Garua, 18th–28th May ..	295
Attack on Garua, 31st May–10th June	297
Capture of Garua, 10th June	298
Advance on Ngaundere	300
Capture of Ngaundere, 28th–29th June..	300
Capture of Koncha, 27th June	301
Cunliffe's Plans	301
Decision to Attack Mora, July	304
Mann's Advance on Gashiga, July	305
Occupation of Tingere, 19th July	305
Cunliffe's Plans, July	305

CONTENTS

CHAPTER VIII—continued

	PAGE
Enemy Attack on Tingere, 23rd July	306
Touch with Lobaye Column, July	307
Progress on Gashiga Line, July	307
Cross River Column, May–July	307
Dobell's Expeditionary Force, July 1915	307–312
Lull in Operations..	307
Nyong River Operations, July	308
Campo Area Operations, July	309
Edea District, July	310
French Affair at Ndupe River, 24th July	311
Northern Railway and Bare, July	311
Question of Future Policy, 19th–26th July	312
Franco-Belgian Operations in the South and South-East, July 1915	313
Oyem Column occupies Bitam, 17th July	313
Lobaye Column captures Bertua, 22nd July; Occupies Dume, 25th July; and Abong Mbang, 29th July	313

CHAPTER IX

AUGUST TO THE BEGINNING OF NOVEMBER 1915. COMMENCEMENT OF THE FINAL ADVANCE ON YAUNDE AND THE CAPTURE OF BAMENDA, BANYO, TIBATI AND CHANG.

Dobell's Expeditionary Force, August 1915	314–321
Question of Future Policy, August	314
British Reinforcements, August	317
Operations in Campo Area, August	317–319
Affair near Njabesan, 8th August	317
Edea and Northern Railway, August	319
Allied Conference at Duala, 25th–26th August.. Plans Agreed Upon.	320
Distribution and Strength, British Contingent, 30th August	321
Franco-Belgian Operations in the South-East, August 1915	321–322
German Counter-Offensive starts at end of August	322
Northern Cameroons, August–September 1915	322–328
Move of Cunliffe to Mora	323
Cunliffe's Dispositions and Intentions	324
Operations at Mora, August–September	324–327
Unsuccessful Attack on Mora, 7th–8th September	326
Abandonment of Further Attacks, 15th September	327
Cunliffe returns to Yola, 26th September	327
Dobell's Expeditionary Force, August–October 1915	328–337
Preparations to Advance on Yaunde and Arrival of Reinforcements	328
Issue of Orders for the Advance, 22nd September	329
Disposition of Gorges' Force, 4th October	329
Second Advance on Yaunde, October 1915	330–337
Advance from Ngwe and So Dibanga commences 6th October	330

CONTENTS

CHAPTER IX—*continued*

	PAGE
Operations of British Column, 6th–9th October	330–332
Capture of Wum Biagas, 9th October	332
Operations of French Column, 6th–13th October	332
Arrangements for British Assistance to French Column, 10th–17th October	333
British Operations, 17th–26th October	334
French Operations, 14th–25th October	335
Sende Occupied, 25th October	335
Combined Anglo-French Advance on Eseka, 26th–30th October	336
Capture of Eseka, 30th October	337
Naval Operations, September–October 1915	337
Franco-Belgian "East Cameroons Force," September–October 1915	337–338
German Counter-Offensive, lasting till 24th September, forces French back to Line Bertua–Dume–Lomie—Aymerich arrives Dume, 18th October, and takes Personal Command—Aymerich commences Forward Movement, 28th October.	
French "South Cameroons Force," and British Force in Campo Area, September–October 1915	338–340
Le Meillour fails to Effect Passage of Ntem River, 24th–25th October	339
Cunliffe's Operations and Co-operation by the Bare Column, October–10th November 1915..	340–350
Cunliffe's Dispositions at End of September	340
His Plan of Action	340
Operations of Bare Column	341–343
Occupation of Chang, 6th November	343
Operations of Column from Ossidinge	343
Capture of Bamenda, 22nd October	343
Operations in Kentu Area, October	344
Advance of Cunliffe and Mann to Banyo, October	344–346
Advance from Tingere and Ngaundere, October	346
Occupation of Tibati, 3rd November	346
Operations against Banyo Mountain	346–350
Capture of Banyo Mountain, 6th November	349
Cunliffe's Future Plans	350

CHAPTER X

NOVEMBER–22ND DECEMBER 1915. STEADY PROGRESS OF THE CONVERGING ADVANCE ON YAUNDE.

Second Advance on Yaunde (*continued*), November–6th December 1915	351–364
Enemy Strength and Dispositions, Beginning of November	351
The Allies at Eseka and Wum Biagas, 1st–22nd November	352
Orders for Advance, 12th November	354

xvi   CONTENTS

CHAPTER X—*continued*

PAGE

Advance of Gorges' Column, 23rd November–6th
   December   356–363
      Affairs at Lesogs, 26th–28th November .. 358–360
      Capture of Puge River Position, 28th November.. 360
      Halt at Ngung, 1st–6th December 362
   Advance of French Column from Eseka, 23rd November
      –6th December   363–364
French Operations from Campo and Bitam, November 1915
   Advance from Campo checked near Akak, 11th
      November   365
   Unsuccessful Attempt by Le Meillour to cross Ntem
      River, 25th–26th November 365
Franco-Belgian East Cameroons Force, November 1915 365–366
   German Counter-Offensive at End of November
      defeated and Aymerich occupies Lembe 366
Cunliffe's Operations in the North, November–December
   1915   366–374
   Advance of Columns under Crookenden and Cotton,
      10th November–4th December   367–371
         Crossing of the Nun River, 27th–29th November.. 369
         Occupation of Fumban, 2nd December 370
   Advance of Cunliffe's Main Column, 8th–9th November 371
   Brisset to Advance on Yoko, 17th November 372
   Cunliffe's Main Column, 19th November–4th December 372–374
      Occupation of Ngambe, 4th December 373
   Brisset occupies Yoko, 1st December 374

Mora, October–November 1915 374

Second Advance on Yaunde (*continued*), 7th–22nd December
   1915   374–383
   General Dobell at Duala, 7th December.. ..   374–376
      Fresh Instructions to Gorges 375
   Advance of Gorges' Column, 7th–22nd December   376–381
      Occupation of Chang Mangas, 17th December .. 381
      Halt at Chang Mangas, 18th–22nd December .. 381
   Advance of French Column, 7th–21st December .. 382
      Occupation of Mangeles, 21st December 383

French Advance on Ebolowa, December 1915 383
   Slow Progress of Column from Campo 383
   Le Meillour forces Passage of Ntem River, 20th
      December, and captures Ambam, 31st December .. 383

Franco-Belgian East Cameroons Force, December 1915 383–384
   Affairs near Lembe, 18th–28th December 384

Cunliffe's Operations in the North, 4th–23rd December
   1915   384–386
   Dispositions on 4th December—Occupation of Ditam
      and Linte, 18th December.

Duala, 8th–21st December 1915 386

Naval Operations, November–December 1915 387

CONTENTS

Chapter XI

23rd December 1915–18th February 1916. The Capture of Yaunde, the Subsequent Abandonment of their Colony by the Germans, and the Surrender of Mora.

PAGE

Second Advance on Yaunde (*concluded*), 23rd December 1915–1st January 1916.. 388–395
    Resumption of Colonel Gorges' Advance, 23rd December 388
    Capture of Yaunde, 1st January 1916 393
French and Franco-Belgian Columns: Situation, 1st January 1916 395
Situation in the North, 1st January 1916 395
The Final Operations, January–February 1916 .. 396–420
    Measures to Pursue the Enemy South of Yaunde .. 396
    4th January: Fresh Instructions to, and Reinforcement of, the French Campo Column 397
    5th January: Haywood's Column leaves Yaunde for Widemenge; British Reinforcements ordered to Campo 399
    6th January: Brisset's Column (of Cunliffe's Force) reaches the Nachtigal Rapids 400
    7th January: Gorges in Touch with Aymerich.. .. 401
    8th January: Aymerich Arrives at Yaunde; Situation of the Allied Forces; Dobell's Suggestions to Aymerich; Release of British Prisoners at Kolmaka; Information Regarding the Enemy 402
    9th–10th January: Coles' Column Marches from Yaunde; Cockburn takes over the British Command at Yaunde from Gorges; Action by Aymerich; Columns of Brisset and Morisson Arrive at Yaunde.. 406
    11th–14th January: Haywood's Column; Faucon's and Coles' Columns; Schmoll's Column leaves Yaunde to Reinforce Haywood; Aymerich assumes Command of Allies in Eastern Area; Dobell sends Reinforcements to Campo 407
    15th–22nd January: Aymerich's Operation Orders of 15th January; Faucon occupies Ebolowa, 19th January; Progress of Coles; Progress of Haywood; Discussion of Plans between Dobell and Aymerich; Action by Le Meillour's "South Cameroons Force" 409
General Cunliffe's Departure and his Past Operations.. 413
    23rd–31st January: Haywood's Pursuit South of Ebolowa; Affair at Mafub, 24th January; Occupation of Abang 25th and Nkan 26th January; Coles moves to Lolo from Ebolowa; Le Meillour in Action against Superior German Force; Haywood Ordered to Withdraw to Kribi; Action of Columns under Le Meillour and Caillet 415
    Final Operations under Aymerich, February 1916; Final German Evacuation of the Cameroons and Retreat into Muni, 15th February 419

CONTENTS

CHAPTER XI—*continued*

	PAGE
Telegraphic Report of German ex-Governor to his Government	420
Allied Naval Forces, January–1st March 1916	421
Surrender of Mora, 18th February 1916	421
End of the Campaign	421
Conclusion	423

TABLE OF APPENDICES

I.—The Terms of Surrender suggested by Major von Doering, and subsequent Correspondence between him and Lieut.-Colonel Bryant	429
II.—Order of Battle of the Anglo-French Expeditionary Force against the Cameroons, 23rd September 1914	432
III.—(A) List of H.M. Ships and Vessels Employed with the Cameroons Expedition	435
(B) List of Nigeria Marine Vessels Employed with the Cameroons Expedition	436
IV.—Captured Enemy Ships and Vessels, armed and used by Cameroons Expeditionary Force	440
V.—Memorandum issued on 7th November 1914	442
VI.—Distribution and Strength of the British Contingent of General Dobell's Expeditionary Force, 30th August 1915	444
VII.—Standing Orders for the Eastern British Force	445
VIII.—Allied Troops (Combatant Units) Operating in the Cameroons on the 1st January 1916	449

MAPS AND ILLUSTRATIONS

Maps

Skeleton Map of West Africa, 1914			*Frontispiece*
Map	1.	Togoland	*In pocket*
,,	2.	Skeleton Map of the Cameroons	,,
,,	3.	Cameroons : Diagrams showing Approximate Altitudes, Healthy and Unhealthy Areas, Distribution of Vegetation, and Annual Rainfall	,,
,,	4.	Duala and Hinterland..	,,
,,	5.	Rough Sketch Map of Mora Mountain	,,
,,	6.	Rough Sketch Map to Illustrate the Affair of Nsanakang, 6th September 1914	*Facing p.* 110
,,	7.	The Anglo-German Frontier in the Vicinity of the Cross River	,, 224
,,	8.	The Muyuka—Chang Area	*In pocket*
,,	9.	Copy of Plan found on the body of Oberleutnant Bachmann after the Attack on Edea, 5th January 1915	,,
,,	10.	Rough Sketch to Illustrate Affair of Harmann's Farm, 4th March 1915. Situation at about 12.15 p.m.	*Facing p.* 242
,,	11.	Sketch Map of Garua	*In pocket*
,,	12.	Edea—Yaunde..	,,
,,	13.	Skeleton Map of the Campo—Ambam Area..	,,
,,	14.	Sketch Map of British Encampment at Wum Biagas. Beginning of November 1915	*Facing p.* 352

Illustrations

Regimental Sergeant-Major Alhaji Grunshi, D.C.M., M.M., Gold Coast Regiment..	*Facing p.*	8
Gold Coast Troops..	,,	8
Wrecked German Train near Ekuni	,,	29
A Typical West African Swamp ..	,,	47
German Native Soldiers ..	,,	54
A Track in the Highland Country of the Cameroons ..	,,	54
A Forest Track in the Cameroons	,,	66
Ambas Bay..	,,	79
Victoria Harbour ..	,,	86
Mora Mountain	,,	90
Obokum and the Cross River	,,	102
On the River Sanga	,,	116
The Nigeria Marine Paddle-Tug *Porpoise*	,,	126
The Yapoma Bridge	,,	140
Yabasi	,,	150

ILLUSTRATIONS

Sanaga River Bridge near Edea	*Facing p.*	163
Sanaga River near Edea	,,	163
Nigerian Troops at Yola	,,	173
Camel Transport, and Watering M.I. Ponies	,,	188
Camp at Sava	,,	192
Nlohe Bridge	,,	200
Nlohe Station	,,	204
Country between Mbo and Chang	,,	216
2nd Nigerians at Muyuka	,,	220
Chang	,,	220
A British N.C.O., Nigeria Regiment	,,	236
A Soldier of the Nigeria Regiment	,,	250
Bridge over Ngwe River	,,	258
A Gun-Carrier, R.W.A.F.F.	,,	264
French Troops arriving at Wum Biagas, 20th May 1915	,,	275
Naval Gun with the Yaunde Column	,,	284
Forts at Garua	,,	295
British Naval Gun at Garua	,,	299
Prisoners taken at Garua	,,	299
Ambulance Convoy crossing a Bridge	,,	320
Nigerian Troops on the Gauala Ridge	,,	326
Machine Gun Section and Signallers, R.W.A.F.F.	,,	340
Nigerian Battery in Action	,,	362
Crossing the Mbam River	,,	386
River Nyong at Olama	,,	408
" A " Company, M.I. Battalion, Nigeria Regiment	,,	421
German Arms collected after the Surrender of Mora	,,	421
Buea	,,	428

BIBLIOGRAPHY

Official War Diaries and Records, Cameroons Expeditionary Force and Governments of Nigeria and the Gold Coast.
Official Records of the Colonial Office, War Office, Admiralty and Committee of Imperial Defence.
Official Despatches on the Operations.
" The Empire at War," Vol. IV.   Sir C. Lucas.
" The Great War in West Africa."   Brigadier-General E. H. Gorges.
" Naval Operations."   Sir Julian Corbett.
History of the Cameroons Campaign, by Commandant Viraud, published in the " Revue des Troupes Coloniales."
" Les Campagnes Coloniales Belges, 1914–1918."   (Belgian Official History.)
" Conquête du Cameroun-Nord (1914–1915)."   Lieutenant-Colonel Jean Ferrandi.
" Der Grosse Krieg, 1914–1918."   Vol. IV.   Edited by M. Schwarte.

BATTLE HONOURS GRANTED FOR THE OPERATIONS IN
WEST AFRICA, 1914–1916.

" Kamina "

" Duala "
" Garua "
" Banyo "
" Cameroons, 1914–1916."

CHRONOLOGICAL SUMMARY OF THE OPERATIONS IN TOGOLAND AND THE CAMEROONS, 1914–1916

TOGOLAND

British summons to Germans to surrender	6th August 1914
British occupy Lome	7th August 1914
Commencement of advance from Lome on Kamina	14th August 1914
Affair of Agbeluvoe	15th–16th August 1914
Affair of Khra	22nd August 1914
German surrender	26th August 1914

THE CAMEROONS

I. *August–September 1914*

Early operations near the Nigerian frontier.

Affair at Mora	27th August 1914
Affair of Tepe	25th August 1914
Unsuccessful attack on Garua	29th–30th August 1914
Affair of Nsanakang	6th September 1914

Early French operations near their frontiers.

Occupation of Singa and Bonga	6th August 1914
Occupation of Wesso	31st August 1914
Occupation of Lobaye river line	by 31st August 1914
Unsuccessful attack on Kuseri	25th August 1914
Capture of Kuseri	20th September 1914
Affair at Mibang (south of Oyem)	6th September 1914
Capture of Ukoko	21st September 1914

Naval operations off Victoria and Duala — 4th–23rd September 1914

Combined naval and military operations against Duala.

Arrival at Suelaba of Dobell's expeditionary force	23rd September 1914
Capture of Duala	27th September 1914

II. *October 1914–January 1915*

Dobell's Expeditionary Force

Consolidation of position at Duala.

Capture of Yapoma	6th October 1914
Occupation of Susa	8th October 1914
Unsuccessful attack on Yabasi	8th October 1914
Capture of Yabasi	14th October 1914
Affair at Kake	19th October 1914
Capture of Edea	26th October 1914

CHRONOLOGICAL SUMMARY OF OPERATIONS

Dobell's Expeditionary Force.

Operations against the Cameroon Mountain and up the Northern Railway.
- Capture of Buea .. .. .. 15th November 1914
- Occupation of Nkongsamba.. .. 10th December 1914
- Occupation of Bare .. .. .. 11th December 1914
- Capture of Chang .. .. .. 2nd January 1915
- Withdrawal from Chang to Bare .. 7th January 1915

Operations in the Edea–Kribi area.
- Affair near Dehane .. .. .. 26th November 1914
- Occupation of Kribi .. .. .. 2nd December 1914
- Unsuccessful enemy attacks on Kribi .. .. 5th and 9th December 1914
- Unsuccessful German attacks on Kopongo and Edea .. .. 5th January 1915

Northern Cameroons and Nigerian frontier.
- Unsuccessful attack on Mora .. 30th–31st October 1914
- Unsuccessful attack on Mora .. 4th–5th November 1914
- Affair at Dukba .. .. .. 16th November 1914
- Occupation of Ossidinge .. .. 1st January 1915
- Junction of French and British columns opposite Garua .. .. 14th January 1915

Under control of Aymerich.

Franco-Belgian operations in the south-east.
- Capture of Nola .. .. .. 17th October 1914
- Occupation of Carnot .. .. 18th October 1914
- Occupation of Baturi .. .. 9th December 1914
- Occupation of Molundu .. .. 19th December 1914
- Occupation of Bertua .. .. 29th December 1914
- Occupation of Yukaduma .. .. 30th January 1915

III. February–March 1915

Dobell's Expeditionary Force.

Operations about Northern railhead.
- Affairs near Mbureku and Harmann's Farm .. .. 3rd February 1915
- Affair at Mbureku .. .. .. 27th February 1915
- Affair of Harmann's Farm .. .. 4th March 1915
- Arrival of French mission at Duala 12th March 1915

Northern Cameroons.
- Affair near Garua .. .. .. 13th February 1915

Under control of Aymerich.

Franco-Belgian operations in the south-east.
- Withdrawal from Bertua to Kadei river line .. .. end of February 1915

French operations in the south.
- Occupation of Oyem .. .. 16th February 1915

CHRONOLOGICAL SUMMARY OF OPERATIONS

IV. April–June 1915

Dobell's Expeditionary Force.
- First advance on Yaunde.
  - Commencement of advance from Edea .. .. 10th April 1915
  - Affair of Ngwe .. .. 14th April 1915
  - Capture of So Dibanga .. .. 14th April 1915
  - Commencement of advance eastward from So Dibanga and Ngwe .. 1st May 1915
  - First affair of Wum Biagas .. .. 3rd–4th May 1915
  - Capture of Eseka .. .. 11th May 1915
  - Concentration at Wum Biagas .. 23rd May 1915
  - Commencement of advance from Wum Biagas .. .. .. 25th May 1915
  - Affair at Ngok .. .. .. 27th–30th May 1915
  - Affair at Matem .. .. 31st May–4th June 1915
  - Withdrawal to Wum Biagas .. 14th June 1915
  - Withdrawal to Ngwe .. .. 16th–18th June 1915

Under Aymerich's control.
- Franco-Belgian operations in the south-east.
  - Capture of Lomie .. .. .. 24th June 1915

Under Cunliffe.
- Northern Cameroons.
  - Cunliffe takes command of Allied force opposite Garua .. .. 18th April 1915
  - German attack on Gurin .. .. 29th April 1915
  - Capture of Garua .. .. .. 10th June 1915
  - Capture of Ngaundere .. .. 28th–29th June 1915
  - Capture of Koncha .. .. .. 27th June 1915

V. July–September 1915

Dobell's Expeditionary Force.
- Operations in the Nyong and Campo river areas.
  - On the Nyong river .. .. .. July 1915
  - Affair near Njabesan (Campo area) 8th August 1915
  - Allied conference at Duala .. .. 25th–26th August 1915

Under Cunliffe.
- Northern Cameroons.
  - Occupation of Tingere .. .. 19th July 1915
  - Unsuccessful attack on Mora .. 7th–8th September 1915
  - Decision to abandon further attacks on Mora .. .. 15th September 1915
  - Affair at Gandua .. .. .. 27th September 1915

Under Aymerich's control.
- French operations in the south.
  - Occupation of Bitam .. .. 17th July 1915
  - Occupation of Akoafim .. .. 3rd September 1915
- Franco-Belgian operations in the south-east.
  - Capture of Bertua .. .. .. 22nd July 1915
  - Occupation of Dume .. .. .. 25th July 1915
  - Occupation of Abong Mbang .. 29th July 1915
  - German counter-attack forces French back to line Bertua–Dume–east of Abong Mbang–Lomie .. .. end of August to 24th September 1915

CHRONOLOGICAL SUMMARY OF OPERATIONS xxv

VI. October 1915–February 1916

Dobell's Expeditionary Force.
- Second advance on Yaunde.
  - Commencement of advance from Ngwe and So Dibanga .. .. 6th October 1915
  - Capture of Wum Biagas .. .. 9th October 1915
  - Capture of Eseka .. .. .. 30th October 1915
  - Resumption of advance from Wum Biagas and Eseka .. .. .. 23rd November 1915
  - Affairs at Lesogs .. .. .. 26th–28th November 1915
  - Capture of Puge river position .. 28th November 1915
  - Occupation of Chang Mangas .. 17th December 1915
  - Occupation of Mangeles .. .. 21st December 1915
  - Occupation of Yaunde .. .. 1st January 1916
- French advance from Campo eastward.
  - Advance checked near Akak .. 11th November 1915

Under Cunliffe.
- Northern Cameroons.
  - Commencement of Cunliffe's advance southward from line Koncha–Tingere–Ngaundere .. .. 14th October 1915
  - Occupation of Bamenda .. .. 22nd October 1915
  - Occupation of Chang .. .. 6th November 1915
  - Occupation of Tibati .. .. 3rd November 1915
  - Capture of Banyo mountain .. 6th November 1915
  - Occupation of Yoko .. .. .. 1st December 1915
  - Occupation of Fumban .. .. 2nd December 1915
  - Occupation of Ngambe .. .. 4th December 1915
  - Brisset reaches Nachtigal Rapids .. 6th January 1916
  - Brisset enters Yaunde .. .. 9th January 1916

Under Aymerich.
- Franco-Belgian operations in the south-east.
  - Advance on Yaunde recommences .. end of October 1915
  - German counter-offensive .. .. end of November 1915
  - German counter-offensive defeated and Lembe occupied .. .. by 4th December 1915
  - Affairs near Lembe .. .. .. 18th–28th December 1915
  - Aymerich arrives Yaunde .. .. 8th January 1916

Under Le Meillour (controlled by Aymerich).
- French operations in the south.
  - Unsuccessful attempt to cross Ntem river.. .. .. 25th–26th November 1915
  - Passage of Ntem river effected .. 20th December 1915
  - Capture of Ambam .. .. 31st December 1915

Under control of Aymerich and Dobell.
- Final operations south of Yaunde, up to Spanish frontier.
  - Occupation of Ebolowa .. .. 19th January 1916
  - Affair at Mafub .. .. .. 24th January 1916
  - Occupation of Banyassa .. .. 15th February 1916

- Northern Cameroons
  - Surrender of German garrison at Mora .. .. 18th February 1916

CHAPTER I

INCEPTION OF THE OPERATIONS AGAINST THE GERMAN POSSESSIONS IN WEST AFRICA, AND THE CAPTURE OF TOGOLAND

(Frontispiece map and Map 1.)

At the outbreak of war, the large navy and the small regular army, which Great Britain had deliberately adopted as the scale of her first line of national defence, were more completely prepared for war and readier for action than at any earlier period of her history. It is true that for the long-drawn-out struggle in Belgium and France and for the major offensive operations undertaken elsewhere our preparations for war proved to be totally inadequate. But, for the security of our overseas Empire the measures of defence proved sufficient; and the integrity of our dominions, colonies and protectorates was scarcely ever in doubt. Relieved of serious anxiety regarding their own security, their British peoples were thus free to devote greater efforts to that organisation of their physical, material and intellectual resources which was to contribute much to the final Allied success. *Imperial Defence.*

It had for many years been accepted that the defence of the British overseas territories against serious attack could be generally assured by a navy of sufficient strength, based on fortified coaling stations held by Imperial troops and supported by local forces. The organisation and strength of the latter had been a matter of discussion by the series of committees, commissions and conferences, which ever since the time of the Crimea and the Indian Mutiny had considered periodically the question of Imperial defence ; and after the South African war the participation in these conferences by representatives of the self-governing Dominions had resulted in their accepting responsibility for their own local defence. In 1911 it had finally been agreed that an Imperial General Staff should be formed to ensure a uniform military doctrine throughout the Empire, and that in each territory forces should be maintained sufficient for self-defence, all organised, trained and equipped on the same lines. But although it was confidently anticipated that in an emergency substantial help would be forthcoming from the Dominions, no pressure had been brought on them to define its form and extent.

Thus when war broke out, though no one could say what forces would be available for any enterprise, there were local forces in every portion of the Empire, each with its own defence scheme prepared to meet local requirements. These schemes legislated primarily for a defensive attitude, though generally, where foreign territory adjoined, projects of offensive operations had been outlined, with the proviso that they were only to be undertaken with the full knowledge and approval of H.M. Government or, in the event of communication with England being cut, when the safety of H.M.'s possessions could not otherwise be secured.

It was certain that these arrangements would not suffice to meet the case of war with Germany. For one thing, this would inevitably mean a conflict for the command of the sea, in which, as always in the past, the navy would look to the army for assistance in capturing points on land whose occupation by the enemy menaced the security of the main sea-routes.

Formation of a Committee to consider operations in foreign territory. It was in these circumstances that, on the 5th August 1914, H.M. Government approved the formation in London of a joint naval and military committee for the consideration of combined naval and military operations in foreign territory. The Committee were instructed that their object was to decide what objectives could be assigned to joint expeditions with a view to producing a definite effect on the result of the war. Having decided on the broad lines of any joint operations, they were to submit their proposals to the Cabinet, and, in the case of those approved, were to work out the details as far as might be necessary.

This Committee, termed the Offensive Sub-Committee of the Committee of Imperial Defence, and composed of representatives of the Admiralty and the War, Foreign, Colonial and India Offices, assembled the same day with Admiral Sir Henry Jackson in the Chair, and with Brigadier-General C. M. Dobell, Inspector-General of the West African Frontier Force among its members.* At this period, owing to the naval

---

* Till the Committee ceased their work in November 1914, the members who attended most of the meetings were Admiral Jackson, Sir George Fiddes (Colonial Office), Major-General C. E. Callwell (War Office), Colonel Sir G. Aston (Admiralty), and the Secretary, Major S. H. Wilson.

IMPERIAL STRATEGICAL REQUIREMENTS

dispositions arranged with the French and to the necessity for concentrating our main naval strength in Scottish waters, the great trade sea-routes were but slenderly protected. This was the more serious since Germany had cruisers abroad and was credited with the intention of arming a large number of fast and powerful liners as commerce destroyers wherever they might happen to be at the outbreak of war. On the 27th July the Admiralty had telegraphed to all foreign stations that, as the European political situation rendered war not impossible, preparations were to be made, as unobtrusively as possible, to shadow ships of the Central Powers and to take other measures of a precautionary nature; two days later, the Admiralty and the War and Colonial Offices had issued their pre-arranged " warning " telegrams for bringing into force the precautionary stage of mobilisation; on the 4th August the Grand Fleet had started to sweep north so as to intercept German commerce destroyers which it was reported were trying to break out of German ports; and on the 5th the five German cables which passed through the English Channel to Vigo, Tenerife and the Azores were cut. The result of these measures, however, still remained to be seen.

As regards the proceedings of the Offensive Sub-Committee, Sir Julian Corbett says in his " Naval Operations ": * " At the outset of its deliberations the Committee recognised the principle that no force must be dissipated on enterprises which would prejudice the Imperial concentration in the main theatre and the safety of the great trade routes, and further that all expeditions for the conquest of distant territory were faulty in conception unless and until we had established a working command of the sea in all quarters. This being so, no objective would be legitimate which could not be dealt with by local forces, and no such objective could have a definite effect on the course of the war unless it tended to confirm our hold upon sea communications. As long as the enterprises were kept within these lines, so far from dissipating force, they would tend to assist and strengthen the main concentration of effort by keeping open the flow of trade and the Imperial lines of passage and communication. Unless this was done effectively a free concentration of effort in the main theatre was impossible.

" The objectives within these limitations were not far to seek. They must all be naval, and of these the most important

---

* Vol. I., p. 129.

were the enemy's foreign bases and centres of intelligence. Long experience had shown that until such positions were in our hands the task of clearing the seas of hostile commerce destroyers must be precarious and indefinitely prolonged. The governing principle, therefore, on which the Committee set out, was that all operations were to be regarded primarily as designed for the defence of our maritime communications, and not for territorial conquest. The single object was to deprive the enemy of his distant coaling and telegraphic stations."

Possible objective in Togoland. Amongst other possible objectives falling within the limitations laid down was the recently completed high-power German wireless station in Togoland, situated at Kamina, about 110 miles north of Lome. Able to communicate direct with Nauen near Berlin, with the German wireless stations in East Africa, South-West Africa, the Cameroons, Monrovia * (Liberia), and with any German ship in the Atlantic, it was the chief receiving and distributing centre for Africa and a pivotal point of naval communication.

Togoland. Togoland, with an area slightly larger than that of Ireland, and with a native population estimated at over a million, was enclosed on its three land sides by British or French territory. Until its annexation by the Germans in 1884, the majority of the tribes inhabiting the districts along or adjacent to the coast and adjoining the Northern Territories of the Gold Coast had regarded themselves as being under the suzerainty of Great Britain. But in 1885-86 both France and Great Britain signed agreements recognising German influence.

From the outset the Germans set themselves to develop thoroughly and systematically the country's natural resources, with the result that Togoland became the one German colony able to dispense with financial aid from the Fatherland. Their methods of administration, however, which replaced the native chief by the European official, and their system of education, which aimed at industrial rather than literary training, showed that they preferred German economic advantage to the country's social, intellectual, and political progress. It is true that there were no important chiefs in Togoland, but the jurisdiction of those there were was greatly restricted, while the German administrators were granted practically unlimited powers; and education, other than industrial, was left to

---

* At that period the three German-owned cables which ran from Monrovia to Pernambuco had not been interfered with by us.

the German missionary societies, whose main object was proselytism. Some of the German administrators had been brutal at times in their relations with the natives and frequently inhumane, while their generally rigid methods, including attempts to Teutonise the people by regulation, had been as unsuitable as they were unavailing. The unpopularity of German control, which had shown itself for some years past in a steady emigration to the Gold Coast, was confirmed by the attitude and behaviour of the Togoland natives after the outbreak of war in 1914.

A range of mountains, rising in places to heights of over 3,000 feet, traverses the country from south-west to north-east, and, dividing it into two approximately equal parts, formed a real barrier to traffic. Owing to this, the northern half of Togoland had not been developed to the same extent as the southern. Here there were three metre-gauge railways and several good roads. One railway ran along the coast from Anekho to Lome, another from Lome to Atakpame, and the third from Lome to Palime. The roads from Lome to Sokode via Atakpame, from Lome to Kete Krachi via Palime, from Palime to Atakpame, and from Kete Krachi to Sansane Mangu were, in 1914, reported to be fit for motors.

The Anglo-German frontier, for more than half its length, was marked by the left bank of the Volta river and by one of its tributaries. But a strip of territory extending about eighty miles along the left bank of the Volta's lower reaches lay in the Gold Coast Colony, forming a pronounced salient in the frontier line. The military significance of this salient was, however, lessened by the lagoons, swamps, and roadless bush country which covered its surface. The Volta, whose channel was all British, was navigable by shallow-draught launches as far as Akuse and up to Yeji by canoes, though these had to be carried past the rapids at Kete Krachi, where the Germans had formed an important inland trading centre. In Togoland canoes could go up the Oti river as far as Sansane Mangu, but with this exception none of the other rivers in the area of the British operations in August 1914 was really navigable. Another noteworthy feature of the frontier line, where it adjoined our Northern Territories Protectorate, was its bisection of the country of the Dagomba and Mamprusi tribes, the whole of which, until the Germans invaded it in 1897, had been recognised by them and by us as neutral territory. Since then, comparisons drawn by its inhabitants between British and German control had generally been favourable to us, and we understood that most of the tribesmen would welcome a re-union under our protection.

Togoland was without a harbour, and had no natural facilities for the construction of one. Even at Lome, where a pier had been built to facilitate landing, steamers had to lie some distance out and transfer passengers and cargo into surf boats.

To the east and south-east of the central mountain range—the area with which we here are mainly concerned—the country rises from the marshes and lagoons of the coastal area through an undulating plateau, which, till it nears the mountains, is seldom more than two or three hundred feet high. For the most part the surface was interspersed with belts of oil palms and scattered cultivated clearings, or was covered with virgin forest and—where this had been cleared or burnt by the natives—with high grass and thick scrub. Many of the numerous small rivers and streams which traverse the area disappear partially or entirely in the dry season, rendering parts of the country periodically uninhabitable for want of water, though after rain they are subject to floods which hamper or stop movement. The rainfall, which is at times heavy, is much greater in the mountain areas than towards the coast, where the month of August is practically rainless. The climate is tropical, and though the temperature seldom rises above 90° F. in the shade, its humidity makes it very trying. The country is no healthier than other parts of West Africa, where even with prudence and precautions it is almost impossible to escape one or other of the major or minor prevalent complaints, most of them water-borne or caused by insects and vermin. Even in peace times under normal conditions the physical and moral strain on Europeans necessitates frequent leave to a temperate climate.

The total number of German native troops and armed police was estimated as about 800, and the majority of the three hundred or so Germans resident in the country were believed to have undergone a military training.

The Gold Coast. The Gold Coast, i.e., the colony of that name, Ashanti, and the Northern Territories, covered an area of rather over twice the size of Togoland. Composed of a number of small, self-contained and independent tribal states, its native inhabitants were prosperous and thoroughly contented with their unity under the British Crown, whose power and jurisdiction had indeed been accepted voluntarily by most of them. Like Togoland, the Gold Coast was enclosed on three sides by foreign territory, that on the north and west consisting of the French possessions of the Upper Senegal and Niger and the Ivory Coast. It had no harbours, and landing, effected generally in surf boats, was difficult and at times dangerous. Except for the Volta, its two or three other partly navigable rivers were of practically no military importance; and until comparatively recent years before the war its roads consisted mainly of tortuous bush paths frequently blocked by fallen trees or swollen streams. The thick forest, heavy rains, lack of skilled labour, and scarcity of material for metalling made road and railway construction and maintenance both expensive and laborious. So that in 1914 there were only about 700 miles of road fit for light motor traffic; and besides the railway line from Sekondi to Kumasi, there was only a branch line from Tarkwa to Prestea, and a short railway from Accra to Koforidua. The alignment of these railways and of the motor roads had been determined mainly by commercial considerations, a drawback from the military point of view, since movement was restricted by the thick forest to the roads or paths practically everywhere but in the Northern Territories; and there for three-quarters of the year the high grass had the same effect. Moreover, the frequency of fly-transmitted disease prohibited the use of animals for transport purposes.

In Equatorial Africa there are practically always twelve hours of daylight, and as the seasonal variation of the hours of sunrise and sunset is slight, they may be taken for the purposes of this history as having always been about 6 a.m. and 6 p.m. respectively.

The only regular troops were the Gold Coast Regiment of the West African Frontier Force. This was composed of a battery, armed with four 2·95-inch Q.F. mountain guns, and of one pioneer and seven infantry companies, armed with short magazine Lee-Enfield rifles and with a machine gun for each company. There were also in charge of the regiment three ·303 Colt automatic guns and a number of obsolete muzzle-loading 7-pounder guns distributed to various posts. Each of the infantry and pioneer companies was about 160 rifles strong; and the total establishment of the regiment was 38 British officers, 11 British warrant or non-commissioned officers, and 1,584 native ranks, including 124 carriers for guns and machine guns. There were also about 330 reservists. Raised in 1865 for service in Lagos and composed of 300 Hausas, it was transferred in 1873 for service in the Ashanti war to the Gold Coast, where it was reorganised and increased in strength by Captain Glover, R.N., and Mr. Goldsworthy. In 1879 it was

The Gold Coast Regiment, W.A.F.F.

constituted as the Gold Coast Constabulary, receiving its present title in 1901, when it was formed in two battalions. The Gold Coast Regiment had an excellent record, and its personnel had shown themselves to be possessed of fine fighting qualities in several local military expeditions. In 1914 the ranks of its single remaining battalion were filled with Hausas, Fulanis, Yorubas, and men from the Northern Territories. In peace time it was administered by the local Government, subject to the control of the Secretary of State for the Colonies, whose military adviser was the Inspector-General of the West African Frontier Force. When on active service it came under the Army Act, and, like all other units of the West African Frontier Force, was liable to serve beyond the territory to which it belonged.

The Northern Territories Constabulary. There was also a semi-military native permanent force termed the Northern Territories Constabulary, which had been formed in 1907 from a nucleus of the then disbanded second battalion of the Gold Coast Regiment. In 1914 it had an establishment of 2 British officers and 321 native ranks, recruited in the Northern Territories, who were armed with Martini-Enfield carbines, a 7-pounder gun, and three machine guns.

Volunteer Corps. The four Volunteer Corps (the Gold Coast Volunteers, the Gold Coast Railway Volunteers, the Gold Coast Mines Volunteers, and the Ashanti Mines Volunteers) had between them a total strength of about 900, and were armed with rifles or carbines, four of the 7-pounder guns, and four machine guns. They could be called out on active service in the event of danger of invasion or rebellion, but were not liable to employment outside the Colony and Ashanti.

Police and Preventive Service. There were, further, about 800 civil police and 400 men of the Customs Preventive Service, who had received, as recruits, a semi-military training and who fired an annual musketry course. Most of them were armed with carbines.

Lack of military administrative services. In one important particular the organisation of the local force departed from normal methods. The duties which, in a military force, are carried out by its own administrative services were, in the Gold Coast, and in all the other British colonies and protectorates in West Africa, performed by civilians in addition to their civil duties. For instance, there were no supply officers, as a money allowance took the place of rations in kind to the native rank and file, who made their own private arrangements for obtaining and cooking their food; transport was provided for civilian and soldier alike by

REGIMENTAL SERGEANT-MAJOR ALHAJI GRUNSHI D.C.M., M.M.,
GOLD COAST REGIMENT, R.W.A.F.F.

On the 12th August 1914, near Togblekove he fired the first shot in the Togoland campaign and apparently the first rifle shot fired by any soldier of the British Army in the Great War.

GOLD COAST TROOPS

two civil transport officers and a few clerks; the personnel of the West African Medical Staff were in medical charge of both civilians and soldiers; and arms, ammunition, and military equipment generally were sent out from England direct to corps by the Crown Agents for the Colonies.

This arrangement provided economically and satisfactorily enough for the normal duty of maintaining internal security. But for operations against a foreign enemy it had several drawbacks. It meant rapid improvisation of staffs who, with all possible goodwill, were not always competent to carry out efficiently the engineer, communication, supply, transport, medical, and ordnance work which a force requires in the field. Moreover, as the civilian staffs were not maintained on a scale to allow for such a contingency, their withdrawal from their normal duties put a considerable strain on those who remained, and, at the same time, might afford a great opportunity to agitators and bad characters generally to create internal strife. The disadvantages of the system were well illustrated by our experiences in 1914–16. Sir Hugh Clifford, when he returned from leave at the end of August 1914 to resume the governorship of the Gold Coast, reported that the administration of its civil departments had been completely disorganised by the defence measures. At that time, it may be noted, there were no less than 73 British and 32 African civil officials from the Gold Coast employed with the columns in Togoland. It was fortunate for us—and a striking tribute to the success of the British administration—that we had a contented native population to deal with, whose goodwill and support we were always able to count on, in spite of straitened conditions, economic depression, and hostile rumours.

The defence scheme, which took into account the special local conditions, was based on the assumptions that, so long as the British navy retained the general command of the sea, any oversea attack would probably take the form of a hasty raid, and that the German forces in Togoland would hardly be capable of offensive action. If, however, they did take such action, they would probably in the first instance try to surprise Keta, Ada, and Yeji, so as to secure the navigation of the Volta, isolate the Northern Territories, and allow of a subsequent advance against Accra, Tamale, and Kumasi. To meet these possibilities, our own dispositions were to be made with a view to precluding espionage, protecting Accra and Tamale, guarding our lines of communication, preventing the isolation of the Northern Territories and safeguarding important coast *Gold Coast Defence Scheme.*

towns. They included a line of observation along the coast and the land frontier, and the formation of small columns at Gambaga, Jimle, Salaga, Krachi, and Ada, with a reserve at Kumasi. Projects of attack, only to be undertaken under conditions already mentioned, were also outlined. These contemplated, in the first phase, a combined movement by the columns at Gambaga, Jimle, and Salaga to cause a German evacuation of Northern Togo, followed by a further advance to drive the German forces southward from the Sokode-Bassari district, and by an attack, if opportunity offered, on Lome by the Ada Column, reinforced by at least 300 men from a neighbouring British colony, and combined with an oversea attack. The Defence Scheme had, however, not been revised since March 1913, when the German wireless station at Kamina was still only in course of construction. Its completion in June 1914 naturally altered the situation.

The scheme laid down the main action to be taken, and in some cases the detailed orders to be issued, by the civil and military authorities, at the precautionary stage and on declaration of war respectively. In case of war the Officer Commanding the Gold Coast Regiment became automatically the Officer Commanding the Field Force, while the officers appointed to command at the different coast towns remained directly under the orders of the Governor.

Generally speaking, at the precautionary stage, which was adopted on receipt of a telegram by the Governor from the Colonial Office, action was taken:—to obtain information regarding enemy dispositions and intentions; for the Constabulary and the Preventive Service to watch the coast and patrol the frontier as well as the navigable part of the Volta river; to mobilise reservists and to increase as far as possible the numbers of the Volunteers; to replace certain military guards by constabulary or police; and to make all necessary preparations for the concentration, on declaration of war, of the troops at their war stations. In nearly all this action civil officials were directly concerned, and a brief outline of the duties allotted to some of them at the precautionary stage is specially relevant. The Principal Medical Officer had to make medical arrangements, including the allotment of personnel, for the columns in the field and the different garrisons; the Transport Officer, assuming the post of Supply and Transport Officer on the staff of the Officer Commanding the Field Force, had to buy up large quantities of food locally, arrange for further periodical supplies, and make preliminary arrangements for the large number of carriers that would be required;* individuals had to be detailed as political officers to accompany each column; the Comptroller of Customs had to arrange for men to watch the coast and the frontier; the Postmaster-General had, in addition to other duties connected with the war, to make preparations to carry out the telegraph and telephone work the soldiers might require; and the Secretary for Native Affairs had to prepare letters, to be sent to the head chiefs of the tribes on the frontier on the declaration of war, notifying them of its causes and existence and directing them not to assist the enemy or give him information, and to communicate immediately to the nearest British official any information regarding the enemy which they might themselves receive or be able to obtain. The only actual military movements to be made at this stage, if Germany was the probable enemy, were:—one company Gold Coast Regiment with a 2·95" gun and ten pioneers from Kumasi by rail and sea to Accra, so as to be ready with the company already there to form the Ada Column; a half-company from Kumasi to reinforce Sekondi; and a detachment by forced marches to watch the frontier at Krachi.

On the 3rd August General Dobell in London drew up a brief appreciation dealing with the employment of the West African Frontier Force in the event of war. The only objectives which seemed to him worthy of attack were Lome and Kamina in Togoland and Duala, Buea and Victoria in the Cameroons. In Togoland the total German force was estimated as being 500–800 strong, ill-armed, and not too well trained. It had just been reported from the Gold Coast that the European reservists had been withdrawn from Lome and had embarked in a steamer to return to Germany,† and also that the Togoland constabulary were abandoning the frontier posts and were concentrating at Kamina and Anekho. The latter concentration seemed to General Dobell to point at anxiety regarding a French attack from Dahomey, though it was just possible that a German evacuation of Togoland and a withdrawal to Duala in the Cameroons was contemplated.

Lome, situated within two miles of the Anglo-German frontier, could, continued General Dobell, be approached by the coast road from Ada via Keta. For the greater part of

General Dobell's appreciation; 3rd August 1914.

---

* It was estimated in the Defence Scheme that a total of 33 " captains," 138 headmen and 3,292 carriers would be required for a defensive rôle only.

† Another report said that this and other German steamers in the vicinity had been ordered to remain at Duala in the Cameroons.

its length, however, this road was practically a causeway between the sea and the Keta lagoon, a serious obstacle at that time of the year; and since the roadless nature of the country rendered impracticable an advance through the area to the north of the lagoon, it might be difficult, without naval co-operation, to overcome the hostile resistance on this very narrow frontage which an enemy force could offer. All things considered, however, it appeared to General Dobell that an advance on Lome from Ada held out a reasonable prospect of success.

Alluding to the project for an attack on Lome outlined in the Defence Scheme, he then proceeded to suggest an alteration in the dispositions which it laid down. He considered that in the circumstances it would be permissible to cancel the proposed despatch of troops from Kumasi to Jimle, Salaga, and Krachi, and, instead, to send two companies of infantry, two 2·95" mountain guns and two machine guns from Kumasi to Ada. With the force already detailed by the Scheme for Ada, this would give a total there of four companies of infantry (640 rifles), three 2·95" guns, and four machine guns. French co-operation from Dahomey would probably be forthcoming if desired, and, even if the British navy were unable to assist, General Dobell came to the conclusion that the project offered sufficient hopes of success to warrant its being undertaken.

On the same day (3rd August) General Dobell discussed the conclusions he had arrived at with the General Staff at the War Office and with the Secretary of the Oversea Defence Committee, with the result that it was decided to include in the " War " telegram—when and if it was despatched—instructions to the Governor of the Gold Coast that those units of the Gold Coast Regiment detailed in the Defence Scheme to move to Jimle, Salaga, and Krachi should instead be held in readiness at Kumasi.

Offensive Sub-Committee; 5th August 1914. At its meeting on the 5th August the Offensive Sub-Committee recommended that, if the local military and naval situation permitted, the British forces in the Gold Coast, reinforced if possible from Sierra Leone, should be used for offensive purposes against Togoland with a view to destroying the wireless telegraph stations in that colony. If H.M. Government approved of the proposed operations, the details would require further consideration.*

---

* General Dobell's views and the Committee's recommendations regarding the Cameroons will be dealt with in the next chapter.

ACTION TAKEN IN THE GOLD COAST

It is necessary now to turn for a time to the action that had been taken in the Gold Coast, where Mr. W. C. F. Robertson was acting Governor in place of Sir Hugh Clifford, at home on leave, and Captain F. C. Bryant, R.A., was acting Commandant of the Gold Coast Regiment, in place of Lieutenant-Colonel R. A. de B. Rose, also at home on leave. The telegram from the Colonial Office saying " Adopt precautionary stage defence scheme ; powers not yet designated," was received at Accra at 11 p.m. on the 29th July by Mr. Robertson, who despatched the consequent telegrams to Captain Bryant at Kumasi and to others concerned as soon as the telegraph offices opened on the morning of the 30th. That day, a meeting was held at Accra of the Executive Council to discuss the action necessary, and all the preliminary measures there and at out-stations were taken without delay " in so far as this was possible," says Mr. Robertson in his despatch of the 12th August 1914, " with the reticence which the situation demanded." On the 1st August, as local supplies of provisions and petrol seemed likely to be restricted, Mr. Robertson appointed a civil committee to go into the question, the arrangements they recommended for taking over necessary stores and for controlling their sale being approved three days later by the Executive Council.

By the 31st July the mobilisation of the Gold Coast Regiment and its reservists had been completed, and Captain Bryant had come to certain decisions regarding the further military action to be taken, having regard to the existing circumstances and the latest intelligence of German movements and intentions. Good and accurate information regarding the German wireless station at Kamina had recently been acquired by the Intelligence Staff at Kumasi, and Captain Bryant was thoroughly alive to the importance of as rapid action as possible to capture or destroy it. Since the European officials, from the acting Governor downwards, and many prominent business men also appreciated fully the urgency of such action, he found himself exceptionally well situated in the matter of the support and assistance he would require. As already remarked, an offensive, with Kamina as its main objective, had not yet been legislated for in the Defence Scheme, and its dispositions were consequently obsolete. But Captain Bryant, coming to much the same conclusion as General Dobell in London was to arrive at two or three days later, decided that the concentration of columns at Jimle and Salaga was unsuitable ; and he proceeded to arrange for a small column at Krachi, a column of two companies at Ada, and his main force at Kumasi, held ready to move to either of these two points as circumstances might dictate.

On the 30th or 31st July he accordingly ordered the following movements :—

> Half " A " Company from Kumasi to Krachi by forced marches,
> Half " A " Company from Obo to Kumasi,
> " B " Company from Zouaragou to Gambaga,
> " C " Company and one 2·95″ gun from Kumasi to Ada via Sekondi and Accra,
> Half " D " Company from Sunyani to Kumasi,
> " F " Company (returning on relief from Zouaragou to Kumasi) to halt temporarily at Salaga,
> " G " Company from Cape Coast and Accra to Ada, and
> " I " Company from Kintampo to Kumasi.

For the concentration of the column at Ada the s.s. *Obuassi* was sent by the civil authorities on the 2nd August to Sekondi. Having embarked here " C " Company and the gun from Kumasi, this steamer, picking up " G " Company at Cape Coast and Accra, proceeded to Ada, where the whole column disembarked on the 5th August. In the meantime, late on the 2nd August, orders from London to establish censorship had been received at Accra and immediately given effect to ; by the 3rd all the necessary proclamations, orders of H.M. The King in Council, etc., had been set up in type ready for issue ; and by the 4th, from a much larger number of applicants, as many Europeans as could be armed and equipped had been enrolled in the existing Volunteer Corps.

On the morning of the 5th August came the telegram from the Colonial Office announcing the declaration of war, some hours after the news had been learnt by the interception of a German message from Berlin to Kamina.* Meetings of the Executive and Legislative Councils on the 5th made the further necessary arrangements,† while a reference to Captain

---

* Intercepted by a small wireless receiving set installed at Accra by the Postmaster-General. From the 30th July to the 25th August a continuous and close watch was kept here to catch interceptions by Messrs. L. C. C. Miles and E. Edginton, the only two British officials available for the duty. The twelve hours' daily duty which this meant for each of them imposed an intense strain, aggravated by the trying climate and endured by a devotion that deserves our admiration.

† Among the proclamations issued was one which endeavoured to secure the German missionaries from rough treatment by drawing attention to the past services in the Colony of the Basel Mission.

Bryant showed that the modifications in the Defence Scheme now ordered from London were practically those which he had already carried out. Then, on the same day, Mr. Robertson informed the Colonial Office by telegram that, in addition to two companies and a section of 2·95" guns already available at Kumasi, a further two companies would arrive there by the 14th. These with the column at Ada would give a total of six companies and three guns available for service outside the Colony by the 15th. Thus, thanks to the promptitude of Mr. Robertson, the initiative of Captain Bryant, and the active and ready support they received on every side, all the arrangements for war were by the evening of the 5th exceptionally well advanced.

Captain Bryant recommended that martial law should be proclaimed in the Gold Coast. But Mr. Robertson considered that this would have unpleasant results, and would be likely to be misunderstood by the native population; and as the Executive Council agreed with him, he decided against such action. Events justified his decision completely, as the attitude of the population proved it to be unnecessary. In fact, their spontaneous expressions of loyalty and offers of active assistance were numerous and so enthusiastic as to be at times embarrassing. Captain Bryant further suggested that native levies should be raised. But Mr. Robertson, considering that to do so might bring about inter-tribal collisions, declined to sanction the proposal in the absence of any news that the Germans were raising such levies.* Several of the chiefs were ready and anxious to assist in this way, the action of the Fia of the Awuna people in the Keta district being a typical example. In addition to sending out spies to obtain information of the German dispositions and having men ready to enter Togoland to cut the German telegraph lines, he offered to deliver a night attack on Lome with his men, of whom he had 12,000, and more if necessary, ready to give us armed assistance.

On the 5th August Mr. Robertson received the following telegram from Major von Doering, the acting Governor of Togoland. " As I understand from home, war has broken out between Great Britain and the German Empire. Having

---

* There was a long record of comparatively recent warfare between Ashantis and other races and of inter-tribal strife among these other races. There consequently still existed a latent feeling of inter-tribal hostility and jealousy, which any attempt to raise levies was calculated to revive, making the danger of collisions almost inevitable.

regard to insecurity of native tribes it is in interests of Togoland and Gold Coast to omit warlike enterprises likely to have no bearing on decision arrived at in Europe. Propose further remain neutral. Should be glad to receive an early reply."
Mr. Robertson at once replied that he could not answer without instructions from London, which he had asked for. With reference to this German request, it is noteworthy that many people in England seem to have gathered the impression from Articles X and XI of the Berlin Act of 1885 (which provided that the protectorates of East Africa and Zanzibar might be placed under the rule of neutrality during a war) that the African dependencies would be declared neutral during a European war. So far as Great Britain, however, was concerned, discussion by the Colonial Defence Committee in the past had always resulted in a conclusion that such action would not be desirable. In this instance, the attitude of the German Government, who ordered Major von Doering to make the proposal, was clearly due to their desire to gain security for the Kamina wireless station.

Mr. Robertson's telegram requesting instructions on the German proposal was received in London between 5 and 6 p.m. on the 5th, at about the time that General Dobell was drawing up his project for an attack on Kamina, and some hours before receipt of the telegram saying that six companies of the Gold Coast Regiment would be available by the 15th.

Dobell's appreciation of 5th August 1914. General Dobell based his project on the force which he then estimated as available, i.e., 640 infantry (four companies), three 2·95" guns and four machine guns of the Gold Coast Regiment, and 315 infantry (two companies) and two machine guns of the Sierra Leone Battalion. The Sierra Leone detachment, he remarked, could only be moved by sea from Freetown under a naval escort, which might subsequently assist in the attack on Lome.

According to the latest information, he continued, the total German force consisted of about 150 Europeans trained to arms and some 1,000 indifferently armed native soldiers and police, of whom about half were said to be well trained. It was not known if they possessed any artillery.

He considered that the difficulties of intercommunication in a strange country and of supplies would render hazardous, if not impossible, any attempt to attack Kamina by columns converging on it from the west. Consequently Lome should be the first objective; and for the advance on this place he estimated that the concentration at Ada of troops from Kumasi and Freetown would take six or seven days. From Ada, he continued, a portion of the force should move in boats along the Keta lagoon so as to outflank any hostile force encountered.

Supplies were said to be short at Accra, and food would have to be carried for the Sierra Leone troops who were rice-eaters, so that supply difficulties would probably be encountered.

After the capture of Lome, the force would possibly be able to utilise the railway to some extent in the advance on Kamina. But before this could be undertaken it might be necessary to attack the German force reported near Anekho, and also to form an advanced base of supply at Lome.

The provision of the necessary carriers would probably present difficulties, and on the assumption that two companies of infantry and one gun would be required to garrison Lome, General Dobell estimated that at least 1,000 carriers would be required.

On the 6th August, the Cabinet in London decided that the Togoland proposal of neutrality could not be entertained,* and, having approved of the project against Kamina, the Offensive Sub-Committee agreed that the War Office should work out in detail, in consultation with General Dobell, a scheme for the proposed operations, including details of the composition of the force and the sea transport required. As these operations would have to depend on the naval situation, the Admiralty should be informed as soon as possible of the date when the force would be ready to start. As it turned out, however, little further action in London was required.

Operations against Togoland; 6th August.

At 6.40 p.m. a telegram was received at the Colonial Office from Mr. Robertson, saying that information had been received that the Germans had mounted three guns at Lome and had mined the landing stage and the principal buildings there; † and at 8.25 p.m. a further telegram arrived, in which Mr. Robertson said that he had learnt by accident that, without informing him, Captain Bryant had instructed the Officer Commanding at Ada to proceed under a flag of truce to Lome to demand the surrender of Togoland. Mr. Robertson asked whether Captain Bryant was to be given a free hand in forward movements. To this a reply was sent at 10.45 p.m. that pending further instructions a forward movement could not be sanctioned.

---

* The telegram acquainting Mr. Robertson with this decision was sent off at 3.40 p.m. on the 6th.
† This information proved to be incorrect.

It appears that Captain Bryant, who had learnt that the French authorities in Dahomey and to the north were anxious and ready to co-operate with us in an offensive into Togoland, decided to clear up the situation by ascertaining the German attitude. He accordingly sent telegraphic orders at 9 a.m. on the 6th to Captain Barker, commanding at Ada, to proceed personally to Lome under a flag of truce and present a demand for surrender to the Governor of Togoland. Captain Barker was to point out that, as we had three strong British columns ready to cross the German western frontier, the French had three columns ready to cross their eastern and northern frontiers, and two important Togoland chiefs were ready to rise and assist us, resistance by the Germans was useless. The German Governor was to be given twenty-four hours within which to reply.

By constant observation the British Preventive Service had by this time learnt that the Germans were concentrating at Lome the men from their frontier posts and patrols, that they were mobilising reservists, impressing prisoners into the ranks, and calling on chiefs for levies. On the 5th August hundreds of refugees crossed the frontier from the Lome district, and, though temporarily stopped by the Germans closing the frontier during the night of the 5th/6th, continued for the next two or three days to come over in great numbers.

Mr. H. S. Newlands, District Commissioner of Keta, who had been appointed Political Officer to the Ada column, and who spoke German fluently, was to accompany Captain Barker to demand the German surrender. Meeting one another between Ada and Keta, the two officers, travelling partly by bicycle and partly by Ford lorry, reached Lome at 6 p.m. on the 6th. As they approached, a mounted patrol of Germans met them and conducted them to the Governor's quarters, where Major von Doering soon appeared, accompanied by Captain Pfaeler, the police * commandant, and Mr. Clausnitzer, the District Commissioner. After hearing Captain Barker read out the British ultimatum, and after the three Germans had retired into another room to confer, a discussion ensued. It having been agreed that the Germans were to be given twenty-four hours for consideration, during which time neither side was to move troops towards the frontier in an

---

* After their surrender the Germans laid stress on the fact that they had only police in Togoland and no soldiers. As, however, the training, arms, and equipment of the police varied little, if at all, from that of native troops in other German colonies, the difference was one mainly of nomenclature.

area south of an east and west line through Akuse, Captain Barker and Mr. Newlands took their departure. But they were almost immediately recalled and asked to confirm this definition of the area within which troops were not to be moved. This was done, and when they left again, at 7 p.m., Captain Barker said that he would return for the German reply at the same hour next day. Neither Captain Barker nor Mr. Newlands had understood why this request for confirmation had been made, but Major von Doering explained it three weeks later to Mr. Newlands. He had been staggered by the discovery, as soon as the two British officers had left the first time, that the line through Akuse ran *south* of Togoland. Having, however, received reports that the British had concentrated 1,000 men opposite Noepe, and that there was a British cruiser off Accra, he jumped to the conclusion that he was being given a hint to evacuate Lome to save it from bombardment. In reality Captain Barker, without a map and knowing that Akuse was sixty miles up the Volta, had defined the area on the spur of the moment, and neither he nor Mr. Newlands realised the mistake. They both arrived back at Keta at 9 p.m., where they remained till next evening.

In describing the journey, Mr. Newlands says that the sight presented that day by the streams of natives along the Lome-Keta road was unforgettable. Thousands of men, women, and children, all carrying their household goods, were fleeing from the probable scene of fighting which would, they were convinced, put an end to German rule.

On the morning of the 7th August there was intercepted at Accra a wireless message in clear German* to Berlin to the effect that the Governor of Togoland was leaving Lome next day with the troops to defend Kamina, and that the District Commissioner of Lome would surrender that place if the enemy pressed. In telegraphing this information to the Colonial Office, where it was received early in the same afternoon, Mr. Robertson said that he gathered that Captain Bryant contemplated action. A few hours later the Colonial Office replied that two companies and two guns were to move from Kumasi to Ada by the quickest land route, and that if Lome surrendered it was to be occupied at once and a base established there for a subsequent advance on Kamina. If Lome did not surrender, Captain Bryant was to use his

7th August.

---

* The probable reason why it was not sent in cipher is that Major von Doering wished us to know that he was taking the hint which he imagined we had given him.

discretion as to awaiting reinforcements from Kumasi before moving forward, but he was not to advance on Kamina without further reference to London.

From Keta, on the morning of the 7th, Captain Barker sent orders to his troops at Ada to cross the Volta at 7 p.m. and march on Lome. By midday Mr. Newlands had received confirmation of the German evacuation of Lome, and also information that their troops were concentrating on Kamina. Learning this, Captain Bryant telegraphed to Mr. Robertson that the news regarding the evacuation of Lome had been confirmed, and he protested strongly against the restriction on a forward movement imposed by the Colonial Office telegram of the 6th. He said that if operations were to be controlled from London, it would be impossible for him to carry out what he considered essential, and he consequently claimed freedom of action. He was of opinion that if Captain Barker received an unsatisfactory reply at Lome, its immediate occupation and an advance on Kamina by a strong column were imperative.

Captain Barker and Mr. Newlands, in the Ford lorry driven by a Krooboy and accompanied only by Mr. Newlands' police orderly, returned to Lome at 7 p.m., and were met by Mr. Clausnitzer. Major von Doering had left with the troops, but had delegated full powers to Mr. Clausnitzer to surrender Lome and the coast-line to Anekho with territory extending for 120 kilometres inland (i.e., as far as Khra village). The Germans, said Mr. Clausnitzer, being outnumbered, desired to save from a bombardment the open and unfortified town of Lome, to which they intended to return in six months' time. But they would resist the Allies if they attempted to penetrate inland. About a hundred Germans remained at Lome, consisting according to him only of missionaries and others not liable for military service, women, and children. The telegraph cable at Lome had been cut, and the telegraph instruments there destroyed by the Germans before their evacuation.

Captain Barker's telegram reporting the above reached Mr. Robertson about midnight on the 7th/8th, when he also received the Colonial Office instructions for the occupation of Lome.

8th August. At an early hour on the 8th * Mr. Robertson telegraphed to the Colonial Office that, having heard from the Governor of Dahomey that the French, whose troops had on the 7th

---

* The telegram was received in London at about 8 a.m.

FRENCH INVADE TOGOLAND

occupied points near Anekho and on the river Mono, proposed co-operation with us to occupy Lome and South Togoland, he had instructed Captain Bryant to place himself in communication with the Governor of Dahomey.

French accounts show that on the 4th August the Governor of Dahomey had also received a proposal of neutrality from Major von Doering, but, treating the message as merely an official notification of a state of war, had forwarded it to the French Governor-General at Dakar without vouchsafing a reply, and had at once taken action to restrain Germans residing in Dahomey and to start the invasion of Togoland. As the attitude of Great Britain was then still uncertain, co-operation from the Gold Coast could not be counted on; and preparations were made to carry out the prearranged plan of seizing the Togoland coast and Lome so as to deprive the Germans of support from the sea. This plan, it is said, had been drawn up in ignorance of the existence of the German wireless station at Kamina, which, being only sixty kilometres from the French frontier, would otherwise have been made the objective of a sudden advance. On the 3rd August the Germans had been reported by the French Intelligence as having concentrated a party of Preventive guards opposite Agoué, but by the next day these men were said to have dispersed again to their ordinary posts. On the 5th the French heard that a German military detachment had arrived at Anekho and had destroyed two important bridges there, and that there was a noticeable movement of German troops towards Lome. Information was also received that there was little enthusiasm among the German native troops. On the 6th it was reported that all the roads leading westward from the Mono were held by German detachments of a sufficient strength to delay a French advance, and that behind these detachments there was a general troop movement towards Atakpame. This change in the German dispositions was evidently due to British entry into the war.

On the evening of the 6th August French police occupied the German Customs posts near Athieme, and on the 7th Major Maroix, commanding the troops in Dahomey, ordered the capture of the frontier post at Agbanake, which was probably strongly held, and the occupation of Anekho, which the Germans were said to have evacuated. Agbanake was occupied at 7 p.m. on the 7th, and a detachment under Captain Marchand entered Anekho at 4 a.m. on the 8th, in both cases without opposition. The French were welcomed by the local

French action.

natives, who, on the previous evening, had shown their feelings by setting fire to the German Government House at Sebe. A French railway detachment started to repair the Anekho-Lome railway, and the French advance, still unopposed, continued, Porto Seguro being occupied at noon on the 8th and Togo at 5 p.m., while the advanced guard pushed on further towards Lome. This advance was stopped, however, when it was learnt that Lome had been surrendered to the British. During the next two or three days the French force consolidated its position by the occupation of important posts on the Mono river up to Tokpli and to the northward of Anekho.

8th August. To Mr. Robertson's telegram of the 8th August regarding French co-operation the Colonial Office at once replied, directing him to ascertain if they would also co-operate in an attack on Kamina and with what strength. If they agreed, the Colonial Office wished to know whether Captain Bryant considered that, after the arrival of the reinforcements from Kumasi, he would be able to undertake offensive action with the British and French troops without waiting for further reinforcements from another colony. At 11.20 p.m. the same day the Colonial Office received an answer from Mr. Robertson saying that the French agreed to co-operate. They had 250 rifles and a railway section about Anekho and the Mono, another 250 rifles and a section of artillery at Savalou and other posts in Dahomey, and they were arranging for reservists to garrison posts in Togoland. Captain Bryant, added Mr. Robertson, was of opinion that he could undertake the offensive without waiting for outside reinforcements.

In the meantime, a proposal by Captain Bryant to move the Kumasi reinforcements from Sekondi to Keta by sea, so as to save the fortnight it would take them to march, had been approved by the authorities in London, subject to local information indicating no undue risk. Thereupon Mr. Robertson arranged for the s.s. *Elele* to proceed from Accra to Sekondi to carry them.

8th-9th August. Lome. Captain Barker and Mr. Newlands spent the night of the 7th/8th August in a German bungalow at Lome. Early on the 8th a Gold Coast telegraph operator arrived there by bicycle from Keta, with an instrument on his back, and with the aid of German native linesmen succeeded, despite the chaos of wrecked instruments in the post office, in opening communication with Keta and Accra. The services of a small party of fourteen Gold Coast soldiers and police, who happened to be at the frontier post of Aflao, were requisitioned that morning by Mr. Newlands to assist in confirming the British occupation. The Union Jack was hoisted on the Secretariat; all Germans remaining in the town were ordered to hand over their arms; proclamations declaring martial law, etc., were printed and posted up; and the services of some friendly natives were procured to patrol the outskirts of the town. The unsupported situation of the two British officers was, however, precarious, and Captain Barker sent urgent telegrams to Keta to accelerate the arrival of his troops. But, in addition to crossing the four miles or so of the Volta river, these men had to cover fifty-one miles on foot; and by the evening none had arrived. A few men of the Gold Coast Preventive Service were then sent from Aflao to Lome, and some more friendly natives were procured to patrol outside the quarters of the British officers, who passed an anxious night, feeling that they might have to beat a retreat at any moment.

At 9 a.m. on the 9th the leading detachment, about thirty rifles strong, of the column from Ada reached Lome, and was followed by the remainder, in successive parties, during the next twenty-four hours.* Their rapid march of over fifty miles in fifty hours had, however, exhausted them greatly, and it was some time before Captain Barker was able to take adequate steps to occupy and secure the town and its vicinity. Fortunately the attitude of the Germans there was courteous and even cordial.

Lome town, with a normal population of about 200 Europeans and 8,000 natives, was well laid out, with a hospital, many Government buildings, and Government railway and other workshops. Dr. Le Fanu, who arrived with the Ada column, took over the hospital, which, with accommodation for 21 Europeans and 60 natives, was well equipped; and he also retained the services on payment of its German nurses and native establishment. The sanitary arrangements, however, had been neglected since the German departure, and the sudden influx of the British detachment with its large number of carriers and other native followers aggravated the bad conditions that had already set in.

During the day a party of civilians, sent off by Mr. Robertson by sea from Accra the previous day, also arrived. Among

---

* The passage of the Volta had been facilitated by the ready and energetic assistance of Captain Fellowes, the Manager of the Volta River Transport Company, and for the march the Awunas assisted greatly by the provision of carriers and of food and water for the troops.

them were Major J. J. F. O'Shaughnessy, telegraph engineer, with half a dozen European and native telegraph operators with telegraph material, Dr. O'Hara May, and a railway engineer with a small party of workmen.

Major O'Shaughnessy at once, in accordance with instructions he had received, picked up, cut, and sealed the German cable between Monrovia and Duala; within twelve hours he had the railway and cranes on the pier working ready for disembarkation work; and he had also started work in the railway and other workshops. Dr. O'Hara May also took prompt and energetic measures to restore and expand the sanitary measures necessary to cope with the abnormal strain of increased numbers.

9th August. At 11 a.m. on the 9th August the Colonial Office telegraphed to Mr. Robertson that he was to instruct Captain Bryant to move, in co-operation with the French commander, against Kamina with the object of capturing the wireless station. Captain Bryant would be in chief command of the Allied force with a temporary higher rank. The same morning Mr. Robertson received a telegram from the Governor of Dahomey saying that a French detachment repairing the railway at Porto Seguro was in touch with Captain Barker, and inquiring whether the French force available—8 French officers, 20 French non-commissioned officers, and 450 Senegalese with two mountain guns—would be sufficient. To this, after consulting Captain Bryant, Mr. Robertson replied in the affirmative, and gave the French Governor particulars of the strength and disposition of the Gold Coast forces. Mr. Robertson also said that he was in communication with the Governor-General of French West Africa in regard to combined operations in North Togoland by British forces from the Northern Territories Protectorate and by French forces from Upper Senegal and Niger.

On receiving sanction for the movement of the Kumasi detachment by sea, Captain Bryant had started to make the necessary arrangements, and with these he made such good progress that his headquarters (Captain C. G. Hornby, adjutant of the regiment, as staff officer, and Lieutenant J. V. Earle, Intelligence Officer), two companies (" I " and " Pioneers "), a section 2·95" guns and 800 carriers, with his civilian medical, supply, and transport staffs, had all embarked 10th August. at Sekondi in the *Elele* by 4 p.m. on the 10th, twenty-four hours earlier than he had anticipated. The excellent work carried out at Sekondi since the 30th July by Mr. R. E. P.

BRITISH OCCUPY KETE KRACHI

Gibson, the acting Chief Transport Officer of the Colony, had facilitated this rapid movement and embarkation.

Receiving the Colonial Office instructions to move against Kamina before he left Kumasi, Captain Bryant had issued orders for the concentration of three companies at Krachi under command of Captain P. E. L. Elgee for an advance towards Kamina by land, preparations for which, in anticipation of such instructions, he had already made.

Kete Krachi had already been occupied by a British detachment. Captain O. H. Warne, an Assistant District Commissioner, while touring his district, had received news from the District Commissioner of Yeji of the possibility of war; and, after making arrangements to facilitate the movement of troops to British Krachi, had started to go there himself by forced marches. On the 4th August, when about ninety miles short of Krachi, he met half "A" Company Gold Coast Regiment (30 rifles) under a British colour-sergeant on their way there, and, pushing on ahead with five of this detachment, he reached British Krachi on the evening of the 7th. At the customs post here there was a small detachment of Preventive men and police, and he learnt that at Kete Krachi there were three Germans and about forty of their native troops. He decided that the situation justified him in stopping all traffic across the ferry, and he posted sentries and took other steps to this end. Early next morning news of the declaration of war reached him from Yeji, and he at once crossed the river with a white flag to demand the surrender of the German post, to find, however, that the enemy troops had retired during the night, abandoning much ammunition and many stores. He at once took possession of the German post, where he was shortly joined by the rest of "A" half-company; and, after sending back word of what had occurred to the Chief Commissioner of Ashanti and to Captain Bryant, he employed himself till Captain Elgee's arrival on the 16th in patrolling the vicinity and gathering information.

Occupation of Kete Krachi.

The *Elele* sailed after dark on the 10th August with lights out from Sekondi to Accra, where she remained during the 11th, and where Captain Bryant landed and discussed arrangements with Mr. Robertson. While they were together, telegrams arrived from the French Governors of the Ivory Coast and Dahomey, with the information that 500 " auxiliary cavalry " with 50 to 60 *gardes cercles* were due to reach Sansane Mangu between the 13th and 15th from Upper Senegal and Niger. This force would guard the district against attack,

11th August.

and a company of *tirailleurs*, about 180 strong, was being sent in support and to prepare for a forward movement in co-operation with the British.

At Accra a contingent of civilians joined Captain Bryant—medical officers, railway officials and personnel, fifty police under a Deputy Commissioner,* members of the Public Works Department, and also several volunteers for work in various capacities. The organisation of the base at Lome and of the onward communications could only be made possible by such means, and Mr. Robertson's readiness to assist was carried to the utmost limits. For instance, on learning that Captain Bryant desired Major O'Shaughnessy to accompany the troops in their advance, he at once lent the services of Mr. S. B. Gosling, the Postmaster-General, to organise telegraphic and telephonic communication at the base. Here, as Captain Bryant reported in his final despatch, his work contributed very largely to the success of the expedition.

12th August. Leaving Accra after dark on the 11th in a dense fog, the *Elele* reached Lome early next morning. Disembarkation commenced at 8 a.m., and thanks to the previous arrangements made by Major O'Shaughnessy and the disembarkation work of Captains R. Minto and Yardley,† all the personnel were ashore by 10 a.m. and all stores by 4 p.m. During the day arrangements with the French were agreed upon for a converging and co-ordinated advance against the enemy in the Atakpame-Kamina area by Colonel Bryant's column reinforced by the French force from Anekho, by a French column under Major Maroix advancing via Cheti, and by Captain Elgee's column from Krachi. The Allied forces in Northern Togoland, acting under orders from Major Maroix, would also move southward.

The total British strength at Lome was now as follows :—

Gold Coast Regiment : British officers, 16 } with three 2·95″ mountain guns and 4 machine guns.
British N.C.Os., 7
Native ranks, 535

Attached to the force : British civil officials or volunteers 34
Native police 50
Native carriers and labourers.. 2,000

---

* Mrs. Bettington, the wife of this Deputy Commissioner, volunteering for nursing duties, also went to Lome a day or two afterwards.

† Captain Minto was Messrs. Elder Dempster & Co.'s agent at Sekondi who had accompanied Captain Bryant, and Captain Yardley commanded the *Elele*.

During the 12th and 13th August Captain Bryant, who was given the temporary rank of Lieutenant-Colonel, was occupied in organising and preparing for an advance and in gaining information of the country and the enemy's intentions and dispositions. Among the staff appointments made the following may be mentioned: Mr. H. S. Newlands as Political Officer; Major S. B. Gosling as Director of Army Signals and Railways, with Major O'Shaughnessy as his Deputy; Dr. W. W. Claridge as Senior Medical Officer; Captain E. C. Spencer as Supply and Transport Officer; and Captain D. R. A. Bettington as Base Commandant. In gaining information and in enabling Mr. Newlands to get into touch with the local chiefs, the Fia of the Awunas was of material assistance.

12th–13th August at Lome.

On landing at Lome, Colonel Bryant learnt that on the 11th the railway bridge and small wireless station at Togblekove, about ten miles to the north, had been destroyed by an enemy party who had come south by train. To prevent further damage, he at once detached a half-company of infantry, reinforcing it on the 13th with a further company and a half.

The advance on Kamina commenced on the morning of the 14th August, "I" Company of the Gold Coast Regiment under Captain H. B. Potter forming the advanced guard and pushing forward from Togblekove. The main body moved in two columns along the road and railway respectively. The road, however, allowed to fall into disrepair since the construction of the railway, was no longer passable for wheeled traffic, and attempts by Colonel Bryant's force to use motor lorries * along it had to be abandoned, though subsequently it was found possible to use light motor-vans obtained from the Gold Coast. Road and railway ran parallel to one another, in some places close together, but in others separated by a considerable distance, the intervening country being swampy and covered with dense high grass or thick scrub. As intercommunication between the two columns was, therefore, generally difficult and frequently impossible, mutual co-operation was much hampered.

14th August. The advance from Lome.

---

* These lorries had been hastily collected along the coast by the prize steamer *Marina*, manned by a scratch crew from the Gold Coast under a District Commissioner—Mr. Heathcote, who had been a lieutenant-commander in the navy—his only European assistants being two schoolmasters without qualifications for the task. As Commander Heathcote was the only man on board who knew anything of navigation, the steamer had many narrow escapes from disaster.

By the evening "I" Company had reached Tsevie without opposition, advanced patrols under Mr. R. S. Rattray * had reported all country south of Agbeluvoe to be clear of the enemy, and the main body had concentrated at Togblekove. At 10 p.m. "I" Company started to advance by road to Agbeluvoe.

15th August. The main body, leaving a section of infantry at Togblekove, moved forward from there at 6 a.m. on the 15th August. About two and a half hours later, on reaching a point about half a mile south of Dawie, Colonel Bryant learnt from some local natives that a train full of enemy troops had come into Tsevie about 6 a.m. and had opened a heavy fire on the railway station.† On reaching Tsevie, however, Colonel Bryant found that the enemy had, at about 8 a.m., retired in his train moving northward. No communication from "I" Company had been received since the previous night, and Colonel Bryant, being anxious to support it, pushed on at once with all speed.

Affair of Agbeluvoe; 15th–16th August. In the meantime, at about 4 a.m., "I" Company, halted on the road near Ekuni, had heard this train pass on its way south. Captain Potter at once detached Lieutenant H. S. Collins with a section to try to cut it off, while he himself with the remainder of the company pushed on as fast as possible to Agbeluvoe. Reaching the railway by a bush track shown them by a local Hausa, Lieutenant Collins's section piled up a barrier of stones across the line about 200 yards north of the Ekuni bridge, and took up a position of readiness there while Lieutenant Collins and Mr. R. W. Kilby ‡ visited the bridge. These two officers, managing to take up a heavy loose iron plate, laid it across the line, and then Lieutenant Collins brought his section down to take up a concealed position in the bush by the bridge. They had not been there long when a second German train from the north stopped at the barrier of stones, but retired before Lieutenant Collins's men, who at once advanced to the assault, could reach it. Meanwhile, Captain Potter's party, who had heard this train pass, had taken up a position to intercept it. But, though they riddled the engine with bullets till it spouted steam in all directions, the train ran through them at full speed.

Captain Potter, who was soon afterwards rejoined by

---

* Of the Gold Coast Civil Service, attached to the Intelligence Staff.
† It appears that the only British troops in Tsevie at this hour were four men of "I" Company rejoining from escort duty.
‡ Of the Gold Coast Survey, attached Intelligence Staff.

To face p. 29]

Wrecked German Train near Ekuni

IMPORTANT BRITISH SUCCESS

Lieutenant Collins's section, then proceeded by road to Agbeluvoe station, where he took up a defensive position across railway and road (here about eighty yards apart) against attack from both north and south. Both the German trains were still south of Agbeluvoe, and, for the last two hours of their march, the escort to "I" Company carriers, who were some way behind the company, had to defend themselves and their convoy against continuous German attacks, their safe arrival in the afternoon at Agbeluvoe station being largely due to the courage and leadership of their commander, Colour-Sergeant Gethin. At an early hour of the evening the enemy in force attacked the British position from the south, but were beaten off; and further attacks they made during the night met with no better success. Early on the 16th the news of Colonel Bryant's advance caused the enemy to retire hastily on his train, where after some further fighting he surrendered to Captain Potter. This gallant and skilful British defence—for which Colonel Bryant in his despatch attributed the greatest credit to Captain Potter, his officers, and men—had completely foiled the enemy attempts to break through, and contributed considerably to his final downfall.

At about 3 p.m. on the 15th Colonel Bryant's advanced guard on the railway had encountered, near the Lili river, enemy troops who, as the British approached, blew up the bridge and took up a defensive position on a ridge behind it. Here, mainly owing to the thick and difficult nature of the country, they succeeded in delaying the British advance till 4.30 p.m., when they were forced to retire, leaving one European and two native dead behind them. This delay obliged Colonel Bryant to give up his intention of joining "I" Company that evening; and his troops, who had sustained four casualties,* did not reach Ekuni—where they found twenty railway vehicles which had been derailed by the obstruction on the bridge—till 5.30 p.m. Trouble and discomfort were experienced that night by the British force, through a stampede at dusk, caused by the fire of a few enemy stragglers, of the whole of its seven hundred carriers, whose dispersion or alarm was so great that in some cases they did not come into Ekuni till 10 a.m. next day.

At 7 a.m. on the 16th August two German prisoners—one, Baron Codelli von Fahnenfeldt, the designer of the Kamina wireless station, and the other the enemy's explosive expert—

---

* One native killed, one European and two natives wounded.

were brought into Ekuni. None of the messengers sent by Captain Potter had managed to get through, and Colonel Bryant, who was consequently still without news of "I" Company, now started again towards Agbeluvoe. No enemy troops were encountered till about half-way there, and even then the opposition they offered was not great, while the arms and equipment of all sorts they had abandoned along the road indicated their demoralisation. As the British approached Agbeluvoe, sounds of heavy firing were heard till Colonel Bryant's force arrived within a mile of the station, when they found that most of the enemy who had come south in the two trains had surrendered. It was subsequently estimated that the enemy's numbers had been at least 200, and Captain Potter had taken prisoner 16 Europeans, who with others previously captured or killed accounted for 25 of the 30 believed to have been with the force. The material captured included two engines, railway vehicles, a machine gun, many arms, and much ammunition. As Colonel Bryant pointed out in his despatch, the moral effect of this German disaster proved to be very great. One of its most important immediate results was that, thanks to the demoralisation of the flying remnant of the enemy, no attempts were made to destroy the railway for thirty miles north of Agbeluvoe, which thus fell intact into British hands.

The British casualties had totalled 6 native ranks killed, including 4 of the Preventive service, and 35 native ranks wounded, including 30 carriers. From the marked contrast between the wounds suffered by the British force and those inflicted by our own ammunition it was evident that the enemy was making extensive use of soft-nosed bullets, and Colonel Bryant protested formally in writing on the 18th August to Major von Doering. This appeared to have little effect, for the nature of the wounds sustained by our men continued throughout the operations to be so destructive that it was found necessary to send urgently for more medical personnel from the Gold Coast. A subsequent expert examination in England of ammunition taken from the German force showed that that used for their machine guns and by their regular native troops could not be regarded as outside the limitations imposed by the Hague Convention, but that many of their European ranks and their levies had been using ammunition which this Convention forbade.*

---

* For Major von Doering's own explanation, see his letter of 25th August, 1914, to Lt.-Colonel Bryant in Appendix I., p. 430.

DEATH OF GERMAN COMMANDER

From an account of the operations written at Kumasi in September 1914 by a German reservist sergeant-major, then a prisoner of war, it appears that the German force at Agbeluvoe consisted of two native companies under the command of Captain Pfaeler. He says that during the attempt to break through Captain Potter's force at night the native troops would not follow their German leaders and, becoming quite demoralised, fired wildly in all directions, endangering the Germans in front of them. Six Germans were killed, including Captain Pfaeler; and the death of this officer, who was the real German commander, appears to have had a considerable moral and material effect both then and subsequently. As the fleeing remnants of the two companies made no attempt apparently to communicate with Kamina, the first news of this disaster reached there from a German engine-driver, whose train had come under fire from Agbeluvoe.

On the 15th August Colonel Bryant, learning that the Germans were compulsorily enrolling native levies and arming them with Mauser rifles, urged Mr. Robertson to enlist levies among the Ashantis and Awunas in the Gold Coast. But he replied that, if further assistance were required, he preferred to ask for detachments of the W.A.F.F. from Sierra Leone and Lagos. The growing needs of his line of communication also obliged Colonel Bryant to apply to Mr. Robertson for the services of more police to guard the line, of more carriers, and of additional transport, railway, and telegraph officers. But the Gold Coast had already furnished all the assistance it could, and Mr. Robertson replied suggesting that Colonel Bryant should use men of the Preventive Service to guard the line.* Even in the matter of material he was unable to fulfil all Colonel Bryant's requirements. At this stage the Fia of the Awunas, in agreement with the Base Commandant at Lome, whom he was personally assisting, started to raise 2,000 levies from his people to guard the railway line, and both he and they evinced great disappointment when told that their services would not be required. On the 17th August, when the inability of the Gold Coast to comply with Colonel Bryant's requests was learnt, instructions were telegraphed from London to Sierra Leone to send two companies W.A.F.F. to Lome; and when a reply from there showed that it would take a few days to make the necessary shipping

margin note: British reinforcements.

---

* Two detachments of Gold Coast Preventive Service men, one under Mr. A. J. Beckley and the other under Supervisor Thompson, had moved to Lome, and were acting as police guards there and at Togblekove.

arrangements, Nigeria was requested on the 21st to despatch a similar detachment by the quickest route, sending on one company independently at once if available. This company, it may be noted, reached Lome early on the 24th, but, as it happened, neither it nor the two companies from Sierra Leone, which arrived three days later, were required.

Events in Northern Togoland.

In Northern Togoland, British and French detachments of troops, police, and irregulars had occupied Yendi and Sansane Mangu respectively, without opposition, on the 14th August; and further Allied detachments, in communication with one another, were moving to confirm and follow up this success. Nearly half of the 400 German native troops in the area had deserted, and the remainder had rapidly retired, while many, if not most, of the local chiefs were offering allegiance to one or other of the Allies. The occupation of Sansane Mangu had been effected by M. Duranthon, who had advanced by forced marches from Fada Ngurma with a small force of 40 police and about 100 irregulars. He was followed by M. Arboussier with a force from Wagadugu of a few police and about 120 irregulars, and by Captain Bouchez with a detachment of 130 rifles of the 2nd Senegalese Tirailleurs. M. Arboussier, it may be noted, arrived at Sansane Mangu on the 23rd and Captain Bouchez, whose detachment covered over 600 kilometres (372 miles) in twenty days, on the 26th August. A British column of details, 104 strong (including 42 Northern Territories Constabulary), from Gambaga, under Lieutenant C.C. Grattan-Bellew, also joined the French at Sansane Mangu on the 18th. Other French detachments of police and irregulars, of a total strength of about 400, also at this time occupied other points in Northern Togoland. The movements of the French forces, though meeting with little or no opposition, were carried out under most trying climatic conditions through a very difficult and little known country.

In the Northern Territories of the Gold Coast, two detachments of the Constabulary, each 20 strong, under Lieutenant W. F. R. Kyngdon,* had been despatched from Tamale on the 4th and 5th August to Zan on the Eastern frontier. But Captain C. H. Armitage, the Chief Commissioner of the Northern Territories, heard with some dismay on the night of the 10th that the officer commanding a company of the Gold Coast Regiment, ordered by Captain Bryant to move to

---

* This officer, who was an artillery officer employed in the Survey Department, had been detailed as Intelligence Officer to the Jimle Column.

BRITISH OCCUPATION OF YENDI

Krachi, had, through a misunderstanding, ordered Lieutenant Kyngdon's detachment to leave Zan and accompany him to Krachi. Captain Armitage feared a raid on Tamale, which had been denuded of constabulary, by a German force, 250 strong, which was reported to have left Sansane Mangu in a southerly direction for an unknown destination; and he had also learnt that the German Commissioner was still in residence at Yendi, though ready to leave if our troops crossed the frontier, and that the Na of Yendi and his people were eagerly awaiting our arrival. Captain Armitage at once sent orders to Lieutenant Kyngdon to return to Zan, and at the same time instructed Major J. Marlow, commandant of the Constabulary, to take all the available trained men at Tamale to Zan and to occupy Yendi if he received favourable reports from our native spies. Major Marlow, with eight N.C.Os. and men, left Tamale on the 12th and occupied Yendi without opposition on the 14th. It appears that the German Commissioner, learning from his spies of the movement of Lieutenant Kyngdon's men on the 11th, had left Yendi on the 12th. Captain Armitage himself followed a few days later, and met with a most gratifying reception from the Na of Yendi and many chiefs, who expressed a wish for the reunion of the Dagomba nation under the British flag. Other small detachments of the Northern Territories Constabulary also entered Northern Togoland at this period, the total number employed in the war area amounting to 139. Further to the south, Messrs. Saich and Cooke of the Gold Coast Service, crossing the frontier with 46 men of the Preventive Service, occupied Ho unopposed on the 17th.

To rest his troops, organise his line of communication, and refit from Lome with ammunition and stores, Colonel Bryant found it necessary to halt at Agbeluvoe till the 19th August. Early on the 17th strong officers' patrols left to secure the important railway bridge over the Haho river, seven miles to the north; and as they sent in reports that the enemy was advancing in strength, " G " Company was despatched that afternoon to join them. They were further reinforced next day by a French Senegalese detachment under Captain Castaing, consisting of 3 French officers, 5 French non-commissioned officers, and 150 men, who had just arrived from Anekho. On the 18th also, Adakakpe, four miles north of the Haho bridge, was occupied by half " C " Company.

Agbeluvoe. 17th–18th August.

To cover the flank of his main line of communication, Colonel Bryant issued orders on the 17th for the detachments of Preventive Service men under Messrs. Beckley and Saich at Lome and Ho respectively to move towards Palime. On the same day Mr. A. J. Beckley proceeded from Lome by motor-cycle, accompanied by a Preventive superintendent, and on the 18th cut the Palime railway line at a point about thirty miles from Lome. The Germans were still occupying Palime, but soon afterwards retired and abandoned the railway after destroying the road and railway bridges near Agu.

By this time, thanks to the efficient and untiring efforts of the railway personnel from the Gold Coast, the bridge at Togblekove had been repaired, and on the 18th railhead was brought up to the Lili river. The telegraph personnel, whose work was equally praiseworthy, had also restored the line as far as Agbeluvoe.

19th August. Colonel Bryant resumed his advance on the 19th August, when his advanced troops occupied Nuatya. That day he notified Major Maroix, commanding the French column at Cheti, and Captain Elgee, commanding the Krachi Column, that he intended to be on the Amuchu river on the 26th, and he requested them both to be within two days' march of Kamina by that date.

These messages, which Colonel Bryant despatched across country by native runners, were successfully delivered in time, a result which he attributed to the universal dislike of the Germans by the natives of Togoland.* Towards the British, on the other hand, their attitude was consistently amicable and helpful. Though in some cases they had been coerced, under penalty of instant death, to take up arms against us, they took every opportunity to evade such action, to obstruct the Germans and to assist us, while the welcome they extended to Colonel Bryant and his men at every stage of the British advance was most marked and obviously sincere. As a typical instance, Colonel Bryant relates how one old chief came out to meet him bearing a Union Jack which he had kept hidden since 1884.

The French column under Major Maroix consisted of 23 French and 345 Senegalese (including reservists) with a section of guns. Concentrating at Cheti on the 19th August, it started to advance against Kamina on the 22nd.

The Krachi Column under Captain Elgee consisted of " A,"

---

* The message to Captain Elgee was actually, it appears, stopped by Germans at Agu on the Lome-Palime railway till Mr. Beckley arrived there and took it on.

"B," and "F" Companies of the Gold Coast Regiment, which all reached Krachi between the 16th and 18th August. Crossing the Volta in canoes collected by the Preventive Service, the column left Kete Krachi on the 19th and advanced down the Kpandu road.*

Colonel Bryant's advanced troops occupied Kpedome and his main body concentrated at Nuatya on the 20th August, both continuing northwards on the 21st. On that day, officers' patrols under Captain A. F. Redfern † reported that the enemy was holding a very strong entrenched position at Khra village, about five hundred yards northward of the railway bridge over the Khra river. This bridge and two mines on the railway line were blown up in the faces of these patrols, and they also came under a heavy fire from two German machine guns. But, being well and boldly handled, the Allied scouts succeeded in gaining sufficient information of the enemy dispositions to enable Colonel Bryant to frame a general plan of attack. 20th–21st August.

Khra village, which stood immediately west of the railway and extended across the road, consisted of an irregular oval enclosure about 400 yards from south-east to north-west and some 150 yards wide. The Germans had dug trenches close to and round this enclosure, as well as some joining and to the eastward of a railway cutting by the village ; and they had emplaced three or four machine guns on their flanks, so as to cover all approaches from the dense surrounding bush.

This denseness of the bush accentuated the difficulties of an attack. The direction the attackers must take could at first only be indicated in general terms, and they would not find it easy to maintain it correctly ; owing to the difficulty of inter-communication and inter-observation, neighbouring units could not expect to arrange mutual support with one another ; and the guns, whose utility was in any case limited by the amount of ammunition they were able to transport on their carriers, would be unlikely to obtain positions from which to range and observe. Moreover, once committed to the attack, units would soon be out of sight of the Force commander, and could only remain in touch with him and one another by messenger.‡ In fact, a co-ordinated advance would be im-

---

* The staff of the column included Captain P. J. Mackesy and Lieutenant Kyngdon as Staff and Intelligence Officers, Mr. L. H. Wheatley as Political Officer, and Dr. W. G. Watt as Senior Medical Officer.
† Assistant Commissioner of Police in the Gold Coast.
‡ The companies had no telephone equipment.

practicable, and success would depend mainly on the initiative and individual action of subordinate commanders.

Affair of Khra; 22nd August. Colonel Bryant planned his attack accordingly. On the morning of the 22nd August his force, covered by an advanced screen, moved forward in two columns. On the right, on the railway, were the Pioneer and half " G " Companies of the Gold Coast Regiment and Captain Castaing's detachment of Senegalese. The Pioneer Company was to hold the enemy in front while the remainder of the column turned the enemy's left flank. The column on the road was composed of half " C " Company, " I " Company, and the three guns of the Gold Coast Regiment, and here, while half " C " Company held the enemy in front, " I " Company was to find a way round the enemy's right flank. The guns were to give such support as they could.

As the half of " G " Company under Lieutenant G. M. Thompson only consisted of twenty-two rifles, seventeen Senegalese were placed under his orders by Captain Castaing. This combined party, leading the advance against the enemy's left, worked their way round through the bush till, at about 11 a.m., they were checked by a heavy rifle and machine gun fire from well-constructed trenches on the German flank. Here they held their ground till about 3.30 p.m., when, as it appeared to Lieutenant Thompson that the enemy's fire was slackening as a result of the British gun fire, he led his men to the assault, well supported by Captain Castaing with the remainder of the Senegalese. But the enemy machine guns had not been really affected; and, in spite of the great gallantry they displayed, the attackers were brought to a standstill at fifty yards' distance from the enemy's trenches, Lieutenant Thompson, the French Lieutenant Guillemart, and many native ranks having been killed or wounded. Further progress being impossible, the attackers retired. The devoted bravery of the seventeen Senegalese under Lieutenant Thompson's orders is specially worthy of mention. All but one of them were killed or wounded, and the position in which, after the fight was over, the bodies of their twelve dead were found showed that to the last they had stood by the British officer whose safety had, they felt, been entrusted to them; and here it was held most fitting to bury them in graves round that of Lieutenant Thompson.

On the left " I " Company had managed, under heavy fire, to work their way right round the enemy's right, but only to find further trenches which it was impossible to assault without further support. Accordingly at nightfall they withdrew and entrenched themselves in the river bed some three hundred yards westward of the village. Two of the British guns under Lieutenant W. L. St. Clair had come into action, in spite of hostile machine gun fire, and had opened fire at a range of 1,300 yards, which " I " Company had sent back word as being the probable distance. But the effect of their fire was unknown at the time, though it was subsequently learnt that their first shell had gone through a high tree, which the enemy then gave up using for observation purposes.

Out of a strength of about 450 combatants actually engaged, the Allies had suffered 75 casualties.* The three enemy machine guns, well concealed and skilfully handled by German ranks, had fired many thousands of rounds and had contributed largely to the successful defence. Their effect on the men of the W.A.F.F., who were facing machine gun fire for the first time, had been distinctly demoralising, and had called for the highest qualities of leadership on the part of their British commanders. Moreover, the old pattern British machine guns, though well handled, had not been nearly so effective.

During the night Colonel Bryant made all arrangements to renew the attack at daybreak on the 23rd. On his own right he entrenched so as to contain the enemy opposite, and he reinforced " I " Company for an assault on the enemy's right. But next morning the German force, of an estimated strength of 60 Germans and 400 natives with three machine guns, was found to have retreated hastily. As the fight on the 22nd August appeared to Colonel Bryant to have gone equally well for both sides, this was quite unexpected; and he could only assume either that the Germans feared that their line of retirement would be cut on the 23rd, or that they had heard of the French advance from Cheti and had decided to concentrate for the defence of Kamina.

According to the German sergeant-major's account, their force of rather over two native companies had been in occupation of the Khra position, digging and camouflaging trenches and clearing the field of fire, for three days before the fight. At first the Germans, he says, feared the effect of the British gun-fire, but found that they were well able to hold their own;

---

* Killed :—1 British and 1 French officer and 21 native ranks (5 British and 16 French);
Wounded :—2 British officers, 1 French non-commissioned officer, 43 native ranks (23 British and 20 French) and 6 carriers.

though the sudden Allied assault against their left flank appeared dangerous for a time, and was only checked by the timely arrival of a third native company by train from Kamina. The order to retire was apparently unwelcome to many of the Germans, whose casualties had only been 13,* and who were by this time convinced of their ability to offer a prolonged resistance in this strong position.

23rd–24th August. Sending out officers' patrols to Glei and the Amu river, where the Germans were said to have rallied, Colonel Bryant with the main body remained at Khra during the 23rd and 24th August, to organise for a further advance and to evacuate his wounded to Lome. The rapid repair of the railway and the improvisation of an ambulance train, both due to the excellent work of the railway officials from the Gold Coast, facilitated these arrangements and saved many lives.† In this connection, it is noteworthy that, apart from bullet wounds, there was very little sickness in the force, though all ranks had frequently to sleep all night in clothes which were wet through.

Though Colonel Bryant did not know it, owing to a storm interrupting telegraphic communication for nearly three days, interceptions at this period at Accra of German wireless messages showed that they had destroyed their cipher codes and that they evidently considered their situation to be desperate. In fact, Colonel Bryant's anticipation of a stubborn German defence of Kamina led him, in view of his own depleted numbers, to send orders to the Krachi Column to move at once via the Palime railway to Lome to reinforce him. The situation round Palime could, he felt, be dealt with adequately by the Preventive service detachments under Mr. Beckley.

25th–26th August. On the night of the 24th/25th loud explosions from the Kamina direction were heard at Khra, and in the morning the masts of the wireless station, which had been clearly visible from Glei, were no longer discernible. By 10.30 a.m. Colonel Bryant had occupied Glei with his main body, and his leading troops were on the Amu river, where the Germans had destroyed the road and railway bridges. At 4 p.m. two Germans (Major von

---

* 3 Germans, 10 natives.
† A few days later the German prisoners at Kamina, on being told to prepare to proceed to Lome by train, declined flatly to believe that the railway could have been repaired. The astonishment and incredulity they displayed affords a good testimony to the efficiency and work of the British railway engineers and their men.

THE GERMAN SURRENDER

Roebern and an under-officer to interpret) came into Glei under a flag of truce to submit terms of capitulation.* Colonel Bryant informed them in reply that any surrender must be unconditional, and that his force was advancing at once on Amuchu. This advance he at once started to carry into effect by occupying the north bank of the Amu river. The river, however, came down in flood that night, and it was not till midday on the 26th that the whole column had passed over by the footbridges which had to be constructed. Colonel Bryant himself reached Amuchu with part of his force at 10.30 a.m. on the 26th August, to be met by two German officers bearing a letter of unconditional surrender. *German surrender; 26th August.*

Mr. Newlands, who had recently rejoined Colonel Bryant from Lome, was sent that afternoon to Kamina to arrange the details of the ceremony of surrender on the following day. There he found that the great wireless station had been wrecked beyond repair. Its nine huge masts lay on the ground twisted and broken, and everything that was breakable, including the storage batteries and the 24-foot marble-faced switchboard, was in fragments. To complete the work, kerosene oil had been poured over all and ignited. All that remained of this most modern and powerful station was a smoking ruin.

Though the use of this station by the Allies would certainly have been an advantage, its loss to the enemy was infinitely more important. Without this direct means of communication, the German ships in the Southern Atlantic, if not elsewhere, would be completely out of touch with current events; and the results of our capture of Kamina must consequently be judged by subsequent naval events in that quarter.

Major Maroix's column from Cheti, after encountering some opposition on the 22nd and 23rd August and incurring a few casualties, also entered Kamina on the 27th. Over 200 Germans surrendered with 3 machine guns, over 1,000 rifles, and about 320,000 rounds of ammunition.

The Krachi Column, advancing via Ahenkro and Liati, reached Palime on the 23rd August, and on the 25th was joined when within thirty miles of Atakpame by Mr. Beckley, who brought the two messages from Colonel Bryant, one of the 19th and the other sent from Khra ordering Captain Elgee to proceed with his three companies to Lome to reinforce the main column. The Krachi Column had met with no opposition, though the area *Krachi Column.*

---

* See Appendix I.

it traversed offered considerable natural facilities for a small force to oppose its advance; and it had met with no other difficulties. The roads it traversed had been good, supplies had been easily obtained locally as it advanced, and the attitude of the natives had been very friendly.

The German Force. The Germans, whose force appears to have consisted of one German and seven or eight native companies, totalling about 300 Germans and 1,200 natives, had been expected to offer a much stouter resistance. The difficulties of the country were all in their favour, and it had never been anticipated that they would surrender without attempting to hold the elaborate network of trenches and dug-outs with which the Kamina station was surrounded.* But their Intelligence system broke down completely with the outbreak of war—they could get no news whatever from the Gold Coast, as no native would proceed there and return—and the only answer they could obtain from Berlin to repeated requests for instructions was an order to protect the wireless station. The rapid invasion of the country by the several Allied columns, whose numbers they invariably over-estimated, consequently combined with the lack of co-operation by their own native subjects † to place them at a grave disadvantage.

To the rapid Allied success several factors contributed. The initiative and skill of Colonel Bryant; the able and energetic action of the local French civil and military authorities; the courage and endurance of all ranks of the Allied forces; and the ready and whole-hearted assistance rendered by civilians from the Gold Coast.‡ The whole operation in fact furnished an exceptional example of fine co-operative effort.

On the 28th August Sir Hugh Clifford reached Lome from England, and after personal discussion with the Governor of

---

* The German sergeant-major's account says that many of the Germans had little or no military training, and also that, though the Kamina position was well entrenched, it was too large for the available force, and was commanded on all sides by surrounding hills.

† Some of the natives, however, remained loyal to their German masters, as the following instance shows. The Germans, before their surrender, announced to their native police and employés generally that they were returning in six months' time. This was so far believed that about February 1915 several of these men came into Lome and asked why the Germans had not returned.

‡ Many names have necessarily been omitted, but Messrs. C. H. Harper (acting Colonial Secretary) and W. L. Townsend (Attorney-General) are specially mentioned by Mr. Robertson as deserving of much of the credit of achievement.

A CONTENTED TOGOLAND

Dahomey, they both proposed that, pending the final post-war settlement, the western districts of Togoland should be administered by the British and the eastern by the French. This was approved.

From the outset the natives of Togoland showed themselves to be so well contented with the change of Governments that most of the Allied military force was soon able to withdraw from the country.

The Gold Coast, shortly afterwards, by the unanimous vote of its Legislative Council, voicing the widely manifested desire of its inhabitants to share the Imperial burden, expressed its desire to bear the whole financial cost of the British share of the operations. By this generous act it crowned fittingly the military achievement of the first capture in the war of a German colony, to which its own efforts had contributed so much.

CHAPTER II

PREPARATIONS TO INVADE THE CAMEROONS

(Frontispiece map and Map 2.)

Local forces in British West Africa. As explained previously, it had been recognised that it would be necessary to restrict the objectives of any joint British naval and military operations in foreign territory to such as could be dealt with by local forces. The forces in the British possessions in West Africa consisted, in 1914, of the Imperial garrison in Sierra Leone and of the units of the West African Frontier Force in the Gambia, Sierra Leone, the Gold Coast, and Nigeria. The Navy was represented only by the gunboat H.M.S. *Dwarf*.

The Imperial garrison in Sierra Leone, which was maintained for the defence of the coaling station at Freetown, comprised the 50th Company, R.G.A., Sierra Leone Company, R.G.A., 36th Company, R.E., 1st West India Regiment, and the West African Regiment, with detachments of the Army Service Corps, Royal Army Medical Corps, Army Ordnance Corps, etc. Of these the Sierra Leone company of artillery, half the Engineer company, and the West African Regiment were composed of locally recruited Africans, trained and commanded by British officers and non-commissioned officers. The Sierra Leone artillery company, with five British officers, four British non-commissioned officers, and eighty-three natives, had a movable armament of six 2·95" mountain guns; the Engineer company had an establishment of 45 native ranks; and the West African Regiment, of a total strength of about 59 British officers, 25 British non-commissioned officers, and 1,415 African ranks, was organised in twelve companies.

The West African Frontier Force. The first units of the West African Frontier Force had been raised by Colonel F. D. Lugard[*] on the Niger in 1897, and had proved such a success that the various armed constabularies in British West Africa had subsequently been organised

---

[*] Subsequently Sir Frederick, and later Lord, Lugard.

THE WEST AFRICAN FRONTIER FORCE 43

on similar lines and embodied in the Force. The different units had, since then, taken part successfully in many local expeditions, in which the West African native had proved himself to be a cheerful, willing, and courageous soldier with great endurance. Though seldom able to read or write, he had responded well and rapidly to training by his British instructors, and his devotion and loyalty to them had been shown by his consistent readiness to follow them in action.

The organisation of the Force differed in each of the four British possessions. In the Gambia, which covers about 4,000 square miles, there was only one infantry company of 3 British officers, 2 British non-commissioned officers, and 130 native ranks. Recruited from local tribes, its smartness and general efficiency had recently been most favourably reported on. The Sierra Leone Battalion was organised in six companies, and had a total strength of about 28 British officers, 1 British non-commissioned officer, and 640 natives, with some 80 reservists. The men were drawn from the same local tribes that furnished recruits for the West African Regiment, about half of them in 1914 being Mendis. The Gold Coast Regiment has already been described. The Nigeria Regiment was practically a brigade group. It consisted of two batteries of artillery, each armed with six 2·95" mountain guns, a mounted infantry battalion of three companies with a total strength of about 380, and four infantry battalions, each with an establishment of 1,100 to 1,200. In addition to this total of about 5,000 combatants, there were some 320 reservists and 400 gun and machine gun carriers, there being eight machine guns with each infantry battalion and four with the mounted infantry. In the past this regiment had been recruited almost entirely from Hausas and Yorubas, races which had earned for themselves a high reputation as soldiers. But, with the cessation of inter-tribal fighting and the general increased security in the country brought about by British administration, trade offered greater inducements than military service; and by 1914 an increasing difficulty had been experienced in obtaining Hausa and Yoruba recruits.

Though Nigeria, with an area of over 335,000 square miles, Nigeria. had a population of eighteen to nineteen millions, only a small proportion were physically fit or suitable for military service. Outside Yorubaland, very few recruits were obtainable in Southern Nigeria, and although recruiting among the pagan hill tribes in Northern Nigeria had recently been resorted to, their backward state of civilisation militated against their enlistment to any great extent. At the outbreak of war, however, three-fifths of the regiment was still composed of Hausas and Yorubas, the remainder consisting of about 400 Beri-Beri, 350 Fulanis, representatives of some twenty-two other tribes, and over 400 unclassified pagans. The commandant of the regiment had a general staff officer, a staff captain, an intelligence officer, and a staff quartermaster to assist him. The lack of military administrative services in the West African Frontier Force has been commented on in the previous chapter, and it is only necessary to point out here that the difficulties and disadvantages due to this system were, as will be seen hereafter, much greater in the case of the invasion of the Cameroons than they had been in Togoland. For a much larger force was involved, with operations of longer duration and more widely extended; Nigeria, from its greater size and its larger extent of recently settled territory, was likely to be more susceptible to disruptive influences than the Gold Coast; and the other three British possessions in West Africa had all to be called on for assistance at the expense of their own administration.

There was also in Nigeria a police force of some 33 British officers and 2,100 Africans who had a semi-military training and were armed with carbines; and a Marine Department with about 90 British officers and 1,000 native ratings, of whom a few of the executive officers had served in the Royal Navy and most of the others in the Royal Naval Reserve. In addition to two sea-going steamers (of 1,500 and 200 tons respectively), the Marine Department had in charge for work on the inland waterways over sixty steamers, launches, or pinnaces, many of which could, if necessary, be fitted with light quick-firing or machine-gun armament. These craft were none too many for the normal administrative work of the country, as, owing to the few railways and roads, the numerous rivers, creeks, and lagoons formed one of the chief means of internal communication in the south.

The armed forces of Nigeria were thus extremely small in relation to its area, while their distribution in numerous widely scattered small detachments had regard only to local political conditions, without consideration of possible aggression from without. It has to be remembered that in 1914 Northern Nigeria had only comparatively recently been freed from the tyranny and terrors of the slave-traders, so that war with an outside Power was calculated to test the British administration severely. As it happened, the war justified completely the policy we had adopted, sometimes termed "Indirect Rule," which, as defined by Lord Lugard, allowed "the largest possible latitude to the tribal chiefs and native rulers to manage their own affairs." In the longer settled regions of the south and west the people generally were wholeheartedly for the British cause, while in the north appreciation of British rule and general contentment led the Mahomedan chiefs and people to give unmistakable proof of their loyalty. Even among the more primitive pagan tribes, where sporadic disturbances normally required a continuous supervision, unrest and outbreaks due to the withdrawal of troops and political officers were local, isolated, and soon suppressed. Another contributory reason for the loyal and law-abiding attitude of the various tribes, especially those living near the frontier, is said to have been their appreciation of the contrast between German and British rule.

In other ways also, Nigeria was less ready for war than most British dependencies. The amalgamation of Southern and Northern Nigeria had only come into being on the 1st January 1914, and there had been little time for the unified services to settle down. An entirely new Defence Scheme had become necessary; and this, when war broke out, was still only in draft form and under consideration by Sir Frederick Lugard, the Governor-General, then on leave in England. Consequently the local civil authorities had generally little idea of what would be required of them, while the military authorities, not knowing if the views they had put forward in the draft scheme had met with approval, were uncertain regarding the preparations to be made. Before dealing further with this point, however, it is advisable to give a brief description of the Cameroons.

Till the German flag was hoisted in the Cameroon river in 1884 no European Power had occupied the country, though European merchants and missionaries had visited it and had settled in various parts of the coast. An English Baptist mission had established itself there in 1845, and other members of the same society had settled in 1858 at Victoria on Ambas Bay, where they had worked so well and successfully that it had become a British possession in all but name. In fact, British influence on and near the coast was such that, at the end of 1882, a number of native chiefs applied for British protection. But H.M. Government took some time to consider the matter. In the meantime, in 1883, some German merchants, realising Bismarck's changed attitude towards

The Cameroons.

colonisation, began to acquire from the chiefs rights in property; and in July 1884 Dr. Nachtigal, ostensibly an Imperial Commissioner sent out to promote German trade, proclaimed a German protectorate, first in Togoland and then in the Cameroons, only just forestalling the British consul then on his way to accept the chiefs' application for British protection. The British protested against the German action, but in 1885 H.M. Government gave up all British claims, except to Ambas Bay and Victoria, in return for some purely nominal concessions by Germany. Lord Granville also agreed to cede Victoria and Ambas Bay provided the Germans could arrange terms with the English missionaries. These, finding themselves with little choice in the matter, consented to be bought out in 1887. But as Sir Charles Lucas says in " The Empire at War," " when the war came, though an interval of nearly thirty years had passed, there were numbers of native Christians whose hearts were with England, the large majority of the native population at Duala were British in sympathy, for purposes of communication between Europeans and natives ' pidgin ' English was the lingua franca of the coast belt, and German military officers gave orders to their Dualese * troops in English."

After hoisting their flag, the Germans at once began to open up the territory by expeditions into the interior, in which they encountered not only resistance by the coast tribes and those in the interior, but also opposition and trouble due to their own tactlessness and lack of consideration or cruelty towards the natives. Several of these expeditions ended in profitless loss of life, there were some mutinies of their native troops, and many of the German administrators were found to be quite unfitted for their tasks. As Great Britain and France were simultaneously taking steps to extend their influence in the interior, international complications also arose; and the last of the series of conventions delimiting the respective protectorates were only signed in 1911-12 with France, and in March 1913 with Great Britain. The territory thus acquired by Germany, some 300,000 square miles in extent, was a rich and valuable section of Equatorial Africa which included some important seaports and an extensive central plateau of sufficient altitude to be healthy enough for prolonged residence by Europeans.

---

* Actually, of course, the German native troops in Duala were almost entirely Yaundes.

To face p. 47]

A Typical West African Swamp

DIFFICULT PHYSICAL CONDITIONS

The climate is tropical. In the zone of dense forest and tropical bush which borders the coastal belt of mangrove swamps, lagoons, and creeks, the temperature is always high and the atmosphere humid. Here there is a considerable rainfall occurring practically throughout the year, though heaviest from May to September; and the climate is not only very trying to Europeans, but, in the origin it gives to the insect life which carries disease, is dangerous to health. As the ground rises towards the interior, however, there is less rain, and the climate becomes cooler and healthier. North of the central plateau the ground falls again, at first somewhat abruptly, to the plains around Lake Chad. The diversity of the physical features and climate is, however, so considerable as to be difficult to describe briefly and at the same time adequately. It has consequently been thought advisable to reproduce in Map 3 four diagrams,* which will enable the reader to grasp generally the main characteristics of the different parts of the area.

The coastal belt with its estuaries, creeks, and swamps; the forest area with its huge trees often rising to a height of over two hundred feet, its dense entanglement of creepers, and its dim obscurity; and the equatorial temperature and humid atmosphere—all combined to offer great difficulties to an invading force faced by a defender with the advantage of local knowledge. It was in these regions that the main fighting occurred, although in the open and healthier country to the north there were also operations of importance.

The frontier between Nigeria and the Cameroons, running from a point in Lake Chad to the sea in a southerly or south-westerly direction, was about 1,000 miles long, and, in places, bisected native tribal and political divisions.† For about 150 miles southward of Lake Chad, as far as the north-western slopes of the Mandara mountains, it ran through country without physical difficulties, except extensive marshes —becoming lakes in the rainy season—near Lake Chad; and in this section an open and easy route connected the British and German military posts of Maiduguri and Mora, both of them converging points for well-used tracks from other parts

The Anglo-German frontier.

---

* These formed annexures to the final report on the work of the Medical Services in the Cameroons from September 1914 to February 1916.
† The territories formerly subject to the Shehu (Sheikh) of Bornu and to the Emir of Yola were thus divided, and although this was regretted by some as detrimental to their interests, to chiefs hitherto subordinate and to their adherents the increased independence and power they gained was certainly welcome ultimately.

of Nigeria and the Cameroons respectively. Maiduguri had the advantage, however, that it was connected with the Nigerian telegraph system, whereas Mora was without such means of communication. The Mandara range itself continued southward alongside the frontier almost as far as the Benue river, which formed the best line of communication between Northern Nigeria and the Northern Cameroons. River steamers could always ascend the Benue as far as Ibi, and during the rainy season up to Yola, though its navigation above that place was restricted by shallows to small craft. These were able to reach the important German trading centre of Garua except in the low-water season between April and June. A Nigerian telegraph line ran along the Benue to Yola, which was thus also better situated than Garua, as the German telegraph system had not yet been extended north of 5° North latitude. From Yola, in addition to a fair road to Garua, there were some other little known tracks leading to Koncha through difficult country.

The Benue river, the chief British line of communication with north-eastern Nigeria, lay for over two hundred miles of its length in Nigeria roughly parallel to and within sixty to one hundred miles of the frontier. On the other hand, the frontier to the south of Yola ran to the sea through extremely rough, mountainous, or bush-covered country, which impassable rivers and streams rendered almost impracticable in the rainy season. There were few good tracks across this section of the frontier and not even many native paths, those there were being generally overgrown and hardly practicable for carriers. The good tracks (i.e., cleared to a width of six feet) were, as far as was known, limited to those running from Ibi on the Benue river to Banyo via Bakundi, from Ibi and Abinsi on the Benue river to Bamenda via Kentu, and along the valley of the Cross river to Ossidinge (Mamfe). The Cross river itself was navigable as far as the German frontier, from May to December, by light-draught steamers or launches. At extreme high-water light launches were also able to reach Ossidinge. South of the Cross river and within about thirty miles of it, two other tracks, cleared of bush to an average width of about five feet, crossed the frontier and joined up with the German road leading south from Ossidinge; and further south again there was a road from Calabar via Rio del Rey to Johann Albrechtshöhe (Kumba).

In the Cameroons, roads or tracks, many cleared to a width of twenty feet, connecting Nkongsamba (the terminus of the

Northern Railway from Duala) with Bare, Chang, Fumban, Banyo, and Koncha, constituted a main lateral communication, which was linked up at several points with other paths or tracks from the plateau in the interior; and though there were frequently no bridges along these tracks, they gave the Germans a means of concentrating their forces for military operations in the Nigeria direction. But beyond the above information little was known in Nigeria, before the war, of the nature and condition of the communications or the country generally on the German side of the frontier. This was mainly due to the fact that the Intelligence Staff in Nigeria had had little time to devote attention to anything but internal conditions and topography, regarding which their knowledge was still incomplete in many respects.

Except in a few places where it is steep and rocky, for instance round the volcanic Cameroon Mountain and between Kribi and Campo, the coast is generally low and bordered by mangrove swamps or lagoons caused by bars of river silt. On the north, at the foot of the Cameroon Mountain, which stands up over 13,000 feet high between two large estuaries, lie a number of small but well-protected bays, among them being Ambas Bay. On the south-eastern slope of the mountain, at a height of 3,000 feet, in a district of prosperous plantations, was Buea, the headquarters of the German Government; and close to it at Zopo ran the narrow-gauge light railway which connected the plantations and the Mungo river with the harbour at Victoria. In the five-fingered estuary of the Cameroon river to the south-east of the mountain is Duala, the best natural harbour on all this part of the West African coast, and a place of which we shall have more to say hereafter. South of Duala and between it and Kribi—at one time a port of some importance —are the mouths of the Sanaga and Nyong rivers, which were navigable only for a short distance inland. Further south again, at Campo, is the mouth of the river of that name, which flows for some distance along the northern frontier of Muni or Spanish Guinea.* This enclave of neutral territory proved to be of material assistance to the Germans. Throughout the war it served them as a base of supplies and intelligence, and after they ceased resistance provided them with a place of refuge. To the south of Muni was a narrow strip of German territory, its coast-line lying along the north-eastern shore of Monda Bay.

The Coast Line of the Cameroons.

---

* It was subordinate to Fernando Po.

50 MILITARY OPERATIONS: THE CAMEROONS

The Franco-German frontier. The French territories of Gabon, Middle Congo, Ubangi-Shari, and Chad enclosed the Cameroons on the south and east, the frontier having been altered considerably by the cession, in November 1911, to Germany, as an equivalent for her recognition of French rights in Morocco, of an area of over 100,000 square miles. This area included the strip south of Muni, the Sanga basin with a frontage on the north bank of the Congo, and an eastern extension to the Ubangi river. The advantages to Germany of this arrangement were obvious. But it had serious drawbacks for the French. The two pronounced German salients which it introduced not only bisected Middle Congo, but separated it from Ubangi-Shari, thus interrupting completely the long line of French communications. As an outstanding indication of German aggressive policy it was, moreover, calculated to cause strife sooner or later. It had also the effect of bringing German and Belgian territory into contact at Bonga on the Congo and at Singa on the Ubangi.*

Communications across the Franco-German frontier were even fewer and less serviceable than those across the Anglo-German frontier. In the regions of forest and swamp which the boundary traversed in the south and south-east native paths were few and far between; and the waterways which formed the main means of communication were generally only passable by canoes, though on some of them long stretches were navigable by river steamer. Even to the north of Singa —where the country was open—as far as 10° north latitude there were few tracks of any importance. It was only in the swampy area between there and Lake Chad that there were tracks of a state and importance to render them useful for military operations. In French territory here the Shari river was navigable by steamers or launches for a considerable distance, and one of its tributaries, the Logone, which either formed the frontier or ran alongside it for about three hundred miles, was also navigable over a large part of its course.

Communications in the Cameroons. In 1914, owing to the difficulties and expense involved in their construction and maintenance, communications in the Cameroons, in the European sense, were of very small extent compared with the area of the country. They consisted of about 240 miles of railway, some 250 miles of carriage roads

---

* In the short German account of the Cameroons campaign included in Vol. IV of *Der Grosse Krieg, 1914–1918*, edited by Herr Schwarte, it is stated that the alignment of the new frontier was arranged entirely in the interests of commerce and that no military considerations were involved.

fit for light motor traffic, and several long stretches of river navigable by shallow-draught vessels. In the open grass-covered country in the north and north-west there was a fairly good system of tracks, but in the coastal and forest areas the paths were few and generally difficult.

The railways and carriage roads were limited to the quadrilateral Victoria-Bare-Yaunde-Campo. In addition to the light line from Victoria serving the plantations, there were two metre-gauge railways. The Northern, from Bonaberi (opposite Duala on the western bank of the Wuri river), ran for one hundred miles through forest country to Nkongsamba at the foot of the rise to the central plateau; and the Midland, designed as the trunk line of the railway system, ran south-eastward from Duala. In 1914 it was under construction to Mbalmajo on the Nyong river, but by the autumn had only been completed to Eseka, a distance of about one hundred and twenty miles. To this point the line ran through tropical forests and was without any steep gradients, so that, except for the important bridges over the Dibamba river at Yapoma and over the Sanaga at Edea, few engineering difficulties had been encountered. Its importance as a means of communication was increased by the fact that the River Nyong was navigable for over one hundred miles above Mbalmajo by small river steamer.

The following roads were fit for light motor traffic for the greater part of the year :—

(i) A system round Victoria, including one to Buea;

(ii) A coast road Campo-Kribi-Longyi, projected to connect at Edea with a still incomplete road from

(iii) Edea to Yaunde; and

(iv) Two roads from Kribi, leading to Yaunde via Lolo, and to Ebolowa, respectively.

In the southern half of the country the river systems were the chief means of communication. But the Germans, not realising at first that an extension of their use was the best practical way of increasing trade intercourse, had until 1914 only recently been paying them much attention. In the coast districts the rains maintain a relatively constant volume of water in the rivers, but though their mouths and estuaries are of considerable use to coastal trade, their navigation inland is much restricted by frequent rapids and falls. Moreover, as many of them fall abruptly over the edge of the central plateau, their upper courses cannot be reached from the sea. They were thus only navigable in stretches, and had little value as through routes, except by light canoes. These the natives used extensively, carrying them over or round the many obstructions, a custom contributed to by the constant care and expense required to keep paths through the forest open and clear of growth.

Until the end of 1912, telegraphic communication with the whole of the Cameroons was via Bonny in Nigeria. But in January 1913 a new German cable was completed from Monrovia to Duala via Lome (Togoland). This connected with a fairly good system of land lines, which do not appear to have extended far outside the quadrilateral in which railways and motor roads had been constructed; and in August 1914 northern and north-western districts still depended to a great extent on Nigeria for telegraphic communication. In 1913 also, a wireless station, with a normal range of 600 nautical miles, was opened at Duala, and was in connection with the German wireless station at Kamina and with one in Fernando Po which had been erected and was operated by a German company.

Population. The native population was estimated by the Germans as less than 3,000,000, the bulk consisting of Sudanese and Bantu-speaking negroes. After them the most important peoples were Fulas and Hausas. The forest zone of the south was very sparsely populated except on the coast, the densest population being in the Lake Chad and Benue basins, on the banks of the Logone river and on the highlands and hill slopes of the north-western portion of the Colony.

In 1913, there were 1,871 Europeans in the Cameroons, of whom 1,643 were Germans, but at the outbreak of war the latter numbered well over 2,000, the increase being largely due apparently to German crews of steamers in Duala harbour.

Administration. The German Governor—in August 1914, K. Ebermaier—was assisted by a Chancellor, a local council drawn from the mercantile community, and a court presided over by a German judge. Of the administrative districts into which the country was divided, those nearest the coast had organised civil governments, but those in the interior were mainly under an arbitrary civil or military rule. In the organised districts the native chiefs or leaders had no real share in the administration, and little latitude in the management of their own affairs; but in the north, where German supervision was not so close, the native chiefs still managed to exercise a considerable measure of control over their people. In such districts our officers frequently found that the less organised the civil

government the more successful had been the administration.*
Generally speaking, the German policy was very much as it
was in Togoland, and led to the idea prevalent in most British
circles at the outbreak of war, that the whole native population was violently anti-German. This appears to have been
true in regard to the Victoria and Duala regions and in a few
other parts; but in the operations of 1914-16 a considerable
number of natives of the central plateau and the north displayed great loyalty and devotion to their German leaders
and administrators. Though this may not have been owing
to any affection the natives bore the Germans, it may well
have been due to the respect, if not admiration, which a
strong government will generally evoke from a virile people.
Moreover, a distinctive characteristic of the West African
native is his traditional or instinctive loyalty towards his
chief or master for the time being.

According to British information at the outbreak of war, the German regular troops in the Cameroons numbered about 200 German officers and non-commissioned officers and 1,650 native ranks, organised in twelve companies each about 120 strong. There was also an armed police force, with a strength of about 30 Germans and 1,500 natives, most of whom had served in the regular forces and were barely distinguishable from them in training and fighting efficiency. The native soldiers and policemen, for the most part Hausas and Yaundes, enjoyed privileges which placed them as a class above their fellow-countrymen, among whom they were thus enabled to practise petty tyrannies without any fear of German rebuke. In fact, instances were known of the Germans having located them as a punitive measure in a refractory village to work their will. The Germans were believed to have nine guns and about thirty machine guns, with a large reserve of rifles and ammunition. As it turned out, they had many more machine guns, each regular company having three, in addition to a number with the police and in reserve. They were also found to have plenty of ammunition, but their reserve of rifles was small and prevented their raising as many new troops as they might otherwise have done.†

Military forces.

---

* In the latter part of 1913, Dr. Solf, then German Colonial Minister, after a tour of inspection to the Cameroons, was readily granted permission to visit Northern Nigeria. As the result of what he saw there, Dr. Solf informed Sir F. Lugard that he intended to introduce the Nigerian system of indirect rule into the Cameroons.
† In the German narrative previously mentioned the total of troops and

In July 1914 the distribution of the regular troops, according to information received from the French subsequently to the outbreak of war, was as follows :—

In the north and north-west.
    Mora—No. 3 Company, with an outpost at Kuseri ; *
    Garua—No. 7 Company and two 7 cm. Q.F. guns, with two outposts to the north-east ;
    Bamenda—No. 2 Company, with outposts at Kentu and Wum.

In the north-east.
    Buma—No. 12 Company.

In the centre and east-centre.
    Ngaundere—No. 8 Company and a 6 cm. mountain gun ;
    Dume—No. 9 Company, with outposts at Buala and Baturi ;
    Bouar—No. 5 Company.

About Duala.
    Duala — Military Headquarters (Lt.-Col. Zimmermann, commanding) ;
        No. 1 (Depot) Company with four 9 cm. and one Q.F. gun ;
    Zopo—No. 4 (Expeditionary) Company.

In the south-east and south.
    Mbaiki—No. 6 Company, with an outpost at Nola ;
    Oyem—No. 10 Company with a Q.F. gun ;
    Akoafim—No. 11 Company.

The police force, located with few exceptions only in the more settled western and central districts, was organised in nineteen companies :—a depot company at Duala ; two companies each 200 strong at Ebolowa and Yaunde ; a company 150 strong at Banyo, the most northerly of their posts ; four companies 100 strong each at Chang, Kribi, Yukaduma, and Ikelemba (on the Sanga river) ; and eleven companies each 50 strong at Fumban, Ossidinge, Bare, Yabasi, Johann Albrechtshöhe, Buea, Victoria, Edea, Dume, Lome, and Ukoko.

This total of about 3,400 fighting men was small in relation to the extent of the country, and, as shown above, their dis-

---

police is given as about 200 Europeans and 3,200 natives, with about a dozen guns of obsolete and diverse pattern. Machine guns were plentiful. A re-armament with magazine rifles in place of the old single-loader was taking place, but had not been finally completed ; and on this account there was no reserve of rifles and ammunition.

* This place has now been re-named Fort Foureau by the French.

[To face p. 54

GERMAN NATIVE SOLDIERS

A TRACK IN THE HIGHLAND COUNTRY OF THE CAMEROONS

persion in peace time was wide. The lack of sufficient rifles prevented any great expansion, and it is doubtful if the total effective strength during the operations ever rose above 5,000. In fact, Germany was no more prepared for international warfare in this region than Great Britain or France.*

The Germans had normally two gunboats, *Eber* and *Panther*,† on the West African station, and it seemed possible that, on the outbreak of war, merchant steamers would be armed and fitted out as commerce destroyers at Duala. There were also small river steamers and launches for inland navigation which were or could be equipped with light armament, but regarding these the British had little definite information.

The draft Defence Scheme for Nigeria, in its preliminary review of the situation, laid down that though the Nigeria Regiment was maintained primarily for the preservation of internal order and defence against external aggression, this did not necessarily imply a passive defence, an exception being made in the case of the ports on the coast, against which a serious overseas attack appeared improbable. A serious German offensive by land, having regard to the numerical inferiority of their force as compared with the Nigerian—even though they had more machine guns per company than the Nigeria Regiment—was also unlikely. Hostilities would probably take the form of raids, for which the most likely objectives were the cable station at Bonny, Insofan on the Cross river, and Yola. Of these the first appeared the only one that could or would be undertaken during the precautionary stage of mobilisation.

The scheme then went on to point out that the German railway and telegraph communications, projected or existing between Duala and the north, ran close to the frontier, and that an early British initiative might cut them, thus interfering with the German concentration and possibly affording an opportunity of defeating the enemy in detail. It was consequently essential that the Commandant of the Nigeria

---

* The account in *Der Grosse Krieg, 1914–1918*, indicates that, in the expectation that the African dependencies would be declared neutral, the Germans had prepared no special plan of mobilisation and operations; and that when the Allies negatived the proposed neutrality of Togoland, orders were issued to the various scattered companies to follow the general instructions given at the time of the Morocco crisis in 1911, namely to fall back fighting on to the central plateau. Here the Germans thought that they would be able to maintain resistance for the few months required to obtain a decision in Europe.

† The *Panther* had left for refit in Germany in May 1914, and at the outbreak of war had not returned to West Africa.

Regiment—who would in absence of orders to the contrary assume chief command in Nigeria—should have the power to cross the frontier. It is noteworthy that, when the scheme was written, little was known of the extent of the telegraph lines in the Cameroons, and the position of the railhead of the German Northern Railway was assumed to be near 6° north latitude, whereas it was really some seventy-five miles south of that. Its actual position was ascertained, however, just before the outbreak of war. The military authorities in Nigeria then came to the conclusion that, as the Germans were liable to be cut off from Duala by a rapid advance from the west via Ossidinge, there was every possibility that their forces would carry out a general retirement from the north and concentrate at Chang, within thirty * miles of their railhead. Here it was estimated that in fourteen days they could concentrate six companies and several guns to cover Duala and the railway, by which they could retire on Duala very rapidly in case of a reverse.

It had been estimated in the scheme that three-quarters of the German troops would be available for operations against us, but it was realised that, owing to the great extent of the Anglo-German frontier and the small forces involved on both sides, the situation at the outbreak of war could not be foreseen. It was consequently considered that the British initial dispositions should be arranged to meet the most probable forms of attack, to hold the seaports, and to be prepared to strike a blow at the enemy's line of communication by a rapid advance from the Cross river of a flying column, which would threaten Buea and Duala, cut off the German troops in the north, and possibly destroy the German Northern Railway. The exact strengths of the various detachments and columns would necessarily be dependent on the garrisons which would have to be maintained at various internal centres, and these would depend again on the local political situation.

For administrative duties with the different columns in the field, and for all duties on the main lines of communication, the scheme pointed out that no military officers would be available, and that the Nigeria Government would consequently have to arrange for these duties to be carried out by civil or Marine Department officers. The action in this and other respects that would have to be taken, at the precautionary and war stages respectively, was then outlined. This varied

---

* It was subsequently found to be over fifty miles by road.

so slightly from that detailed in the previous chapter as having to be taken in the Gold Coast that recapitulation of it here seems unnecessary.

On the 30th July 1914, the "warning" telegram from the Colonial Office was received at Lagos; and a reference to the commandant of the Nigeria Regiment at Kaduna elicited the information that approval of the Defence Scheme had not yet been received from H.M. Government. This had been realised in London three or four days previously, and the Colonial Office had obtained the draft scheme from Sir Frederick Lugard on the 31st, and had passed it to General Dobell for scrutiny in consultation with the other military authorities concerned. Mr. A. G. Boyle, who was acting as Governor-General of Nigeria during Sir Frederick Lugard's absence, decided, however, that the draft scheme was to be acted on, and telegraphed to that effect to Sir F. Lugard, his action in this respect being confirmed on the 3rd August, when a telegram from him to the Colonial Office asking if the scheme had been approved was answered in the affirmative.

In his appreciation regarding the employment of the W.A.F.F. in the event of war, written on the 3rd August,[*] General Dobell suggested Duala, Buea, and Victoria as points worthy of attack. An attack on Duala without naval co-operation would in his opinion have to be made from the direction of Insofan and Calabar, but he considered that the difficult country, lack of supplies, and absence of information regarding the communications beyond our frontier would render such an operation too hazardous. With naval co-operation, on the other hand, he estimated that it would be possible to embark at Lagos, Forcados, and Calabar a force of the Nigeria Regiment amounting to six guns, fourteen companies (1,680 rifles), and fourteen machine guns. He estimated that the Germans in the Cameroons had four 9 cm., two 6 cm., and three 3 cm. guns, thirty machine guns, twelve infantry companies (1,500 rifles), 120 mounted infantry, 1,200 native police, and 800 Europeans who had been trained to arms. As the loss of Duala, Victoria, and Buea would strangle the Cameroons, and would deprive Germany of the only possible naval base on the West Coast of Equatorial Africa, General Dobell anticipated that they would concentrate about 2,400 of their trained armed forces to defend those places. But, as Duala was forty-five miles from Victoria, which was

Dobell's appreciation of 3rd August.

---

* See p. 11, *ante.*

fifteen miles from Buea, some dispersion of those forces could be counted on. Germany had, further, two warships, *Eber* and *Panther*, on the West African station besides a small flotilla in the Cameroons of launches armed with light quick-firing guns; and General Dobell came to the conclusion that an attack on Duala would only be possible with very effective naval co-operation. He had not taken into account co-operation by the French, who might be in a position to assist with troops drawn from the French Congo, embarking them at Libreville, which was only three hundred miles from Duala.

Decision of Offensive Sub-Committee; 5th August 1914. With these views before them, the Offensive Sub-Committee of the Committee of Imperial Defence, at their first meeting on the 5th August, came to the conclusion that, for an offensive against the Cameroons, the British troops in Nigeria would probably require both naval and military reinforcements from elsewhere, and that, in the circumstances, the initiation of such offensive operations should be deferred for the time being.

Action in Nigeria; 30th July–8th August. In Nigeria the incomplete state of the Defence Scheme naturally delayed action. On receipt of the " warning " telegram precautionary measures were taken, including the detention of postal and telegraphic correspondence passing through to the Cameroons. But it was not till the 3rd August that definite instructions were issued to the civil officers in charge of districts along the eastern frontier to organise an intelligence system and to watch the frontier, or that warning orders were issued for the concentration of four groups of troops near that frontier. These, which were practically what had been proposed in the Defence Scheme, were as follows :—

Maiduguri Column, a company each of mounted infantry and infantry at Maiduguri, with two companies of infantry at Nafada ;

Yola Column, a company of mounted infantry, two guns, and four companies of infantry at Yola ;

Ikom (or No. 2) Column, four guns and four companies of infantry ;

Calabar (or No. 1) Column, two guns and two companies of infantry.

On receipt of the " war " telegram, orders were issued for the concentration of the above (commanded by Captain R. W. Fox, Lieutenant-Colonel P. R. Maclear, Lieutenant-Colonel G. T. Mair, and Lieutenant-Colonel A. H. W. Haywood respectively) and of other troops at points in rear. At the same time the Resident at Maiduguri was requested to ascertain what German troops were at Dikwa and Kuseri, and also to try to get into touch with the French at Fort Lamy; and the Resident at Yola was asked to find out the German strength at Garua. Colonel C. H. P. Carter, the commandant of the Nigeria Regiment, planned offensive operations, commencing with an early advance by the Maiduguri and Yola columns against Mora and Garua respectively, where success would, he anticipated, enable him to free other troops to reinforce the southern columns—which would meanwhile carry out reconnaissances and organise preparations—for an advance on Duala.

Among the various proclamations and Orders in Council issued in Nigeria at this period was one of the 5th August, creating a marine and a land contingent for combatant duties, both composed of Europeans. The Marine Contingent, which included the whole of the Marine Department, had at once much to do in the measures necessary for protection against sea attack at Lagos, Forcados, Bonny, and Calabar, and in the organisation at Calabar of a light transport service for the Cross river. The Land Contingent was a volunteer force recruited from officials and business men, and was practically limited to those residing at Lagos and Calabar.

On the 5th August Mr. Boyle telegraphed to the Colonial Office that the Commandant proposed to invade German territory, if circumstances were favourable, with Duala as the objective. Colonel Carter, said Mr. Boyle, seemed more impressed with the offensive than the defensive part of the Defence Scheme. Mr. Boyle added that the French were reported to have 2,000 men at Fort Lamy.* To this telegram the Colonial Office replied on the 6th that, for the time being, the general policy of H.M. Government was that no offensive action was to be taken without instructions from London. Mr. Boyle and some of the other civil officials in Nigeria were at this time somewhat concerned lest the withdrawal of most of the troops and several officials from their normal stations should give rise to internal disturbances; and on the receipt of this telegram he questioned the necessity of concentrating on the frontier to the extent ordered. But Colonel Carter would not agree to any alterations. Reports were reaching him that in the northern half of the Cameroons the Germans were still unaware of the outbreak of war, and he hoped to be

---

* This was evidently meant for 200 men. Actually, the normal French strength at Fort Lamy had been much depleted owing to operations in the extreme north of the Chad Territory.

able to take advantage of this.* But he warned the officers commanding the columns that though they were to obtain all possible information and watch the frontier, their troops were not to cross it. This difference of opinion was reported by Mr. Boyle to the Colonial Office in a telegram on the 8th August, which did not, however, give in detail Colonel Carter's reasons.

<small>British plans and preparations; 8th–17th August.</small> The Offensive Sub-Committee, on the same day (8th), decided that consideration of an offensive against Duala should be deferred till the Colonial Office, War Office, and Admiralty had worked out the details of the force that would be required. The Committee also recommended that, in the meantime, the Foreign Office should ascertain in what way, if any, the French Government would be prepared to allow their forces on the West Coast of Africa to co-operate.

To assist in working out the details of the force required, the Colonial Office telegraphed to Mr. Boyle on the 9th inquiring if Colonel Carter considered that an attack on Duala without naval co-operation held out any reasonable chance of success, and, if so, what force would be necessary. Mr. Boyle was also asked to report, after consultation with Colonel Carter, what troops could safely be spared from Nigeria for employment on this object, and, further, to ascertain the views of the French Governor-General at Dakar with regard to co-operation. The French Government, said the telegram, were being asked whether French troops could co-operate.

On the 10th August the British Ambassador at Paris replied, to the instructions sent him by the Foreign Office, that the French Government had already been considering an attack on Duala and were prepared to give naval co-operation for its occupation and that of any other ports in the Cameroons, which would be simultaneously invaded from the north-east by French troops. Information as to numbers would be given later.

Mr. Boyle telegraphed on the 12th August that Colonel Carter considered naval co-operation necessary for an attack on Duala, and that the force required and available from Nigeria would be 2,000 infantry with ten guns. As distance would make impossible French co-operation by land, Mr. Boyle had not communicated with Dakar. With a view to

---

* The German orders for concentration, sent by telegram through Nigeria, had been intercepted, decoded, and stopped by the British, who realised that the confirming copy of these orders sent by native runners would take some time to reach Garua and Mora.

freeing certain troops for the Duala attack, Colonel Carter was anxious to advance at once on Garua, so as to clear the north before any advance was made across the southern part of the frontier. Our war dispositions on the Bornu frontier were as follows. Maiduguri column, one company of mounted infantry and one company of infantry; Nafada column, two companies of infantry; and Yola column, one company of mounted infantry, two guns, and four companies of infantry. According to reliable information the German garrisons at Kuseri, Mora, and Garua consisted of 16, 30, and 170 men respectively. Colonel Carter advocated the engagement of 2,000 carriers from Sierra Leone, as he did not consider the local carriers suitable. For the Duala project Colonel Carter suggested an advance by one or two columns by land, combined with a strong attack from the sea to be made by landing parties formed from the 2,000 men from Nigeria, provided that the Admiralty would ensure their safe passage to and up the Cameroon river. Ships drawing up to twenty-one feet could at high water, according to the local Marine Department, lie within four or five thousand yards of Duala. After saying that it was absolutely essential to make preliminary reconnaissances on the frontier in connection with the operations, Mr. Boyle asked for a telegraphic reply as soon as possible, both concerning them and an advance on Garua.

It will be noted that the French Government had offered no land force to co-operate in an attack on Duala, and that the Nigerian authorities considered that distance would render such assistance impossible. But M. Ponty, the Governor-General of French West Africa, had, on the 10th, on his own initiative, asked the French Government for authority to prepare battalions for the Cameroons in addition to those which he offered for Morocco.

In a note written on the 9th August the Admiralty Staff expressed the opinion that an attack by sea would probably be the quickest means of capturing Duala, as lack of communication and difficult country would render co-operation between a joint expedition by sea and a force advancing by land from Nigeria practically impossible. At the same time military action in the interior should, they said, precede an attack by sea, so as to induce the enemy to reduce his coast defences. Such defences at Duala were unlikely to be formidable, and they concluded that the *Dwarf* would probably suffice for the naval work if no German armed ships were present. That day, however, the Admiralty received information from Lagos, obtained from the master of a British steamer just arrived from Cameroon ports, that a native rising there was feared ; that food was scarce and expensive ; that Germans had taken control of the wireless station at Fernando Po ; and that the enemy cruiser *Dresden* was expected momentarily at Duala. The information about the *Dresden* might, it was considered at the Admiralty, be correct, but it seemed to them improbable that the Spanish authorities would allow the Germans to control the wireless station at Fernando Po. On the 10th the Admiralty learnt that the *Dwarf* was cleaning boilers and could not be ready till the 14th, by which time it was expected that the naval situation would be clearer ; and on the 12th they heard that the *Dresden* had been met off the Amazon.

On the 12th August the Colonial Office proposed to the Governor of Sierra Leone that, in view of the improbability of an attack on Freetown, four companies of the West African Regiment, four companies of the W.A.F.F., and two 2·95" guns should be moved from there for operations elsewhere. After consultation with the General Officer Commanding, the Governor replied next day pointing out that this would mean serious modification of the defence arrangements, but that, if H.M. Government were fully satisfied that an attack was improbable, the General Officer Commanding was ready to detach four companies West African Regiment, two companies W.A.F.F., and two 2·95" guns. In view of possible unrest in the Protectorate, it was considered undesirable to move more of the W.A.F.F.

On the 14th August the Offensive Sub-Committee came to the conclusion that further information was necessary regarding the situation in the Cameroons and at Fernando Po before any definite decision to commence offensive operations against Duala could be given. General Dobell should, however, prepare plans in conjunction with the Admiralty, and the War Office should communicate direct with the General Officer Commanding Sierra Leone regarding the withdrawal of troops from there.

That evening the Colonial Office telegraphed instructions to Nigeria for Colonel Carter to ascertain and report if any definite movement of German troops was in progress. He was further given sanction to conduct the reconnaissances he had proposed, but he was to avoid serious hostilities and ensure ability to recall his troops at short notice. The War Office also, informing the General Officer Commanding Sierra

ALLIED CONFERENCE IN LONDON

Leone that the Admiralty were satisfied that no maritime attack was probable and that there was no fear of a hostile landing, inquired if he still thought that only two companies W.A.F.F. should be moved. To this he replied next day that six companies West African Regiment, two companies W.A.F.F., and two guns could be spared.

Early on the 15th August the Colonial Office received a telegram from the Gold Coast summarising information obtained the previous day from 800 Krooboys whom the Germans had found it advisable to deport from Duala.* They reported that steamers had been sunk to block the channel at Duala, which was also believed to be mined and was defended by guns mounted on land; the native population and the 250 native troops at Duala were disaffected and a recent rising of natives had occurred; there were 100 Germans there exclusive of crews of steamers, of which there had been about a dozen in the harbour on the 8th; the *Eber* had left Duala some days previously for an unknown destination, and a German warship was reported to be in the vicinity of the Congo river; and food for natives was scarce.

General Dobell, who had by this time come to the conclusion that the numbers of West African Frontier Force available would not suffice for an attack on Duala without French military assistance, attended on the 15th August a conference at the Admiralty, at which French officers were present, to discuss a joint offensive against Duala. This conference recommended that cruisers should be sent to Fernando Po to blockade the Cameroons coast, and, as this would warn the Germans and give them time to prepare, that the attack should not be unduly delayed. The assistance of the French gunboat *Surprise* and a French military force of 2,000 men with six guns from Dakar was promised; small steam launches should be requisitioned in the neighbouring British possessions and armed with 3-pounders and machine guns; Victoria would probably be the best place to land for the attack, for which 3,500 troops with artillery should suffice; † and, though everything should be prepared, more definite information

---

* The German crew of the small steamer *Marina* were compelled by the Krooboys, whom it was intended to land on the Kroo coast, to put in at Accra. Here the steamer—at first in the distance taken for a German gunboat—was seized and her crew interned.

† To make up this force Sierra Leone could spare 600 men if required, and Nigeria about 1,700 with ten 2·95" guns. The troops from Dakar would be ready in three weeks and the others very shortly.

from the blockading cruisers should be awaited before any troops were moved.

The Admiralty thereupon issued orders to Rear-Admiral A. P. Stoddart, commanding the 5th Cruiser Squadron in the mid-Atlantic area, to send a cruiser to Fernando Po to ascertain whether reports of German cruisers near Duala were true and to gain intelligence. He was told that there were mines off the entrance to Duala; that thirty German merchant ships were said to be taking refuge there; that one entrance was blocked; and that an expedition was ready to proceed to Duala, but awaiting the cruiser's report. The Rear-Admiral directed the *Cumberland* (Captain C. T. M. Fuller) to proceed to Fernando Po to search for and gain intelligence of German cruisers reported near the Cameroon river; and, having dealt with them, to turn her attention to thirty-two German steamers stated to be at Duala.

It had been decided on the 15th August to move two companies W.A.F.F. from Sierra Leone to Lome, for use either in Togoland or, if not required there, to be in a position of readiness for employment against Duala; and on the evening of the 17th August, the Offensive Sub-Committee having agreed, orders to move these two companies and 300 carriers, when the naval situation permitted, were sent to Sierra Leone by the Colonial Office.

General Dobell's appreciation; 16th August. On the 16th August General Dobell wrote a further appreciation of the situation, and, in forwarding it for the consideration of the Offensive Sub-Committee, suggested that before troops were concentrated the Germans should be called upon to surrender Duala, if only to obviate any chance of a native rising in which Germans might be massacred.

Taking Duala as the primary objective, he said that the nature of the country prohibited a landing below that place, on the Cameroon river, or on the banks of the many creeks forming the delta. He then proceeded to describe briefly, and as far as the imperfect information at his disposal permitted, the approach to Duala from the sea, the landing place at Victoria, and the land and river communications in the area between south-eastern Nigeria and Duala. He pointed out that when the rains ceased in the middle of September military operations would be easier and healthier, and that there were persistent reports that great dissatisfaction with German rule existed among the natives in the Duala region, and that its overthrow would be popular.* Recent information, apparently

---
* The cause of the disaffection was the arbitrary seizure by the Germans

reliable, that there was a shortage of native food in the country, indicated that the expedition must be self-contained in that respect.

Though he was evidently unable to give the dispositions of the German military forces, General Dobell estimated the total number of armed troops and police as 235 Germans and 3,100 natives with 9 guns and 17 machine guns. Natives other than troops or police were not allowed fire-arms of any description, but the Germans were believed to have a considerable reserve of rifles and ammunition, and most, if not all, of the 1,600 German males in the country were said to be in possession of sporting rifles, which probably fired service ammunition. In addition to these 1,600 must probably be added the crews of the several steamers taking refuge at Duala. Of the nine guns, six were reported to be at Duala. The Germans were said to be engaged with the French in the south-east Cameroons, so it was difficult to estimate what numbers they could make available to defend Duala. But it was certain that the numbers would include a large proportion of Europeans. The German gunboats *Panther* and *Eber* and the Governor's yacht *Spearber* (mounting six Q.F. guns) might, some or all, be at Duala. It appeared to be the German policy, in defending their colonies, to abandon the coast ports and after destroying everything of value to retire inland, possibly with the idea that no effective pursuit would be made, and that consequently at the conclusion of hostilities they would be able to plead a continuous occupation of the country. Their apparent intention to defend Duala might only be to keep out our cruisers, and it was very doubtful if they would offer serious opposition to a superior land force.

Taking all this into consideration, General Dobell came to the conclusion that a total Allied force of 3,500 with a proportion of artillery would suffice to capture Duala. The British could make available 2,000 men with ten 2·95″ guns;* and, in view of the distance the French would have to come and of their employment of native troops in Europe, it was possible that they might prefer to send only 1,600 men and

---

of the ground on the river front at Duala. The Dualese appealed through Chief Bell to Germany, but war broke out before their case had been heard. Shortly after the outbreak of war, the Germans arrested and hanged Chief Bell on the grounds that he had been conspiring with the British.

* i.e., Nigeria W.A.F.F. 1,650 with 8 guns, Sierra Leone W.A.F.F. 200, and the Gold Coast W.A.F.F. (Pioneer Company) 180 with 2 guns.

6 guns. He estimated that the British force would require some 3,300 carriers (from Sierra Leone 1,400, the Gold Coast 500, and Nigeria 1,400) : the scale of ammunition to be taken by our forces should be 150 rounds per gun, 500 rounds per rifle, and 5,000 rounds per machine gun ; the difficulties of disembarkation and the nature of the country rendered it undesirable to take riding horses ; and the local British Governments in West Africa would have to provide personnel for supply, transport, railway, telegraph, and medical duties, and the Nigeria Marine to supply steam launches, surf-boats, and lighters.

Concluding that, whatever the German action might be, our first object must be the occupation of Duala and Buea, it appeared to General Dobell that there were three courses open to us :—

(*a*) To move by sea and effect a landing near Duala ;

(*b*) To move part of the force by the Cross river and thence by road, combining with a simultaneous attack by sea on Duala ; and

(*c*) To land the whole force at Victoria, occupy Buea, and thence advance on Duala with such naval co-operation as might be possible.

The very unsuitable country to the south and east of Duala and the reported obstruction of the channel militated against (*a*) and (*b*), while for the latter a great number of carriers would be required, and it would be most difficult to synchronise the land and sea attacks. General Dobell consequently discarded these two courses and advocated (*c*), which, for the following reasons, offered a good prospect of success. Landing at Victoria was said to be very easy at all seasons of the year, and could be assisted, if required, by the guns of the escorting cruisers ; Buea and Zopo offered facilities for a base depot and hospital ; except for a landing at Duala this offered the shortest available line of advance, thus facilitating supply arrangements ; and it would keep the whole force concentrated for subsequent operations, the nature of which must depend on reconnaissance after landing.

Offensive Sub-Committee ; 17th August. At its meeting on the 17th August the Offensive Sub-Committee concurred generally in General Dobell's appreciation, and agreed that, as soon as H.M. Ships were in a position effectively to blockade Duala, it would be desirable to summon the garrisons of Buea, Duala, and Victoria to surrender. It was also agreed that the French Government should be informed that General Dobell would command the British

[*To face p.* 66

A Forest Track in the Cameroons

PRELIMINARY ARRANGEMENTS

expedition, and that they should be invited to place any co-operating French forces at his disposal.

The French, it was learnt two days later, proposed that while the superior naval command should be British, the military command should be French. But on the 23rd, in view of General Dobell's special qualifications, they agreed to the British proposal.

Sierra Leone, the Gold Coast, and Nigeria were instructed on the 18th August by the Colonial Office that in three or four weeks' time they would probably be required to embark the following troops and carriers :—

From Sierra Leone: 1,200 carriers in addition to those ordered on the 17th. No decision had yet been come to, they were told, regarding the West African Regiment;

From the Gold Coast: the Sierra Leone troops and carriers sent to Lome, a section of mountain guns and the pioneer company of the Gold Coast Regiment, and 500 carriers;

From Nigeria: Headquarters Staff, two batteries of four guns each and three battalions of four companies each of the Nigeria Regiment, also 1,500 carriers.

All these detachments were to be accompanied by adequate transport and medical staffs, and Nigeria was also to send personnel for railway and telegraph work. Sierra Leone might, and the Gold Coast and Nigeria would, be required to make arrangements for the necessary sea transport, the voyage being made under naval escort. Nigeria was, further, to provide sufficient boats and launches for the expeditious landing of the force, which might take place on an open beach. They were all asked if they foresaw any difficulties in carrying out these arrangements, regarding which definite instructions would be sent them as early as possible.

The Admiralty sent further instructions on the 19th August to Captain Fuller, informing him that a blockade of the Cameroons followed by combined Franco-British operations was contemplated, their main object being the destruction of the wireless station and naval base at Duala. He was told what troops would participate, and that the *Dwarf* and the French gunboat *Surprise* would be under his orders. He was to obtain the latest local intelligence at Lagos, and to be ready to act in co-operation with the military forces.

The *Cumberland* joined the *Dwarf* at Sierra Leone on the 21st August, and from there they both sailed on the 23rd August, escorting the transport carrying two companies

68 MILITARY OPERATIONS: THE CAMEROONS

Nigeria; 13th–19th August. W.A.F.F. and 300 carriers to Lome and Lagos, where they arrived on the 28th and 29th respectively.

It is necessary now to turn for a time to Nigeria. On the 13th August Colonel Carter with Regimental headquarters had arrived from Kaduna at Lagos, so as to be in close touch with Government headquarters; and on receipt of the instructions of the 14th from London he ordered special reconnaissances by the Maiduguri, Ikom, and Calabar columns. The mounted infantry, on arrival at Maiduguri, were to reconnoitre towards Mora, where the German strength was reported to be 70; and from Ikom and Calabar reconnaissances eastward were to try to ascertain if any German movements were in progress. No special reconnaissances from Yola were ordered, as they appeared to be unnecessary, owing to the expected immediate arrival from Garua of Major A. H. Festing, a retired officer employed by the Niger Company. He reached Yola on the 15th August, and reported that, when he left Garua on the 11th, the Germans knew nothing of the declaration of war. He also confirmed the information previously obtained that the German garrison of Garua consisted of about 10 Germans and 70 native rifles, with two machine guns.

As the result of the various reconnaissances, Colonel Carter reported to Mr. Boyle as follows on the 19th August. Concentration was in progress at all German company headquarters in the vicinity of the frontier; a company of Nigerian mounted infantry, supported by a company of infantry, was in close observation of Mora, but, as telegraphic communication with Maiduguri was interrupted, no actual report had been received; and German troops in small numbers were observing the whole frontier from the tenth parallel to Okuri, fifty miles north-east of Calabar. The following were reliable estimates of German posts on the frontier: Kuseri evacuated; Mora, 60 rifles; Garua, 10 Germans, 2 machine guns, and 70 rifles; from Kentu 2 Germans and 30 rifles had recently withdrawn to Bamenda; Ossidinge, 100 rifles; and Okuri, 20 rifles. Regarding the British dispositions, Colonel Maclear had two guns and four companies with four machine guns on the frontier east of Yola, and was being joined that day by a company of mounted infantry. This force, said Colonel Carter, was held in readiness to take the offensive against Garua; and he requested sanction to undertake it before German reinforcements could reach Garua, so as to clear the situation in the north of the Cameroons and free certain other British troops for service in the south. At Ikom, he

THE GARUA PROJECT

continued, Colonel Mair had four guns and 500 rifles with five machine guns, and was equipped with the necessary carriers ready to advance on Ossidinge if required.*

Mr. Boyle, who had just received the Colonial Office instructions regarding the probable utilisation overseas of troops from Nigeria, telegraphed to London on the 19th, in reply, that he foresaw no difficulties in making the necessary arrangements. He also said that though the channel in the Cameroon river was said to be blocked, it was believed that landing could be effected elsewhere. In a second telegram sent about the same time he informed the Colonial Office of the reports regarding the concentrations at German company headquarters and the size of the Garua garrison. He gave the strength of the British column at Yola and said: "Commandant urges and I entirely agree that it is advisable to occupy Garua in order to clear situation in North Cameroons before forces for embarkation are concentrated." † In reply, on the 20th, the Colonial Office authorised Colonel Carter, while bearing in mind the general plan, to use his own discretion in the case of Garua and any other similar post.

In England the preparations for the proposed operations continued. By the 25th August General Dobell had obtained further information, and his inferences from this and from the reports of the fighting in Togoland led him to inform the Offensive Sub-Committee on that day that some modification in his appreciation of the 16th was necessary. He estimated that, including reservists and police, the German armed forces in the Cameroons numbered from 1,500–2,000 Germans and well over 3,000 natives, all well trained and armed with modern rifles. He also estimated that they had 9 field guns, 12 to 15 quick-firing guns off ships, and 30 machine guns. Though it was unlikely that the whole of this force would be concentrated for the defence of Duala and Buea, General Dobell considered it possible that the enemy's strength there might amount to 1,200 Germans and 1,600 natives with a large proportion of the guns. He had accordingly come to the conclusion that the expedition would require more ammunition than he had anticipated. It had been decided that the contingent from Sierra Leone was to include two

Offensive Sub-Committee; 25th August.

---

* An idea, prevalent in Nigeria at the time, that the German native soldiers would rise in rebellion in case of a British invasion, contributed to Colonel Carter's desire to advance into the Cameroons.

† It is noteworthy that this telegram did not give more of the information in Colonel Carter's report.

2·95″ guns of the Sierra Leone Company, R.G.A., and four companies West African Regiment, which would bring the total of the Allied expeditionary force up to about 4,000 native ranks, with 16 guns and 30 machine guns. This strength was not excessive, but General Dobell considered that the difficulties of supply and the nature of the country rendered its increase undesirable. He considered that, though the result was in no way a foregone conclusion, there were good prospects of success. He was unable to suggest any means of making the attainment of our object more certain.

The Offensive Sub-Committee, evidently satisfied that everything possible had been done, agreed that Departments should be responsible for the following duties in connection with the operations. The Admiralty for all the naval and sea transport arrangements: the War Office for the provision and administration of the detachment from the Imperial garrison in Sierra Leone; for advice regarding the composition of the military force, the organisation of the Staff, and the numbers of the medical personnel; and for the provision of maps and any additional military equipment required: the Colonial Office for the provision and administration of the Colonial forces participating, including medical, accountant, and political personnel: and the Foreign Office for all necessary communication with the French Government regarding the progress of the arrangements and operations and French co-operation. The Committee also agreed that it would not be advisable to summon the surrender of Duala until the military expedition was in a position to commence active operations.

All the arrangements in London were completed within the next three days, and on the 28th August definite instructions were issued to the Gambia, Sierra Leone, the Gold Coast, and Nigeria. General Dobell, with several staff officers,* leaving Liverpool on the 31st in the transport *Appam*,† was to call at

---

* General Staff Officer (2)
  (Senior G.S. Officer) .. Lieut.-Col. A. J. Turner, Royal Artillery.
  General Staff Officer (2) Major J. Brough, Royal Marine Artillery.
  D.A.A. & Q.M.G. .. Captain R. H. Rowe, Royal Artillery.
  Chief Engineer and
  Director of Signals .. Captain F. L. N. Giles, Royal Engineers.
  Political Officer .. K. V. Elphinstone, Esq. (of the Nigerian Civil Service).
  Financial Officer .. H. St. J. Sheppard, Esq. (of the Nigerian Civil Service).

† For this vessel, Messrs. Elder Dempster & Co., who owned the steamer, were to arrange for two Masters who had a thorough knowledge of the Cameroons coast, especially in the vicinity of Duala.

Bathurst to pick up a signal section of the Gambia Company, W.A.F.F., about the 9th September, and at Freetown the next day to embark the Sierra Leone contingent. The Gold Coast was to have its necessary transports ready, and all the troops, carriers, etc., detailed for the expedition (including the detachment from Sierra Leone at Lome) prepared to embark on the 14th September. By the 15th Nigeria was to have ready at Lagos one battalion and one battery, together with light-draught vessels carrying a good supply of surf-boats. The remainder of the Nigerian contingent was to be ready with transports at the most convenient ports. The *Appam* with its naval escort was also to call at Dakar, to escort thence the French contingent.

The written instructions of H.M. Government to General Dobell, issued to him on the 29th August by the Colonial Office, were as follows. The initial objective of the joint British and French expedition, which he had been selected to command, was to be the capture of Victoria, Buea, and Duala. He was to make no formal proclamation of the annexation of any occupied territory, for the administration of which he was given discretion to take the necessary measures. He was given authority to call upon the Governors of the British Colonies and Protectorates in West Africa for reinforcements, munitions of war, supplies, or other requirements. He was to use his discretion as regards summoning the German garrison in the Cameroons to surrender before the actual initiation of an attack. He was to acquaint the senior British naval and French naval and military officers with his instructions, and to arrange for an interchange of British and French officers on the staffs of the respective commanders. He was to keep the Secretary of State for the Colonies informed of the progress of the operations and the Governor-General of Nigeria of any political developments. Finally, he was informed that a copy of these instructions was being communicated to the French Government, the Governor-General of Nigeria, and the Governors of the Gambia, Sierra Leone, and the Gold Coast.

<small>Government instructions to General Dobell.</small>

In transmitting these copies to the different British Governors the Colonial Office requested them to comply, to the best of their ability, with any requisitions received from General Dobell. The Governor-General of Nigeria was also informed that the entire responsibility for the military operations and for provisional measures of civil administration in the Cameroons rested with General Dobell.

Offensive Sub-Committee; 29th August. On the 29th August General Dobell received information from Mr. D. McCallum,* a Consular Assistant, who had recently returned from the Cameroons, which showed him that the country between Victoria and Duala would be almost impracticable for military operations during the next two months.

On hearing this, the Offensive Sub-Committee met at once to consider whether it would be advisable to issue any further instructions regarding the operations. They agreed that, if this information proved to be correct, some modification in the plan of attack would be necessary, probably involving a larger measure of combination between the naval and military forces. In view, however, of additions which were being arranged for to the naval force participating, it was considered unnecessary to issue any further instructions or to alter existing arrangements, the actual method of attack being left to General Dobell to decide in consultation with the Senior Naval Officer.

Few people are likely to question the soundness of this decision, as even though our information was defective, the project offered sufficiently good prospects of success. To deprive the Germans of the use of Duala as a base for raids was essential, and to occupy it ourselves was obviously the best plan. That there was no pre-war plan for this operation and insufficient information at the outbreak of war on which to base a plan was one of many instances of our national unpreparedness.

---

* Volunteering to accompany the expedition, he sailed at forty-eight hours' notice, and throughout the operations in the Cameroons performed invaluable services as an officer of the Intelligence Staff.

CHAPTER III

AUGUST—17TH SEPTEMBER 1914

THE PREPARATIONS TO ATTACK DUALA; AND OPERATIONS UNDERTAKEN BY THE ALLIES IN THE NORTH-WEST AND SOUTH-EAST OF THE GERMAN COLONY

(Maps 2, 4, 5, 6, 7 and 11)

Duala town, consisting of a European and a native quarter (Bell Town), extended for about two and a half miles along the southern bank of the Wuri river and possessed a floating dock, good quays, roads and buildings, artesian wells, a modern system of sanitation and an ice factory. Two telegraph cables connected it with Europe : a British line via Lagos and Bonny, and a German one, which had been cut at the outbreak of war, via Lome. There was also a small wireless station. In August 1914 Duala was the actual seat of German government.

The estuary, at the head of which it stands, is formed by several rivers—the Wuri (or Cameroon) and the Dibamba (or Lungasi) being the most important—and by a number of mangrove-bordered creeks, most of them navigable by small craft to a greater or less extent. The navigable entrance, lying about midway between Cape Cameroon and Suelaba Point, was of a width of about one and a half miles, and there were three bars; an outer one, extending from seven to ten miles outside Cape Cameroon with a general depth of four fathoms, with some considerably shallower patches; a middle bar, reaching from about four miles eastward of Cape Cameroon to the flats on the east of Rugged Point; and an inner bar, about a mile south-westward of Duala, with a depth of nine feet and a dredged channel of twenty-one feet. Of other channels little was known to the Allies except that the depth of the various waterways leading into the estuary varied with the rainfall and that bars existed at the mouths of most of them. Immediately inside Suelaba Point there was anchorage for deep-draught vessels.

74 MILITARY OPERATIONS: THE CAMEROONS

For vessels the difficulty in approaching the West African coast, owing to the numerous shallows, the flat coast and the lack of well-defined features, was at all times enhanced by the constant shifting of shoals and channels. Charts were consequently unreliable, and the only safe guides were buoys, beacons and other artificial aids to navigation. The removal of these would obviously be one of the first measures of the German defence, combined probably with other active measures, such as mines laid and guns mounted to block and protect navigable channels.

<small>British naval progress; 28th–29th August 1914.</small> For the ten days preceding the *Cumberland's* * arrival at Lome on the 28th August, Captain Fuller and his officers studied all documents on board bearing on the situation. But, as the information gained was scanty, old and probably in many cases unreliable, no definite plan of action could be formulated. It seemed certain that Duala harbour would be defended, possibly with mines at the entrance, though if German cruisers were operating from there the outer channel might be clear. In this case it might not be possible to do more than reconnoitre; and the *Cumberland*, unable to get within range of Duala, might have to act as a base for smaller vessels capable of exploring and blockading the many subsidiary waterways. If this were so, natives would have to be engaged to act as pilots and guides, and also Europeans accustomed to work with them.

At Lome, examination of the log of the *Marina*—in which the Krooboys had been deported from Duala †—showed that all buoys in the fairway had been removed and that steamers had been sunk to block the channel. But interrogation of the Krooboys failed to show whether this was the inner or the outer channel, whether mines had been laid, or the position, number and size of the German guns said to have been mounted on land.

At Lagos, on the 29th August, Captain Fuller gained further and more reliable information. The definite instructions issued by H.M. Government the previous evening had also just reached there, and he received a telegram from the Admiralty which, after instructing him to co-operate with General Dobell—who was expected to reach Lagos on the 15th September—informed him that his immediate duties

---

* *Armament* :—Fourteen 6-inch, eight 12-pounders, three 3-pounders, also a field gun and two machine guns.

† See p. 63, *ante*.

were to gain intelligence and to prepare to assist in the attack on Duala with light-draught vessels. He was handed by the Nigerian authorities copies of the latest available maps and charts, as well as two memoranda which had been specially prepared for him. One by Major Wallace Wright, General Staff Officer of the Nigeria Regiment, contained the latest information regarding Duala and its vicinity, and the other an appreciation drawn up on the 13th August by the Acting-Director of Marine, Lieutenant J. Percival, R.N.R.

The latter, which outlined a plan of attack assimilating closely to that which was subsequently adopted, deserves mention in some detail. It appeared to Lieutenant Percival that the objective of combined operations should be Duala, as if this place was captured the enemy would probably retire to the north, in which case the other ports west of Duala could easily be blockaded, and supplies, of which the enemy was already said to be short, cut off. Discarding the idea of landing the attacking force west of Duala owing to the difficult and little known nature of the intervening country in which the enemy would have the advantage, as well as to the fact that it would not be easy to protect and maintain communication with the open sea base which such a landing place must at first provide, he considered that troops should land quite close to Duala itself. For this a good sea base could be found just within the entrance to the Cameroon estuary. Here the narrowness of the entrance would facilitate protection against sea attack, while hostilities from within could only be carried out by light-draught and lightly armed vessels with which similar vessels of our own should be able to cope.

To afford the necessary protection to our transports against the German warships likely to be encountered, Lieutenant Percival considered that one British cruiser drawing not more than twenty-one feet and one gunboat of the *Dwarf* class should be sufficient. The cruiser could get within two miles of Duala, and he suggested that, under cover of her fire, the transport flotilla, escorted by the gunboat, could cross the inner bar and land troops at Duala without much opposition. The gunboat could give covering fire at close range and also ensure protection against attacks by lightly armed enemy vessels sheltering upstream from the cruiser's fire. Landing at Duala would present no difficulties, as, in addition to a good government wharf, there were four smaller ones belonging to commercial firms. It would be necessary to guard against mines, though there was nothing to show that the Germans had either vessels or facilities for laying these. Also, after the British flotilla had anchored at a base within the mouth of the estuary, a thorough reconnaissance of the surrounding waterways would be necessary, not only to search for and hunt down armed enemy vessels, but to look for a suitable landing place on the Dibamba river for a subsidiary attack on Duala from the south-east.

For inshore protection and reconnaissance work and for the transport of troops up creeks and inlets, Lieutenant Percival recommended certain vessels, which he named, belonging to the Nigeria Marine; and he outlined his proposals for protecting and arming them.

The General Staff memorandum, drawn up with the assistance of Nigeria Marine officers, gave a précis of the information obtained up to date bearing on an attack on Duala (a) via the Cameroon estuary, (b) via the Sanaga river and Edea, and (c) via Victoria and Zopo. The general conclusions which the General Staff had arrived at from this information were as follows :—

(i) That the Germans were prepared for, and feared, an attack on Duala, but that they had been emboldened by the favourable war news from Europe to hope for assistance from there if they could hold out long enough.

(ii) That they could not rely on their native troops or the natives generally, who were as likely to assist the British as the Germans.

(iii) That buoys had been removed from the channel of the estuary, that it had been blocked at various places by sunken vessels, and that mines had probably been laid.

(iv) That entrenchments had been made and guns mounted round Duala and to the south but not far from it, though their exact position was uncertain (one report mentioned a battery at Rugged Point); that the guns probably consisted of four 4-cm., and a few others of old pattern, with possibly one or two landed from ships; but that the defence arrangements generally were not of a formidable nature.

(v) That the Duala garrison, consisting possibly of 700 Germans and 400 natives, was capable of opposition which must not be underestimated.

The memorandum gave information which showed that a route for launches to Duala existed via Manoka Bay, Dibamba river and Doctor Creek; that coastal steamers could cross the bar of the Sanaga river to Malimbe, whence to Edea (where a waterfall stopped navigation) steamers drawing twelve feet could navigate without difficulty, and that from Edea to Duala the best way was by the 100-foot clearing made for the railway, which crossed the Dibamba by a bridge; and as regards an advance via Victoria, where landing would be easy—especially as the German troops at Zopo were believed to have been withdrawn to Duala—there were two or three routes to Bonaberi, where launches to cross the mile of river to Duala would, however, be probably unprocurable. The General Staff concluded that successful operations against Duala were possible by any of these three routes, but that, in view of transport difficulties in an unknown country, an advance by the Cameroon estuary and a landing between Duala and Doctor Creek would be the easiest operation, provided that the guns from naval vessels could cover the landing.

In a paper giving the British and German dispositions near the Anglo-German frontier, the General Staff estimated that the Germans were in some strength at Ossidinge but that they did not appear to be in any force to the east of Calabar.

That day Captain Fuller with some of his officers attended a conference with the local civil, military and marine authorities at Government House, to discuss plans. Here, as the writer of an article in *Blackwood's Magazine* for December 1915 [*] points out, the naval officers realised how much had to be learnt about Africa before any enterprise was likely to be attended with success. In this case they were able to count, for the local knowledge and experience required, on the Nigeria Marine contingent, to the great value of whose work all accounts of the subsequent operations pay tribute.

The conference confirmed the opinion which Captain Fuller had formed before his arrival that an advance by the Cameroon estuary offered the best method of attacking Duala. It was clear, however, that the lines of the proposed operations could not be settled pending both investigation and reconnaissance by the *Cumberland*, and the arrival of General Dobell. But Captain Fuller considered it essential that immediate steps should be taken to prepare light-draught vessels; and, after he had personally inspected and approved those recommended by Lieutenant Percival, work on them was at once put in hand and continued day and night. Except for officers and crews for the guns, which the Navy would provide, they were all to be manned by natives under officers of the Nigeria Marine contingent.

---

[*] " Doing her Bit," by Guns, Q.F.C. To this article the author is indebted for much useful information.

For the purposes of the expedition Captain Fuller also took a number of Nigeria Marine native ratings on to the books of his ship, twenty of them as stokers and twenty with a surf-boat for use in landing over bars. Mr. Bell—uncle to Chief Bell of Duala, recently executed by the Germans—who was anxious to assist us as a means of gaining the throne to which he was heir, also joined the *Cumberland* with twenty native guides, pilots and intelligence agents.

Having arranged that the Nigerian flotilla of light craft under command of Commander R. H. W. Hughes, R.N.R., who was captain of the Government yacht *Ivy*, should join him at Ambas Bay on the 6th September, Captain Fuller sailed in the *Cumberland* on the evening of the 29th August for Fernando Po, the *Dwarf** (Commander F. E. K. Strong, R.N.) remaining at Lagos to clean boilers.

Naval progress. Arriving off Fernando Po on the 31st August, the *Cumberland* searched the coast but found no signs of enemy ships beyond two small steamers in Santa Isabel harbour. She then proceeded to the Cameroons coast and examined Ambas Bay and the entrance to the Cameroon estuary, where an enemy merchantman acting as guardship was driven in. As the *Cumberland's* signals were being continually jammed by the German wireless station at Duala, she returned to Calabar to communicate by land wire with her collier and with Lagos and to report progress to the Admiralty. She then proceeded to San Carlos Bay in Fernando Po, arriving there on the evening of the 2nd September.

Captain Fuller thus missed a telegram sent him by the Admiralty on the 2nd † informing him that H.M.S. *Challenger* ‡ and a French cruiser would join the Allied flotilla of troop transports, probably reaching Sierra Leone on the 10th, and would then proceed to join him at Ambas Bay or any other rendezvous he selected. Before taking action, Captain Fuller was to discuss the scheme of operations personally with General Dobell and the French senior naval officers. He was further instructed that, as military operations by land from Victoria to Duala seemed impracticable, a direct attack on Duala from the river would probably be necessary. He was accordingly to try to find a safe passage over the outer bar for the *Challenger* and was to prepare to arm launches and light-draught steamers.

---

* *Armament* :—Two 4-inch and four 12-pounders.
† It does not appear to have reached him till the 10th.
‡ *Armament* :—Eleven 6-inch and eight 12-pounders.

To face p. 79]

Ambas Bay

Captain Fuller had telegraphed from Calabar to the Governor-General of Nigeria that he considered a base at Ambas Bay essential, and he suggested that Victoria, which the enemy was reported to have evacuated, should be occupied by troops as soon as possible. Sir Frederick Lugard, who had just arrived back at Lagos from England to find that Nigerian troops in the north-east had sustained reverses, did not agree to a military occupation of Victoria and referred the matter to London. From here on the 4th September the Colonial Office replied that, pending General Dobell's arrival, no attempt should be made to occupy Victoria.

In the meantime, the *Cumberland*, after coaling on the 3rd and being rejoined by the *Dwarf*, had sailed with her at midnight (3rd/4th) for Ambas Bay, with the object of gaining the sheltered base which the Nigerian flotilla would require in bad weather.

The two warships arrived off Ambas Bay at daybreak on the 4th September and, in spite of a heavy swell which made sweeping by *Cumberland's* boats difficult, the channel to the anchorage was reported to be free of mines by 4 p.m. About an hour later a party of seamen and marines landed at Victoria, the German official in charge having stated, in answer to an ultimatum, that his lack of troops prevented his offering any opposition. Captain Fuller's object was to cut telegraphic communication, collect supplies, secure any steamboats, lighters or surf-boats and gain information of the enemy. Most of the stores and provisions had, however, already been removed, but a guard of marines was left on shore for the night to prevent any further removals. A few telephone wires were cut and some lighters were found there, but the efforts to obtain reliable information were not very successful.

Ambas Bay: 4th–7th September.

Next morning landing parties began to remove the stores. But at 8 a.m. an ultimatum demanding an instant British evacuation was received from the commander of some German troops who, coming from the direction of Buea and Duala, had surrounded Victoria during the night. They were estimated to be about 500 strong, and their dominating positions in the surrounding bush made it clear that no advantage was to be gained by attempting to offer resistance. The British landing parties consequently re-embarked; and the *Cumberland*, after sending a warning message ashore, shelled the food store, which in a few minutes was wrecked and burning furiously.

Reporting to the Admiralty on the 6th September, Captain Fuller said that Victoria was strongly entrenched against an attempted landing and that it could be reinforced in nine hours from Duala, where there were reported to be 1,000 armed Europeans. That day the *Cumberland* and *Dwarf* were joined, at a rendezvous some six miles south of Ambas Bay, by the Nigerian flotilla under Commander Hughes. This consisted of the yacht *Ivy*, the steam lifeboat *Moseley*, two steam-launches (*Vigilant* and *Vampire*), two motor-launches (*Alligator* and *Crocodile*), two steam tugs (*Walrus* and *Balbus*), and a lighter filled with stores, explosives and mines. The *Ivy* was armed with an old muzzle-loading 7-pounder gun of no value and two machine guns, but the launches and tugs, though protected with iron plates, were not as yet armed.

The sudden appearance of the German troops at Victoria had prevented the British from removing the lighters found there, but Captain Fuller now organised a cutting-out expedition to gain possession of them during the night of the 6th/7th September. Twenty men from the *Cumberland*, wearing indiarubber-soled shoes, with their faces and hands blackened and armed only with revolvers, were embarked in the *Walrus* and the *Vampire* (each towing a cutter) in charge of Lieutenant A. W. Hughes, R.N.R., and Lieutenant G. F. Carlton, R.N.R., the whole operation being under the direction of Commander Strong in the *Dwarf*. Three lighters and a water-boat were anchored within one hundred yards of the shore, but the cutting-out party in the two cutters succeeded in reaching them, apparently unobserved, and in removing them without any opposition. Heavy rain was falling at the time; and it was subsequently learnt that the German commander, observing their approach and believing that it implied a surprise landing, had given his men orders not to fire till the attackers left their boats. The departure of the British craft was also observed, but was taken to mean that the attempt to land had been abandoned. It was not till daylight that the enemy realised what had occurred.

Off the Estuary; 7th–9th September. On the 7th September the *Cumberland* and *Dwarf*, with the flotilla, arrived at a position about twenty miles south-west of Cape Cameroon and anchored. They had been sighted by a German merchant ship acting as guardship; all the fairway and channel buoys had been removed; it was possible that mines had been laid in the fairway and guns mounted at Cape Cameroon and Suelaba Point; and the Germans had at least two armed vessels in the estuary without counting the *Eber* and *Panther*, of whose whereabouts nothing was known. As the British small craft for minesweeping were unarmed, they

NAVAL RECONNAISSANCE

could not safely work beyond the range of the warships' guns; and consequently the advance would have to be carried out by stages.

Sweeping and surveying operations were commenced on the 8th and, the position of the outer fairway buoy having been determined and marked by a lighter at a point about twelve miles south-west of Cape Cameroon, a second temporary base was formed there. From here the channel was gradually found, swept and buoyed; and after dark on the 8th, a third base was established at a position well within the warships' gun range of the two headlands. That evening the small steamer *Trojan* arrived from Nigeria, loaded with buoys, sinkers and moorings. During the night of the 8th/9th, Mr. Bell and three of his men were landed on the beach to the west of Cape Cameroon, to try to make their way to Duala, to gain information and to persuade the natives to assist us, arrangements being made to pick them up at the same place after dark on the 11th September.

Meanwhile the sweeping operations progressed. By the 9th September no mines had been found and no opposition had been encountered, but, to ascertain if there were guns mounted on shore, the two headlands were searched with gun-fire by the *Cumberland*. This had no result and parties of marines, previously embarked in the *Dwarf* and *Ivy*, landed in surf-boats. They found Cape Cameroon unoccupied, and captured on Suelaba Point a German signalling party of three men. In the afternoon the *Dwarf* entered the estuary and reported that a barrage had been formed of sunken merchant vessels and lighters across the fairway off Rugged Point, about seven miles below Duala. Shortly afterwards the German armed yacht *Herzogin Elisabeth* appeared. She was promptly engaged by the *Dwarf* at a range of 6,000 yards and was quickly forced to retire, apparently on fire, revealing, as she went, the existence of a passage on the south side of the wreck barrage.*

On the 10th September the *Cumberland* proceeded into the estuary and established a base on the north side of Suelaba Point. There the small craft, after several days of discomfort, were able to lie comfortably. This position, where the main base remained till the fall of Duala, had many advantages. Sufficient depth and room existed to anchor a number of vessels; it afforded a clear view of the entrance to the various rivers and

Naval operations from base at Suelaba; 10th–23rd September.

---

* According to *Der Grosse Krieg, 1914–1918*, this navigable passage had been excavated by the force of the strong current.

creeks at a sufficient distance to thwart surprise attacks; the *Cumberland*, covered by the land, could command with her guns the entrance to the outer channel and thus control it without establishing a distant patrol; and it was far enough out from the surrounding land to be comparatively free of mosquitoes. Communication with Lagos was, however, difficult, as the Duala station jammed all wireless signals and necessitated the use of a despatch boat to carry telegrams to Calabar.

Steps were now commenced to arm the light craft. A 12-pounder was mounted in the *Ivy*, and arrangements made for the remainder (except the *Cumberland's* picket boat, whose armament was a 3-pounder and a machine gun) each to carry a machine gun on an improvised mounting when employed at any distance.

The German steamer *Kamerun*, which had been stationed at the entrance to give warning by wireless of an enemy's approach, was found abandoned off Manoka Point and was taken possession of.*

To examine a route which appeared from the chart to lie up the Dibamba river and Doctor Creek and which might allow of a landing to destroy the Duala wireless station, a successful reconnaissance was carried out that day by two steamboats from the *Cumberland* under Lieutenant-Commander R. S. Sneyd. On their way they sank a large German steam launch, whose crew ran her ashore and escaped into the bush; and at Pitti, after dispersing a small enemy party which opposed them, they landed a party which destroyed a telephone apparatus and captured some important papers relating to the defence of the Midland Railway. But there were no signs of a practicable way into Doctor Creek, and any idea of landing by this route was dismissed.

In the meantime sweeping operations past both sides of the wreck barrage had cleared the channel to within six miles of Duala; and the *Dwarf* passed the barrage.

This consisted of eight sunken steamers and, in the gaps between them, lighters filled with sand or concrete. Work was at once commenced to clear a channel through it for the passage of the *Challenger* and the transports of the expeditionary force. No salvage plant was available, and the necessary demo-

---

* She was undamaged, and all her modern and valuable gear was intact. After being salved with much labour and ingenuity, she was taken to Suelaba and used as a depot for prisoners. Her wireless set was subsequently used on board one of our own armed craft.

lition was undertaken by the *Cumberland's* divers and torpedo staff under the direction of Commander Hughes of the Nigerian Contingent, the work, owing to the strong current, being both dangerous and difficult. About this time a telegram was sent to Lagos asking the authorities there to prepare a large lighter and a dredger, each to take a 6-inch gun. These did not arrive, however, till after the fall of Duala.

The *Dwarf* and *Ivy* took turns as guardship at the wreck barrage in order to protect the diving and salvage party from German attacks and to prevent them sinking any more ships; and by the 22nd September, this party had succeeded in clearing a passage sufficient for a ship of nineteen feet draught to pass through.*

In the meantime and till the fall of Duala the British light craft were constantly employed in sweeping, surveying and reconnaissance operations, which were full of exciting incidents, but of which space forbids more than the relation of a few typical examples. The necessary exploration of the various creeks, which afforded innumerable hiding places for enemy craft of all descriptions, was particularly hazardous and trying. The width of these creeks varied from about forty to six hundred yards, and their waters were apt to shoal so suddenly that vessels reconnoitring were constantly grounding. Practically throughout their course, moreover, these waterways were bordered by an almost impenetrable belt of mangroves rising some fifteen feet above high-water level; and this made ambushes easy and generally impossible to discern till they were disclosed by a sudden burst of fire at close range, fortunately as a rule—owing to the enemy's bad marksmanship—with no very great effect. The boats employed had frequently to be away for several days at a time and, as their small accommodation included no protection from the torrential rains and the bites of mosquitoes, the crews suffered considerably, few of them escaping without malaria. The daily temperature was very high, flies were a constant source of irritation, and, as fresh food would not keep and was unprocurable locally, diet was generally unsuitable and monotonous. The water in the creeks was unfit for consumption, so all drinking water had to be carried from the start; and at night time, when navigation was impossible, the continual torment from insects, the noises of wild animals on shore and the danger of a surprise

---

* Bad weather, strong tides and the failure of the first locally made mines to detonate had all impeded progress.

attack at close quarters left little chance of sleep. There were in fact many sources of trouble and difficulty in these regions, most of them affecting equally operations by land and by water. But sufficient has been said to show that the strain on officers and men by day and night was quite abnormal.

Much valuable help in these operations was obtained from the natives of the Duala region. Their readiness to give us assistance was asserted by Mr. Bell on his return on the 11th, when he brought information regarding the enemy dispositions and also several natives who volunteered as pilots. A number of canoes also came out full of natives with evidence of their harsh treatment by the Germans and with expressed desire by many of them for means to retaliate. By their prohibition, under severe penalties extending even to death, of the use of canoes, the Germans had stopped fishing; and when the invariable request to be allowed to resume this was as invariably acceded to by us, the people's gratitude was unbounded and showed itself frequently in active assistance.

On the 11th September, while covering sweeping operations towards Duala, the *Dwarf* was fired upon by a well-masked battery of field guns on Yoss Point. The *Dwarf* turned sixteen points and retired, replying vigorously, and succeeded in completely silencing the battery. But she received one shell hit on her bridge, which wounded five men, one mortally.* By the evening the channel had been swept and surveyed as far as Doctor Creek, no trace of mines having been found.

On the 13th September, at 10.30 p.m., the *Ivy*, then guard-ship at the barrage, was subjected to a brief and unsuccessful attack by the armed merchant ship *Nachtigal*. Next day, the *Cumberland's* picket boat, while reconnoitring the Mikanje Creek, encountered the *Nachtigal* and was forced to retire under fire; but on the *Ivy* arriving to assist her the *Nachtigal* retreated into the Bimbia river, where the *Ivy* could not follow owing to the state of the tide.

On the 16th September, the *Dwarf* commenced a search for the *Nachtigal*, anchoring at sunset in the Bimbia river near Tiko. As it happened, she and the *Nachtigal* had unknowingly anchored within a mile of one another, and three hours later the latter appeared steaming at full speed round a bend less

---

* In commending the work in this action of the *Dwarf's* officers and men, Captain Fuller drew special attention to the conduct of Lieutenant E. F. L. Jones, R.N., the navigating officer, who, as the result of this shell and owing to the Captain being in the spotting top, found himself single-handed on the bridge in a narrow channel and shallow water.

than a hundred yards away from the *Dwarf*. The latter switched on her searchlight and at once opened fire, literally blowing the *Nachtigal's* foremost gun and crew into the water. But this was not sufficient to stop her and she rammed the *Dwarf* abreast the foremast, though, as she had already slipped her cable and had started going astern, the blow was lessened somewhat. Disengaging herself, the *Dwarf* continued to fire at point blank range till it was realised that the *Nachtigal* was making no reply and was on fire and drifting. She sank half an hour later. The *Nachtigal's* captain, three other Germans and ten natives—all that had not been killed out of a complement of 12 Germans and 25 natives—had jumped overboard and were rescued, all the Germans and some of the natives having been wounded. The *Dwarf* herself was badly holed by the special ram which had been fitted to the *Nachtigal*, but was able to return next day to Suelaba, where her repair was taken in hand by *Cumberland's* artificers and completed within a week—in the circumstances a very fine piece of work. In describing the fight, Captain Fuller commended specially the conduct of Commander Strong and Lieutenant Jones and of some half dozen others of the ship's company.

On the previous night, i.e., 15th September, when acting as guardship at the wreck barrage, the *Dwarf* had been attacked successively between 10.30 and 11.15 by two enemy launches. They were driven off and next morning one of them was seen derelict and ashore on an adjacent sandbank. Attached to her bow was an infernal machine, fashioned out of two gas cylinders and percussion fuzes, with which it had been hoped to ram the *Dwarf*. But the German coxswain had jumped overboard prematurely, the launch went wide, and he himself—the boat which was to pick him up having retired when the *Dwarf* opened fire—took refuge on the wreck barrage, where he was taken prisoner next morning.

A similar infernal machine, intended for a second attack on the barrage guardship, was found on the bow of one of two launches encountered and sunk on the 19th by the *Cumberland's* steam pinnace under Lieutenant B. F. Adams, R.N.; and on the 22nd the picket boat under the same officer, reconnoitring the Mungo Creek, attacked an enemy party entrenched at Boadibo. Lieutenant Adams and an able seaman were wounded, and after an action lasting twenty minutes the picket boat retired, having accounted for several of the enemy.

Between the 19th and 21st September a line of flag buoys

was observed across the river below Duala, and the supposition that the enemy had laid a line of mines there proved subsequently to be correct.

On the 16th the powerful tug *Remus* had arrived from Lagos, protected by iron plating and prepared to take 12-pounder guns. Three of these from the *Cumberland* were then mounted in her, and she was finally commissioned for service on the 22nd. On that day the old paddle-wheel tug *Porpoise*, similarly prepared, also joined from Lagos, and by the 25th had been armed with two 12-pounders and one 3-pounder. A 3-pounder had also been mounted in the *Vigilant*. With this accession to the flotilla and the successful accomplishment of the greater part of the preparatory work, all was ready for the arrival of the troops.

On the 23rd September, H.M.S. *Challenger* (Captain C. P. Beaty-Pownall, R.N.) arrived with six transports containing the British contingent of the expeditionary force under General Dobell. The *Challenger* at once commenced the work of lightening ship, so as to enable her to pass through the barrage to within effective range of Duala. Here for the time we will leave the naval operations and return to occurrences in Nigeria.

Lagos; 20th August 1914. Acting on the latitude accorded him by the Colonial Office telegram of the 20th August, Colonel Carter issued instructions that day to the commander of the Maiduguri Column to attack and capture Mora if he considered that his force was adequate. Colonel Carter also telegraphed to the officer commanding at Nafada to send a company to the frontier to get into touch, by native runners, with the Maiduguri Column.

Maiduguri Column; 6th–16th August 1914. After sending orders on the 6th to " C " Company, Mounted Infantry, at Geidam to move to Maiduguri, Captain Fox had left that place on the 9th August with " A " Company, 2nd Battalion Nigeria Regiment, and had moved out along the road which led to Mora (some 85 miles distant) over open and park-like country. On the 10th he camped at Konduga and pushed forward a small detachment to Awulari, a village near the frontier. Two days later he telegraphed to Lagos that a German force of unknown strength was near Bama ; and that, pending further orders, he would remain entrenched at Konduga. On the 13th August he obtained fairly reliable information that the German garrison of the small brick loopholed post at Mora consisted of less than 100 native soldiers with six Germans. They were said to have a large quantity of

[*To face p.* 86

Victoria Harbour

grain stored there. On the 15th, the day before the mounted infantry company left Maiduguri to join him, he received Colonel Carter's order to use them in a reconnaissance towards Mora, where the latest reports indicated that the Germans had taken up an entrenched position on the Mora mountain.

From the diary of Captain von Raben, commanding the German 3rd Company at Mora, it appears that no telegraphic or postal communications reached there or Kuseri from across either the British or the French frontiers after about the 31st July. On the 10th August he received a report, sent on the 7th by Lieutenant Kallmeyer, commanding the detachment at Kuseri, that French military activity along the frontier had obliged him to order the local native chiefs to post men to watch and guard against surprise. Considering that this meant war with France, and probably with Great Britain also, Captain von Raben, who combined with his military duties those of Resident at Mora, declared a state of war. The German official notification, it may be noted, did not reach him till the 23rd August. The German garrison at Mora consisted of nine German officers and non-commissioned officers and sixty native troops with two machine guns. Raben at once enlisted sixty recruits and ordered the Marua detachment of the 7th Company (whose headquarters were at Garua), consisting of two Germans and thirty-four natives with a machine gun, to come into Mora. He also instructed Kallmeyer to hold Kuseri as long as possible; and, in addition to despatching small parties of native levies to scout in all directions, sent out two mounted patrols under German non-commissioned officers, one towards Maiduguri and the other to Kuseri. In the expectation that the enemy would attempt to occupy the whole of the Northern Cameroons, Raben decided that it would be better for him to hold Mora and Kuseri than to leave the way open to the enemy by marching to Garua.

The Germans at Mora; 10th–19th August 1914.

Instead of holding the defensive post, which was situated in the plain about a mile east of the native town, Raben also decided to occupy and entrench a position overlooking the town on a ridge, some three miles long by one mile wide, at the north-eastern extremity of the Mandara range. This ridge, termed the Mora mountain, is connected with the main range by a neck of land covered with a tangled network of intricate, rugged and steep ravines, and on the east and south its rocky and boulder-covered slopes descend abruptly and precipitously to the plain.*

* See Map 5.

On the north an underfeature, known as Wacheke, is joined to the main crest of the mountain by a col, having deep and precipitous ravines on either side. Rising above this col, still precipitously, the main crest line ascends in a south-easterly direction from Dabaskum for about 1,500 yards before turning southwards to Molugve—the highest point on the mountain and some 1,600 feet above the plain. The position which Raben had entrenched lay along the Dabaskum spur as far as the point where the crest turns southward, and was thus overlooked by the ground about Molugve. To the west of the main crest line and some 1,200 yards distant lies the Gauala ridge, somewhat lower than the main crest line and separated from it by a deep valley containing a few villages, a number of wells, and some arable land.

On the morning of the 19th August a strong British mounted patrol was seen close to Mora, and Raben, moving out with a detachment, drove it back. Its mere appearance, however, caused all the Mora carriers with the Germans to desert; and Raben then finally abandoned the permanent post, destroying its walls and the stores he was unable to remove to the partial extent that his available explosives permitted.

Maiduguri Column; 20th–29th August 1914. This British patrol reported to Captain Fox that the enemy strength was about seventy, that the *moral* of the native ranks was low and that the local natives were strongly pro-British. On the 20th Captain Fox advanced with his whole column across the frontier, encountering and driving back the German patrol sent out by Raben on the 10th. Telegraphic communication between Lagos and Maiduguri had been interrupted since the 16th, and Colonel Carter's instructions of the 20th August did not reach Captain Fox till the 29th. But, in accordance with the order received on the 15th, he decided to make a thorough reconnaissance of the German situation.

On the 21st August Captain Ferrandi and fifteen Senegalese tirailleurs, who had crossed the northern part of German territory from Fort Lamy, arrived at Maiduguri with information that Colonel Largeau, Commanding in Chad, did not wish to assume the offensive till September, owing to his inability to concentrate sufficient troops before then. Next day Captain Ferrandi and his party left Maiduguri to join Captain Fox.

In the meantime the Maiduguri Column had been gradually advancing and reconnoitring. From the 21st to the 26th August its mounted patrols were observed daily from Mora by the Germans, who also learnt that a British infantry company had established itself in camp not far from Mora on the 23rd.

By the 26th Captain Fox had moved round to the east of the Mora mountain and was encamped at Sava, about four thousand yards to the south-east of the German position. There he was joined in the afternoon by Captain Ferrandi and his party.

From the reports he had received and from personal observation Captain Fox realised that the German position was overlooked and commanded by Molugve and, having in mind the reported unreliable attitude of the German native troops, he decided to reconnoitre closely with his whole force so as to be able to take full advantage of any favourable opportunity. Leaving his camp in charge of a small detachment of mounted infantry, with one machine gun, Captain Fox marched out at 8 p.m. on the 26th August with the remainder of his force, Captain Ferrandi and the small French detachment accompanying him.

Guided by two local natives, the Allied troops after a strenuous climb reached Molugve at 4 a.m. on the 27th August, and about an hour and a half later, as it was getting light, opened fire. Their position certainly overlooked that of the enemy, but this was 1,500 yards away and most of it on the further side of the deep valley between the main ridge and Gauala. The Germans had manned their trenches; they were maintaining a steady fire with two machine guns in action; and there was no sign of any demoralisation among them. Surprise was out of the question, and there was little prospect of success for a British attack, supported by only one machine gun, over difficult ground against a strong position. Captain Fox therefore decided to withdraw from the mountain. He would in any case have found it impossible with the means at his disposal to transport up the precipitous slopes the water, food and ammunition which his men would require for a further stay.

Just before Captain Fox gave the order to retire the whole mountain top became enveloped in a thick mist and, although the bulk of the British column carried out the retirement successfully and without molestation, three small parties encountered misfortune. A machine gun crew under Sergeant Studley, following the main column, had gone by mistake too far to the left and had been followed by Dr. P. T. Fraser with medical equipment and by Sergeant Taylor with reserve ammunition. After these parties began to retire following the main withdrawal, some native troops wearing red fezes were seen advancing towards them and were fired on. But this firing was at once stopped as the advancing troops were taken to be French troops, who also wore red fezes; and before it was realised that they were German, they had rushed the British parties, seizing the machine gun before it could be mounted. This enemy party was in fact one which Raben had detached to move round via the Gauala ridge and counter-attack the British left flank, and this it had managed to do unobserved under cover of the mist.* Sergeant Studley and some of the British party escaped; Dr. Fraser, two native soldiers and five machine gun carriers were killed; Sergeant Taylor and one native soldier were taken prisoners; and the machine gun, twelve boxes of ammunition and some stores were captured.

Withdrawing to Sava, Captain Fox formed an entrenched camp on a small rocky hill in the plain. In this position he felt secure against attack, he could maintain contact with the enemy and he had no difficulty in obtaining supplies from the local natives, who were most friendly. Captain Ferrandi sent a message to Fort Lamy asking for mountain guns and as many men as possible; and on the 29th August Captain Fox reported to Lagos that he intended to remain at Sava till these reinforcements arrived. Without them and without guns he considered it inadvisable to attempt an attack on the German position, whose garrison he estimated at eight Germans and one hundred natives with three machine guns. In point of fact the German strength was twelve Germans and 154 rifles (including sixty recruits) with three machine guns.

With Captain Fox's two companies there were five British officers, two British non-commissioned officers and about 210 rifles, in addition to four British civilians carrying out intelligence, medical and supply and transport duties. In addition to those already mentioned, his force had only incurred three casualties. The number of German casualties had also been very small. On 2nd September Captain Ferrandi left Sava to return with his party to Fort Lamy.

Yola Column; 18th–22nd August. The Yola Column, commanded by Lieutenant-Colonel P. R. Maclear, 2nd Battalion Nigeria Regiment, was composed of headquarters and "B" Company Mounted Infantry, one section 1st Battery, headquarters and "C," "G," and "H" Companies 2nd Battalion and "H" Company 3rd Battalion, with a total strength of two guns and about 600 rifles with five

---

* Captain von Raben in his diary attributes, wrongly, the British retirement to this counter-attack.

[*To face p.* 90

MORA MOUNTAIN

ORDER TO ATTACK GARUA

machine guns. None of these units except " C " Company 2nd Battalion were stationed in peace time at Yola, but by the 18th August, when Colonel Maclear reached there, all but the mounted infantry and " H " Company 3rd Battalion had arrived. The Germans at Garua would probably, it was understood, have learnt of the declaration of war on the 13th August, and it was estimated that by the end of the month they might be able to concentrate there a force of about fifty Germans and 420 natives with one gun and seven or eight machine guns.

Colonel Maclear at once started preparations for an early advance, but experienced difficulty in collecting the number of carriers required. On the 19th August he received a telegram from Colonel Carter saying that an offensive must await sanction from London but suggesting that the column, while concealing its intentions as far as possible, should move forward to a position from which it could strike quickly as soon as sanction had been received. Next day Colonel Maclear received notification that an attack on Garua had been sanctioned by the Colonial Office, and he was instructed that, if he considered his force sufficient, without the mounted infantry and " H " Company 3rd Battalion which had not yet arrived, he was authorised to carry out the attack. He was also informed that the Maiduguri Column had been ordered to capture Mora. To these instructions Colonel Maclear replied the same day that he proposed leaving Yola on the 22nd. In the summary of intelligence he telegraphed at noon from Yola on the 20th August to Lagos, he reported that German natives were actively patrolling the frontier and that many carriers were said to have left with loads from Garua to Ngaundere. Colonel Carter took this to mean that the Germans were evacuating Garua and accordingly telegraphed to Colonel Maclear, urging him to start before the 22nd so as to assist Colonel Carter's plan of action in the south by striking a severe blow in the north as quickly as possible. On the 22nd another telegram from Colonel Carter reached Colonel Maclear asking if he had received the previous message and saying that the sooner he reached his objective the better.

Garua was about ninety miles by road from Yola, and supplies were reported to be practically unprocurable *en route*. By the 19th August sufficient grain had been collected at Yola by Captain C. F. Rowe (the civilian appointed to take charge of supply and transport duties), but it was not till the 21st that he had succeeded in obtaining all the 1,400 odd carriers and thirty-three donkeys* required for the transport of the necessary stores, ammunition and seven days' supplies.

At 1 p.m. on the 22nd August Colonel Maclear commenced his advance, crossing to the north bank of the Benue river, along which the mounted infantry—already on that side—moved off eastward during the afternoon. "H" Company 3rd Battalion only reached Yola at noon that day and did not cross the river till next morning to join the remainder of the column, which had camped for the night two miles from the ferry.

Affair of Tepe; 25th August 1914. After two long marches on the 23rd and 24th, the frontier was passed on the 25th August and the enemy was encountered at Tepe, the German customs station on the Benue river. Reports had placed an observation post of one German and about ten native rifles here, but the mounted infantry under Major Lord Henry Seymour, forming right flank guard to the column, encountered opposition there from a party obviously stronger. Concealed by the high grass, corn, thick scrub and trees, the Germans, allowing the scouts to pass through and round the village, withheld their fire until the head of the advanced guard was within fifty yards. Under this sudden fire the leading British troops fell back slightly and were reinforced by the remainder of the mounted infantry, who dismounted and carried the line slightly forward on both flanks. There ensued a fire fight at close range in which Captain T. S. Wickham was shot dead. It was very difficult to observe or control the fire, however, and Major Lord Henry Seymour, leaving the remainder of the company under Captain J. T. Gibbs to contain the enemy in front, soon moved to the more open country on his right with two sections and charged home with great dash. No casualties were incurred till the British troops were right among the enemy, but then Lord Henry Seymour was wounded severely and shortly afterwards Lieutenant G. L. S. Sherlock and a German officer were killed. The enemy had by this time ceased firing and his detachment, numbering apparently three Germans and possibly as many as fifty natives, retired towards Garua.

The casualties among the British officers had been very heavy, four out of the six having been killed or wounded,† but of the native ranks, who had behaved admirably, only two

---

* The rain and their slow pace rendered the use of more donkeys undesirable.
† Captain D. H. Macdonell, in charge of the machine gun detachment, had also been wounded.

ADVANCE ON GARUA

had been hit. The enemy casualties included two Germans and two natives killed.

At 10.45 a.m. Colonel Maclear, receiving a message from Captain Gibbs which reported these casualties and asked for assistance, first sent one and a half infantry companies to Tepe and subsequently camped there with his whole column, establishing an advanced base, to which further supplies were brought by river from Yola in a flotilla of barges and canoes collected by Major Festing.

On the 26th August, after a difficult march over a road much cut up and rendered very slippery by rain, the column reached Saratse, where it halted on the 27th to allow the transport to close up. On the 28th, still without opposition, the column camped at Bulungo, four miles west of Garua. Little or no reliable information had been obtained of the German strength or dispositions at Garua, but, impressed by Colonel Carter's instructions to act with rapidity, Colonel Maclear decided to attack next day.

Advancing from Bulungo at 6 a.m. on the 29th August, Colonel Maclear halted his column under cover of a low ridge, running roughly north and south, which the road crossed at a point less than three miles west of Garua town. Some of the mounted infantry on the left flank, on topping this ridge, came under an accurate fire, apparently from three German guns. To this the British guns, coming into action on the ridge, replied with a few rounds, which it was subsequently ascertained fell short of the enemy's position though causing a number of casualties among labourers collected by the Germans. *First attack on Garua; 29th–30th August 1914. (Map 11.)*

From a commanding point on the ridge, about one and a half miles north of the road, christened Observation Hill, Colonel Maclear obtained a good view of an entrenched enemy position, but could not see their permanent post or the native town. He sent for his artillery and company commanders and with them examined the entrenched position. This lay along a ridge to the north of the native town, three knolls or peaks, separated from each other by a few hundred yards, having been entrenched to form three detached forts, of which the centre was the highest and largest and evidently commanded the other two. The permanent brick-built post, it may be noted, was about half a mile south-east of the southern entrenched knoll and overlooked the native town.

In the generally open and park-like country the grass was about two feet high, while the slopes which ran down to the river between Observation Hill and the enemy's position were intersected by two rocky ravines, narrow on the British left but opening out to the southward; and between these ravines, flat-topped low ridges lay parallel to the enemy's position at distances from it of approximately 1,200 and 500 yards.

Colonel Maclear decided to attack the position by night and marched the column back to camp. At 4 p.m. Colonel Maclear and Major T. N. Puckle, accompanied at their own request by Captains G. S. C. Adams and J. T. Gibbs, proceeded to Observation Hill to make a further inspection of the position, the northern detached fort of which was found by the range-finder to be 4,300 yards from Observation Hill. No close reconnaissance appears to have been made, probably to avoid disclosure of the British intentions.

Colonel Maclear's plan of attack was to assemble his infantry and guns at Observation Hill at 10 p.m.; to advance from there with three infantry companies directly against the northern enemy fort; and, after capturing it, to reorganise and capture the centre fort by a second assault. The fourth company, all the machine guns and the guns were to entrench themselves on Observation Hill; and the mounted infantry, taking up a position to the right front, were to open fire at twelve midnight.

"H" Company, 3rd Battalion, under Captain Adams, was to lead the attack, followed by "C" and "H" Companies, 2nd Battalion, with a distance of one hundred yards between companies. These companies and the guns all arrived punctually at Observation Hill; but "G" Company, 2nd Battalion, with the machine guns was late and delayed the start till about 11 p.m. The three attacking companies then advanced about three thousand yards to the position of deployment, formed into line and extended to one pace interval. The further advance, which was to be carried through without a halt, then commenced, but had only proceeded for a short distance when the mounted infantry on the right flank opened fire, in accordance with their orders. In a moment all three enemy forts opened a heavy fire and sent up numerous rockets which lit up the ground over which the British were advancing.

When the firing commenced, Colonel Maclear moved up from his position with the rear company to the leading line, which he ordered to halt and lie down. Some confusion ensued, but the men of the right section, under Lieutenant C. G. Bowyer-Smijth, not hearing this order, continued to advance steadily without firing. Finally, with bayonets fixed, they dashed up the slope and drove the enemy out of the northern fort, killing a German officer and seven men and capturing a machine gun. No one, however, arrived to support Lieutenant Bowyer-Smijth's men and they were shortly forced to retire behind the fort, whence, after a long wait for support which did not arrive, they finally withdrew to camp. In the meantime, unaware of the success gained by the right section, the progress of the remainder of the line had been slow as, on Colonel Maclear's orders, they halted from time to time for considerable periods, getting mixed up with the two companies in rear which overtook them. In the dark this caused further confusion. Eventually a part of all three companies succeeded in occupying the northern fort. Here several British officers urged Colonel Maclear repeatedly to advance against the centre fort while there was still darkness to cover the movement, but he decided to rest the men and to wait till dawn before assaulting.

From dawn, when he sent Sergeant-Major Steed with a verbal message to the reserve at Observation Hill and the mounted infantry to move round by their left to the Demsa road near the captured fort, his troops were subjected to a heavy concentrated fire from rifles, four machine guns and guns from the centre fort at about four hundred yards range. Crowded together in a space some fifty yards in diameter, without covering fire to help them and in too exposed a situation to reply effectively themselves, his troops found themselves in a most insecure situation; and at 7.30 a.m., were subjected to a counter-attack, which the enemy, under an intense covering fire, launched with a force of about twenty Germans and sixty natives. The British native troops broke and fled; all the efforts of their officers and non-commissioned officers failing to rally them till they reached camp. The reserve saw what was happening but was too far away to assist.

On arrival in camp the British officers found soldiers and carriers much demoralised. Colonel Maclear had been killed and Captain Adams, the senior surviving officer, decided to withdraw to Tepe. This retirement commenced at 12.30 p.m., the severely wounded being left behind in charge of Doctors W. A. Trumper and J. Lindsay, to be taken prisoner later by the Germans.

The total British casualties were 63, including four British officers killed, one mortally wounded and captured, and two wounded.* Those of the enemy, whose force appeared to have consisted of the bulk of their 7th Company and a section of

---

* *Killed*—Lieut.-Colonel P. R. Maclear, Major T. N. Puckle, Captain A. C. Aubin, Lieut. A. H. Stewart; *mortally wounded and captured*—Lieut. H. W. Brown; *wounded*—Lieutenants R. Scott-Moncrieff and E. E. Loch.

their 8th Company from Ngaundere, were said to have amounted to 21, including two Germans.

The series of apparent tactical errors or omissions that contributed to this unfortunate result cannot, owing to the death of Colonel Maclear, be satisfactorily explained. The native ranks, according to the testimony of their surviving British officers, displayed steadiness and courage in the initial stages of the attack—their first encounter with European-led troops and their first experience of modern gun and machine gun fire; and, in the circumstances, it seems reasonable to assume that a loss of confidence in their leaders had as much to say to the panic which seized them as the strain of the final bombardment. Captain Adams, commanding the leading company, subsequently stated his opinion that, had the mounted infantry not opened fire, his men could have got quite close to the enemy position unobserved, as the Germans had no piquets out.

After an exhausting march over roads swamped by heavy rain, the British column reached Tepe on the morning of the 1st September, one of its piquets that day successfully driving off a German mounted patrol—the only attempt made by the enemy to interfere with the retirement.* Captain Adams, having already decided that it would be necessary to return to Yola to reorganise, embarked the sick and wounded in barges and canoes at Tepe and marched with the remainder of the column to Bilarchi. Here, finding Major Festing with the Niger Company's stern-wheeler *Kampe*, he sent his guns, most of his ammunition and supplies and a large number of carriers in her to Yola, where with the rest of the force he arrived on the 3rd September. The next three days were spent in reorganisation. On the 7th the column, depleted in numbers by about a fifth through battle casualties and sickness (mainly cut feet),† recrossed the river *en route* for Bilarchi.

---

* Captain von Crailsheim, the German commander at Garua, informed Colonel Cunliffe in June 1915, after the fall of Garua, that shortage of ammunition had precluded any German pursuit in force.

† The natives, troops and carriers, did not wear boots and generally marched with bare feet. Before the war the exceptionally good marching powers of the native soldier of the West African Frontier Force were ascribed to the fact that he did not wear boots, although on active service he carried a pair of chupplies or light leather slippers for use in rough places. The tendency had been for the construction of these chupplies to become heavier, until they resembled heavy ventilated brogues instead of the original light skin sole with a string between the toes. During the Cameroons campaign the number of casualties from foot trouble (especially those caused by jiggers, a local flea which burrows under the toe-nail) became a sufficiently serious drain on the forces

CUNLIFFE SENT TO YOLA

As subsequently reported by Lieutenant-Colonel F. H. G. Cunliffe, Assistant Commandant of the Nigeria Regiment, Captain Adams, himself suffering from ill-health at the time, had conducted the retreat with skill, coolness and courage under very trying circumstances.

On receiving, on the 1st September, the news of the reverse at Garua and also Captain Fox's report of the 29th August, Colonel Carter telegraphed to the commander of the Yola Column that a resumption of the offensive against Garua was left to his discretion, and that he was to get into communication with Captain Fox. The latter was instructed that, if he gained success at Mora and Marua, he was to co-operate as quickly as possible with the Yola Column ; and that he was, in any case, to prevent a junction of the German troops from Mora with those at Garua. At the same time Colonel Carter directed Lieutenant-Colonel Cunliffe to proceed as rapidly as possible to Yola to take command of all the British troops operating in German Bornu, i.e., the Maiduguri and Yola Columns and " B " Company, 1st Battalion, then moving eastward from Nafada to the frontier via Gumsuri. The objectives of the Maiduguri and Yola Columns were, he was told, the enemy about Mora and Garua respectively, while the company near Gumsuri was to act as a reserve. His general instructions were to operate against the enemy in German Bornu from Garua (inclusive) northward. Colonel Cunliffe reached Ibi on the 6th, having taken on with him, in a river steamer from Lokoja, " B " Company of the 2nd Battalion.

Action at Lagos and in London; 1st–6th September 1914.

On the 3rd September, Sir Frederick Lugard, who had arrived at Lagos the previous day, received telegraphic instructions, despatched by the Colonial Office after learning of the Garua reverse, that pending the arrival of General Dobell the efforts of the British troops on the frontier were to be confined strictly to gaining information, and that they were to avoid, as far as possible, any serious engagement. The Colonial Office presumed that the incident at Garua would not affect the number of troops that Nigeria would place at General Dobell's disposal for the offensive against Duala. Sir Frederick Lugard replied on the 4th that the necessary orders had been

---

to cause much thought and investigation of this question. Various medicaments for the feet to keep out jiggers were tried without success. The French native soldiers wore boots, and experiments were tried of equipping some British native troops with boots. While many officers were converted to the necessity of boots for native troops, there was much disagreement on the point. After the war the troops reverted to bare feet and the heavier type of chupplies.

issued to the Calabar, Ikom and Yola Columns, but that Colonel Carter and his staff considered it most inadvisable for the Maiduguri Column to retire, especially as the French were co-operating. As Colonel Carter considered the number of Europeans with the column to be inadequate, he was sending instructions to defer the offensive. To replace the British casualties Sir Frederick Lugard was calling for European volunteers; and he concluded his telegram by saying that the number of Nigerian troops for Duala would not be affected.

<small>Colonel Cunliffe to Yola; 6th–13th September 1914.</small> He telegraphed on the 6th September to Colonel Cunliffe at Ibi that Colonel Carter had been recalled to England and that Colonel Cunliffe would be required to join General Dobell, who was due at Lagos on the 15th. Sir Frederick Lugard said that he would be glad to have Colonel Cunliffe's report on the situation at Yola, but left it to him to decide whether to proceed there or to return at once to Lagos. Information from Major Festing at Ibi decided Colonel Cunliffe to push on to Yola at once and to order " H " Company, 1st Battalion, at Abinsi to follow him to Yola as quickly as possible. He reached Yola on the 10th, and after a personal inspection came to the conclusion that the *moral* of the troops who had taken part in the fight at Garua was not as low as might have been surmised and that, under good leadership and stimulated by the reinforcement of fresh troops, they were quite fit to take the field once more. He reorganised the column, now comprising two guns, one company of mounted infantry and six companies of infantry, appointing Major W. I. Webb-Bowen to command it, and also placing under his control the other British forces operating in German Bornu, i.e., the Maiduguri Column and the reserve company which had then reached and occupied the German frontier post at Mubi.

On the 13th September, when he left Yola to return to Lagos, Colonel Cunliffe gave Major Webb-Bowen instructions to the following effect. The chief object of the Yola Column was the defeat and subjection of the German forces in the neighbourhood of Garua and the seizure of that place; the aim of the Maiduguri Column was to defeat the enemy forces near Mora and Marua; and the company at Mubi was to act as a reserve. Unless forced to do so, Major Webb-Bowen was not, pending further orders, to undertake any active offensive operations against the enemy; and before the Yola Column crossed the frontier for offensive action, Major Webb-Bowen was to take steps to ensure the safety of Yola against a possible

AFFAIR AT TAKUM

enemy attack or raid, leaving behind him for the purpose such troops as he considered necessary.

At this time, the police in the district were doing excellent work, patrolling the frontier, blocking the roads and collecting information. The Emir of Yola was thoroughly loyal and had given material assistance by supplying remounts, carriers and grain for the column; and with this assistance, supplies for all troops and carriers for at least three months had been collected at Yola by Captain Rowe. More could be sent up from Abinsi and Lokoja if required.

The news of the British reverse at Garua caused a considerable amount of unrest among the natives of the Benue river districts. But this lessened considerably after the 17th September when an attack by a German detachment on Takum, a native town about seventy miles south of Ibi, was successfully beaten off. Takum was held by fifty-seven Nigerian police under Lieutenant B. E. M. Waters, R.N. (a political officer), Major A. E. Churcher (a political officer doing intelligence work), being also present. The German force, of about the strength of a company with three Germans (their No. 3 Reserve Detachment under Captain Adametz), crossed the frontier from Kentu; and when its attack on Takum failed completely, causing no loss to the British, it retreated hurriedly across the frontier, having itself suffered a number of casualties, including two Germans. *Affair at Takum; 17th September 1914.*

In accordance with Colonel Carter's plan for one or two columns to cross the southern part of the frontier and advance on Duala in conjunction with an attack from the sea, Lieutenant-Colonel G. T. Mair, commanding the 3rd Battalion of the Nigeria Regiment, arrived at Ikom on the 10th August with instructions to organise a column, reconnoitre, and prepare for an advance by the Cross river route. On the previous day he had been told that no offensive movements were to be undertaken pending orders from England, and that he was not to cross the frontier; and on the 10th he received further instructions to observe the frontier and ascertain all possible roads eastward. The whole Cross river area, it may be noted, was covered with dense forest, and the available information regarding roads and geographical conditions generally in the trans-frontier portion was scanty. *Ikom Column; 10th August– 6th September 1914. (Map 7, facing page 224.)*

From Ossidinge (or Mamfe), where it is joined by the Bali river, the broad, swift and unfordable Cross river flows westward to the frontier past Old Ossidinge and the then German customs post at Nsanakang. Near the British village of Obokum, by the frontier, it bends to the south-west and, for about ten miles, formed the frontier line till it joined with the Awa river, along which the frontier continued. From the Awa junction, the Cross river forms a southerly bend across which a direct road, some seventeen miles in length, led from Ikom to Obokum. On the German side of the frontier, two tracks, which joined at Old Ossidinge, led to Ossidinge; one from nearly opposite Obokum, and the main track, whose seven-foot wide clearance was reported to be well maintained, from Nsanarati, a German village on the Cross river between Obokum and the Awa junction.

As soon as he reached Ikom, Colonel Mair commenced to make thorough preparation for an advance. Special staff officers, including a marine transport officer, were appointed; arrangements were made to accumulate a large stock of supplies and to collect carriers; and intelligence arrangements were organised and supplemented by local reconnaissances. On the 11th August Captain C. R. T. Hopkinson with "G" Company, 3rd Battalion, left Ikom for Obokum with instructions to watch the frontier, gain information regarding the enemy and the neighbouring country, and obtain guides for use across the frontier. Steps were also taken to extend the telegraph line from Obubra to Ikom and Obokum.

On the 13th August Colonel Mair was given discretion to send officers across the frontier, his instructions from Colonel Carter suggesting that it would be essential to do this to gain the information required, but emphasising the necessity of their avoiding contact with hostile troops. By this date "A," "E" and "F" Companies, 3rd Battalion, and the right section of the 2nd Battery (composed only of two sections) had reached Ikom; and on the 14th "A" Company under Captain J. Crookenden was sent to reinforce Captain Hopkinson at Obokum. On the 16th telegraphic instructions reached Colonel Mair that, as information was urgently required as to whether there was any definite movement of German forces in progress, he was authorised to conduct reconnaissances across the frontier. He must, however, retain ability to recall at short notice any troops so employed, and they must avoid serious hostilities. Colonel Carter was anxious, said the telegram, to know if the Germans were occupying Old Ossidinge and Ossidinge.

Colonel Mair then started a series of active reconnaissances across the frontier. His own information showed that there were only a few very small German parties near the frontier. But he now received information from Calabar, believed there to be reliable, that the Germans were concentrating five or six hundred troops at Nsanakang; and Colonel Mair, informing Captain Hopkinson of the instructions and information received, directed him to ascertain definitely if there were any German troops at Nsanakang, as a necessary preliminary to a wider reconnaissance. Under Captain Hopkinson's orders, a detachment of one and a quarter companies with two machine guns under Captain Crookenden crossed the river after dark on the 17th August and occupied Nsanarati without opposition, the three or four German police or soldiers there escaping into the bush. Next morning a British officer's patrol from Nsanarati reconnoitred to Nsanakang, finding no signs of German troops.

On the evening of the 17th Colonel Mair received from Lagos a telegram informing him that there was as yet no question of a general advance, and next morning he forwarded a copy of this telegram to Captain Hopkinson with orders that no advance was to be made in force beyond Nsanarati, but giving permission for reconnaissance by small patrols from there. On the morning of the 17th, the left section of the 2nd Battery had reached Ikom, and on the morning of the 18th the right section of this battery and " F " Company, 3rd Battalion, left Ikom by river steamer for Obokum. That night Colonel Mair received telegraphic instructions that his column would be completed to a strength of five companies, and that Lieutenant-Colonel Haywood's* column from Calabar would also be completed to a strength of five companies and would concentrate at Ikom. A section of the 1st Battery and two infantry companies would remain to garrison Calabar. Colonel Mair was also instructed that, if the enemy made any offensive movement against him, he could disregard any previous instructions to avoid hostilities.

On the 20th August, the British troops under Colonel Mair were disposed as follows :—

Ikom .. .. One section 2nd Battery.
" E " Company, 3rd Battalion.
" D " Company, 4th Battalion (for Lieut.-Col. Haywood's Column).

---

* Lieutenant-Colonel Haywood was the commanding officer of the 4th Battalion Nigeria Regiment.

Advanced troops under Captain Hopkinson

North of Obokum ..	One section " A " Company, 3rd Battalion.
Obokum	Half " G " Company, 3rd Battalion, with one machine gun.
	Half " F " Company, 3rd Battalion, with one machine gun.
Nsanarati, left bank Cross R.	" A " Company, 3rd Battalion (less one section).
	One section " G " Company, 3rd Battalion.
	Two machine guns.
Do., right bank ..	One section 2nd Battery.
	One section " G " Company, 3rd Battalion.
At the Awa—Cross rivers junction.	Half " F " Company, 3rd Battalion, with one machine gun.

Next day " B " Company, 3rd Battalion, reached Ikom, completing the five companies for Colonel Mair's column.

On the evening of the 20th, Mr. Croxford, the British consular agent at Duala, reached Ikom from Ossidinge.* He gave information regarding the German dispositions at Duala, which proved to be by no means correct, and he stated that the natives were hostile to the Germans. Those round Ossidinge would, in his opinion, rise against the Germans as soon as they learnt that Nsanarati had been taken by the British. Guns in wooden cases and a stern-wheeler launch in sections had been sent to Ossidinge overland, and the latter was then on the river. The Germans were concentrating as many troops as possible at Nsanakang, but only for purely defensive measures.

That a German concentration at Nsanakang was in progress had already been reported, and British officers' patrols had recently reported two German companies, each about one hundred strong, near Old Ossidinge.

Late on the 21st August Colonel Mair received a telegram despatched the previous day by Colonel Carter, saying that all previous orders for the formation of columns were cancelled; that three battalions, of four companies each, with the batteries of artillery, would be formed for oversea attack; that Colonel Mair would command No. 3 Battalion; and that, pending further orders, no change in the dispositions of the Ikom Column was to take place. In a further telegram he received at the same time referring to the information that two German companies had been observed at Old Ossidinge, Colonel Mair was instructed to do everything he could to lead the enemy to believe that a main advance towards Ossidinge was to be

---

* The Germans had arranged for him to leave the country by this route.

[*To face p.* 102

OBOKUM: AUGUST 1914

THE CROSS RIVER

undertaken, and also to deceive him as to the actual strength of the British troops. Next day Colonel Mair sent copies of these telegrams to Captain Hopkinson and directed him to instruct Captain Crookenden at Nsanarati to obtain by officers' patrols, etc., all possible information about the two roads leading to Nsanakang and about any others that existed, in order to give the enemy the impression that the reconnaissances were preparatory to an advance. Captain Hopkinson was at the same time given permission, if he considered it necessary, to reinforce Captain Crookenden with another half-company.

At midday on the 24th August Colonel Mair heard from Captain Hopkinson that a British patrol reported that enemy troops in force had reached Old Ossidinge after dark on the 22nd; that on the 23rd patrols from Nsanarati reconnoitring towards Nsanakang had been attacked by enemy troops; that in the evening Captain Crookenden had advanced from Nsanarati with two companies and three machine guns, and that Captain Hopkinson with another detachment including one gun had gone up the river by night, but had been heavily fired on and had been forced to retire on the morning of the 24th. Two further reports reached Colonel Mair during the afternoon of the 24th from Captain Crookenden, who after a night advance had occupied Nsanakang at 6.30 a.m. that day at the cost of three men wounded. A German detachment of three Europeans and forty natives had been driven back and pursued to the Munaya river, where they were holding the bridge. There were large quantities of rice, etc., stored at Nsanakang, which was a big place and required more British to hold it in view of the possibility of the Germans attempting to retake it. Sniping was still going on, but the natives appeared to be friendly.

That evening Colonel Mair wrote to Captain Hopkinson that the advance on Nsanakang was scarcely justified by the instructions to reconnoitre with patrols, but that as Captain Crookenden was in occupation he was to remain there till Colonel Mair obtained further instructions from Lagos. To assist Captain Crookenden, who was to take precautions against the enemy getting round his right to Nsanarati, Captain Hopkinson could reinforce him if necessary, but was to send him only three days' supplies, to obviate any great quantity falling into enemy hands in case a retirement became necessary. Reporting this occupation of Nsanakang to Lagos and his instructions to Captain Crookenden to remain there pending further orders from Colonel Carter, Colonel

Mair attributed Captain Hopkinson's order to advance to the instructions sent from Lagos on the 17th, permitting hostilities if an enemy offensive was encountered. He himself, he said, was proceeding to Obokum to investigate the situation.

Taking with him from Ikom " D " Company, 4th Battalion, Colonel Mair went by steamer on the 25th to Obokum, and from there with his staff officer (Lieutenant E. L. Salier) and Captain Hopkinson he paid a visit to Nsanakang, where the garrison comprised one section 2nd Battery, eight sections of " A," " E " and " G " Companies, 3rd Battalion, and three machine guns. In the evening at Obokum he received a report from Lieutenant J. C. Blackburn—who with a section had for some days been reconnoitring the country on the north side of the Cross river towards Ossidinge most successfully—that there were 200 German troops at Old Ossidinge.

On the 26th August, taking some troops with him,* Colonel Mair again visited Nsanakang and held a conference there to discuss the situation. On the 27th morning—after instructing Captain Hopkinson to take over command at Nsanakang and to make all preparations, in anticipation of orders from Lagos, for a withdrawal—Colonel Mair returned to Ikom. On arriving there he found orders for " D " Company, 4th Battalion, to move to Calabar, as well as a telegram from Lagos replying to his report of the occupation of Nsanakang. This telegram was to the following effect: no further withdrawal of troops from Ikom was contemplated for at least ten days, and Colonel Carter would await Colonel Mair's report before issuing any further orders. As, however, the main British objective was elsewhere, Colonel Mair was to do his best to avoid casualties.

From these instructions Colonel Mair inferred that the occupation of Nsanakang was concurred in, and he sent Captain Hopkinson further instructions to demonstrate towards Old Ossidinge in order to deceive the enemy, but to avoid casualties.

Such a demonstration was carried out on the 30th August by Lieutenant A. Milne-Home with one gun, two infantry sections and a machine gun. They crossed the Munaya river in canoes at 8 a.m.,† and on approaching Old Ossidinge fired a few shells into the town. Some Germans were seen and fired on by the machine gun, and the British detachment then withdrew,

---

* In the next few days some movements took place, leaving " E " and " G " Companies complete at Nsanakang.

† The enemy had destroyed the bridge.

DELAY IN EVACUATING NSANAKANG

arriving back at Nsanakang, after a halt at night, without incident at noon on the 31st. That day " D " Company, 4th Battalion, left Obokum for Calabar.

On the 2nd September Colonel Mair went by river to Obokum, and to Nsanakang on the 3rd. He had just received intimation from Lagos that No. 3 Battalion would probably embark at Calabar for oversea service on the 15th, and that, after the departure of its four companies, " B " and " D " Companies would be responsible for the defence of the frontier near Ikom. He consequently instructed Captain Hopkinson to make arrangements to withdraw from Nsanakang. The intelligence reports for the last three or four days had indicated a definite increase in the German strength at Ossidinge.

One section 2nd Battery left Ikom for Calabar on the 4th, and on that day Colonel Mair issued orders for Nsanakang and other advanced posts to be evacuated in accordance with instructions from Headquarters. But he countermanded these orders shortly afterwards on receiving a telegraphic enquiry from Lagos for his opinion regarding the ability of two companies *plus* a reservist company to guard the frontier near Obokum. He at once replied recommending strongly that three companies instead of two should be detailed, as this would enable Nsanakang to be held by one of them. On the evening of the 5th a report reached him from Captain Hopkinson saying that the Germans appeared to be advancing, and shortly afterwards he received a telegram from Lagos saying that, for the time being, only two companies would be available for the defence of the frontier, and that the four companies of the 3rd Battalion for overseas were to leave Ikom for Calabar on the 10th. He at once sent messages, i.e., early on the 6th, to Obokum and Nsanakang that he was coming up that day by steamer to superintend the withdrawal, which was to be carried out on the morning of the 9th. But he was too late, as the Germans were already attacking Nsanakang.

The dispositions of Colonel Mair's force on the 6th September were as follows :—

Ikom	Half " B " Company and " D " Company, 3rd Battalion.*
At the Awa river junction	Half " F " Company, 3rd Battalion.
Nsanarati	Half " F " Company, 3rd Battalion.
Obokum	" A " Company, 3rd Battalion (less one section).

* " D " Company had just arrived from Calabar.

106   MILITARY OPERATIONS: THE CAMEROONS

Abia..	.. ..	One section " A " Company, 3rd Battalion.
Abunorok	.. ..	Half " B " Company, 3rd Battalion.
Nsanakang	.. ..	One section 2nd Battery, and " E " and " G " Companies, 3rd Battalion, with five machine guns.

Affair of Nsanakang; 6th September 1914. (Map 6, facing page 110.) In the dense bush on the south bank of the Cross river, to the westward of Nsanakang village, the British had entrenched the two small hills on which the German customs house and factory were situated. These hills were eight hundred yards apart and were separated from one another by a creek spanned by a canoe bridge, Customs Hill to the west being some forty feet higher than Factory Hill, which stood about twenty feet above the river level.

On Factory Hill, which was garrisoned by six infantry sections with four machine guns, the trenches faced east, south and south-west; and on Customs Hill, which was held by two infantry sections with a machine gun and the artillery section, they faced south and west. It had only been possible to clear a field of fire extending from one hundred and fifty to three hundred yards round these trenches.

At some distance south of Factory Hill the road to Nsanarati branched off from the road to Eomodyo, and the only other British means of communication with their base was by river or by a native path along the river bank. The road to Ossidinge led from Factory Hill through Nsanakang village and across the Munaya river ferry. On each of these two roads the British had posted piquets, one of six men about Nsanakang village, and the other of twelve men about six hundred yards south of Factory Hill.

At about 2 a.m. on the 6th September, hearing a short, sharp burst of firing in the vicinity of Nsanakang village, the British on Customs and Factory Hills manned their trenches. Some three hours later a heavy rifle and machine gun fire was opened by the enemy from the surrounding bush, at ranges of two to three hundred yards, directed against Customs Hill and the southern trenches of Factory Hill.

The German force, about five hundred strong, was composed of three companies * with six German-manned machine guns; and it appears that its primary objective was the high ground close to the river lying to the westward of Customs Hill. On the 5th two of these companies had moved to Eomodyo, and the third, under Captain von Sommerfeld, to the eastern bank

---

* No. 2 Company from Bamenda, the police depot company from Duala, and a company apparently formed of police from the Chang-Ossidinge district.

AFFAIR AT NSANAKANG

of the Munaya river ferry. Both parties advanced during the night. Sommerfeld's company, crossing the Munaya river a mile or two above the ferry, pushed forward two patrols which apparently overwhelmed the British piquet at Nsanakang village at about 2 a.m. The two companies from Eomodyo appear to have accounted for the British piquet on that road without giving it an opportunity of sending in warning of their approach, and, by 5 a.m., had reached and extended along the edge of the cleared ground, with their right south of Factory Hill and their left near the bank of the Cross river. Here they endeavoured to establish a fire superiority. But finding that the fire of the two British guns, which were separated and fighting singly, was too effective, the Germans gradually moved larger numbers round through the forest to the high ground on their left, whence they enfiladed and took in reverse many of the trenches on Customs Hill and also, at long range, those on Factory Hill.

The British on Customs Hill under Captain Hopkinson suffered severely, more especially the guns' crews who were insufficiently protected by the low parapets required by their guns. By about 6.30 a.m. two successive German attempts to rush the British right on Customs Hill had been repulsed by the section and machine guns under Lieutenant W. G. Yates; and Captain Hopkinson apparently saw an opportunity for a counter-attack. But the message he is believed to have sent to Factory Hill for reinforcements to carry it out never reached its destination; and the configuration of the ground prevented Lieutenant Milne-Home, who was commanding there, from seeing how the fight on Customs Hill was proceeding. The enemy then concentrated the fire of two machine guns which took in reverse the trenches held by Lieutenant Yates' section; all the British gun ammunition —only thirty rounds per gun—was expended; their rifle and machine gun ammunition was also running short; and many of their trenches had become untenable. Consequently, soon after 7 a.m., Captain Hopkinson gave the order to fall back on Factory Hill. During this movement he himself was killed and Lieutenant Yates was wounded. The enemy at once occupied Customs Hill.

In the meantime at about 6.15 a.m. Sommerfeld's company had come into action astride the Nsanakang road and engaged Factory Hill, whose garrison, however, continued to hold its own easily till Customs Hill was lost. Then, surrounded closely on three sides with most of their trenches under enfilade or reverse machine gun fire, the British situation became desperate. Considering that further resistance was hopeless, Lieutenant Milne-Home issued orders which resulted in attempts by practically his whole remaining force to break through the enemy cordon and gain the shelter of the forest. Only 62 of the original 220 succeeded. Three British (Captain C. R. T. Hopkinson, Lieut. A. C. Holme and Sergeant J. Dennis) and 39 native ranks were killed, one British (Lieut. W. G. Yates) and 24 natives were wounded and captured, and four British (Lieutenants O. G. Body, A. L. de C. Stretton and R. R. Taylor, and Sergeant J. Mannion) and 36 natives were taken prisoner. The Germans, who captured the two guns * and five machine guns, had also lost heavily, their casualties totalling, it is understood, 8 Germans † and 118 natives killed or wounded. All British accounts testify to the courageous and generally admirable behaviour of the Nigerian troops, and their opinion was endorsed by the German officers present.

That day at 1.30 p.m. Colonel Mair, coming up the river in the *Jackdaw* with " D " Company, 3rd Battalion, met the *Sandfly* from Obokum bringing a message from Captain Crookenden there. Hearing heavy firing he had proceeded at an early hour in the *Sandfly* to reconnoitre and had anchored some five hundred yards below the British position. But, after remaining some time in observation, he had come under fire and, having no force with him, had returned immediately to Obokum, learning soon afterwards from fugitives that the Nsanakang position had been lost. He also attached a report from the commander of the detachment at Nsanarati, stating that in consequence of the news from Nsanakang, he had evacuated Nsanarati and was returning to Ikom in the *Hornbill* after picking up the detachment at the Awa river junction.

---

* The two British guns had to be abandoned on Customs Hill. After their gun ammunition was exhausted the gunners fought with their rifles to the last, the gallant conduct of Sergeant J. Dennis, R.A., who was in charge of one gun, being specially worthy of mention. Though wounded by machine gun fire through both thighs, he retained charge of his gun to the end and was eventually found bayoneted beside it.

After the action was over, the Germans—in expectation of a British counter-attack—pushed the two captured British guns over the edge of Customs Hill into the Cross river, whence one of them was later recovered by the Germans and taken away. The other gun was eventually retrieved from the river by the British and now surmounts the War Memorial erected at Calabar.

† Captain Rammstedt, commanding the German ¡force, was among the wounded.

NEUTRAL HOSPITAL AT NSANAKANG

Continuing upstream, the *Jackdaw* met the *Hornbill*, and soon afterwards both steamers returned to Ikom, the *Hornbill* carrying three sections of " F " Company, the fourth section having been left on the right bank of the river opposite Nsanarati. Colonel Mair had decided to leave the three sections of " F " Company to hold the Ikom defences and to march himself that night with " D " Company to Obokum, to be followed the next day by half " B " Company with ammunition.

Colonel Mair with " D " Company left Ikom that night at ten o'clock, and after a very trying march reached Obokum at 8 a.m. on the 7th. On his way he received a letter from one of the British officers captured, conveying a request from Captain von Sommerfeld that he would proceed by river under a flag of truce to Nsanakang to discuss the establishment of a neutral zone, so as to admit of the treatment there in a joint German-British hospital of the many wounded. Colonel Mair and two officers accordingly went to Nsanakang, and an agreement was signed to the effect that Nsanakang and an area of four miles round it were to remain neutral till hostilities ceased.

On the 8th September Colonel Mair, telegraphing to Lagos an account of what had occurred, gave his dispositions : half a company at Abia, one section each at Obokum and opposite Nsanarati, and the remainder of his force at Ikom. The advanced detachments, he said, had orders to fall back on Ikom, if the enemy advanced in force against any of them.

In his official report on the action at Nsanakang, written subsequently from accounts given by surviving British officers and from information supplied by German officers who were present, Colonel Mair commended Lieutenant R. R. Taylor, Colour-Sergeant J. Mannion, Dr. W. S. Clark, and a few native ranks for their gallantry.

Colonel Mair had never liked the occupation of Nsanakang, as, although it offered a comparatively strong defensible position, the configuration of the ground made a retirement on Nsanarati very difficult ; and there were insufficient launches or other river craft for a retirement by water. Its retention was, he felt, only justified by his instructions to do everything possible to lead the enemy to believe that he was about to undertake an advance on Ossidinge. When Colonel Mair visited Nsanakang on the 3rd September, he arranged with Captain Hopkinson that, in case of attack, the main defence should be concentrated on Customs Hill and that Factory Hill should be abandoned. But on the evening of the 5th, on news of the German approach, Captain Hopkinson decided not to abandon Factory Hill, though pressed to do so by Lieutenant Milne-Home. This was all the more unfortunate as at that early stage of the war neither he nor his officers anticipated that the trenches they had dug would provide insufficient protection against the machine gun fire they would encounter.

Colonel Mair's reports of the Nsanakang disaster reached Lagos on the 7th September, when instructions were issued arranging that Colonel Haywood should comply with any demand for reinforcements from Calabar which Colonel Mair deemed absolutely necessary. Further, on the 8th, Colonel Mair was informed that the withdrawal from Ikom of the four companies of No. 3 Battalion for service overseas would remain in abeyance for the time being.

The Calabar Column; 3rd August– 6th September 1924. Previous to Colonel Haywood's arrival from Lagos on the 13th August to assume command of the Calabar Column, the orders, to prepare the column for an advance against Duala by the shortest route and to gain information regarding this route, had been restricted for some days by the instructions of the 7th August not to cross the frontier. But they had been subsequently amended by permission to reconnoitre across the frontier subject to the proviso that serious hostilities were to be avoided.

By the 13th August a section of the 1st Battery, and " B," " C " and " D " Companies, 3rd Battalion, had been concentrated at Calabar. On the 18th, however, Colonel Haywood received orders from Lagos altering the plans for, and the composition of, the Calabar Column, which was thereafter to consist of " B " and " E " Companies, 2nd Battalion, and " D," " E " and " F " Companies, 4th Battalion, and was to concentrate at Ikom. One company of the 3rd Battalion from Calabar was to move to Ikom to join Colonel Mair's column and the other two companies of this battalion and the section 1st Battery at Calabar were to remain there as its defensive force. These orders were again cancelled on the 21st August, when the order for the organisation of the force for oversea service was received. In this force Colonel Haywood was appointed to command No. 2 Battalion, consisting of " A," " D " and " E " Companies, 4th Battalion, and " B " Company, 3rd Battalion, the last named company being subsequently replaced by " F " Company, 4th Battalion.

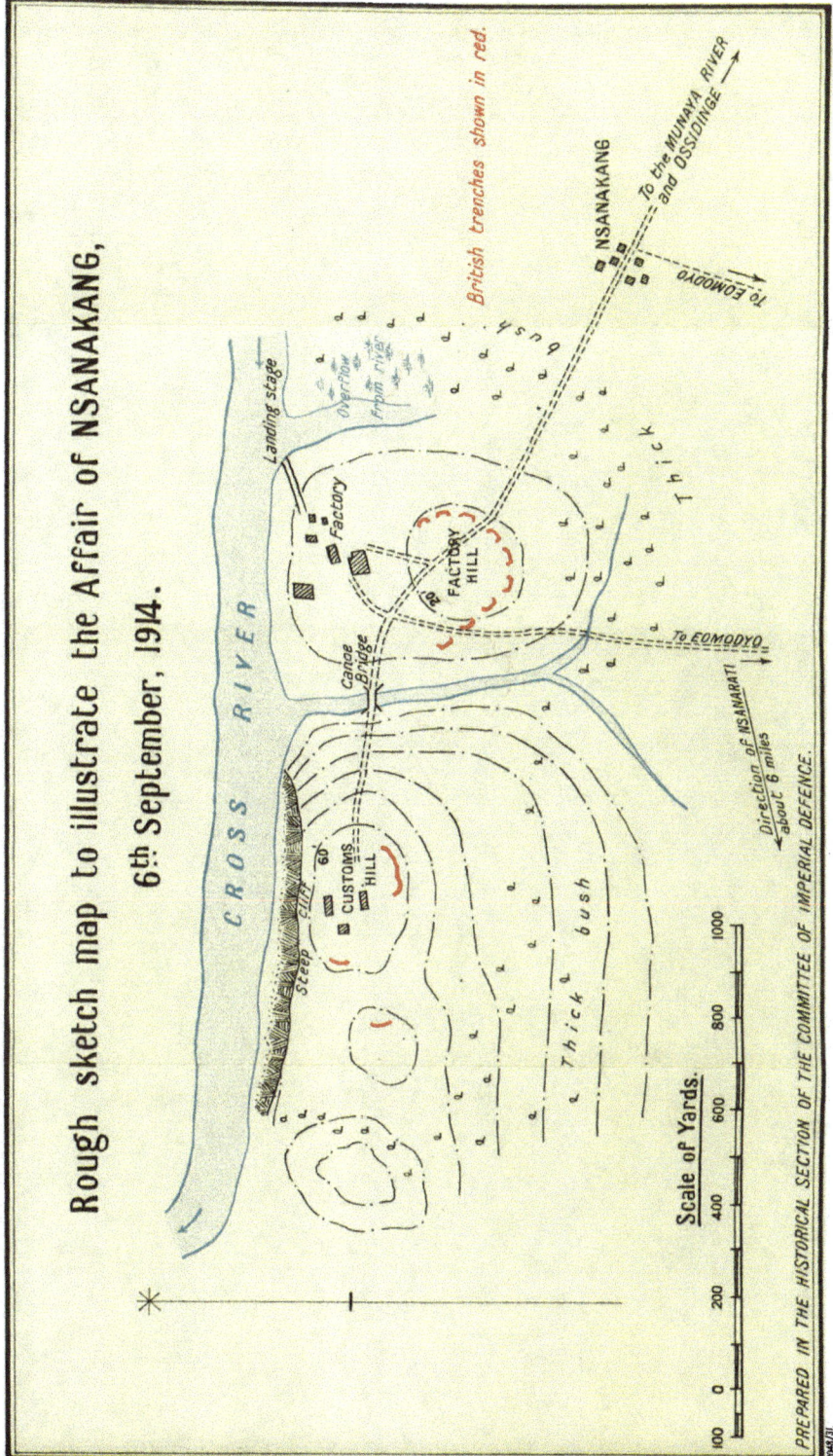

TWO FALSE ALARMS

During the last week or so of August there were some patrol encounters with the enemy in the area between Calabar and Rio del Rey, in which a few casualties were incurred. On the 29th a British detachment occupied, after slight opposition, the German station of Archibong; and subsequent reconnaissance disclosed the evacuation of Rio del Rey, which the Germans had apparently abandoned in some haste on the 30th.

On the 27th August Colonel Haywood's force comprised only one section 1st Battery, "C" and "D" Companies, 3rd Battalion, and "E" Company, 4th Battalion. But by the 6th September one section 2nd Battery had arrived and also "A," "D" and "F" Companies, 4th Battalion, all to form part of the force for oversea service. Some 180 reservists had also been concentrated at Calabar.

At 6 p.m. on the 8th September, Colonel Haywood with one section 2nd Battery and "A" and "D" Companies, 4th Battalion, left Calabar in the steamers *Bansara*, *Jackdaw*, and *Hornbill*, and proceeded at full speed to Ikom. One of the steamers reached there in twenty-six hours, and all had arrived by the 10th. Calabar & Ikom Columns; 8th–16th September, 1914.

Information from Calabar that a strong German force, joined probably by troops from Nsanakang and Ossidinge, was marching towards Calabar was received on the 11th at Lagos, whence instructions at once issued giving Colonels Mair and Haywood a free hand to deal with this threat as they considered best. Accordingly, on the evening of the 12th, Colonel Haywood left Ikom by river with the force he had just brought from Calabar and arrived back there on the 13th. No. 1 Battery (less one section), waiting at Forcados to join General Dobell, had also been ordered to Calabar and reached there on the 16th. In the meantime, however, the news of a German advance on Calabar had proved to be false and Colonel Haywood had reported that the alarm at Calabar was unwarranted.

On the 16th, news from Ikom of a German advance against the force under Colonel Mair reached Colonel Haywood and he again proceeded by river with reinforcements for Ikom consisting of one section 1st Battery and "A" and "D" Companies, 4th Battalion. This news also proved to be false and, on reaching Obubra on the 18th, he received orders to return to Calabar, where he arrived on the morning of the 19th.

On the 16th September a telegram dated the 13th from Maiduguri Column:

112 MILITARY OPERATIONS: THE CAMEROONS

28th August –13th September 1914. Captain Fox, commanding the Maiduguri Column, was received at Lagos. This reported that the German force at Mora had extended its position to include Molugve on the summit of the mountain where it was maintaining a passive defence; that nothing else of importance had occurred since the 27th August; and that Captain Fox had no definite news of the French at Fort Lamy, but had heard that they were experiencing difficulty in overcoming the German resistance at Kuseri. Another telegram received at Lagos on the 16th from the Resident at Maiduguri stated that the French had suffered considerable casualties in an abortive attack on Kuseri and were awaiting reinforcements before taking further action. The news of the French failure to capture Kuseri had been received some days previously by Sir Frederick Lugard, accompanied by a request for British assistance.

General Dobell's progress; 31st August–17th September 1914. The transport *Appam*, conveying General Dobell and some of his staff, sailed from Liverpool on the 31st August. She was to act as depot and hospital ship for the expedition and also carried three nursing sisters. On the 7th September, her escorting warship was relieved off Las Palmas by the *Challenger*.

Bathurst was reached on the 10th September, and the small detachment of the Gambia Company W.A.F.F. was embarked. Here General Dobell received messages acquainting him with the action of the Maiduguri Column and with the repulse at Garua of the Yola Column. He also heard that Colonel Carter, who was to have commanded the British (land) contingent of the Expeditionary Force, had been recalled to England.

On reaching Sierra Leone on the 12th news of the reverse at Nsanakang was received, as well as information that the French from Fort Lamy were encountering strong resistance. Under instructions from England the strength of the detachment to be drawn from Sierra Leone was increased to a total of four mountain guns, a small detachment R.E., six companies West African Regiment, some officers and other details (including Medical, Supply and Transport staffs) and 1,275 carriers. All these, with ammunition, stores and supplies, were embarked in the *Appam* during the day.

Five French transports from Dakar, carrying six mountain guns and approximately 2,000 infantry under Colonel Mayer, escorted by the French cruiser *Bruix*, had arrived at Freetown two days previously ; and General Dobell held a conference with Colonel Mayer and the senior French naval officer. General Dobell also obtained, from the General Officer Commanding Sierra Leone, the services of Colonel E. H. Gorges (Commandant, West African Regiment) to command the British contingent *vice* Colonel Carter. The French ships left that evening and the British the next morning.

Accra was reached on the 16th September and General Dobell discussed the situation with Sir Hugh Clifford. Being then of opinion that an additional two companies of the Gold Coast Regiment would not be required, and learning that Sir Hugh Clifford deprecated their withdrawal from the Gold Coast in view of possible requirements there, General Dobell said that he would only ask for them if he felt that it was absolutely necessary to do so. At the same time, as a precautionary measure, he telegraphed to the General Officer Commanding Sierra Leone that, as further men of the W.A.F.F. might not be available, he considered it advisable to ask that a further contingent from Sierra Leone should be prepared. Both the Governor and the General Officer Commanding Sierra Leone, however, telegraphed to London deprecating the withdrawal of more troops.

The *Challenger* and *Appam* arrived at Lome at 11.30 p.m. on the 16th. Here the transport *Elmina*—carrying Lieutenant-Colonel R. A. de B. Rose, " C " and " E " Companies, Sierra Leone Battalion W.A.F.F., one section Gold Coast Battery, the pioneer company Gold Coast Regiment, and 800 carriers—joined the convoy. Lagos was reached on the morning of the 17th September.

The distribution of the troops in Nigeria was then as follows :—

Maiduguri Column	" C " Company, Mounted Infantry, and " A " Company, 2nd Battalion.
Nafada detachment (at Mubi)	" B " Company, 1st Battalion.
Yola Column ..	" H " Company, 1st Battalion.
	" B," " C," " G " and " H " Companies, 2nd Battalion.
	" H " Company, 3rd Battalion.
	" B " Company, Mounted Infantry.
	One section 1st Battery.
Ikom Column * ..	" A," " B," " D," " E," " F " and " G " Companies, 3rd Battalion.
	One section 2nd Battery.

---

* The artillery section and " E " and " G " Companies had been practically destroyed at Nsanakang ; " A," " E," " F " and " G " Companies had been designated for No. 3 Battalion for service overseas.

Calabar *	.. ..	No. 2 Battalion for oversea service (i.e., "A," "D," "E" and "F" Companies, 4th Battalion). No. 1 Battery for oversea service (i.e., two sections, 1st Battery). 2nd Battery, less one section, i.e., two guns. "C" Company, 3rd Battalion. 193 reservists.
Forcados	.. ..	No. 1 Battalion for oversea service (i.e., "A" and "F" Companies, 1st Battalion, and "D" and "F" Companies, 2nd Battalion).
Lagos	.. ..	"C" Company, 1st Battalion. "B" Company, 4th Battalion (less half company at Abeokuta). Depot, 4th Battalion. Reserve section artillery (two guns). European Land Contingent (187 strong).
Birnin Kebbi	..	(internal security) "D" Company, 1st Battalion.
Sokoto	.. ..	(internal security) "E" Company, 1st Battalion.
Lokoja	.. ..	(internal security) "G" Company, 1st Battalion.
Ogoja, Ohwoja and Abakaliki.		(internal security) "E" Company, 2nd Battalion.
Udi and Okigwi	..	(internal security) "C" Company, 4th Battalion.
Kano	.. ..	(internal security) "A" Company, Mounted Infantry.

Operations by the French; 31st July–September 1914.
Local French Forces.

Before concluding this chapter it is advisable to give a brief account of the French action in the Cameroons previous to General Dobell's arrival at Lagos.

The regular military forces in the four French territories bordering the Cameroons consisted, at the outbreak of war, of the following units, all under the orders of General Aymerich, the Commander-in-Chief in French Equatorial Africa, whose headquarters were at Brazzaville in Middle Congo. In Chad there was the 4th Regiment (of Chad), organised in three battalions, comprising ten infantry and two *méharistes* † companies, a cavalry squadron, a mountain artillery section and a section of machine guns, with a total strength of 220 French and 2,300 native ranks; in Ubangi-Shari were the 3/3rd Senegalese Tirailleurs, their six companies mustering 90 French and 1,160 natives, but being without either guns or machine guns; in Middle Congo the six companies of the

---

* As shown previously, Colonel Haywood's detachment was between Calabar and Obubra.

† i.e., men mounted on camels.

FRENCH EQUATORIAL AFRICA

2/2nd Senegalese Tirailleurs had a strength of 115 French and 1,190 natives with one mountain gun, but no machine guns; and the 1st Regiment of Gabon, totalling 150 French and 1,370 natives, was organised in eight companies, but was also without guns or machine guns.

These units, which were barely sufficient for the maintenance of internal order and security, were all so widely dispersed in small detachments that concentration of even a few companies took a very long time and was beset with difficulties and risks. Consequently war with Germany presented a difficult problem. The frontier was nearly 2,000 miles long; the enemy held a central position; and the territorial changes of 1911–12 placed him in an advantageous position to sever the long line of French communications. The French had devoted much study to the question, but when mobilisation was ordered in 1914, their plans were still under consideration, nothing definite beyond certain principles having been decided upon. These enunciated that, in view of the time required for French concentration, the security of their long line of communication could only be assured from the outset by forming groups wherever possible—and especially at vulnerable points—which by taking the offensive would oblige the enemy to conform and thus abandon his own offensive projects. This action would, further, cover and gain time for the general French concentration. To carry these principles into action, the following measures had been proposed. In Gabon, to place the principal points on the coast in a state of defence and to prepare specially for an offensive with two or three companies against Oyem; to remain on the defensive along the frontier from Mvahdi to the Komo river; and, in order to secure the Ubangi river line of communication, to undertake an offensive as early as possible with two or three companies from Ubangi-Shari towards the Lobaye river.

French plans.

The Lobaye valley offered the Germans a better line of advance than the Sanga salient, which was covered with pathless dense forest or marsh. But as the Germans could transport troops rapidly down the Sanga river in steamers to the Congo, the French decided on the 1st August to send a detachment to Mossaka to command the Sanga-Congo confluence and to form a base for a subsequent advance on Wesso, a point which, by its dominant position towards the Sanga salient, offered important advantages for covering the Congo and the frontier of Middle Congo.

Action at outbreak of war.

On the 29th July, on receiving the warning telegram from

France, M. Merlin, Governor-General of French Equatorial Africa, sanctioned the immediate issue by General Aymerich of the following instructions: Gabon was to ensure the defence of Libreville and Cape Lopez, as well as the maintenance of telegraphic communication with Brazzaville and France, using, if possible, the gunboat *Surprise*; and Ubangi-Shari was to prepare for an offensive, on the declaration of war, against Singa and Mbaiki with the object of covering the French telegraphic and river communications. For this purpose a company of the 2/2nd Senegalese Tirailleurs from the area in Middle Congo near Singa was placed at the disposal of Lieutenant-Colonel Morisson, commanding in Ubangi-Shari. Colonel Largeau, commanding in Chad, was at the same time given a free hand to act as if he were in an independent colony.

On the 1st August the local Council of Defence agreed on certain other measures, including the rapid transportation of troops to the Sanga-Congo confluence, both to protect the line of the Congo and to form a base for a possible offensive up the Sanga. The general result of these measures during August was as follows:—

Gabon. In Gabon, Libreville and other points on the coast were placed in a state of defence, and by the 28th August the Oyem Column of three companies was concentrated near Midsik.

Middle Congo; 2nd–31st August 1914. In Middle Congo, on the 2nd August the requisitioned river steamer *Largeau*—armed with a quick-firing gun and equipped with a portable wireless—and a detachment of 130 infantry with a mountain gun, were sent to Mossaka. This detachment, learning of the declaration of war before the Germans, occupied Bonga without opposition on the 6th, and by the 19th had been brought, by reinforcements, to a strength of 375 rifles with three mountain guns. Including the *Largeau*, they had several steamers, including two captured from the Germans; and the officer commanding, hearing that the Germans had been late in learning of the declaration of war,* decided to make a rapid advance up the Sanga to Wesso.† On the way he heard that Germans from Ikelemba had destroyed a party of French militia near Wesso and had occupied that place. But they evacuated it again on the 29th on hearing of the advance up

---

* The French had captured a German steamer taking the first news of this up the river.
† The Sanga was navigable by river steamers up to Nola. Those drawing 6 feet of water could reach Wesso at all seasons, but during the low-water season only vessels drawing 3 feet could get to Nola.

[*To face p.* 116

On the River Sanga

FRENCH OPERATIONS

the Sanga of the French detachment from Bonga, which was thus able to occupy Wesso without opposition on the 31st August.

A detachment from Bangui, the military headquarters of Ubangi-Shari, occupied Singa on the 6th August, this being the first intimation the Germans there received of the declaration of war; and on the 12th three companies of Senegalese infantry under Lieutenant-Colonel Morisson occupied the fortified German military post of Mbaiki. The headquarters of the German 6th Company here had only learnt of the declaration of war after the loss of Singa and, receiving information that the French were advancing in force, evacuated Mbaiki precipitately without attempting to defend it. Colonel Morisson pursued rapidly, and by the end of the month, when forced to halt by lack of carriers, had established posts along the banks of the Lobaye river extending as far north as Kolongo. In the meantime 100 police rifles had been detached towards Yakonendji to cover the communication northward from Bangui from attacks by the German 5th Company at Bouar. *Ubangi-Shari; August 1914.*

The news of the declaration of war reached Fort Lamy (in Chad), where there was a French garrison of about 200 rifles, at the beginning of August. Learning from Colonel Largeau that he could not undertake operations on a wide front without evacuating a portion of French territory, the French Colonial Office, after consulting M. Merlin and General Aymerich, issued instructions that garrisons required to retain control of all the French districts were to be maintained, and that the available remainder were to be organised in detachments to co-operate with the British from Nigeria in an offensive in the Northern Cameroons. Colonel Largeau consequently arranged for the concentration at Fort Lamy of 350 rifles by the end of August and of 470 rifles and a mountain gun section by the end of September. Further, as the French frontier post at Lai, some two hundred miles to the south of Fort Lamy, was threatened by the German 12th Company from Buma, he arranged to concentrate at Lai by the 10th September, 180 rifles, who would also cover his communications with Bangui. As already noted, Colonel Largeau, with a view to co-operation with the British, had detached Captain Ferrandi with a small escort to get into touch with Maiduguri. But before the main French detachment from Fort Lamy effected a junction with the British it was obviously advisable to seize Kuseri. This the French attacked on the 24th-25th August with a detachment of 250 rifles and one gun. But the gun, *Chad; 2nd-25th August 1914.*

which was an old one, was soon put out of action, and the French, after suffering some 23 casualties (5 French and 18 natives), decided to postpone the attack till they received further reinforcements.

Germans at Kuseri; 15th–25th August 1914. Captain von Raben's diary shows that his orders to Lieutenant Kallmeyer to hold Kuseri as long as possible before retiring on Mora reached that officer on the 15th August, when he also received local news indicating an imminent French attack. The Kuseri garrison consisted of two Germans and 35 natives with a machine gun, and they at once began to improve their defences. On the evening of the 24th a native post opposite Fort Lamy signalled that the French were crossing the river, and, not long afterwards, as it was getting dark, the French opened a heavy fire on the post from the right bank of the Logone river. This lasted for about forty-five minutes, but the garrison did not respond. Next morning, at 6.25 a.m., after a night of continuous rain, the French commenced their attack, at once suffering several casualties (in a gallant though premature attempt to break through the German thorn abattis *) by fire from a strong outlying German entrenchment of whose existence they were evidently unaware. By 8.15 a.m., when the German machine gun opened fire, the French had practically surrounded the post but were unable to make much progress and their gun, which came into action at 11 a.m., had practically no effect and soon ceased fire. The French appear to have abandoned the attack shortly afterwards. Lieutenant Kallmeyer, in a report quoted by Captain von Raben, pays tribute to the courage and endurance shown by his men in face of superior numbers and under a hostile fire to which they were unaccustomed.

The Sanga and Lobaye Columns; September 1914. By the 3rd September, the columns at Wesso and on the Lobaye river had each reached a strength of between 500 and 600 rifles. General Aymerich had just received instructions from Paris that the troops under his command should aim, by prudently conducted operations, at containing the German troops in the interior of the Cameroons and so facilitate the Allied attack on Duala. He consequently decided on an offensive by the Wesso and Lobaye Columns towards the Upper Sanga, both as fulfilling his instructions and at the same time covering the frontiers of Ubangi-Shari and Middle Congo. In the meantime the Wesso Column had advanced towards

---

* The Germans had constructed two low thick hedges of this at 220 and 550 yards respectively from their main post.

Molundu. But, failing to capture on the 11th September a strongly entrenched German position at Ngoko, it returned to Wesso. Here the column commander received instructions to direct his efforts to an advance towards Nola in co-operation with the Lobaye Column.

By the 28th August the Oyem Column of three companies under Commandant Dubois de Saligny had concentrated about Midsik and, crossing the German frontier a few days later, attacked, on the 6th September, a strong German detachment at Mibang. De Saligny was killed, all his carriers fled and his column was forced to retire, arriving back at Midsik on the 9th September. The news of this reverse did not, however, reach Libreville and Headquarters for some time.

Gabon; August–15th September 1914.

Two companies were holding the coast defences at Libreville, but as the Allies held command of the sea it seemed in little danger. It was consequently decided on the 15th September to utilise these companies to attack, in conjunction with the gunboat *Surprise*, some Germans who with some armed steamboats were endeavouring to create trouble in the area between Muni and Gabon. By this time the three other companies of the Gabon Regiment had been concentrated, two at Ndjole and one at Mvahdi.

CHAPTER IV

THE CAPTURE AND CONSOLIDATION OF DUALA, AND FRENCH ACTION ELSEWHERE; 17TH SEPTEMBER–17TH OCTOBER 1914

(Maps 2 and 4)

Lagos; 17th–20th Sept. 1914. At Lagos, where he conferred on the 17th September with Sir Frederick Lugard, General Dobell heard further details of the recent unsuccessful operations on the German frontier and learnt that there was some unrest among the natives in the British districts of Abeokuta, Bassa, Nassarawa, and the Benue river. Thus in several respects the situation in Nigeria was distinctly unsatisfactory; and this fact, in conjunction with the reports of the progress made in the Cameroon estuary, served to confirm General Dobell in his previous opinion that Duala must be his immediate objective.

Nigeria was obviously unable to spare as many troops as had been previously arranged, and it was decided that the Nigerian contingent of the Expeditionary Force should consist only of No. 1 Battery and Nos. 1 and 2 Battalions.* To make good the deficiency General Dobell telegraphed to Accra asking for the two companies of the Gold Coast Regiment which he had previously intimated that he might require. Sir Hugh Clifford's reply, that these would be sent at once, enabled General Dobell to form a composite battalion comprising these two companies and the two companies of the Sierra Leone Battalion that had joined the force at Lome.

The control of the operations on the Nigeria-Cameroons frontier was also discussed with Sir Frederick Lugard. General Dobell appreciated their relation to his main operations, but considered that the distance of his headquarters from the scene of action and the lack of rapid means of inter-communication would make it very difficult for him to exercise efficient control over them. On the other hand, Colonel Cunliffe and the whole of the headquarters staff in Nigeria

---

* For their composition see Order of Battle in Appendix II.

were required to accompany the force to Duala, and there was no one to replace them at Lagos without withdrawing officers, who could ill be spared, from the columns on the frontier. In deference to Sir Frederick Lugard's wishes, General Dobell therefore consented to assume responsibility for these operations. To issue orders in his name in Nigeria, he obtained the services of Major H. C. Moorhouse, who was the Secretary of the Southern Provinces and a reserve artillery officer who had served in the Nigeria Regiment.

After discussion with Colonel Cunliffe, who returned to Lagos from Yola on the 20th September, General Dobell before his departure issued the following general instructions for the conduct of these frontier operations. Colonel Mair was to take command of all the troops on the Cross river, including Calabar, and was to act on the defensive till he heard that the expeditionary force had reached the Cameroons. He could then take such offensive action as seemed to him advisable. The Yola Column, when joined by the Maiduguri Column from the vicinity of Mora, was to attack Garua with all possible strength.*

These instructions were, however, modified after news had been received on the 25th September that the French had captured Kuseri on the 20th. The movement of the Maiduguri Column to join the Yola Column was countermanded, the attack on Garua was postponed, and Colonel Mair was told to delay an assumption of the offensive.

On the 18th September the French transports, escorted by the *Bruix*, arrived at Lagos, and on the 19th Captain H. A. Child,† Director of the Nigeria Marine, returned from a visit to the Cameroon estuary, bringing reports of the situation there and of the progress made by Captain Fuller. The safety of the sea passage being assured, General Dobell decided to sail for the Cameroon estuary next day, and that afternoon

---

* The regular troops remaining in Nigeria after General Dobell's departure were distributed as follows :—

Maiduguri Column ..	One company mounted infantry and one company infantry.
Mubi	One company infantry.
Yola Column	Two guns, one company mounted infantry and six companies infantry.
Ikom Column	Two guns and six companies infantry.
Calabar, or under orders for there	Two guns and two and a half companies infantry.
Internal garrisons ..	One company mounted infantry and five and a half companies infantry.

† He was a retired Lieutenant, R.N.

held a conference on board the *Appam* with the French naval and military commanders.

In addition to Colonel Cunliffe and the headquarters staff of the Nigeria Regiment, there embarked at Lagos, in the *Appam*, personnel for the medical and other ancillary services, and also some forty European members of the Nigerian Land Contingent, whose services had been especially arranged for by Sir Frederick Lugard. As all these forty had previous experience of active military service, they formed a valuable addition to the force, enabling General Dobell to increase the number of British ranks with each native company to five or six and so partly counterbalance the large number of Germans under arms.

Preceded by the French convoy, which was to call at Calabar to take in fresh water and provisions, General Dobell, with the British transports under escort of the *Challenger*, sailed from Lagos in the afternoon of the 20th September. Next day the British convoy was joined off Forcados by the transports *Niger* and *Lokoja*, carrying No. 1 Battalion Nigeria Regiment; and, on the 22nd, the transport *Boma*, carrying No. 1 Nigerian Battery and No. 2 Battalion Nigeria Regiment, was picked up off Calabar. The whole British flotilla entered the Cameroon estuary on the 23rd and anchored at the Suelaba base.

Organisation of the Allied Force. The Order of Battle of the Allied Expeditionary Force is given in Appendix II. Its total combatant strength amounted to approximately 4,250 rifles and 16 guns, of which the British contingent furnished 2,400 rifles and 10 guns. The British rank and file were entirely African, but the French force included a company of Europeans; and it is noteworthy that General Dobell's experiences led him to recommend the inclusion in future similar expeditions of a detachment of British European rank and file for orderly and other such duties and also to furnish guards over European prisoners. The British native companies were much weaker in strength than the French and had a lower proportion of European ranks, the higher number of French non-commissioned officers being especially noticeable. A further point of difference was that the French guns and ammunition were carried on mules: an arrangement which, in the frequent embarkations and disembarkations of the first stages of the operations, compared unfavourably with the British system of gun and ammunition carriers.

The British administrative and departmental organisation for the force was an improvisation, commenced and completed in essential details while the troops were still in their transports. The task was not at all an easy one. But, in Captain R. H. Rowe, General Dobell had, to carry out his instructions, a chief administrative staff officer whose combination of tact, ability and powers of organisation contributed greatly to the creation and maintenance throughout the operations of an efficient and satisfactory administrative system. The personnel employed, mostly volunteers, were neither homogeneous nor experienced from a military point of view. Collected from the various ports as the convoy moved down the African coast, they either came from the Colonial civil services—political, medical, engineer, postal, railway, telegraph and other departments—or were merchants, mining prospectors or otherwise engaged in private enterprise. They had the advantage, however, that they knew West Africa and realised the difficulties they were likely to encounter ; and they all brought to their tasks unbounded enthusiasm and energy. The material was similarly collected ; the stores and equipment, generally embarked in some haste, being of varying pattern and quality and on differing scales.

For the *Signal Service* under Captain F. L. N. Giles, R.E., a headquarters signal detachment was formed from the party of the Gambia Company W.A.F.F. and from some regimental signallers from Nigeria and the Gold Coast. After arrival at Duala, however, it was found that the denseness of the forest prevented signalling on any large scale and these detachments were detailed for duty with regimental units.

The *Engineer Services* at first consisted of the small Sierra Leone field section, and a telegraph section and railway detachment formed of personnel drawn from the Nigerian services.

There was no officer of the Army Service Corps to take charge of the *Supply and Transport* arrangements. But General Dobell applied for and obtained the services of Captain D. A. Wallbach, whom he had known first as Mess Sergeant of the Royal Irish Regiment in 1891, and then as Senior Transport Officer in Nigeria. His work as Director of Supply and Transport during the operations showed that no better appointment could have been made.

The scale, composition and character of rations varied in each colony, and all units had to improvise arrangements for messing. The only means of transport were carriers who belonged to various tribes in Sierra Leone, the Gold Coast and Nigeria. They were formed into tribal units, and during the campaign considerable and frequent replacements became necessary owing to sickness. Altogether, before the conclusion of hostilities, over 14,000 carriers from the three Colonies were employed in addition to well over 10,000 recruited locally.

Major J. C. B. Statham, R.A.M.C., who joined the *Appam* at Freetown, was appointed Director of Medical Services. He had at first a total of one R.A.M.C. officer, twenty-four doctors of the West African Medical Staff, six nursing sisters, four non-commissioned officers and twenty dressers to assist him, few of the doctors except the R.A.M.C. officer having previous experience of a military organisation larger than a company. Before arrival at Duala, in anticipation of the considerable casualties to be expected in the landing operations, four field ambulance sections were organised. Each consisted of three medical officers, one N.C.O. and two dressers with a stretcher division of thirty-two to forty-eight bearers and a tent division (for the formation of dressing stations) equipped with from thirty-two to forty-eight carrier loads of medical stores and equipment.

The further development of the administrative services will be referred to later.

The Cameroon Estuary; 23rd–26th Sept. 1914. Captain Fuller proceeded on board the *Appam* on her arrival at the Suelaba base on the morning of the 23rd September, and reported that a passage had been cleared through the wreck barrage. It was, however, barely 20 feet deep at high tide, whereas the *Challenger* was drawing 21 feet 6 inches. General Dobell consequently decided not to attempt to land troops until it had been definitely ascertained that she could be lightened sufficiently to pass through the barrage passage. By working day and night this was effected by the morning of the 25th, when her draught had been reduced to 19 feet 7 inches.

During the 23rd and 24th the work of re-sweeping and surveying the main channel, through and above the barrage, continued; the *Dwarf* and *Remus*, who covered the operations, trying unsuccessfully to draw the fire of the German battery on Yoss Point.

On the morning of the 24th September Lieutenant-Commander Sneyd, Captain H. G. Howell and Lieutenant D. McCallum of the Intelligence Staff proceeded in the *Cumberland's* picket boat to reconnoitre for a practicable landing place on the north bank of the Dibamba river, where the latest map showed a small road leading from Yansoki to Duala. The whole area between the outskirts of Duala and the Dibamba river appeared to be mangrove swamp,* covered with palm trees and rendered almost impenetrable by dense undergrowth. No sign of any road coming down to the river bank could be discerned, and only at one point on the river bank near Mbenga, a mile or so below Yansoki, was the ground at all firm. It seemed to Captain Howell that here it might be possible to land a small force to cut its way forward through the bush and gain the path shown on the map. Further upstream the picket boat came under fire from an enemy detachment of about sixty men near Pitti and again on the return journey from some enemy troops near Yansoki, but in neither case did she suffer any casualties.

After receiving Captain Howell's report, General Dobell arranged with Captain Fuller on the evening of the 24th that the *Challenger* should pass through the wreck barrage next day and should try to reach a point about 5,000 yards from Duala, but should not open fire unless opposed by shore batteries. General Dobell had decided to call on the Germans to surrender Duala, and, if they did not do so, to threaten their line of retreat by the Midland Railway by landing a small force near Mbenga early on the morning of the 26th. This was also calculated to bring about some dispersion of their forces.

The *Challenger*, skilfully piloted by Commander Hughes, passed through the barrage successfully, though touching bottom, on the morning of the 25th, and by the afternoon had moved up-river and anchored at a point about 7,000 yards from Duala, just short of what was correctly supposed to be a line of mines. At 9.30 a.m. the French convoy arrived and anchored at the Suelaba base, the French commander, who visited General Dobell, being given a verbal explanation of next day's programme. At about noon General Dobell and Captain Fuller went on board the *Challenger* and a message was then despatched under a flag of truce to the German Governor informing him that the Allies intended to bombard Duala, preparatory to landing troops, unless he should desire to surrender the town. To this message a totally irrelevant reply was received from the German commandant at Duala, and con-

---

* To those who have never seen a mangrove swamp a short description may be of interest. The tree grows in water and has dense foliage, but seldom reaches a height of over 15 feet. Its main characteristic lies in the number of its roots, which grow above the water and form with the lower branches of the tree a close and intricate network of limbs above the muddy water or, at low tide, black slime. To traverse these swamps, which are the haunt of biting insects and reptiles, it is in practice necessary to walk along upon this slippery network of branches and roots.

sequently the *Challenger* was ordered to bombard the town at daylight on the 26th and prevent the enemy escaping across the river. It was hoped that the bombardment would also divert the enemy's attention from the Dibamba river landing.

It has to be remembered that most of the British steamers had been necessarily taken up in a hurry on the coast. They were inadequately fitted and equipped for transport work, had insufficient condensing plant, and were generally overcrowded. The condition of his troops in the British transports had, in fact, already forced General Dobell to the conclusion that an early disembarkation was imperative, when reports he now received from Colonel Mayer showed the arrangements in the French transports to be even more defective. General Dobell could consequently not afford to spare much time on preliminary reconnaissance before disembarkation and had to accept the military risks involved.

Attempted landing in the Dibamba river; 26th Sept. 1914. Preparations for the Dibamba river landing were made during the 25th September. A covering force was to land near Mbenga, capture or destroy the enemy detachment at Yansoki, cut a track from the river bank to the road shown on the map, and improve the landing place to provide a base for the disembarkation of further troops. Colonel Gorges was placed in control of the operation, with discretion to withdraw if the physical difficulties rendered it unlikely that an advance on Duala from the landing place could be carried out successfully. The *Cumberland's* picket boat and the *Vigilant* were detailed to cover the advance of the covering force to the landing place, whilst the *Remus* and *Porpoise*, each carrying half a company of troops, were at daylight to proceed up the Dibamba river, engage the enemy detachment at Pitti, cut the telegraph wire there and subsequently reconnoitre as far as the Yapoma bridge.

Colonel Gorges detailed the Sierra Leone Battery (less one section), detachment R.E., and the West African Regiment, all on board the *Appam*, as the covering force; and as first reinforcements, to be landed later, one section Sierra Leone Battery and No. 1 Battalion Nigeria Regiment. The pioneer company of the Gold Coast Regiment was to proceed, under naval control, in the *Remus* and *Porpoise*. The covering force would be commanded by Lieutenant-Colonel E. Vaughan and would be accompanied by Lieutenant-Colonel Cunliffe [*] (to represent Colonel Gorges) with two staff officers and signallers.

---

[*] Second-in-Command of the British contingent.

[*To face p.* 126

THE NIGERIA MARINE PADDLE-TUG "PORPOISE"

ADVANCE UP DIBAMBA RIVER

Colonel Gorges with the remainder of his staff would be with the first reinforcements.

Colonel Vaughan, who was warned that considerable opposition might be expected, was at first only to land two companies. Having effected a landing he was to send out reconnaissances in both directions along the river bank, and also towards the railway.

The covering force was to embark in the ex-German s.s. *Marina* and in the *Walrus*, *Crocodile* and *Alligator*, each with a lighter in tow.

The naval instructions were that the *Vigilant*, showing a light, was to be at anchor before dawn on the 26th off the entrance to the Dibamba river. The *Remus* and *Porpoise*, in which the Pioneers were to embark on the afternoon of the 25th, were to enter the river at dawn, ahead of the covering force, and proceed to carry out the duties allotted to them. The *Cumberland's* picket boat was to pilot the covering force flotilla, leaving the *Appam* at 4 a.m., the *Vigilant* following up the river as rear guard. On approaching Mbenga the picket boat and *Vigilant* were to anchor and cover the landing.

Early on the 26th September the *Remus* went aground at the entrance to the Dibamba river, and it was not till 8.30 a.m. that she was able to get off and proceed upstream with the *Porpoise*. At 10 a.m. a bombardment at 2,000 yards range of the enemy position at Pitti elicited no reply, but, when the *Remus* advanced and arrived within about seventy yards, the enemy from a well-concealed position in the bush opened a heavy rifle and machine gun fire. Lieutenant F. Q. Champness, R.N., in command, withdrew his craft about one thousand yards and, after twenty minutes further bombardment, silenced the enemy. Again advancing and, as they passed Pitti, sending a dinghy ashore to destroy the telephone post, the *Remus* and *Porpoise* proceeded a short distance upstream to destroy a boom obstructing the channel. But as the dinghy got close to the bank a very heavy rifle fire was opened on her, wounding two out of four native soldiers she was carrying and causing the native paddlers to jump overboard. Leading Seaman W. Norman, the one naval rating in the dinghy, displayed great coolness and paddled into cover under the bank until a further bombardment by the *Remus* and *Porpoise* enabled him to pull back to the *Remus* in safety. She and the *Porpoise* then withdrew out of range and Lieutenant Champness informed Lieutenant-Commander Sneyd, who had come up in the picket boat to see what was happening, that to capture Pitti it would, in his opinion, be necessary to land military reinforcements well below to take the enemy position in flank and rear. Lieutenant-Commander Sneyd at once went back with this information to Mbenga, where it was decided soon afterwards to abandon the whole project. The *Remus* and *Porpoise* commenced their return journey at about 4 p.m., being fired on near Yansoki. They had incurred a total of 17 casualties; 13 naval (11 in the *Remus* and 2 in the *Porpoise*) and 4 in the Gold Coast Regiment.

In the meantime the covering force, leaving the *Appam* at 4.50 a.m., had reached the landing place near Mbenga at about 7 a.m. No opposition was encountered, but some difficulty was experienced in mooring the *Marina*, and it was not till 7.45 a.m. that "E" and "I" Companies, West African Regiment, disembarking in surf-boats, had both started off to capture Yansoki and to reconnoitre to the westward respectively. By this time "A," "B" and "D" Companies had landed from the other craft and, with carriers to assist them, now began to clear the ground so as to provide a landing base. Colonel Vaughan then went forward to make a personal reconnaissance. He found that the whole ground in the vicinity was swamp, covered with dense undergrowth and much intersected with creeks and morasses. Convinced that the place was quite unsuitable as a base for a force of any size, he returned to the landing place to find that no reports had come in from "E" or "I" Companies and that Colonel Cunliffe had sent off "A" Company to support "E" in its attack on Yansoki.

At 10.20 a.m. Colonel Cunliffe sent a message by the *Vigilant* to Colonel Gorges informing him that the landing place was quite unsuitable and that no news had yet been received from the two companies sent to capture Yansoki. If they succeeded Colonel Vaughan would take the whole force to try to effect a landing there. Heavy firing, he added, had been heard from the Pitti neighbourhood.

Neither had any reports been received from "I" Company. But it returned to the landing place at 11.30 a.m., having found the country very difficult and having come across no signs of paths or villages.

At 12.35 p.m. Colonel Cunliffe sent a further message to Colonel Gorges saying that a report from Captain H. Goodwin, commanding the Gold Coast Pioneer Company, brought by Lieutenant-Commander Sneyd, estimated the enemy strength in a well-concealed position at Pitti as about two hundred.

SURRENDER OF DUALA

Colonel Cunliffe said that he was still without news of the two companies sent to capture Yansoki and that, as long as this place was held by the enemy, it seemed inadvisable to send reinforcements to Pitti.

At 1.45 p.m. Colonel Gorges arrived himself in the *Vigilant* at the landing place and agreed that it was unsuitable as a base for a further advance. There was still no news of " A " and " E " Companies. But about 3.15 p.m. signals from them, from a point on the river bank about half a mile upstream, were observed; and arrangements were made to bring them down by water. They had not only failed to reach Yansoki, but had completely lost their way. At 3.30 p.m. Colonel Gorges issued orders for the whole force to withdraw. The *Marina, Crocodile* and two lighters had, however, gone aground and were not all refloated till 9.45 p.m., when the last of the troops were re-embarked and the flotilla started to return to Suelaba.

Meanwhile, in the morning the *Challenger*, opening fire on Duala, had found the wireless station to be out of range; and, not desiring to damage the town unnecessarily, had ceased fire after a few rounds pending the result of the Dibamba river operations. To ascertain this result, General Dobell proceeded during the afternoon to the mouth of the Dibamba river, where he met Colonel Gorges and learnt that a landing was impracticable. General Dobell thereupon decided that early next morning he would carry out a personal reconnaissance of the main channel to Duala.

Early in the morning of the 27th September General Dobell, accompanied by Captain Fuller and the officers commanding the British and French contingents, proceeded in the *Ivy* towards Duala, primarily to examine the vicinity of Doctor Creek near Yoss Battery with a view to effecting a landing there. The *Ivy* anchored in a position from which a clear view of the town and its outskirts was obtained.

The surrender of Duala; 27th Sept. 1914.

At 9.30 a.m. several loud explosions were heard; the wireless mast was seen to fall; and the Germans ran up a white flag over Government House. Shortly afterwards a German representative came on board the *Ivy* to surrender Duala and the surrounding area. This included Duala and Bonaberi; a point $1\frac{1}{2}$ kilometres to the north-west of Bonaberi; Bonabela to the north; and a point on the railway $3\frac{1}{2}$ kilometres to the east of Duala. Within these limits all arms, ammunition and government property were to be surrendered, as well as all shipping in the harbour, and all German and Austrian male subjects were to be made prisoners of war.

The town of Duala stood on ground terminating towards the estuary in abrupt cliffs 30 feet high, along which the Germans had dug a series of trenches and gun emplacements, constituting a formidable position and one which it would have been very difficult to carry by assault. That they had not attempted to hold this position was surprising, but subsequent information showed that the fear of a successful landing by the Allies in the Dibamba river had contributed materially to their decision to surrender.

Landing at Duala. General Dobell at once ordered up some of his troop transports from Suelaba, but there was not time for them to arrive before dark. He himself, with Captain Fuller and the French commander, landed at Duala, with an escort of fifty marines, at 3 p.m. At the same time a party of fifty seamen from the *Challenger* landed to garrison Bonaberi. At both places steps were at once taken to safeguard life and property and both districts were covered by the *Dwarf's* guns. The short bombardment had done little damage, but the Germans had blown up the magazine and the wireless station; they had destroyed all the telegraph and telephone instruments and had cut all the wires; and they had also removed most of their armament* and considerable quantities of stores and provisions. But much valuable property remained—left, it is said, by the Germans under the conviction that their forces in Europe were well on the way to victory and that they would consequently recover everything undamaged after a very brief interval. About four hundred European Germans, including seventy women and children, were at first said to be still in Duala and Bonaberi.

Immediately prior to the surrender, the German troops in Duala and the immediate vicinity appear to have consisted of a European detachment about seventy strong, No. 1 (Depot) Native Infantry Company, a section of the Police Depot Company and No. 2 Reserve Detachment. The two depot units had apparently withdrawn from Duala on the 26th and No. 2 Reserve Detachment, which had occupied the positions at Yansoki and Pitti, withdrew to Yapoma on the 27th September. The only troops remaining at Duala were the seventy men of the European detachment, and these were made prisoners. The Governor had left there on the 25th for Eseka, and next day the military commander, Colonel Zimmermann, had left for Edea. The direction in which the main

---

* We captured four 9-cm. guns.

German forces had withdrawn was doubtful, but reports indicated that they had retired in two portions, one towards Yabasi in the north and the other towards Edea in the east. Small detachments still remained in the vicinity, however, and a force of some importance was reported to be at Nkongsamba, the Northern Railway terminus.

Before describing the operations undertaken to clear up the local situation and to consolidate the position at Duala, it will be convenient to mention some of the administrative measures carried out at Duala before and during the first few days of its occupation. *Administrative measures at Duala.*

No. 1 Battalion Nigeria Regiment landed on the 28th September and relieved the naval detachments occupying Duala and Bonaberi. But the disembarkation of the remainder of the Allied force was not completed for several days, until the mines laid by the Germans had been recovered.* As they had been laid close to the surface, this work was exceptionally difficult and hazardous, its execution reflecting great credit on Lieutenant L. H. K. Hamilton, R.N., and those working under him.

Separate areas of occupation were allotted to the British and French contingents. British troops occupied Bonaberi and were quartered in Duala to the south of the Midland Railway, the area to the north of it being allotted to the French.

General Dobell had already arranged that Lieutenant K. V. Elphinstone † should administer the civil goverment of the occupied area. The immediate necessity for measures of control over the several thousand natives there was, however, impressed on General Dobell, the moment he stepped ashore, by a request for European guards to protect the six or seven hundred Germans remaining. When the enemy troops had retired, the Germans had also withdrawn all the personnel who had hitherto exercised a very firm, not to say harsh, control over the natives. These had a reputation for turbulence; and as many of them were imbued with a desire for revenge it was clear that the Germans in Duala would not be safe unless guarded. There was also a shortage of food. In the circumstances General Dobell decided that he had no option but to *Civil administration.*

---

* Thirty-four mines had been laid, and under German guidance thirty-three were recovered and destroyed by the 1st October. One was never found.

† He and other civilians with the expeditionary force had been given military or naval rank.

deport all Germans and other white aliens. On the evening of the 27th September their collection and embarkation commenced, and within a week 684 in all, including the crews of various ships and many women and children, were sent off in transports, in the first place to Lagos or Kotonu (Dahomey). The Governors of the British possessions on the coast could not accommodate such large numbers nor, with their reduced garrisions, safeguard them, and many, not taken over by the French, were finally sent to England.

Lieutenant Elphinstone, assisted by two British and two French civil officers, at once started the work of pacification and administration of the native population. Further, in addition to assisting the Provost-Marshal of the force in maintaining law and order, he took over control of the convict prison and of the prisoners of war information bureau. The Dualese in general fortunately favoured a British accession and behaved satisfactorily, restraining themselves well in circumstances which must have tried their self-control severely; and some slight plundering that at first took place was quickly suppressed without much difficulty. The shortage of local supplies was also soon overcome, as the natives in the vicinity were not long in regaining sufficient confidence to bring them in for sale.

Naval arrangements. In the river off Duala and Bonaberi and in neighbouring creeks, nine large sea-going steamers, six smaller vessels, a trawler, four dredgers, nearly thirty steam or motor launches and about fifty lighters were captured. These were in addition to the *Kamerun* and the seven steamers, dredger and steel lighters which had been sunk to obstruct the main channel. The nine large steamers, of a tonnage ranging from 1,500 to 3,500, were all in full commission, ready for sea and with general or homeward cargoes of valuable produce; and on one of them were found thirty-two British and French prisoners of war. Of the six smaller vessels four had been sunk in creeks, but they were raised, armed and commissioned for British service, among them being the armed yacht *Herzogin Elisabeth*, which was rechristened *Margaret Elizabeth* and armed with 12-pounders. The remaining two, found in working order, were the stern-wheel gunboat *Soden* and a powerful tug. Rechristened *Sokoto* and *Sir Frederick* respectively, they were at once armed and commissioned for river work.*

Lieutenant-Commander Percival of the Nigeria Marine was

---

* The Germans had removed the guns from all the vessels.

NAVAL AND ADMINISTRATIVE WORK 133

appointed King's Harbour Master, and under his direction the dockyard and workshops were put into working order. Other steps were taken to form at Duala an effective naval base for further operations. The floating dock, accommodating ships up to 1,200 tons displacement, had been sunk; but it was soon raised and proved to be of great value to us during the subsequent operations.

On the 2nd October, after the minefield had been cleared, the *Challenger* proceeded to a buoy off Duala where she commanded all the water approaches and where she could render assistance to the troops with her searchlights. Work was then commenced to prepare, arm and man the available steam and motor launches for operations up creeks and rivers. Including work previously done, altogether two 6-inch, six 12-pounders, four 3-pounders, eight machine guns and three small French guns were mounted in various craft, all being manned by the *Cumberland* and *Challenger*, except the French guns, which were manned by the *Bruix*.*

Captain Giles, the Director of Signals, was, on the 8th October, appointed Chief Engineer, his manifold duties being apparent from the diagram below.

Engineer and Communication Services.

Chief Engineer
(one staff officer and one officer for general duties)

Field Section R.E. (Sierra Leone Det.).	Officer i/c Northern Railway (R.E. at Bonaberi & Nigerian Railway Det.).	Officer i/c Midland Railway (French Railway Section).	Pioneer Coy. G.C. Regt.	Director of Signals (H.Q. Signal Co., Survey & Drawing Office).	Director of Posts & Telegraphs (Nigerian P. & T. Section).	Director of Works.

The railway stations at Duala and Bonaberi were found in good condition, and the stores and workshops reasonably well equipped, though the workshop engine, steam cranes, etc., had been partly dismantled and portions of them removed.

Only one small shunting engine and no rolling stock were found at Bonaberi. But at Duala there were ten locomotives, though all required extensive repair or replacement of essential parts, for which there were no spares available; and there were thirty trucks in running order or nearing completion.

---

* For detailed lists of British and captured vessels and craft employed during the operations, see Appendices III and IV.

The Nigerian railway section disembarked on the 30th September and the shops started work next day, a number of local native engine-drivers and workmen being employed. By the 7th October one small engine had been put in running order, seventeen wagons were completed, three armoured trucks (one with a naval 12-pounder mounted on it) nearly completed and two ambulance coaches improvised.

Between the 2nd and 8th October trucks were man-handled between Duala and the Yapoma bridge for the transport of naval guns, supplies, water, ammunition and wounded. On the 9th, the day that the first train left Duala, this railway was handed over to a newly arrived French railway section, and the Nigerian section moved to Bonaberi to deal with the Northern Railway.

Lieutenant H. M. Woolley and his Nigerian telegraph section at once set to work to establish telegraphic communication between Duala and the outposts, as well as telephonic communication within the town. Despite the chaos of wrecked instruments and of damaged lines, telegraphic communication was opened with Yapoma by the 4th October, and two days later with Maka on the Northern Railway. By the same date a fourteen-line telephone system was working in Duala.

Both the submarine cables had been cut near Duala by the Germans at the outbreak of war. But, on the 17th September, the cable ship *Transmitter*, which had come to Suelaba at the request of Captain Fuller, had picked up the Duala-Bonny cable and established communication with Bonny and Lagos. The *Transmitter* now started to put the cable through to the Duala shore station, which, though its instruments had been removed, was otherwise undamaged. This work was completed by the 7th October, and the shore station was manned by the African Direct Telegraph Company.

The main water supply of the town, which was pumped from six wells through filters into the supply mains and a reserve tank, appeared to be in good order. But as the Germans had either removed or hidden all plans, some difficulty was experienced for the first two or three days both with the water supply and with the town's drainage system. The Works directorate had, from the outset and throughout the British stay in Duala, much work to do and innumerable services to organise and maintain in connection with the provision of accommodation, maintenance of existing roads and buildings and in a multitude of miscellaneous work.

Supply and Transport. The removal from Duala of large quantities of supplies by

SUPPLY AND TRANSPORT ARRANGEMENTS 135

the Germans made little difference. For it had been anticipated that local supplies could not be depended upon and arrangements were made to obtain regular consignments from England and from the different Colonies in West Africa. During the subsequent operations it was found that, though columns in the field were in a few cases able to obtain fruit and vegetables in the districts where they were operating, they were never able to depend wholly on local supplies.

The main base supply depot was established at Duala in good offices and stores, previously belonging to a German shipping company, and remained throughout the campaign the main distributing centre, advanced supply depots being formed as the operations progressed.

Owing mainly to the number of different native tribes represented in the force, the authorised scale of rations varied greatly; and to avoid complication of supply it became essential to standardise a ration. This was not easy, and only after many experiments were two scales standardised. No. 1 was for issue during halts of any duration, and No. 2, for issue during movement, was specially designed to be of light weight so as to reduce the length of the transport columns. The native soldier was able himself to carry six days' supply of No. 2 Ration and, though it was of much lower calorific value than would have been required by Europeans, he was able to march and fight well on it and at the same time maintain his health and strength.

The system and method of the French Supply and Transport were so different to those of the British that assimilation of the two was impossible. This naturally complicated matters.

On first landing at Duala there was a great lack of local labour. Carriers subsequently engaged there were of poor physique, with generally but little idea of carrier work. Some engaged in other parts of the Cameroons were somewhat better, but on the whole they compared unfavourably with the carriers from Sierra Leone, the Gold Coast, and Nigeria. The 3,600 or so carriers who landed at Duala with the force rendered it, however, to a great extent independent, and as the operations progressed their numbers were supplemented by further importations.

No Ordnance Department officer was available. Major H. W. G. Meyer-Griffith, a reserve officer, and private secretary to the Governor of Sierra Leone, was appointed Chief Ordnance Officer, and a depot was established at Duala. A number of

Ordnance.

German stores in good order were found in the well-equipped German barracks.

<small>Medical.</small> The buildings of the Duala general hospital, from which the Germans had removed the equipment, were utilised for the establishment of three Allied base hospitals. Some equipment was found in the German war hospital at Deido, near Duala, and this was utilised with the equipment brought by the force. The French contingent, with a medical staff only sufficient to provide one field unit and to perform regimental duties, could furnish no personnel for duty with the Allied base hospitals. These were accordingly entirely staffed by the British, and were gradually enlarged to accommodate, by the 10th October, 12 European and 130 native patients. In addition, the British staffed the *Appam* (which was rapidly transformed to take 80 European and 300 native cases), as well as an ambulance train and a hospital boat, both of which were improvised within a few days of landing.

The conditions with which the medical staff had to deal were unusual. The area was peculiarly unfavourable for the employment of large bodies of men, the climate was unhealthy,* and there was generally a lack of fresh food. A high sick rate was, therefore, to be anticipated, and there was a constant danger of serious epidemics. As, moreover, it would be difficult to obtain reinforcements, and as there were no large hospitals, medical staffs or hospital ships in the neighbouring colonies, it would be necessary to retain on the spot, for return to the ranks, every possible fighting man, European or native.

Considerations of space have limited the description of the administrative services to a bare outline. But it is evident that, in the circumstances, the rapid improvisation of an organisation to cope efficiently with the problems before them was a notable feat. For the area of operations presented unusual obstacles to the maintenance of inter-communication and to the provision of the daily requirements on which the mobility and effectiveness of the force would depend.

<small>Duala vicinity and Dibamba river; 28th–30th Sept. 1914.</small> In addition to taking steps at once to secure law and order in Duala and Bonaberi and for local defence, General Dobell had to consolidate his occupation by clearing the immediate vicinity of enemy troops. This involved, in the first place, the clearance of the swampy, creek-intersected areas surrounding the estuary, the capture of the Yapoma bridge, reconnais-

---

* In particular, the prevention of water-borne diseases and anti-mosquito measures involved much hard work and care.

SOME LOCAL CONDITIONS

sance of the Wuri river and the occupation of Maka on the Northern Railway.

To illustrate the unusual nature of the operations the account of some of them at this period is given in considerable detail. The denseness of the forest was the dominating factor. It restricted movement absolutely to difficult waterways or narrow paths,* which themselves limited the strength of an advancing column; it rendered the enemy invisible till the last moment or, as more usually happened, till he disclosed his presence by a sudden burst of heavy fire at a few yards range; even then it concealed his dispositions and accentuated the difficulty of turning movements; and it made the maintenance both of intercommunication and the proper direction extraordinarily difficult. The usual result was that, after groping forward for the enemy, an advancing column found itself suddenly under fire at point blank range in a situation which was bewildering and which afforded little opportunity of judging of the hostile dispositions. In this "blind" warfare officers and men had consequently to maintain an attitude of constant watchfulness and self-control which imposed a continuous strain on nerves already weakened by the trying climate.

On the 28th September the 1st Nigerians † (Lieutenant-Colonel J. B. Cockburn) disembarked at Duala at 8 a.m., and sent a company to occupy Bonaberi, thus setting free the seamen and marines. During the day reconnaissances were carried out on both banks of the Wuri river, a party sent towards Yapoma encountering an enemy detachment with machine guns. In the evening the 2nd Senegalese Battalion also disembarked. Native reports still asserted that the enemy had retired in two parties towards Edea and Yabasi respectively.

On the 29th General Dobell established his headquarters at Government House, being joined there by Captain Fuller, who maintained his naval headquarters under the same roof for the remainder of the campaign. The 2nd Nigerians (Lieutenant-

---

* Off the paths, numerous quagmires and hidden fallen trunks of trees added to the slowness of progress, which was only possible, through the high undergrowth thickly tangled with creeping canes, by the constant use of axe or machete.

† To avoid confusion with the parent battalions of the Nigeria Regiment operating in the north of the Cameroons, the composite battalions from Nigeria accompanying General Dobell will hereafter be referred to as the 1st and 2nd Nigerians, instead of as No. 1 and No. 2 Battalions as they were called at the time. Their component companies are shown in Appendix II.

Colonel A. H. W. Haywood) and the Nigerian battery disembarked at Bonaberi, relieving the company of 1st Nigerians, which rejoined its battalion at Duala. An officer of this company had previously reconnoitred the Bomono creek, reporting the railway bridge at Bapele to be partly destroyed and also the presence of a small enemy detachment at Maka. Colonel Haywood was instructed to safeguard Bonaberi and to drive the enemy out of Maka.

By this time reports showed that there were small enemy detachments on all the river communications leading from Duala, including both banks of the Dibamba about Yapoma. To deal with the latter, instructions were issued on the morning of the 29th September for two companies of the 2nd Senegalese with a section of artillery to move to Yapoma and to reconnoitre Lobesu, about four and half miles north-west of the Yapoma bridge. This detachment moved out in the afternoon.

On the previous day the *Porpoise* (Lieutenant F. H. G. Dalrymple-Hamilton, R.N.), carrying twenty-five men of the Gold Coast Regiment under Lieutenant H. R. Greene, had proceeded up the Dibamba river to break through the boom above Pitti and reconnoitre the Yapoma bridge. After a short bombardment of the Pitti position had elicited no reply, a patrol was sent ashore and found many corpses in the trenches but no sign of an active enemy. The patrol also found a track which appeared to lead inland. The *Porpoise* then advanced again and, after negotiating without difficulty an obstruction of logs just above Pitti, encountered a strong log boom stretching right across the river. By the time this was destroyed it was dark and she anchored for the night. Advancing again early next morning the *Porpoise* was stopped by shallows some 1,200 yards below the Yapoma bridge, which the Germans had partly destroyed. No enemy could be seen, and Lieutenant Greene landed on the right bank with two men to reconnoitre closer, but was recalled at 7 a.m. when fire was opened on the *Porpoise* from the left bank. The *Porpoise* shelled and silenced the enemy and then retired downstream, making for Suelaba.

Disembarkation at Duala continued throughout the 30th September. A company of the 2nd Nigerians, reconnoitring that morning towards Maka, found that the Bapele railway bridge, though badly damaged, was just passable and that, at its northern end, an enemy detachment of about fifty men with a machine gun in an armoured truck was strongly entrenched. From native reports Colonel Haywood also learnt that a German force of about three hundred men was holding an east and west line through Maka extending to the Mungo river. That evening Colonel Haywood was reinforced by two companies of the composite W.A.F.F. battalion and received orders to attack Maka.

The Senegalese detachment sent to gain possession of the Yapoma bridge had established itself, by the evening of the 30th September, on the right bank of the river near the bridge in touch with the enemy, who was entrenched on the opposite bank apparently in some strength.* Two of the five spans of the bridge, which was 352 yards long, had been cut by explosives.

During the 30th General Dobell arranged with Captain Fuller for various naval reconnaissances to be carried out.

Colonel Haywood moved out from Bonaberi at 9.30 a.m. on the 1st October with a column consisting of one gun of the Nigerian battery, "D" and "E" Companies of the 2nd Nigerians, "B" Company of the Gold Coast Regiment, "E" Company of the Sierra Leone Battalion, and 470 carriers. In addition to the detachment of 50 men at the Bapele bridge, the enemy was now reported to have 150 men about Maka. The flat bush country was covered with extensive swamps and the column advanced along the railway line.

The capture of Maka; 2nd October, 1914.

At the same time a detachment of fifteen men of "A" Company, 2nd Nigerians, with a machine gun, under Captain J. Sargent, proceeded towards Bapele in a launch up the Bomono creek to create a diversion; and from Bonendale station Colonel Haywood sent an infantry section from his column to the creek to collect canoes and co-operate with Captain Sargent.

On approaching the Bapele bridge Colonel Haywood made a personal reconnaissance and posted his gun in a good covered position. From here, at about 3 p.m., when the sound of firing against Captain Sargent's party was heard, this gun opened fire at a range of one thousand yards. Twenty minutes later the enemy retired and the British troops, pushing forward, crossed the bridge. By 4.15 p.m. they had entrenched themselves at the northern end.

"D" Company, 2nd Nigerians, was then sent forward to reconnoitre, and shortly afterwards Captain J. P. D. Underwood, commanding the company, sent in a report that from a

---

* The German force here seems to have actually consisted of No. 2 Reserve Detachment and a section of the Police Depot Company.

point about one thousand yards short of the town he could see a white flag displayed at Maka. Thereupon Colonel Haywood ordered firing to cease and went forward with Captain Underwood and half " D " Company to take over the town, where two white flags were flying. But when they arrived within four hundred yards of it, fire was suddenly opened on them from three sides. The other half of " D " Company was some five hundred yards in rear and the main body about a thousand yards further back; the country was swampy and completely concealed the enemy; and it was getting dark. Colonel Haywood decided to withdraw his advanced troops who, fortunately, had only suffered two casualties; and the column bivouacked for the night by the bridge, suffering great discomfort from continuous torrential rain.

Next morning, after a bombardment of the enemy's position, the British advanced and occupied the town at 10 a.m., without further opposition, the enemy—apparently No. 4 (Expeditionary) Company—retiring to the northward. In this direction information acquired during the day indicated that the Germans had a force of some 50 Europeans and 450 natives about Susa and Mbonjo.

Maka was a tactically strong position, and General Dobell approved Colonel Haywood's proposal to leave two companies and a gun to hold it and to return with the remainder of his column on the 4th October to Bonaberi. On the 3rd there was a patrol encounter with the enemy about six miles north of Maka, and on the 4th Colonel Haywood returned to Bonaberi.

Tiko and Misselele Plantation; 1st October 1914. Two simultaneous combined naval and military operations under naval direction were also carried out on the 1st October at Tiko and the Moewe Lake, where the presence of an enemy detachment about one hundred strong and of an armed party of German colonists, respectively, were reported.

The expedition to Tiko, under Lieutenant Champness, R.N., comprised the *Remus, Cumberland's* picket boat, the *Alligator* and *Vigilant*, carrying one and a half companies of the West African Regiment under Captain A. C. Taylor. The troops landed unopposed at Tiko island wharf, but two miles beyond encountered an enemy detachment entrenched at the further end of the long bridge or viaduct connecting the island with the mainland. Attacking this position, Captain Taylor drove the enemy out after a short engagement, being assisted in the final stages by covering fire from the picket boat which had come up the creek. One German officer was killed, but there were no

THE YAPOMA BRIDGE

British casualties; and after destroying the telephone line to Victoria and a high wooden observation tower, the flotilla returned to Suelaba.

The other expedition, under Lieutenant F. H. G. Dalrymple-Hamilton, R.N., consisted of the *Porpoise, Crocodile, Walrus* and *Cumberland's* steam pinnace, carrying one and a half companies of the West African Regiment under Captain J. R. Robertson. The colony of thirteen Germans at the Misselele plantation had made preparations to defend themselves. But the British landing took them by surprise and they surrendered without fighting. The large stocks of provisions previously reported there were secured and also a useful map showing all the plantations and roads in the vicinity as far as Buea and Victoria. In the evening the expedition returned to the *Appam*.*

That day the *Dwarf*, reconnoitring up the Wuri river, found it obstructed some distance up by trees which had been cut down from both banks. She again proceeded up this river on the 2nd, making a survey *en route* and, after reaching a point between five and six miles above Bonaberi, returned to Duala on the 3rd.

The French force near Yapoma was increased in strength on the 1st and 2nd October to a total of one battery (six mountain guns) and one battalion (2nd Senegalese); and the Sierra Leone Field Section R.E. (Lieutenant C. V. S. Jackson) was also sent to join them. But they were unable to force the passage of the wide and deep river, and on the 2nd General Dobell arranged with Captain Fuller to assist them by sending (i) two naval guns in trucks along the railway to join them, (ii) the *Remus* to co-operate from the Dibamba river, and (iii) a small party of Gold Coast Pioneers by water to land at Pitti to move round and cut the railway in the German rear. *The attack on Yapoma Bridge; 1st–6th Oct. 1914.*

Two 12-pounder guns from the *Cumberland* and *Challenger*, under Lieutenant L. H. K. Hamilton, R.N., each gun escorted by one section of the West African Regiment, were pushed out in railway trucks and joined the French in the afternoon of the 2nd. Next day was spent by the Allied detachment in reconnaissance, in the selection of a position for the guns, and in the clearance by the West African Regiment escort of a track through the bush to this position from the railway.

The *Remus* (Lieutenant Champness), with thirty marines (Captain J. Goldsmith, R.M.L.I.), proceeded up the Dibamba

---

* The West African Regiment had not yet disembarked.

river in the evening of the 2nd, accompanied by the *Alligator* carrying the R.E. officer and the Pioneer party detailed to cut the railway. This party landed at Pitti, encountering some opposition, but, finding the raid on the railway to be impracticable, returned to Duala. The *Remus*, anchoring below Pitti for the night, continued upstream next morning till she was stopped by shallow water at 8 a.m. about 2,200 yards from Yapoma bridge and within sight of it. Both banks of the river were covered with dense forest and no signs could be seen of any troops, either Allied or enemy. To get into touch with the French and to examine the bridge, Captain Goldsmith embarked in a surf-boat with ten of his men and reached a position right under the bridge without having seen any signs of an enemy. It was not till about 10 a.m., when he landed three marines on the right bank to try to locate the French, that the enemy opened fire on the marines and the surf-boat. All but one of its native paddlers promptly jumped overboard, and, after unsuccessful attempts to recall his patrol from the bank, Captain Goldsmith took two of his men who had been wounded back to the *Remus*. Her fire effected some reduction in the enemy fusillade, and Captain Goldsmith went off again in the surf-boat and picked up two of his patrol, a long search failing to find the third man.* One of the other two had meanwhile been wounded in the boat, and Captain Goldsmith finally returned to the *Remus*.

At 3 p.m. Lieutenant Champness decided to return to Duala so that his wounded—two marines and a Nigeria Marine deckhand who had bravely remained in the surf-boat when the others went overboard—might be treated. On his way downstream he was met off Yansoki by natives in a canoe with a message from Lieutenant Hamilton saying that the French commander wished to meet Lieutenant Champness to discuss the situation. Giving the natives a reply which explained his day's action, asked for further instructions and said that he would be back off Yapoma at nine o'clock next morning, Lieutenant Champness resumed his journey downstream.

That evening, however, his orders were changed. General Dobell came to the conclusion that it would not only be less costly in casualties but would facilitate the river crossing if the

---

* This man (Lance-Corporal Saxton) had lost touch but remained on the river bank for about six hours, when his ammunition gave out. Then, after climbing on the bridge and lashing there a small Union Jack, with which the patrol had been provided for recognition purposes, he walked back along the railway till he met a French piquet.

flank or rear of the German position at Yapoma were threatened or attacked. He accordingly directed the French commander to despatch two companies by water to seize Pitti and to move from there, by a bush path which had been reported, towards the railway in rear of the Germans. To allow time for this movement to develop it was subsequently arranged that the French frontal attack should be postponed till the morning of the 6th October.

By the evening of the 4th October two French companies, in a small steamer and three launches, escorted by the *Remus* and *Porpoise* and with a dozen surf-boats for disembarkation, reached the mouth of the Dibamba river. They started to move up the river at 4 a.m. on the 5th, and by 8 a.m. all the troops had disembarked without opposition at Pitti. But the native guides failed altogether to find any path towards the railway, although the German troops who had previously occupied Pitti must have retired by land in that direction; and next morning at about 9.30 fifty of the French troops were embarked in the *Porpoise* to be landed at a point one and a half miles upstream where the native guides reported that there was a path leading to the railway. While they were landing at this point the *Vigilant*, which had been sent up the previous day to a position near the Yapoma bridge with surf-boats to assist the crossing, arrived with the news that the French had successfully crossed the bridge and that the French commander wished all the French troops at Pitti to be landed on the left bank near the bridge.

The French had carried this by a purely frontal attack. Opening fire at 5 a.m. on the 6th October the French infantry twenty minutes later, under cover of the French and British gunfire, started climbing across the bridge, moving with great coolness and courage in face of a heavy fusillade. By 6 a.m. they had made good the far side of the bridge, which in one place they had only been able to cross by means of a single rope ladder. The *Vigilant* then conducted the transfer of the remainder of the French troops, including the mountain battery,* across the river in surf-boats. The Germans retired slowly, and one of their machine guns in an armoured truck on the railway kept up a continuous fire until forced to retire by the fire of the naval 12-pounder. Soon after this the French commander informed Lieutenant Hamilton that the naval guns were no longer required, and they returned to Duala by rail on

---

* It crossed on a raft made on two surf-boats fastened together.

the evening of the 7th. In this exploit the French only incurred fourteen casualties, a surprisingly small total in the circumstances.

For some days after this the French were engaged with small hostile forces to the eastward of Yapoma, but were able to withdraw three companies and four guns on the 7th October to Duala.

Naval reconnaissances. In the meantime several naval reconnaissances had been carried out elsewhere. On the 3rd, 4th and 5th October, Commander Strong in the *Sokoto* (late *Soden*) reconnoitred the Wuri river to within one and a half miles of German entrenchments at Yabasi, finding on the way up that an entrenched position at Nsake had been hastily evacuated. He also reconnoitred the tributary river Abo and generally, in addition to making a rapid survey of the rivers, obtained much useful information regarding the enemy. On the 4th and 5th Lieutenant-Commander Sneyd with the *Cumberland's* picket boat and steam pinnace reconnoitred up the Mungo river as far as Mbonjo, engaging there with an enemy detachment whose presence rendered a further advance inadvisable.

On the 1st October the *Ivy* visited Victoria and, finding it free of German troops, Commander Hughes placed all the Germans there on parole after giving them the option of being removed as prisoners of war. He also arranged that, for the information of ships subsequently visiting there, they should display a white flag at the end of the pier, only removing it if German troops reoccupied the town.

After proceeding to Fernando Po, to inform the Governor of the surrender of Duala, Commander Hughes sailed in the *Ivy* to reconnoitre the mouth of the Sanaga river, arriving off the Benge entrance at daylight on the 5th October. A landing party removed or destroyed telephones and other useful stores without opposition, and the *Ivy* proceeded to reconnoitre the Bungo mouth. The German observation station here had been evacuated, and the natives reported sufficient water in the river to allow coastal steamers to reach Edea.

To avoid constant repetition, mention has been omitted of the heavy rain that fell continuously, by day and night, during these operations round Duala*. It not only rendered

---

* The following figures show the extremely heavy rainfall on the Cameroons coast. At Duala the approximate average rainfall per annum is 155 inches, at Kribi 125 inches, at Victoria 171 inches, at Buea on the Cameroon mountain 106 inches; while at Debunsha (on the coast some twenty miles north-west of Victoria) it is no less than 412 inches.

FUTURE BRITISH PLANS

many of the tracks and paths impassable but it kept all ranks in a constant state of being wet through. But they bore the discomfort cheerfully and their health remained generally good.

While these steps were being taken round Duala, the authorities in London had been considering what further action should be taken in the Cameroons. On the afternoon of the 27th September, the Admiralty, considering that the naval objective had been attained by the surrender of Duala, and anxious for the return to the trade routes of the *Cumberland*, telegraphed to Captain Fuller inquiring when she could safely leave the Cameroons. To this he replied next day that, as the enemy was still in force on all sides, he was unable to give a probable date. On the 29th the question of the Cameroons was considered by the Offensive Sub-Committee of the Committee of Imperial Defence. The enemy, evidently hoping that the war would be brought to a successful conclusion in Europe before the Allies could overcome him in the interior of the Cameroons, seemed bent on offering considerable resistance there; the reverse sustained on the frontier by the Nigerian columns rendered German attacks on Nigeria possible, if not probable; and the French from Fort Lamy had apparently only captured Kuseri with some difficulty. Although territorial conquest was not our aim, it seemed obvious that the best, if not the only possible, method of rendering our occupation of Duala secure and of protecting our own frontier at the same time was for General Dobell to push on into the interior. The Committee consequently agreed that General Dobell should be informed that the ultimate object of his operations was the complete reduction of the German colony and that he should be asked to give his views and proposals to this end, bearing in mind his own strength and that of the enemy. H.M. Government, however, were not prepared to approve this recommendation without further consideration; and in telegraphing to General Dobell on the 30th September, the Colonial Office asked for his proposals on the assumption that the complete reduction of the Cameroons would be his objective, intimating at the same time that he was not expected to do more than he considered safe with the force at his disposal.

General Dobell replied on the 2nd October that he was engaged in driving back the small German parties which were in the vicinity of Duala and Bonaberi on all sides. His information indicated that the enemy was in strength at Edea and Yabasi, with smaller numbers at Nkongsamba. The

Instructions of H.M. Government; 30th Sept. 1914.

country was very dense bush in all directions. For the time being he did not intend to occupy Buea and Victoria as this would entail serious dissemination of his force.

<small>Colonel Cunliffe to control the operations from Nigeria; 3rd–7th Oct. 1914.</small>
On the 3rd October General Dobell informed Sir Frederick Lugard that Colonel Cunliffe was being sent back to Lagos to direct the operations on the Nigerian frontier. Major Moorhouse had kept General Dobell well informed of the situation, which at this juncture seemed to call for the presence of a senior officer, and, having secured Duala, he found himself able to spare Colonel Cunliffe's services.

Sailing from Duala on the 4th, Colonel Cunliffe reached Lagos on the 7th October, having received the following instructions from General Dobell. He was to assume charge of all troops in, or based on, Nigeria which were not under General Dobell's immediate command. Colonel Cunliffe was to avoid unnecessary dispersion of his forces, keeping General Dobell acquainted with their distribution and with the information he collected of enemy movements. For the time being the general rôle of his forces would be defensive, the offensive being undertaken only when the chances of success were much in our favour. An attack on Garua would, it was hoped, fall within this category. In distributing his troops Colonel Cunliffe should pay special attention to the protection of Calabar and the safeguarding of the Cross and Benue rivers. He should also make efforts to obtain French co-operation to undertake a systematic clearance of the country from the north. But it was understood that the French would not be able to move south from Fort Lamy in any strength before the 15th October.

<small>Operations against Yabasi and Susa; 5th Oct. 1914.</small>
On the 5th October General Dobell turned his attention to the north of Duala, where two German detachments, each consisting of about sixty Europeans and three hundred natives, were reported to be holding positions at Yabasi and at Susa (about eight miles beyond Maka on the Northern Railway) respectively. To deal with these General Dobell issued orders for two columns to move out and attack on the 8th. Information also pointed to another German concentration at Nyamtam, to the east of Yabasi, and operations in this direction from Yabasi were also contemplated. The Yabasi Column, composed of naval and military detachments, was to be commanded by Colonel Gorges and the attack on Susa was to be carried out by a force under Lieutenant-Colonel Haywood.

<small>The first advance of</small> The military portion of the Yabasi Column consisted of two mountain artillery sections (Sierra Leone and Gold Coast), the

ADVANCE ON YABASI

West African Regiment (six companies and two machine guns),* two companies 1st Nigerians, half the Gold Coast pioneer company, telephone and medical detachments, and 688 carriers. The naval force, under Commander the Hon. B. T. C. O. Freeman-Mitford, included a detachment of one hundred seamen and stokers, a 12-pounder gun and one hundred carriers. In the flotilla of fifteen steam or motor vessels and twelve lighters the following were armed. The *Mole* † (a dredger from Nigeria) and the *Dreadnought* lighter each mounted a 6-inch gun; the *Balbus* towing the latter carried three French 1-pounders; the *Cumberland's* picket boat was armed with a 3-pounder; and the *Mole*, the *Cumberland's* picket boat and steam pinnace, the *Sokoto* and the *Crocodile* and *Alligator* each carried a machine gun.

the Yabasi Column; 6th–10th Oct. 1914.

Embarking in the evening on the 6th October, Colonel Gorges' combined force started to move up the Wuri river at 5.30 a.m. on the 7th, the picket boat and steam pinnace leading, followed by the *Mole*, in which Colonel Gorges and his staff accompanied Commander Mitford. The river banks were covered with dense forest, interspersed with a number of native villages and occasional cultivated clearings.

Just after 4 p.m., as the picket boat and steam pinnace approached the bend where Nsake stood on the left bank, a few rifle shots were fired from a hill there which commanded the river both ways. This firing ceased, however, when the boats replied; and a company of the West African Regiment landed and occupied the hill without opposition. This company, and a small detachment which was landed on the right bank of the river, covered the flotilla for the night. But before dark Colonel Gorges and Commander Mitford reconnoitred upstream for about a mile and found the country on the right bank to be low-lying and cultivated though steep and densely vegetated on the other bank.

Delayed by a mist, the advance on the 8th October did not commence till 6.15 a.m. Some forty minutes later the *Mole* reached a point from which the German buildings on the high ground at Yabasi, some three miles distant, were clearly visible. These and the native town were on the right bank, where also, according to the rather indefinite information received, was the whole of the German force. Reports that the left bank was covered with impenetrable forest appeared to be correct; and

* The West African Regiment, with no machine guns with companies, had only this section.
† The *Mole* was fitted with W/T.

Colonel Gorges decided to land the whole of his force on the right bank, a contributory factor to this decision being his desire to keep his force intact.

A covering force of two companies West African Regiment under Colonel Vaughan disembarked about 7.30 a.m., and within an hour the whole force—except a small infantry detachment and the Sierra Leone gun detachment left to guard the transport flotilla—had landed. At 9 a.m. the advance commenced, the covering force forming advanced guard. The main body was composed of the Gold Coast gun section, four companies and the machine gun section West African Regiment, and the half-company Gold Coast Pioneers, while Colonel Gorges kept the hundred seamen, the naval 12-pounder and the two companies 1st Nigerians as a reserve in his own hands. Leaving the rest of the flotilla anchored near the landing place, the picket boat and steam pinnace, the *Mole*, *Crocodile* and *Balbus* with the *Dreadnought* proceeded slowly upstream abreast of the land advance, which followed a muddy path through dense elephant grass near the river bank.

At 9.20 a.m. the British 6-inch guns opened fire, but the enemy made no reply, and twenty-five minutes later the *Mole* shelled the forest on the left bank as Germans were reported there by native canoes. About 10 a.m., on a signal from Colonel Gorges, Commander Mitford stopped firing and, as natives reported Germans close by on the left bank, made arrangements to open rifle fire on any European or armed native appearing there. These reports of enemy on the left bank do not appear to have been passed on to Colonel Gorges. In any case, their full significance does not seem to have been grasped and no attempts were made to take active counter-measures against enemy action from this direction.

By about 10.30 a.m. Colonel Vaughan with the main body had reached a hill near the river bank some 1,500 yards short of Yabasi, closing up on the two advanced companies. They had located the enemy as holding an entrenched position on the hill on which stood the buildings, termed Government Hill.*
Planning his attack on the information these two companies had obtained, Colonel Gorges ordered Captain E. S. Brand (West African Regiment) with two companies West African Regiment, the half-company Gold Coast Pioneers and the two Gold Coast guns, to make a turning movement and attack the

---

* The German force was subsequently ascertained to have consisted of No. 1 (Depot) Company of infantry supported by the local European and police detachments.

enemy's right flank, while Colonel Vaughan, with the remaining four companies and machine gun section West African Regiment, made a frontal attack. Colonel Gorges established his own headquarters on the hill 1,500 yards short of Yabasi.

At 11.20 a.m. Colonel Gorges ordered his reserve up to this hill. By this time the troops of the frontal attack under Colonel Vaughan, emerging from thick bush and elephant grass which had hitherto confined their advance practically to the path, had reached a low hill, where they were at once checked by a heavy rifle and machine gun fire from Government Hill at a range of about eight hundred yards. They also found that an unfordable swamp lay in front of them, which could only be crossed by a bridge near the river, while their difficulties were further increased by rifle and machine gun fire directed on them from the left bank of the river. In a short time both their machine guns were put out of action, the British officer and N.C.O. with them being both wounded.

Some ten minutes later, as the reserve reached the headquarters hill, it and the naval vessels came under a heavy rifle and machine gun fire from the left bank of the river. The reserve was able to obtain good cover, but the naval vessels were fully exposed to a cross fire at one hundred yards range, and only the enemy's erratic shooting saved them from heavy casualties.* The naval guns at once turned their fire on to the left bank but could see nothing definite to aim at. Nevertheless by noon the enemy fire on the left bank died down. But Commander Mitford deemed it necessary to go astern and secure cover from an island about a thousand yards downstream.

Just before this Colonel Vaughan, who had moved his men some five hundred yards to his left where the swamp in front was passable, had received orders from Colonel Gorges to push in his attack so as to co-operate with Captain Brand, whose flanking movement should by then have been making itself felt; and to cover this movement the naval 12-pdr. was brought into action on headquarters hill. But, seeing no sign of an advance by Colonel Vaughan's men, Colonel Gorges went forward with his staff to see the situation for himself. He found the state of affairs to be most unsatisfactory. Many of the men of the West African Regiment had become demoralised under the constant bursts of machine gun fire of which this was their first real experience; tactical unity had been lost in the thick and high elephant grass; and, as it was an in-

---

* The naval casualties totalled only five, including one Frenchman.

tensely hot day, officers and men were all very much exhausted. The whole line had thus become considerably disorganised.

Hoping to get a party across the swamp by the bridge near the river under a covering fire from the left of his line and from the guns, Colonel Gorges ordered a reorganisation for a further effort. He also reinforced Colonel Vaughan with one company 1st Nigerians from the reserve. The flank attack came up soon after this, but, not having made a sufficiently wide detour, emerged from the bush in rear of the frontal attack instead of well to the left; and attempts to carry the line forward all proved fruitless. Colonel Gorges then decided as a last resort to call on the detachment of sailors. But they were in heavy marching order and their exertions in hauling their 12-pounder into action, in the great heat, had so exhausted them that they were quite incapable of advancing. As Commander Mitford pointed out in his report, it had been a mistake to send them in heavy instead of light marching order and to use them instead of native carriers to drag the gun. As the exhaustion of his force might lead to a disaster, Colonel Gorges, at 3.15 p.m., ordered a general retirement out of range; and at the same time sent his staff officer to inquire from Commander Mitford whether the flotilla would be safe if the troops held on to their position so as to renew the attack next morning. A fall of water in the river was causing Commander Mitford some anxiety, the *Balbus* and *Dreadnought* had gone aground, and he also felt that unless the troops occupied both banks of the river his craft would be dangerously exposed. Colonel Gorges thereupon decided to re-embark his force and move down the river to below Nsake. The total British casualties had amounted to three British and twelve natives killed and one British and nineteen natives wounded, all but two having occurred in the West African Regiment.*

By 3.15 p.m. the *Dreadnought* had been refloated; but all efforts failed to free the *Balbus* and it was decided to abandon her, removing her guns, ammunition and stores. The retirement by the troops was carried out in good order without special incident, and all had re-embarked by 6 p.m. But the voyage downstream was carried out in a tornado, the wind and rain making navigation extremely difficult and causing the utmost discomfort to the force generally. At 10.30 p.m. the flotilla anchored for the night some four miles below Nsake.

The heavy rain continued throughout the night, and by

---

* *Killed*—Captain E. S. Brand, Sergeants H. McQuirk and F. C. Wade; *wounded*—Lieutenant R. D. Bennett.

[*To face p.* 150

YABASI (looking downstream)

SECOND ATTACK ON YABASI   151

the morning the condition of the men, wet through, crowded together and unprotected from the weather, decided Colonel Gorges to seek a spot further downstream where he could land to rest, reorganise and await reinforcements and supplies. Wuri island was the first suitable point reached, and here on the 10th October, while preparations were in progress to disembark, General Dobell arrived from Duala. He had received a report on the previous evening from Colonel Gorges suggesting that, as he had been unable to find a suitable spot on which to land and recuperate, he should return to Duala. General Dobell consequently decided to go upstream to see for himself how matters stood. After a discussion with Colonel Gorges and Commander Mitford, General Dobell ordered the force to return to Duala. The water in the river appeared to be falling so fast as to jeopardise the safety of some of the heavier craft, and many of the troops were urgently in need of rest.

That evening, however, finding that the Wuri river was not falling as fast as had been feared, General Dobell gave instructions for the preparation of a fresh expedition under Colonel Gorges to drive the enemy out of Yabasi. The military portion of the force consisted of the 1st Nigerians (Lieutenant-Colonel Cockburn), the Composite Battalion (Lieutenant-Colonel Rose), the Gold Coast Pioneer Company, the Nigerian Battery (less one section), the Gold Coast artillery section, medical and telephone detachments, and 450 carriers. The naval force, under Commander Mitford, included a 12-pounder field gun and crew with 100 carriers, *Cumberland's* picket boat, steam pinnace, the *Walrus* towing the *Dreadnought*, the *Sokoto* fitted with a wireless installation, eleven launches and fourteen lighters.* All the heavier draught vessels had been excluded.

The second advance on Yabasi; 12th–16th Oct. 1914.

The troops embarked before daylight on the 12th October and the flotilla left Duala about 5.30 a.m., Colonel Gorges with his staff and Commander Mitford embarking in the *Crocodile*.

The small towing power of the launches, however, delayed progress, and at 5 p.m. a halt for the night was made three miles below Nsake to allow vessels to close up. As it was, the *Dreadnought* did not arrive till 7 a.m. next day.

Advancing again on the 13th, and profiting by previous experience, the bulk of the Composite Battalion was landed at Nsake at about 10 a.m. on both banks of the river— Lieutenant-Colonel Rose with two and a half companies on the

---
* The picket boat and *Vigilant* each had a 3-pdr., and two of the launches each a French 1-pdr.; and the picket boat, steam pinnace, *Walrus*, *Vigilant*, and four other launches had one machine gun each.

left bank and one company on the right bank. An impassable creek on the left bank half a mile north of Nsake and the non-arrival of half the 1st Nigerians owing to a breakdown caused, however, a postponement of a further advance till next day. But patrols reconnoitred forward on both banks. On the left bank two officers' patrols, driving back a German patrol, got within two miles of Yabasi, where they found that the enemy was holding positions on both banks of the river, and that on the left bank the country near Yabasi was dense bush.

Colonel Rose's detachment having been transferred by river to the northern side of the impassable creek before daybreak, the whole force commenced its advance on Yabasi at 5.30 a.m. on the 14th October. Covered by the detachments on either bank, the flotilla, led by the *Walrus* with the *Dreadnought*, in which Colonel Gorges had his headquarters, proceeded slowly upstream. In addition to protecting the flanks of the force the detachments ashore had orders to gain contact with the enemy and obtain information.

At 9.20 a.m. the 1st Nigerians (less one company), one section Pioneer Company, the Nigerian artillery section and the naval 12-pounder landed on the right bank at the point where the force had disembarked on the 8th. Here a section of infantry and the Gold Coast artillery section were left to guard the fleet of transports; and a reserve of one company 1st Nigerians, half a company Composite Battalion and the Pioneer Company (less one section), remained in three vessels to follow the *Dreadnought* upstream in readiness to reinforce the troops on either bank.

With much fuller information than he had possessed before his previous attack, both regarding the enemy and the country, Colonel Gorges issued orders for the attack. On the left bank Colonel Rose was to attack the two factories which the enemy was said to be holding. On the right bank, where the main attack was to be made, Colonel Cockburn, with his 1st Nigerians, the Nigerian artillery section and the Pioneer section, was to make a turning movement to his left and come in from the west on to the heights above Yabasi. To protect his rear and right flank the company of the Composite Battalion and the naval 12-pounder were to take up positions on the former headquarters hill near the river.

At 11 a.m., disembarkation having been completed, the troops on both banks moved forward covered by the fire of the *Dreadnought's* 6-inch gun. Little opposition was encountered, and the advance, progressing steadily and smoothly,

OCCUPATION OF SUSA

resulted in both banks at Yabasi being cleared of the enemy before dark at a cost of only two men wounded.* Ten Germans were taken prisoners by Colonel Cockburn.

Reconnaissances on the 15th October gained touch with the retreating enemy, most of whom were moving towards Nyamtam, and there was some skirmishing in dense bush.

The *Balbus* was successfully salved on the morning of the 16th, but had been so much damaged by the enemy that she had to be sent back to Nigeria to refit. On that day, leaving the 1st Nigerians to hold Yabasi, the remainder of the force started to return to Duala.

Colonel Haywood's advance on Susa had meanwhile met with immediate success. For this attack on the 8th October he was instructed to take with him the strongest possible force, leaving minimum garrisons at Bonaberi and Maka. After capturing Susa he was to reconnoitre the vicinity, especially Mbonjo.

Operations up the Northern Railway; 6th–12th Oct. 1914.

Being anxious to capture some railway rolling stock, General Dobell detailed a small party of engineers to accompany Colonel Haywood to try to cut the railway behind the enemy and also, on the 7th October, sent another small party of engineers up the Abo river to Miang, whence they were to move inland and cut the railway near Kake. This they succeeded in doing early on the 8th, but the enemy had already passed to the northward.

Leaving a half-company Composite Battalion at Bonaberi and a company 2nd Nigerians at Maka, Colonel Haywood assembled the remainder of his force, i.e., the Nigerian Battery, three companies 2nd Nigerians and one and a half companies Composite Battalion at Maka on the 7th October. An enemy armoured train was reported to be south of Ndale, and the engineer party with an escort was sent out that evening by Colonel Haywood to cut the railway north of Ndale. This it did successfully, but the train had unfortunately already retired.

On the 8th October, advancing in two columns, one by a bush path to the west and the other along the railway, Colonel Haywood occupied Susa practically without opposition, only a few enemy scouts being encountered. His whole force had reached Susa by 3.30 p.m., and, learning that the Germans with three armoured trains, two or three guns, and two to three hundred infantry had only recently retired to Kake,

---

* A British non-commissioned officer died from the effects of the sun.

Colonel Haywood pushed on at once. Kake was reached at 5.30 p.m., but there were no signs of the enemy, who had evacuated a strongly entrenched position between Susa and Kake and had done some damage to the permanent way. The column bivouacked for the night at Kake railway station.

Reconnaissances on the 9th showed that the country was clear of the enemy as far as Miang on the Abo river, Muyuka on the railway, and Mpundu on the Mungo river. Mbonjo had been burnt and evacuated.

On the 10th October Colonel Haywood received orders from General Dobell not to advance north of Susa and to send back to Bonaberi two guns and two companies Composite Battalion which were required to join the new Yabasi Column. Next day he received instructions to leave a garrison at Susa—sufficient to hold it and to carry out local reconnaissances—and to return himself to Bonaberi with the remainder of the force. This he did on the 12th, leaving one company 2nd Nigerians at Susa. On the 11th October, before he left Susa, two officers' patrols, which he had sent out from Kake on the 9th, returned and reported Muyuka to be held by an enemy force of twenty to thirty Europeans and two hundred natives with two or three "Rexer" guns in armoured trucks. The patrols also reported that three trains were ready at Muyuka to convey troops northward. The enemy's main body in this area was believed to be at Nkongsamba.

General remarks. In one of his periodical reports to the Colonial Office written at this period General Dobell drew attention to the good embarkation and disembarkation work which had been carried out under quite abnormal circumstances, the officers and crew of the *Appam* meriting special mention. He also said that the administration and military control of the occupied area was progressing most satisfactorily. In fact, he was likely to be embarrassed by the rapid way in which the native population was coming in as, until the Mungo river area had been cleared of the enemy, food supplies for them were likely to be insufficient. This remark affords a good illustration of one of the many unusual problems with which he was faced.

Interrogation of prisoners of war as well as of natives had by this time elicited some indication of what the enemy intended to aim at. For instance, the Force Headquarters war diary of the 16th October states that Lieutenant McCallum had formed the opinion from the information he had thus obtained that the enemy intended to make Yaunde their point of final concentration and that, if they lost this, they would abandon the colony.

On the 6th October the Admiralty, anxious for more cruisers to secure the trade routes, telegraphed again to Captain Fuller asking when either the *Cumberland* or the *Challenger* could be spared. To this Captain Fuller replied on the 10th that both would be required till Edea had been captured, which it was hoped would be before the end of the month. He continued that, until the whole colony capitulated, a cruiser guardship off Duala would be required, as well as a cruiser and two gunboats for the protection of Duala and to patrol the coast.

Naval operations; 6th–16th Oct. 1914.

On the 7th October Commander Hughes in the *Ivy*, when examining the coast north of the Cameroon estuary, found that the Germans had evacuated Rio del Rey. Next day a landing party placed on parole fifteen Germans on plantations at Bibundi, took three away as prisoners of war, and removed all arms, ammunition, telephones, etc. The *Ivy* then visited Victoria and, seeing that no white flag was flying, Commander Hughes landed under a flag of truce to find that German troops, whose headquarters were at Buea, were in the vicinity. Returning to Duala to report, Commander Hughes received instructions to return and remove all Germans from Bibundi, except the manager and one assistant for each plantation, and also to endeavour to remove from Victoria all Germans on parole. These instructions were carried into effect at Bibundi on the 10th. But on arrival at Victoria that evening the German flag was found to be flying and, in answer to a British request sent in under a flag of truce, the Germans on parole declined to surrender. Commander Hughes then returned to Duala to report.

With a view to an advance on Edea the *Ivy* carried out, between the 12th and 16th October, a survey of the channels at the entrances to the Sanaga and Nyong rivers, the existence of bars rendering the work both difficult and dangerous. The Bungo or southern entrance of the Sanaga river was found to be navigable by small steamers. But the water near the entrance of the Nyong river was found in several places to be only six feet deep at high tide. An observation and telephone station here was destroyed, and the telephone line across the river cut.

Some enemy had been reported at Lobetal, the point where the Kwa-kwa creek from the Cameroon estuary joined the Sanaga river. The *Porpoise* accordingly proceeded on the 9th October to ascertain if any enemy were there and also whether the Kwa-kwa creek would afford a practicable passage for a flotilla of small craft proceeding from Duala to the Sanaga river. Next day the *Porpoise* returned and reported that the creek, which was navigable only by vessels of very light draught, was obstructed by sunken lighters and fallen trees.

French operations elsewhere. To enable the French authorities in Gabon to deal with two German armed vessels which were reported to be doing much damage about the Rio Muni in Corisco Bay, the *Surprise* left Lagos on the 15th and arrived at Libreville on the 19th September. Next day a company of infantry under Major Miquelard embarked in her with the object of seizing Ukoko (Cocobeach) and of advancing inland against the German troops there. To co-operate in these operations, a platoon of another company was to advance by land across the frontier from Médégué, while the Oyem Column—the news of whose reverse had not yet been received—was to send a company to cut off the German retreat from Muni.

Gabon; 19th–21st Sept. 1914.

Under cover of a bombardment by the *Surprise*, Major Miquelard's company landed at Ukoko at daybreak on the 21st September and met with an obstinate resistance from an enemy detachment, numbering apparently about twenty Europeans and fifty natives with two machine guns. After a sharp engagement, in which the French suffered thirteen casualties (including four Europeans), the enemy was driven out and his two vessels sunk. By the evening Ukoko had been occupied.

On the 20th September another company of the Gabon Regiment, which had crossed the frontier from Mvahdi, attacked a portion of the German 11th Company at Minkebe but was repulsed, while simultaneously a part of the same German company from Ngara Binzam made an equally unsuccessful attack on Mvahdi, which was held by forty French native infantry.

The operations of the Gabon Regiment continued in this area, but the further account of them will fit better into the next chapter.

On the 7th October the *Bruix* left Duala to join the *Surprise* and, if the situation in the vicinity of Libreville was satisfactory, to bring her to Suelaba, reconnoitring on the way there and dispersing, as far as possible, any enemy concentrations on the coast south of the Nyong river. Both vessels started to return from Libreville on the 10th, and on their way up the coast demanded the surrender of Campo and Kribi, bombarding both places when no reply to their demands was received. No landing was made as, although these places appeared to be clear of troops, it was thought probable that they had only withdrawn to the shelter of the surrounding bush.

In accordance with instructions from General Aymerich, the commander of the Sanga Column, leaving about 310 rifles at Wesso to hold off the German force at Molundu, left Wesso on the 4th October with a strength of 360 rifles and four guns to advance up the Sanga river. That day his advanced guard captured a small German post at Djembe. Leaving sixty rifles to hold this post, the main column continued its advance, and after several minor engagements with hostile detachments captured Nola on the 17th October, taking twenty prisoners (six Europeans and fourteen native ranks). On the previous day news had been received that German troops from Molundu had surprised and re-captured Djembe. *The Sanga Column; 4th–17th Oct. 1914.*

During the third week in September the Germans, concentrating their 6th Company, which had originally retired from Mbaiki, and their 5th Company from Bouar, made unsuccessful attempts to force a crossing of the Lobaye river, whose passages, from Kolongo to Loko, were defended by the Lobaye Column. Its advance had been stopped pending the arrival of carriers from Bangui, but on the 9th October Lieutenant-Colonel Morisson, with about five hundred rifles and a gun just arrived from Brazzaville, effected a crossing at Kolongo and advanced, in two columns, on Carnot. He left some hundred rifles on the Lobaye river, and his right flank towards Yakonendji was covered by a detachment of about one hundred men, which was about to be reinforced by a company from the interior of Ubangi-Shari. Carnot was occupied on the 18th October, having been abandoned by the enemy. *The Lobaye Column; 18th Sept.–18th Oct. 1914.*

In the northern Cameroons Captain Ferrandi with his party of Senegalese left the Maiduguri Column on the 2nd September to return to Fort Lamy, where he arrived on the 8th, accompanied by Lieutenant C. W. T. Lane and a small escort of Nigerian mounted infantry.* *Chad area; 2nd–21st Sept. 1914.*

Having received the required reinforcements, Colonel Largeau captured Kuseri on the 20th. But Lieutenant Kallmeyer managed successfully to withdraw his force to Mora, evading an attempt to intercept him by a British detachment, with a total loss at Kuseri and *en route* of about half his party.

---

* Lieutenant Lane only stayed a few days at Fort Lamy.

CHAPTER V

OCTOBER—NOVEMBER 1914

THE CAPTURE OF EDEA AND BUEA, AND OPERATIONS IN THE NORTH AND SOUTH OF THE CAMEROONS

(Maps, 2, 4, 5 and 7)

The Edea project. With the capture of Susa and Yabasi the area to the north had been cleared sufficiently to secure General Dobell's position at Duala and to give him room for manœuvre in that quarter. He now turned his attention to extending his hold in a south-easterly direction, where the capture of Edea offered considerable advantages, especially if, as appeared likely, the Germans made Yaunde their chief centre of opposition. For Edea, which is situated on the left bank of the Sanaga river at a distance of fifty-two miles by railway from Duala, was both an important German administrative centre and a pivotal point of communications. Up to it the Sanaga river was navigable by coastal steamer; it was connected with the Nyong river and the coast road from Kribi by a good track from Dehane; and from it to the eastward ran the railway to Eseka and a main road to Yaunde.

German attempt to retake Susa. While engaged in his preparations for this project General Dobell learnt, on the 17th October, that the Germans seemed bent on an attempt to retake Susa, whose importance lay in its connection, by a track and a telegraph line through Mbonjo, with Mpundu on the Mungo river and the light railway from Victoria.

Susa was held by a company and a half ("F" and half "D") 2nd Nigerians, with two machine guns, the remainder of the battalion (less a detachment at Maka) and one section Nigerian Battery being at Bonaberi, which had by this time been connected by telephone with Susa. On the 15th October Colonel Haywood, receiving a telephone message from Susa to say that German parties and an armoured train were in the vicinity of Kake and that a British post on the Kake bridge had sustained two casualties, had sent half " D " Company with a machine gun to reinforce Susa. Next day no special incident occurred, but on the afternoon of the 17th the officer commanding at Susa reported that German troops in some strength had reached Kake and had driven British patrols from Kake bridge. Receiving instructions from General Dobell to act on his own initiative, Colonel Haywood left Bonaberi to march to Susa at 11 p.m., taking with him a section of the Nigerian Battery and " A " and " E " Companies 2nd Nigerians. Rain and darkness reduced the pace of his column; the damaged Bapele bridge took an hour and a half to cross; and it was not till 8 a.m. on the 18th October that the column reached Susa.

Learning that the Germans were burning Kake village, Colonel Haywood pushed forward with a gun and two companies. One company and the gun advanced along the railway and the other company by a path through the forest to the east of the railway. A small enemy party was quickly driven from the Kake bridge and then, after a brisk engagement lasting about half an hour, the Germans were pushed out of the village and the station at a cost of two British casualties. The German force, whose strength was estimated at three to five Europeans and 50 to 100 natives, retreated rapidly along a bush path on the western side of the railway.

Next morning, before daylight, Lieutenant E. B. Wesche with half " F " Company 2nd Nigerians and a machine gun was sent out to reconnoitre along this path and ascertain if it was feasible to ambush the enemy's armoured train. The Germans themselves, however, attacked Susa that day with a force which was subsequently estimated at 50 Europeans and 300 natives.* Reaching Kake at an early hour on the 19th, the enemy was engaged with British patrols to the north of Susa by 10 a.m., while another German party, found subsequently to have come from the Buea area, had driven in a British patrol from the Mbonjo track. These enemy parties then pressed on and attacked Susa; but, after about four hours' fighting, were finally driven back with some loss.

The men of Lieutenant Wesche's detachment, passing through Kake station at 5.15 a.m., and then advancing by the path to the west of the railway, did not hear the German troop train pass, and eventually emerged on the railway line at a point about three miles north of Kake station. Here they

---

* It included the German 4th Company.

were passed by the empty enemy train going northward, and their machine gun opened fire on it before they started to return by the western path. This firing evidently betrayed their presence to the Germans to the south, for they laid an ambush for the British party about a mile northward of Kake. Faced here by superior numbers, the Nigerians displayed great gallantry, their machine gun being well and boldly handled by the native soldier in charge. Lieutenant Wesche was killed, and there were other casualties, but the detachment gradually fought its way to the clearing round Kake station. Its ammunition then gave out, the enemy opposition increased, and, after three gallant but fruitless charges with the bayonet, its men were forced to scatter and seek the shelter of the forest, abandoning their machine gun after removing its essential parts. Several hours later, rather more than half the detachment under Lieutenant K. S. Grove succeeded in rejoining at Susa. Including the numbers this half company had lost, the total British casualties during the 19th October amounted to twenty-nine.

The Germans withdrew northward up the railway, having, as subsequently ascertained, sustained nearly fifty casualties. That evening, when reporting the affair to General Dobell, Colonel Haywood said that his position was satisfactory, but suggested that he should be reinforced by three companies. The troops for the Edea expedition were, however, on the point of starting, and General Dobell decided not to reinforce Colonel Haywood unless he was hard pressed. The necessity did not arise, and active patrolling by Colonel Haywood's troops round Susa revealed no signs of hostile troops. The enemy's headquarters on this line were at Muyuka, and it appears that he was nervous lest the British should advance from Yabasi direct on Nkongsamba in conjunction with an attack along the railway on Muyuka.

Allied estimate of enemy dispositions; 18th Oct. 1914. On the 18th October, when General Dobell issued his orders for an advance against Edea, his information led him to locate the enemy's total forces, estimated at a European detachment, twelve regular companies, four reserve detachments and nine police companies, as follows : *—

(i) *In the north about Mora, Garua, etc.:* four regular companies (Nos. 3, 7, 8 and 12);

(ii) *Farther south, along the Nigerian frontier and in the*

---

* German returns captured in December 1914 showed that this estimate was approximately correct, some of the peace-time police companies having apparently been amalgamated.

PLAN TO ATTACK EDEA

Ossidinge area: a regular company (No. 2), a reserve detachment (No. 3), and one and three-quarter police companies;

(iii) *Victoria-Buea-Muyuka-Yabasi area:* a European detachment, two regular companies (Nos. 1 and 4), and two police companies;

(iv) *on the railway east of Yapoma:* a reserve detachment (No. 2) and a section of a police company; *at Edea:* military headquarters and a police company, with a detachment at *Lobetal* on the Sanaga river; *at Yaunde* (Government headquarters): a police company and recruits; *in the Kribi-Lolo-Ebolowa area:* a reserve detachment (No. 4), and two police companies; and

(v) *engaged with the French in the south and south-east of the Cameroons:* five regular companies (Nos. 5, 6, 9, 10 and 11), a reserve detachment (No. 1), and a police company.

The enemy was evidently prepared for an allied advance on Edea by the railway or by the Sanaga river, but not, apparently, for one by the Nyong river, which—as not even the smallest coastal steamers had been known to enter it— was deemed unnavigable. But the *Ivy's* recent reconnaissance showed that its main navigation difficulties after crossing the bar lay in the three miles of delta above its mouth, where, in places, a depth of six feet only could be relied on at high water. Above the delta, where the mangroves ceased, natives reported plenty of water up to Dehane.

Plan for the advance on Edea.

General Dobell decided, after discussion with Captain Fuller, to send the main column of his attacking force by sea from Duala to move up the Nyong river and disembark at Dehane for an advance from there by land; and, in order to divert the enemy's attention from this column, to make two other simultaneous advances along the railway and up the Sanaga river respectively.

Colonel Mayer of the French Contingent was to command the main column, consisting of the French European company, 1st Senegalese, two French artillery sections, a French engineer section, and one and a half companies West African Regiment, i.e., a total of about 1,000 rifles and 4 guns.* Under escort of the *Cumberland*, *Dwarf* and *Surprise* this column was to be conveyed from Duala in six transports and, for work in the river, was to be accompanied by the *Ivy* with six small

---

* This was the maximum force with carrier transport that could advisably move along one track.

armed craft towing a steam lifeboat and a number of lighters.*
Fifteen days' supplies would be taken.

The naval flotilla detailed by Captain Fuller to advance up the Sanaga river was in two portions. One, of light-draught vessels, was to move through the Kwa-kwa creek and, driving the enemy out of Lobetal, was to join there the heavier draught vessels which were to enter the river from the sea. The former portion, under command of Lieutenant R. D. B. Haddon, R.N., consisted of *Cumberland's* picket boat, *Sokoto, Keka, Wuri* and *Vampire*, with lighters and one and a half companies West African Regiment; while the latter portion, under Commander L. W. Braithwaite, R.N., was composed of the *Remus, Porpoise, Sir Frederick, Mole* and *Dreadnought* lighter, the two last-named each mounting a naval 6-inch gun.

The advance along the railway was to be carried out by a column under Commandant Mathieu, consisting of two companies 2nd Senegalese with a machine gun section, a French artillery section, a British naval 12-pounder on a railway truck, with an escort from the West African Regiment, and the Sierra Leone field section of engineers.

Lieutenant Haddon received orders to attack Lobetal if possible on the afternoon of the 20th October, before the arrival of Commander Braithwaite's flotilla. This was to enter the Sanaga river at daylight on the 21st, and the combined flotilla was then to endeavour to reach the vicinity of Edea that evening, by which time it was hoped that the main column would be commencing to disembark at Dehane. Commander Braithwaite was to do everything possible to co-operate with and assist the main column; and this, he was instructed, he could probably do best by attracting the enemy's attention on the 21st and 22nd and by giving as much supporting fire as possible when the main column attacked Edea, directing his attention especially to preventing the passage of hostile troops across the river.

The *Remus* on the Sanaga river, and the *Ivy* and *Vigilant* on the Nyong river, would communicate by wireless with the *Cumberland*, which would be off the coast between the two rivers; while, after disembarkation at Dehane, Colonel Mayer would communicate with the vessels on the Nyong and the Sanaga by means of messengers. The *Dwarf* and *Surprise* were to cover the landing off the Nyong river.

---

* The six transports were the *Niemen, Hausa, Forcados, Lagos, Boma* and *Fullah*, and the six small armed craft were the *Vigilant, Alligator, Crocodile, Bonaberi, Forelle* and *Walrus*.

To face p. 163.

Northern Arm of the Sanaga River Bridge near Edea

Sanaga River near Edea

The operations commenced on the 20th October, but, as will be seen below, unavoidable delays affected the prearranged sequence of events. *Edea operations; 20th Oct. 1914.*

Information that an enemy force had established itself on the Dibamba river at Butu, about twelve miles above Yapoma, caused Commandant Mathieu to postpone his advance along the railway pending the result of an expedition by *Cumberland's* steam pinnace (Midshipman H. J. M. Ashby, R.N.), sent on the 20th October to reconnoitre and patrol the Yapoma-Butu stretch.

Lieutenant Haddon's flotilla, proceeding down the Kwa-kwa creek at an early hour on the 20th, was delayed by shallows and obstructions in the channel and anchored for the night about six miles short of Yadibo.

At 6.30 p.m. that day the Nyong river flotilla, followed by that under Commander Braithwaite, put out to sea from Suelaba under naval escort.

The *Cumberland's* steam pinnace on the Dibamba river encountered on the 21st October a small hostile party entrenched on both banks near Butu and engaged it successfully, driving it off with about fifteen casualties, including a German officer and four native soldiers drowned after jumping overboard from a canoe under fire. *Edea operations; 21st Oct. 1914.*

The Kwa-kwa flotilla that day encountered opposition, in the vicinity of Yadibo, from enemy posted in the dense forest on both banks of the creek, and suffered eight casualties (including Midshipman L. J. Bidwell, wounded) before succeeding in driving the enemy away. In addition, two British military officers received accidental injuries. Owing to the delay that had occurred it was necessary to refill with coal and water ; none of the guns of the Sanaga flotilla had been heard firing ; and it was advisable to replace the officer casualties. The officer in command, therefore, decided to return to Duala, and the flotilla consequently retired for the night to the anchorage it had left that morning.

Commander Braithwaite's flotilla, arriving off the southern entrance of the Sanaga river at daylight on the 21st, was forced by bad weather to postpone any attempt to cross the bar till 9 a.m. The *Mole*, only just able to make headway against the strong current, was then safely piloted across by the *Ivy's* boatswain (Mr. E. Wallace). But after that the swell on the bar increased so much as to make it unsafe for any of the other vessels to attempt the crossing. Consequently, during the day, operations were limited to a reconnaissance upstream by the *Mole*.

The *Cumberland*, *Dwarf*, and the transports conveying the Nyong column, arrived off the mouth of that river at daylight on the 21st, the handling of the convoy, which consisted of ships of all descriptions, including recent captures and some with officers and men of little sea experience, having proved no light task in the bad weather, which delayed the arrival of the *Ivy* and the small craft. This bad weather also created a heavy swell on the usually calm bar, though, after a preliminary reconnaissance by Commander Hughes (*Ivy*) in a motor boat, two transports and the *Alligator* crossed it successfully, but about 11 a.m. the *Fullah* and *Bonaberi* both went aground; and about noon, when it was near low tide, the surf on the bar became heavy and dangerous.

Shortly after this hour Captain Fuller, Captain Child (the Director of the Nigeria Marine), Commander G. S. B. Gray, R.N.R. (transport officer to the expedition), and Captain A. A. Franqueville (Colonel Mayer's staff officer) left the *Ivy* in a steamboat, towing a whaler, to enter the river. The steamboat broke down outside the bar and the party transhipped into the whaler. This, which was unsuitable for such work, was unfortunately soon capsized by a heavy roller; and despite prompt and gallant attempts at rescue, Captain Child, Commander Gray, Captain Franqueville and two of the native crew were drowned.* The death of these three officers was a great loss to the force, that of Captain Child being felt especially owing to the invaluable and prominent part he had hitherto taken in the operations.

The *Bonaberi* had to be abandoned, but the *Fullah* was refloated on the flood tide and entered the river in the early afternoon followed by the *Hausa* and the small craft. At 5.30 p.m. three of the small armed vessels, each towing two lighters, started up river towards Dehane carrying an advanced party of French troops.

<small>Edea operations; 22nd Oct. 1914.</small> During the night 21st–22nd October, the German force near Yapoma retired along the railway, and on the morning of the 22nd the column under Commandant Mathieu began to advance, being accompanied, till breaks in the line stopped its further progress, by the *Challenger's* 12-pounder gun mounted on a railway truck.†

---

* Captain Fuller, himself exhausted and at considerable personal risk, managed to save two of the native crew. For this action he and seven other officers and ratings of the Royal Navy and Nigeria Marine were awarded the Bronze Medal of the Board of Trade.

† This truck was on the eastern bank of the river, the bridge over which

On the 22nd the Kwa-kwa flotilla arrived back at Duala, and General Dobell inquired from Captain Fuller if he wished it to return to join the force on the Sanaga river. Here an improvement in the weather enabled the *Remus*, *Porpoise* and *Trojan* to cross the bar that morning by 8 a.m. But the *Sir Frederick*, towing the *Dreadnought*, went ashore through the tow parting, though fortunately the lighter itself drifted out on the ebb-tide. This unwieldy gun lighter had been a constant source of trouble and delay from the outset of the expedition and, as there seemed little chance of being able to get it across the bar, Commander Braithwaite requested the *Dwarf*, which had just arrived, to take charge of it and tow it back to Duala. The *Sir Frederick* was soon refloated, and during the afternoon the *Porpoise* and *Remus* started to proceed upstream. But both went aground, and were only refloated after considerable trouble as it was getting dark. All the vessels then anchored for the night about a mile and a half above the mouth of the river.

On the Nyong the French advanced party reached Dehane early on the 22nd, its unopposed disembarkation indicating that its advent had surprised the enemy. The *Fullah* and *Hausa*, carrying troops, started up river at 5.30 a.m., and though the former reached Dehane successfully at 9 a.m.* the latter went ashore and remained aground all day. By utilising the small craft and lighters, however, all Colonel Mayer's troops were concentrated that night at Dehane.

A report that all the troops of the main column were expected to arrive at Dehane by 6 a.m. on the 23rd, and that Colonel Mayer hoped to reach Edea on the 24th, was received by General Dobell at Duala during the night of the 22nd–23rd.

On the 23rd October the British naval 12-pounder on the railway was moved back to Yapoma and a field gun (Lieut. C. Hamilton, R.N.R.) from the *Challenger* was sent up to replace it. That night Commandant Mathieu's force bivouacked at a point about twenty-eight miles from Duala.

At Captain Fuller's request, the Kwa-kwa flotilla left Duala again on the morning of the 23rd, but was delayed by several of its vessels going aground. Lieutenant Haddon learnt, however, from friendly natives that the bulk of the enemy party on the creek had now concentrated on its eastern bank

---

had not yet been re-opened, and the gun had been mounted during the previous week by artisans from the *Challenger*.

* The *Fullah*, whose net tonnage was 177, was the first ship of its size to navigate to that point.

at Ngogotunda; and, on receiving a request for news that evening, after anchoring, from Commander Braithwaite, he replied giving this information and his own programme for the next day. He would land troops on the west bank, he said, to get into touch with the *Remus*, and he asked that Ngogotunda should be bombarded as a preliminary to his landing troops there also.

During the 23rd Commander Braithwaite's flotilla made very little progress, as the *Remus* went aground and was not refloated till evening. As there seemed some doubt about finding sufficient water for this vessel, Commander Braithwaite then transferred to the *Mole* to avoid further delay.

After Colonel Mayer's troops landed at Dehane, Captain Fuller, leaving the *Surprise* with a transport and two armed launches off the Nyong river and sending the *Ivy*, the steam lifeboat and the *Vigilant* to assist in the Sanaga river, returned with the remaining vessels to Duala.

Colonel Mayer, leaving the British portion of his column to guard stores and supplies at Dehane, marched off towards Edea with the remainder at noon on the 23rd. The Dehane-Edea track, twenty-five miles in length, was a good one, but the forest it traversed was particularly dense. About 4 p.m. the French advanced guard was checked by heavy hostile rifle and machine gun fire, and fighting continued until dark, when the Germans retreated, leaving numerous dead, including three Europeans. The French column then bivouacked, having advanced about seven and a half miles from Dehane.

Edea operations; 24th Oct. 1914. On reaching a point about thirty-seven miles from Duala on the 24th October, Commandant Mathieu's column encountered considerable opposition from the enemy in a prepared position. The French, who incurred about sixteen casualties, were definitely checked, and orders were issued for a reinforcement of one hundred men to be sent them from Yapoma.

On the Kwa-kwa creek, a party of the West African Regiment, landing on the western bank, occupied Lobetal on the morning of the 24th without opposition, and at 11.30 a.m. established communication with Commander Braithwaite in the *Mole*. After bombarding the entrance to the Kwa-kwa creek with the 6-inch gun and then proceeding a short way up the creek and firing a few more shells in the direction in which Ngogotunda appeared to lie, without eliciting any reply or seeing any sign of the enemy, Commander Braithwaite gave the pre-arranged signal for Lieutenant Haddon to advance.

EDEA OPERATIONS

The latter's vessels arrived without encountering any opposition at about 5.30 p.m., and the combined flotilla anchored for the night off Lobetal. The enemy, whose strength was subsequently ascertained to have been about forty rifles, had retreated north-eastward.

During the 24th Colonel Mayer's troops made only slow progress. They encountered obstructions, including trenches and wire entanglements, across the track, and at about 2 p.m. the advanced guard was stopped by heavy rifle and machine gun fire. The Senegalese found themselves unable to make their way through the dense forest in a turning movement, and an attempt to bring their mountain guns into action on the track was unsuccessful. Fighting continued until dark, when, the Germans still holding to their position, the French troops bivouacked for the night. During the fighting on the 23rd and 24th October they had sustained twenty-four casualties, including two French officers and four French non-commissioned officers. The Germans, they estimated, had suffered even more, including at least a dozen Europeans.

On the 25th the *Challenger's* field gun and crew, after a difficult march in which they had many obstacles to surmount, joined Commandant Mathieu, whose column was still confronted by the enemy's position at the 37th mile.

Edea operations; 25th Oct. 1914.

On the Sanaga river the British flotilla, with troops landed on both banks to move ahead, proceeded up river at 8 a.m. on the 25th. The banks were flooded, however, and progress on land was so slow that the troops were re-embarked and proceeded alongside the banks in boats, landing small piquets at intervals to cover the flotilla while it passed. Navigation no longer presented much difficulty, as there was plenty of water and the native pilots did exceptionally well. The mission station at Marienberg was visited, its German members being sent downstream to Lobetal, and the flotilla, again proceeding, anchored for the night near Dibonga island. A communication by messenger from Colonel Mayer had been expected at a pre-arranged point, but was not received, and Commander Braithwaite sent off a messenger to try to get into touch with the French, but without success. An attempt by Commander Braithwaite to get a wireless message through to one of the naval vessels off the coast was equally unsuccessful. This failure to get a wireless message through from a station in the forest was one of the first of many similar ineffectual attempts during the operations, and was, apparently, due either to the humidity of the atmosphere or to the deadening effect of the surrounding foliage.

On the morning of the 25th, finding that the enemy had retreated during the night, apparently towards Edea, Colonel Mayer's column resumed its advance. It halted at noon at a point about eight miles from Edea, and Colonel Mayer sent off a situation report to General Dobell. This was the only message sent by Colonel Mayer during his march from Dehane to Edea which General Dobell received, and it did not reach its destination till the 27th. In the meantime, the arrival at Duala of French wounded from Dehane gave General Dobell some indication of the French progress. This general failure in communication—which, as it happened, appears to have had little effect on the operations—was probably due, to a great extent, to the unfortunate death on the 21st October of the French staff officer, Captain Franqueville.

Edea captured; 26th Oct. 1914. Commandant Mathieu, evidently unable to overcome the enemy opposition, remained halted on the 26th October and renewed previous applications for the naval 12-pounder to be sent back to him.

A thick mist delayed the resumption of its advance by Commander Braithwaite's flotilla till 7.30 a.m. on the 26th, though the picket boat proceeded before that hour to reconnoitre and shell a look-out station which the enemy was said to be holding. This station was, however, found to have been evacuated. When the flotilla began to advance the strong current made progress slow till enemy trenches were sighted on both banks of the river a short distance below Edea. Commander Braithwaite was still without news of Colonel Mayer's column—though information received from natives indicated that the enemy was retiring—and he proceeded to reconnoitre the trenches with a view to bombarding them. This he was preparing to do at 2.30 p.m., when a canoe came alongside with a message from the French saying that they had been in possession of Edea since 9 a.m.

The British flotilla then proceeded upstream, progressing slowly against the strong current caused by two waterfalls, one on either side of the midstream island which connected the two railway bridges spanning the river. Edea was reached at 4.30 p.m. The Germans, who had broken one of the railway bridges, were said to have retired in three parties, i.e., along the Yaunde road, the railway towards Eseka, and to the northward, but the French had not considered it necessary or advisable to attempt to pursue them. Subsequent information showed that their strength had been practically as estimated by Allied Headquarters and that the main factors determining their retreat from Edea had been the totally unexpected approach of the heavy naval gun up the Sanaga river and the unforeseen advance from Dehane. General Dobell had, in fact, appreciated the situation correctly; and his plan to deal with it, though slightly delayed in execution by bad weather, had attained success at a surprisingly small cost.

Colonel Mayer does not appear to have at once communicated the news of his capture of Edea to Commandant Mathieu, for at 7 a.m. on the 27th October, on request by the French, Commander Braithwaite ferried a party of twenty-five of their men across the river to take a message to the Yapoma column. That night at 9.15 p.m. General Dobell at Duala received a report from Commandant Mathieu that Colonel Mayer had occupied Edea.* It was not, however, till the morning of the 28th that Commandant Mathieu discovered that the enemy opposing his advance had retired. He then proceeded to march to Edea.

Colonel Mayer informed Commander Braithwaite that he would not require the British flotilla at Edea. But he asked for a launch and a lighter for ferrying purposes and also that Lieutenant McCallum of the British Intelligence Staff might remain with him. These requests being complied with, Commander Braithwaite left that day and arrived back at Duala on the 31st October.

Colonel Mayer was detailed to hold Edea with his European company, the 1st Senegalese and four French mountain guns; the railway from there to Duala was guarded by detachments of the 2nd Senegalese; and the remainder of the troops were withdrawn to Duala.

Despite inclement weather the health of the troops had been satisfactory, though malaria was beginning to affect the European ranks. Since the arrival in the Cameroon Estuary of General Dobell's force there had been 23 deaths from disease, in addition to 170 battle casualties.†

To turn now for a time to Nigeria and the operations in the north. On his arrival at Lagos on the 7th October Colonel Cunliffe found little change in the general situation. Captain

The Anglo-German frontier and Nigeria; 7th Oct. 1914.

---
* The indefinite nature of this report is indicated by an entry in the Force Headquarters war diary saying that it required confirmation.
† 51 killed, 111 wounded, and 8 missing.

Fox at Sava, in close observation of the Germans on the Mora mountain, was awaiting the arrival of a French force from Fort Lamy to attack the enemy. At Yola, Major Webb-Bowen—with a mounted infantry company, two guns and six companies of infantry—was constructing defences pending the capture of Mora; after which it was intended that he should advance and, joining the Allied force from Mora, attack Garua, where the Germans were said to have received strong reinforcements and to have greatly improved their defences.

German parties had made a few raids across the frontier to the south-west of Yola, and, as exaggerated reports of these had caused some alarm among the natives, two companies of infantry (one from Lokoja and one from Yola) had been sent to Takum to watch the frontier and restore confidence. Farther to the south, a threatened German raid had caused the despatch to Obudu from Ikom of two infantry companies and a gun under Captain G. D. Mann.

At Ikom itself, where Colonel Mair had at his disposal four and a half infantry companies and three guns, the situation was quiet. Nsanakang was to remain neutral territory till the 19th October, when the question was again to be considered. Calabar was garrisoned by the two infantry companies which had lost so heavily at Nsanakang.

Beyond some unrest in the Udi district, which was being dealt with by the company stationed there, the internal situation was generally satisfactory.

Mora; 9th-31st Oct. 1914. (Map 5.) On the 9th October Captain Fox heard from General Largeau * that a French detachment would reach Sava in a few days' time, that its commander, Lieutenant-Colonel Brisset, had instructions to co-operate with Captain Fox for the destruction of the German force at Mora and that, when that had been accomplished, the combined force would be available to attack Garua if the British authorities agreed.

Colonel Brisset reached Sava and assumed control of the Allied operations in the area on the 13th October. Next morning a French company and a Nigerian section moved out to the westward of Mora mountain to ambush an enemy party seen in that direction. This party, of about twenty rifles, which had been sent out from Mora to meet a reported reinforcement from Garua, was successfully intercepted. The premature opening of fire by some of the French infantry, however, not only destroyed all chance of surprise but enabled

---

* He had just been promoted.

SITUATION AT MORA

the Germans to despatch a relief party from the mountain which, by taking the Allied detachment in reverse, enabled the returning enemy detachment to rejoin without loss and caused sixteen casualties to the Allies.

Reconnaissances during the next two or three days resulted in Colonel Brisset reporting to General Largeau on the 17th October that the German position was very strong with no apparent weak points. From it the only three possible positions for French guns were completely dominated at a range of 3,300 yards; the Germans carried out daily target practice and their marksmanship had become very good; they had ample supplies and water; and the *moral* of their native troops appeared to be excellent.

Between the 17th and 26th October Colonel Brisset was joined by further French troops, the arrival of some being due to the retirement to Garua of the German 12th Company from Buma. These reinforcements gave Colonel Brisset a force of four French infantry companies, a French machine gun section, a French mountain gun section, a British mounted infantry company, and a British infantry company, with a total effective strength of about 830. By the end of the month the Mora mountain, where the German position had been extended to include Molugve, was invested, the Allies being disposed as follows: a French section at the former German post in the plain; a French company with a gun and two machine guns at Wacheke; the Nigerian infantry company at Padiko, a mountainous bluff some 2,500 yards west of Dabaskum but separated from it by a deep and rocky valley; a French infantry company on the foot of the southern spur of the mountain; and the remainder of the force at Sava.

On the 29th October Colonel Brisset and Captain Fox reconnoitred Dabaskum from Wacheke. The boulder-covered slopes above them were everywhere precipitous, and there were deep and rocky ravines on either side of the col connecting the two localities. But Dabaskum appeared to be held by only about a dozen enemy rifles; and its importance to the Germans, as assuring them supplies and especially water from the adjacent village and wells, was such that its capture might well hasten their surrender. Colonel Brisset decided, therefore, with Captain Fox's concurrence, to attack it on the night of the 30th/31st October.

To divert attention from the main attack, which was to be carried out from the west by the Nigerian company from Padiko, demonstrations were to be made by two French companies, one advancing from the east of Mora mountain and the other from the south. Further, a small French detachment from Wacheke was to take up a position of readiness, from which it would advance south-westward after the Nigerians had delivered the final assault. No attempt could be made to synchronise the times of the different movements, as it was obviously impossible to forecast how long any of them might take by night to traverse the difficult ground.

From Padiko, after dark on the 30th October, Captain Fox led his company, seventy-six rifles strong, down into the intervening valley, and at 10 p.m. started on the difficult ascent. At 1 a.m., when some distance below Dabaskum, enemy outposts were encountered. Heavy firing broke out, and the Nigerians, extended for a further advance, could only be restrained with great difficulty by Captain Fox and his subaltern, Lieutenant A. C. L. D. Lees, from useless firing in reply. The advance continued, but the precipitous ground strewn with large boulders made it very hard to maintain touch; and when Captain Fox, on the right of the line, gained the crest near Dabaskum he found that he had only seven of his men with him and had lost touch with the remainder. A party of the enemy was heard talking close by, but no more of his men arrived, and Captain Fox, after a time, descended a short distance and, moving along the slope, joined Lieutenant Lees and the remainder of the company. Reorganising, Captain Fox then advanced with the whole company direct on Dabaskum under a heavy fire, only, however, to be stopped at a short distance from it by an impassable precipice. Here Lieutenant Lees was wounded.

By this time it was nearly 4 a.m.; his men were much exhausted; and Captain Fox realised that it would be light by the time they moved round and advanced by the line which he himself had previously taken. He accordingly gave the order to retire. In addition to Lieutenant Lees, twelve native ranks had been wounded, but the withdrawal was successfully carried out without further loss.

In accordance with its orders the French detachment at Wacheke, lacking any indication that the Nigerians had assaulted, had not advanced. According to German accounts the French demonstration from the east achieved its object, but the French advance from the south caused them no uneasiness.

His experience that night showed Captain Fox how deceptive was the aspect of the mountain slopes; his previous reconnaissances, even from a short distance, having given him

To face p. 173]

NIGERIAN TROOPS AT YOLA

CONSTRUCTING DEFENCES

YOLA AND IBI COLUMNS

an imperfect conception of their real character and practicability. He expressed his conviction, however, to Colonel Brisset that, with the knowledge and experience he and his men had gained, a second attack would be successful.

At Yola, pending success at Mora, Major Webb-Bowen's force was mainly occupied during October in constructing defences and in constant local reconnaissances and minor enterprises, German detachments being active along the frontier in the vicinity and continually making raids across it. In one instance they succeeded in cutting the telegraph line fifty miles west of Yola, thus severing all communication for some days. The weather was very hot, water was running short, and most of the British officers went sick at times. This and the fact that half of his officers had insufficient military experience, added considerably to the difficulties of Major Webb-Bowen, who was not himself in the best of health. At the end of October an infantry company was withdrawn from Yola to deal with internal trouble in the Udi and Okigwi districts. By this time the defences at Yola had been completed, and Major Webb-Bowen was expecting orders at any moment to move and join the French in an attack on Garua.

Nigeria; 7th–31st Oct. 1914.

One of the infantry companies was withdrawn from Takum to Lokoja soon after Colonel Cunliffe's arrival. But, owing to reports of a German concentration at Koncha, from where parties threatened Bakundi, Colonel Cunliffe sent orders on the 14th October to Captain Mann at Obudu to reinforce Takum with his whole detachment and to take over command there. After a long and difficult march Captain Mann reached Takum on the 25th and assumed command of what became known as the Ibi column, amounting to three infantry companies, one gun and sixty-five police. As German troops were reported to be in some strength near Bakundi, Captain Mann at once detached a company to occupy that place and reconnoitre its vicinity.

On the 19th October, at an Anglo-German conference at Nsanakang, it was agreed that its neutrality should terminate on the 30th. The Ikom column—or the Cross river column as it was now termed—whose patrols had several encounters with German parties near the frontier during the latter half of October, was reduced in strength after the 21st October by one and a half companies withdrawn to deal with disorder in Southern Nigeria.

Altogether at this period four and a half infantry companies had to be employed in putting down native risings in the

Kwale, Udi and Bassa districts. Clear evidence that the disorders were due to the instigations of German emissaries, or of German traders who had been left at liberty on parole, obliged Sir Frederick Lugard to take steps to collect all enemy subjects for deportation.

French action and intentions in the south and south-east, and the arrival of a Belgian detachment. Oct. 1914. At the end of October General Dobell received, from the authorities in Gabon, the first information he obtained direct from the French regarding the action and intentions of their troops operating in the south and south-east of the Cameroons. Their object, he was told, was to capture the territory ceded to Germany in 1911, and at the same time to occupy the attention there of as many German troops as possible and so prevent them increasing their strength against General Dobell. Owing to the distances involved and communication difficulties, the information sent to General Dobell was, however, out of date.

During October Major Miquelard had advanced eastward through German Muni and had arrived at Essone on the 28th with orders to take over command of the Oyem column. This column had meanwhile been instructed to send forward a company to cut off the Germans retreating to Oyem from Ukoko. But it had not succeeded in doing so. The Germans, concentrating their 10th and 11th Companies to cover this retreat, had advanced towards the frontier about Ebom and had successfully driven back the different detachments, into which the company of the Oyem column had been split up, to Essone. The German force in Muni had thus withdrawn successfully and their 10th and 11th Companies had returned to Oyem. In addition to these two companies, the German force in the Oyem area comprised No. 1 Reserve Detachment and about 115 police. The information given General Dobell was that a French column of some 680 rifles was concentrating about Midsik to take the offensive against Oyem in November.

The French company at Mvahdi (160 rifles) had made no move during October and was, General Dobell was told, observing Minkebe. This place, as well as Ngara Binzam, had as a matter of fact been by then evacuated by the Germans.

The news that Germans from Molundu had captured Djembe caused Lieutenant-Colonel Hutin, commanding the Sanga column, to start back from Nola—leaving a company with two guns to hold that place—on the 23rd October to re-establish his line of communication. In the meantime,

General Aymerich, on a visit to Wesso, hearing of the loss of Djembe, hurried French and Belgian * reinforcements to Wesso. The Belgian detachment, consisting of the steamer *Luxembourg* with three guns, a machine gun and 136 rifles under Lieutenant Bal, had come up the Congo from Leopoldville, and on the 21st October was near the mouth of the Sanga river. On the 26th and 28th October a French detachment from Wesso attacked the Germans, who had moved from Djembe to a well-fortified post at Dzimu (south of Djembe and about thirty miles north of Wesso), but failed to dislodge them. On the 29th, however, a further attack carried out in combination with Colonel Hutin's column achieved its object, the Germans being driven out and forced to retire on Molundu. In the course of this fighting both sides incurred somewhat heavy casualties. The information sent General Dobell was that the Sanga column, of a total strength of 720 rifles with 4 guns,† was holding Wesso and was advancing against Nola. The German force at Molundu comprised the 9th and a police company, with a strength of about 400 rifles with machine guns.

On the 21st October the Lobaye column had established touch with the Sanga column at Nola. The strength of the Lobaye column was 600 rifles, and it was shortly to be reinforced by another 350 rifles. Opposed to it were the German 5th and 6th Companies, retiring from Gaza on Baturi.

Operations northward of Duala; Nov. 1st 1914.

To return to the operations from Duala. The Bapele bridge on the Northern Railway having been temporarily repaired, a daily train service, with rolling stock from the Midland Railway, had been started between Bonaberi and Susa during the last week of October. At Susa Colonel Haywood, with an advanced detachment holding Kake bridge, had three companies of the 2nd Nigerians with which he was carrying out constant reconnaissances. Opposing him on the Northern Railway was a German force of about 60 Europeans and 400 natives with several machine guns and an armoured train ; while guarding the approaches to Buea, with outposts at Victoria, Tiko and Mpundu, was another German force of

---

* The Belgian Government had at first tried to arrange with Germany that Belgian Congo should remain neutral during the war. But following a German attack on the eastern frontier of Belgian Congo at the end of August, the Belgians decided to assist the French against the Cameroons.

† The actual strength by this time was nearly 900 rifles.

about 50 Europeans and 300 natives with five or six machine guns.

At Yabasi, Colonel Cockburn's force of the 1st Nigerians and one gun of the Sierra Leone Battery had opposite to it two German detachments; one at Nyanga, about twenty miles to the north-west, consisting of about 20 Europeans and 150 police with a machine gun, and the other about Nyamtam, some fifteen miles to the eastward, composed of some 20 Europeans and 150 natives with several machine guns.

General Dobell had decided, after the capture of Edea, to deal with the enemy forces round Buea, whose situation appeared to lay them open to capture or destruction if their attention could be sufficiently diverted while British troops from the Northern Railway moved across and cut them off from the north. For the operations which he planned with this object, General Dobell would require troops—which he could only make available by reducing the size of the Yabasi garrison—and fuller information regarding the topographical features of the Susa-Mpundu area. On the 1st November he started to put into force the preliminary measures designed to fulfil these requirements.

Yabasi; 1st–9th Nov. 1914. Despatching three companies West African Regiment under Major J. P. Law and a gun of the Sierra Leone Battery to reinforce Yabasi, he instructed Colonel Cockburn, after clearing up the situation round there by active and aggressive measures, to return to Duala with the 1st Nigerians, leaving the West African Regiment companies with the two guns to hold Yabasi.

The Germans round Yabasi became very active on the 31st October, and during the next two days reports that Colonel Zimmermann and some of the German troops from Edea had arrived in the vicinity reached Colonel Cockburn. He consequently expected to be attacked at any moment, and when the first of the boats conveying the West African Regiment approached his position at about 6.30 p.m. on the 2nd November, some of his outposts mistook them, in the dark and the rain, for the enemy and opened fire on them. Finding that the shouts of his men that they were British had no effect, Lieut. B. F. Adams, R.N., at Major Law's request, ordered his flotilla to drop downstream and anchored for the night about two miles below Yabasi. Here at 11 p.m. Colonel Cockburn's adjutant, taking an urgent message to Duala, found Major Law and informed him that the presence of his detachment at Yabasi was urgently required. He thereupon landed the bulk of his party on the right bank of the river and marched into Yabasi, arriving there at 1.30 a.m. There his men, tired and wet through, occupied trenches ready to meet the expected attack. But it did not materialise.

On the 4th November Colonel Cockburn with the 1st Nigerians and one gun advanced towards Nyamtam. His advanced guard was continuously engaged, the difficulties and strain of the fighting being accentuated by the particularly dense forest and the stifling atmosphere of an exceptionally hot day. In the next two days' advance Colonel Cockburn encountered no opposition, and entered Nyamtam on the 6th to find that the enemy had retreated leaving only a few missionaries. On the 7th he moved out against a large enemy camp eight miles to the eastward, but this the enemy evacuated after offering only slight opposition, and Colonel Cockburn returned to Nyamtam before dark. On the 8th, after clearing the mission station of everything of use to the enemy and taking with him the missionaries, Colonel Cockburn moved back to Yabasi, covering the whole march in one day.

On the 4th November also, the motor launch *Keka*, in charge of Leading Seaman W. Mitchelmore, R.N., and with a small escort of African troops on board, engaged at Dibombe the larger enemy launch *Vogel* and a party of Germans on the bank, landing and pursuing till all the enemy escaped in the *Vogel* up the Dibombe river. One of the *Keka's* native crew was wounded and the Germans are believed to have suffered at least two casualties.

In the meantime General Dobell, learning that the seasonal fall might shortly render the Wuri river so difficult to navigate as to jeopardise the supply of Yabasi, had sent his senior general staff officer (Lieutenant-Colonel Turner) on the 6th to report on the situation. Colonel Turner found a position, at the mouth of the Dibombe river twelve miles below Yabasi, which steam craft could reach at all seasons, which could be defended by two companies and from which the passage of both the Wuri and Dibombe rivers could be denied to the enemy. Yabasi was consequently evacuated and a post at Dibombe established on the 9th November. Leaving there two companies West African Regiment as garrison, Colonel Cockburn moved down that day to Duala with the remainder of his force.*

---

* On the way downstream Colonel Cockburn made a very gallant, though unfortunately unsuccessful, attempt to rescue a British bluejacket who fell overboard. For this action he was awarded the Silver Medal of the Royal Humane Society.

Susa;
1st–8th
Nov.
1914.

From Susa on the 1st November, Colonel Haywood sent a company to reconnoitre the tracks from Mbonjo to Mpundu on both banks of the Mungo river, evidently in anticipation of the orders sent him the next day by General Dobell to carry out a complete topographical reconnaissance of the routes to Mpundu. Headquarters and two companies of the Composite Battalion would, Colonel Haywood was told, reinforce him on the 4th, when, to avoid arousing the enemy's suspicions that an attack on Mpundu was contemplated, he was to advance up the railway and reconnoitre towards Muyuka. His whole force was to concentrate again at Susa not later than the 8th.

Colonel Haywood directed Colonel Rose to take a company of his Composite Battalion and, with the company of 2nd Nigerians already at Mbonjo, carry out the required reconnaissance towards Mpundu. Colonel Haywood himself, with one company 2nd Nigerians, one company Composite Battalion and two guns, would advance towards Muyuka.

Colonel Rose carried out his task successfully and returned to Susa on the 8th November. Mpundu was occupied, he estimated, by about a company of the enemy, and an advance on that place was practicable by land, though it would be facilitated by the provision of a launch with some lighters for use on the Mungo river. This was about one hundred and fifty yards broad at Mpundu and would, it was said, have a depth of at least four feet of water till the end of the month. In obtaining this information Colonel Rose's column encountered some opposition and incurred seven casualties. One of his patrols had the unusual experience of having to disperse to escape from a wild elephant, which had just put a hostile patrol to flight.* These animals not only added to the dangers to be encountered, but were a constant source of trouble owing to the damage they did to telephone lines, etc.

Colonel Haywood's column moved northward on the 4th November, the necessary scouting through the dense forest on either side of the railway rendering its progress slow. It bivouacked at Nkongpina, where it was attacked that night in rather a half-hearted fashion by a small enemy force and incurred one casualty. Next day, reaching a point some two

---

* The presence of numbers of these elephants had led to the issue of instructions to the force to disperse on meeting them without attempting to fire. During the campaign the increase in the activity of herds of elephant became marked. Complaints received from farmers round Victoria, as to damage by herds with which they were becoming increasingly unable to deal, were so numerous that a special expedition was sent to the area in an attempt to help the villagers to defend their farms.

and a half miles short of Muyuka, Colonel Haywood entrenched a camp, where he left half his force while he reconnoitred, that night and the next morning, with the remainder towards Muyuka.

Just before dawn on the 6th November the enemy outposts were encountered and Colonel Haywood disposed his small force so as to give an impression of strength and to induce the enemy, by opening fire, to disclose his dispositions. With his company consequently divided into small parties extended over a wide front with both flanks advanced, Colonel Haywood gave his men orders to cut their way through the bush towards Muyuka station, carrying out sudden sharp bursts of fire as they moved forward. In reserve he retained a small party with the gun at a point two thousand yards from the station, which could not be seen, but whose position he fixed by a bearing obtained from a German railway map.

The enemy was gradually driven back to the station, at which three shells were then fired. This at once caused the German troops, about 100 in number, to retreat hurriedly in a waiting train; and the British occupied the station. Further reconnaissance disclosed the enemy, apparently about 300 strong with machine guns, entrenched in a position on a hill fifteen hundred yards to the north-west. Colonel Haywood, having attained his object, now decided to retire. His only casualty during the day had been one man wounded, and his withdrawal to his entrenched camp was effected without incident. On the 7th he returned to Susa.*

For some time past General Dobell and Captain Fuller had been receiving reports that small vessels were carrying communications and trafficking between the Cameroons and the islands of Fernando Po, Sao Thome, and Principe; and on the 29th October the *Ivy* and *Forelle* left Suelaba for patrol duty with special instructions to try to intercept these vessels. Visiting Fernando Po, Commander Hughes formed the opinion that the Germans had many Spanish sympathisers there, an important factor, having regard to the regular steamer service between Santa Isabel and Bata in Spanish Muni. Shortly afterwards the capture of a letter written on the 6th November by the German consul at Fernando Po to the German consul in Monrovia confirmed the impression that the Germans

Naval coast operations; 31st Oct.- 7th Nov. 1914.

---

* As a result of the previous six weeks' fighting, Colonel Gorges—commanding the British Contingent—on the 7th November 1914 issued a memorandum of special tactical instructions to his officers and men. As military students may find this useful, it is reproduced in Appendix V.

in the Cameroons were communicating through Fernando Po. For this letter sent a narrative of the operations in the Cameroons up to the capture of Edea for report by telegram to Berlin, promised further definite information shortly, and said that telegrams from Monrovia were sent regularly by a secret way to the Cameroons.

Picking up the *Forelle* with her engines disabled on the 30th October, the *Ivy* had to tow her back to Suelaba, sailing again in the evening with the *Vigilant* (Lieut. L. J. Hall, Nigeria Marine). The *Bruix* also left then to visit Principe and Sao Thome.

Having sent the *Vigilant* to reconnoitre Campo, the *Ivy* reached Bata on the 1st November. Here it was ascertained that two rowing boats, under the Spanish flag but really German property, carried mails and passengers weekly between Campo and Bata, connecting with the Spanish steamer which carried the German mails. Leaving Bata, the *Ivy* proceeded to Campo, where she anchored at 1 a.m. on the 2nd and learnt that on the previous day a landing party from the *Vigilant* had found that the German station at Campo, which was protected with extensive entrenchments and barbed wire, had been recently evacuated. Both vessels then visited Great Batanga, Kribi, Plantation, Longyi, and Little Batanga on the 2nd and 3rd November, and with slight opposition destroyed the German telephone stations. At these places large numbers of natives, whose canoes the Germans had destroyed to prevent the Allies getting information or assistance, besought the naval officers to protect them not only against the Germans but against Yaundes, whom the Germans had armed knowing that they had a feud with the coast natives. Campo was visited again on the 4th, and the landing party, despite opposition, succeeded in destroying the large telephone exchange there. The *Vigilant*, with Commander Hughes on board, then reconnoitred up the Campo river for seven miles. After again going to Bata and visiting Concepcion, the two vessels arrived back at Suelaba on the 7th November. In addition to gaining much other useful information they had ascertained that the German military headquarters from Kribi and all stores and material from the coast factories had been removed inland to Makure, which was connected by telephone and by roads passable for motors with other German centres. It had also been discovered that a German wireless station at Nsiki * was receiving messages from an unknown source.

---

* Nsiki cannot be traced on the map. It was apparently in the vicinity of Makure.

QUESTION OF THE NAVAL COMMAND 181

About this time a circular in Arabic, calling on Moslem soldiers in the British and French forces—in the name of their religion—to side with the Germans, was found by the British, who at later periods came across a few other similar documents. But, as the Germans themselves must have realised, this variety of propaganda had no success whatever in these regions. Neither the entry of Turkey into the war nor Turkish attempts to declare a *Jahad* had any effect on the attitude of local Mahomedans, or on the loyalty of the soldiers of this religion.

Meanwhile a discussion had taken place between London and Duala concerning the naval strength and command in the Cameroons. Learning on the 2nd November that the French were about to relieve the *Bruix* by the *Pothuau*, whose commander, Captain Cheron, was senior to Captain Fuller, General Dobell telegraphed to the Colonial Office urging that Captain Fuller should remain Senior Naval Officer, a position which it was imperative that a British officer should hold. But the British Admiralty were anxious to complete their naval distribution to meet Admiral von Spee, who might well consider the situation in South Africa, South-West Africa or the Cameroons worthy of his attention; and on the 3rd November they telegraphed to Captain Fuller that, on the arrival of the *Pothuau*, he was to hand over the duties of Senior Naval Officer to Captain Cheron and proceed with the *Cumberland* to Sierra Leone, whither the *Challenger* was shortly to follow. On the 4th November General Dobell again telegraphed to the Colonial Office and said that the presence of not less than two gunboats and two cruisers, one of them capable of anchoring off Duala, was necessary, and that for the successful conduct of the operations it was imperative that the Senior Naval Officer should be British. Captain Fuller also telegraphed in a somewhat similar strain to the Admiralty.

Naval strength and command; 2nd–9th Nov. 1914.

Next day, after further consideration, General Dobell sent another telegram pointing out that there were twenty guns from the *Cumberland* and *Challenger* mounted in small vessels and that, exclusive of landing parties and the crews for field guns, the average number of naval ratings regularly employed from the two cruisers was 220. These could not be replaced by native soldiers, and the French were only able to provide three small guns with crews. As the communications were practically all water, the operations were essentially amphibious, and the withdrawal of armed craft would make it difficult to supply, and dangerous to hold, some of the posts then occupied by the Allies. Though the capture of Duala had achieved the main Allied object, the clearance of its vicinity, where the Germans maintained great activity, was necessary, but would be impossible of attainment without efficient British naval co-operation. The captain of the *Bruix* agreed with General Dobell and the senior British naval officers that a change of naval command was undesirable. In conclusion General Dobell expressed the hope that in no circumstances would the *Cumberland* be withdrawn before the completion of the operations which he hoped to commence on the 9th November.

This telegram, as will be seen below, had the desired effect. A further explanation, as given in the written report which General Dobell sent the Colonial Office on the 6th November, will, however, make the position clearer. Owing to the absence of roads, the closest co-operation and mutual understanding and confidence between the local naval and military commanders and services generally were essential and had, in fact, been maintained from the outset of the operations; while the complex nature of these would make harmonious relations much more difficult if commanders and personnel were of different nationalities. French naval ranks made no attempt to conceal their dislike to work in small vessels and boats; very few of them were able to make themselves understood by the English-speaking natives (either of the Nigeria Marine or locally engaged) who formed the crews of the various craft, which were all British; and, besides having no small vessels to replace these, the French would apparently be unable to supply suitable guns or mountings. The linguistic difficulties must inevitably cause confusion and might lead to disaster; and it was probable that the work of the natives would deteriorate if they came under foreign officers whose methods they did not know and whose instructions they could not understand. The French were thus in no way able to replace the British, whose practical experience would also be lost to the force if they were withdrawn. Finally, as regards Captain Fuller, General Dobell pointed out that his unsparing energy, his intimate knowledge of the capabilities of the various craft and of the intricate network of local creeks, and the confidence he inspired in all members of the force and in the native pilots made his services invaluable.

General Dobell's telegram of the 5th November received full and sympathetic consideration at the Admiralty. It was realised that von Spee could not arrive upon the scene before the end of November; and representations to the French authorities resulted in an agreement that the *Pothuau* should, for the time being, do no more than pay a flying visit to the Cameroons. In informing Captain Fuller of this arrangement of the 9th November, the Admiralty informed him that the *Cumberland* would have to be withdrawn before the end of the month.

On the 9th November General Dobell issued his military orders for a combined operation against the enemy in the Cameroon Mountain district. The German strength was reported to number approximately 400, and he hoped to defeat and capture the majority. A demonstration was to be carried out by a naval force near Bibundi to induce any enemy in that vicinity to withdraw eastward or north-eastward; another naval force was to occupy Victoria; an attack was to be made on Buea by two columns of troops, advancing via Tiko and from Susa via Mpundu respectively; and a third column of troops was to advance up the Northern Railway to Muyuka, and from there, besides reinforcing the Mpundu column if necessary, was to move troops to Bombe on the Mungo river so as to intercept any enemy who might try to escape by the Johann Albrechtshöhe road. The demonstration at Bibundi and the attacks on Victoria, Tiko, Mpundu and Muyuka were to take place simultaneously on the 13th November. *The Cameroon Mountain; 9th–17th Nov. 1914.*

At Bibundi on the 13th the *Dwarf* with the transport *Boma*, pretending to put ashore a number of Krooboys, succeeded in making the enemy believe that a considerable force had actually landed. Off Victoria on the same day, the *Ivy*, *Porpoise* and *Vigilant*, with some small vessels and the transport *Niemen* carrying a company of marines, arrived at an early hour, the *Bruix* being also in attendance to cover the landing. The German commander refused a summons to surrender; and then, under cover of a short bombardment, the marines landed well to the west of the town and, after very slight opposition, occupied it at about 11.30 a.m. *13th Nov. 1914.*

For the attack on Tiko, the column, under the personal command of Colonel Gorges, consisted of two naval 12-pounders (Lieut. L. H. K. Hamilton, R.N.), the Nigerian Battery, 1st Nigerians, half the Gold Coast pioneer company and one company 2nd Senegalese. With field cable * and medical detachments, etc., the total personnel numbered 70 Europeans, 1,077 natives, and 1,015 carriers, i.e., the maximum force that could advantageously move along one track. It left Duala early on

---
* Among the signallers were men of the West India Regiment from Sierra Leone, who had joined the force on the 26th October.

the 12th November in four small steamers towing lighters, accompanied by the *Remus*, *Sir Frederick* with the *Dreadnought* and two despatch vessels, the whole flotilla being under the command of Captain Beaty-Pownall. Anchoring for the night in the Bimbia river, the flotilla arrived off the Tiko island pier at 8 a.m. on the 13th, and landed a covering force. A small body of enemy troops was entrenched at Tiko commanding the 600-feet long bridge connecting the island with the mainland, but, with the aid of the *Dreadnought's* 6-inch gun, the covering force drove them off successfully by 10 a.m. The whole column then disembarked, concentrating by 2.30 p.m. at Tiko, where it bivouacked for the night.

The column to advance via Mpundu was also under Colonel Gorges' orders. It consisted of the Composite Battalion, two guns, half the pioneer company from the Gold Coast, field cable and medical detachments, and 550 carriers, and concentrated under command of Colonel Rose at Mbonjo on the 11th November. Here it was joined next day by a flotilla under Lieutenant-Commander Sneyd—consisting of *Cumberland's* picket boat and steam pinnace, *Sokoto*, three motor launches, a lighter and five surf-boats—which had successfully overcome considerable navigation difficulties in the voyage up the Mungo river. On the 13th the column advanced on Mpundu, troops moving along both banks of the river with the flotilla in between. No opposition was encountered; on approaching Mpundu the enemy was seen evacuating his strong position on the right bank; and his retirement was accelerated by fire at short range from the picket boat, steam pinnace and the troops on the left bank. Having occupied Mpundu by 11.30 a.m., Colonel Rose decided to push on towards Ekona, leaving half a company to guard stores and the flotilla. But some slight opposition he encountered and the intricate nature of the country—covered with cocoa and rubber plantations intersected by light railways and numerous paths—made progress slow, till darkness forced him to bivouac after advancing about three miles. The capture of Mpundu had been most timely, for that day the river began falling so rapidly that Lieutenant-Commander Sneyd was obliged to send the deeper draught vessels some distance downstream.

On the Northern Railway the arrival of one and a half companies West African Regiment, to take over the garrison duties from Bonaberi to Susa, set free the 2nd Nigerians to accompany Colonel Haywood together with a section of the Sierra Leone Battery, and some R.E. and telegraph details;

ADVANCE ON BUEA

and he marched off from Susa on the 12th November. Next day, without opposition, he occupied Muyuka and camped there for the night, incurring two casualties in reconnoitring the enemy's entrenched position about fifteen hundred yards to the north-west. He also succeeded, by tapping the German telephone line, in learning that the enemy intended to hold Muyuka as long as possible, that its garrison consisted of 120 rifles, No. 4 Company, with two machine guns, and that there were reserves of unknown strength at Mbanga and Mundek.

Thus, with the completion of the carefully organised preliminary concentrations and the successful occupation of Victoria, Tiko, Mpundu and Muyuka, the operation had commenced well.

Detaching a right flank guard of a company with two guns to move via Boanda, Colonel Gorges advanced on the 14th November towards Buea by the main road through Dibamba and Molyko. At 9.40 a.m., near Dibamba, his advanced guard encountered hostile scouts and, after reconnaissance, pushed on with vigour and dash supported by the fire of two mountain guns. They proceeded to carry a series of entrenched positions on the lower slopes of the mountain which the enemy, numbering about fifty natives with four Europeans,* made little attempt to hold, inflicting only two casualties on the British. At 3 p.m., when a short distance from Molyko, his men began to show signs of fatigue after their nine hours of ascent against opposition through dense forest, and Colonel Gorges decided to bivouac for the night. His right flank guard, which he then called in, had reached Boanda, also after only slight opposition. 14th Nov. 1914.

In its advance on Ekona, Colonel Rose's column was opposed throughout the 14th by a small enemy party of about thirty native troops with one or two Europeans, which took up a succession of entrenched positions, and the British advance was hampered even more by the intricate network of roads and light railways which intersected the numerous plantations. These, both then and subsequently, served to facilitate the escape of the enemy's small parties. With two casualties, the British reached Ekona, whence Colonel Rose detached a portion of his column to hold Lisoka. Nine German non-combatants surrendered to the British at Ekona.

On the same day Colonel Haywood occupied the hostile position immediately north-west of Muyuka. The Germans

---

* These Europeans were all eventually captured, one of them having been wounded.

had evacuated it during the night—an unexpected movement, as the position was so well sited and entrenched that a stubborn resistance would have made its capture anything but easy.

Capture of Buea; 15th Nov. 1914. Colonel Gorges reached Molyko without opposition on the morning of the 15th November, and learnt there from an officer with a patrol from Colonel Rose's column that he was at Ekona blocking the roads leading northward from Buea. Continuing his march and still unopposed, Colonel Gorges reached Buea at 1.45 p.m. The German District Commissioner handed over the keys of Government House, and with due ceremony the British and French flags were hoisted. The whole place was found to be undamaged and intact—not even the silver, cutlery and linen at Government House having been removed—and there had been no time for the natives to plunder. Colonel Gorges at once took steps to take over the various offices and to safeguard life and property.

The occupation of the Cameroon Mountain. From Ekona that day Colonel Rose sent out patrols in various directions, one of them taking prisoner near Lisoka the local German commandant (Captain Gaisser) and another capturing a German official mail from Yaunde which afforded some useful information. On the 16th November, leaving near Lisoka a detachment of fifty men with a machine gun under Lieutenant J. F. P. Butler to try to capture some enemy parties reported to be sheltering in the neighbouring forest, Colonel Rose's column marched into Buea.

An episode in the Lisoka area next day deserves special mention. Lieutenant Butler, with Dr. D'Amico and a party of thirteen soldiers, surprised the rear guard of a German detachment, some fifty strong with a machine gun, and caused it to retreat precipitately, abandoning stores and ammunition. Following the enemy up so rapidly that about half his party had dropped behind, Lieutenant Butler suddenly came under machine gun fire at about thirty yards range and found that the Germans had rallied But Lieutenant Butler was not to be deterred, and he and Dr. D'Amico,* taking cover on either side of the path, before long caused the enemy, with the loss of three Europeans killed, to retire once more by shouting out orders to imaginary companies to fix bayonets and charge.†

Colonel Haywood, after reconnoitring to the northward and westward of Muyuka on the 15th and 16th November,

---

* Dr. D'Amico, for his temporary rôle as a combatant on this occasion, had previously taken off his red-cross armlet.

† For his conduct on this, and on a subsequent occasion, Lieutenant Butler was awarded the Victoria Cross.

advanced westward on the 17th with two companies and a gun, and occupied Bombe on the Mungo river on the 18th after a skirmish with a small enemy party.

For the next few days parties from here and from Buea searched the intervening country and brought the total number of enemy troops captured, killed and wounded to 56, including 16 Europeans. The enemy's success in avoiding greater losses with a minimum of resistance had been mainly due to his intimate knowledge of the difficult country and its intricate network of paths.

At Buea itself, over 170 Germans, including 68 women and children, had been captured or taken charge of, and by the 26th November all had been transferred to Duala. This brought the total number of Germans who had fallen into our hands in the Cameroons up to about 1,200. Many of them were members of religious bodies or women and children; and the deportation of these non-combatants to England or to British and French colonies evoked strong German protests. But as it was impossible to feed them or to assure their safety locally General Dobell had really no option in the matter.

In view of German allegations of harsh treatment, it is interesting to note that Sir Frederick Lugard, who paid a flying visit with General Dobell to Buea on the 27th November, reported to the Colonial Office how some of the German ladies from there had expressed to him, in the very strongest terms, their gratitude for the treatment they had received.

Signal communication from Buea was quickly opened up. By the 16th November communication by telephone with Victoria and by runner with the *Remus's* wireless at Tiko was established, and by the 19th communication by telephone had also been established with Muyuka via Mpundu and Susa and thence with Duala.

Traffic on the light railway was also soon restored, the first train to Victoria leaving Zopo on the 18th. This well-laid line, ascending from sea level to an altitude of nearly 3,000 feet at Zopo and traversing the whole plantation area, was intact, and most of the rolling stock was undamaged.

A Nigerian political officer, Mr. St. C. E. Stobart, was placed in executive charge of the district, full control being taken of the plantations.

Their short residence at Buea was a welcome incident for the force; the Europeans, especially, appreciating the coolness and fresh food, including good meat, milk, butter * and European

---

* There was a German dairy with imported Prussian cattle.

vegetables and fruit. The district had been little affected by the war, as the Germans had treated the natives with much greater consideration than round Duala and Yabasi, where burnt villages and evidence of natives shot or hanged had revealed the very harsh nature of the German repressive or retaliatory measures.

<small>Edea and Dibombe; 1st–17th Nov. 1914.</small> While the Buea operations were in progress, little of importance occurred in the Edea and Yabasi directions. To reconnoitre hostile concentration points in the vicinity, Colonel Mayer sent out several strong detachments, and these inflicted some loss on the enemy at but little cost to themselves, while at Dibombe the post had not been molested.

<small>Question of the local naval command.</small> On the 14th November the *Pothuau* arrived at Duala for Captain Cheron to confer, before proceeding to visit Libreville, with Captain Fuller, with a view to taking over from him about the end of the month. But, after discussion with General Dobell and Captain Fuller, Captain Cheron reported to the French Admiralty that the principal naval task was to control a flotilla, whose personnel and material the *Pothuau* could only inadequately replace; and he suggested that the *Cumberland* should remain, with Captain Fuller on shore to control the flotilla, while he himself in the *Pothuau* took charge of the naval forces on the high sea. In London and Paris the retention of Captain Fuller as Senior Naval Officer at Duala was agreed to. But the British Admiralty required the *Cumberland* and she sailed for England on the 4th December, Captain Fuller then exchanging commands with Captain Beaty-Pownall of the *Challenger*, which remained and took on her books the personnel and guns of the *Cumberland* serving in the light craft.

<small>Franco-Belgian operations in south and south-east; 1st–16th Nov. 1914.</small> In the south and south-east of the Cameroons, the French, during the first half of November, made practically no attempt to advance. In Gabon, the Oyem column at Midsik was being reinforced by an infantry company, a draft of 280 recruits and a section of Nordenfeldt guns borrowed from Belgian Congo but manned by French troops. The Lobaye column had to reorganise its supply and transport arrangements, and French efforts on the Upper Sanga generally were directed to consolidating the positions gained by this and the Sanga column. To deal with the threat constituted by the German force at Molundu, which had two steamers on the Ja river, and also to prevent the diversion of men from there to oppose General

[*To face p.* 188

CAMEL TRANSPORT

WATERING MOUNTED INFANTRY PONIES

In the dry season in the North

MORA MOUNTAIN ATTACKED

Dobell, General Aymerich had decided on an offensive against Molundu.

To turn to events in the Northern Cameroons and on the Nigerian frontier.

At Mora, Colonel Brisset decided to make another attempt to capture Dabaskum on the night of the 7th/8th November. But, learning on the 2nd that a German force from Garua was moving towards Mora, he ordered the attack to be made on the night of the 4th/5th. It was carried out by the French company under Captain Thibault from Wacheke, while the Nigerian company to the westward of the mountain and the French company to the southward remained in observation. To free the whole of Captain Thibault's company, about 120 rifles strong, for the assault, two sections of the French company at Sava were sent to hold Wacheke.

The Northern Cameroons and the Nigerian frontier: Attack on Mora; 4th–5th Nov. 1914.

The advance from here commenced at 7 p.m. on the 4th November, three sections in the firing line and one in support. Two of the leading sections were directed against the east of the post and the other was to attack its northern side. The French were very short of gun ammunition, and about 8.30 p.m. their mountain gun at Wacheke fired four shells at Dabaskum, and after that, during the next hour or two, another seven or eight shells in the direction of the main German position.* In the meantime, under the light cast by signal cartridges fired from enemy pistols, those troops of the leading sections who had not missed their way among the boulders and precipitous ground had lost heavily; and small numbers of them, approaching their objective, had made gallant but unsuccessful attempts to assault the eastern and north-eastern sides of the post. About 10.30 p.m. the reserve section, led by Captain Thibault—supporting the section attacking from the north, which had lost its direction—found itself alone at the foot of the rock on which the enemy post was situated. From here with about twenty of his men Captain Thibault made a successful assault, making good his hold after some hand-to-hand fighting. He failed completely, however, to gain news of, or touch with, the rest of his company, while the position he occupied was completely dominated by two commanding points within two hundred yards to the southward which he did not feel himself strong enough to capture and hold. He

---

* This was about midway between Dabaskum and Molugve.

consequently decided between 3 and 4 a.m. that he must retire, and this he did, his company dribbling back to Wacheke in parties, having incurred a total of 37 casualties. It is noteworthy that Raben's account shows that the German hold of Dabaskum had, by midnight, become so precarious that a very slight further French effort would probably have assured success. Both the German non-commissioned officers in the post had been killed and, with the exception of a handful of native soldiers who clung to one of the commanding points mentioned above, the remainder of the troops had retired. The French troops, says Raben, displayed great gallantry.

After this failure, Colonel Brisset's efforts were directed mainly to tightening the blockade of Mora mountain, and to preventing communication between the Germans there and those to the south. On the night of the 13th/14th November, he occupied Gauala ridge with forty French rifles. From this position the Allies were able to harass the German position by day and night, utilising for the purpose the machine gun belonging to Captain Fox's company.

Marua, the Yola Column and Mora; 1st–30th Nov. 1914. A small party of Nigerian mounted infantry were holding Marua; and on the 6th November—in anticipation of endorsement by Colonel Brisset, who was temporarily absent from Sava on reconnaissance—Captain Fox telegraphed to Major Webb-Bowen at Yola urging him to advance at once on Marua with as strong a force as possible.

Major Webb-Bowen had received a telegram on the 1st November from Colonel Cunliffe saying that General Dobell considered the Allied force at Mora ample to deal with the Germans there and, subsequently, to attack Garua in conjunction with the Yola column. Major Webb-Bowen was to pass on to Colonel Brisset all the information he received regarding the enemy. On the 3rd Major Webb-Bowen informed Colonel Cunliffe that the Germans at Garua, reinforced and having evidently completed their defences, were becoming active and had sent a force of about 200 men to Marua, presumably to hinder a southward movement by Colonel Brisset. Major Webb-Bowen considered that his column should move out to prevent hostile raids and to take action to counter the German advance on Marua. Colonel Cunliffe thereupon asked General Dobell if he considered it advisable for Major Webb-Bowen to send half a mounted infantry company, two guns and three infantry companies to intercept the Germans moving to Marua. This would leave half a mounted infantry company and two infantry companies to hold Yola. At the same time

ACTION OF YOLA COLUMN

Colonel Cunliffe sent Major Webb-Bowen instructions to take action to prevent hostile raids, especially against Yola town, Garua, said Colonel Cunliffe, was the main Allied objective in the north, and Colonel Brisset's force should be sufficient to deal with the German detachment moving on Marua. Major Webb-Bowen was to keep in touch with Colonel Brisset, join him when his force moved south and act under his orders. On the 6th November Colonel Cunliffe telegraphed further instructions, just received from General Dobell, saying that Major Webb-Bowen should show activity in the direction of Garua and also—in order to stop raiding, prevent German movements northward and inspire confidence in troops and inhabitants—attack vigorously any hostile parties encountered. An attack on Garua would, however, probably have to be postponed till a junction with Colonel Brisset had been effected. Next day Colonel Cunliffe sent Major Webb-Bowen another telegram pointing out that by these instructions he was given a free hand to advance, using his own discretion.

It was not till the 8th November that the telegram sent on the 6th by Captain Fox reached Major Webb-Bowen, who at once commenced preparations to move northwards. On the 11th, while still engaged in these preparations, he received a message dated the 9th from Colonel Brisset suggesting that the Yola column should advance towards Garua and pin the enemy there by taking up a position in the vicinity, so as to harass him and restrict his liberty of movement, till the Mora force was able to join the Yola column for an attack on Garua.

On the 12th November, leaving two companies to hold Yola, Major Webb-Bowen marched out with one company of mounted infantry, two guns and three infantry companies,* crossed the Benue river and moved northward along the frontier. His intention is shown by telegrams he sent that day to Colonel Brisset and Captain Fox. To Colonel Brisset, in reply to his message of the 9th, Major Webb-Bowen said that he was moving out to operate in the vicinity of the frontier and would make every endeavour to get into communication with Colonel Brisset. To Captain Fox he telegraphed that as the strength of the German garrison at Garua—consisting according to reliable reports of 57 European and 675 native ranks,

---

* " B " Company, M.I., one section 1st Battery, " H " Company, 1st Battalion, " B " Company, 2nd Battalion, and " H " Company, 3rd Battalion. Total strength of column was 45 European and 384 native ranks and 205 followers, with 52 gun and machine gun carriers, 1,300 other carriers, 113 donkeys, and 240 slaughter cattle.

with three or four guns—made a raid on Yola probable, he doubted his ability to reach Marua.*

These telegrams were received by Colonel Brisset and Captain Fox on the 14th November about the same time that information reached them of the forced evacuation, by the Nigerian mounted infantry, of Marua and its occupation by the German 12th Company (Captain von Duhring) with an estimated strength of 175 rifles (about half of them mounted). On the 16th Colonel Brisset sent Captain Rémond's company of Senegalese to join the Nigerian mounted infantry and investigate the Marua situation, at the same time informing Colonel Cunliffe and Major Webb-Bowen of his action and asking that 200 men of the Yola column should be sent to Marua via Mubi and Gauar.

Captain Rémond reached Dukba, sixteen miles south of Sava, on the 16th November and continued his southerly advance next morning with a detachment of Nigerian mounted infantry, under Lieutenant A. R. Peel, moving several miles in advance. Encountering a small German party near Kosseva, Lieutenant Peel attacked impetuously with most unfortunate results. He himself, Lieutenant M. Percival and three natives were killed and three natives wounded; and the remainder of the detachment, seeing both their British officers killed, retreated. On reaching Kosseva Captain Rémond found that the Germans had retired. Next day he was joined at a point three miles north of Marua by Colonel Brisset, who had hurried southward, on hearing of the Kosseva affair, to clear up the situation with Captain Fox's company and part of a Senegalese company.

Colonel Brisset's telegram of the 16th reached Colonel Cunliffe on the 18th, and Major Webb-Bowen—who had halted for reasons mainly connected with his supplies since the 15th—on the 19th November. In reply to Colonel Brisset, Colonel Cunliffe telegraphed that the Yola column had left on the 12th with orders to move in the Garua direction and to act vigorously so as to stop raiding and prevent German movement northwards; and at the same time he instructed Major Webb-Bowen to move with his column on Marua.

Major Webb-Bowen, himself, sending word to Colonel Brisset that he would make every endeavour to join him as rapidly as his supply difficulties permitted, started off for Mubi on the 20th November. By the 30th, however, he had only got as far as Pella and had received no further communica-

---

* The war diary says Mora, but this is obviously a clerical error.

[To face p. 192

CAMP AT SAVA

SITUATION IN THE NORTH

tion from Colonel Brisset. That officer had been for some days in some doubt as to the best course to pursue. Reconnaissance showed that the German post at Marua was a very strong one, and that Duhring was well served and assisted by the local native population. With the idea of attacking the post Colonel Brisset at first sent for a gun from Sava. But his supply of gun ammunition was limited; an attack might take some time; and he finally decided that it would be unwise to be drawn into operations round Marua until he had dealt with Mora. He consequently started back there with his whole force on the 23rd November. On his arrival there on the 24th he found that the Germans from Mora had that day surprised and killed practically the whole of a French detachment of twenty-four rifles (including one French officer) occupying a position near Gagadema village on the eastern slopes of the mountain.

Duhring from Marua followed cautiously northward after Colonel Brisset's force, but was kept at bay by the Allied mounted troops, now strengthened by the recent arrival of a troop of French cavalry. There was some skirmishing for a few days, but, on the 29th November, having apparently failed in his attempts to get into communication with Raben and evidently learning of the movements of Major Webb-Bowen's column, Duhring withdrew again to Marua.

"C" Company, 2nd Nigeria Regiment, sent by Captain Mann to occupy Bakundi, reached there on the 3rd November and at once came into contact with parties of the enemy. On the 16th a patrol of 30 Nigerian rifles under Lieutenant E. E. Loch moved out to eject an enemy party from Gazabu, some twelve miles to the south-east. But the British were repulsed and forced to retreat, having incurred seven casualties, including Mr. H. Q. Glenny (a political officer) mortally wounded. To restore the situation, Captain Mann, whose force had been reduced by a company ordered to Ikom, marched out from Takum with half "D" Company, 3rd Nigerian Regiment, and a gun, and averaging over twenty miles a day reached Bakundi on the 25th November. Next day with the whole force at Bakundi, i.e., one and a half infantry companies, a gun and some police, he advanced on Gazabu to find it evacuated. Continuing his advance he came into contact with the enemy near Karbabi at an early hour on the 29th. For the next five hours his force advanced slowly through dense bush, driving the enemy back till the fort of Karbabi, strongly situated on a high rock, came in view. This he shelled and, having dispersed the enemy

Ibi Column; Nov. 1914

parties in its vicinity, he withdrew again to Gazabu. His total casualties had been only six, and the results he had obtained had been generally satisfactory.

Cross River Column; Nov. 1914. (Map 7, facing page 224.) After the termination of the neutrality of Nsanakang, the German troops in the area, of a total approximate strength of 25 Europeans and 300 natives, showed great activity and carried out several raids across the frontier. In one of these on the 8th November the German 2nd Company captured a British outpost at Danare held by half a company, its native ranks dispersing into the bush and abandoning a machine gun after its commander, a British non-commissioned officer, had been killed; and in another, on the 12th, a British patrol was ambushed near Abunorok, losing half its strength. Within two or three days of this last episode Colonel Mair's column was reinforced by two and a half companies, bringing it up to a strength of five and half companies with three guns, and so better able to watch all approaches.

Internal situation in Nigeria. The internal situation in Nigeria had improved greatly as the result of the action taken in October; and on the 22nd November, accepting an invitation from General Dobell, Sir Frederick Lugard left Lagos and paid a visit to Duala, returning to his headquarters again on the 29th.

CHAPTER VI

NOVEMBER 1914—JANUARY 1915

OCCUPATION OF THE NORTHERN RAILWAY AND DESTRUCTION OF CHANG; GERMAN COUNTER-ATTACKS IN EDEA AREA; AND FRANCO-BELGIAN ADVANCE IN THE SOUTH-EAST

(Maps 2, 4, 7, 8 and 9)

The disinclination to hold their strong positions covering Buea and at Muyuka which the Germans had displayed, the fact that their men were beginning to surrender in small numbers and the dispirited tone of several German letters recently captured, all seemed to show that enemy resistance was beginning to crumble. It was estimated that, including reserve and police companies, there were four German companies at Mora and Garua in the north, one company near the Nigerian frontier in the Karbabi-Banyo-Bamenda sector, two or three companies in the Ossidinge area and four between Bamenda and the Muyuka-Yabasi line; in the Edea-Kribi-Yaunde area there were apparently about six companies; and another seven or eight were facing the Franco-Belgian troops acting under General Aymerich's orders in the south and south-east. The internal situation in Nigeria had improved, and General Dobell hoped shortly to hear that Colonel Brisset had disposed of the German force at Mora, or had arranged to contain it by a detachment, and was well on his way with Major Webb-Bowen's column to capture Garua. If, therefore, General Dobell could strike an effective blow at the enemy force between Bamenda and the Muyuka-Yabasi line, he would not only secure the Northern Railway and relieve pressure on the Nigerian frontier, but would have taken a distinct step forward towards obtaining a final decision in the northern half of the country. On the 22nd November he telegraphed to Colonel Cunliffe that the enemy at Buea and on the Northern Railway had been scattered and demoralised and that a general British advance up the Northern Railway was to commence shortly. With this advance

The general situation after the capture of Buea.

General Dobell suggested that the Ikom and Ibi columns should co-operate by a vigorous advance, the former moving on Ossidinge and Tinto.

Proposal to make the Sanaga river the dividing line for main British and French operations.

The French troops from Equatorial Africa had recovered a great part of the territory ceded to Germany in 1911 and were about to advance on Oyem. If their successful operations continued at anything like the same rate as hitherto, it would not be long before it should be possible to co-ordinate to some extent their movements with those of General Dobell's force. General Dobell accordingly proposed to Colonel Mayer that all operations between the Sanaga river and Nigeria should henceforth be carried out by the British force, leaving all those south of the Sanaga river to the French troops under Colonel Mayer based on Edea and Kribi. They should, suggested General Dobell, first seize Sakbajeme, Sende, Lolo and Ebolowa, then try to establish touch with the French forces from Equatorial Africa, and ultimately carry out a concentric advance on Yaunde.

Colonel Mayer replied that the programme assigned to the French appeared feasible with some modifications. He pointed out that a concentric advance on Yaunde through Edea and Kribi would mean a subdivision of force for which his troops were insufficient, that Ebolowa was too far away in a wrong direction and that it was doubtful if touch could be established with Oyem. He proposed that Commandant Mathieu with two infantry companies, two guns and a section of machine guns should hold Kribi, where they would be supplied by sea and whence they should look after Ebea and finally Lolo, and that all the other French troops should be concentrated under him at Edea for an eventual advance on Yaunde. It would, however, he said, be necessary in the first place to clear the area Edea-Dehane-Kribi of all hostile troops.

Operations in the Edea-Dehane-Kribi area; Nov. 1914.

On the 19th and 20th November a reconnaissance up the Nyong river by naval vessels had verified the presence of German troops at Dehane and Ebea; and the early clearance of this area was also called for by information, recently confirmed, that the enemy was communicating with, and obtaining stores from, Fernando Po via Muni. On the 24th November General Dobell, after consultation with Captain Fuller, issued orders for operations to clear the country about Dehane, Ebea and Longyi as a preliminary to occupying Kribi.* Two

---

* On the same day Captain Fuller recommended to the Admiralty that a naval blockade of the Cameroons coast should be declared; but this step was not as yet approved.

companies of Senegalese with two mountain guns and two machine guns under Commandant Mathieu were to land at daybreak on the 27th at Longyi—covered by the *Surprise*—and from there were to move and attack Ebea in co-operation with an armed flotilla under Commander Braithwaite, carrying the *Cumberland's* and *Challenger's* marines. This flotilla was to be in position off the mouth of the Lokundje river at daybreak on the 27th in readiness to move up that river in close co-operation with Commandant Mathieu's force. Further, a French force from Edea—one and a half companies of Senegalese with two machine guns under Captain Salvetat—was to move against Dehane, reaching there about 9 a.m. on the 28th, when it was to be met by the *Crocodile* with two surf-boats to transport it across the river if necessary. After the completion of these operations, the Longyi column was to occupy Kribi, supported by the *Dwarf* and *Surprise*, and to carry out operations from there to clear the vicinity up to and including Lolo.

On the 25th November a report from Colonel Mayer reached General Dobell to the effect that the Germans were displaying considerable activity in the neighbourhood of Edea. Three separate German attacks on that place had been repulsed on the 23rd with a loss to the enemy of at least a dozen killed. This report caused General Dobell to review the situation afresh. On the 24th, for the advance up the Northern Railway, he had issued orders for a concentration of troops which, after the departure of Commandant Mathieu's column to Longyi, would leave him no disposable reserve at Duala unless, instead of sending it to Edea, he retained at the base the other half of Commandant Mathieu's battalion. This he decided to do, informing Colonel Mayer on the 26th that the latter's movement towards Yaunde would consequently be somewhat delayed.

At daybreak on the 26th November Captain Salvetat's column, when camped about ten miles north of Dehane, was heavily attacked. The action continued till 3 p.m., when the Germans withdrew. Casualties on both sides were heavy, those of the French totalling eight French and forty-two Senegalese Captain Salvetat himself being among the killed. In view of these serious losses, the French officer on whom the command devolved considered it imprudent to continue the advance on Dehane and marched back to Edea.

The *Crocodile*, just entering the Nyong river, was consequently recalled on the morning of the 27th November, and was directed to join Commander Braithwaite's flotilla off the mouth of the Lokundje river, which she reconnoitred during the day, encountering hostile patrols about twelve miles up. Commander Braithwaite, informed by Commandant Mathieu that he would commence his advance on Ebea at daybreak on the 28th, embarked on the 27th all the marines in the small craft, which then proceeded up the river for five miles before anchoring for the night. Next morning, however, Commandant Mathieu decided to postpone his advance till the morning of the 29th to enable him first to carry out a reconnaissance of the Longyi district; and during the 28th Commander Braithwaite with Captain C. L. Hall, the commander of the marines' detachment, took the opportunity to proceed in the *Vigilant* and reconnoitre towards Ebea, where he shelled the enemy look-out station without eliciting a reply.

In the meantime, Commandant Mathieu had reported to General Dobell that, owing to the presence of hostile detachments near Longyi, he would require reinforcements before he could advance on Ebea. Being unable to furnish these, General Dobell directed Commandant Mathieu to march to Kribi and occupy that place. This he did on the 2nd December. On the 1st, Commander Braithwaite's flotilla returned to Duala, his officers and men much disappointed at the abandonment of the attack on Ebea, which they were convinced could have been carried out successfully without any reinforcement. On this opinion it is of course impossible to pass judgment, though it is noteworthy that it was subsequently learnt that the German 1st Reserve Company had recently arrived in the Dehane-Ebea area from Oyem. Whether it was owing to this or to the encouragement which the abandonment of this attempt to clear the Dehane-Ebea area gave the Germans is uncertain, but for some time afterwards their activity increased greatly in this quarter.*

Operations up the Northern Railway; Dec. 1914. (Map 8.) For the advance up the Northern Railway, the striking force—composed of a naval 12-pounder from the *Challenger*, two machine guns manned by seamen, the Nigerian Battery, section Gold Coast Battery, Field Section, R.E., 1st and 2nd Nigerians and half the Gold Coast pioneer company—concentrated under the command of Colonel Gorges at Muyuka on the 2nd December; the 1st Nigerians arriving from Buea after a trying and difficult march over the densely covered foothills. The administrative details included two and a half field ambulance sections and railway and telegraph detach-

---

* Subsequent events tend to show that the Germans sent forces into this area to cover their communications with Spanish Muni.

PLAN TO CLEAR NORTHERN RAILWAY   199

ments; and, for duty on the line of communication from Bonaberi inclusive, two companies Composite Battalion, one company West African Regiment and one gun of the Sierra Leone Battery had been placed at Colonel Gorges' disposal. The train service between Bonaberi and Muyuka was still restricted by there being only one engine available, and that a shunting engine. On the 4th December, however, another engine arrived from French Guinea and was at once put in service.

To cover the right flank of Colonel Gorges' striking force against a possible attack from the south-eastward, a force of seventy-five rifles West African Regiment under Captain W. S. Browne and two armed motor launches under Lieutenant R. D. B. Haddon, R.N., was sent from Dibombe Post to occupy Nyanga and patrol up the Dibombe river from there. A German detachment with a motor launch had, on the 23rd November, been driven out of Nyanga by a skilful raid carried out by Major J. P. Law with a company of the West African Regiment with the assistance of Lieutenant Haddon's launches. But the enemy had since re-occupied both Nyanga and Yabasi.

General Dobell's instructions to Colonel Gorges were that the general direction of his advance was to be along the railway, that he was to march with all possible speed to railhead, attacking the enemy wherever found, and that he was to try to gain communication with Colonel Mair, commanding the Ikom column, who had been instructed to advance on Tinto.* Supplies up to the 12th December had been collected at Muyuka, but, as it would be necessary to cut down the number of carriers to the minimum, General Dobell left Colonel Gorges discretion to decide the amount of supplies and ammunition he would carry with him. Colonel Gorges was given a summary of available information regarding the enemy, and Captain H. G. Howell of the General Staff, who dealt with Intelligence at Force Headquarters, was attached to Colonel Gorges' staff. Little definite, however, was known of the enemy's numbers and dispositions, though it was understood that he meant to retire to Lum before offering much opposition and also that he intended to blow up the bridge which spanned the Dibombe river near Nlohe.

Colonel Gorges decided to advance at first with the bulk of his column along the railway, while to cover his left flank two

---

* General Dobell realised, and informed Colonel Cunliffe, that co-operation between the Northern Railway column and the Ikom column would be impossible, owing to the intervening distance and difficult country.

small detachments advanced up either bank of the Mungo river,* where small enemy parties had been located.

3rd–4th Dec. 1914. The advance started on the 3rd December, the main column reaching Mundek that day without opposition. On the Mungo river patrols exchanged a few shots with enemy scouts. On the Dibombe river Captain Browne's detachment, transported as far as the low state of the river allowed in the naval launches, surprised and drove out of Nyanga an enemy force of about fifty rifles. Continuing on the 4th, Colonel Gorges' column, faced by a few enemy scouts, camped at Penja station; and the Mungo river detachments also advanced without special incident. From Nyanga a patrolling detachment moved up the Dibombe river.

5th Dec. 1914. To try to take by surprise a small enemy detachment and an armoured train reported to be at Lum station, one company 1st Nigerians was sent off at 12.15 a.m. on the 5th December to move round by a path east of the railway. After five hours' march through dense bush this company surprised and dispersed the enemy detachment at a cost of two casualties, but was unable to intercept the armoured train. At 10.30 a.m., Colonel Gorges' main column reached Lum and bivouacked; and at midday a company of the 1st Nigerians under Captain J. W. Chamley, accompanied by a party of R.E. under Lieutenant H. H. Schneider, was sent forward to reconnoitre the bridge and Dibombe river crossing at Nlohe. The bridge was found to be destroyed and the swift flowing river appeared to be unfordable.† In the course of his reconnaissance, Captain Chamley's party fell into an ambush, the enemy with machine guns having occupied skilfully selected positions, for the most part on the further bank of the river. With the loss of two killed, including Lieutenant Schneider, and nine wounded, including Lieutenant C. Luxford, Captain Chamley succeeded by good leadership in extricating his men. The enemy did not press the pursuit and, after retiring for about a mile, Captain Chamley sent back for reinforcements, which shortly reached him in the shape of a second company of the 1st Nigerians. Both companies then took up a position for the night. On the Mungo river that day only slight opposition was encountered and the British detachments there bivouacked

---

* On the west bank, one company 2nd Nigerians, one section Gold Coast Pioneers and a Gold Coast gun, under Captain C. Gibb; on the east bank, one company 2nd Nigerians and one section Gold Coast Pioneers, under Lieutenant R. H. Poyntz.

† Fords were subsequently found about three feet deep.

[*To face p.* 200

Nlohe Bridge, as left by the Enemy

Nlohe Bridge, after Repair

ADVANCE UP NORTHERN RAILWAY

that night north of Etam and at Nsuke, on the west and east banks respectively. The party from Nyanga moved up to Nsake.

On the morning of the 6th December no enemy was encountered; Colonel Gorges occupied Nlohe; and a covering detachment gained the northern bank of the Dibombe river without opposition. A native "tie-tie"* suspension bridge was found intact a short way upstream, and during the day another footbridge, to carry both troops and guns, was constructed by the engineers and pioneers. The permanent bridge— an iron girder structure, 226 feet long, in three spans—had been badly damaged,† stopping railway traffic beyond Nlohe and restricting onward transport to the carriers. On the Mungo river, the east bank detachment reached Ngushi that evening, while the detachment on the west bank, after driving before it small parties of the enemy, began to cross the river to make for Ngushi. But the swift current and the absence of canoes made the passage difficult and it was not till the evening of the 7th that the two detachments united at Ngushi under Captain C. Gibb.

6th Dec. 1914.

Taking from 6 a.m. to 8.30 a.m. on the 7th December to cross the Dibombe river, and after a slow and trying march under a very hot sun, in face of incessant enemy sniping, Colonel Gorges' column reached Manengoteng at 3.15 p.m. and bivouacked for the night. On the right flank the party from Nyanga reached the junction of the Dibombe and Tinga rivers. During the ensuing night the Germans sent down the railway line a truck of dynamite timed to explode on reaching the British bivouac. But it was derailed, and exploded, at a point above, where the British had taken the precaution of removing some rails. A German patrol on a railway trolley was also dispersed, a German and a native soldier being taken prisoner. That day Colonel Gorges issued orders for his advanced base to be moved forward from Muyuka to Nlohe.

7th Dec. 1914.

On the 8th December Colonel Gorges' main column marched to Manengole, encountering some slight opposition. Before leaving camp three Germans came in and surrendered; during the day some railway rolling stock was found at sidings; and the retiring Germans left nearly all telephone instruments and installations intact. It thus looked as if the enemy,

8th Dec. 1914.

---

* The native bridges are made from long lengths of stout creepers known generally by this name.
† Its repair, commenced on the 16th December, was completed in eighteen days—a noteworthy piece of work.

whose force retiring northward in front of the two British columns was estimated at a total of about 30 to 40 Europeans and 150 to 200 natives, was becoming demoralised. Captain Gibb's detachment started eastward that day from Ngushi and moved over the foothills of the Kupe mountain to within four miles of the railway, while on the right flank the detachment on the Dibombe river remained halted, having completed its task.

9th Dec. 1914. On the 9th the main column, advancing through hilly and difficult country, which made progress slow, occupied Ndunge after brushing aside some slight opposition near that place at the cost of two casualties, including Lieutenant L. C. Paterson wounded. Some more rolling stock was found *en route*, and the German members of a mission station were placed on parole pending deportation. While the camp was being entrenched the enemy opened fire from the surrounding hills, but was soon driven out of his positions by gun fire, including that of the naval gun, which came into action for the first time. Captain Gibb, whose column, after a difficult march, camped about four miles to the north-west of Ndunge, received orders that night from Colonel Gorges to co-operate, as closely as the difficult country permitted, with the main column next day, and endeavour to strike the enemy in flank or rear if he took up a position covering Nkongsamba.

10th Dec. 1914. Occupation of Nkongsamba. On the 10th December the advance of the main column met at first with some slight opposition. But about 10.30 a.m. a German officer came forward under a white flag with a message from Lieutenant von Engelbrechten, the German commander in this area, surrendering Nkongsamba and the country up to and including Bare. Colonel Gorges then occupied Nkongsamba, where he was joined by Captain Gibb's column. Five damaged locomotives, a quantity of rolling stock and many stores of all kinds were captured here, while twenty-three Germans (including one woman) fell into our hands. The locomotives, it may be noted, were soon repaired, and on the 3rd January, after the Nlohe bridge had been re-opened, a through railway service was established between Bonaberi and Nkongsamba.

The country-side had changed completely a few miles short of railhead, and the force experienced great relief at leaving behind it the interminable and insect-infested forest with its gloomy and stifling atmosphere. Nkongsamba, lying a few hundred feet above sea level, is within two days' march of the central plateau and, although it is somewhat overshadowed by neighbouring heights, is in comparatively open country and generally enjoys a cool breeze from the hills. These rise steeply to the plateau, with their summits often wrapped in mist and their thickly timbered slopes intersected by waterfalls and many swiftly flowing streams. To a stubborn defence they certainly offered many points of vantage; and coming operations held out probabilities of much arduous piquetting and climbing. But, as the horizon would no longer be limited and the climate would be drier and cooler, such warfare would be far preferable to that of the past few weeks.

The country round, moreover, was fairly well populated and cultivated, and fresh supplies were obtainable. The European station of Nkongsamba had a good water supply, and the good road running northward from it to Bare and Chang was well drained, being about fifteen feet wide, with a good surface and bridges over the numerous streams.

Taking with him one section Nigerian Battery, a party of R.E. and the 2nd Nigerians under Colonel Haywood, Colonel Gorges occupied Bare on the 11th December, about forty more Germans, including some women and children, falling into our hands there. Many stores and two aeroplanes in packing cases —the first to reach West Africa—were also captured.

Occupation of Bare; 11th Dec. 1914.

Bare, which was the headquarters of a German district, had a Government House and other good buildings, and supplies and water were good and plentiful. The station stood on a rise, the surrounding country being mostly palm bush, but more open to the north and west.

Owing to the slight opposition offered by the enemy the total British casualties in the operations which concluded with the capture of Bare had been under twenty. But, although there had been little fighting, the nine days' advance had entailed much hard and exhausting work, not to mention the constant nervous strain inseparable from the " blind " operations which the forest entailed. In congratulating Colonel Gorges and his force on their success General Dobell expressed his appreciation of the way in which the advance had been carried through.

On the 11th December a telegram from General Dobell reached Colonel Gorges instructing him, when he was in a position to do so, to pursue the enemy northward with the utmost vigour. Colonel Mair, he was told, had been informed of these instructions. Next day Captain Browne's detachment was withdrawn from its isolated position on the Dibombe river—where it was almost impossible to keep it supplied—to Dibombe post.

Preparations for a further advance northward; 12th–24th Dec. 1914. Before the further advance could commence it would be necessary for Colonel Gorges to collect supplies, a slow business owing to the break in the railway at Nlohe. In the meantime, he occupied Melong, a road junction fourteen miles north of Nkongsamba, established supply depots there and at Bare, and constructed defensive posts at these two places and at Nkongsamba. Reconnaissances northward were also carried out.

The attitude of the local natives, who were of a much more virile type than those of the forest and coastal regions, proved to be friendly, and many presents of food were brought in by chiefs from the surrounding country.

General Dobell, who had previously impressed on Colonel Gorges the desirability of moving northward as quickly as was prudent, gave his reasons in a letter written on the 15th December. The chief reason was that the troops with Colonel Gorges might be required elsewhere at any time, though General Dobell hoped that the necessity would not arise. He explained that the situation at and round Kribi was unsatisfactory and that he had not a man to spare from Duala, while the French at Edea were immobilised owing to the sickness of practically all their French ranks. General Dobell then went on to say that he realised that Colonel Gorges would experience difficulty in collecting supplies, but must remember that every day's delay would give the enemy confidence and time to concentrate troops and prepare defences. In the advance to Chang, General Dobell did not consider that Colonel Mair would be able to co-operate, though, till it was seen what action the enemy took in the Ossidinge area, it was difficult to forecast what the Cross river column might be able to do. Having regard to food difficulties, the men required for line of communication duties, wastage from sickness, etc., it seemed unlikely to General Dobell that Colonel Gorges would be able to get beyond Chang; and while General Dobell regretted that he had not another two companies available to send for line of communication duties, it seemed to him doubtful if it would be possible to feed any larger force than Colonel Gorges already had with him.

On the 21st December, a party of the 1st Nigerians under Major R. G. Coles, sent to clear the right front for Colonel Gorges' coming advance, dispersed, at the cost of two casualties, a small hostile force which was holding the point where the Bare-Bana road crossed the Nkam river.

On the 24th December Colonel Gorges concentrated his

[*To face p.* 204

NEAR NLOHE

NLOHE STATION

column (including 1,400 carriers) at Melong, in readiness to commence the advance northward next day. The units of General Dobell's force had received no reinforcing drafts since their arrival in the country, and the wastage from casualties and sickness was mounting up. For instance, the strength of the 1st Nigerians at Melong was down to 450, and that of the 2nd Nigerians still lower, being only 330.

Before describing the further advance of Colonel Gorges' column, it is advisable to turn to the situation elsewhere, as this had a definite effect on the extent of the advance northward.

With the departure from Duala of the *Cumberland* on the 4th December under the command of Captain Beaty-Pownall, the force lost the services of many officers and men whose fine and gallant work had contributed much to the successes of the previous three months. The *Challenger* and *Dwarf* remained, and with them Captain Fuller, as well as a party of the *Cumberland's* officers and men for duty with the Nigeria Marine contingent in the several small vessels operating in the various waterways.* As most of their channels were now steadily falling in depth with the cessation or diminution of the rains, the work of these craft increased in difficulty. On the Wuri river the armed launches co-operating with the Dibombe post found the enemy still in occupation of Yabasi on the 8th December; but, four days later, the continued fall in the river necessitated the withdrawal of all these launches to a point five miles below Dibombe post. The only vessel that could remain there was a flat-bottomed steel canoe obtained from Nigeria, which mounted a 3-pounder gun. Patrol work still continued, though with difficulty, on the Dibamba river, the Kwa-kwa creek, the Sanaga river and in other waterways connected with the Cameroon estuary, while south of there coastal patrol work was mainly carried out by the larger vessels, both British and French.

<small>Naval operations; Dec. 1914.</small>

Information acquired from native sources during November indicated that the German detachments in the Edea and Kribi neighbourhoods had received strong reinforcements, most of them apparently from Yaunde, where the Germans were said to be recruiting and training a considerable number of natives. Many of these the Germans had armed with spears,

<small>Kribi-Edea area; Nov.-Dec. 1914.</small>

---

* The French cruiser *Pothuau* and gunboat *Surprise* did not at that time furnish any personnel or armament for these craft.

swords, and bows and arrows and had sent them out to the area round Edea and on the coast south of the Nyong river to carry out punitive measures against villages suspected of sympathising with and assisting the Allies. As these levies had apparently been given a free hand, this action resulted in many villages being pillaged and burnt and their inhabitants outraged or murdered; with the consequence that many of them fled to the Allies for refuge, while the others became too terror-stricken to give the Allies any sort of information or assistance.

This was first noticeable round Kribi, where Commandant Mathieu, with half his Senegalese battalion and two mountain guns, was inactive, expressing his inability, unless he received reinforcements, to undertake the active operations which General Dobell desired. Such reinforcements General Dobell was in no position to send.

On the 5th December the *Ivy* relieved the *Surprise* as guardship at Kribi, which was attacked by a German party next morning. It was only a weak attack, however, and was easily repulsed. There was another and a more serious attack on the morning of the 9th, but this also was repulsed without very much difficulty with the assistance of the *Ivy's* guns, the Senegalese garrison suffering only half a dozen casualties. After this attack, in response to a further request from Commandant Mathieu for reinforcements, the *Pothuau* sent fifty-six of her marines as well as two field guns and two machine guns with crews, who landed at Kribi and joined the garrison on the 11th and 12th December. The local defences were further strengthened and a larger field of fire cleared, the *Ivy's* crew assisting in the work.

The French force at Edea and in posts along the railway back to Duala consisted of their European detachment, a Senegalese battalion, and four mountain guns. By the beginning of December enemy activity was on the increase, but the natives round Edea were so afraid of German retaliatory measures that they dared not give the French any notice of enemy movements; and Colonel Mayer, who had given up his policy of strong reconnoitring patrols as producing insufficient results, found a system of ambuscades equally ineffective owing to lack of information. The German activity and the retention at Duala of half Commandant Mathieu's battalion led Colonel Mayer to reorganise his defences. The strong system of entrenchments round Edea which he constructed and the clearance in the surrounding forest of a good field of fire proved, however, such arduous work that it affected the health of his European personnel, whose strength generally was already below normal from a prolonged residence in Africa. Moreover, with the cessation of the rains Edea had become most unhealthy. The many streams running between the small knolls on which the station was built had become semi-stagnant and marshlike, forming many breeding places for mosquitoes, while with little or no breeze reaching it through the forest the area had a distinctly higher temperature and a more oppressive atmosphere than Duala. In consequence Colonel Mayer's force had become immobilised by the sickness of his French ranks.

In the third week of December a massacre of villagers by German native levies caused a sudden influx into the French position at Edea of some 2,000 refugees from the surrounding villages. At first they were settled in the town, but their insanitary habits seemed likely to affect the health of the troops, and they were soon transferred to an island in, and a camp on the other side of, the river.

By a fine piece of work on the part of the French engineer and railway detachments, the Yapoma bridge over the Dibamba river was repaired and through railway communication—from Duala to the Sanaga river bank opposite Edea—restored by the 18th December. At Edea itself, still only foot passengers could cross the Sanaga river.

Learning of the strength of the German position at Mora, General Dobell, as far back as the 30th October, had telegraphed to General Largeau at Fort Lamy suggesting that Mora should be contained by a detachment, while Colonel Brisset with the bulk of his force and the column from Yola marched against Garua. As already shown, however, Colonel Brisset maintained hopes throughout November of capturing Raben's company. At the beginning of December, after the withdrawal of the German 12th Company to Marua, Colonel Brisset again considered the question of attacking Mora mountain, but, finding no means that appealed to him, finally abandoned the idea and decided to conform with the wishes of Generals Dobell and Largeau. *Northern Cameroons; Dec. 1914.*

The attempts to bring about co-operation between Colonel Brisset's force and the Yola column had all hitherto failed, mainly owing to the difficulty of inter-communication. This difficulty still existed. A message sent on the 22nd November by Colonel Brisset from near Marua—informing Major Webb-Bowen that, as his co-operation against Marua would be useless, he should operate round Garua with a view to preventing further German detachment to Marua—was never received at all by Major Webb-Bowen; and a second message sent from Sava on the 29th November, repeating the instructions of the 22nd and saying that the Yola column should immobilise the German garrison at Garua by operating round there without actually attacking the German position, only reached Major Webb-Bowen on the 5th December. The latter, faced by considerable supply and transport difficulties in his march northward along the frontier, had reached Pella, about thirty miles south-west of Mubi, on the 1st December, having received no message from Colonel Brisset since the 19th November. On the 30th November, however, news reached him from Maiduguri that Marua was in enemy, and not Allied, possession and that Colonel Brisset's force had returned to Mora to reduce its German garrison. On the 1st December, therefore, Major Webb-Bowen sent off a message to Colonel Brisset saying that he would advance northwards along the frontier with a view to moving, if necessary, on Marua via Gauar and asking for further instructions. This message was not received by Colonel Brisset till the 6th December.

In the meantime, on the 3rd December Major Webb-Bowen had reached Uba, where, as it was a convenient point from which to advance either on Marua or Mora, he halted and sent word, of his intention to await there further instructions, to Colonel Brisset. On the 5th, however, receiving Colonel Brisset's instructions of the 29th November, he started to move southward towards Garua. The report he sent off that day of his action does not appear to have reached Colonel Brisset till the 17th December.

Moving southward through German territory, Major Webb-Bowen reached Demsa on the 9th December and halted to reconnoitre. On that day Colonel Brisset, finally deciding to march on Garua with the bulk of his force, sent off a company of Senegalese infantry under Captain Simonet to join Major Webb-Bowen near Gauar and to give him instructions, not knowing that he had already started southward. On the 11th December Colonel Brisset was reinforced by a squadron of French native cavalry, which he sent on the 13th to occupy Marua, recently evacuated by the Germans, probably owing to Major Webb-Bowen's southerly movement. On the 17th Colonel Brisset marched off southwards, leaving Captain

THE CROSS RIVER COLUMN

Rémond's Senegalese company and Captain Fox's Nigerian detachment to contain Mora. Colonel Brisset reached Marua on the 19th December and, continuing his advance towards Garua two days later, was rejoined by Captain Simonet's company on the 22nd. The strength of his force then totalled 34 French and 478 native soldiers.

By the 12th December Major Webb-Bowen had arrived at a point about fourteen miles north of Garua.

At Ikom, on receiving a repetition of General Dobell's telegram of the 22nd November to Colonel Cunliffe, Colonel Mair at once commenced preparations for an advance. But it took a little time to obtain the necessary carriers and to organise the supply arrangements. On the 30th November General Dobell sent Colonel Cunliffe a second telegram saying that, as it would be impossible to count on co-operation between the force advancing up the Cameroons Northern Railway and the Cross river column, Colonel Mair's action must be independent and he should not undertake more than he felt he was strong enough to carry out.* On the 2nd December Colonel Mair learnt from an intercepted message that the German commander at Ossidinge had received instructions to evacuate that place if the British combined an advance up the Northern Railway with one from Nigeria on Ossidinge.

It had at first been Colonel Mair's intention to make a wide flanking movement to the north in his advance on Ossidinge. But, after further reconnaissance, he decided instead to advance by a route well to the south of the Cross river with four companies and four guns, leaving two companies to cover the frontier and Ikom.†

There was considerable outpost and patrol activity, with several minor encounters along the frontier about Obokum, during the first ten days of December. On the 7th, Major J. Fane marched off southward via Nsarum with an advanced detachment of "F" Company, 3rd Battalion, and "B" Company, 4th Battalion, and, crossing the frontier on the 10th, occupied Otu after surprising and dispersing an enemy piquet. Next morning, while half of Major Fane's detachment was

The Cross River Column; Nov.–Dec. 1914. (Map 7, facing page 224.)

---

* On receiving this telegram Colonel Mair was in some doubt as to what he was intended to do, and there was a further exchange of telegrams before it was made clear to him that his objectives were to be Ossidinge and Tinto if possible.

† The striking column comprised, "C," "E" and "F," Companies, 3/Nigerian Regiment, "B" Company 4/Nigerian Regiment, and the 2nd Battery, while "A" and "B" Companies, 3/Nigerian Regiment, held the line about Obokum.

out on topographical reconnaissances, the camp at Otu was heavily but unsuccessfully attacked by a hostile force of some strength. The enemy left eight dead behind him, and his other losses were believed to have been heavy. Finding no good road beyond Otu, however, Major Fane recrossed the frontier on the 13th December and next day selected some high ground near Nkami as suitable for the formation of an advanced base. Here the whole column was concentrated in the next few days, while Major Fane carried out reconnaissances eastward across the frontier, Colonel Mair himself arriving on the 19th. A further halt to organise the supply and transport arrangements was, however, necessitated by the bad road over difficult country between Nsarum and Nkami, and it was not till the 22nd December that Colonel Mair was able to commence his advance eastward. He then took with him three companies with six machine guns, his men carrying two days' rations on the person. A further three days' supply was transported by carriers. Major Fane, with the battery and one company, was to follow not later than the 28th, escorting a carrier column with seven days' supply of grain.

The Ibi Column; Nov. 1914. It was during his movement to Bakundi, which has been described in the preceding chapter, that Captain Mann received his copy of General Dobell's telegram of the 22nd November; and his subsequent successful dispersal of the enemy round Karbabi has already been related.

Franco-Belgian operations in the south and south-east; Nov.-Dec. 1914. The French force from Gabon under Major Miquelard had established itself strongly during November in a position on the southern Cameroons frontier north-east of Midsik. The Germans about Oyem were holding the line of the Wola river, and throughout December Major Miquelard's force remained in its position awaiting reinforcements before assuming the offensive. At the end of the month Major Miquelard received information that the Germans were moving stores northward from Oyem.

In the middle of November the authorities in Gabon decided to reinforce their company at Mvahdi to enable it, first to assume the offensive against Minkebe and then to co-operate either with the Oyem or the Sanga column as circumstances dictated. These reinforcements, however, could not concentrate at Mvahdi till the end of February. While awaiting them, the company at Mvahdi was generally inactive till the end of December, though on the 24th of that month one of its detachments occupied Minkebe and reconnoitred towards Akoafim, ascertaining the presence there in a strong position of an enemy force about 140 strong with three machine guns.

To the north-eastward of Mvahdi, General Aymerich had, as previously mentioned, decided on an offensive against Molundu; and, on the 17th November, in furtherance of this plan, he issued instructions for the Lobaye column to seize Yukaduma. To attack Molundu, the Sanga column under Lieutenant-Colonel Hutin—composed of two French companies, a Belgian company with two Nordenfeldt guns and the armed Belgian steamer *Luxembourg*, with a total combatant strength of 62 Europeans and 515 natives—started from Wesso up the Ja river on the 24th November. Arriving before Molundu on the 29th, Colonel Hutin made a detailed and careful reconnaissance of the strong position confronting him. On the 1st December reinforcements reached him bringing his total strength up to 71 Europeans and 659 natives; and on the early morning of the 4th he started to put into execution a carefully prepared enveloping attack. At the same time the enemy launched a counter-attack and, driving back a portion of the Franco-Belgian force, threatened the security of their river transport. This forced Colonel Hutin to withdraw his whole column down the Ja river, pursued by the Germans as far as Ngoko, where some heavy fighting occurred which obliged the Germans to retreat. Shortly afterwards a reinforcement of 225 Belgian native troops reached Ngoko and enabled Colonel Hutin to advance again on the 17th December, with the result that, after two days' fighting, the Germans evacuated Molundu.

The Lobaye column, under Lieutenant-Colonel Morisson, after its recent rapid advance, was obliged to halt during November to reorganise its supply and transport arrangements. At the end of the month 457 of its rifles with three mountain guns were at Gaza and Naho, with another 210 rifles about Binge, while in front of them, about sixty miles south-westward of Gaza, the German 5th and 6th Companies were holding a position covering Baturi. General Aymerich's instructions to seize Yukaduma had not yet reached Colonel Morisson. But, understanding that his main object was to hold and occupy the enemy troops in front of him, he decided to undertake an offensive against Baturi, advancing on three converging lines from Binge, Gaza, and Naho. With a total strength in his three columns of 610 rifles and three guns, his advance commenced on the 3rd December. Some opposition was encountered and overcome on the 7th; and on the 9th he occupied Baturi, which the Germans, finding their flanks threatened by the French converging movement, evacuated without fighting. Next day Colonel Morisson advanced to the Kadei river, where the Germans opposed his further advance for about ten days, until movements against their flanks forced them to retire. At this stage Colonel Morisson, receiving totally incorrect information that General Dobell had occupied Yaunde, decided on a further advance. This he carried out on two lines. His northern column—360 rifles with one gun—occupied Bertua on the 29th December, after three days' fighting in which fairly heavy casualties were incurred; and the other column—about 230 rifles with two guns—seized Nyassi on the 2nd January 1915.

The general situation; Dec. 1914. From the foregoing it will be seen that the various Allied columns, with a total strength probably about double that of the enemy, were operating over a vast area and were widely separated from one another by large tracts of difficult and frequently roadless country. Co-ordination of their movements was precluded by the impracticability of reliable and rapid means of communication; supply and transport difficulties limited the extent to which any of them could advance and caused frequent halts; and the nature of the country necessitated the maintenance of strong garrisons to assure the retention of important centres gained. Reliable intelligence was, moreover, becoming increasingly difficult to obtain. The guerilla tactics which the enemy had adopted and his knowledge of the country enabled him not only to cope successfully with the Allied numbers but also to escape severe loss. His superiority in machine guns * was especially useful in these tactics and placed the Allies at a great disadvantage, for they were seldom able to use their mountain guns effectively; they found it very difficult or impossible to deploy sufficient numbers at the point of contact; and to make turning movements not only took them a long time but entailed arduous work, often beset with hardships, which had its effect on the health and strength of their officers and men.†

---

* These machine guns were of a lighter and generally better type than those of the Allies.
† From the German point of view, according to the account in *Der Grosse Krieg, 1914–1918*, the situation at this time was not altogether discouraging. Duala, indeed, had fallen; and in the south-east the French had made some progress, making good use of the navigable waterways in that area. But on other parts of the Cameroons frontier Allied progress was either slight or

The recrudescence of German activity round Edea and Kribi, at the time that the bulk of the British contingent was employed along the Northern Railway and that the French at Edea were suffering from the cumulative effects of the bad climate, showed that the enemy's resistance was far from crumbling. It also made clear to General Dobell that his existing strength would not permit him to continue to pursue a very active policy. On the other hand, the destruction on the 8th December of Admiral von Spee's squadron at the Battle of the Falklands removed a menace which had caused the retention of many British troops on the coast of our African possessions. General Dobell felt justified, therefore, in telegraphing on the 13th December to the Colonial Office asking that, with this change in the situation, reinforcements should be sent him. He suggested that these should consist of four companies Sierra Leone Battalion and half the Gambia Company, both of the West African Frontier Force. *Duala; mid-Dec. 1914.*

Hardly had General Dobell sent off this telegram when he was presented with a further cause for uneasiness by reports, whose accuracy remained in doubt for some days, of the presence of a German cruiser off the Angola coast. It was known that cases, apparently of ammunition, had recently passed into German territory at Campo from Muni, and it was also known that the German consul at Fernando Po had sent messages via Monrovia to Berlin urging the despatch of naval assistance to cover the supply of munitions to the Cameroons. To prevent such supply the Allies had, in addition to the vessels at and off Duala, some ten gunboats or other small armed vessels and three transports cruising off the coast. As the Admiralty had negatived the declaration of a blockade, General Dobell recommended to the Colonial Office that a British consul should be appointed to Bata to watch our interests; and he also arranged with Captain Fuller for the immediate despatch of two flotillas of armed small vessels to watch the approaches by the Nyong, Lokundje, and Campo rivers.

It will be convenient here to describe briefly the operations of these flotillas, which, with the transport *Lagos* carrying all the available marines under Captain C. L. Hall (R.M.L.I.), *River flotillas south of Duala; Dec. 1914– Jan. 1915.*

had been definitely checked. The German plan of campaign was, perforce, strategically defensive. Ngaundere had been selected as the concentration point in the interior for the final resistance; but for the time being it was important to hold on to Yaunde and the area south of the Sanaga river. For this was within reasonable distance of the coast (and also of Spanish Muni), and the Germans found it still possible to obtain munitions from oversea —especially a much needed supply of small-arm ammunition.

left Duala on the 18th December under Commander Sneyd in the *Remus*. During the next two days the entrances to the Nyong and Lokundje rivers were reconnoitred and the German trenches there filled in by the marines, no enemy being encountered. On the 20th two launches, under Lieut. L. H. K. Hamilton, R.N., reconnoitred up the Nyong, engaging enemy patrols near Dehane. The Germans had burnt the villages along the river banks, and a considerable number of their inhabitants had taken refuge at Little Batanga. On the 22nd another reconnaissance was made up the Lokundje river to near Ebea without encountering any enemy.

Leaving Lieutenant Hamilton, with the *Alligator, Crocodile, Cumberland's* late picket boat and *Fullah* (as depot ship) at the Nyong mouth, whose immediate vicinity was clear of the enemy, Commander Sneyd proceeded on the 23rd December, with the *Remus, Vigilant, Sir Frederick* and *Lagos*, to Campo.

Lieutenant Hamilton displayed great activity in reconnoitring the Nyong and Lokundje rivers as far as they were navigable, i.e., up to Dehane and Ebea. Opposition from enemy patrols or marksmen was usually encountered, but the flotilla succeeded in burning Ebea and in doing considerable damage at Dehane. On the 26th December Lieutenant Hamilton reported that a temporary enemy evacuation of Dehane and Ebea seemed to indicate a possible big concentration elsewhere. Within the next few days he was reinforced by the light-draught launches *Wuri* and *Roy* and a steel canoe mounting a 3-pounder gun.

Commander Sneyd, arriving with his flotilla off Campo on the 24th December, landed the marines above that place to advance along the beach, and sent the *Vigilant* into the river. Here she was fired on, but her gunfire soon dispersed the enemy and the marines entered Campo without opposition. At Campo Commander Sneyd established a strong defensive base, from which constant reconnaissances were carried out—for about ten miles up the Campo river by the flotilla to the Dipikar waterfalls, which stopped a further advance, and on land by the marines. These accomplished much useful work in filling in enemy trenches and destroying enemy look-out posts, telephones, etc., before they were recalled to Duala on the 2nd January. But they were sent back again on the 17th, following an unsuccessful enemy attack on Campo three days previously.

On the Sanaga river, as the dry season came on, the steam launch detailed for patrol work found its radius of action greatly limited by the low state of the water. As a patrol of this river was essential to gain early intelligence of any hostile movement across it threatening the Duala-Edea railway, a lighter launch, *Lala*, was armed and protected and was sent under Lieutenant H. T. W. Pawsey, R.N., early in January by way of the Kwa-kwa creek. The passage of this creek proved very difficult and took five days, entailing the excavation of channels through numerous sandbanks. The *Lala* reached Edea on the 17th January.

At Duala on the 19th December General Dobell learnt from Colonel Cunliffe that Major Webb-Bowen had arrived fourteen miles north of Garua on the 12th with instructions from Colonel Brisset to operate round, without attacking, the German position. But it was not till four days later that General Dobell heard of Colonel Brisset's departure from Mora to join Major Webb-Bowen. In the meantime, on the 20th, not having received a reply to his request for reinforcements, General Dobell telegraphed to the Colonial Office that he trusted they had been sanctioned and would be despatched shortly. To this, on the evening of the 24th December, the Colonial Office replied that the Army Council were not aware that General Dobell's force was insufficient to hold the enemy territory already occupied. They deprecated the further depletion of the Sierra Leone garrison without cogent reasons, as the continued absence of hostile craft capable of endangering the security of the coaling station could not be considered absolutely certain and it would be impracticable to move troops back there from the Cameroons at short notice. The Army Council would, therefore, like to know General Dobell's reasons for requiring reinforcements when he had already established himself firmly in those portions of the Cameroons which were of strategical importance. In conclusion, the Colonial Office said that the Governor of the Gambia had been instructed to arrange, unless he saw grave objections, for the despatch to Duala of a half-company.

To this telegram General Dobell replied on the 26th December. He said that since the receipt of the Colonial Office telegram of the 30th September * he had kept in view the

---

* See Chapter IV, page 145. In this telegram the Colonial Office had asked General Dobell to state his views and proposals on the assumption that the ultimate object of H.M. Government was the complete reduction of the Cameroons. They further gave him to understand that he was not expected to do more than he considered safe with the forces at his disposal. Though General Dobell had kept the Colonial Office regularly acquainted with the progress of his operations, these had not yet, in his opinion, reached the stage when he could formulate the required proposals.

possibility, by constant activity, of effecting the surrender of the whole of the Cameroons and that, after accomplishing the strategic objects of his expedition, he had felt it incumbent on him, in absence of further instructions, to bring the maximum amount of pressure on the enemy. This limit had now been reached without the aid of further reinforcements; and he asked for the decision of H.M. Government in regard to his future action, submitting that those natives who had associated themselves with us must be protected against brutality by the Germans. He went on to say that, if the campaign were protracted and he failed to obtain the surrender of the colony, his force would become immobilised through wastage among its Europeans. This was practically the case already with the French, as he had reported to the Governor-General of French West Africa. He asked for an early decision, as on it depended the direction of the operations in progress. Next day General Dobell telegraphed to Colonel Gorges instructing him that, in making his supply arrangements, he must bear in mind the possibility that orders from home might necessitate the early return of his force to railhead, after defeating and dispersing the enemy in front of him and visiting Chang.

Advance on Chang; 25th Dec. 1914. (Map 8.) Colonel Gorges had commenced his advance northward on Chang on the 25th December, his main column moving along the main road up the Nkam valley through country covered with elephant grass twelve feet high. A left flank column under Colonel Haywood, consisting of two and a half companies 2nd Nigerians and the two Gold Coast guns, advanced by the alternative and much steeper road leading, between rugged and thickly timbered heights, to Chang via Mbo, a fortified post on a spur of the Manenguba mountains. Both columns were to re-unite at the road junction seven or eight miles south-west of Chang.

26th Dec. 1914. After some skirmishing through the thick and high elephant grass the main column bivouacked on the 26th December at a point near Fongwang, where it spent a restless night owing to intermittent enemy sniping and the bites of mosquitoes and ants. On the left flank Colonel Haywood's column had encountered serious opposition but had eventually driven the enemy back with somewhat heavy casualties at a cost to the British of twelve killed and wounded, including Colour-Sergeant J. J. Winter of the Nigerians killed. On the right flank Lieutenant J. F. P. Butler of the Gold Coast pioneer company,

[*To face p.* 216

CARRIERS ON THE ROAD FROM MBO TO CHANG

COUNTRY BETWEEN MBO AND CHANG

who had been sent out from the main column on the previous day with a patrol to disperse a hostile detachment which had been harassing the column, returned on the 26th having successfully performed his task. Two of his men had been wounded and he himself, by his coolness and gallantry in swimming an unfordable river under fire to reconnoitre single-handed, had performed another of the feats which gained him the Victoria Cross.*

The vanguard of the advanced guard of the main column, under Lieutenant H. D. S. O'Brien, 1st Nigerians, found itself opposed, on the 27th December, by the enemy at the bridge over the Nkam river one and a half miles north of Fongwang. The banks of the hundred-foot wide river were covered with elephant grass and were fifteen feet high, and along them the enemy had constructed by the bridge and to the northward a series of well-sited trenches. But from all these in succession the enemy was driven by the British vanguard, skilfully led by Lieutenant O'Brien, at a cost of four casualties, including Lieutenant O'Brien himself wounded. [27th Dec. 1914.]

Colonel Haywood that day, having to evacuate his wounded, moved only to Sanchu, whence he carried out forward reconnaissances.

Next day, passing through a country covered for a considerable distance by swamps in addition to the elephant grass, the main column reached a point about a mile south of Fonelas. The road had now definitely begun its ascent to the plateau, and native reports attributed to the enemy the intention of resisting a further British advance in a strong position on the Fongdonera (or Fondola) ridge. On the left Colonel Haywood moved to a camp about two and a half miles north of Sanchu without encountering opposition. [28th Dec 1914.]

Enemy opposition and difficult country combined on the 29th December to make the main column's progress slow. The road ascended steadily through mountainous country, and the enemy had destroyed stretches of it and all the bridges over the many streams. Throughout the day the advanced guard was engaged with the enemy, whose presence on the thickly wooded mountain slopes was only revealed by his periodical and sudden bursts of rifle and machine gun fire. The British were necessarily advancing on a narrow front, and the turning movements they had to make against the invisible enemy were very difficult and took up much time. By the evening Colonel [29th Dec. 1914.]

---
* See page 186, *ante*. He was subsequently killed in the operations in East Africa.

Gorges' troops had reached a point about a mile short of the enemy's position at Fongdonera, having incurred only three casualties—a surprisingly small number in the circumstances—and having taken two prisoners, one a German.

The mountainous and thickly wooded country had proved even a greater obstacle to Colonel Haywood's column, and though the opposition he encountered had been slight, the difficulty of scouting and reconnaissance had prevented his advancing much over a mile.

The British post at Bare, held by a half-company, was attacked that day by an enemy force of an estimated strength of 100 rifles and two machine guns, which came from the Bana direction. After two hours' fighting, however, the attack collapsed, without loss to the garrison, apparently after the two German leaders of the detachment had been killed. Telephone communication between Bare and Colonel Gorges' column was also severed at the same time in several places, apparently by enemy action. The reports of this affair which reached General Dobell the same day combined with the severance of communication to cause him considerable anxiety. He felt that in his desire to exercise all possible pressure on the enemy he had exceeded the capacity of his force with the result that its positions in more than one direction had become insecure. On the 30th December he accordingly deemed it necessary to remind Colonel Gorges that he was not expected to undertake more than he could safely perform with the troops at his disposal.

30th Dec. 1914. The Fongdonera position was situated on a spur running from west to east with deep and thickly timbered ravines on either side of it. But on the 30th the enemy, finding himself outflanked by part of the British main column, evacuated it without attempting further resistance. Thereupon Colonel Gorges took up good positions on the hills some two miles to the north.

That night Colonel Haywood, his progress still greatly hindered by the difficult country, camped in a position which the enemy had entrenched strongly but which he had made no attempt to hold.

31st Dec. 1914. Halting on the 31st December to repair roads and bridges for the passage of the naval 12-pounder and to restore the telephone line in the Nkam valley, for the destruction of which a herd of wild elephants had been partly responsible, Colonel Gorges sent forward a detachment to occupy positions covering the road junction south-west of Chang. On that day Force

ADVANCE ON CHANG

Headquarters at Duala received confirmation of the presence of an enemy force, some 300 strong, east of Bare and in a position to operate against Colonel Gorges' line of communication. This force was taken to be Sommerfeld's company from the Nsanakang area, and General Dobell, out of communication with Colonel Gorges and feeling compelled to assist, reduced his already small reserve by arranging for a company of the West African Regiment to move next day to Nkongsamba, its place at Duala being taken by a company withdrawn from Dibombe post.

Telephonic communication having been restored, General Dobell heard on the 1st January from Colonel Gorges that he had reached the road junction south-west of Chang, where he hoped to be joined shortly by Colonel Haywood—who had that morning taken Mbo—for the advance on Chang. General Dobell then telegraphed to Colonel Gorges informing him of the confirmation of the presence east of Bare of a German company from Nsanakang, and also of the despatch of the West African Regiment company to Nkongsamba. General Dobell went on to say that, as it was impossible to send more reinforcements, the presence of these hostile troops caused grave anxiety. Colonel Gorges was consequently to return to railhead as soon as the situation permitted. If the capture of Chang was to be a long-drawn-out affair or presented great difficulty Colonel Gorges might, at his discretion, withdraw without effecting its capture. If he took Chang he was to destroy it and return to railhead as soon as possible. *1st Jan. 1915.*

Colonel Haywood had occupied Mbo fort without opposition, the series of strong entrenched positions covering it having been evacuated by the enemy without fighting, evidently owing to the turning of his flank by the advance of Colonel Gorges' main column.

Being joined at the road junction at an early hour on the 2nd January by Colonel Haywood, Colonel Gorges decided to advance at once against Chang. The road in that direction ran up a narrow valley, though the surrounding country was easier and more open. But it was not till they got near Chang and could see the German flag flying over the fort that the British advanced troops were fired on from the surrounding hills. When about a mile from the fort Colonel Gorges halted his main body and made his dispositions for attack. Covered by the fire of the naval and Nigerian guns his infantry started to advance soon after midday and were making good progress when suddenly the German flag over the fort was replaced by a *2nd Jan. 1915; Capture of Chang.*

white one. For the next hour or so, however, in spite of the white flag, the advancing British troops were subjected to an intermittent fire from the surrounding hills, due, in Colonel Gorges' opinion, to the German native troops being out of control.* By 5 p.m. the fort, Residency, mission station, the many other buildings and the surrounding hills were all in British occupation. All Germans save ten—seven of them priests or sisters—had gone.

The majority of the enemy forces appeared to have retired on Fumban. The lack of resolution they had displayed in opposing the British advance and their sudden evacuation of Chang had been unexpected. They had apparently been unpleasantly surprised by the skill with which Colonel Gorges' column had overcome the physical difficulties of the advance; and the evacuation of Chang fort, which was better fitted to withstand a native attack than an artillery bombardment, had probably been hastened by the presence of the British naval 12-pounder, the advance of which the Germans had hoped to stop by their destruction of roads and bridges. Colonel Gorges now gained the impression that the Germans had not meant to fight; while their removal from Chang, evidently some time before, of all stores, furniture, etc., combined with the likelihood that its capture would make the natives less inclined to help them, led him to assume that there was little chance of further extended active operations in this quarter by the enemy.

Its high-lying situation in the midst of open and undulating country made Chang a pleasant place of residence. The temperature by day, though hot, was dry and a considerable fall after sunset brought refreshingly cold nights. There was an ample supply of good drinking water, its coolness being especially attractive, and supplies of fresh food were assured by the existence in the neighbourhood of many goats and cattle and of vegetable fields and gardens.

3rd–12th Jan. 1915; Withdrawal from Chang to railhead. British patrols along the Bamenda road encountered the enemy in some strength on the 3rd January. But, having regard to his definite orders to withdraw, Colonel Gorges contented himself with sending out a column under Colonel Cockburn to engage the enemy, while the remainder of the force carried out the demolition of Chang. On the 5th Colonel Cockburn returned, having successfully dispersed the enemy detachment, which was estimated at a strength of 20 Germans

---

* This had happened on previous occasions.

[To face p. 220

2ND NIGERIANS AT MUYUKA

CHANG

and 250 natives. The demolition of Chang had been completed and, receiving a telegram sent that day by General Dobell, after the German attack on Kopongo,* ordering as early a withdrawal as possible, Colonel Gorges made arrangements to commence this next day. Colonel Haywood, with his 2nd Nigerians and two guns, moved southward on the 6th January, escorting prisoners, sick and wounded; and the remainder of the force started to follow him long before dawn on the 7th. By the 10th January the whole force, unmolested and without special incident, had arrived back at Nkongsamba, having left a company of the 1st Nigerians to garrison Bare.

In his report Colonel Gorges brought to notice the good work of his officers and men. That carried out by the Royal Engineers and pioneers, the party laying out the field telephone and the naval gun detachment under Commander W. H. Davies, R.N.R., had been particularly noticeable, and Colonel Gorges also praised the patience and cheerfulness of his African carriers, who had suffered the fatigue and exhaustion induced by their unusually arduous duties without complaint.

By this time an increasing sick rate showed that many of the officers and men were beginning to feel the effect of the bad climate and of their exertions of the last five months. On the 12th January Colonel Gorges reported that his men were footsore and tired and that their ranks were depleted by sickness; and his senior medical officer recommended that, before undertaking further operations, officers and men should have a period of rest, if this was at all possible.

It was unfortunate that General Dobell had insufficient troops to maintain his hold on Chang. He had concluded that the destruction of this German station, which was regarded generally in the Cameroons as second only in importance to Yaunde, would have an important moral and political effect; and he was of opinion that its loss combined with that of Ossidinge indicated that the German troops opposing him northward of Nkongsamba were unlikely to undertake much more in the nature of serious active operations. It was not till the beginning of February that he found that the British withdrawal from Chang had given a totally false impression to the local natives and the Germans. Neither apparently grasped the real reasons for it, and some of the Germans seem to have jumped to the conclusion that it was caused by an adverse change in the situation, probably due to a German naval

---

* See later, p. 225.

222 MILITARY OPERATIONS: THE CAMEROONS

victory in Europe and the arrival off the African coast of a superior German naval force.

From Nkongsamba Colonel Gorges with his staff and all units of his column and on the line of communication, excepting the Nigerian battery and the two Nigerian infantry battalions, proceeded to Duala. The 1st Nigerians and the Nigerian Battery were left to hold Nkongsamba and Bare, and the 2nd Nigerians garrisoned the line of communication back to Bonaberi.

Reinforcements; 9th-27th Jan. 1915. In the meantime on the 9th January the Colonial Office had telegraphed to General Dobell that the Army Council had instructed the General Officer Commanding Sierra Leone to send to the Cameroons the remainder of the Sierra Leone Battalion, W.A.F.F., consisting of Battalion headquarters and four companies (strength, 9 officers, 397 rank and file) under the command of Lieut.-Colonel G. P. Newstead. These, with the half-company from Gambia, arrived at Duala on the 27th January.

The Cross River Column; Occupation of Ossidinge and move to Tinto; Dec. 1914– Jan. 1915. (Map 7, facing page 224.) On the 4th January General Dobell had heard from Colonel Cunliffe that Colonel Mair had occupied Ossidinge on the 1st and proposed moving to Tinto. He had met with no very serious resistance. His column, crossing the Nigerian frontier on the 25th December, had soon encountered the enemy, who fell back keeping in touch with the British but offering only slight opposition. Moving via Araru without further opposition, Colonel Mair reached, at an early hour on the 27th, the Munaya river at a point which, he had ascertained, was not being watched by the enemy. The river here, eighty yards wide with rapids, was a considerable obstacle; but, assisted by rocks in the rapids, a bridge over it was rapidly constructed, and the British, all having crossed by 2.15 p.m., bivouacked for the night on the further bank. Next day reconnaissances were made but no advance, as Colonel Mair awaited the arrival of Major Fane, who had left Nkami on the 27th. His column, consisting of the battery, half "C" Company 3rd Battalion with two machine guns and the supply column, joined Colonel Mair in the afternoon (28th). The whole column moved northward towards Ajundep on the 29th December, its advanced guard ("B" Company, 4th Battalion) soon encountering opposition from an enemy party, which it drove back to the right bank of the Bakori river. Though fordable, this river was about forty yards wide with a very swift current flowing through dense bush; and its further and higher bank was held by the enemy, whose strength was subsequently found to have been eight Germans and sixty natives with two machine guns. Crossing the river in small parties under cover of fire from the main body, the advanced guard drove the enemy out of his position and so enabled the main column to cross unmolested during the afternoon. Throughout the day the British casualties only totalled six, those of the enemy being about the same.

Continuing its advance past Ogomoko on the 30th and 31st December, the British column found that enemy resistance, in the shape of delaying tactics, gradually decreased. Casualties on either side were slight and on the 1st January Ossidinge was found unoccupied by the enemy, though as soon as the leading British company emerged into the open there it came under heavy fire from high ground on the right bank of the Cross river. From these heights the enemy was driven after two hours' fighting, at the cost of six British casualties.

Colonel Mair now changed his line of communication to the main road via Nsanarati, and ordered " B " Company about Obokum and half " C " Company about Nkami to move up to Ossidinge, where they arrived on the 5th January. On the previous day, leaving a small garrison at Ossidinge, Colonel Mair had started with the bulk of his column to march south-eastward. He met with no opposition and on the 8th January occupied Tinto, in which vicinity he remained till the 15th, when he received instructions, sent on the 12th by General Dobell to Colonel Cunliffe, that as Colonel Gorges had successfully accomplished his task, the Cross river column could be withdrawn. Colonel Mair at once replied that he would move back with all speed to Ikom via Ossidinge. But after arriving back at Ossidinge he telegraphed on the 17th January to Colonel Cunliffe advocating the retention of Ossidinge and, as General Dobell had also just telegraphed to the same effect, the column remained at Ossidinge, constructing there a defensive position on both banks of the Cross river.

Throughout December and January the Ibi column, under Major Mann,* in its active patrol work along the frontier of the Muri province, had many minor encounters with the enemy, but no serious fighting. At the end of December, when his strength was brought up to two and a half companies and one gun by the arrival of half " G " Company, 2nd Battalion, from Lokoja, Major Mann reported that the Germans had small

The Ibi Column; Dec.1914- Jan. 1915.

---

* His headquarters were still at Takum.

parties along the frontier, evidently to give warning of any British advance on Kentu or Banyo, at neither of which places did the Germans appear to be in any great strength. It had previously been the intention that Major Mann should advance and seize Kentu and should endeavour from there to get into touch with Colonel Mair's column operating in the Ossidinge-Tinto area. But supply and transport difficulties and the distances involved caused delay; and finally, apparently after the withdrawal from Chang, the idea was abandoned.

<small>2nd-8th Jan. 1915. German attacks on Kribi, Kopongo and Edea.</small>
At the end of December the German forces round Edea—excluding their badly armed native levies—were estimated at about 800 rifles with eight machine guns. They appeared to be distributed in four approximately equal bodies, i.e., about Sakbajeme (some forty miles to the north-east), Ngwe (thirty miles to the east), a point on the railway twenty-five miles to the south-eastward, and in the Dehane-Ebea area. Learning of the despatch up the Northern Railway of a large Allied contingent and believing that the Edea garrison had been reduced, the Germans about this time seem to have come to the conclusion that the moment was favourable for a serious counterstroke in the Edea area.* They consequently decided to attack not only Edea, but also Kopongo—a French railway post fourteen miles north of Edea—and Kribi. The attack on Kopongo was evidently undertaken with a view to cutting Edea off from Duala, while that on Kribi was probably made with the idea of creating a diversion.

Two consecutive attacks on Kribi were the first to occur. One on the 2nd January, when a portion of the garrison had proceeded in the *Dwarf* to operate against an enemy party reported near Great Batanga, was repulsed easily with a loss to the Germans of three killed and several wounded; and the other, made during the night 3rd/4th January, was also beaten off without difficulty and with further loss to the enemy.

On the 4th January, Colonel Mayer at Edea, having received

---

* In *Der Grosse Krieg, 1914–1918*, the German attack on Edea is stated to have been undertaken with a view to inducing General Dobell to abandon his advance on Chang. It appears that the Germans were apprehensive of a hostile advance via Chang towards Ngaundere on the central plateau; for a hostile occupation of the central plateau would not only deprive the Germans of an important supply area, but would also separate their forces operating in the Northern Cameroons from those in the south. Moreover, Ngaundere was still the focal point on which the German forces in all parts of the Cameroons were eventually to fall back when hard pressed by the enemy.

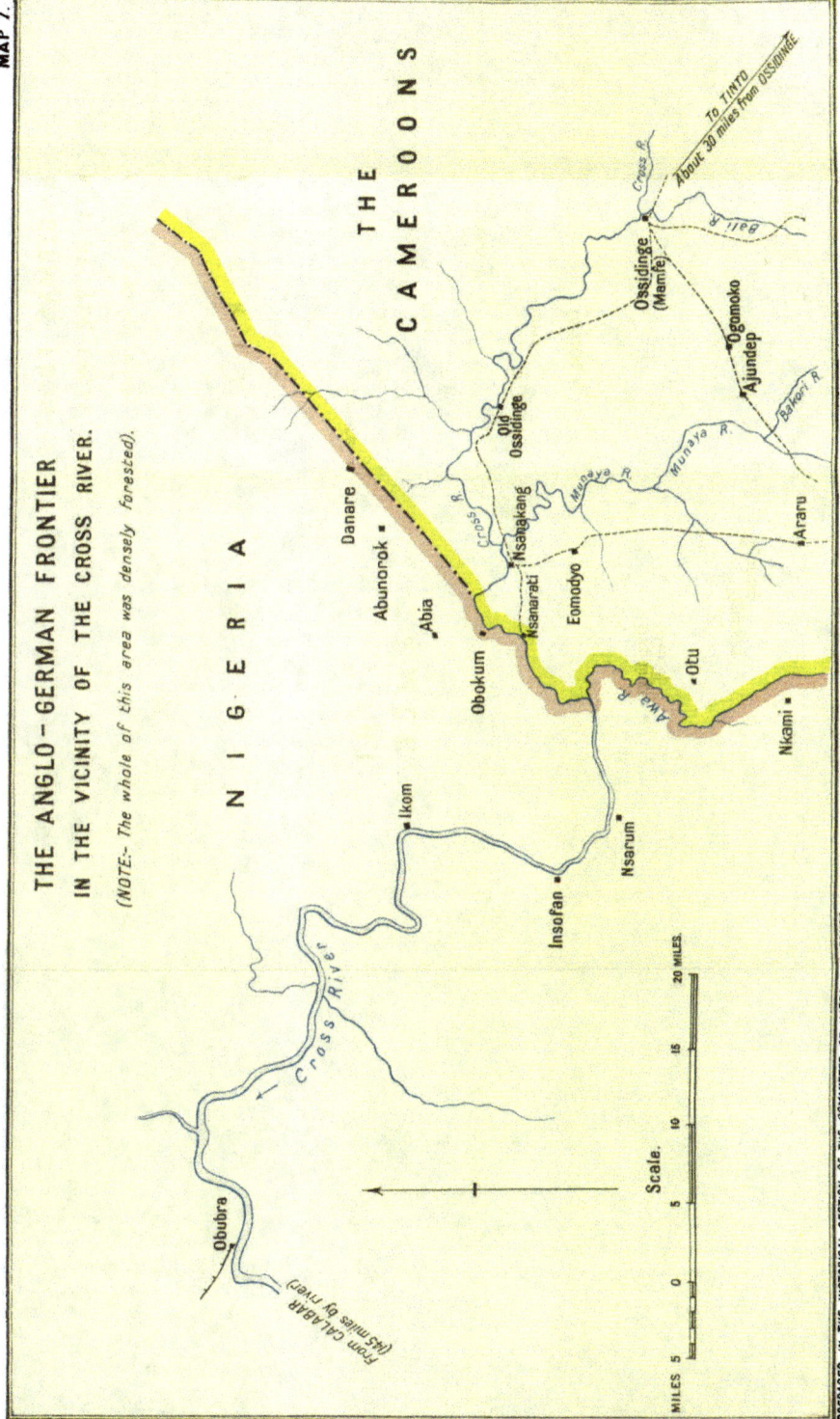

GERMAN DEFEAT AT EDEA

information on the previous day of an enemy concentration ten miles east of Kopongo, reinforced that post with 90 men, bringing its total strength to 130; and he also took increased precautions at Edea itself. Next day the Germans attacked both places.

The attack on Kopongo lasted from 4.45 to 7.30 a.m., when it was finally repulsed at a cost to the garrison of ten casualties and to the attackers of nearly double that number. Learning that an attack was in progress, General Dobell sent out a train from Duala with reinforcements; but they did not arrive till the fight was over and then returned to Duala.

Edea, owing to its scattered alignment, the inequalities of its ground area and the proximity of the forest, was not at all an easy place to defend. But in laying out his line of defence Colonel Mayer displayed great skill, and the enemy's attack on the 5th January came to naught. It commenced at 5.15 a.m., the enemy—who advanced in three distinct converging movements—having managed, under cover of the darkness and a mist, to approach close to the French positions. The attack from the eastward, along the road and railway from Yaunde, was conducted with considerable vigour, but was completely checked and then finally repulsed with loss by twenty Senegalese in a blockhouse about a mile outside Edea. The Germans killed here included Lieutenant Bachmann, the commander of their No. 2 Reserve Company. The attack from the south was weak and never dangerous. But that from the south-west was pressed with great vigour, and it was here that the Germans suffered most. *See Map 9.*

By 8.30 a.m. all fighting was over, and the enemy was in full and disorderly retreat. The French, who had displayed great courage and tenacity, suffered a total of 15 casualties, while those of the Germans were very heavy. They left behind them 20 German and about 80 native dead; and they also lost 6 natives, a machine gun, 52 rifles and much ammunition and equipment, captured by the French.

This defeat had been the heaviest that the Allies had hitherto been able to inflict on the enemy, and it was a matter of satisfaction to General Dobell that the enemy's attack had taken the direction it had. They might instead have cut off Edea by holding the right bank of the Sanaga river and destroying all the French posts on the railway. This would have placed General Dobell at Duala in a difficult and dangerous situation. For, even though the enemy might not have been able to attack Duala, the Allied troops there were too few, until reinforced by men from Colonel Gorges' force, to furnish a relief column for Edea ; and by the time these reinforcements had arrived the food at Edea might have given out.*

The Germans made a further attack on Kribi on the night of the 8th/9th January, only, however, to suffer another repulse and further loss.

Edea-Kribi area; 9th–31st Jan. 1915. For the remainder of January the French garrisons in the Edea-Kribi area were practically undisturbed. To place Colonel Mayer, however, in a position to adopt such offensive measures as he considered feasible and especially to display greater activity in a southerly direction, General Dobell decided to reinforce Edea. With the return of troops from the Northern Railway the force at Duala now consisted of the Sierra Leone Battery, the section Gold Coast Battery, the West African Regiment (less one company), two companies Composite Battalion, half the Gold Coast pioneer company † and two companies of Senegalese. Further, the reinforcements from Gambia and Sierra Leone were due to arrive in the near future. Consequently, on the 21st January General Dobell ordered Colonel Vaughan with two Sierra Leone guns and four companies West African Regiment with four machine guns (two manned by naval personnel) to relieve the two French guns and two Senegalese companies at Kribi.

Disembarking at Kribi on the 24th January, Colonel Vaughan moved out next day with his own troops and a Senegalese company towards Plantation to deal with an enemy detachment which had been giving trouble for some time past. Driving the enemy back before him throughout that day without much difficulty and at a cost of only four casualties, Colonel Vaughan found on the 26th that the enemy had evacuated the whole vicinity. On the 27th Commandant Mathieu's detachment left Kribi for Duala as a preliminary to the concentration of the whole French contingent at Edea and along the Midland Railway.

During January Colonel Mayer started, with General Dobell's sanction, to enlist and arm a small body of local natives as levies. Hitherto these natives had been enrolled by the Allies only as pilots or guides and for civil police work ; and the decision to raise and arm them for employment against

---

* The German account previously referred to claims that the attack on Edea, though repulsed with heavy loss, achieved its object—namely, the British abandonment of Chang, the key to the central plateau.

† One company West African Regiment was at Dibombe Post, and the Composite Battalion (less two companies) and half the Gold Coast pioneer company held Buea, Zopo and Victoria.

the Germans was only taken after the Germans themselves had organised armed levies, whose activities and outrages Colonel Mayer's Senegalese, unaccustomed to movement and warfare in such dense forest, were unable to cope with effectively. The work of recruitment and organisation at Edea was carried out by Lieutenant McCallum;* the men being provided with a simple uniform, armed with captured German rifles and bayonets and equipped with captured bandoliers and pouches. Care had to be taken, however, to limit their amount of ammunition as cases occurred of individuals using this to pay off old scores against their neighbours instead of in their legitimate duties. While certain of the men proved of considerable value as Intelligence agents, many of the others were not very reliable; but they sufficed to show the way through the bush to the French troops and to cause, by their guerilla tactics, some concern and anxiety to the German forces. The numbers of those with the Edea column never exceeded sixty. A similar procedure was followed by the French at Kribi, where the levies were raised and organised by Lieutenant W. S. Taylor of the British Contingent, whose services had been placed at Commandant Mathieu's disposal for Intelligence duties. At both places the levies were paid by the British Intelligence service.

The constant patrol work by naval vessels along the coast and the numerous waterways still involved many minor encounters with enemy parties; but raiding continued. Some missionaries, of American or other neutral nationality, had remained at their stations in the Kribi area, but in January, owing to the enemy raids on their stations, they requested facilities for removal to Spanish Muni; and on the 11th January they were given passages in the *Remus*. [Naval coast and river patrols; Jan. 1915.]

In the middle of January attacks on Bare and on a railway post ten miles south of Nkongsamba, as well as a patrol encounter to the west of that place, indicated a revival of German activity near the Northern railhead. The attack on Bare, which was carried out on the 16th January by an enemy force estimated at 150 rifles with two machine guns, was unsuccessful, causing the garrision only two casualties. On learning that an attack was in progress Colonel Cockburn despatched two companies to Bare from Nkongsamba, but they did not arrive till the fighting was over and returned next day to railhead. [Bare and Northern Railway.]

---
* He was still attached to Colonel Mayer's headquarters for Intelligence duties.

Enemy activity in the neighbourhood continued to increase, however, and there were a number of raids attempted against the railway. To ease the situation it became necessary to take the offensive and defeat the main enemy body in the vicinity. A contributory factor was also General Dobell's desire to release a number of troops from that area for operations elsewhere. The necessary arrangements were consequently put in hand; and the four companies of the Sierra Leone Battalion, West African Frontier Force, who had just arrived from Sierra Leone, reached Bare between the 30th January and 2nd February, under the command of Lieutenant-Colonel G. P. Newstead.

It was subsequently ascertained, from captured documents, that Engelbrechten, believing that a victory over Allied vessels off Duala by German cruisers had caused the British withdrawal from Chang, requested permission on the 9th January to pursue with at least four companies, and that two or three days later an advance of all the German troops at Bamenda, Chang and Bana was ordered to take place immediately with all speed.

Allied casualties; General Dobell's force. The total casualties so far incurred by General Dobell's force had not been heavy, considering the country, the difficult nature of the operations and the enemy's tactics. Including those killed, died of disease, wounded and missing—but excluding those invalided—they amounted to 11 British, 29 French, and 389 African natives (210 of the British contingent and 179 of the French contingent).

The replacement of casualties among Europeans, both British and French, was, however, causing General Dobell some difficulty and anxiety. The authorities in French West Africa had intimated their inability, at any rate for the time being, to do anything in this respect; and the Governor-General of Nigeria and some of the other British Colonial Governors were pressing him to send back, generally for duty in their own Colonies, several of the civil, medical and marine officials whose services they had lent. On the other hand General Dobell's requirements for the administration of occupied territory were increasing rather than decreasing.

The Northern Cameroons; 1914– Jan. 1915. In the Northern Cameroons, after Colonel Brisset's departure from Sava, the Allied investment of the German position at Mora continued for many weeks without important incident. The delay and inconvenience caused by the difficulties of rapid communication between Colonel Brisset and Major Webb-Bowen continued. On the 17th December Major Webb-Bowen moved northward again from Demsa towards Mubi, in compliance with a request from Captain Simonet from Uba to join him near Gauar. Next day, hearing that a hostile detachment had occupied Demsa, Major Webb-Bowen sent back his mounted infantry; and a skirmish ensued, after which the enemy, who had two men killed, withdrew from Demsa during the night.

Continuing his northward movement, Major Webb-Bowen on the 22nd December when near Mubi received instructions dated 13th December from Colonel Brisset. These, after announcing the retirement of the German company from Marua towards Garua, stated that Colonel Brisset's column would advance southward and that the detachments of Captain Simonet and Major Webb-Bowen were to join Colonel Brisset independently on the Marua-Garua road at the points nearest them

Again Major Webb-Bowen retraced his steps and missed another message which Colonel Brisset had sent on the 17th giving a definite rendezvous. On the 26th December, at Dembo (about twenty-five miles west of Golombe), Major Webb-Bowen heard that the French were near Golombe and sent off there a British officer, who returned a day or two later with Colonel Brisset's instructions. Major Webb-Bowen was to move to Demsa and there await further instructions. Colonel Brisset said that he himself would have to halt awhile at Golombe to consolidate his line of communication and to ensure the protection from the Germans of the natives of the territory traversed, but would probably arrive in the vicinity of Garua about the 5th January. On the 3rd Colonel Brisset sent Major Webb-Bowen instructions to reconnoitre from Demsa but to avoid a general action.

It was not till the 1st January that Colonel Brisset's column reached Golombe, and a further ten days elapsed before it established itself in an entrenched camp at Nassarao, some three miles to the north-east of the German position at Garua. During his move southward Colonel Brisset had met with practically no opposition, and the slowness of his progress was almost entirely due to the importance he attached to consolidating his political relations with the local inhabitants as he advanced.

Meanwhile Major Webb-Bowen had found no enemy in the vicinity of Demsa, where there was a scarcity of water and which was too far from Garua for reconnaissance. He reported to Colonel Brisset to this effect on the 8th January and, in the belief that supply difficulties were delaying the French advance, offered to help with supplies from Yola. In reply he learnt that the French were able to get locally all the supplies they required, and he received instructions to proceed to Nassarao. Here on the 14th January he at last effected a junction with Colonel Brisset's force.

The French and British contingents, now united under Colonel Brisset's command, were approximately equal in strength. That of the French consisted of a cavalry squadron, two guns and three infantry companies, while Major Webb-Bowen's column was composed of a mounted infantry company, two guns and three infantry companies.* The total Allied strength was about 900 rifles, with four guns but only five machine guns.

The German defences at Garua had by now been made very strong, and to hold them they had a garrison of 40 Germans and 537 natives with four guns and ten machine guns. Colonel Brisset, seeing little chance of capturing this position by a speedy assault, kept it under close observation, establishing the French contingent at Nassarao and the British contingent in another entrenched camp at Bogole, about three miles south of Nassarao and on the south side of the Benue river. To the French fell the duty of watching the approaches northward towards Mora, while the British observed those between Garua and Ngaundere.

By this time Sir Frederick Lugard, who was very anxious for the early capture of Garua so as to free the Nigerian frontier from raids and to sustain the *moral* of the local inhabitants of his frontier districts, had become dissatisfied with the progress of the Allied operations in the Northern Cameroons. He accordingly sent Colonel Cunliffe to Duala to ascertain General Dobell's wishes regarding the conduct of the campaign in the north and to place beyond doubt the question as to who was responsible for the command of the columns operating on the Nigerian frontier and at Garua.

Colonel Cunliffe arrived at Duala on the 27th January, and General Dobell explained his views. The difficulties of communication and the great distances involved precluded him from controlling the movements of any forces other than

---

* " B " Company, M.I., section 1st Battery, " H " Company, 1st Battalion, " B " Company, 2nd Battalion, and " H " Company, 3rd Battalion, Nigeria Regiment.

those actually forming part of the force based on Duala. All troops in Nigeria and those which had crossed the Nigerian frontier into the Cameroons must be under Colonel Cunliffe's orders, as he alone was in a position to control their operations. Where co-operation was desirable between Colonel Cunliffe and himself he was always prepared to offer suggestions or give advice if asked. As regards Colonel Brisset, who took his instructions from General Largeau, General Dobell felt debarred from interference.

As a result of this discussion and with a view to the maintenance of closer touch and to a better representation of the British point of view, General Dobell agreed to send Major W. D. Wright from the staff of his British contingent at Duala to join Colonel Brisset's staff at Garua. Captain Fuller also agreed to strengthen the Allied forces in the Northern Cameroons by sending from Duala to join them a naval 12-pounder gun, manned by a Petty Officer and four able seamen under Lieutenant Hamilton, R.N. Major Wright and this gun with its crew accordingly accompanied Colonel Cunliffe to Nigeria when he left Duala on the 1st February. At Forcados the gun crew was augmented by Nigerian artillery gunners.

Franco-Belgian operations in the south and south-east; Jan. 1915.

During January the French column near Midsik, having been brought up to a strength of five companies with a section of Nordenfeldt guns, commenced a cautious advance on Oyem, where the Germans were reported to have two or three companies. The Mvahdi Column was still awaiting its reinforcements, but during the month communication was established between it and the Sanga Column.

The latter column had to remain at Molundu to replace by carriers, for its further operations towards Lomie,* the water transport it had hitherto used. On the 30th January one of its detachments moved from Nola and occupied Yukaduma without opposition.

Colonel Morisson, commanding the Lobaye Column on the line Bertua-Nyassi, received orders to remain temporarily on the defensive. He had been undeceived regarding the reported capture of Yaunde and had learnt that the German force opposite him had received reinforcements which brought its strength up to five companies.† On the 27th January

---
* Lomie was reported to be held by a German company under Marwitz.
† The German 9th Company had come from Molundu, their 11th Company from Oyem, and another company from the westward

Colonel Morisson's outposts were attacked by the Germans, who retired again, however, two days later, after attaining little or no success.

On the 22nd January the Commander-in-Chief in French West Africa forwarded his views, with extracts from Colonel Mayer's report, regarding the division by the Sanaga river of the area of operations between General Dobell's French and British contingents. Colonel Mayer had offered the opinion that his contingent would have the hardest task, and the French Commander-in-Chief considered that it would be beyond the strength and capacity of Colonel Mayer's force. He also queried the desirability, from a post-war settlement point of view, of withdrawing all the French troops from Duala.

On the previous day the French Foreign Office had addressed the French Ambassador in London offering the opinion that the time had come for closer co-operation between the operations based on French Equatorial Africa and those of the force under General Dobell; and they offered certain suggestions for that officer's consideration. It appeared to them very important that the Midsik and Mvahdi Columns should assume a vigorous offensive against Oyem and along the frontier of Spanish Muni, with a view to preventing the Germans obtaining supplies or taking refuge there and to supporting the French contingent about Edea so as to bring about eventually an encirclement of the Germans at Yaunde. To settle the new objectives and to obtain, as soon as possible, a general combined decisive result, the French Foreign Office proposed that the Chief of Staff in French Equatorial Africa should proceed to Duala and confer with General Dobell. This communication, handed by the French military attaché to the British War Office on the 25th January, was passed on next day to the Colonial Office, who informed General Dobell on the 28th that they had agreed to the proposed conference.

CHAPTER VII

FEBRUARY—APRIL 1915

INDECISIVE OPERATIONS FROM NKONGSAMBA, LEADING TO ABANDONMENT OF ENEMY COUNTER-OFFENSIVE; AND DECISIONS TO ACCELERATE CAPTURE OF GARUA AND TO CO-OPERATE FROM EDEA WITH FRENCH ADVANCE FROM SOUTH-EAST

(Maps 2, 8, 10, 11 and 12)

At the beginning of February German parties were still displaying great activity in the areas adjoining the terminus of the Northern Railway, devoting much of their attention to procuring food and carriers. Reports indicated that the bulk of their forces were encamped at various villages along the line Mbureku-Harmann's Farm-Ekom, and that their headquarters were at Melong. But their scattered and varying distribution, governed apparently by their food and transport requirements, made it difficult to assess their exact dispositions, though their total strength was evidently not more than about 50 German and 500 native troops, with four machine guns. Information was, in fact, becoming increasingly difficult to obtain, as the harsh and severe German retaliatory measures, similar in method to those pursued in the Edea and Kribi areas, made the natives chary of assisting the British. As a counter-measure General Dobell authorised Colonel Cockburn to arm a small number of trustworthy local natives for use as scouts, etc. *[margin: Affairs near Mbureku and Harmann's Farm; 3rd Feb. 1915.]*

To ease the situation, and particularly to free the railway line of communication from raids, Colonel Cockburn issued orders on the 2nd February for an offensive against the enemy's main force. Attacks were to be carried out simultaneously in the early morning of the 3rd, on Mbureku by a column from Nkongsamba and on Harmann's Farm by a column from Bare. After gaining these positions, the two columns, communicating with one another by heliograph and runner, were to unite for an advance against Melong.

The Nkongsamba column, composed of two Nigerian guns and the 1st Nigerians (400 rifles) under Colonel Cockburn's personal command, moved out at 10.30 p.m. on the 2nd February. There was moonlight, and Colonel Cockburn hoped to get within striking distance of Mbureku by daybreak on the 3rd. At about 3.30 a.m. the column reached a point—about four miles south of the enemy's supposed position—where Colonel Cockburn proposed to halt and rest his men. But a sudden rifle shot, which killed the leading man of the " point " of the advanced guard, heralded a heavy burst of enemy rifle fire and a concentrated fire from three of his machine guns. This fire caught the British at a particularly awkward moment, as the path they were following had just bent round at right angles under ridges, which commanded the British front and left flank at close ranges and which, in fact, constituted the enemy's position, four miles south of where Colonel Cockburn had expected to find it.

For a short time there was confusion in the British ranks, contributed to in no small degree by carriers dropping their loads, rushing through the troops and stampeding the carriers in rear. The surrounding high grass and hilly country also added to the British difficulties. But the officers, rising well to the occasion under Colonel Cockburn's resolute leadership, quickly restored order and confidence. The British guns came into action and Colonel Cockburn, reinforcing his advanced guard, sent out detachments to turn both the enemy's flanks. At this critical stage many did well, and in his report Colonel Cockburn mentions Captain A. H. Giles (commanding the advanced guard) and Sergeant-Major Shearing (whom he sent up with a machine gun to reinforce the advanced guard) as specially worthy of praise.

As day broke the enemy began to retreat, and at about 6.30 a.m. the British occupied his position, finding that in his camp he had abandoned a large quantity of dynamite,* 10,000 rounds of rifle ammunition, tents, equipment, stores, and many supplies, including livestock. His casualties were unknown, but he had left eleven dead behind him.

The British were unfortunately in no condition to pursue. Their casualties had been 65 in all, including Colour-Sergeant H. R. G. Hooker killed; and a halt was necessary for

---

* This dynamite was presumably intended for use in raids against the railway.

BRITISH ADVANCE CHECKED

reorganisation and rest. While this was in progress, at about 10.30 a.m. heavy firing was heard from the direction of Harmann's Farm, and Colonel Cockburn decided to proceed there as soon as possible by the quickest route, i.e., via Bare. A company had to be detached to escort the wounded back to Nkongsamba, but the remainder of the column marched off towards Bare at 1 p.m., reaching there at 6.15 p.m.

The Bare Column, consisting of a gun of the Nigerian Battery and three and a quarter companies of the Sierra Leone Battalion under Lieutenant-Colonel G. P. Newstead, had moved out from Bare at 6 a.m. on the 3rd February. Three days previously Colonel Newstead, reconnoitring from Bare, had found the enemy in unexpected strength at Harmann's Farm, in a position entrenched behind a field of fire cleared for about six hundred yards. This position Colonel Newstead's troops, advancing under cover of the fire of his mountain gun, captured on the 3rd, with little loss, at about 9.30 a.m. An hour later the enemy, reinforced from the Melong direction, launched a vigorous counter-attack supported by the fire of two or three machine guns. This was met by the Sierra Leone men with steadiness and courage, but they had no machine guns and were in an exposed situation. Consequently, after suffering considerable casualties, they were forced by 11 a.m. to evacuate the position they had won ; and they retired in good order on to the position where the mountain gun was in action. The German troops did not advance beyond Harmann's Farm, and by noon all firing had ceased. At 11.20 a.m., while the retirement was in progress, Colonel Newstead had received a message which Colonel Cockburn had sent off about seven hours previously, asking for assistance. But, soon after midday, a second message from Colonel Cockburn arrived announcing his success, and from this Colonel Newstead gathered that no assistance was required. He was, however, unable to get into communication with Colonel Cockburn and, deciding to return to Bare, he started to march there at 3.30 p.m. His column had suffered a total of 55 casualties, including Lieutenant M. J. Parker severely wounded and made prisoner.*

At Bare Colonel Cockburn decided to reorganise before renewing the offensive. He had several difficulties to contend

---

* Gallant attempts were made by Lieutenant G. Dawes and some of his men to carry Lieutenant Parker out of action. But these were abandoned after Lieutenant Parker had been twice wounded again (apparently mortally) and Private Monde Yeraia, one of his rescuers, had been severely wounded. For their gallantry Lieutenant Dawes and Private Monde were awarded the M.C. and D.C.M. respectively.

with. The weather was atrocious, there being constant rain by day and night; he had recently lost all the permanent company commanders in his own battalion; and a large proportion of his men were lame owing to " jiggers." *

On receiving reports of these operations, General Dobell at once despatched reinforcements to Nkongsamba, and also sent Colonel Gorges there, both to assume control of further operations and to report on the advisability of withdrawing from railhead to a point on the railway farther to the south. The physical condition and reduced numbers of his troops, both British and French, seemed to General Dobell to indicate the advisability of reducing his commitments; and he had just heard that Sir Frederick Lugard proposed to withdraw the Nigerian column from Ossidinge to the frontier.† In the meantime, pending Colonel Gorges' arrival, Colonel Cockburn was instructed to postpone any further offensive.

The reinforcements, consisting of the section Gold Coast Battery and of two companies West African Regiment withdrawn from Kribi, reached Nkongsamba on the 6th and 8th February respectively, Colonel Gorges also arriving there on the latter date. On the 10th, General Dobell, hearing that a company of Senegalese infantry was being sent from Dakar to reinforce him, and also that a draft from the Gold Coast would shortly reach Duala, decided that it would not, after all, be necessary to consider a withdrawal from railhead.

Changes in distribution and organisation; Feb. 1915.
He also decided on certain changes in the distribution and organisation of his British troops. The 1st Nigerians were withdrawn from the Northern Railway to quieter areas to rest, their headquarters and two companies being sent to garrison Buea, Victoria and Zopo, and their remaining two companies to Kribi. The Composite Battalion, after the relief of its headquarters and two companies in the Buea area, was to be broken up,‡ its two Sierra Leone companies joining the Sierra Leone Battalion under Colonel Newstead, and its two Gold Coast companies with the Gold Coast pioneer company—the three brought by the coming draft up to a total strength of about 500 rifles—forming a Gold Coast Battalion under Colonel Rose.

---

* Unless these fleas, which burrow into the flesh to lay their eggs, are promptly and properly extracted, they cause bad sores or ulcers. The men from Northern Nigeria suffered especially.
† This proposal was, as explained hereafter, subsequently abandoned.
‡ It was broken up on the 26th February.

[*To face p.* 236

A British N.C.O., Nigeria Regiment

NORTHERN RAILHEAD SITUATION 237

By the 15th February the troops at Nkongsamba and Bare consisted of: Northern Railway: 15th Feb.– 3rd March 1915.

    Nigerian Battery (less one section).
    Section Gold Coast Battery.
    One section Sierra Leone Battery.
    Headquarters and four companies West African Regiment.
    Headquarters and four companies Sierra Leone Battalion.
    One Sierra Leone company, Composite Battalion.
    Gold Coast pioneer company.

i.e., a total of 6 guns and about 900 rifles.

In spite of patrol activity and the efforts of his Intelligence staff, Colonel Gorges found it impossible to gain really reliable information concerning the enemy, whose main force was reported to be at Melong. On the 19th February, reports having reached him that a party of about 200 German troops had occupied Mbureku, Colonel Gorges sent out two small columns from Nkongsamba and Bare to attack and, if possible, capture the enemy camp there. But, beyond a small patrol, no enemy was encountered, and Mbureku village was found to have been burnt recently.

Further strong reconnaissances were carried out during the next few days. On the 23rd February British patrols reported Mbureku, Harmann's Farm and Ekom to be held by the enemy, the patrol reconnoitring Mbureku having had a sharp fight in which it had suffered ten casualties. From this and other reports Colonel Gorges estimated the hostile strength, at and south of Melong, at about 60 German and 500–600 native troops.

General Dobell, being of opinion that the enemy should be attacked and driven away from Melong, arranged to reinforce Colonel Gorges for the purpose. But, before these reinforcements arrived, it appeared to Colonel Gorges that the growing enemy concentration at Mbureku threatened Bare, and he decided to strike at the Germans there before they were reinforced further.

This intention he carried out on the 27th February, meeting with only partial success. A column—consisting of one gun each of the Sierra Leone and Gold Coast Batteries, two companies and the machine-gun section West African Regiment, and a company of the Sierra Leone Battalion—under command of Lieutenant-Colonel Vaughan, moved out from

Nkongsamba at 5 a.m. to attack Mbureku from the south; while to co-operate with it from the eastward a column, of two companies Sierra Leone Battalion with a machine gun under Lieutenant-Colonel Newstead, left Bare at 6 a.m. A company of the West African Regiment was also despatched from Nkongsamba through Bare towards Harmann's Farm and Ekom, to engage the enemy's attention in that direction; and as a report from Bare, received late on the 26th, indicated increased enemy strength and activity near Harmann's Farm and Ekom, Colonel Newstead was instructed to leave an extra half-company with a machine gun at Bare itself.

Having previously received a message from Colonel Newstead that he would be in the vicinity of Mbureku at 11 a.m., Colonel Vaughan came into action to the south of that place at 11.15 a.m. The enemy, with at least three machine guns in action, offered a vigorous resistance, and it was not till about 1.45 p.m. that Colonel Vaughan's men gained possession of the German position. This lay along a razor-backed ridge covering Mbureku from the south, and soon after its capture patrols from Colonel Newstead's column, which was not far away to the east, met Colonel Vaughan's patrols. About 2.30 p.m., however, the enemy—apparently reinforced from Melong—delivered a counter-attack against Colonel Newstead's right flank. At the same time communication between the two columns was broken and remained interrupted for over an hour, leaving Colonel Vaughan without any indication of the direction in which to turn the fire of his guns so as to shell the enemy attacking Colonel Newstead. At 3.20 p.m. a company which had been sent by Colonel Vaughan in Colonel Newstead's direction was stopped by the enemy's enfilading fire; and twenty minutes later Colonel Vaughan received word that Colonel Newstead was unable to locate the enemy's machine guns. At this stage the British gun ammunition gave out; and the enemy, who had managed under cover of the dense high grass to work round, opened fire on Colonel Vaughan's left flank and rear. Feeling that he had no other alternative, Colonel Vaughan then ordered a general retirement. This was carried out in good order; and, except for a small party which retired direct on Bare, Colonel Newstead's column joined Colonel Vaughan about 6 p.m. and returned with him to Nkongsamba. The total British casualties had been eighteen, including 2nd Lieutenant F. E. Andrew killed.

Colonel Gorges continued his preparations to advance on

HARMANN'S FARM AFFAIR

Melong as soon as the reinforcements arrived. This they had done by the 3rd March, when the following troops were concentrated at Nkongsamba and Bare:

> One section each, Sierra Leone, Gold Coast and Nigerian Batteries.
> Four companies West African Regiment.
> Five companies Sierra Leone Battalion.
> Three companies Gold Coast Battalion.

The enemy's main body was still reported to be at Melong, with strong advanced posts at Mbureku and Harmann's Farm, and a small detachment at Ekom.

On the 2nd March Colonel Gorges issued orders for the advance. It was to commence on the 4th, when one column, moving direct from Nkongsamba, was to seize Mbureku, and another, the main column, its right flank covered by a detachment operating against Ekom, was to capture Harmann's Farm. On the following day both columns were to advance against Melong. *Affair of Harmann's Farm; 4th March 1915. (Map 10, facing page 242.)*

The main column, under Colonel Gorges' personal command, comprised one section Nigerian Battery, headquarters and two and a half companies West African Regiment with two machine guns, and four companies Sierra Leone Battalion with two machine guns (one manned by naval ratings), i.e., a total of 2 guns and 550 rifles with 4 machine guns; the detachment to operate against Ekom consisted of another half-company West African Regiment; and the left column, under Lieutenant-Colonel Rose, was composed of the Gold Coast artillery section and the Gold Coast Battalion with three machine guns, i.e., a total of 2 guns and 450 rifles with 3 machine guns. This left one company and one gun at each of the posts at Nkongsamba and Bare.

Leaving Nkongsamba at 5.30 a.m. on the 4th March with part of his column, Colonel Gorges picked up the remainder at Bare some two hours later, and the whole column moved forward from there at 8.30 a.m. A halt was made at 8.45 a.m., while Colonel Gorges and his staff and commanding officers went on to a hill termed " Gun Hill," from which they obtained a clear view, over undulating country covered with elephant grass, of the enemy entrenchments about Harmann's and Stoebel's Farms. These farms were on the west and east of the main road respectively and not far from it, Stoebel's Farm being a few hundred yards to the south-eastward of Harmann's Farm. To cover the further advance of the column the Sierra Leone gun from Bare was posted on " Gun Hill," with orders to bring a cross fire to bear on Harmann's Farm in conjunction with the Nigerian guns when they opened fire, and to remain in position till Harmann's Farm had been captured.*

The column then resumed its march, the Nigerian guns pushing ahead of the main body to cover the advance of the advanced guard, which consisted of two companies of the Sierra Leone Battalion with two machine guns. At 10 a.m. hostile patrols, encountered at the road junction one and a half miles north of Bare, were driven off by the advanced guard; and shortly afterwards the Ekom detachment moved off eastward along the Bana road.

At 11.30 a.m. Colonel Gorges heard from Colonel Newstead, commanding the advanced guard, that his vanguard had cleared Stoebel's Farm fifteen minutes earlier; and at 11.35 a.m. Colonel Gorges received a second message saying that the advanced guard had occupied Stoebel's Farm, that no enemy had been seen at Harmann's Farm and that the hostile outposts appeared to be one thousand yards to the north of it. Colonel Newstead, from recent visits to the ground round Harmann's Farm, was presumably well acquainted with its neighbourhood, and no question of the accuracy of his rather rapidly made report appears to have occurred to Colonel Gorges. He at once sent orders to Colonel Newstead to make good his position at Stoebel's Farm and to clear Harmann's Farm. To assist him in this action Colonel Gorges, at the same time, sent forward to Stoebel's Farm a Nigerian gun under Captain C. F. S. Maclaverty, and moved himself with the main body to about six hundred yards south of Stoebel's Farm, where a wooded gully afforded a covered reserve position.

At 12 noon the advanced guard came under a sudden and heavy enemy fire from positions about five hundred yards north and nine hundred yards westward of Harmann's Farm; and a few minutes later Colonel Gorges received a request from Colonel Newstead for reinforcements. Colonel Gorges ordered a company of the Sierra Leone Battalion from the main body to advance and reinforce Colonel Newstead; and, lacking a definite indication of where it was most required, sent it forward by the least exposed line of advance to the right flank of the advanced guard.

---

* This gun actually returned to Bare at 10.30 a.m., apparently without further orders and under a misapprehension.

The available accounts of the subsequent fighting are not very clear; and, as two of the British officers most concerned were killed or wounded, the following description may not be quite complete or accurate. There is, however, ground for supposing that the enemy had received previous warning of the coming attack. He appears to have pushed out a screen of native riflemen, who, as the British approached, fell back, uncovering the front of a German European detachment skilfully posted behind a deep and densely wooded gully with at least three machine guns. When these opened fire, though the British vanguard held to its ground, a part of the advanced guard became unsteady and fell back, the machine gun carriers discarding their loads. To add to the British difficulties many of the shells from Captain Maclaverty's gun failed to explode and their gun carriers also fell back. The gunners, however, stuck gallantly to the gun until compelled to abandon it.

Influenced by the unsteadiness in front, the company sent from the main body to reinforce the right made no progress and began to retire. The British officers and N.C.Os. made vigorous and gallant attempts to restore the situation, but their efforts were unavailing, and in making them Colonel Newstead and his adjutant, Lieutenant H. S. Finch, were wounded. In the meantime Colonel Gorges, seeing troops and carriers retreating down and alongside the road in front of him, had pushed out, to take up a position to his left front, a half-company Sierra Leone Battalion under Lieutenant de Miremont.* Colonel Gorges and his staff were on the road on the northern bank of the gully, where they strove to stem the tide of retreating troops and carriers, exposing themselves in doing so, with the result that Captain C. H. Dinnen, on Colonel Gorges' staff, was killed. While working his gun at close range Captain Maclaverty had also been severely wounded and, though his native gunners continued to serve the gun with courage and devotion, they had no option but to abandon it when the vanguard, finding its position untenable without reinforcements, retired past them.

To retrieve the situation and to secure the gun and the machine guns dropped by their carriers, Colonel Gorges sent forward part of the West African Regiment to Stoebel's Farm. They carried out their task with steadiness and courage, their advance being facilitated by a lessening in the

---

* The actual time when this half-company was pushed out is doubtful.

hostile fire, due, as was subsequently ascertained, to the enemy having begun to retire.

By this time, thanks in great measure to the strenuous efforts of Lieutenant-Colonel A. J. Turner of the General Staff,* backed by the coolness and action of other British officers, a certain measure of confidence had been restored among the native troops and the ammunition and medical carriers. But most of them were so badly shaken as to be incapable of offensive action, and Colonel Gorges decided that he must withdraw. As already mentioned the enemy had actually begun to retire. But Colonel Gorges was not aware of this, and the British retirement proceeded. It commenced at 1.15 p.m. and was carried out without molestation, Bare being reached at 3 p.m. The British casualties totalled twenty-seven, mostly in the Sierra Leone Battalion, and included four British officers and one British seaman, Colonel Newstead unfortunately dying of his wounds.

From Bare Colonel Gorges sent orders to Colonel Rose to withdraw with his column to Nkongsamba. He had occupied Mbureku without opposition and his retirement was carried out without special incident. The Ekom detachment had also been ordered back to Bare and arrived there at 7 p.m., having driven the enemy detachment from Ekom across the Nkam river.

Northern Railway; 5th–31st March 1915. During the next few days there was a redistribution of the troops on the Northern Railway. The Sierra Leone Battalion was withdrawn to garrison posts between Nkongsamba and Bonaberi, the latter place being held by two companies 1st Nigerians withdrawn from Kribi on the 1st March. The Gold Coast artillery section and two companies of the Gold Coast Battalion, under command of Colonel Rose, were posted to Bare; the section of the Nigerian Battery went to Duala; and the headquarters and four companies West African Regiment, one company Gold Coast Battalion and a section of the Sierra Leone Battery were stationed at Nkongsamba, where Colonel Gorges established his headquarters.

By the 10th March British reconnoitring parties had discovered that the Germans had evacuated the Mbureku-Harmann's Farm-Stoebel's Farm line, the state of their camps disclosing signs of a hasty retreat.† On the 13th a

---

* General Dobell had lent Colonel Gorges his services for the advance.
† It was learnt, several months later, that the succession of British attacks had caused such inroads on the German ammunition as to render their leaders apprehensive of a shortage if they continued to hold this line.

MAP 10.

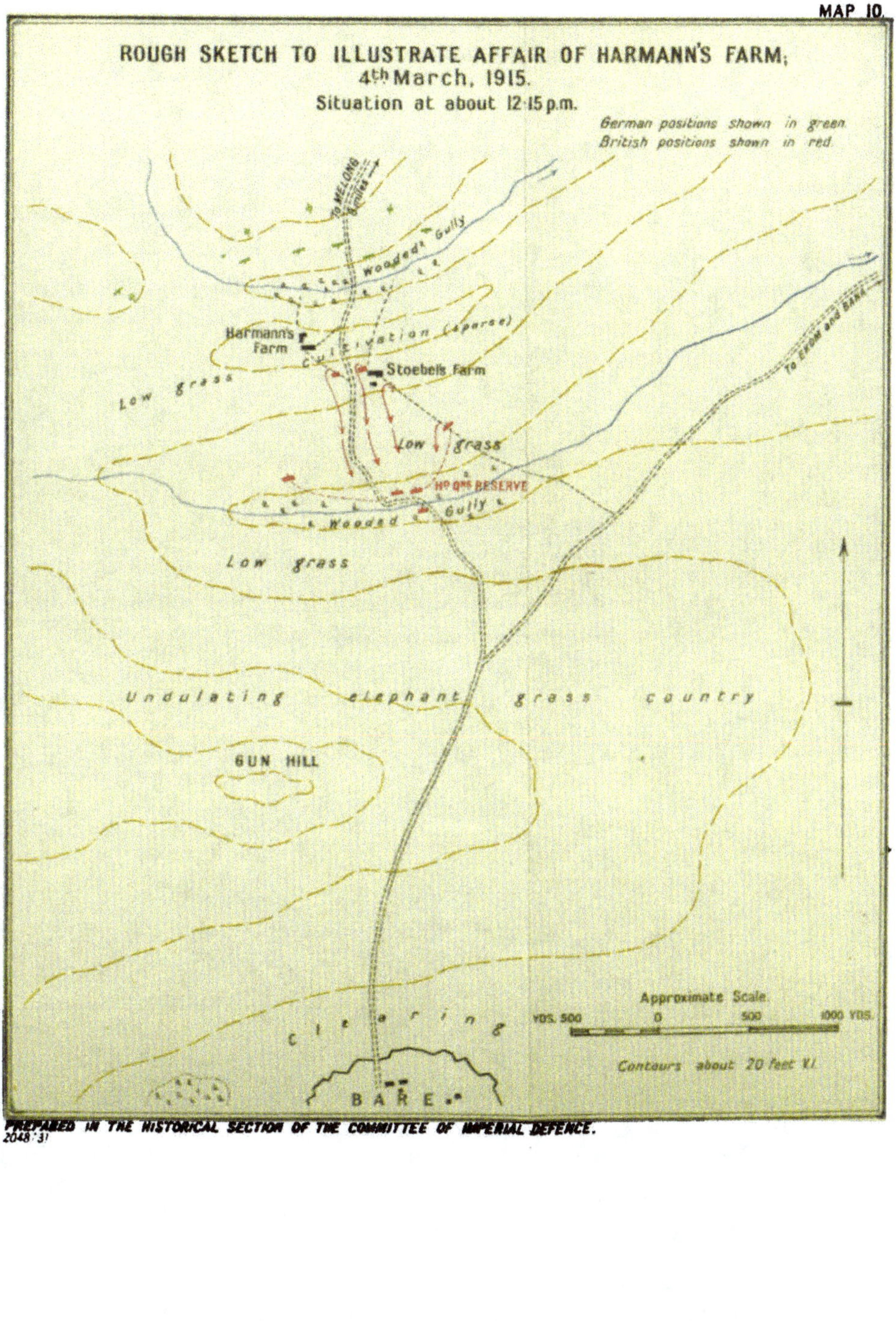

PREPARED IN THE HISTORICAL SECTION OF THE COMMITTEE OF IMPERIAL DEFENCE.
2048/31

strong reconnoitring detachment found Melong also clear of enemy troops and three days later another British party drove an enemy observation post of about one hundred rifles out of Melong without difficulty. The enemy's main body was evidently some distance to the north, and to obtain information of it Colonel Gorges proposed that he should occupy Melong temporarily with a company. But General Dobell deprecated the idea unless information was otherwise unobtainable. He was contemplating an advance eastward from Edea and, although he had no intention of withdrawing from the Northern Railway, his general policy there for the time being was to hold railhead and Bare, limiting offensive movements to those necessary to avert threats against those places and the railway line of communication. This policy he directed Colonel Gorges to carry out by maintaining touch with the enemy by means of patrols and armed native partisans and so obtain information of any transference of enemy strength from the vicinity.

On the 18th March, in a report to General Dobell, Colonel Gorges summarised the information he had acquired by the various means at his disposal. The enemy's main body was at Fongdonera, with a covering detachment patrolling as far south as Melong, and he also had detachments at Sanchu (covering Mbo and the Tinto road) and at the bridge over the Nkam river near Ekom (covering a force based on Bana). The total German forces at and south of Chang were estimated at a strength of 80 to 100 Germans, 600 natives and 7 machine guns. A fairly large German force was also reported to be in the Dibum district (about thirty miles eastward of Bare), but they were too far off the railway to cause much concern. All the German detachments were reported to be short of provisions and to be living on the country. The local chiefs were giving the British much useful information, and the many natives who had taken refuge at Nkongsamba and Bare from the Germans were being employed on work on roads, etc. It appeared evident, said Colonel Gorges, that the Germans had never meant to hold Melong and had fallen back anticipating a second British advance on Chang. Their native troops were said to have been shaken by the fighting on the 4th March, but they were well organised and their fire tactics were excellent.

Towards the end of March it was reported that the Germans had concentrated a force of about four hundred men on the

Bana-Yabasi road about one and a half day's march from the Nkam river.

<small>The Duala-Kribi-Edea-Yabasi area; Feb. 1915.</small>
At Duala at the beginning of February, General Dobell found it rather difficult to interpret German action. Though showing more enterprise, they were avoiding serious engagements and were evidently taking great care of their lives.

On the 6th February, the German activity near the Northern railhead caused the withdrawal, for transfer to Nkongsamba, of the headquarters and two companies West African Regiment from Kribi; the remaining two companies being also withdrawn about a week later, on relief by two companies 1st Nigerians under Major R. G. Coles.

By the 9th February the greater part of the French contingent was concentrated at Edea and Kopongo, with detachments, each 100 strong, at Butu and Yapoma.* On the 14th February the reinforcing Senegalese company from Dakar reached Duala and was also sent to Edea.

On the 13th February the enemy made two unsuccessful attacks on the post at Dibombe, and on the 15th information was received that Ebermaier and Zimmermann, the German civil and military chiefs in the Cameroons, had recently left Yaunde with 400 troops for the Yabasi district. In the next two days various reports indicated considerable hostile activity on a line running roughly north-west and south-east through Yabasi, and on the 17th the British post at Dibombe was consequently reinforced by 150 rifles, viz., one company West African Regiment and the Gambia detachment under Captain V. B. Thurston. But they had hardly been despatched when further and persistent reports were received that a strong German force was at Ndokama (about twenty-five miles north-eastward of Duala) and had pushed forward its advanced troops to Lobesu, within seven or eight miles of Duala. As these reports attributed to the enemy the intention of advancing against Duala, precautions were taken there for the night of the 17th/18th February, the Gambia detachment being recalled from Dibombe, one company 2nd Nigerians being brought across the river from Bonaberi and a naval armed party with a gun being landed from the *Challenger*. Early on the 18th, however, a French patrol from Yapoma found that there were no enemy troops at or near Lobesu.

Colonel Mayer then came in from Edea to Duala to discuss the situation and informed General Dobell that there was

---

* There was also a French depot, of about 100 men, at Duala.

every indication that the railway from Edea to the Kele river was still held by the enemy in some strength.

To clear up the position it was decided that a column under Colonel Rose, acting in co-operation with a company from Dibombe under Captain Thurston, should reconnoitre towards Ndokama, and that Colonel Mayer should push out strong reconnoitring parties from Edea to the eastward and southeastward. Between the 21st and 24th February Colonel Rose's and Captain Thurston's columns carried out a close examination of the country on the left bank of the Wuri river, but without encountering any enemy, and on the 25th a French column from Edea under Commandant Mathieu reached a point twenty-three miles to the south-east, also without opposition. On the Yaunde road and railway, however, another French column had been stopped at about eight miles from Edea by an enemy detachment. But it was soon driven back, Commandant Mathieu returning to Edea on the 1st March after turning the enemy out of Ngwe with loss at a cost of ten French casualties.

It was subsequently learnt that the reports of a German intention to attack Duala had been based on fact. In the belief that German cruisers had recaptured the entrance to the Cameroon estuary they imagined for a short time that Duala lay at their mercy. But they discovered their mistake in time.*

It was a rather significant coincidence that, on the 24th February, General Dobell received information from the Allied naval authorities that four German cruisers might be concentrating off the coast near the Equator. As a hostile naval attack would isolate Kribi, General Dobell thereupon decided to withdraw its British garrison and the many native refugees there. The two companies 1st Nigerians accordingly returned to Duala on the 1st March, after some 1,900 native refugees, including men, women and children, had been embarked for transference to the plantation area on the Cameroon mountain. As a matter of fact these reports of German naval movements proved to be incorrect.

On the 28th February the French European company, its members being generally ineffective from sickness, reached Duala from Edea on its way back to Dakar.

The Nyong flotilla, under command of Lieutenant W. McC.

The Nyong and Campo flotillas; Feb. 1915.

---

* It is possible that they were enlightened by the sight of the searchlights of the *Challenger*, who was assisting in the defence.

Lunt, R.N.R., till the arrival of Commander Sneyd in the *Remus* about the 5th February, was still carrying out constant reconnaissances up the Nyong and Lokundje rivers, in the course of which hostile parties were frequently encountered. On two of these occasions, on the 14th and 19th February, eight casualties were incurred, including Lieutenant Lunt and four British naval ratings wounded. During the month it became impossible to feed the large number of native refugees who had come into the Nyong base, and all but about five hundred old men, women and children were removed along the coast road to settlements on the right bank of the Sanaga river.

At the end of January, no enemy having been encountered in the vicinity for some time, the detachment of marines at Campo had been transferred to Kribi and the construction of blockhouses surrounded by stockades at Campo and Dipikar was commenced. On the 4th February Commander Hughes relieved Commander Sneyd in charge of the Campo flotilla. Enemy activity in this area was mainly confined to raids by parties of armed native levies; and, to deal with these and also to collect information, Commander Hughes was authorised to enrol and arm trustworthy natives, no troops being available for the purpose. It became clear at this period that German agents in Muni had arranged an elaborate system of convoys between Bata and the German-occupied parts of the Cameroons.

Dobell's need of reinforcement; March 1915. On the 5th March, the day after the fight at Harmann's Farm, General Dobell telegraphed to the Colonial Office that he had, for the time being, only two battalions fit for active duty. It was strategically essential, he continued, to maintain his hold on Nkongsamba so as to protect the Cameroon Mountain district and the country adjoining the Northern Railway. But, though he had placed six guns and some 1,300 rifles at Colonel Gorges' disposal to deal with the menace presented by the German force near Bare, the recent fighting had gone against our troops and General Dobell had no more men he could send. In fact, he could but ill spare the services, for any length of time, of those already there. The exhausted condition of all ranks of his force and the inability of the West African colonies to supply the large reinforcements necessary for replacements led him to urge strongly that, if possible, Indian troops should be sent him. In conclusion he pointed out that the climate made it impossible for Europeans and natives to continue constantly engaged with the enemy for more than six months.

THE QUESTION OF REINFORCEMENTS

The inability of the West African colonies to comply with General Dobell's requirements was quite intelligible. Local recruitment for military service had always been on a small scale and had been handicapped by the limited numbers of men suitable and fit for military service. The withdrawal, for the operations in the Cameroons, of officials, officers, troops, carriers, etc., had taken nearly all who could have recruited and trained reinforcing drafts, while those who remained had in most cases to do double duty, including that of maintaining internal security. Ex-soldiers had come forward well for re-engagement, but were frequently too old or unfit for service and generally incapable of up-to-date training, while those who were capable made it clear that they had re-enlisted to fight and not to train recruits. In Nigeria, where men of the right type were most plentiful, the requirements of the forces operating on and across her own frontier had also to be considered. All the colonies, moreover, were finding it increasingly difficult to provide, under war conditions, for the upkeep of the contingents they had already furnished.

On the 9th March the Colonial Office informed General Dobell that there was no possibility of Indian troops being sent him and that the Gold Coast and Nigeria were being asked what they could do to assist. In a second telegram of the same date the Colonial Office inquired whether, in view of the importance of a thorough co-ordination of the various operations in the Cameroons, General Dobell considered that any of the forces operating from Nigeria could be employed to better advantage if they were with him. They also inquired the result of his conference with the delegates from French Equatorial Africa.

Replying on the 10th, General Dobell said that the French delegates were due at Duala in a few days' time. The difficulties of co-ordinating all the operations by the various Allied forces were, as he had explained in December, very great, and he went on to say that, in his opinion, the existing distribution of the troops operating from Nigeria allowed of their being employed to the best effect. Garua was their main objective, and its reduction would undoubtedly influence the course of the campaign. He concluded by asking if the French Government could be approached with a view to strong reinforcements being sent to Duala.

The Colonial Office, after consultation with the War Office, replied the same day instructing General Dobell to make the best defensive arrangements possible with the force at his disposal, as a vigorous offensive was not expected of him. He was asked to telegraph his proposals in detail.

On the 11th March Sir Frederick Lugard replied to the Colonial Office telegram of the 9th asking him if he could assist. He was doing all he could, he said, to re-enlist old soldiers, and recruiting was very successful. But he was without officers to train men. In his opinion, the best solution of the existing deadlock would be to strike a vigorous blow in the Northern Cameroons, where very large Allied forces had been inactive for many months. He trusted that the despatch there of Colonel Cunliffe with the naval gun and reinforcements would prove successful and would assist General Dobell by liberating a large body of troops.

In the Gold Coast arrangements were made to send a strong draft to Duala, and General Dobell was informed accordingly.

In London the War Office, as a result of their discussion with the Colonial Office, requested the French military attaché to telegraph to Paris urging the necessity for sending French officer reinforcements to Edea. The War Office also agreed to furnish a number of British officers and non-commissioned officers for whose services General Dobell had recently applied.

Arrival of French Mission at Duala; 12th March 1915. The mission sent by the Governor-General of French Equatorial Africa to confer with General Dobell arrived at Duala on the 12th March. Its members were Monsieur Fourneau (Governor of Middle Congo), Commandant Joly (Chief of Staff to General Aymerich), and Monsieur Damiens (Civil Staff). Before giving an account of the resulting conference, however, it will be advisable to bring the description of the operations in the south, south-eastern and northern Cameroons up to date.

Franco-Belgian operations in the S. and S.E. Cameroons; Feb.–March 1915. The future policy to be adopted by the French troops operating in the south and south-east Cameroons was considered by the Council of Defence of French Equatorial Africa on the 6th February. It was evident that a continued French advance on a wide arc would bring about increased communication difficulties and a reduction in the size of their striking forces, while, on the other hand, the farther the enemy retired the stronger the opposing forces that he would be able to concentrate. The Council had, therefore, to determine a general line to which the French could advance without undue risk pending co-operation by the force under General

Dobell. After full consideration, it was decided that this line should be the Ntem river north of Oyem-Akoafim-Lomie-Dume.

Three days later, i.e., on the night of the 9th/10th February, the Oyem Column (Major Miquelard) forced the passage of the Wola river and encountered considerable resistance on the 10th, when it incurred a number of casualties and its advance was checked. On the 16th, however, the Germans evacuated Oyem, and the French occupied it the same day. Here they remained for many weeks after pushing forward a covering force of two companies some twenty miles to the north and north-eastward.

The Mvahdi Column (Lieutenant-Colonel Le Meillour), its concentration completed, pushed forward in the middle of February and joined its advanced detachment at Minkebe. From here a column of 250 rifles with a Nordenfeldt gun started on the 5th March to advance on Akoafim; but, after arriving within eight miles of that place, was forced by the rain and by supply difficulties to return to Minkebe.

The Sanga Column spent February in reorganisation, its distribution at the end of the month being as follows :

Sembe	..	300 rifles and 1 mountain gun.
Ngoila	..	300 rifles and 3 Nordenfeldt guns.
Molundu	..	150 rifles and 2 mountain, 2 Nordenfeldt and 1 machine, guns.
Yukaduma	..	225 rifles and 2 mountain guns (a detachment of 250 rifles had been sent from here in the middle of the month to reinforce the Lobaye Column).

General Aymerich then arrived at Molundu on a tour of inspection and gave orders for an immediate advance on Lomie by three columns : one of 275 rifles advancing from Ngoila via Eta, a second of 400 rifles advancing from Molundu via Besam, and a third of 170 rifles advancing from Yukaduma. General Dobell was informed by the French Mission at Duala that it was anticipated that these columns would capture Lomie by the end of March.

At the beginning of February Colonel Morisson, commanding the Lobaye Column—which was in occupation of the line Bertua-Nyassi—found the increasing German activity so threatening that he called for reinforcements from the Sanga Column. But these proved insufficient, and at the end of the month he was forced to retire under enemy pressure to the line of the Kadei river, where supply difficulties prevented his attempting to re-assume the offensive.

Nigeria and the Northern Cameroons; Feb.–March 1915.
After Colonel Cunliffe returned to Nigeria at the beginning of February he discussed with Sir Frederick Lugard the possibility of sending some troops to reinforce General Dobell. The release, for this purpose, of a company from the Cross River Column would be possible if the British force were withdrawn from Ossidinge, and Sir Frederick Lugard proposed that this should be done. But, as General Dobell deprecated such withdrawal as likely to encourage the enemy and discourage our own troops and subjects, the idea was eventually abandoned. Moreover, Sir Frederick Lugard and Colonel Cunliffe had come to the conclusion that the latter must proceed to Garua to examine the situation and that he should take with him the naval gun and all possible reinforcements. The naval gun, its passage up-country much delayed by the low state of the Benue river, did not reach Yola till the 12th March, and Colonel Cunliffe and his staff arrived there three days later. His advent to Garua had been announced to Colonel Brisset, who had agreed to Major Wright remaining on Colonel Cunliffe's staff when the latter, as senior officer, assumed command of the Allied forces in the Northern Cameroons.

The Cross River Column; Feb.–March 1915.
At Ossidinge the Cross River Column maintained contact, for the first half of February, with an enemy force at Tinto, both sides incurring a few casualties in a series of patrol encounters. Here as elsewhere the Germans were endeavouring to establish a reign of terror among the local inhabitants, but after the middle of February they appeared to have evacuated Tinto, as touch with them was then lost. At the end of the month Colonel Mair was invalided and command of the column was taken over by Captain Crookenden and about the same time two companies (" G " Company, 3rd Battalion, and " B " Company, 4th Battalion) were withdrawn from the column to go to Yola.

In the middle of March there were four companies (" A," " C," " E " and " F " of the 3rd Battalion) and two guns of the 2nd Battery at Ossidinge, and one company (" B " of the 3rd Battalion) holding the line of communication back to the frontier.

Ibi Column; Feb. 1915.
Except for an abortive attack on a camp near Beli on the 4th February,* the Ibi Column, in its watch on the frontier

---

* Lieutenant E. A. Sandilands was wounded in this affair.

[To face p. 250

A Soldier of the Nigeria Regiment

of the Muri province, was undisturbed by the enemy during February. Towards the end of the month Major Mann and the gun of the column were ordered to Yola, the local command then devolving on Captain H. W. Green, his headquarters remaining at Takum with a company detached to Beli.

At Garua the strength of the German force and position made such an impression on Colonel Brisset that he decided he would have to act with prudence if he was not to lose, at one stroke, much of the territory he had already gained. It seemed to him that it would be hazardous in the extreme to attempt to assault the German position until he had stronger artillery. Garua; Feb.–March 1915.

In his instructions to Major Webb-Bowen he said that his immediate aims were a careful reconnaissance of the whole of the hostile position, the stoppage of all communications and supplies for the garrison from outside, the rupture of German relations with natives of the surrounding districts, and the seizure by the Allies of every opportunity to weaken and wear down the enemy.

Colonel Brisset had selected the French and British positions at Nassarao and Bogole respectively as cutting the German garrison off from a rich and populous district and at the same time placing the Allies in a situation to hinder hostile movements towards Mora in the north or to the south, where the Fulanis were said to be pro-German. At Bogole the British were, it is true, cut off from their line of communication with Yola, but to Major Webb-Bowen's consequent objections Colonel Brisset had replied that if the British were located to the westward of Garua communication with Nassarao would be very difficult and combined operations impossible. He promised French co-operation to secure the British communication with Yola and to escort convoys from that direction. A great advantage of the two Allied positions, in Colonel Brisset's opinion, was that, being three miles approximately apart from one another and from the German position, they could afford one another mutual support.* So that, once these Allied positions had been fortified, they could be held by small garrisons, thus freeing the maximum numbers for frequent reconnaissances in strength to harass the enemy and impel the natives to leave Garua town.

By such action Colonel Brisset hoped to force the Germans to attack the Allies instead of themselves awaiting attack.

---

* The Benue river would normally remain fordable till September.

He also hoped that the Germans at Mora would shortly have to evacuate their position and so set free another Allied column for location near Jambutu Manga, to the north-west of Garua. In the meantime he asked General Largeau if arrangements could be made for a heavy gun to be sent him from Dakar via Nigeria. This was agreed to.

After establishing himself at Bogole Lieutenant-Colonel Webb-Bowen * changed his line of communication with Yola to a route running south of the Benue river via Gurin.

The Germans in the meantime had shown no intention of seriously attacking the Allies, but pursued harassing tactics with constant patrols and shelled the Allies at every opportunity with guns, of which at least one outranged any with the British or French.

German documents captured about, and after, this period show that up till the 9th February the garrison were still receiving messages from outside, one that reached them on that date from Banyo informing them that German war vessels had arrived at Duala!

On the night of the 12th/13th February, in fulfilment of a plan he had made to entice a part of the German force out of its entrenchments so as to defeat it in the open, Colonel Brisset moved out with a French detachment 250 strong and marched round the north of Garua to Jambutu Manga. He had instructed Colonel Webb-Bowen to move out with a British detachment of similar strength so as to arrive by daybreak on the 13th at a place, the description of which in Colonel Brisset's orders, as translated into English, signified an area rather than a fixed point. Hoping that the Germans would move a force out to attack him about Jambutu Manga on the morning of the 13th, Colonel Brisset intended, as soon as this attack commenced, to send word to Colonel Webb-Bowen to ford the Benue and advance northward so as to take the German force in reverse. The plan, however, miscarried. For, though the Germans attacked as expected, the message from Colonel Brisset did not find Colonel Webb-Bowen where it had been expected that he would be. Colonel Brisset consequently broke off the action and withdrew, retiring by a route to the south of the Benue river as he had originally intended to do. His force had suffered twenty-three casualties, including two French killed.

During the next few weeks hostilities on both sides were

---

* He had just been promoted.

limited to minor operations by patrols and detachments, and there were no incidents of importance. Smallpox broke out in Garua town, and the Germans were said to have attempted to drive those infected into the areas occupied by the Allies, but without success. The weather was very hot and its effect on the health of Europeans was noticeable, while it combined with the shortage of water, due to the usual dry season, to make operations and movement trying and difficult.

On the 9th March Colonel Webb-Bowen left to confer with Colonel Cunliffe at Yola, for which purpose also Colonel Brisset, deeming it inadvisable that both he and Colonel Webb-Bowen should be away together, sent there Captain Ferrandi (his staff officer) and Lieutenant Ozier.

On the 13th March Colonel Brisset heard that a 95-mm. gun with five hundred shells was being sent him from Dakar via Nigeria.

At Mora, during the period under review, there had been no change in the situation and no special incident of importance. *Mora; Feb.–March 1915.*

The French Mission had come to Duala to arrange, if possible, for co-operation by the force under General Dobell in an advance on Yaunde. This place, the temporary seat of German Government, was regarded by the military authorities in French Equatorial Africa as the most important objective they could aim at. Since the enemy would almost certainly endeavour to defend it he must lay himself open to defeat, and this, with its capture, was calculated to hasten the end of the campaign. The French delegates informed General Dobell that French troops would probably have occupied Lomie and Dume by the end of the month and that co-operation from General Dobell was desired in their intended advance on Yaunde from those localities. *The French Mission at Duala; March 1915.*

We now know—and the reader may have surmised from the previous account of French operations in that quarter—that this estimate of future French achievement in the south and south-east was unduly optimistic. At the time, however, General Dobell, who fully realised the importance of Yaunde, had no grounds for questioning the accuracy of the French forecast. But he foresaw other difficulties to prevent his acceding to the French request. It took a month for telegrams from the Lobaye Column to reach Edea, so that any close co-ordination of movement would be impossible; Colonel

Mayer's contingent was in no condition to provide a sufficient force for the advance of 120 miles; the rainy season would shortly set in; and the strength and physical condition of the troops of the British contingent rendered it unlikely that they could assist by protecting Colonel Mayer's line of communication. In deference, however, to the representations of the French delegates, General Dobell agreed that, if reinforcements for Colonel Mayer's contingent were provided, he would co-operate in the French advance from the south and south-east by despatching a force of 1,000 rifles from Edea to move against Eseka; otherwise his forces would only be able to display local activity. It was understood on both sides that exact co-ordination of the movements from the south and south-east with those from the west would not be possible, and that the rôle of the force from Edea would be to prevent the enemy transferring troops from the west to the east.

On the 18th March General Dobell heard from Dakar that a reinforcement of two Senegalese companies with two machine guns and some other details were leaving there for Duala on the 22nd. As the arrival of these men would enable Colonel Mayer to form a column of the necessary strength, General Dobell arranged with the French Mission, which was leaving Duala that day,* that the combined advance should start on the 20th April, preliminary movements to establish advanced bases being commenced about twelve days earlier. The approach of the rainy season made it desirable to start as soon as possible, but General Dobell did not consider that Colonel Mayer would be able to do so before the date he fixed. On the 19th March he telegraphed to the French Governor-General at Brazzaville that he was prepared to co-operate in the proposed advance on Yaunde with a force of 1,000 French and 600 British troops, including line of communication troops. General Dobell's ability to find the British troops for this purpose was due to information that a strong draft from the Gold Coast and a small one from Nigeria would shortly reach Duala, and also to the receipt of reports from Colonel Gorges confirming the retirement of the enemy's main forces to an area about thirty miles north of Nkongsamba.

There had so far been no direct indication that the French Government approved, or contemplated fulfilment, of the

---

* The French cruiser *Pothuau*, which had brought the French Mission from the south, took them back again.

evident desire of the local authorities in French Equatorial Africa for territorial gain in the Cameroons. The instructions to General Dobell, the Allied commander, recently issued by the British Government showed that, for the time being or pending the result of the Allied conference at Duala, no more was contemplated than the occupation of points of strategical importance. On the 19th March, however, the French military attaché in London handed to the Director of Military Operations at the War Office a memorandum by the French Colonial Office on the situation in the Cameroons, which made it clear that the French Government had in mind the conquest of the whole German colony.*

Reports in the third week of March that a force of 150 to 200 Germans had re-occupied Yabasi led General Dobell to despatch two small columns to advance, from Dibombe Post and from Penja on the Northern Railway respectively, against Yabasi. These two columns, under Colonel Haywood, gained touch with one another on the 19th March close to Yabasi and found next day that it had been evacuated. After spending two more days patrolling the district without encountering any enemy, both columns withdrew downstream. *Duala; March 1915.*

A reinforcing draft of two British officers and 160 native ranks of the Gold Coast Regiment arrived at Duala from the Gold Coast on the 31st March, and were formed into a fourth ("D") company for incorporation in the Gold Coast Battalion. A draft of thirty reservists arrived at the same time from Nigeria.

On the 3rd April General Dobell received a telegram from the Colonial Office informing him that the direction of military operations in the Cameroons had been transferred to the War Office, though on political, civil and commercial matters he would still receive his instructions from the Colonial Office. He was further told that troops on or adjacent to the Nigerian *War Office assume control of operations; April 1915.*

---

* It is noteworthy that this memorandum showed that the French Colonial Office had gathered a wrong impression of the respective efforts of the Allied contingents in the Cameroons. From reports they had received from Equatorial and West Africa the French Colonial Office concluded that with the reinforcements recently ordered from Dakar to Duala the French troops would be bearing almost the entire burden of conquest. This opinion was based mainly on the larger numbers of the French land contingent—now totalling, they said, 7,500—over those of the British land contingent—just under 5,000—and on the greater physical difficulties of the forest area in which most of the French troops were operating. The memorandum omitted, however, to take into account the considerable assistance rendered by the British naval and marine contingents, and also the greater immunity from German aggression which, owing to their location, the French African possessions enjoyed as compared with Nigeria.

frontier were not to be diverted from their existing sphere of operations without the concurrence of the Colonial Office, unless by arrangement between General Dobell and Sir Frederick Lugard.

The reason for this transfer of control was the growth in magnitude of the task in the Cameroons. The West African colonies were no longer able to meet its financial cost or its demands in personnel and material; and the conduct of the operations had also, on more than one occasion recently, necessitated requests by the Colonial Office for advice by the General Staff at the War Office.* As the operations extended more assistance would be required from the War Office to comply with demands for the necessary personnel and material, while their expert advice on strategical and tactical questions, especially those affecting military co-operation with the French, would be more than ever necessary. They were, moreover, the proper agency to control a campaign for which the Imperial Government had assumed financial responsibility.

Operations east of Edea; April 1915. (Map 12.) The withdrawal of the enemy from the neighbourhoods of the Northern Railway and the Dibombe post facilitated the readjustment of his dispositions which enabled General Dobell to free a part of his British contingent to act in conjunction with the French in their coming advance eastward from Edea. For this purpose he placed at Colonel Mayer's disposal the following column under Lieutenant-Colonel Haywood:—

> One section Nigerian Battery,
> One company 1st Nigerians,
> Headquarters and three companies 2nd Nigerians,
> One company Sierra Leone Battalion,
> The Gambia Detachment,

i.e., a total of two guns and about 600 rifles with six machine guns. By the 10th April they and approximately 1,000 carriers had reached Edea by train. For the forthcoming operations under Colonel Mayer it was arranged that a French column of 1,000 rifles with four guns should move by the line of the railway from Edea to Eseka and that Colonel Haywood's column should advance along the Yaunde road on the French left flank in readiness to co-operate as required.

The first objective was the line of the Kele river, where the French and British columns were to establish advanced

---

* After the dissolution, at the end of November 1914, of the Offensive Sub-committee of the Committee of Imperial Defence, the Secretary of State for the Colonies had assumed, as a member of the Cabinet, the responsibility for military policy in the Cameroons.

bases, at So Dibanga and Ngwe respectively, from which, as arranged with the French delegates, their further advance was to commence on the 20th April.

Starting from Edea on the 10th April a French column under Commandant Mathieu—consisting of two guns, 460 rifles and a party of Sierra Leone R.E. under Captain Jackson—moved forward along the railway line, and on the 14th, after a fight in which the French incurred some fifteen casualties, forced the passage of the Kele at So Dibanga.

Colonel Haywood's column, leaving Edea on the 11th April, encountered continuous enemy opposition and found its progress much hampered by the denseness of the forest. On the evening of the 13th the column bivouacked about one thousand yards to the west of the still intact bridge over the Ngwe river. The enemy was entrenched on the further bank, but his position was so well concealed that its exact nature and location could not be discerned. It was subsequently found to consist of trenches and a redoubt with overhead cover, wire entanglement, abattis, and a field of fire cleared for about three hundred yards on all sides except the north, where there was dense bush.

In his attack at daybreak on the 14th April Colonel Haywood's preliminary movements were screened by a thick mist. The three companies of the 2nd Nigerians, forming the main attack, advanced along both sides of the road with the two guns following in support, while the company of the 1st Nigerians moved southwards so as to cross the river two miles downstream and from there fall upon the enemy's rear.

Affair of Ngwe; 14th April 1915.

By 7 a.m. the company 2nd Nigerians forming the firing line of the main attack was hotly engaged, having drawn the fire of two hostile machine guns, one on each flank of the enemy's position. There for some time progress was delayed by the failure to find a suitable position for the British guns to come into action. By about noon, however, a hill on the west bank of the river was occupied, and from this the guns were able to bring a heavy fire to bear on the enemy's redoubt, just as the approach of the turning movement by the 1st Nigerians was making itself felt. The enemy began to retire, and shortly afterwards his position was taken at the point of the bayonet. The British casualties had, in the circumstances, not been heavy, totalling thirteen, all in the 2nd Nigerians, including Colour-Sergeant R. Dokes wounded. The German force apparently consisted of their No. 2 Reserve Detachment, about 150 strong, with their No. 1 Depot

(25) K

Company in reserve on the Sakbajeme road. Their losses were believed to have been only slight.

In the meantime, on the 12th April, General Dobell had received a telegram from Brazzaville informing him that the French troops could not reach Lomie much before the end of the month, and requesting him to postpone Colonel Mayer's advance from the Kele river till the 1st May. General Dobell replied that this would be done.

In order to clear his left flank before a further advance, Colonel Haywood despatched, on the 16th April, a column of 200 rifles to reconnoitre Sakbajeme and its vicinity. This column returned to Ngwe on the 21st, having encountered little or no opposition and bringing back with it some German missionaries and a quantity of live stock. The remainder of the month was spent in forward reconnaissances and in building up a stock of supplies at Ngwe. The Sierra Leone company in the column was replaced by one from the Gold Coast Battalion.

Thanks to the skilful work of the French engineers the Edea bridge was ready for railway traffic by the 15th April; and on the 18th the arrival of the French reinforcements from Dakar, consisting of 14 French and 550 native combatants and 500 carriers,* removed all doubt regarding Colonel Mayer's ability to commence his advance on the 1st May. On the 22nd April General Dobell went to Edea to discuss arrangements with Colonel Mayer.

On the 24th April General Dobell received another telegram from Brazzaville saying that supply difficulties would cause a further delay in the advance by the troops under General Aymerich's orders. To this General Dobell replied that his plans would not be affected, as a halt would be necessary on the line Eseka-Wum Biagas till the 10th May at least, in order to organise for the further advance. General Dobell hoped that by then definite information would have reached him of General Aymerich's advance, so that the Allied movements could be regulated accordingly.

<small>Dobell's appreciation of the situation; April 1915.</small> While these operations were proceeding some telegraphic correspondence had taken place between Duala and London following the assumption by the War Office of the control of the military operations. The duality of control envisaged by the Colonial Office telegram of the 3rd April caused General Dobell some apprehensions and, before sending the War Office the summary of the general military situation they had

---

* They brought three months' supplies for the whole French contingent.

[*To face p.* 258

BRIDGE OVER NGWE RIVER

(2nd Nigerians crossing)

asked for, he requested the Colonial Office to define more exactly whence his instructions and requirements were to come. Having obtained this information he telegraphed to the War Office on the 11th April that his despatches and telegrams to the Colonial Office showed the military situation clearly and that his reserves of ammunition, equipment, clothing and supplies, as well as their maintenance under the existing arrangements, were sufficient. He went on to say that if no marked result was produced by the operations eastward from Edea it would be necessary to withdraw the troops taking part, as the rainy season and transport difficulties would, for the time being, prevent further offensive action. He had hitherto, he said, received no very definite instructions as to the military policy to be pursued, but he had always tried to engage the enemy wherever possible. His forces were showing the effect of the trying local conditions and, though there appeared to be no means of replacing the African ranks, he recommended the gradual relief of many of his British Europeans.

The War Office replied on the 14th April that they were only able to make out an outline of the existing situation and asked for further details. They would, they said, make every endeavour to relieve the British officers who required a change of climate. General Dobell answered on the 15th giving the dates of three recent despatches to the Colonial Office which would afford the information required and he telegraphed in addition the details of the force advancing eastward from Edea. He followed this up by post on the 21st April with a detailed appreciation of the situation, dealing with the operations under three headings, i.e. those in the south and south-east Cameroons, those in the Duala hinterland, and those based on Nigeria, the first and last named being under the control of General Aymerich and Colonel Cunliffe respectively.

He gave the disposition of the Allied forces, as far as he knew them, as follows, the figures being in round numbers:

S. and S.E. Cameroons	French Rifles	French Guns	Belgian Rifles	Belgian Guns
Kadei river (Colonel Morisson)	1,215	3	—	—
Lomie (Colonel Hutin)	781	5	560*	4*
,, (Colonel Le Meillour)	535	2		
Oyem (Colonel Miquelard)	719	2		
Total	3,250	12	560	4

* Believed by General Dobell to be on the line of communication.

Opposing these columns, the Germans were estimated to have the following troops, *excluding partisans, levies and recruits whom they had enlisted in considerable numbers*:

Facing the French advance from the east	500 rifles
In the south-east and south	470 ,,
Total	970 ,, *

It was the French intention, said General Dobell, that their columns on the Kadei river and at Lomie should advance on Yaunde under the direction of General Aymerich, who hoped to reach Lomie towards the end of April and to start the forward movement on the 1st May.†

The Duala Hinterland.

The distribution of General Dobell's military (i.e., excluding the naval and marine contingents) force was as follows:

	British		French	
	Rifles	Guns	Rifles	Guns
Duala	650	4	200	—
Midland Railway and Edea	—	—	1,050	4
Yaunde Column	600	2	1,000	2
Dibombe Post	150	—	—	—
Nkongsamba and Bare	850	4	—	—
Northern Railway line of communication	350	—	—	—
Buea district	250	—	—	—
Total	2,850	10	2,250	6

These numbers included 300 French sick, but excluded the British sick. They also included 100 recruits from Nigeria under training at Duala.

The troops at Duala were the minimum considered necessary to provide for its safety and to furnish the many guards required for stores, ammunition and prisoners.

Opposing the French at Edea there had been normally 400 to 600 German troops, capable of being reinforced up to about 800, and Edea itself required 600 to 800 French troops for defensive purposes.

The Dibombe post was maintained to keep in touch with hostile movements between the Wuri and Sanaga rivers and

---

* The French estimated the total German strength in this area at between 1,100 and 1,500.

† This was written before General Dobell heard that the advance was delayed.

DOBELL'S APPRECIATION

to gain information of any general movement of the enemy between Bare and Yaunde. It also safeguarded thousands of natives and enabled them by cultivating their farms to supply a large proportion of the requirements of the native population of Duala.

The troops on the Northern Railway had recently been reduced slightly—to free troops for the Yaunde column—but they and those at Nkongsamba and Bare were still in sufficient strength to protect those places and the line of communication and to provide a column of 300 to 400 for offensive action.

The garrison in the Buea district was retained solely for political and commercial purposes and was formed by troops requiring rest or temporarily unfit for military operations. They prevented minor raids and kept order among the plantation labourers.

The Allied naval and marine forces, which General Dobell did not give in detail, were very active all along the coast, visiting places where the enemy could land stores and ammunition and taking all possible precautions to prevent supplies reaching the enemy through Spanish Muni.

Opposing General Dobell's force, the Germans were estimated to have the following troops, *excluding partisans, levies and recruits* :

Yaunde-Edea line	890 rifles
Hitherto operating between Chang and Yaunde, but now probably on the Yaunde-Edea line	200 ,,
Total	1,090 ,,

South of Fumban-Chang facing the Northern Railway	600 rifles
Tinto	300 recruits

The Yaunde column was to commence its advance on the 1st May in two parties, the French moving along the railway line and the British along the Edea-Yaunde road. After the capture of Eseka, the first objective of the French, it was intended that the two parties should unite, the further advance taking place in one column, probably along the Edea-Yaunde road, under the orders of Colonel Mayer.

The force available at Northern railhead for offensive action was insufficient for extended operations. But the enemy opposite had been inactive for some time and avoided any decisive action by retiring whenever the British advanced.

Operations based on Nigeria.

The distribution of the Allied troops was as follows:

	British Rifles	British Guns	French Rifles	French Guns
Ossidinge and line of communication	600	2	—	—
Ibi column	230	—	—	—
Garua column	1,000*	3*	700	2
Yola garrison	200	2†	—	—
Mora	200	—	130	—
Total	2,230	7	830	2

The primary object of the Ossidinge column was the protection of the Nigerian frontier about the Cross river. It also acted as a deterrent against hostile movements from the west against the Northern Railway. Though three companies had recently been withdrawn from this force to reinforce the Garua column, the retention of Ossidinge was necessary apart from other reasons to prevent the enemy concentrating against the Northern Railway at a moment when it would be impossible to send reinforcements there without interfering with the movement on Yaunde.

The Ibi column was maintained to prevent raids across the Nigerian frontier.

The strength and distribution of the German troops in the Northern Cameroons was estimated as follows:

 Garua   600 rifles and 3 guns.
 Mora   120 rifles.‡

The situation in the Northern Cameroons had been most unsatisfactory for months past. The Allied troops had effected nothing, as attacks on either Mora or Garua had not been considered feasible. Shortly, however, nearly 2,000 troops with the naval 12-pounder would be concentrated under Colonel Cunliffe's command round Garua and would, it was hoped, effect its capture in the course of the next six weeks.

General Dobell, in considering the enemy's probable future action, said that it appeared to be his object to hold out as long as possible. With the sole exception of his attack

---

 * Including recent reinforcements.
 † Including naval 12-pounder.
 ‡ We now know that the German strength at Mora was rather more than this, and General Dobell omitted mention of the two German companies, each 120 to 150 rifles strong, which the Nigerian authorities had located opposite the frontier between Garua and Bamenda.

DOBELL'S APPRECIATION

on Edea on the 5th January, he had consistently avoided any decisive action and had always retired when the Allies pressed. With an enormous area to retire into and with established depots to fall back on, it was difficult to see how he could be forced to fight except on his own terms. It appeared likely, however, that he would offer strong opposition to any threats against Garua and Yaunde. The latter was the more important; it had always been considered the last ditch of the German resistance; the enemy could concentrate at least 1,500 men to hold the strong earthworks by which it was said to be protected; and although he had probably no artillery there he had a very large number of machine guns. If the enemy stood at Yaunde its fall would bring to an end all organised resistance except in the Garua district. There were, however, indications that he might intend to retire from Garua and Yaunde, directly these places were seriously threatened, into the Ngaundere district, where he probably had depots of supplies. In such a case distance and transport difficulties would preclude his being followed by forces from Duala or the South Cameroons, though a strong force based on Yola might attempt such a movement. There seemed little ground, in this eventuality, for supposing that lack of food or ammunition, or disaffection among his native troops, would cause the enemy to surrender; and the only chance of this appeared to lie in the recognition by the German leaders that the ultimate fate of the Cameroons would be settled by the issue in Europe, and that it would be hopeless for them to continue the struggle locally.

General Dobell said that no effort would be spared by his force to crown the movement against Yaunde with success. But, if the enemy retired without decisive results being obtained, the impracticability of undertaking a prolonged movement after him into the interior would impose on us a strategically defensive attitude. For, since it was hard to see how any form of offensive action would produce tangible results, a process of attrition would have to be relied on to effect a capitulation. If in these circumstances Yaunde was to be held permanently, the garrison and line of communication troops should be furnished by French forces under General Aymerich supplied through Edea.

In referring to some of the peculiar local conditions, General Dobell described briefly the nature of the country and the climate with their effect on the operations and the health of his men. He emphasised the need of relief for his Europeans, but, owing to the impossibility of replacing them by men with the requisite experience of West Africa,* he admitted that such relief could only be carried out very gradually. For infantry duties he recommended that, for the time being, fifteen British officers and five British N.C.Os. should be sent to Duala every month. For other duties he would specify vacancies as they occurred. He also recommended that he should send home, on three months' leave, as many British as he could spare.

As regards intelligence General Dobell thought it probable that the German commanders, owing to their cruel methods of dealing with the natives, were much better served than the Allies. It was mainly for this reason that he had commenced to enrol and arm native partisans.

In conclusion General Dobell pointed out that except for the limited railway service he was dependent for transport on carriers. Those obtained locally had proved most unreliable in the field and others had consequently to be imported to replace the serious casualties among the 4,500 † who had originally come in with his force.

Northern Railway; April 1915. During April there were no events of importance near the Northern railhead. The enemy had apparently abandoned all intention for the time being of an offensive or of raids against the British line of communication, and both sides remained in their respective areas on either side of the Nkam river.

Naval operations; March–April 1915. During March and April the Allied naval forces continued to carry out a systematic patrol of the Cameroons coast and the adjoining trade routes.‡ From midnight 23rd/24th April a formal blockade of the whole of the Cameroons coast—except the entrance to the Cameroon river § and the coast of the territory to the south of Spanish Muni—was declared, in accordance with instructions from London and Paris. This was fully justified by the clear evidence, gained during

---

* It is noteworthy that General Dobell stated, as an undoubted fact, that no European was of real value in the country till he had at least six months' experience and, in the case of company commanders and other senior appointments, much longer. Moreover, African troops had no confidence in officers they did not know.
† British, 3,500; French, 1,000: of the British 1,100 had been invalided.
‡ On the 8th March Lieutenant A. M. P. Ford, R.N., in the *Alligator* was severely wounded whilst reconnoitring up the Nyong river.
§ Duala had been previously declared an open port.

[*To face p.* 264

A Gun-Carrier, R.W.A.F.F.

the past few months, that German agents, with the assistance of German sympathisers in Fernando Po and Spanish Muni, had established between there and the Cameroons a system of regular communication and convoys. After the declaration, moreover, the Allies had the satisfaction of finding as time went on, from captured German letters and other sources, that cargoes seized had indeed been intended for the Cameroons.

To assist the Allied advance from Edea arrangements were made by Captain Fuller to create a diversion on the coast by raids, conducted between the 9th and 17th April, by armed naval craft carrying landing parties of marines and levies. The vessels employed were the *Margaret Elizabeth*, *Ivy* and *Fullah*, all under Commander Sneyd; and landing parties from them carried out successful raids at Kribi, Longyi, Plantation, and in the Nyong river.

On the 21st April the cruiser *Astræa* arrived at Suelaba to relieve the *Challenger*, the latter leaving the Cameroons on the 6th May under Captain A. C. Sykes, R.N., of the *Astræa*, who had exchanged commands with Captain Fuller.

The Campo and Nyong flotillas continued their work throughout these two months, having several minor encounters with hostile parties. At Campo, after the completion of the blockhouse, a large number of refugees gathered, necessitating the clearance of a larger area and the construction of a second blockhouse. In the Sanaga river Lieutenant Pawsey (*Lala*) succeeded in salving two launches which the enemy had sunk prior to our capture of Edea.

In the south and south-east Cameroons the Franco-Belgian columns made much less progress during March and April than General Dobell had been led to expect. The Oyem Column, which drove back a hostile advance during March without difficulty, remained stationary, as did the Mvahdi Column at Minkebe on its return from the Akoafim direction. **South and South-east Cameroons: March–April 1915.**

The three groups of the Sanga Column made some progress in their advance towards Lomie during March, the left group, after several engagements with the enemy, reaching Eta by the end of the month. But, after that, all three groups were obliged by supply difficulties to remain halted throughout April.

In March the Germans facing the Lobaye Column took the initiative and attacked the French right, threatening Carnot and forcing Colonel Morisson to remain on the defensive. His supply difficulties also stood in the way of an offensive, and his column, with a strength of about 925 rifles and 3 guns, remained throughout April about the line of the Kadei river.

Nigerian frontier; March–April 1915. The Ibi Column. In Nigeria the Ibi Column was only disturbed during March and April by one serious raid, carried out by an enemy force (5 Germans, 75 natives and a machine gun) from Banyo against Mutum Biu on the 12th April. On its approach the District officer, taking with him the telegraph instruments, withdrew to Amar; and the raiders had to content themselves with destroying the telegraph line and doing some damage in the place. Their boast in their official report—which we subsequently captured—that it would scarcely be possible to repair the telegraph line during the war, was quite unjustified, for they only caused an interruption of telegraphic communication for fourteen days (12th–26th April).

At the end of April the Ibi Column had one company (C/2nd Bn.) at Takum, half a company (G/2nd Bn.), and 25 police at Beli, and 25 police at Kasimbila. But, owing to reports that the enemy intended further raids, a company (C/1st Bn.) in the interior was held ready to reinforce the column.

The Cross River Column. The Cross River Column, reduced by the end of March to a strength of four companies, held Ossidinge with three of them (A, C and F/3rd Bn.) and the line of communication back to the frontier with the fourth (E/3rd Bn.). Captain Crookenden had instructions to maintain an active defence at Ossidinge if possible, but to fall back on Ikom if seriously pressed. As, however, the enemy limited his activities to minor patrol enterprises, Captain Crookenden experienced no difficulty in maintaining his position.

Nigerian recruiting. Special steps taken in April in Nigeria to obtain more recruits by the offer of a bonus had an excellent effect and, in view of the lack of instructors in Nigeria, General Dobell arranged to take a certain number of recruits and complete their training at Duala. The first batch of 100 sailed for there on the 10th April and was followed some two weeks later by another batch of the same strength.

The Northern Cameroons. Garua. (Map 11.) At a conference, which he held at Yola on the 17th March, Colonel Cunliffe explained to Captain Ferrandi that his chief object was to effect the capture of Garua and thus set free a number of Allied troops to co-operate in the operations farther south.

Assuring Colonel Cunliffe of the French readiness to serve under and co-operate fully with him, Captain Ferrandi said that Mora was impregnable; and both he and Colonel Webb-Bowen agreed that stronger guns would be required to take Garua. Here Colonel Brisset's dispositions which Captain Ferrandi detailed appeared to the British to be better adapted to establishing a hold on the territory occupied in rear than to investing Garua closely. For the Allied positions there blocked little more than the exits from Garua to the east, and there was hardly anything to prevent the Germans marching out to the northward, westward or southward. If they did so and effected a juncture in the Ngaundere district with German forces from the south, the Allied difficulties of bringing them to battle would be much increased and the danger to Nigeria itself would be far greater.

Convinced that to bring about the fall of Garua would be the greatest assistance he could render General Dobell, Colonel Cunliffe started to concentrate at Yola as many troops as possible. In addition to the two companies from the Cross River Column already on their way to Yola, he ordered the transfer of a third company, and also the withdrawal to Yola of a company from the Ibi Column.

During the next four weeks, while these troops were concentrating, Colonel Cunliffe remained at Yola engaged in preparations which included a reorganisation of the Intelligence service and the despatch of an infantry company (less a section) and a mountain gun to reinforce Colonel Webb-Bowen, who had returned to Bogole. The excessive heat which heralded the approach of the rainy season delayed matters slightly; and several enemy raids on the frontier to the southward brought about some minor engagements, in which, among other casualties, Lieutenant C. J. Hebblethwaite was killed.

On the 12th April Colonel Cunliffe left Yola with the naval gun and three infantry companies (less one section), arriving on the 18th at Bogole. The British contingent here now comprised the naval 12-pounder, three mountain guns, one mounted infantry, and six and a half infantry companies.*

---

* B/Mtd. Infy., B and H/1st Battn., B and H/2nd Battn., D and H/3rd Battn., and B/4th Battn.; B/1st and H/2nd Battn. being each less one section. B/3rd Battn. from the Cross River Column did not join the force till the end of May.

One company (G/3rd Bn.) and some police had been left to garrison Yola; a small detachment of some forty soldiers and police held Gurin, near the frontier, on the line of communication between Yola and Bogole; and another small detachment of about fifty soldiers and police watched the frontier to the southward.

After discussion with Colonel Brisset, Colonel Cunliffe started on the 20th April to move British troops from Bogole to the south-westward, so as to tighten the investment and especially to close the enemy's line of retirement by the roads to Koncha and Ngaundere. Next day there were three infantry companies at Bogole, two infantry companies and the guns at Bilonde, and one infantry and the mounted infantry companies at and about Tondere. Colonel Cunliffe established his headquarters at Bilonde, which was the best observation point near Garua. He also contemplated a movement of French troops to the westward from Nassarao. But, owing to their dispersion in detachments at Golombe, Lere and on political missions in the surrounding districts, Colonel Brisset had at the moment no men to spare for the purpose. However, he took steps at once to comply with Colonel Cunliffe's wishes by bringing in his detachments as soon as possible.

The necessity for tightening the line of investment became clear on the morning of the 22nd April, when news reached Colonel Cunliffe from his mounted infantry that during the previous night a party of the enemy from Garua had passed southward, fording the Benue river well to the west of Tondere and getting a start which enabled it to elude pursuit. This enemy party was reported to be commanded in person by Captain von Crailsheim, the commander of the Garua garrison. But no definite or reliable information concerning his movements and intentions was obtainable for the space of the next week, and Colonel Cunliffe decided that, lacking such information, any attempt at pursuit was unsound as likely to be unprofitable. First reports said that Crailsheim had gone south to meet and escort back to Garua a party of troops from Ngaundere; but subsequent information indicated that he had joined this party and was moving with it towards Ngaundere. This led Colonel Brisset to offer the opinion that these two parties might be contemplating an attack on the French Sanga Column about Carnot.

German attack on Gurin; 29th April 1915. It was not till 5 p.m. on the 29th April that Colonel Cunliffe got definite news from Major C. A. Booth, who was on his way from Bilonde with six hundred carriers, escorted by twelve soldiers, to bring supplies from Yola. He had received information that morning, when about seven miles from Gurin, that the Germans were attacking the British post there. After sending in this information to Colonel Cunliffe at Bilonde, Major Booth marched on with his tiny force to the help of the Gurin post, where he arrived at 11 p.m. to find that the Germans had withdrawn a few hours previously after an unsuccessful attack.

Colonel Cunliffe had at once despatched troops under Colonel Webb-Bowen to Gurin, the forty-seven miles there being covered by the mounted infantry by 9 a.m., and by one and a half companies of infantry by 2 p.m., on the 30th —a particularly fine performance.

The small circular fort constructed at Gurin by Colonel Webb-Bowen had a good field of fire, and its garrison of forty-two soldiers and police had defended it stoutly against the attack which commenced at daybreak on the 29th April. Lieutenant D. W. Pawle, in command, was killed early in the action and the command then devolved on the only other officer present, Lieutenant J. F. J. Fitzpatrick of the Intelligence Staff. The attacking force consisted of three hundred rifles under Crailsheim, and the fire of his five machine guns was very effective, causing the garrison a number of casualties—mainly head wounds from bullets coming through the loopholes—and actually, in places, cutting away the top of the wall. But the garrison maintained a steady fire; and, his force having suffered thirty casualties, Crailsheim broke off the action about midday. The British garrison had incurred thirteen casualties, including Lieutenant Pawle killed and Colour-Sergeant J. H. Fraser wounded.

It was subsequently ascertained from captured documents that Crailsheim, with a force of about 250 rifles with machine guns, had first proceeded to Chamba—about thirty-five miles south of Gurin—with a consignment of ammunition and had been joined there by a party of troops under Captain Schipper, who had come from Banyo via Koncha. From Chamba the combined parties, of a strength of three hundred rifles and five machine guns, had marched north to attack Gurin, their right flank and rear being covered against attack from the Garua direction by a detachment from Ngaundere under Captain Fuchs.

The last-named detachment was encountered at Kone on the 29th April by a section of Nigerian mounted infantry reconnoitring from Cheboa, whom it forced to withdraw with a loss of three casualties, and then, apparently, withdrew itself. Believing Fuchs to be still at Kone, Crailsheim moved southward from Gurin for about fifteen miles on the 29th, and reached Chamba on the 1st May. From there Schipper, taking the severely wounded, seems to have moved to Banyo, but Crailsheim started to return to Garua. This, in spite of attempts made by Colonel Cunliffe's troops to intercept him, he succeeded in doing by skilful and rapid movements across country, reaching Garua on the 8th May. While we can admire the skill and daring of this enemy exploit, it is impossible, without further information than we at present possess, to say how far it was justified by the results achieved.

Mora;
March–April
1915.
There was no change in the situation at Mora. In March, Raben sent to Garua a party of about a dozen rifles under Lieutenant Weyse and they succeeded in making their way safely past the investing forces at both places. A suggestion by Colonel Cunliffe that the investing force at Mora might be reduced in strength was deprecated strongly by Colonel Brisset, one of his reasons being that General Largeau, who was much embarrassed by hostile propaganda and attempts to raise a *Jahad* in Darfur and Tripolitania, regarded the retention of the Allied force round Mora as necessary to the security of Chad.

CHAPTER VIII

MAY—JULY 1915

THE FIRST AND UNSUCCESSFUL ADVANCE ON YAUNDE; THE CAPTURE OF GARUA AND NGAUNDERE; AND FRANCO-BELGIAN PROGRESS IN THE SOUTH-EAST

(Maps 2, 11, 12 and 13)

When he decided that Colonel Mayer's columns should adhere to the arrangement to start eastward from So Dibanga and Ngwe on the 1st May, General Dobell had no reason to suppose that the supply difficulties hampering the French in the south-east were other than temporary. In fact, as he told them, the slight delay which he anticipated on this account would give Colonel Mayer time to consolidate positions at Eseka and Wum Biagas and to prepare for a further advance. *The advance on Yaunde; 1st May 1915.*

At Ngwe post, with a force of two Nigerian guns, one company 1st Nigerians, the 2nd Nigerians less a company, one company Gold Coast Battalion and the Gambia Detachment, Colonel Haywood had collected supplies to last his column till the middle of June. From So Dibanga most of the French, having constructed a bridge and a blockhouse, had returned to Edea before the end of April. But on the 28th Commandant Mechet left Edea for So Dibanga with a French artillery section, engineer detachment, six hundred Senegalese rifles, and two machine gun sections. Colonel Mayer remained for the time being at Edea.

On the 1st May, in pouring rain, both Commandant Mechet and Colonel Haywood started to advance, moving along railway and road respectively.

Colonel Haywood, whose transport consisted of 512 carriers, left the Gold Coast company to hold the post at Ngwe. His column encountered opposition, on the 1st and 2nd May, which

First affair of Wum Biagas; 3rd–4th May 1915. he brushed aside without difficulty. But on the 3rd he found the enemy at the crossing of the Mbila river immediately west of Wum Biagas, holding a position which proved to be more formidable than any Colonel Haywood had yet encountered in the course of the operations. The bridge had been destroyed, the waist-deep stream was filled with stakes and abattis, and a field of fire had been cleared on the banks to a depth of about three hundred yards. Well concealed and skilfully sited trenches, on a practically continuous frontage of 1,600 yards, had been constructed on the eastern side of the river and were connected with the rear by an ample system of covered approaches or communication trenches. Both flanks, moreover, were strong, the right resting on a steep forest ridge about eight hundred feet high and the left on the unfordable Kele river, here about one hundred and twenty feet wide and running south of, and parallel to, the road. From a personal reconnaissance Colonel Haywood concluded that a purely frontal attack would be costly and that the enemy's right flank would be the least difficult to turn. He accordingly decided to make a strong holding attack in front and to send Captain C. Gibb with two companies 2nd Nigerians (less two sections) to turn the enemy's right.

In face of a heavy enemy fire, the frontal attack, supported by the British guns, succeeded before long in advancing to within two hundred yards of the enemy's line and establishing a distinct fire superiority. About 2 p.m. Colonel Haywood received a message that Captain Gibb was heavily engaged with the enemy's right, but, some two hours later, learnt from a second message that the strong enemy opposition and the steep ascent in front of Captain Gibb would prevent his completing his task by daylight. He was thereupon sent orders to draw his men out of action before dark. This he accomplished successfully, and by 5.45 p.m. the bulk of the British column had withdrawn behind a screen of outposts.

During the night there was a good deal of firing between the outposts, and at an early hour on the 4th Colonel Haywood sent out a company to reconnoitre for a crossing over the Kele river, and another company to push on as far as possible against the enemy's front. By 8 a.m. the enemy's fire had slackened so much that Colonel Haywood called for volunteers to cross the Mbila and reconnoitre up to the enemy's trenches; with the result that the enemy was found to have retired, for the most part apparently before daybreak.

The British column had sustained twenty-two casualties,

WUM BIAGAS AND SENDE CAPTURED 273

including Lieutenant K. Markham-Rose killed and Lieutenants J. F. Warren and A. E. Beattie and Sergeant O. Dwyer wounded. The enemy force, whose casualties were unknown, had, it was reported, been commanded by Major Haedicke of No. 1 Depot Company.* His strength was estimated at 300–350 rifles with three machine guns, and his failure to offer a more protracted resistance indicated that the enemy was still pursuing the policy of avoiding battle.

Occupying Wum Biagas, Colonel Haywood started, in accordance with his orders, to construct a defensible post and to build up a reserve of supplies. He had also received instructions to assist the French in their advance on Eseka. But, since from the 1st till the 7th May he received no news from Commandant Mechet, he could do no more than reconnoitre to his front, to gain information and to occupy the enemy's attention in that direction. He had been given to understand, however, that the French would probably be in front of Eseka on the 7th or 8th, and he therefore despatched on the 7th a column of two hundred rifles with three days' supplies to threaten the German position at Eseka.

That afternoon a message reached him from Colonel Mayer at Edea requesting the despatch of two companies, if possible, from Wum Biagas to assist Commandant Mechet, who had been stopped by strong enemy opposition at Sende. To this message Colonel Haywood sent the reply that the column he had just sent towards Eseka would probably have the desired effect. As a matter of fact Commandant Mechet, who had attacked the hostile position at Sende on the 3rd and 4th May without success, had been enabled by an enemy retirement to occupy it on the 6th. In these attacks, carried out through dense bush, which hampered operations and stopped turning movements, the French had incurred thirty-seven casualties.† *French capture of Sende; 3rd–6th May 1915.*

The British column sent towards Eseka returned on the 9th May to Wum Biagas bringing in some useful information, and on the 10th Colonel Haywood, receiving intimation that Commandant Mechet expected to attack Eseka on the 12th or 13th, arranged to co-operate with a detachment from Wum Biagas. Colonel Haywood's camp at Wum Biagas was attacked *French capture of Eseka; 11th May 1915.*

---

* This information was correct. Haedicke's group had lately been withdrawn from the Yabasi area to reinforce the German troops on the Edea—Yaunde road. (*Der Grosse Krieg, 1914–1918, Vol. IV.*)

† The Senegalese troops had displayed great gallantry. But, like all who came from Dakar where they were accustomed to desert warfare, they had no previous experience of bush fighting.

during the night of the 11th/12th in rather a half-hearted fashion, by a party of about 150 of the enemy; and on the 12th May a British detachment moved out to co-operate in the attack on Eseka. Commandant Mechet had, however, captured that place on the previous day by a skilful attack, in face of which the Germans, surprised by a French turning movement, had retired in some disorder and with considerable loss, the French casualties only totalling two.

At Eseka, the terminus of the railway, seven engines and over two hundred wagons were captured. But the demolition by the enemy of the bridges and part of the line east of the Kele river—which had denied the use of the railway to the French and hampered their advance—made it unlikely that the Allies would be able to utilise this rolling stock for a considerable period.

Aymerich's co-operation delayed; 11th May 1915. On the 11th May General Dobell received intimation from Brazzaville that General Aymerich's columns had been unable to make sufficient progress to occupy either Dume or Lomie by the 25th April, that no date could be fixed for their advance beyond those places, and that consequently their effective co-operation in an immediate advance on Yaunde should not be counted on. But General Dobell decided not to stop Colonel Mayer's eastward movement. The *moral* of the German troops was reported to be deteriorating, and it appeared likely that hostile resistance to Colonel Mayer's advance would not be serious. It was not easy, however, to gauge the German intentions. Reports of General Dobell's intelligence agents credited the Germans at Garua and elsewhere in the north with the intention of moving towards Yaunde. On the other hand—as General Dobell had stated in his appreciation of the 21st April—there were also indications that the enemy intended to retire and concentrate in some locality between Garua and Yaunde as soon as those places were seriously threatened; and these indications were somewhat strengthened by the perusal of certain German documents captured at Eseka, which mentioned the formation of a supply depot to the north of Yaunde on the road to Yoko.

In any case, if Colonel Mayer's advance was carried out rapidly, it appeared that enemy opposition would not be serious; and even if enemy opposition proved too great, Colonel Mayer's force was quite strong enough to be able, if necessary, to retire in safety. Realising, however, that if the advance were much delayed, the rain would render it impracticable, General Dobell sent his senior general staff officer

To face p. 275]

FRENCH TROOPS ARRIVING AT WUM BIAGAS; 20TH MAY 1915

CONCENTRATION OF MAYER'S COLUMN

(Lieutenant-Colonel Turner), on the 12th May to Edea to discuss any difficulties which Colonel Mayer might anticipate.

Colonel Mayer, who intended to advance in one Allied column along the Yaunde road from Wum Biagas, apparently anticipated no special difficulties, though he asked for, and obtained, the assistance of a British naval 12-pounder gun. As regards supplies he was informed that sufficient for about four weeks was being collected for Colonel Haywood's column at Wum Biagas. On his part he said that the French would only collect there sufficient for fifteen days as their troops relied on living on the country.*

On the 18th May General Dobell issued instructions to Colonel Mayer to advance as rapidly as possible, emphasising that the hostile resistance would probably not be serious, and that it was of the greatest importance to gain early possession of Yaunde so as to prevent the Germans removing from that place all the supplies and munitions that had been accumulated there.

On the 19th May Commandant Mechet's force reached Wum Biagas, where during the previous night Colonel Haywood's column had again been half-heartedly and unsuccessfully attacked by a German detachment; and on the 20th Colonel Mayer, with 300 Senegalese troops and the British naval 12-pounder (from the *Astræa* under Lieutenant R. A. Clark, R.N.) left Edea, arriving at Wum Biagas on the 23rd. The rains had recently been heavy, the weather was still intensely hot, and the health of Colonel Haywood's troops was far from good. Despite precautions, malaria was rife and dysentery had developed among both British and Africans. In view of the necessity for special medical care and precautions, General Dobell lent the services of Lieutenant-Colonel Statham, his Director of Medical Services, to Colonel Mayer for the coming operations; and also collected every available carrier to place at Colonel Mayer's disposal.

Concentration at Wum Biagas.

By this time the Sierra Leone R.E. detachment had repaired many of the bridges which the enemy had destroyed and had improved the road between Edea and Ngwe sufficiently to allow the use along it, for the transport of supplies, of three Ford cars which were available. Telephonic communication between Edea and Ngwe had also been established. But

---

* The French arrangements for this collection failed however. Fortunately, Colonels Turner and Haywood had realised the difficulties which might be met with and had taken steps to remedy a possible deficiency. Their action prevented delay in the Allied advance from Wum Biagas.

traffic along the railway was still stopped by the broken bridge over the Kele river, where the heavy repairs required were in course of execution by the French engineers. Consequently the captured rolling stock had perforce been abandoned at Eseka when Commandant Mechet left that place for Wum Biagas.

After detaching about 300 rifles * for duty on the line of communication at and beyond Ngwe, Colonel Mayer had available for his forward movement from Wum Biagas one British naval and four mountain guns (two British and two French) and about 750 French and 540 British rifles.

<small>Advance from Wum Biagas; 25th–26th May 1915.</small> The advance commenced on the 25th May, the British contingent, who were leading, encountering strong opposition from the outset. Along the road were many good defensive positions which favoured delaying tactics, as turning movements meant cutting a way through the dense forest and took a long time. From a position about two miles eastward of Wum Biagas the enemy was forced to retreat with some loss by a turning movement carried out by a company and a half † under Captain V. B. Thurston; but at such a late hour that the British column, having only incurred one casualty, was forced to camp for the night about a mile farther on.

Resuming his advance at 5.45 a.m. on the 26th, Colonel Haywood very soon again encountered strong opposition, and by 9.30 a.m. the whole of his two companies in advanced guard were heavily engaged. It was not till some two hours later, after one of the British mountain guns had been able to find a position from which to open fire, that the enemy was driven back. But he took up another strong position on a hill about half a mile east of Ntim village from which he was not turned out till 4.30 p.m. In this vicinity the British bivouacked for the night, having suffered eight casualties, including Captains Thurston and C. J. Maclaverty wounded. Their total progress in two days had amounted only to about five miles.

<small>Affair at Ngok; 27th–30th May 1915.</small> On the 27th May the French troops, taking over the lead, were stopped in front of a hostile position at Ngok about half a mile from the British bivouac. Fighting went on all day; but the French, who sustained fourteen casualties, gained no success. Next day a turning movement round the

---

* Two hundred Senegalese, one company Sierra Leone Battalion, and a detachment Gold Coast Battalion.
† One company 2nd Nigerians and the Gambia half-company.

ALLIED DIFFICULTIES

enemy's right by three French companies was also unsuccessful; and at daybreak on the 29th Colonel Haywood was sent with one of his guns and three and a half of his companies * to make a further attempt to turn the enemy's right. The physical difficulties were very great. In the dense pathless forest there were many rocky hills and numerous deep ravines. The heavy rain had converted large areas into deep swamps; ascents and descents were made so difficult that steps had frequently to be cut in the slippery mud, and the conveyance of the gun was particularly arduous. But by skill and endurance Colonel Haywood and his men finally succeeded, after a skirmish with the enemy, in getting in rear of the hostile position, though at too late an hour to make an attack. They bivouacked, therefore, where they were, to find next morning that the enemy had retired. In the afternoon of the 30th, Colonel Haywood followed up the enemy for about two miles, being opposed stubbornly for the whole way by the German rear guard. During these two days, though actual fighting had only caused the British the surprisingly small total of four casualties, progress had been laborious and tiring in the extreme. This had the result of aggravating the sickness latent in the force; and between the 25th and 31st May the British alone evacuated ten European and fifty African sick, suffering chiefly from dysentery.

In the meantime, on the 28th May, the enemy, who had evidently been reinforced, had struck at the Allied line of communication, which the dense forest rendered particularly vulnerable. An empty Allied convoy, returning westward, was driven back to Wum Biagas; the British commander of the line of communication, Major H. W. G. Meyer-Griffith,† who had moved out from Wum Biagas with a small party of men to the convoy's assistance, was killed; and communication between Ngwe and the main Allied column became interrupted. *Attack on Allied L. of C.; 28th May 1915.*

On the 31st May the French troops, whose turn it was to lead the advance, were checked at Matem, about 7½ miles eastward of Wum Biagas, in front of a strong enemy position. Its flanks were covered against turning movements by extensive swamps, and the French incurred *Affair at Matem; 31st May–4th June 1915.*

---

* From the Nigerian Battery, 2nd Nigerians and Gold Coast Battalion, with two days' supplies.
† He was killed gallantly leading a handful of men in a charge, five French Senegalese, who followed him closely with devoted bravery, being wounded at the same time.

twenty-two casualties without making any impression on the enemy. Next day a French detachment strove to turn the enemy's left, but lost its way and returned to camp on the 2nd June without having achieved any success. That afternoon another flanking detachment, composed of one British and two French companies under the French Captain Deslaurens, was sent out and proved more successful, its movements causing the enemy to evacuate his position at an early hour on the 4th June. Movement through the forest in this area was so beset with difficulties that even the Germans, who knew the country, lost their way. For instance, during the afternoon of the 2nd June, the rear face of Colonel Mayer's camp was suddenly fired into by a German detachment of about eighty rifles under Captain Priester, which, coming up from the southward to reinforce Major Haedicke, had lost its direction and blundered into the Allied outposts.

The Allied advance was resumed from Matem at 2 p.m. on the 4th June, the British leading. Strong opposition was at once encountered, and it was not till just before dark that Colonel Haywood succeeded in driving the enemy from his position on a hill and in gaining a point on the main Bafia-Eseka road about two miles east of Matem. The British battle casualties during the last four days had again been slight, only amounting to six.

Duala; 27th May–6th June 1915. Meanwhile, at Duala General Dobell had received a telegram on the 27th May from Brazzaville saying that Colonel Hutin had resumed his advance on Lomie on the 15th, moving in three columns from Eta, Ngato and Yukaduma, that Colonel Morisson was to co-operate in the movement, and that Commandant Le Meillour's column from Minkebe was also to move on Lomie if possible. On the 29th May General Dobell heard from Colonel Mayer that the enemy was disputing every yard of ground and that the country was extremely difficult. But no further reports from Colonel Mayer's force were received till the 1st June, when a message from Captain Thurston arrived reporting the convoy affair of the 28th May and the death of Major Meyer-Griffith. A reinforcement of 400 French Senegalese from Dakar reached Duala that day (1st June) and in consequence of Captain Thurston's report General Dobell ordered a hundred French rifles from Edea to reinforce Wum Biagas. On the 2nd June he received a message from Colonel Mayer explaining the difficulties which were likely to delay progress and asking for more carriers and reinforcements. General Dobell thereupon decided to

FURTHER ADVANCE IMPRACTICABLE 279

reinforce Colonel Mayer by a French company from Edea, a company of the Gold Coast Battalion under Colonel Rose, and by drafts of Europeans and Africans for the companies with Colonel Haywood. He also took measures to obtain, with the least possible delay, more carriers from the British West African colonies.

On the 4th June General Dobell received a further report, written on the previous day by Colonel Mayer, saying that, in his opinion—and Colonel Haywood and Commandant Mechet agreed with him—the sickness among his troops, the difficulties of the country accentuated by the torrential rain, and the enemy's stubborn resistance, all combined to render impracticable any further attempt to advance on Yaunde. Pending further instructions, he proposed to establish himself on the Puge river, eight miles east of Matem, and await there the approach of General Aymerich's troops from the south-east.

On the 5th June General Dobell telegraphed to the Governor-General of French Equatorial Africa acquainting him with the state of affairs and adding that unless General Aymerich was making progress it would be necessary to withdraw Colonel Mayer's troops to the line of the Kele river. From a reply received on the 7th General Dobell learnt that the French authorities at Brazzaville had no further news to impart. On the same day he heard again from Colonel Mayer that he not only estimated the enemy force opposite him at a strength of four companies or more, but that he found the increasing sickness in his own force most disquieting. General Dobell thereupon sent instructions to Colonel Mayer to withdraw to the Ndupe river, as a preliminary to holding either the Sende-Ndupe or the So Dibanga-Ngwe line till news of General Aymerich's advance justified a resumption of the advance. These instructions were sent by the hand of Colonel Rose, who had left on the 6th June with reinforcements to join the Yaunde column. *Decision to withdraw; 7th–8th June 1915.*

Since the 4th June the progress of Colonel Mayer's column had been very slight. On the 5th the British, who were leading, had been stopped by a strong hostile position less than a mile from their previous night's bivouac, and they had only managed to capture it after five hours' fighting. They had incurred eight casualties, including Colour-Sergeant J. L. Burgess killed. Next day Colonel Haywood's men again encountered such strong opposition in dense bush among swamps that they only managed to advance for about a *The Yaunde Column; 5th–13th June 1915.*

mile, incurring three casualties. On the 7th June the French took over the lead in their turn also to encounter stubborn opposition. After some hours' hard fighting they drove the enemy back for about a mile, but only to another strong position on the Puge river. Here, in spite of a series of gallant attempts to dislodge the enemy, the French were checked till the 10th June.

Colonel Rose joined the column on the morning of the 11th, but Colonel Mayer, who had already directed Colonel Haywood to carry out a turning movement round the enemy's position, decided to proceed with it before complying with General Dobell's instructions to withdraw. To carry out this turning movement Colonel Haywood detailed a force of 300 rifles with three machine guns under Colonel Rose. Carrying four days' supplies, they were to march round the enemy's northern flank and debouch in his rear,* while the French infantry continued to occupy his attention in front. On the morning of the 12th June the French found that the enemy had evacuated his position, evidently owing to the movement by Colonel Rose's column, which was not completed till the 13th. The denseness of the forest had hitherto prevented use of the British naval gun. But, a clearing having been made, it came into action on the 12th-13th with good effect at a range of 2,500 yards.

On the 12th June, however, the enemy had again struck at the Allied line of communication and with considerable success.† A force estimated at about 200 of his rifles with two machine guns had attacked, at about 2 p.m., at a point some six miles to the west of Colonel Mayer's camp, a convoy of 500 carriers, escorted by only 33 rifles. A larger escort had not been available at the time and the convoy had only been despatched as the French troops at the front had run completely out of rice. The escort made a very gallant stand, but the carriers all dropped their loads and bolted and the escort, having sustained nine casualties,‡ was forced to retire, leaving the loads in the hands of the enemy. §

---

* To guide the column through the bush the Intelligence Staff had compiled a sketch map based on native information.

† On the previous day, 11th June, a British transport officer—Lieutenant E. J. D. Bussell—was killed by an ambuscade whilst on convoy duty between Ngwe and Wum Biagas.

‡ Eight in the 2nd Nigerians.

§ The enemy's attack, actually carried out by three companies, was intended by the Germans as a flanking counter-stroke and more than a mere raid on the Allied L. of C. (*Der Grosse Krieg, 1914-1918, Vol. IV.*)

An indication that the enemy contemplated some counter-stroke of this sort had been afforded by the receipt, by Colonel Mayer that morning, of a message from Colonel Rose saying that he had found traces of the passage of a large enemy detachment evidently making north-westward. Colonel Haywood suggested detailing troops to cut off this detachment. But it was too late to recall Colonel Rose, and Colonel Mayer could not spare other troops for the purpose. All he felt able to do was to send out at 11 a.m. a party of 50 rifles to meet the convoy. This party was stopped by a hostile detachment two or three miles from camp at 3.30 p.m.; and being unable to make much progress its commander broke off the action in time to allow of his arriving back in camp before dark. His party had suffered four casualties.

Next morning (13th) Colonel Mayer sent out a column of 200 rifles with a gun to clear up the situation and to re-open communication with Wum Biagas. A report from this column, and a message received at an early hour on the 14th from Wum Biagas, acquainted Colonel Mayer with the total loss of the food in the convoy. His French troops had now no supplies at all, and the British, who had already from their own stock supplied the French with two days' rice, had only enough left for two days. Colonel Mayer thereupon decided on an immediate retirement by his whole force to Wum Biagas. This was carried out during the day without molestation by the enemy, the distance of twelve miles, laboriously gained in the last nineteen days, being covered without difficulty in five hours. *Withdrawal to Wum Biagas; 14th June 1915.*

In the meantime General Dobell had gone himself to Edea on the 8th June. He telegraphed that day to the War Office informing them of the circumstances in which he had decided to order Colonel Mayer to halt and which made it necessary for his force to withdraw now to Edea to be housed and fed. Returning to Duala on the 10th General Dobell next day sent Colonel Mayer instructions to withdraw to Edea, leaving posts at Sakbajeme, Ngwe, and So Dibanga. On the 13th General Dobell received a report from Edea which indicated that a hostile attack at Ndupe had broken communication with Colonel Mayer. On the 14th he learnt of the total loss of the convoy and, in the absence of any report from Colonel Mayer of events later than the 6th, he decided to send out every available man from Duala and Edea to clear the road and re-open communication. Two companies of the 1st Nigerians under Colonel Cockburn were accordingly ordered *General Dobell at Edea and Duala; 8th–14th June 1915.*

282 MILITARY OPERATIONS: THE CAMEROONS

to move next morning from Duala to Edea and to take on from there a French company. General Dobell himself would also proceed next day to Edea.

A telegram from Brazzaville received on the 14th June at Duala showed that, on the 25th May, the French columns under Colonel Hutin were approaching the vicinity of Besam and Assobam, that Colonel Morisson had previously received orders to support Colonel Hutin's right by a movement towards Ngangela and Nyassi, and that General Aymerich was expected at Brazzaville shortly for a few days' visit. This made it clear that no pressure from the French in the south-east on the Germans around Yaunde was to be expected in the near future.

<small>Attack on So Dibanga and Wum Biagas; 15th June 1915.</small> On arrival at Edea General Dobell heard that So Dibanga was being attacked and had called for reinforcements. To enable these to be sent from Edea he at once ordered up from Duala 150 Nigerians, who, though not fit for active work in the field, would be able to do garrison duty at Edea. It was soon learnt, however, that the attack on So Dibanga, which had been vigorously carried out from daybreak till 1 p.m. on the 15th, had failed with considerable loss to the enemy.*

That day Colonel Mayer halted at Wum Biagas to rest his tired force. Two strong attacks on his outposts, in which the Gold Coast companies sustained six casualties, indicated the enemy's determination to follow up the Allied retirement.

<small>Retirement from Wum Biagas to Ngwe and Edea; 16th–18th June 1915.</small> On the 16th June, after a long and exhausting march of about twenty miles in pouring rain, Colonel Cockburn's column reached a point well to the east of Ngwe; and on the same day the main force under Colonel Mayer retired to Nkonjok. His French rear guard was harassed the whole way by the pursuing enemy and lost about a dozen men killed and wounded. His British advanced guard also encountered some opposition. But Colonel Haywood had taken the precaution to send a company, on the previous evening, to secure the Ndupe bridge, and the enemy encountered between there and Nkonjok were brushed aside without much difficulty.

Colonel Mayer continued his retirement on the 17th to Ngwe, his British advanced guard again encountering slight opposition and his French rear guard again considerably harassed by the enemy. But he was joined at an opportune moment by Colonel Cockburn's column, whose vigorous intervention caused the hostile pressure to cease. The Allied

---

* The enemy had left eight dead and two prisoners behind him, while the French garrison had only lost seven men slightly wounded.

casualties during the day totalled ten, of which nine were French.

Colonel Mayer's Allied troops were by this time completely worn out. Since the 25th May they had been in constant conflict with a determined and resourceful enemy, favoured by his knowledge of the difficult country; and they had encountered the most adverse and trying conditions. The admirable spirit which animated all ranks, however, had remained unbroken in spite of sickness, torrential rain, continual torment of insects, a shortage of supplies, and the constant strain and exasperation of hidden fire.

Colonel Mayer now received instructions from General Dobell to leave a garrison at Ngwe under Colonel Cockburn —of sufficient strength to clear up the local situation and also to provide if necessary a strong column for Sakbajeme—and to return himself with the remainder of the force to Edea.

Leaving at Ngwe under Colonel Cockburn three guns, seven companies and a machine gun section,* Colonel Mayer with the remainder of the force moved on the 18th June to Edea, whence the British contingent went by railway to Duala.

The enemy near Ngwe displayed considerable activity on the 18th June. He attacked the Allied outposts with vigour, but was repulsed with considerable loss and then forced to retire by a skilful counter-attack. The Allied casualties only totalled four. Next day Colonel Cockburn sent out a French detachment (under Captain Tibout) to make a detour through the bush and get behind the enemy, who had taken up a position at Nbokelen. This movement Captain Tibout executed with considerable success, killing over twenty of the enemy—at a cost to his own force of only nine casualties—and capturing 8,000 rounds of ammunition and some valuable documents.

Ngwe; 18th June–1st July.

The enemy, meanwhile, had begun to interrupt communication between Ngwe and Edea, and on the 20th June Colonel Rose was sent out with 300 rifles † to clear the road for a convoy coming from Edea. He encountered a hostile force of between two and three hundred rifles with machine guns in position across the road rather over a mile

---

* One gun Nigerian Battery, one company Gold Coast Battalion, and two companies 1st Nigerians, under Lieutenant-Colonel Rose; and a section each of French guns and machine guns and four French companies under Commandant Mathieu.

† One company Gold Coast Battalion, one company 1st Nigerians, and a French company.

from Ngwe, and a brisk action ensued, the brunt of the fighting falling on the Gold Coast company, which behaved with conspicuous courage. The enemy was skilfully handled and held on stubbornly till a couple of well-directed shells from the camp at Ngwe and the arrival in his rear of the escort to the convoy from Edea forced him to beat a hasty retreat. The Allied casualties totalled twenty-three, including Lieutenant J. V. Earle and sixteen of the Gold Coast company.

After this, as the result of a week's operations, in which strong parties moved out from Ngwe in all directions, Colonel Cockburn reported on the 26th June that the road to Edea was clear. The enemy was reported to have suffered heavy losses in the recent fighting and, as it was evident that the bulk of his force had retired, Colonel Mayer requested permission to withdraw the British detachment from Ngwe, where there was much sickness. To this General Dobell agreed, provided that Colonel Mayer did not consider it advisable to send a force to visit Sakbajeme. Colonel Mayer thereupon ordered Colonel Cockburn and the British troops to withdraw to Edea on the 1st July, leaving a French garrison at Ngwe.

Retrospect. In these abortive operations in the Yaunde direction the Allied force under General Dobell had incurred, in the last two months, a total of 301 battle casualties * and at least 600 from sickness. The hopes that pressure by General Aymerich's troops would have prevented the enemy reinforcing his Edea front had not been fulfilled. Captured documents showed that, by bringing in two companies from the north-west, a detachment from the Kribi-Lolo district, and a batch of recruits from Yaunde, he had concentrated about 600 rifles in addition to the 600 which had previously opposed Colonel Mayer. With these numbers he had offered a resistance to the Allied advance from Wum Biagas which had been as stubborn as it was unexpected. The area traversed had also proved to be less practicable and more affected by the heavy rain than had been anticipated; and the enemy, realising the advantages which the physical difficulties and the Allied advance by one road † conferred on him, concentrated his

---

* *Killed* 13 Europeans and 83 natives, and *wounded* 6 Europeans and 199 natives.

† The lack of experience in bush warfare of the French led them to regard the difficulty and delay involved as prohibiting an advance off the main road, and consequently, at the moment of contact with the enemy, the column almost invariably found itself without sufficient room to deploy.

[*To face p.* 284

Naval Gun with the Yaunde Column

opposition and at the same time struck by short lines at the Allied communications.

Much of the sickness which occurred was undoubtedly due to the arduous labour which all movement had entailed and, in the absence of tents of any kind, to constant exposure to torrential rain. The whole force was badly in need of rest for recuperation.

In a telegram of the 12th June to the War Office, requesting guidance regarding the future policy he was to adopt, General Dobell outlined briefly some of the main factors governing the situation. After pointing out that the rainy season prohibited extensive operations till November he drew attention to the unsatisfactory state of health of his force. At the moment few of his experienced European officers were capable of sustained effort, and his Nigerian troops, suffering from dysentery, were unfit for hard work. Unless Europeans and Africans were sent on leave to their homes to recuperate he considered that few would be fit for active service in November.

The question of future policy; 12th–23rd June 1915.

He then went on to express doubts as to whether, having regard to the difficulties he was likely to experience, General Aymerich would be able to reach Yaunde, the capture of which, in any case, appeared to have lost its importance, as the German Government was said to have left it and to have moved to Yoko. For a successful advance on Yaunde, independently of General Aymerich, General Dobell said that he would require a reinforcement by at least 1,000 men, as well as the improvement and repair of the road and railway leading in that direction, the provision of motor vehicles and a large number of additional carriers.

In view of the doubtful effect of such an advance and the great expenditure in men, money and material involved, General Dobell was not prepared to recommend it. He proposed instead that the Allies, while holding the territory already gained, should endeavour to bring about a German surrender by stopping the import of all food supplies, which apparently came through Spanish Muni; and he suggested certain action to make the blockade more effective.

Next day General Dobell heard of the surrender of Garua to Colonel Cunliffe, and on the 14th June received the telegram from Brazzaville, previously mentioned, which showed that General Aymerich's progress was slow.

The War Office replied on the 15th June, agreeing to the relinquishment for the time being of the advance on Yaunde, to the direction of efforts to stop the import of food supplies and to such measures as General Dobell deemed feasible for the recuperation of his troops' health. His difficulties were fully recognised, and it was realised that extended operations would be barely feasible till November. Should energetic measures by General Dobell—to harry the remaining German posts and to cut off supplies—not succeed, however, in effecting a surrender, the War Office hoped that he would be able later to renew the offensive with increased vigour and success. They would do what was possible to maintain his supply of officers and towards tightening the blockade.

At the beginning of the month, learning that the 5th Light Infantry of the Indian army was being sent to Duala,* General Dobell had suggested to the War Office that it should, instead, be sent to Garua, where the country and climate were more suitable for its employment than the forest region. After the fall of Garua the War Office telegraphed on the 18th June suggesting its employment in the Bare-Chang area, where it could relieve African troops accustomed to bush warfare. General Dobell agreed to carry out this suggestion if possible.

On the 23rd June General Dobell sent a letter to the War Office in which he replied at some length to their telegram of the 15th. In addition to an active defence of the occupied territory, including the Kele river-Ngwe line, his main efforts during the rainy season, he said, would be directed to preventing the transit of supplies and ammunition through Spanish territory, by which route he had reason to believe that the enemy had recently received fresh supplies of munitions.

The fall of Garua would have a great moral effect, and he understood that Nigerian troops from there were moving south and clearing the country north of Ngaundere. General Aymerich's troops, though unlikely to get within striking distance of Yaunde, would presumably show such activity as was possible at that time of year. This pressure on the enemy from all sides, combined with a tightened blockade, would, he hoped, produce the enemy's surrender in due course. But to meet the possibility of this not occurring by the close of the rainy season in the middle of November, he considered it advisable to enter into the question of an offensive.

The only apparent objective was Yaunde, an advance on

---

* Part of this battalion had mutinied at Singapore in February, and the remaining portion had petitioned to be sent on service anywhere to prove its loyalty and wipe out the stain on the regiment.

which the enemy would probably oppose with all his strength, though he was also likely, in view of the move of the German Government to Yoko, to retire from Yaunde if an adequate Allied force was sent against it. In such a contingency little but moral success and possession of the enemy's main recruiting area would be gained.

There were two lines of advance to Yaunde : one, the railway to Eseka and thence, either by the carrier road to Chang Mangas or by a light railway track to a point about thirty miles south of Yaunde ; and the other, the main Edea-Yaunde road. By both the distance from Edea was about 110 miles, though if the light railway track were followed another thirty miles must be added. For an advance it would be necessary to construct a motor road to Wum Biagas, and to repair the railway to Eseka. This motor road should not be difficult to construct, but its extension beyond Wum Biagas would be prevented by the mountainous nature of the country. On the railway the enemy had already destroyed several bridges and might do further damage.

The difficulties of an advance were accentuated by the dense forest, in which any movement off the road was only possible by cutting a way through the bush. As far as Wum Biagas and Eseka the country was hilly, but beyond became almost mountainous with impassable marsh in the valleys. Defensive positions abounded, and at every bend of the road a few men with a machine gun could hold up an advance for hours. The advantages to a defender with modern armament were obvious and facilitated ambushes and attacks on convoys. In consequence, an unusually large proportion of troops would be necessary to protect the lines of communication.

By November the enemy might be able to concentrate for the defence of Yaunde a force of 300 Germans and 1,500–2,000 natives with two field guns and thirty to forty machine guns. He had organised his resources well, and was said to have a 50 per cent. trained native reserve, for whom he had no rifles, but who could replace casualties as they occurred.

It would be necessary for the Allies, on each line of advance, to arrive in front of Yaunde with at least 1,000 good troops, accustomed to bush warfare and led by experienced Europeans, with artillery ; and a similar number of troops would be required on each line of communication. By sending his British officers and African troops on leave to recuperate during the rainy season and with the aid of reinforcements from Nigeria, General Dobell hoped to be able to provide a sufficient force for one line of advance. For the other the French would require considerable reinforcement.

With a motor road to Wum Biagas and the railway to Eseka there would still, however, be about sixty-five miles along which carrier transport must be employed; and he estimated that 3,500 carriers for the French and 4,000 for the British would be required. Most of those for the French, moreover, would have to be procured from the British West African colonies. Carriers were very vulnerable to attack and prone to panic, so that if the enemy concentrated on attacks on convoys he might cause such demoralisation as to make the use of carriers impracticable.

The ease with which the lines of communication could be dislocated and the other great difficulties, presenting so many chances of failure, made General Dobell unwilling to recommend an offensive. He considered that the only alternative was to continue with the policy then in progress—for which sufficient native troops were available—during the further period of the war or until the Germans surrendered.

If General Aymerich's troops were able to carry out an advance on Yaunde, continued General Dobell, he himself would always be able to prevent the withdrawal of hostile troops from his own front; and he would, in any case, continue to act vigorously against any enemy within striking distance.

General Dobell concluded by saying that if the Allied Governments, disagreeing with his view, decided on an offensive on the scale outlined, he would like an intimation by telegraph, as there would be little time available to obtain his requirements, which included three or four wireless telegraph sets with personnel, motor lorries, railway personnel and material, some light howitzers, and a large number of additional carriers. The collection of the last would take a considerable time.

The Northern Railway and the Cameroons coast; May–June 1915. Elsewhere than on the Edea-Yaunde line, General Dobell's troops had only been engaged in operations of a minor character during May and June. The Allied naval force had continued its blockade of the coast and its constant patrol of the inland waterways and neighbouring seas.*

During the continual reconnaissances from Nkongsamba

---

* Commander W. C. G. Ruxton, R.N., from England relieved Commander F. E. K. Strong, R.N., in command of the *Dwarf* on the 3rd June.

NAVAL OPERATIONS

and Bare, and the energetic patrolling to keep the surrounding districts clear of hostile parties, there had been occasional minor encounters with the enemy. But he had attempted no serious interference with the British line of communication nor with the British patrols, who on several occasions penetrated well to the east of the Nkam river. Towards the end of May information had been obtained of the movement of a strong enemy detachment from Bana to Yabasi, apparently on its way towards Yaunde.

Naval patrols on the Wuri and Dibombe rivers, which were extended as soon as the state of the water allowed, had continued practically without incident. The enemy had made no attempt to re-occupy Yabasi, though he occasionally visited a point a few miles above that place, to which point our patrols also penetrated.

For most of the period low water rendered the Kwa-kwa creek impassable. On the Sanaga the patrol had to pay constant attention to natives on both banks and prevent the enemy fording the river at places where the water was exceptionally shallow.

At the beginning of May the approach of the rainy season had rendered it necessary to reconstruct the shore base of the Nyong flotilla and to send for duty there a party of fifteen marines from Duala. The native levies there, recruited from the Kribi district, were also replaced by men enrolled from among the local refugees. During the latter half of May hostile parties were encountered near Dehane by patrolling vessels on several occasions, and by the middle of June the enemy strength in this district had increased considerably. The harassing tactics he adopted towards the local population led to such an influx of refugees to the shore base that it became very difficult to supply them with food; and it became necessary at the beginning of July to transfer over 1,400 of them to the plantation district near Victoria. On the 28th May three vessels of the Nyong flotilla proceeded up the river as far as Dehane and successfully drove an enemy party out of its trenches at Etima; and in another affair on the 9th June at Rocky Point in the Lokundje river Lieutenant-Commander A. B. McCullagh was wounded.*

---

* Owing to the shortness of officers and the necessity of arranging for various duties in the different areas of operations, Lieutenant W. McC. Lunt, R.N.R., Lieutenant R. A. Clark, R.N., Lieutenant-Commander C. J. R. Learmonth, R.N., and Lieutenant-Commander A. B. McCullagh, R.N., successively took command of the Nyong flotilla and native levies.

The Campo River flotilla, carrying out reconnaissances inland and along the Muni frontier, engaged in numerous minor patrol encounters, one of more than usual duration on the 14th June heralding an increase in the neighbourhood of enemy activities. Steps had to be taken here also to improve the shore bases at Campo and Dipikar.

Naval Blockade Force; June 1915. There had been an access of various vessels to assist in the blockade. In April and May the *Lagos* and *Uromi* of the Elder-Dempster line had been taken up and armed with 3-pounders; the French armed trawler *Vauban* from France had joined on the 22nd May; and H.M. ships *Sirius* and *Rinaldo* from England on the 6th June. By the end of that month the force employed on blockade duty and patrol duty on the high sea comprised H.M. ships *Dwarf, Sirius* and *Rinaldo*, the Nigerian armed yacht *Ivy*, the French warships *Friant*,* *Surprise* and *Vauban*, and the armed merchant ships *Lagos* and *Uromi*, besides several smaller vessels.

Distribution of British land contingent; June 1915. At the end of June the distribution of the British troops under General Dobell was as follows:—

Northern Railway and Bare..	Sierra Leone Battery, Section Gold Coast Battery, West African Regiment, Gold Coast Battalion (less one company).
Buea, Victoria and Zopo ..	Sierra Leone Battalion Headquarters and two companies.
Dibombe Post	Two companies Sierra Leone Battalion.
Duala (or en route there from Ngwe)..	Nigerian Battery, 1st Nigerians, 2nd Nigerians, Recruits from Nigeria (209), One company Gold Coast Battalion, Two companies Sierra Leone Battalion, Gambia Detachment.

The West African Regiment and Sierra Leone Battalion each comprised six companies; the Nigerian battalions each four companies; and the Gold Coast Battalion, an additional company having been formed of a reinforcement of 150 men which had arrived on the 16th June, five companies.

The rifle strength of battalions was as follows; but of this strength a considerable number, especially in the Nigerian battalions and the Gambia Detachment (as will be seen below), were undergoing medical treatment:

---

* *Friant* relieved *Pothuau* in June.

CIVIL ADMINISTRATION

	Rifle Strength		
	Effective	Sick	Total
Gambia Detachment	34	27	61
West African Regiment	682	34	716
Sierra Leone Battalion	514	65	579
Gold Coast Battalion	789	87	876
1st Nigerians	437	224	661
2nd Nigerians	291	286	577
	2,747	723	3,470

On the 27th June, the British officer and sergeant of the Sierra Leone Field Section R.E. having previously been invalided, the African ranks were sent back to Sierra Leone, being relieved by a new detachment of a British sergeant and thirteen native ranks. On the 16th June Colonel C. C. J. Pery, R.E., arrived at Duala and became Chief Engineer.

A brief reference may here be made to the civil administration which had been re-established wherever it was possible, i.e. in the occupied territory up to the southern Nigeria border and also along the military lines of communication leading inland. *Civil and Political administration.*

A civil police force, recruited largely from ex-German police and soldiers, had been raised and was doing good work; two or three British officers who had had previous administrative experience had been granted magisterial powers; the native courts had been re-established; and no difficulty had been experienced in collecting the poll tax which was payable by all adult males.

After the German evacuation, the native population as a whole settled down to live their old lives as far as possible, though in some areas they suffered considerable hardship from the lack of foodstuffs and clothing resulting from the cessation of trade. In those districts in which in the past there had been a knowledge of the British protectorates, the Allied occupation brought a feeling of relief which induced a general desire to give as little trouble as possible to the Allies; and in many other districts there was evidently a widespread wish for a change from the harsh and unsympathetic German rule. The cold hard facts of warlike operations, entailing serious danger to life, soon, however, put a stop to any inclination to assist the Allies openly and created a universal desire for a cessation of hostilities. The general apathetic attitude which ensued, and which extended throughout the daily life of the population, made it difficult, however, to reconstruct an administration which might, they felt, be put a stop to at any moment by one of the recurring irruptions of warring troops.

On the 26th June, Mr. W. F. Gowers of the Colonial Civil Service, who, since his arrival on the 26th February, had held the post of Political Adviser to General Dobell, was invalided, and it became necessary to alter the following channel of civil administration which had been laid down in March:

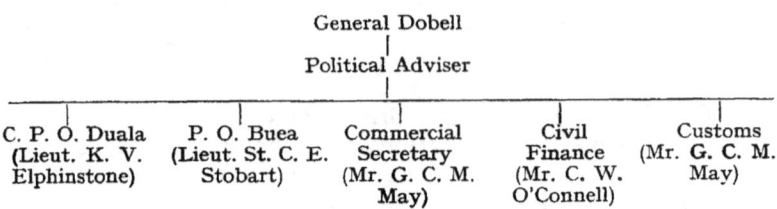

After Mr. Gowers' departure, the Political Officer, Buea, and political officers who had been appointed at Nkongsamba and Rio del Rey were made subordinate to the Chief Political Officer, Duala, while the Commercial Secretary, Collector of Customs and Financial Officer came directly under General Dobell.

Franco-Belgian operations in the south and south-east; May–June 1915.

As already mentioned, General Aymerich's troops had been unable to make as much progress as the French authorities had anticipated.

Oyem Column. The Oyem Column, immobilised by the rain and unable to get news of General Dobell's offensive, remained in occupation of Oyem till the 24th of June, when it advanced northward, but found itself checked a few days later by a German force in position at Bitam. Major Miquelard had sent a message, asking for news of General Dobell's offensive, which reached the British at Dipikar (on the Campo river) on the 5th May. But he never received the reply, as the messenger carrying it was stopped in Spanish Muni.

Mvahdi Column. The Mvahdi Column, then still at Minkebe, was broken up on the 1st June, one of its companies with a Nordenfeldt gun being sent to join the Sanga Column at Eta and arriving there on the 20th.

Sanga Column. In a telegram received on the 7th May General Aymerich, who was with the Sanga Column, was requested by the Governor-General of French Equatorial Africa to accelerate his forward movement as General Dobell was starting his advance on Eseka on the 1st May. General Aymerich thereupon issued instructions to the Sanga Column to advance as soon as its supply situation permitted and to the Lobaye Column to co-operate by moving on Nyassi and Ngangela.

The Germans had so devastated the country, however, that the French were unable to obtain anything locally, and before the Sanga Column could advance, a total of 3,000 carriers had to be recruited in, and brought from, the Middle Congo.

The Sanga Column was divided into three groups. The right group, roughly halfway between Yukaduma and Lomie, consisted of one French and one Belgian company (300 rifles)* with a section of Nordenfeldt guns and a party of 100 Belgian rifles detached to try and gain touch with the Lobaye Column about Ngangela. The centre group, at Ngato, was composed of one French and one and a half Belgian companies (400 rifles), a section each of mountain and Nordenfeldt guns and a machine gun. There was also a reinforcement of 150 rifles on its way to join the group. The left group, *en route* from Eta to Ngato, consisted of one French and half a Belgian company (270 rifles), a mountain gun and a machine gun.

Commencing its advance from Ngato on the 24th May, the centre group encountered stubborn resistance by the enemy from a series of defensive positions. The most serious fighting occurred during a three days' attack (30th May–1st June) on the Monso position, in which, before gaining success and capturing nine Germans, the French lost sixteen killed and a considerable number wounded. Lomie was finally entered by them on the 24th June, the Germans having burnt the place before evacuating it. In the meantime the right group had commenced to advance on the 4th June and reached Assobam on the 22nd, practically simultaneously with a detachment from the centre group.

The Lobaye Column, with its headquarters at Baturi, was distributed along the Kadei river in three groups, their strengths from north to south being, respectively, 200 rifles, 365 rifles with two mountain guns, and 350 rifles with a mountain and a machine gun. The column was opposed by four German companies (Nos. 5, 6, 9 and 11); it was confronted with serious supply and transport difficulties; and, to enable it to assume the offensive, required reinforcement.

Lobaye Column.

On the 22nd May General Aymerich sent instructions to Colonel Morisson to despatch his southern group to occupy Nyassi and Ngangela so as to gain touch with the Sanga Column. The enemy was strongly posted, however, in a

---

* The figures here and those below are only approximate.

region of forest and swamp, and in several actions at the beginning of June the southern group suffered considerable loss without attaining success. Colonel Morisson was then able to reinforce it to a strength of four companies (470 rifles) with a mountain and two machine guns. Taking over command of the group himself on the 22nd June he resumed the offensive and, fighting a series of successful actions, occupied Ngangela on the 30th. Three days later he gained touch with the Sanga Column.

<small>Northern Cameroons; May 1915. German position at Garua.</small>
To turn now to the operations in the north. The enemy's position at Garua extended northward from the slopes above the native town for about two thousand yards and, in a breadth of about half that distance, included the German military post and the ridge running alongside it and to the northward (see Map 11). From this position—whose height above the Benue river varied from about eighty to about two hundred and thirty feet—the ground fell away in all directions and afforded an uninterrupted view and field of fire, within effective field artillery range, of the surrounding open and grass-covered country. To fortify this naturally strong position the Germans had been at work since the outbreak of war and, by the continuous employment for five months of two thousand native labourers,* had built up a most formidable group of defensive works.

Five small rocky peaks on the ridge, marked A, B, C, D and F on the map, had been converted into self-contained redoubts with parapets and traverses solidly constructed and revetted with sandbags. In each there was a command post protected by armoured plates, a central bomb-proof shelter, a cement water-tank and stores for food and ammunition, while the three largest at A, B, and C were sited and specially organised to afford each other the fullest mutual support. The military post, marked E on the map, had been even more strongly fortified to serve as a *reduit* or keep. Its walls had been strengthened by mud to a thickness of fourteen or fifteen feet ; loopholes had been cut along the ground level in addition to those above and along the strengthened verandahs ; below there were large cellars to shelter reserve troops, women, and children ; and infantry redoubts at D and F, with another at G, served as outworks and to flank its walls.

---

* Their own figures.

To face p. 295]

Forts at Garua

THE ATTACK ON GARUA

All these separate works were connected with one another and with the keep by telephone; and all were surrounded by a triple belt of deep military pits, wire entanglements or thorn abattis and a continuous deep and wide ditch. An immense amount of labour had been expended on this line of obstacles, by which the whole position—as well as the separate works—was surrounded. The military pits were five or six feet deep, and most of them had been excavated in the rock, the barbed spears or stakes they held being concealed by a thin covering of mud and thatch. The ditch had also in a great part been cut in the rock and its scarp rendered more inaccessible by planks covered with spikes.

Reconnaissance during April led Colonel Cunliffe to agree with Colonel Brisset that the northward would be the best direction from which to launch the main Allied attack. This would certainly leave the line of retreat to the southward more open to the enemy. But the progress of the rains, which had already commenced, would decrease the risk by filling the Benue river. On the other hand, the attacking force would in this way be exposed to the minimum amount of hostile fire as, owing to the configuration of the ground, its advance would almost amount to an attack on the enemy's flank. *Cunliffe's plans; April–May 1915.*

Colonel Cunliffe also agreed to a request by Colonel Brisset to await the arrival of the French 95 mm. gun from Dakar, a prudent decision in view of the strength of the German position. As there was no news of this gun's progress, the date of the attack was still in doubt when the return to Garua on the 8th May of Crailsheim's party enabled Colonel Cunliffe to concentrate his whole attention again on the capture of Garua and its garrison. He proposed to encircle the enemy completely by placing his British troops astride the Benue river in positions to the south and west of Garua and by moving a great part of the French troops round to its north and north-west from Nassarao. But the retention in strength of this place by the French till the last moment before the attack, so as to ensure the safety of his communications with Fort Lamy, was so strongly urged by Colonel Brisset that Colonel Cunliffe abandoned his proposal.

A few days later, on the 18th May, news that the French gun was expected to reach Yola that week enabled Colonel Cunliffe to start his final preparations for the attack. One of the first steps was to concentrate, without arousing the enemy's suspicions, the bulk of his British contingent at *Preparations to attack Garua; 18th–28th May 1915.*

Jambutu Manga, which had been fixed as a suitable concentration point near the position of deployment. For some days the British infantry had been holding the line Bilonde-Tondere, with their mounted infantry some sixteen miles farther west covering fords by which Colonel Cunliffe had proposed to move his troops northward, passing well to the west of Garua. But a sudden rise in the Benue river forced him to abandon this idea and he then arranged to utilise the route via Bogole and Nassarao, which were both held by the French.*

The task of transporting, by carriers, the British supplies, ammunition and material generally, was a laborious one, especially as to escape enemy attention it had to be carried out entirely by night. A commencement had been made on the 15th May and the whole movement was successfully completed by the morning of the 25th when, except for a company of infantry left at Bilonde to cover the main crossing over the Benue, the whole British force with all its impedimenta had reached Jambutu Manga. Till then the Germans had no idea that such a movement was in progress. In fact, Crailsheim had decided to move out westward next day with his whole garrison, abandoning Garua and proceeding south to join hands with the main German column opposing General Dobell.† But the new British dispositions obliged him to abandon his intention; and for the next few days he restricted his activities to shelling the British outposts.

By the 28th May, when the French 95 mm. gun arrived, Colonel Cunliffe had selected his line of attack and next day issued orders for the move by night of the bulk of the Allied forces to their battle positions, and to a camp due north of Garua. Eighty French rifles were to remain at Nassarao, while their cavalry squadron watched the country and the crossings over the Benue river between there and Bilonde. From this place, which was occupied by " B " Comapny, 4th Battalion Nigerian Regiment, the British mounted infantry were to watch the river crossings and the country to the westward and north-westward up to the main Allied camp.

The transportation of the French heavy gun, from the railway at Baro in Nigeria, up 750 miles of river fallen almost below canoe draught, had been a fine feat, which reflected the greatest credit on the Nigeria Marine. With it there arrived

---

* Colonel Brisset had insisted on occupying Bogole when the British evacuated it.
† A week previously Colonel Cunliffe's Intelligence staff had informed him that the Germans contemplated such action.

THE ATTACK ON GARUA

a large convoy of British war material and "B" Company, 3rd Battalion Nigeria Regiment, from the Cross River Column. This brought the total Allied strength at Garua to :—*British*, 78 Europeans, 1,130 native ranks, one naval and three mountain guns and ten machine guns; and *French*, 46 Europeans, 580 native ranks, one heavy, two mountain and two Hotchkiss guns.* The British contingent of artillery and one mounted and seven and three-quarters infantry companies † was organised into headquarters troops and two columns, the latter being commanded respectively by Lieutenant-Colonel Webb-Bowen and Major G. L. Uniacke. To garrison Yola and its vicinity there had been left a section "B" Company, 1st Battalion, "G" Company, 3rd Battalion, and a few details and police.

At daybreak on the 31st May the Germans, discovering that the Allied firing line ‡ was entrenched about 3,000–3,500 yards north of Fort A, at once opened fire with their artillery. The Allied heavy guns, however, did not reply till four hours later, when they soon succeeded in silencing the German gun in Fort A, and in enabling the British mounted infantry on the Allied right to drive in the hostile outposts and occupy points within two thousand yards of the enemy's main position. The artillery duel ceased at 11.15 a.m. The German fire had been accurate, but the Allies were well entrenched and only one of their men had been wounded. On the other hand, according to native information, the enemy had sustained several casualties, and the loss of a machine gun and a considerable amount of ammunition destroyed in Fort A.

Attack on Garua; 31st May–10th June 1915.

The artillery duel recommenced on the 1st June, but the German fire was much reduced in volume, and the Allies were able to carry out reconnaissances to determine their future line of attack, sustaining only three casualties during the day. By the morning of the 2nd the Allied line had advanced another thousand yards. But Colonel Cunliffe had come to the conclusion that the great strength of the enemy's position rendered an immediate attack too hazardous and that he could only hope to cross the open space still intervening, and destroy the

---

* The French force was composed of a squadron of cavalry, three infantry companies and two detachments of *gardes regionaux*.

† "B" Mounted Infantry, "B" (less one section) and "H" 1st Battalion, "B" and "H" 2nd Battalion, "B," "D" and "H" 3rd Battalion, and "B" 4th Battalion, all of the Nigeria Regiment.

‡ The firing line was composed of two British companies (Lieut.-Colonel Webb-Bowen's column) and one French company, which was on the left of the line. Echelonned to its left rear, to guard against a counter-attack, were the two other French companies.

enemy's obstacles prior to an assault, by sapping his way forward to close quarters. This he proceeded to do, and in the next few days the Allies made good progress.

By the 6th June the enemy had been completely cut off from all sources of supply, and native information indicated a definite food shortage in Garua. The Allied trenches had reached to within 1,500 yards of Fort A, and by the morning of the 10th they had progressed a further five hundred yards with an efficient service of communication trenches to the rear. The German defenders had displayed little enterprise, and the Allies, whose casualties were very small, had experienced more difficulty from the rain and from the lack in the vicinity of a supply of drinking water.*

Enemy attempt to escape; 9th–10th June 1915. Early on the 10th June Colonel Cunliffe learnt that during the previous night the enemy had moved out with his whole force, his baggage and munitions, and had tried to cross the Benue river. This was in flood, however, and he had abandoned the attempt after fifteen of his men had been drowned. Colonel Cunliffe at once ordered his mounted troops to close in round the enemy position, his heavy guns to search it with fire, and the British company from Bilonde to line the southern bank of the Benue.

Surrender of Garua; 10th June 1915. The Allied heavy artillery opened fire soon after 1.15 p.m., that of the French 95 mm. gun being very effective, and arrangements were made for all the Allied mountain guns to join in the bombardment next morning. But suddenly, at about 3.30 p.m., white flags were run up on several prominent points in the enemy position and shortly afterwards a mounted German in white uniform was seen coming from Fort C towards the Allied lines. This was a Captain Wanka, and Major Wright and Captain Ferrandi, who were sent to meet him, were surprised to learn that he had come to discuss terms of capitulation. He informed Colonels Cunliffe and Brisset that Crailsheim was prepared to surrender Garua, provided its garrison were allowed free passage southward with all the honours of war, i.e., with their arms and baggage. In reply he was told that only an unconditional surrender could be accepted; and his further request for a twenty-four hours' armistice in which to consider this reply was answered by the intimation that a two hours' truce only could be accorded. He accordingly returned to Garua, but arrived back about 6 p.m. with Crailsheim's acceptance of an unconditional surrender.

---

* Two thousand natives had to be employed daily to bring up the necessary water.

To face p. 299]

British Naval Gun at Garua

Prisoners taken at Garua

SURRENDER OF GARUA

He was thereupon instructed that Crailsheim and four other German officers were to come immediately to the Allied lines as hostages and to conduct the Allied detachments which would occupy Forts A, B and C and the keep E during the night. Captain Wanka demurred and suggested a postponement of these measures till daylight, urging the danger of moving through the German lines of obstacles in the dark. His real reason, as well as that of the German commander for surrendering his stronghold so easily, became apparent, however, when his request for a horse (to replace his own which had been stolen in Garua) disclosed the fact that the German native troops had mutinied.

From subsequent statements by German officers it appears that, from its outset, the Allied bombardment had greatly demoralised the garrison and that the increased intensity of the shell-fire on the 10th June created such panic as to snap all the bonds of discipline. By about 5 p.m. many of the German native soldiery were beyond control and started to pillage prior to seeking safety in flight. In the attempts they made to break to the south and south-west across the Benue a large number were drowned, others were killed by the cordon of Allied troops and only a certain percentage managed to escape, most of them without arms or equipment.

Crailsheim and the four officer hostages arrived at the Allied lines between 10 and 11 p.m., and shortly afterwards Allied detachments proceeded to occupy the main points in the German position. At seven o'clock next morning the Allied force made its formal entry.

The prisoners numbered 37 Germans, including 17 reservists, but only 212 native combatants, an uncertain number having managed to escape.* But, as most of them had abandoned or lost their arms and equipment, their escape can have done the Germans little good. Many stores of all kinds, four guns, ten machine guns, over two hundred rifles and a large amount of ammunition, all practically undamaged, were also taken. The capture of all the Germans and of these arms and ammunition which the enemy could not replace was for the Allies one of the most beneficial results of the operations.

At the time of the surrender Colonel Cunliffe's information *Situation after surrender.*

---

* Their total strength, according to Crailsheim, had originally been 317 trained soldiers and 187 recruits. But about 50 of the recruits had deserted before the attack and, taking into account those killed and drowned since, Colonel Cunliffe came to the conclusion that not more than 70 had escaped. Subsequent information indicated that this may have been an underestimate.

showed that, in addition to small posts and parties of enemy troops based on Koncha, Banyo, and Bamenda, and operating northward from those places towards the Nigerian frontier, the only German troops between the Bamenda-Chang-Fumban area and Garua were a body of some seventy native rifles about Ngaundere and a small party in a post near Tibati. Some reports had been received in May of enemy movements towards an impregnable position on a plateau southward of Tingere, but the information was very indefinite and could only be taken as indicating the site of a possible position for a final stand by the Germans in this area.

The advance on Ngaundere.
The news of the capture of Garua spread rapidly and freed Nigeria of all anxiety by causing the immediate retirement to the southward and eastward of all the German troops operating near the frontier. The fugitives from Garua had apparently made for Ngaundere; and to keep them on the run, to anticipate any enemy concentration and to secure a good base for an Allied advance southward, Colonel Cunliffe decided to seize at once the northern edge of the Ngaundere plateau. He accordingly ordered a column under Colonel Webb-Bowen to move from Garua against Ngaundere and arranged, as he thought, for Colonel Brisset to remain at Garua ready to move out with reinforcements to support Colonel Webb-Bowen if necessary. Colonel Cunliffe decided to go himself to Yola with a part of his British contingent and to send detachments from there to occupy Koncha and Chamba. His main reason for going there himself, however, was to get into direct telegraphic communication with Sir Frederick Lugard, from whom he took his instructions,* and with General Dobell, with both of whom he wished to discuss future plans and the best means of co-operation. Colonel Cunliffe had at first suggested that, for this purpose, he and Major Wright should visit Lagos, but their continued presence on the spot was considered necessary by Sir Frederick Lugard, who was himself proceeding shortly on leave to England.

Capture of Ngaundere; 28th–29th June 1915.
Leaving Garua on the 17th June, Lieutenant-Colonel Webb-Bowen's column encountered no opposition till it reached, on the 28th, the very steep ascent to the main central plateau, at the northern edge of which lies Ngaundere. The German outposts were strongly posted across all the steep or precipitous paths leading upward. But, by moving forward during a very heavy tropical storm, Colonel Webb-Bowen's

---

* Sir Frederick Lugard received his instructions from the Colonial Office, who issued them after consultation with the War Office.

advanced guard under Captain C. H. Fowle surprised these outposts completely and drove them all in. Their retreat uncovered several strong positions in rear which had been constructed on the last 2,000 feet of the ascent; and that evening the French cavalry, after pursuing the enemy for several miles, established themselves on the summit. Next morning (29th) the main body occupied the forts and Ngaundere without opposition, though, during the ensuing night, a hostile force of about four Germans and one hundred natives from the southward opened a heavy fire on the Allies in the forts and barracks. This enemy force soon retired again, however, in the direction of Tibati, having effected nothing beyond inflicting nine casualties on the Allies.

From Yola on the 20th June Captain C. E. Roberts started with a section of mounted infantry and " B " Company, 3rd Battalion, to occupy the German fort at Koncha; and, at the same time, a section of mounted infantry and a mixed detachment of troops and police were sent to take possession, respectively, of Chamba and the enemy post at Maio Kaleh. Both these were occupied without opposition, and Koncha—a strong fort with accommodation for four companies—was captured on the 27th after a bloodless skirmish. On the 29th its late garrison of about three Germans and thirty natives, fleeing towards Banyo from the pursuing Nigerian mounted infantry, lost five men (one a German) drowned or killed by local natives. *Capture of Koncha; 27th June 1915.*

Colonel Cunliffe had come to the conclusion—and Sir Frederick Lugard agreed with him—that the best way in which he could assist General Dobell was by co-operating with him in an attack on the German troops in the Bamenda-Chang-Fumban area. They were estimated to be about six hundred in number and formed the largest German force remaining in the northern half of the Cameroons. While awaiting a reply from General Dobell, Colonel Cunliffe heard on the 19th June from Colonel Webb-Bowen that Colonel Brisset intended to proceed at once to Ngaundere with the greater part of the troops at Garua. Colonel Brisset's letter of the 19th June informing Colonel Cunliffe of this intention appears to have gone by mistake to Fort Lamy and it only reached Colonel Cunliffe five weeks later. He was, therefore, unaware of Colonel Brisset's reasons for the step he was taking.* Colonel Cunliffe *Cunliffe's plans.*

---

* The main reason given by Colonel Brisset was that he was convinced that the presence of a strong Allied force with artillery at Ngaundere would have a great moral effect on the German forces at Banyo and about Bertua.

himself was much averse to this movement to Ngaundere as there were evidently only inconsiderable German forces in that direction. On the other hand, Colonel Brisset had been placed under Colonel Cunliffe by General Largeau for the operations to capture Garua, and though at their conclusion Colonel Brisset had given no indication that he considered himself an independent commander again, it might be that this was the case. Feeling doubtful, therefore, if he was justified in giving orders, Colonel Cunliffe wrote to Colonel Brisset on the 19th June that he did not wish any British troops or carriers to move from Garua to Ngaundere, except in case of real emergency. Colonel Cunliffe also suggested that as future military plans were under discussion with M. Merlet,* Sir Frederick Lugard and General Dobell, Colonel Brisset might feel it advisable to await the result before leaving Garua.

Colonel Brisset replied on the 21st that he had hitherto thought that Colonel Cunliffe agreed with him as to the imperative necessity of activity and of an immediate movement in strength to the southward so as to deprive the enemy of time to dig himself in. In view of Zimmermann's † known intention of retiring to the central plateau from Yaunde and the distance of the enemy forces from Garua, Colonel Brisset felt that his force was wasted there and he was starting for Ngaundere next day,‡ leaving at Garua three French infantry sections and the two British infantry companies.

On the 22nd June Colonel Cunliffe received information from General Dobell that the advance on Yaunde had been abandoned as General Aymerich's troops, hard pressed in a difficult country, were not within two hundred miles of Yaunde; that General Dobell's force was to hold the territory gained but would not resume the general offensive or be able to co-operate with the Allied forces in the north during the rainy season, i.e., till November; that the German force east of Edea and about Yaunde had been reinforced, had not retired into the interior or to the northward and were better supplied than before with food and ammunition; and that General Aymerich's troops from the south-east had not been able to reach Bertua and would find it most difficult, owing to the supply and transport difficulties and the hostile opposi-

---

* M. Merlet was at Lagos on his way to take over the administration of Chad.
† The German military commander in the Cameroons.
‡ He actually left on the 23rd.

tion they were encountering, to co-operate with an Allied force at Ngaundere. General Dobell also intimated that he did not feel in a position to offer advice regarding the operations to be undertaken by Colonel Cunliffe in the near future.

Replying on the 24th June to Colonel Brisset's letter of the 21st, Colonel Cunliffe explained that, feeling it undesirable to move all available troops southward before they were required to co-operate with the Allied forces operating from the south and south-east, he had restricted himself to occupying Ngaundere and Koncha with flying columns. He had now received information of the situation of the forces under Generals Dobell and Aymerich, which he repeated and which, as he felt sure Colonel Brisset would agree, showed that it would be premature to send a large force to occupy Ngaundere. For there was no enemy force of any size within many miles of that place, and its situation on the central plateau was such that if the enemy had ever intended to fall back on it from Yaunde the fall of Garua must have caused him to abandon the idea. In conclusion, Colonel Cunliffe expressed the opinion that, during the period of inactivity (i.e., the rainy season) in the south and south-east, the Allied forces in the north should apply themselves to reducing Mora, so as to free more troops to co-operate subsequently with Generals Dobell and Aymerich, and to occupying the Koncha-Banyo-Bamenda line. On this plan Colonel Cunliffe invited Colonel Brisset's views.

But Colonel Brisset was already well on his way southward and did not receive this letter till the 4th July, three days before he reached Ngaundere. On the 29th June, feeling strongly that the force at Ngaundere could do little or no good and was rather isolated, Colonel Cunliffe wrote again to Colonel Brisset and asked him to instruct Colonel Webb-Bowen to return with his British troops to Garua unless the local situation demanded their presence at Ngaundere for a short time longer. Colonel Cunliffe also inquired when Colonel Brisset himself expected to be back in Garua. On the same day, in a telegram to General Largeau at Fort Lamy describing the general situation, Colonel Cunliffe stated that he was recalling the British troops from Ngaundere. He went on to inquire whether the French troops under Colonel Brisset were still under his (Colonel Cunliffe's) orders ; as if so, he proposed that Colonel Brisset, taking with him as many of his French troops as he considered necessary to join the investing force already there, should attack Mora, while he himself proceeded to operate with all available troops in the direction of Banyo.

Brisset's views. Colonel Cunliffe's letters to Colonel Brisset of the 24th and 29th June crossed one from that officer sent on the 3rd July in which he advocated an Allied advance to the line Kentu-Banyo-Tibati-Kunde as a first step towards co-operating and gaining touch with Generals Dobell and Aymerich. This letter reached Colonel Cunliffe on the 10th July, by which time he had been forced to the conclusion that an advance from the Nigerian frontier through the thick and mountainous country in the Bamenda-Banyo direction would be very difficult if not impossible during the rainy season; and he replied the same day concurring in the occupation of Ngaundere till he and Colonel Brisset could discuss the whole situation together, preferably at Yola. Colonel Cunliffe went on to mention some objections to Colonel Brisset's plan and concluded by saying that if an advance towards Banyo and Bamenda proved to be physically impossible, and if Brisset wished to remain with the bulk of his troops at Ngaundere, Colonel Cunliffe himself might undertake an attack on Mora * with British troops.

Decision to attack Mora; July 1915. On the 13th July Colonel Cunliffe received a telegram sent on the 4th by General Largeau saying that subject to General Aymerich's approval—and this was practically certain—Colonel Brisset and his troops would remain under Colonel Cunliffe's orders. In sending a copy of this on to Colonel Brisset next day, Colonel Cunliffe announced his intention of proceeding at an early date to reduce Mora. He would take two British companies from Yola and wished to take also a British and a French company and the French 95 mm. gun from Garua. Colonel Brisset would remain at Ngaundere, unless he wished to come to Mora, but no offensive would be undertaken from Ngaundere to the southward for the time being. Two days later, Colonel Cunliffe received a reply to his letter of the 24th June, despatched by Colonel Brisset on the 4th July. This showed that Colonel Brisset, considering himself independent of Colonel Cunliffe after the fall of Garua, had moved to Ngaundere with the idea of communicating and co-operating with General Aymerich's troops and that his action was in accordance with instructions which he had since received from General Largeau. Colonel Brisset also intimated that he regarded the Mora position as practically impregnable and consequently considered that it would be better to continue to contain it than to incur heavy casualties by attempting an

---

* The rains in the Mora district were much less than in the central and south Cameroons.

assault. He also again advocated the early occupation of the Koncha-Banyo-Bamenda line by the British while he prolonged the line eastward from Ngaundere towards Kunde.

In view of this intimation that Colonel Brisset's advance to Ngaundere was in accordance with General Largeau's instructions, Colonel Cunliffe at once withdrew his objections and cancelled his orders to Colonel Webb-Bowen to move back to Garua. At the same time he expressed the opinion to General Largeau that the despatch of a column from Ngaundere to Kunde would, for the time being, be premature. Colonel Cunliffe also informed General Largeau of his intention of proceeding personally with a force to reduce Mora.

In the meantime, in accordance with Colonel Cunliffe's modified plan of limiting his activity in the Banyo-Bamenda direction during the rainy season to operations of a preparatory nature, the Ibi Column, brought up to a strength of three and a half companies,* had moved forward across the frontier along the Bakundi-Gashiga road. Major Mann had been placed in command and had received instructions on the 5th July to reconnoitre topographically as well as to gain information regarding the enemy and to avoid committing himself to extended operations without reference to Colonel Cunliffe. Karbabi had been occupied without opposition, and by the 22nd July one of Major Mann's companies had reached Barua; a company and a half were between there and Bakundi; and another company was in the Takum district of Nigeria. On that day Major Mann received further instructions not to go beyond Gashiga, where he was to construct a fort, and to consolidate his line of communication. *Advance on Gashiga; July 1915.*

From Ngaundere Captain Fowle with "H" Company 2nd Nigerian Regiment and a French cavalry troop had been sent westward to occupy Tingere and establish touch with the British at Koncha. He occupied Tingere on the 19th July, its small German garrison retiring towards Tibati without offering opposition. *Occupation of Tingere; 19th July 1915.*

Before sailing for Europe Sir Frederick Lugard had informed Colonel Cunliffe that General Dobell was preparing a memorandum on the situation for submission to the Governors-General at Brazzaville, Dakar, and Lagos. On the 22nd July Colonel Cunliffe wrote, referring to this memorandum, to General Dobell and asked for as early an intimation as possible of the way in which, in his opinion, Colonel Cunliffe's troops could *Cunliffe's plans; July 1915.*

---

* C/1st Battalion, C and half G/2nd Battalion and H/3rd Battalion.

best co-operate when the general offensive was resumed. This intimation Colonel Cunliffe desired to enable him to make the necessary arrangements. He himself was moving very shortly to reduce Mora; and his column across the south-east frontier was making satisfactory progress along the Banyo road. But he did not propose to commit himself to an occupation of Banyo until he was sure of being able to maintain himself there. This would depend on enemy action. Consequently, until the situation developed, he would retain his hold on Koncha and on Ngaundere, where Colonel Brisset had an Allied force of one squadron, five companies, and five guns (including two of the German guns from Garua).

The misunderstanding which had arisen between Colonels Cunliffe and Brisset had been mainly due to the difficulty and delay of inter-communication,* and Colonel Cunliffe decided to postpone his departure for Mora until all misapprehension between them had been removed and a complete understanding arrived at regarding operations in the immediate future. Such slight delay should not matter, as General Dobell did not propose to resume operations till November. It was accordingly not till the 9th August that General Cunliffe † left for Mora, immediately after receipt of a letter of the 25th July in which Colonel Brisset said that he would not, for the time being, take the initiative beyond Ngaundere and Tingere. Colonel Brisset, it may be noted, still urged General Cunliffe not to attempt to assault Mora, on the ground that its capture was impossible. General Cunliffe, however, considered that the advantages of its capture outweighed the risks of failure, though all accounts agreed that the position was a formidable one.

Enemy attack Tingere; 23rd July 1915. In the meantime, at Tingere, Captain Fowle had been attacked at daybreak on the 23rd July by the former German garrison reinforced from Tibati to a strength of four Germans and one hundred and fifty natives. But they met with such a reception that they soon began to withdraw and were then driven to headlong flight by a bayonet charge of Nigerian infantry initiated and led by its native section commander. The enemy sustained at least a dozen casualties, including a German N.C.O. wounded and captured, who stated that the attacking force was a newly formed company, composed

---

* A proposal by Colonel Cunliffe to extend the telegraph line from Nigeria and also to provide his force with telephone equipment had been negatived on the score of its impracticability.

† He was gazetted Brigadier-General on the 26th July.

OPERATIONS IN THE NORTH

largely of fugitives from Garua. Shortly afterwards the garrison at Tingere was reinforced from Ngaundere by the other British company and mountain gun under Colonel Webb-Bowen.

From Ngaundere by the end of July Colonel Brisset's messengers had gained touch with the right flank of the Lobaye Column, and thereafter communication between Colonels Brisset and Morisson was maintained by means of a French company detached from Ngaundere to a point about fifty-five miles to the south-east whence it kept up connection with a flank detachment of the Lobaye Column at Kunde. *Touch gained with Lobaye Column; July 1915.*

Further progress had also been made by the advanced company (H/3rd Battalion) of the Ibi Column. Learning that an enemy party was holding a river crossing about two miles east of Gashiga, Captain C. G. Bowyer-Smijth, commanding the company, obtained permission from Major Mann to attack it and secure the canoes there. Taking with him a half-company and a machine gun, Captain Bowyer-Smijth started off on the 29th July. The country was most difficult, but, after twelve hours' marching in a wide turning movement over hills and rivers, he surprised the enemy completely and got astride his main line of retreat to Banyo. But, by using another route, the enemy, who fled hurriedly abandoning all his property, managed to escape. Neither side had many casualties, those of the British being only three. Gashiga itself, however, was not occupied by Major Mann until the 16th August, when no enemy opposition was encountered. *Progress on Gashiga line; July 1915.*

The Cross River Column under Major Crookenden was still at Ossidinge, where it was immobilised by the rain. Beyond occasional patrol encounters it had remained practically undisturbed since May. *Cross River Column.*

The lull in the active operations between the end of June and beginning of October was of distinct benefit to General Dobell's troops. It enabled many of the British ranks and most of the rank and file from Nigeria and the Gold Coast to proceed to their homes on leave, and it gave those who remained in the Cameroons a period of comparative rest; in both cases affording a badly needed chance of recuperation. *Lull in operations; July 1915.*

It also released troops to assist the naval forces in tightening up the blockade measures. For this purpose, at the beginning of July General Dobell detailed two detachments, of a company each, to proceed respectively to the Nyong and Campo rivers, where for some weeks longer the rain would be less heavy than at and above Duala.

Small hostile detachments, composed mainly of levies under German leadership, had for some time past been pursuing tactics calculated to harass the vessels of the Nyong flotilla; and it was with a view to clearing up the situation and destroying hostile positions and camps that a company of the 1st Nigerians under Captain M. E. Fell arrived on the 5th July at the Nyong shore base.

Nyong river; July 1915 — On the 7th, *Fullah, Alligator, Crocodile,* and the picket boat, carrying some marines and levies in addition to the Nigerians, started for Ebea. Some distance up the Lokundje river the soldiers were transferred into boats and canoes to proceed up a creek, land at its head and move thence by a bush path to a point south of Ebea on the Longyi-Ebea road. News that they had successfully arrived at this point reached the flotilla at midnight. Next morning the flotilla proceeded up river and reached Ebea without opposition, the enemy scattering in the bush to evade an attempt made by a landing party of marines (Captain E. Tootell, R.M.L.I.) and levies (Lieutenant-Commander McCullagh), who had been landed, to cut off his retreat. Practically the only opposition was encountered by Captain Fell advancing from the south, and he reached Ebea without much difficulty with the loss of only two casualties. The enemy's defences and habitations were then destroyed, and the expedition, having accomplished its object with skill and despatch, returned to its base.

On the 9th July, the force moved up the Nyong river, and the troops, landing below Etima, captured and destroyed the enemy position there after slight opposition. Next morning the Nigerians, advancing by land, with the flotilla moving upstream in support, captured and destroyed the enemy position at Dehane, encountering some opposition and suffering seven casualties.

To oppose Captain Fell's further advance the enemy now concentrated at Etjahe (some three miles north-eastward of Dehane), where he had a strongly entrenched position. The *Fullah*, with Commander Sneyd on board, had gone aground, and in his absence Lieutenant-Commander McCullagh agreed with Captain Fell that the British force was too weak to risk an attack on Etjahe. The force, therefore, returned by river to its base, and Captain Fell asked for reinforcements from Duala.

Before he learnt of this withdrawal General Dobell had

already arranged for a reinforcement of one hundred and twenty rifles (a half-company each of the 1st Nigerians and Gold Coast Battalion) under Major R. G. Coles to move to the Nyong river and also for a French company from Edea to move direct to Dehane. The whole force concentrated at Dehane on the 13th July and advanced next day, under command of Major Coles, against Etjahe. The enemy, however, made no really serious attempt to hold his strong position there, and it was captured and destroyed with no great difficulty. Having thus successfully carried out their object, the troops—except a half-company Gold Coast Battalion left at the Nyong base to assist the naval flotilla—withdrew to Duala and Edea.

The mission of the (Pioneer) company of the Gold Coast Battalion under Captain H. Goodwin, which arrived at Campo on the 9th July, was to assist the Campo detachment in clearing the district of hostile detachments, ascertain if convoys were plying between Spanish Muni and the Cameroons and intercept, and if possible capture, any such convoys. To gain information the detachment was accompanied by Captain E. Davidson of the Intelligence Staff. *Campo river; July 1915. (Map 13.)*

The enemy had constructed a series of strongly entrenched positions astride the road which led inland from Campo to Ambam. To deal with these effectively and to cut off the enemy's retreat by taking them in reverse Captain Goodwin decided to make a wide turning movement to the south; and Commander Hughes (Nigeria Marine) arranged to send at the same time a party to the north to Bodje, to cut off the enemy's retreat in that direction.

The troops were landed at Dipikar on the 10th July, and on the 12th moved out at an early hour, accompanied by Commander Hughes and Lieutenant Clark with a naval machine gun and crew and thirty-five levies. The enemy, evidently aware of the British movement, evaded capture and, being apparently unprepared to resist an advance from this direction, applied himself for the next few days to guerilla tactics. On the 17th July, after passing through and destroying two strongly entrenched positions, which he found empty, Captain Goodwin arrived back at Campo. He had inflicted some slight loss on the enemy and had taken several prisoners, his own casualties only amounting to two levies wounded. To prevent the enemy's return he had established a British post at Akak, twelve miles from Campo on the Ambam road.

Next day (18th) the column marched to Bitanda on the Bongola river, where a further strong hostile position was found unoccupied and was destroyed. Another British post was established here, and to support it a small armed vessel (*Manatee*) was stationed nearby on the Bongola river at Randad und Stein. A third British post was established at Moloko, five miles south-east of Dipikar.

The Campo area having been cleared and rendered secure, Commander Hughes proceeded in the *Ivy* to visit the Spanish port of Bata, where he arrived on the 20th July and found the Spanish authorities well disposed towards the Allies. The information obtained here indicated that beyond luxuries, such as wine and tobacco, little food was being sent to the Cameroons from Spanish Muni. It was understood that there was no shortage of food at Yaunde.

A report just received, however, of the landing at Fernando Po under suspicious circumstances of a quantity of ammunition * appeared to confirm previous information which had reached General Dobell that the Germans were obtaining munitions by this route. He consequently decided to reinforce Campo by two more companies (1st Nigerians and Gold Coast Battalion) under Lieutenant-Colonel Rose. On the 26th July, the day that this detachment left Duala, General Dobell, hearing from Brazzaville that the French Oyem Column was investing Bitam and that the Germans were despatching reinforcements there from Ebolowa,† gave Colonel Rose instructions to do what he could to relieve the pressure on the Oyem Column by vigorous action on the Campo-Ebolowa road. Colonel Rose with his troops disembarked at Campo on the 28th July.

Edea district; July 1915. In the Edea area the exceptionally heavy rain and sickness among the French ranks prevented extended operations. The enemy also displayed little activity, and it was ascertained that the bulk of his force had retired from the neighbourhood, leaving posts at Sakbajeme and Eseka, with covering detachments in observation of the French posts at Ngwe and So Dibanga. On the 11th July the French carried out a very successful reconnaissance from Ngwe to the north-east, in which they inflicted considerable casualties on the enemy at no loss to themselves. A few days later, in view of the possi-

---

* That this ammunition was intended for the Germans is borne out by a statement made to a British officer prisoner of war on one occasion by a German officer, who said that he with several of his brother officers had volunteered to try and get across in canoes to Fernando Po to bring over twenty cases of rifles and a lot of ammunition which were lying there.

† As a matter of fact this news was out of date, as the French had occupied Bitam on the 17th July, after it had been evacuated by the Germans.

A FRENCH EXPLOIT

bility of the Germans establishing a stronger post at Sakbajeme—where it would be a constant menace to Ngwe and the road between there and Edea—General Dobell instructed Colonel Mayer to send out a strong column to drive the enemy out of Sakbajeme and to destroy his position there. Commandant Mathieu with a column of three hundred Senegalese effected this without difficulty on the 21st July and also obtained evidence that the enemy had no intention of holding the place permanently.

Leaving Sakbajeme on the 23rd July, the French returned via Nkonjok and encountered hostile patrols to the east of that place on the 24th. Deciding to pursue these parties, Commandant Mathieu sent his carriers back to Ngwe and advanced eastward pushing the enemy in front of him. On approaching the Ndupe river he found the enemy in some strength,* with machine guns, entrenched on the further side of the river, which was about three feet deep. At about 10 a.m., his advanced guard having become hotly engaged, Commandant Mathieu decided to push home an attack. This he did successfully with vigour and determination, putting all his men into the front line, as soon as fire superiority had been gained, to assault the position. At the critical moment both' French machine guns jammed. But the French troops were not to be denied and charged with great courage and dash across the river and up the further slope, when the enemy, hardly waiting to meet them, retired hastily. The French, who had incurred twenty-nine casualties and were without carriers or food and over twenty miles from their post, pursued for a short distance before marching back to Ngwe, where they did not arrive till 10 p.m. the same day.

Northern Railway and Bare; July 1915.

In the Nkongsamba-Bare area the continuous heavy rain of the period was accompanied by cold thick mists, which made patrolling both difficult and arduous, while the Nkam river, in heavy flood, was a serious obstacle to movement. The enemy also, though attempting an occasional raid, was generally inactive; and in consequence the British troops enjoyed a period of comparative rest. There were only a few patrol encounters and, largely owing to this and the general enemy inactivity, the British gained little fresh information regarding the enemy's strength and dispositions. There appeared to

---

* The enemy force was reported subsequently to have consisted of about two companies under Major Haedicke.

be little appreciable change in these. The enemy's main force was still reported to be at Chang and Bana, with strong detachments at Mbo and Fongdonera covered by outposts to the south; and a detachment of about six Germans and one hundred natives was reported to have arrived at Bana from Bamenda, towards the end of June, with news of the fall of Garua.

News of French progress in the south-east and the question of future policy; 19th–26th July 1915.
On the 19th July General Dobell received a telegram from Brazzaville informing him that all the French troops in the south-east were acting on the offensive and expressing the hope that General Dobell would be able to prevent the transfer from his own front of enemy troops to oppose the French.

Four days later, on the 23rd July, General Dobell telegraphed to the War Office that his views had undergone a change since his letter of the 23rd June. The unopposed occupation by the Allies of Ngaundere and Koncha and the few troops the enemy was retaining in that neighbourhood indicated his intention of concentrating in the south. The importance of Yaunde as an objective had consequently increased and, while the difficulties of an advance against it remained no less than he had previously stated, its occupation appeared more likely to bring about a surrender. Moreover, the prevention of the importation of supplies, other than ammunition, appeared unlikely to have a decisive effect. General Dobell felt, therefore, that any operations undertaken in the dry season must be in the direction of Yaunde, their scope being dependent on the resources placed at his disposal.*

On the 26th July a further telegram from Brazzaville gave General Dobell news of the occupation of Lomie a month earlier by the Sanga Column and of the establishment of contact between this and the Lobaye Column, which was at Ngangela and Baturi. The telegram also said that Colonel

---

* According to the account in Volume IV of *Der Grosse Krieg, 1914–1918*, the German command definitely decided to make Yaunde the central and final point of their defence when they received news, in the middle of June, of the fall of Garua. Work on strengthening the strong natural defensive positions in the mountainous area surrounding Yaunde had already been begun a month earlier. An improvised arms and munition factory was also set up in Yaunde; its output was crude, but certainly—it is said—helped to prolong the German resistance. Apart from military reasons, there was a strong political reason for making Yaunde the final point of defence. For the Yaunde tribe was intensely loyal to German rule, provided the largest proportion and best material of their native soldiers, and was unstinting in its provision of carriers and in service of all kinds to the Germans.

Morisson was endeavouring to get into touch with Ngaundere and again repeated the out-of-date information that the Oyem Column was investing Bitam.

The command of the French Oyem Column—its strength by this time about 850 rifles—was taken over on the 6th July by Lieutenant-Colonel Le Meillour and its designation changed to South Cameroons Force. On the 17th it occupied Bitam, which the Germans had evacuated.

Franco-Belgian operations in the south and south-east; July 1915.

The Lobaye Column, with a strength of four guns, about 930 rifles, and two machine guns, on a line extending north-eastward from Ngangela, adopted a defensive attitude for the first half of July whilst regrouping its troops and reorganising its supply arrangements. After beating back a vigorous German counter-offensive delivered between the 14th and 16th July, Colonel Morisson resumed his advance with complete success. Bertua was captured, after a series of engagements, on the 22nd July and, three days later, Dume was occupied without opposition. Then, moving forward to the south-west in expectation of co-operation by the Sanga Column, Colonel Morisson gained possession of Abong Mbang on the 29th July.

This place Colonel Hutin had been instructed by General Aymerich to gain after the capture of Lomie. But Colonel Hutin was faced by considerable supply and transport difficulties; and his apprehensions lest the Germans should concentrate to the west and south-west and attempt to sever his communications caused further delay. In the meantime Abong Mbang had fallen to the Lobaye Column.

Thus, by the end of July, the successful operations of General Cunliffe in the north, General Aymerich's progress in the south and south-east, and the blockade measures along the coast and in the Campo district had brought about a change in the situation which held out a prospect of drawing round the Germans at Yaunde an Allied net which would force them to fight or surrender.

CHAPTER IX

AUGUST TO THE BEGINNING OF NOVEMBER 1915: COMMENCEMENT OF THE FINAL ADVANCE ON YAUNDE AND THE CAPTURE OF BAMENDA, BANYO, TIBATI, AND CHANG

(Maps 2, 5, 8, 12 and 13)

Question of future policy; August 1915.
A telegram of the 2nd August from the War Office drew General Dobell's attention to a recent French *communiqué*—announcing the occupation of Lomie and the establishment of contact between their Lobaye and Sanga Columns—which stated that German troops and natives alike were reported to be disaffected and to be welcoming the French. The War Office telegram then went on to say that the considerable traffic in supplies, shown by intercepted German letters to be in operation between Spanish territory and Yaunde, appeared to be the main prop to further German resistance. These German letters showed that, owing to native hostility, the convoys moving via Ambam and Ebolowa required armed escorts; that the Germans were apprehensive of a native rising in the Kribi and coastal area; and also that one writer (in a responsible mercantile position) queried the German ability to maintain resistance for long. In conclusion the War Office requested General Dobell to give his views, after consulting General Cunliffe, on the best method of bringing about a junction of their respective forces, which it seemed important to effect as early as possible.

Replying on the 4th August General Dobell said that whatever disaffection there was among German troops and the natives in the east, it did not by any means obtain in the Yaunde district. He appreciated the importance of the Ambam-Ebolowa route and thought that the enemy convoys using it would be interfered with by the French advance towards Ambam and the small force he himself had sent to operate temporarily in the Campo district; but even if all supplies were cut off a German surrender would not necessarily ensue. This could only be effected by the capture of Yaunde, and he considered that the force advancing from Edea should be strong enough to carry this out without relying on the co-operation of the French eastern columns. To make it strong enough he would require the additional personnel and material mentioned in his appreciation of the 23rd June. With his existing resources he could certainly advance as soon as the weather permitted, but he was doubtful whether he could reach Yaunde. Since in either case preparations for an advance should be commenced without delay, he would like to know soon whether his demands could be met or whether he could only count on his existing resources. In conclusion, General Dobell said that General Cunliffe's advance south was of great moral value, but was unlikely to make such progress as to come into the sphere of the move on Yaunde. General Dobell had, however, requested him and General Aymerich to come and discuss the situation at Duala.

The War Office, answering on the 10th August, concurred in the importance of Yaunde as an objective and accepted General Dobell's proposed method of reaching it. They could not send him reinforcements, but, if a battalion could be placed at his disposal by General Cunliffe, the War Office would arrange with the Colonial Office. Wireless sets for pack transport could be supplied, but their range of thirty miles might be diminished if altered for carrier transport; the only howitzer lighter than a 5-inch or a 4·5-inch field howitzer would be a trench mortar; and the employment by General Dobell of either aeroplanes or seaplanes was considered impracticable. General Dobell was to telegraph his exact requirements for motor transport and railway construction. In conclusion General Dobell was asked what reinforcements he considered Colonel Mayer should have.

General Dobell replied on the 11th that he was asking if Nigeria could provide another battalion. Colonel Mayer would require an additional 1,200 infantry, three machine gun sections, 2,500 carriers, many more medical personnel and a large quantity of medical stores. General Dobell had asked Sierra Leone for 1,200 carriers, the Gold Coast for 1,200 and Nigeria for 700, in view of the projected advance. He would like a 4·5-inch field howitzer, fitted with drag-ropes and accompanied by a gun detachment, and was sending a statement of his other requirements in a separate telegram.

In the course of a discussion between the British and French Governments regarding the operations in the Cameroons, the

War Office at this period received a copy of a memorandum dated the 5th August in which M. Delcassé (the French Foreign Minister) said that the French Government, desirous of attaining a quick decision by Allied co-operation, suggested that it was undesirable for General Dobell's force to remain inactive at the moment that General Aymerich's columns in the east were making good progress. The French Government were evidently anxious for General Dobell to resume the offensive towards Yaunde, and among other arguments they urged that the general defeat of the enemy, on which the defence of Nigeria depended ultimately, could only be realised by constant Allied co-operation.

In this connection, it is noteworthy that Sir Frederick Lugard (in England) addressed, on the 10th August, to General Dobell a proposal which the War Office repeated to him by telegram on the 14th for his considered opinion. Sir F. Lugard suggested that, as a preliminary to the advance on Yaunde, General Dobell should first, in co-operation with General Cunliffe, deal with the enemy in the Bamenda-Tinto-Bare area. This would free a considerable portion of the column at Ossidinge and of the troops in posts in the Bare area to take part in the advance on Yaunde. It would also have the political advantage of clearing the enemy from the Western Cameroons. After completing the operations, the forces employed could concentrate at Bare and rail to Bonaberi. If, however, General Dobell considered this plan inadvisable, General Cunliffe should still be able to send him strong reinforcements for the prosecution of his original plan, though Kentu would have to be held in some strength and the column at Ossidinge could not be reduced.

General Dobell replied on the 17th August that the proposal could not, in his opinion, be undertaken without impairing considerably the success of the operations against Yaunde. General Aymerich's columns were making progress, and the earlier co-operation they might require from General Dobell would be impossible if he was operating against Bamenda. General Dobell went on to point out that, except in the unlikely contingency of the capture of the enemy troops in the Bamenda district, the reduction of the garrison on the Northern Railway seemed impracticable; that if any resistance was encountered the proposed operations would take two months to complete, and would call for some of the units required for the advance on Yaunde; while, judging from past experience, all the troops and carriers employed would need at least another month in which to rest before starting on further extended operations. In conclusion, General Dobell said that the Governor-General of French Equatorial Africa and General Aymerich were coming to Duala on the 23rd August for a conference.

To this telegram the War Office at once replied that, in the circumstances, they concurred in General Dobell's view that the advance on Yaunde should take precedence of all other considerations.

On the 20th August General Dobell informed the War Office that General Cunliffe could not spare any more troops from Nigeria. His intention was to occupy Banyo and Tibati and so close the Northern Cameroons to the enemy, a plan with which General Dobell was in agreement. Colonel Mayer, he added, had already received reinforcements of two companies and two machine guns.*

The following British reinforcements had also arrived at Duala: a machine gun section of the West India Regiment from Sierra Leone on the 4th August; one hundred rifles from Nigeria on the 6th; and the 5th Light Infantry (Indian Army), with a strength of seven British officers and 588 Indian ranks, organised in three double-companies, on the 11th. During the month a number of new officers also arrived from England, but as many of them had little or no military or African experience, a school of instruction for them had to be formed.

<small>British reinforcements; August 1915.</small>

The force operating from Campo had encountered, in the meantime, unexpectedly strong resistance. Colonel Rose, with his two reinforcing companies, had disembarked at Campo on the 28th July and, preparatory to advancing towards Ambam, had concentrated his whole force at Ngat, about twenty-five miles inland. In addition to his troops, Colonel Rose had at his disposal a naval machine gun detachment (Lieutenant J. P. R. Thompson, R.N.) and three parties of twenty levies, each commanded by a naval officer,† with Commander Hughes of the *Ivy* as naval commander and intelligence officer.

<small>Campo operations; August 1915</small>

Till its arrival on the 7th August at Manimanji Colonel Rose's column encountered only slight opposition. On the 8th it moved out towards Njabesan—the junction of a road leading southward towards Spanish Muni—where the Germans

---

* They reached Duala on the 18th August.
† Commander Hughes, Lieutenant W. R. J. White, R.N., and Lieutenant de Vaisseau Prechac.

had formed a convoy depot. Five miles out the enemy in some force, with two machine guns, was encountered in a particularly strong position. Colonel Rose attacked, but in the dense bush the attempt to turn the enemy's position failed after some severe fighting. Colonel Rose then decided that his instructions did not justify him in incurring the heavy casualties involved in a continuance of the attack; and, breaking off the action, withdrew to Manimanji, his losses having been twenty-nine, including three British.* Reconnaissances of the enemy's position were carried out on the 9th and 10th August when nine more casualties were incurred, and on the 11th Colonel Rose withdrew to Ngat to await reinforcements which General Dobell was sending him.

Colonel Rose's report of the action on the 8th reached Duala on the 10th August, when General Dobell—in view of the information contained in the War Office telegram of the 2nd August, the enemy's evident anxiety to prevent any advance on Njabesan † and the French request for co-operation from Campo with their column advancing from Bitam—decided to reinforce Colonel Rose immediately. A double-company of the 5th Light Infantry and one company Sierra Leone Battalion left Duala for this purpose on the 14th August and were followed on the 16th, at Colonel Rose's request, by a gun of the Nigerian Battery. On the 15th August General Dobell telegraphed to Brazzaville that the reinforced Campo column would act vigorously till the 3rd September, when it would commence to withdraw, though some troops would be left in the Campo district till the middle of September. Eight days later, however, on hearing from General Aymerich that he had ordered the Oyem Column to halt on the line of the Ntem river till the general advance on Yaunde commenced, General Dobell sent Colonel Rose instructions that active operations were only to continue till the end of August, when the column was to withdraw and the three original companies under Colonel Rose were to return to Duala, to proceed on leave to recuperate for subsequent participation in the advance on Yaunde.

Colonel Rose, meanwhile, in an operation order issued on the 17th August, had defined his object as being to show all

---
* Lieutenants J. Leslie-Smith and T. B. C. Piggott (Gold Coast Regiment) and Able Seaman A. M. Pratt wounded.

† Information obtained in the next few days showed that a large convoy had left Spanish Muni on the 6th August for Ebolowa, where the Germans had concentrated a strong force and where the presence of Ebermaier and Zimmermann was also reported.

CAMPO OPERATIONS

possible activity in order to withdraw pressure from the French column operating in the vicinity of Ambam. The strength of the enemy in the Campo hinterland was estimated at about 400 rifles with two machine guns, more than half this total being on the Campo-Ambam road. To carry out his task Colonel Rose divided his force into two columns: the northern column, to operate along the main road, comprising a naval machine gun detachment, one company Gold Coast Battalion, one company 1st Nigerians and half a company Sierra Leone Battalion,* under command of Lieutenant-Colonel W. C. N. Hastings (Sierra Leone Battalion); and the southern column, to operate along the line of the Campo river, under Colonel Rose's personal command, consisting of the Nigerian gun, the 5th Light Infantry double-company and one company Gold Coast Battalion. Communication between the two columns would be maintained by the Ngat-Bipa road.

The two columns commenced their advance eastward from Afan and Moloko respectively on the 19th and 21st August, and operations continued until the 29th. Throughout this period the northern column was in contact with hostile troops, which in every case were driven back; but Colonel Hastings never felt himself strong enough to attack the enemy still holding the position near Njabesan. The southern column, following a very difficult bush track along the Campo river, surprised on the 28th August a hostile detachment holding the ford near Nguambang and advanced to Nkweiteng, but found no enemy there. On the 30th, in accordance with Colonel Rose's instructions, the column started its return march.

Both columns, having apparently sustained only a few casualties, arrived back at Campo on the 1st September, when all the troops except the 5th Light Infantry and Sierra Leone companies returned by sea to Duala. The force remaining, under command of Colonel Hastings, held, with naval support, the line Afan-Randad und Stein-Dipikar.

As General Dobell pointed out in his despatch of the 18th September, these Campo operations might have been more fruitful in results had he not been obliged to withdraw most of his troops to give them the period of rest they required to fit them for the coming advance on Yaunde.

Neither in the Edea nor the Northern Railway areas did any **Edea and Northern Railway; August 1915.**

---
* The other half-company was to garrison Campo.

hostilities of importance occur during August. On the 8th, the necessary repairs to the Midland Railway—including the reconstruction of one large bridge—were completed, and it was opened for traffic as far as the Kele river.

Allied Conference at Duala; 25th–26th August 1915. M. Merlin, Governor-General of French Equatorial Africa, and General Aymerich arrived at Duala on the 24th August and during the next two days discussed the plan of future operations with General Dobell, Colonel Mayer being also present.

It was decided that all the available troops under Generals Aymerich and Dobell should advance on Yaunde from the east and west respectively.

General Aymerich's troops, totalling about 2,000, would advance, between the 15th October and 1st November, from the line Bertua-Dume in three columns; the right column following the road along the Sanaga river, the centre and main column by the Bertua-Nanga Eboko road, and the left column along the Dume-Mendang road. General Aymerich hoped to effect a junction of all three columns on the Yaunde-Yoko road and then approach Yaunde from the north.

General Dobell's troops would advance to, and make good, the line Eseka-Wum Biagas about the 7th October, and, having repaired the railway to Eseka and made the road to Wum Biagas fit for motor traffic, would (it was hoped) continue the advance from these places in two columns about the 15th November.* Taking his total effective strength at about 4,000 British and 1,800 French rifles, General Dobell estimated that, after allowing for obligatory garrisons in occupied territory up to and including the Kele river, he could make available about 1,800 British and 1,100 French rifles for the advance east of the Kele river. If the French reinforcements asked for were provided, another 800 French rifles would be available.

As regards the Campo-Muni area, the French delegates said that the column under Colonel Le Meillour would make such effort from the Ntem river line towards Ebolowa as its strength permitted, and since General Dobell, requiring all his available

---

* This date, as General Dobell reported at the time, was dependent on developments; and the progress or difficulties of General Aymerich's column might necessitate a forward movement before then. General Dobell anticipated, however, that General Aymerich would experience greater difficulties as he approached Yaunde and, if the enemy resisted, General Dobell doubted the French ability to reach Yaunde unsupported. He consequently regarded his own advance from the west as the decisive movement.

[*To face p.* 320

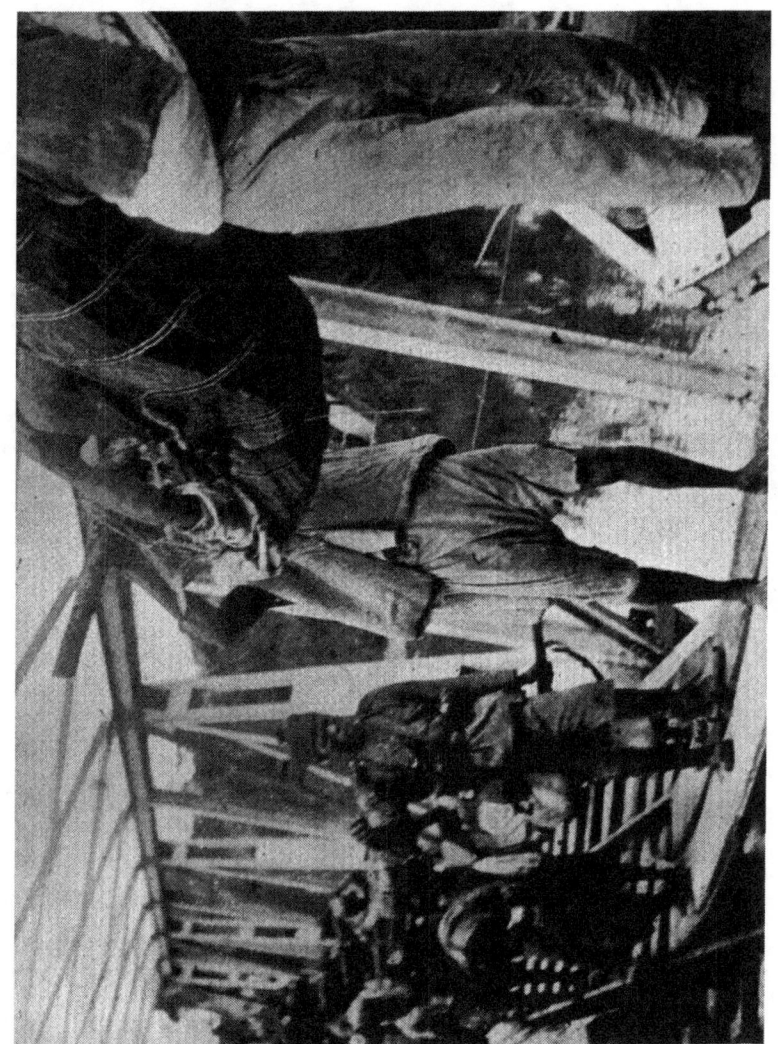

Ambulance Convoy Crossing a Bridge

troops for the advance on Yaunde, would be unable to provide any to co-operate from Campo with Colonel Le Meillour, M. Merlin decided to ask for a half-battalion from Dakar for the purpose.

As regards General Cunliffe's troops, General Dobell informed General Aymerich that their next objective would be the line Banyo-Tibati and that from there they would no doubt continue their advance southward when they were in a position to do so. General Dobell's intention to reduce to a minimum the strength of his own troops on the Northern Railway precluded his co-operating by any extended movement northward with the Allied troops in the Northern Cameroons. But he informed General Cunliffe, when acquainting him with the details of the plan arranged with General Aymerich, that, as far as the situation at the Northern railhead was concerned, there was no reason why General Cunliffe should not utilise the Ossidinge Column to co-operate in any operations in the Bamenda-Tinto-Chang district.

General Dobell telegraphed the general result of this conference to the War Office on the 27th August. Most of General Dobell's British officers had had short spells of rest and change and Lord Kitchener now telegraphed to General Dobell suggesting that if he himself took a short sea voyage (to Dakar and back) before the recommencement of operations he might find it beneficial. General Dobell decided, however, that it was not an opportune time for him to be absent, as his arrangements were reaching an advanced stage.

The distribution and strength of the British contingent of General Dobell's expeditionary force on the 30th August, 1915, is shown in Appendix VI. *Distribution and strength British Contingent; 30th August 1915.*

East of Yaunde Colonel Morisson, whose troops were on the line Bertua-Dume-Abong Mbang, had not heard by the beginning of August that General Dobell's troops had abandoned their advance on Yaunde; and, while keeping his main strength at Dume, he pushed forward reconnaissances to the west. On the 6th August, having been instructed by General Aymerich to assume charge of the operations of both the Lobaye and the Sanga Columns, he directed Colonel Hutin to detail a company to relieve the garrison at Abong Mbang. Colonel Hutin reached Abong Mbang with a Belgian company on the 17th August and the two column commanders then discussed their future action. Pending the receipt of instruc- *Franco-Belgian operations in the south-east; August 1915.*

tions resulting from the conference at Duala the following dispositions were agreed upon :—

The left, or Sanga, Column, whose future objective would be Akonolinga, would hold Abong Mbang, covered by an observation detachment in the direction of Akoafim.

The right, or Lobaye, Column, whose objective would be the enemy forces between the Nyong and Sanaga rivers, would hold the line Dengdeng-Gele Menduka, which was already held by outposts.

On the 23rd August, when Colonel Hutin arrived back at Lomie, his troops were distributed as follows :—

Abong Mbang	One Belgian company.
Yaposten vicinity	Two French companies.
Lomie	Headquarters, artillery and one French and one Belgian company.
Alade Makei	One French and one Belgian company.

At the end of August the Germans commenced a vigorous counter-offensive against the French right column.

Northern Cameroons; August 1915. To turn now to the operations in the Northern Cameroons. On the 6th August, in reply to a telegram from General Dobell inquiring how far southward he hoped to advance in the immediate future, General Cunliffe said that he was leaving for Mora on the 9th, that he hoped to be back at Yola by the middle of September, and that his next objective would be the line Kentu-Banyo.

On the 8th August General Cunliffe issued instructions to Major Mann, commanding the Ibi Column operating on the Gashiga road, and to Major H. A. Porter, who had been appointed to command the troops in the Yola-Maio Kaleh-Koncha-Chamba area,* that during General Cunliffe's absence their rôle was to be that of an active defensive.

General Cunliffe took with him from Yola on the 9th August, when he started for Mora, two guns (1st Battery) and two infantry companies (D and G/3rd Battalion).† A Nigerian infantry company (H/1st Battalion) and the French 95-mm. gun from Garua were to join him at Sava (near Mora), where the investing force of " C " Company Mounted Infantry and

---

* Major Porter had at his disposal B mounted infantry company (less one section) and one and a half infantry companies (half B/1st Battalion and B/3rd Battalion).

† B/4th Battalion had been withdrawn in July from Yola to do garrison duties in the Southern Provinces of Nigeria.

"A" Company 2nd Battalion Nigeria Regiment and a French infantry company had recently been reinforced by another French infantry company (Captain Popp) and a detachment of thirty rifles (Captain Lamouroux), the former of which had marched from Zinder through Northern Nigeria.

On the 9th August General Dobell telegraphed to Nigeria asking whether the Governor-General and General Cunliffe considered it probable that a battalion from there would be available in October for service at Duala, and also whether the situation would allow of the transfer to Duala, to command the West African Frontier Force contingent in General Dobell's force, of General Cunliffe accompanied by Major Wallace Wright. Replying on the 17th, Mr. Boyle, who was acting for Sir Frederick Lugard,* said that General Cunliffe considered it impossible to send 600 men to Duala, as to do so would deprive him of about half his available force and oblige him to retire behind the frontier, leaving the French stranded. Under the latest arrangements, Colonel Brisset would move to Tibati when the Nigerian troops occupied Banyo; and, as General Cunliffe was of opinion that it would be a mistake to abandon the proposed subsequent combined movements with the French, he did not consider that he ought to go to Duala.

General Cunliffe and the troops with him from Yola, as also the troops from Garua, reached Sava on the 23rd August. The blockade of Mora had continued without special incident for several months under the control of the French Captain Rémond. Captain Fox had in April been promoted Major, but, as Colonel Brisset had represented the hardship of Captain Rémond's supersession by an officer of less service, Colonel Cunliffe had recalled Major Fox to Yola and had sent Captain J. F. Badham to take his place.

Cunliffe arrives at Mora; 23rd August 1915.

It appears from Captain von Raben's diary that the first report which he received on the 30th June of the capture of Garua was not confirmed till nearly a month later; and that some of the messengers he sent out were able to evade the blockade and return with information which gave him a general idea of current events of importance in the Northern Cameroons. For instance, towards the end of August, he received news of the advent of a heavy enemy gun from Garua.

During the first few days after arriving at Sava, General Cunliffe carried out a series of reconnaissances of the enemy position. Before, however, entering into an account of these

---
* He had gone on leave on the 4th July to England, where he still kept in touch with the operations.

324 MILITARY OPERATIONS: THE CAMEROONS

and of his subsequent attack on Mora it will be convenient to give a summary of the dispositions of his force and of his future intentions, as given in a letter he wrote on the 28th August, i.e., before he learnt of the result of the Duala conference, to M. Merlet, the Administrator of Chad.

Excluding the column under Colonel Brisset, his troops were disposed as follows:—

(a) Based on Yola and disposed at Sava, Garua, Tingere and Koncha.	Two mountain guns, two coys. mounted infantry, eight coys. infantry.	=1,100 effectives.
(b) Based on Mutum Biu and operating towards Banyo via Gashiga.	One mountain gun, three coys. infantry.	=330 effectives.
(c) At Takum, observing enemy at Kentu.	One coy. infantry.	=110 effectives.
(d) At Ossidinge	Two mountain guns, four coys. infantry.	=450 effectives.

and he hoped to get another company to reinforce Takum from the interior of Nigeria.

After the fall of Mora he intended to form a strong column at Koncha and advance against Banyo in co-operation with force (b) from Gashiga, while force (c) moved against Kentu to hold it as long as there was an enemy force at Bamenda.

After capturing Banyo, he proposed to make it his main base for future operations and to direct Colonel Brisset to move from Ngaundere against Tibati, assisting him by a demonstration from Banyo.

His subsequent action, after occupation of the Kentu-Banyo-Tibati line, would depend on the development of the German situation in the Chang area. The British force at Ossidinge would, he said, be ready for an offensive in the dry season in co-operation with General Dobell's troops on the Northern Railway; and he personally favoured a direct advance on Yaunde from the Banyo-Tibati line provided he could make his line of communication with Banyo secure.

Operations at Mora; August–September 1915. (Map 5.) General Cunliffe carried out his first reconnaissance of the enemy's position on the 25th August, when he rode from Sava right round the Mora mountain and visited the British post at Padiko, covering a distance of about twenty-seven miles. Next day he rode a further sixteen miles, reconnoitring Dabaskum and the enemy's main position from Wacheke; and on the 27th he and his officers, in two parties, made more detailed reconnaissances from Padiko and Wacheke. He had been warned that the enemy's position was very strong, but he

ATTACK ON MORA MOUNTAIN

found it to be even stronger than he had supposed. Only in a few places was an ascent of the precipitous slopes of the mountain at all possible and then only by slinging rifles and using both hands and feet. These approaches, moreover, were well known to the enemy, who had constructed numerous stone breastworks to command them. Everywhere, moreover, in the hostile position, besides numbers of these breastworks, huge boulders provided the enemy with practically unlimited cover against the effects of artillery fire.

General Cunliffe finally came to the conclusion which Colonel Brisset had arrived at nearly a year previously, namely that the best chance of success lay in launching an attack by night on Dabaskum from Wacheke. The summit of Wacheke was nearly on the same level as Dabaskum and, though separated from it by a deep and precipitous ravine about six hundred yards wide, offered greater tactical advantages in the way of space for manœuvre and positions for covering fire than any other locality. General Cunliffe disposed his force accordingly. The French heavy gun, with Captain Lamouroux's detachment as escort, was posted at Padiko and the two British mountain guns took up positions on Wacheke. Here General Cunliffe established his own headquarters and concentrated " H " Company 1/Nigeria Regiment, " D " and " G " Companies 3/Nigeria Regiment and Captain Rémond's French company, i.e., the force with which it was proposed to carry through the assault. " A " Company 2/Nigeria Regiment was detailed to hold posts on the Gauala ridge; Captain Popp's French company was posted to Vami; and the Nigerian mounted infantry company retained its headquarters at Sava.

The Allied bombardment of the enemy's position commenced on the 1st September, when General Cunliffe issued secret operation orders for the attack. That night (1st/2nd) Captain Popp with his company was to occupy the Gosinda under-feature as a preliminary to further activity northward, the actual nature and extent of this being left to his discretion. The attack on Dabaskum was to be carried out during the night of the 2nd/3rd, when " D " and " G " Companies 3/Nigerian Regiment were to push forward without firing and establish themselves in the Dabaskum position by daybreak. Their advance would be covered by fire from Gauala and from Wacheke, where the remaining two companies would be held in reserve and would assist by covering fire and by a feint attack from Ndala directed against the enemy's main position. A dismounted detachment of Nigerian mounted infantry would attempt to create a further diversion by pushing up the mountain slope immediately south of Gagadema.

Having occupied Gosinda as ordered, Captain Popp carried out a demonstration towards Sidoue on the morning of the 2nd September, incurring about seven casualties before withdrawing to Gosinda. After dark the advances from Wacheke, Ndala and Gagadema commenced according to plan. But, owing to the difficulty of maintaining direction over the precipitous ground in the darkness, none of the detachments engaged succeeded in achieving their object. The two Nigerian companies advancing on Dabaskum only managed by daybreak to establish themselves under cover in the ravine below that place ; and the ineffectiveness of this and other movements is shown by Raben's diary, which makes it clear that he was quite unaware of any attempt to attack his position that night either from the Wacheke or any other direction.

An attempt to resume the advance on the night of the 3rd/4th September was also unsuccessful, the troops engaged again losing touch and direction in the darkness. The British incurred seven casualties, though Raben's diary again makes no mention of any sign of an attack. A further attempt to assault was postponed, at first to the night of the 6th/7th and then, owing to unfavourable weather, to the night of the 7th/8th. In the meantime the bombardment continued intermittently, but evidently had little effect.

Attack on Mora; 7th–8th Sept. 1915. This time the advance was more successful, and some of the British troops succeeded by daybreak on the 8th September in gaining a footing on the northern edge of the Dabaskum spur. The Allied guns and machine guns then started a bombardment to cover an assault, which several groups attempted to deliver at about 7.30 a.m. But the enemy post,* well protected against hostile bombardment, maintained a steady and heavy fire, which first brought the British assault to an absolute stop within sixty yards of the German breastworks and then forced the attackers to retire.

In his diary Raben pays tribute to the bravery of the assaulting troops. Most of them appear to have belonged to "H" Company 1/Nigeria Regiment, who were commended by General Cunliffe for their outstanding gallantry ; and conspicuous among them was Captain R. N. Pike, General Cunliffe's Intelligence officer, who was shot dead while acting as guide in the last stages of the assault. One section of this company fell

---

* Raben gives their numbers as two Germans and thirty-eight native rifles and says that they incurred only five casualties.

[*To face p.* 326

Nigerian Troops on the Gauala Ridge

back only a few yards, and throughout the 8th clung tenaciously to a point little more than sixty yards from the enemy's post, while other troops remained in scattered positions lower down the slopes. As soon as it got dark, General Cunliffe attempted to reorganise them and to consolidate the positions gained. But by daylight on the 9th September there was still considerable confusion and all endeavours to get food and water up to the advanced troops had failed. General Cunliffe, therefore, ordered a general retirement to a position farther back, where the men could be provisioned by night with less difficulty.

During this fighting the British incurred thirty-eight casualties, including Captain Pike and sixteen natives killed, and Captain A. Gardner and Lieutenant A. J. L. Cary wounded.

General Cunliffe now felt that, without much more ammunition for the French heavy gun, the reduction of the hostile position could only be effected by more deliberate methods; and, thinking that he had ample time, he was proceeding to inaugurate these when the receipt, on the 15th September, of a telegram from Lagos forced him to reconsider the whole situation.

In this telegram, dispatched on the 12th September after receipt of a letter from General Dobell detailing the results of the Duala conference, Mr. Boyle said that M. Merlin had telegraphed urging very strongly that General Cunliffe should co-operate with the advance on Yaunde by occupying the Banyo-Tibati-Kunde line so as to threaten Yoko and Fumban, cover the right and rear of the French eastern columns and contain the German troops in the north. General Dobell, continued Mr. Boyle, proposed making his first advance on the 7th October and was reducing his troops on the Northern Railway, so could not promise to undertake any extended movement northward from Bare. Mr. Boyle inquired when General Cunliffe would be returning to Yola. *Decision to abandon further attacks on Mora; 15th September 1915.*

General Cunliffe at once discussed the change in the situation with the French leaders in his force and they agreed with him that it was more important to move troops southward, so as to co-operate with the advance on Yaunde, than to attempt further attacks on Mora. There was little time to spare and General Cunliffe, with the section of mountain guns, " H " Company 1/Nigeria Regiment, " A " Company 2/Nigeria Regiment and " D " Company 3/Nigeria Regiment left the Mora vicinity on the 17th and 18th September to return to Yola, where General Cunliffe himself arrived on the 26th.

The force left at Mora to continue the investment consisted

of " C " Company Nigerian Mounted Infantry, " G " Company 3/Nigeria Regiment, the French heavy gun and two French companies and detachment. The heavy gun was also withdrawn to Garua about a fortnight later.

Preparations for the advance on Yaunde; August–October 1915. General Dobell commenced to prepare for his operations against Yaunde immediately after the conclusion of the August conference. The advance from Edea was to be carried out under his personal direction on two distinct lines, each with its own line of supply. A British column under Colonel Gorges would move along the Edea-Yaunde road; and a French column under Colonel Mayer would advance along the railway to Eseka and thence by the light railway track to a point on the Kribi-Yaunde road about thirty miles south of Yaunde. The first objectives of these columns would be, respectively, Wum Biagas and Eseka, where advanced bases would be established. From these, as arranged at the conference, the further advance of the two columns would commence about the 15th November.

During September no active operations, beyond constant reconnaissances from Bare, So Dibanga and Ngwe, were undertaken against the enemy's main forces by the troops under General Dobell. A certain number of his officers and men were absent on recuperative leave till the middle of October and by that time General Dobell had received some important accessions in strength. At his request, the remaining half of the Gambia Company, West African Frontier Force, joined him at Duala in September, followed by two companies of the West India Regiment and a second detachment of the 36th Company, R.E., from Sierra Leone on the 13th October. On this date there also arrived from England a 4·5-inch field howitzer with a detachment R.A., a W/T detachment and a postal section R.E., and No. 581 Mechanical Transport Company, A.S.C. With this company there were one armoured car, two Ford cars, twenty-five Ford vans, four Ford ambulances with two Ford vans for first aid, etc., and a large stock of petrol. The carriers asked for had also arrived from neighbouring British colonies, and their Governors had undertaken to maintain the necessary numbers by monthly drafts. Reinforcements for the French contingent under Colonel Mayer arrived on the 12th October, including a number of French officers, a complete Senegalese battalion and drafts for units already present.

The enemy at this period was devoting most of his attention to offensive action against the French eastern columns and displayed little activity in the western area, though he carried out two successful minor raids there during September. In the first, on the 18th September, he damaged a railway bridge to the west of So Dibanga, thereby causing some dislocation of the French line of communication; and in the other, during the night 27th/28th September, he drove a party of eleven rifles of the West African Regiment temporarily out of its post about five miles north of Bare with a loss of six killed and wounded.

Work was commenced at the end of August on the bases at Edea and Ngwe and on the improvement of the road, of which the section between those places was ready by the 3rd October for motor van traffic, subject to suspension in wet weather.

Good progress was made in the administrative preparations, and on the 22nd September General Dobell issued orders for a simultaneous advance by French and British columns, from So Dibanga and Ngwe respectively, on the 6th October. As a preliminary, British troops relieved the French at Ngwe on the 24th September, and a British detachment under Lieutenant-Colonel Rose occupied Sakbajeme without opposition on the 3rd October. *Orders for the advance issued; 22nd September 1915.*

On the 4th October Colonel Gorges' force was disposed as follows :—

Ngwe (under Lieutenant-Colonel Haywood):
    One section Nigerian Battery.
    One gun Gold Coast Battery.
    One field section 36th (Sierra Leone) Company, R.E.
    2nd Nigerians.
    Two companies Sierra Leone Battalion.
    Gambia Company.

Sakbajeme (under Lieutenant-Colonel Rose):
    One gun Gold Coast Battery.
    Machine gun section, West India Regiment.
    Three companies, Gold Coast Battalion.

Edea-Ngwe line of communication:
    One company, Sierra Leone Battalion.

Duala (in reserve):
    One section Nigerian Battery.
    1st Nigerians.
    Two companies, Gold Coast Battalion.

To the Gold Coast Battalion was attached a contingent of 37 volunteers, drawn from the educated African classes in the Gold Coast, who at their own special request on arrival were at once sent to the front.

Colonel Gorges, who remained with his headquarters at Duala * till the 18th October, when he proceeded to Edea, had issued instructions to Lieutenant-Colonels Haywood and Rose on the 27th September to the following effect. The enemy was believed to be holding strong positions astride the Yaunde road at the Ndupe and Mbila rivers. Colonel Haywood was to advance from Ngwe against Wum Biagas on the 6th October with one section Nigerian Battery and the 2nd Nigerians. On the same day Colonel Rose, leaving a company to garrison Sakbajeme, was to advance with the remainder of his detachment and co-operate with Colonel Haywood. Colonel Rose was to select his own route, bearing in mind that his assistance might be required to force the hostile position at Ndupe as well as to attack and turn the enemy's right at Wum Biagas. He would act under Colonel Haywood's orders as soon as a junction between them had been effected.

Advance commences; 6th October 1915. Operations of British column. Leaving a Gold Coast gun, the Gambia Company and two companies Sierra Leone Battalion to garrison Ngwe and taking with his column a telephone detachment, a few levies or partisans as guides and intelligence agents and 1,100 carriers, Colonel Haywood moved out on the morning of the 6th October. Only slight opposition from small enemy parties was encountered and Colonel Haywood camped for the night about four miles west of Ndupe. Learning early on the 7th that the enemy was not holding the line of the Ndupe river, Colonel Haywood pushed on in pouring rain which continued throughout the day. He found that the bridge over the river was broken and that the river itself was shoulder deep and flowing very swiftly. After repairing the bridge all baggage was got across by 2 p.m., but all attempts to communicate meanwhile with Colonel Rose had failed. Colonel Haywood consequently decided to camp at Ndupe to await news of him. Late that evening Colonel Haywood received a message from Colonel Rose, who had reached Lissege, having encountered no opposition, but having experienced difficulty in moving along the overgrown bush tracks and negotiating the numerous streams. It appeared that previous messengers had all been stopped by hostile patrols between Ndupe and Lissege.

The instructions which Colonel Haywood then sent Colonel Rose—to try to reach by 4 p.m. on the 8th October the right flank and rear of the enemy's position at Wum Biagas—did

---

* Lieut.-Col. Turner, his senior general staff officer, proceeded to Edea on the 5th October.

not reach him till 8.30 a.m. on the 8th, though Lissege was only about six miles from Ndupe by a good track. Colonel Rose pushed forward at once. But an extensive swamp, the overgrown track and rain, which made inclines slippery and dangerous, delayed his progress. He was consequently forced, some three miles north-west of Wum Biagas, to camp at a point which his gun and supply column only reached at 8.45 p.m. with their carriers in a state of exhaustion. In the meantime, leaving sixty rifles to garrison a post at Ndupe, Colonel Haywood had arrived, about midday on the 8th, in front of the Mbila river position. Hearing, however, from Colonel Rose that he would probably be unable to reach that day the rear and right of the enemy's position, Colonel Haywood spent the remaining hours of daylight in careful reconnaissance.

The hostile position was much as it had been when Colonel Haywood had attacked it in May. The strongly entrenched line—lying along the east bank of the river and about one hundred yards from it—extended for some sixteen hundred yards from a high ridge on its right to the Kele river, six hundred yards south of the road, on its left; and the thick bush and forest by which the position was surrounded on all sides, had been cleared in front of the trenches to a depth of about five hundred yards to afford a field of fire.

There were considerable exchanges of fire during the afternoon of the 8th and by the outposts during the night. On the 9th October Colonel Haywood started his attack at 5.30 a.m., when his firing line—divided on a wide front into a right, centre and left section— attempted to push forward over the cleared ground. They found progress very difficult, however, in face of the volume of hostile fire, which was skilfully concentrated against each part of the British front in turn and against which the fire of the British guns proved to be ineffective. These had come into action in a position selected and cleared of a number of trees the previous day, but one gun was now moved forward towards the centre of the line and the other to the right flank. On this flank, however, it was found that the swift-flowing Kele river was ten or twelve feet deep, so that all idea of a turning movement in this direction was abandoned.

About midday a message arrived from Colonel Rose saying that he would be within striking distance of the enemy by 2 or 3 p.m.; and Colonel Haywood, deciding to contain the enemy's left and centre and to extend his own left to try and gain contact with Colonel Rose, reinforced his left.

Capture of Wum Biagas; 9th October 1915. Hearing the fire of Colonel Rose's gun at about 3 p.m., Colonel Haywood, after a pre-arranged signal,* ordered a heavy bombardment by his guns, followed by an advance and assault by his whole line. By 4 p.m. the enemy's fire had been mastered to a great extent and a portion of the British centre had managed to wade across the waist-deep Mbila (the bridge having been destroyed). This body was quickly supported and the German trenches were rushed. The enemy, however, had made good his retreat and the British, who pursued till dusk, only encountered small hostile parties.

Colonel Rose, who had marched from his bivouac at 5.30 a.m., had been much delayed by the difficulties of the ground. Reaching the Mbila river at 9.30 a.m, he sent his baggage and supplies under escort to Ndupe and pushed on eastward, as fast as possible, into the hilly area lying to the north of the enemy's position. Here, at about noon, he encountered, to his front and on his left, German parties, whom he engaged till 4.15 p.m., when they retreated. Sending a party to communicate with Colonel Haywood, Colonel Rose then bivouacked for the night on the scene of his fight.

The British casualties totalled thirty-one, of which eleven occurred in Colonel Rose's column and the remainder, including five British officers,† among Colonel Haywood's troops. The losses of the enemy, whose strength was estimated at three companies (No. 1 Depot, No. 4, and No. 3 Reserve) with three machine guns, were not known.

Colonel Haywood now started to organise an advanced base at Wum Biagas and to consolidate his line of communication. Colonel Rose took over charge of the Ngwe-Wum Biagas section on the 11th October with a detachment composed of one Gold Coast gun, two Gold Coast companies and the machine gun section of the West India Regiment. He established his headquarters at Ndupe and placed one company in a post at Nkonjok. At Wum Biagas there remained with Colonel Haywood the section Nigerian Battery and the 2nd Nigerians.

Operations of French Column; 6th–13th October 1915. The French column, under Commandant Mechet, composed of 750 rifles with two guns and four machine guns, had moved out as arranged on the 6th October from So Dibanga, where a further force—of six Senegalese companies with two guns and

---

* The firing of two star shell.

† Lieutenant H. W. Cathie (2nd Nigerians) killed; Lieutenants H. N. Steptoe and R. V. Trengrouse (2nd Nigerians), Lieutenant T. Vise (Nigerian Battery) and Dr. K. K. Grieve (W.A.M.S.) wounded.

three machine guns under Commandant Mathieu—concentrated to support Commandant Mechet and to protect the line of communication.

Commandant Mechet encountered strong and stubborn opposition from the outset, while his operations were also much hampered by rain, swollen rivers and difficult country. His progress was consequently very slow. On reaching and crossing the Makota river on the 8th October, he had to turn his attention southward to deal with hostile detachments at Sukudukuki and Hagbes, which were not finally cleared of the enemy—with the aid of troops from So Dibanga—till the 12th October. Next day, when Commandant Mechet reached a point on the railway only about ten miles from So Dibanga, he was instructed that it was important to lose no time and that he was to push on to Sende as quickly as possible.

It was subsequently learnt from captured German documents that the Allied advance from Edea obliged Zimmermann to cancel an offensive against the rear of the French eastern columns, which he had planned for the middle of October, and to transfer two German companies from the eastern area to oppose the advance west of Yaunde.

On the 10th October, on hearing of the capture of Wum Biagas, General Dobell informed Colonel Gorges that the time appeared ripe for the movement from there of a force to the south to cut off the enemy opposing Commandant Mechet and so relieve the pressure on the French. This plan Colonel Turner had previously been directed to discuss in anticipation with Colonel Mayer; and that evening, in reply, General Dobell learnt that Colonels Mayer, Turner and Gorges were all of opinion that Colonel Haywood was not strong enough to undertake more than a movement to create a diversion. General Dobell was still of opinion, however, that the situation at Wum Biagas admitted of two companies being detached from there to move on either Sende or Eseka, whichever Colonel Mayer might select. Inquiry from Colonel Haywood having elicited the opinion that he could do what was required if he was reinforced by a half-company, orders were issued to him on the 14th. These, after informing him that Commandant Mechet expected to attack Sende that day and that a company of the Gold Coast Battalion would leave Edea on the 15th to reinforce him,* instructed him to send, as soon as

Arrangements for British assistance to French column; 10th–17th October 1915.

---

* Actually two companies Gold Coast Battalion left Duala on the 14th for the purpose, one of them to remain for the time being at Edea.

possible, a detachment of two companies with one gun towards Eseka to cut the enemy's line of retreat, acting in co-operation with Commandant Mechet, who would continue his advance on Eseka from Sende.

Colonel Haywood at once made arrangements for this movement. On the 17th October, when the reinforcing Gold Coast company (" B ") reached Ndupe, Colonel Rose took it on, with a Gold Coast gun and the West India Regiment machine gun section, to Wum Biagas. Here he learnt that the Field Section R.E. and " A " Company 2nd Nigerians—which, with the Gold Coast gun, " B " Company Gold Coast Battalion and 320 carriers with six days' supplies, were to form his column for Eseka—had left that morning to instal a flying bridge over the Kele river and to hold the crossing.

<small>British operations; 17th–26th October 1915.</small> After a night of torrential rain, Colonel Rose reached this crossing with the remainder of his column early on the 18th October. But he found that the river was in flood and that the flying bridge, which had only been constructed after great difficulty, had been carried away. A fresh bridge was erected, but was also carried away by the flood, and it was not till the 20th that Colonel Rose was able to get the whole of his column across and advance for about five miles to the south of the river. Moreover, the country proved so difficult that all the fine efforts of his gun-carriers failed to get the gun along and he was obliged to send it back, receiving in its place the machine gun section of the West India Regiment.

On the 21st October he advanced a further eight miles to the southward and reached, without opposition, a locality called Pookapi, whence good tracks led in three directions: south-westward to Sende; southward to Eseka, about eight miles distant; and south-eastward to Bog Nso on the main route between Eseka and the German Puge river position on the Edea-Yaunde road.

At Pookapi Colonel Rose obtained native information that the French were a few miles west of Sende, which the Germans were still holding with the aid of strong reinforcements which had recently passed through Bog Nso. Considering that, in these circumstances, it would be imprudent to risk an immediate advance on Eseka, Colonel Rose decided to remain for the time being at Pookapi and, in reporting the situation and his intention to Colonel Haywood, he asked for reinforcements. Next day native information still indicated that the Germans were holding Sende, while all attempts to get messages through to Commandant Mechet proved fruitless.

On the 23rd October, Colonel Rose, being reinforced by "E" Company 2nd Nigerians (less posts dropped on the way to secure the line of communication with Wum Biagas), sent his Gold Coast company southward to occupy Song Mandeng, about four miles to the north of Eseka. This it effected without incident. Colonel Rose also sent word to Commandant Mechet that he was in a position to co-operate as soon as the French advanced from Sende. At an early hour on the 24th Colonel Rose sent instructions to the commander of the Gold Coast company at Song Mandeng to make a dash on Eseka if the situation permitted. But his patrols, advancing and engaging enemy patrols to the north of Eseka on the 24th and 25th, found that the enemy was in too great strength to justify an attempt. In the afternoon of the 25th October Colonel Rose, who received information that there was an enemy detachment of two hundred men at Bog Nso, dispatched one section "A" Company 2nd Nigerians with a machine gun to reinforce Song Mandeng.

A message, written by Commandant Mechet at 4 a.m. on the 25th in reply to Colonel Rose's communication of the 23rd, reached Colonel Rose on the morning of the 26th October and informed him that Commandant Mechet hoped to occupy Sende on the 26th, but that the distance between him and Colonel Rose was too great to make co-operation possible. A further message from Commandant Mechet, however, received at 3 p.m., announced his occupation of Sende on the previous day (25th).

Since the 14th October, the enemy opposing Commandant Mechet, estimated at a strength of 300 rifles with 3 machine guns, had offered a stubborn resistance, disputing every bend of the road and taking up three or four strongly entrenched positions. The rain, the thick country and extensive marshes all contributed to make progress slow and difficult and Commandant Mechet, in reply to the instructions impressing on him the necessity of pushing on as quickly as possible, said that his troops were doing all they could and that a more rapid advance was impossible without incurring a very large number of casualties. On the 20th October he forced a crossing of the Lingen river (two to three miles west of Sende) in face of opposition and started to attack Sende itself on the 24th, his entry thereto next day being practically unopposed. This was evidently due to the enemy's fear of being cut off by Colonel Rose's movement, which they do not appear to have discovered till the 23rd or 24th.

French operations; 14th–25th October 1915.

Combined British and French advance on Eseka; 26th–30th October 1915. On hearing on the 26th October of the French occupation of Sende, Colonel Rose at once dispatched a message inquiring how he could best co-operate with Commandant Mechet's advance on Eseka. A few hours later Colonel Rose learnt that the Gambia Company was on its way from Wum Biagas to reinforce him, and that the Germans had vacated their large camp at Bog Nso. Next morning he commenced to concentrate forward by despatching a Nigerian company to Song Mandeng and ordering the Gold Coast Company from there to Bog Nso. This it occupied the same day without difficulty, driving out a few hostile troops. Reports indicated that the bulk of the enemy force which had opposed the French on the railway was retiring in a north-easterly direction.

The Gambia Company, with a supply convoy, reached Pookapi on the afternoon of the 27th and next day Colonel Rose moved south and concentrated the bulk of his column at Song Mandeng, sending from there at midday an officer's patrol to gain touch with the French on the railway. This had only been gone a few hours when messages reached him from Commandant Mechet who, when he wrote, was about six miles west of Eseka and who, believing Colonel Rose to be still at Pookapi, asked him to advance at once. British patrols sent out from Song Mandeng during the day reported that about fifty hostile rifles were holding positions at Kwang-le-Bong and on the Eseka-Bog Nso road. The country was still very difficult, the bush in the whole of this area being exceptionally thick and difficult to penetrate.

The enemy position at Kwang-le-Bong was captured, on the morning of the 29th October after a skirmish with a small enemy party, by a detachment of 120 rifles with four machine guns, under Captain Thurston, at the cost of only two casualties;[*] and Colonel Rose, moving forward with the remainder of the force, occupied a point to the south of Kwang-le-Bong. He received information during the morning from the officer's patrol sent the previous day to communicate with the French that Commandant Mechet had intended to advance that morning (29th).

Anticipating that the enemy would expect him to advance direct on Eseka, Colonel Rose, on the morning of the 30th, moved forward by a bush path which he understood would bring him out in rear of the enemy's Eseka position. The

---

[*] Lieutenant W. H. Ramsden, machine gun section West India Regiment, was wounded.

path, however, soon disappeared completely and progress became very slow till 11.30 a.m. when, from a point to the north-eastward of Eseka, the French were seen to be in occupation of the enemy's position. They had met with very slight resistance from the enemy rear guard and their casualties that day had only been three men wounded. In fact, since their occupation of Sende the enemy opposition had been always feeble, the bulk of the 116 casualties the French had suffered in the course of their advance from So Dibanga having been incurred to the west of Sende. The enemy was reported to have suffered serious losses in the same period.

Eight railway engines, all much damaged, fifty wagons and a quantity of useful railway stores were captured at Eseka, from which place Colonel Rose marched off with his column on the 31st October to rejoin Colonel Haywood at Wum Biagas.

During September and October the Allied naval forces were as active as ever. They maintained the blockade of the coast with a considerable measure of success, and in the Mungo, Wuri and Dibamba river areas their efforts had to be specially directed to frustrating attempts by natives to smuggle food through to the enemy in the Bamenda district. Vessels patrolling the Nyong, Lokundje and Sanaga rivers encountered few signs of the enemy. *Naval operations; September–October 1915.*

The counter-offensive launched by the Germans at the end of August forced the French Lobaye Column to retire for some distance. By the 18th September, however, Colonel Morisson, having arrested the enemy advance, had commenced to reorganise his troops. His main force was then on the line Bertua-Dume, with advanced posts to the westward and a detachment at Kunde to maintain touch with Colonel Brisset at Ngaundere. *Franco-Belgian eastern columns; September–October 1915.*

The Sanga Column also had to meet a German counter-offensive, lasting from the beginning till the 24th of September. After a considerable amount of fighting the Franco-Belgian troops were driven out of Abong Mbang for a short distance, and were also compelled to yield ground to the north-west and south-west of Lomie.

Meanwhile, on the 1st September, orders (dated 7th July) had been received at Dume constituting, under the command of Colonel Morisson, the East Cameroons Force. This was to include the Lobaye and Sanga Columns under the new titles of Right and Left Columns respectively.

Farther south, on the 3rd September, a French company from Minkebe occupied Akoafim, which the Germans evacuated after setting fire to it.

General Aymerich, arriving back at Brazzaville from Duala on the 7th September, left again five days later for Dume, which he reached on the 18th October to assume personal command of the East Cameroons Force. As arranged at Duala, he was to advance before the end of the month, moving westward towards Nanga Eboko so as to avoid the marshes and forests of the Nyong valley.

Though his left column was still feeling the effect of its recent fighting and had not yet concentrated all its scattered detachments, General Aymerich commenced his forward movement on the 28th October, when his force was disposed as follows :—

Dengdeng	100 rifles (Capt. Staup), in touch with Colonel Brisset.
Bertua vicinity ..	Right Column (Col. Morisson) consisting of eight companies (1,000 rifles) with four guns.
Dume	Left Column (Comdt. Thomas) one French and one Belgian company (350 rifles) and one gun.

By the 4th November, after some stiff fighting to overcome considerable enemy opposition to General Aymerich's passage of the Long river from Tina southward, his Right and Left Columns had made good the western bank of the river.

French South Cameroons Force and British force in the Campo area; September–October 1915.

The French South Cameroons Force, five companies strong, under Colonel Le Meillour, remained throughout September in the vicinity of Bitam and at Mimwul.

It had been arranged at the Duala conference that this force, which was to receive reinforcements to bring its total strength eventually up to 940 rifles, two machine gun sections and three guns, was to advance via Ambam on Ebolowa, getting into communication with the French column from Campo which was to attempt to gain Njabesan so as to cover Colonel Le Meillour's left flank.

At Campo, when the company of the 5th Light Infantry (Indian Army) withdrew to Duala on the 11th September, the only British troops remaining were a company of the Sierra Leone Battalion, though Commander Hughes, who was in command of the district, still had at his disposal some naval and marine detachments and levies to hold the line Dipikar-Randad und Stein-Ebabomwode, and advanced posts at Moloko and Afan. He was also assisted by the *Vigilant* (Lieutenant-Commander P. V. Kilgour). During September there were frequent patrol encounters, but no fighting of importance. Before the end of the month the rainy season had set in in earnest, with the result that by the middle of October most of the rivers in the district became unfordable. Communication with Colonel Le Meillour was established in the middle of September and maintained thereafter till the 23rd October by runners. At the beginning of October the enemy displayed special activity, and on the 6th delivered a sharp attack on the post at Moloko, only, however, to withdraw again after $2\frac{1}{2}$ hours' fighting without success and with some loss. On the British side the only casualty was one marine wounded.*

On the 11th October a party of 150 refugees arrived at Campo from Mabenaga, near Great Batanga, where according to their statement the Germans had made a new camp and were evicting and killing many of the natives. Refugees continued to arrive at the British camp in numbers at intervals.

In the middle of October Colonel Le Meillour concentrated his troops near Bitam for the advance on Ambam, but failed in an attempt he made on the night of the 24th/25th to cross the Ntem river, which the enemy was watching with great care.

On the 25th October the two Senegalese companies, sent from Dakar in response to M. Merlin's request, arrived at Duala under command of Captain Blum. Here the situation was explained to him † and he was instructed to advance from Campo on Njabesan, after establishing communication with Colonel Le Meillour and placing himself under that officer's orders. The British force at Campo had already prepared a rest camp and temporary base for his force and would, besides, he was told, render him all further possible assistance. To strengthen his force Commandant Carré, commanding the

---

* This was Pte. A. F. Hammond, R.M.L.I., who with five levies on outpost duty had held up the enemy advance to give the main post time to prepare for the attack.

† The War Office had recently telegraphed to General Dobell that intercepted letters indicated the establishment of a considerable German supply depot at Ebolowa.

French cruiser *Friant*, also arranged to place at his disposal a naval machine gun section.

Captain Blum with his two companies arrived at Campo on the 27th October.

General Cunliffe's operations and co-operation by the Bare Column; October–10th November 1915.

To turn to the operations of General Cunliffe's troops, who—apart from the force investing Mora—were, at the end of September, disposed as follows:—

With General Cunliffe at Yola	Headquarters, three guns (1st and 2nd Batteries), one section mounted infantry ("B" Company), and three infantry companies (H/1st Bn., A/2nd Bn., and D/3rd Bn.).
Under Major Mann (based on Ibi)	*Takum*—two half-companies (C/and E/2nd Bn.).
	Karbabi—one half-company (G/2nd Bn.).
	Barua—one company (H/3rd Bn.).
	Gashiga—one company (C/1st Bn.).
Under Major Porter at Koncha, with an advanced post at Dodo	"B" Company Mtd. Infantry, less one section.
	A company and a half of infantry (B/1st Bn. and half B/3rd Bn.).
Garua	One half-company (B/3rd Bn.).
Under Lt.-Col. Brisset—	
Tingere (Lt.-Col. Webb-Bowen)	Two companies (B/and H/2nd Bn.).
Ngaundere	One squadron French cavalry. Four French guns (including two captured from Germans).
	Two Senegalese infantry companies. (Another Senegalese company was about fifty-five miles south-east of Ngaundere keeping touch with Colonel Morisson.)
Under Major Crookenden at Ossidinge	Two guns (2nd Battery).
	Four companies (A, C, E, and F/3rd Bn).

Information regarding the strength of the German forces opposed to him was rather indefinite, but General Cunliffe estimated that they had (i) about three hundred men holding Banyo and the passes to the north and west of it, (ii) between one and two hundred men at Tibati with an outpost at Galim, and (iii) a stronger force in the Bamenda-Fumban-Chang area with outposts at Kentu and Wum.

By the 2nd October General Cunliffe had decided to move against Bamenda, Banyo, and Tibati, setting all his troops in

[*To face p.* 340

MACHINE GUN SECTION, R.W.A.F.F.

SIGNALLERS, R.W.A.F.F.

CUNLIFFE'S PLANS 341

motion so as to threaten the enemy simultaneously from every direction. His plan was as follows.

Major Crookenden was to advance from Ossidinge on the 12th October against Bamenda, moving via Widekum, and on the same day the company at Takum was to advance against Kentu. To assist Major Crookenden and enable him to push on subsequently against Fumban, General Cunliffe on the 2nd October asked Mr. Boyle to inquire if General Dobell would allow his Bare force to occupy Chang. General Dobell replied on the 5th that Colonel Cotton had been instructed to move from Bare on the 12th and that General Dobell hoped that this would relieve the pressure on Major Crookenden, but that as Colonel Cotton's column would not be strong enough to engage and contain any large number of the enemy, too much must not be expected.

General Cunliffe himself, after concentrating the troops from Yola at Koncha by the 9th October, would advance from there on the 14th against Banyo, with one mounted infantry company, two guns and four infantry companies (leaving half a company to garrison Koncha). To co-operate with him Major Mann would advance from Gashiga, timing his movement so as to reach Gandua at the same time as General Cunliffe reached Mba. From these two places a combined advance would be made on Banyo, the mounted infantry company then being detached eastward to cover the left flank and cut the enemy line of retreat from Galim.

On the 15th October, Colonel Brisset was to advance from Ngaundere on Tibati and Colonel Webb-Bowen was to advance from Tingere on Galim.

When General Dobell, on the 5th October, received the telegram from Nigeria asking for co-operation from Bare, his troops on the Northern Railway and in the Bare area consisted of the Sierra Leone Battery, the 5th Light Infantry (now organised in six companies, each about 100 strong) and the West African Regiment, the whole under command of Lieutenant-Colonel W.L. Cotton (5th Light Infantry). On the same day General Dobell sent Colonel Cotton instructions to move out on the 12th October from Bare towards Chang with a column of three companies 5th Light Infantry, two companies West African Regiment and one section Sierra Leone Battery, i.e., a total of about 500 rifles with four machine guns, two guns and 800 carriers.* His object, he was told, was to hold the enemy in Chang or draw him southward.

Operations of the Bare Column; October–6th November 1915.

---

* The Indian troops required more transport than the African.

Colonel Cotton moved out with the Bare Column on the 12th October and, camping that night at Melong, started next morning towards Chang by the westerly road leading past Mbo. On the 14th, after crossing the Mwu river in face of some slight opposition, he formed a camp a short distance to the north of it. Next day one company went back to bring up supplies from Melong and three companies, reconnoitring to the Nkam river, left an advanced post to hold the crossing there. This post was attacked during the night of the 15th/16th October, but two companies from the main camp, moving to its assistance, found that the enemy had retired. On the 16th a company of the West African Regiment reconnoitring Fongwang was fired on by enemy scouts, and had one man wounded.

On the 18th Colonel Cotton resumed his advance and, crossing the Nkam river by a temporary bridge which his men had constructed, occupied Sanchu after driving out a few enemy troops. On the 19th he occupied Mbo without opposition, and decided that the nature of the surrounding mountainous country rendered it necessary to halt for a few days to reconnoitre.

On the 21st October Major C. S. Stooks (5th Light Infantry), with one company 5th Light Infantry and one company and two machine guns West African Regiment, moved out to reconnoitre towards Chang. He encountered a good deal of opposition which, in the difficult country, delayed his progress and obliged him to bivouac short of the junction with the main Bare-Chang road, where it had been intended that he should encamp for the night. He advanced again next morning and, after reconnoitring thoroughly and sighting several enemy parties whose total strength he estimated at about two hundred, he bivouacked a short distance south-west of the enemy position covering the road junction. On the 23rd he was joined by Colonel Cotton with the remainder of the column, less a detachment left to garrison Mbo.

The enemy was estimated at a strength of between two and three hundred with two machine guns, and Colonel Cotton attacked his position covering the road junction on the 24th October. After a lively engagement, in which the British sustained thirty casualties,* the enemy was driven out and the road junction occupied. The enemy retired to Chang, but

---

* Lieutenant E. F. Fielding (West African Regiment) was killed and Captain R. V. Morrison, Indian Medical Service (5th Light Infantry) was wounded.

ADVANCE FROM OSSIDINGE

Colonel Cotton, who did not consider his force strong enough to occupy Chang and at the same time keep open his line of communication with Bare, felt that he could best fulfil his instructions by holding a position covering the road junction and by reconnoitring actively from there.

Here he remained till the 6th November, when, having heard that Chang was only weakly held, he advanced and captured it without loss and almost without opposition. News of Major Crookenden's occupation of Bamenda on the 22nd October was received at Duala on the 29th and presumably reached Colonel Cotton two or three days later; but it was not till the 9th November that a message by native runner reached Chang from Major Crookenden at Bamenda.

Advance from Ossidinge and capture of Bamenda; October 1915.

Major Crookenden advanced from Ossidinge towards Widekum on the 12th October with his four companies, eight machine guns and one gun * and at once began to encounter opposition. The enemy parties, however, were weak in strength and retired whenever their flank was threatened. The country, on the other hand, rendered progress both arduous and slow, being intersected by numerous streams and torrents and in the last stages hilly or mountainous, while its difficulties were aggravated by the constant rain. The Germans evacuated two very strongly entrenched positions on the 18th and 20th October, and on the 22nd a party of about fifty of their troops made only a show of disputing Major Crookenden's entry into Bamenda. The British casualties were consequently small, apparently totalling, in the eleven days' advance, only five, including one man drowned. The greater part of the German force previously at Bamenda, estimated at a strength of two or three hundred, was reported to have retired on the 21st October towards Banyo.

Having established himself in a defensive position at Bamenda, but being without news of the advance on Chang from Bare, Major Crookenden decided to advance and reconnoitre Bagam, the point of junction of the main roads from Bamenda and Chang to Fumban. Leaving Bamenda on the 27th October with a column of 200 rifles with five machine guns, he encountered at Bali Bagam, two miles north of Bagam, an enemy detachment about one hundred strong. This he drove back to and through Bagam, the fighting being carried out under difficult conditions among large, straggling and bush-grown native towns. His casualties, however, only totalled

---

* The other gun followed later.

four, including Captain G. N. Heathcote wounded, and he took prisoner a wounded German.

He camped that evening north of Bali Bagam. On the 29th October he learnt that the enemy near Bagam had been reinforced from Fumban and that his strength now amounted to about 15 Germans and 200 natives. Major Crookenden was still without news of the Bare Column and on the 30th he marched back to Bamenda.

Operations in Kentu area; October 1915. The company at Takum under Captain B. C. Parr advanced on the 12th October as ordered. On the 16th one of its patrols surprised a German piquet, killing six of them, and next day, after overcoming slight opposition at the cost of two casualties, Captain Parr occupied Kentu. From there the enemy withdrew southward to a precipitous hill commanding the Bamenda road. Reconnoitring this hill in strength on the 20th October Captain Parr found the Germans posted in a strong position, which was only assailable with the aid of scaling ladders. His force had incurred thirteen casualties and, judging that a further advance would be too costly, Captain Parr withdrew; but learning soon afterwards that the enemy had evacuated his position Captain Parr occupied it on the 24th October.

Advance of General Cunliffe and Major Mann to Banyo; October 1915. Prior to General Cunliffe's arrival at Koncha on the 9th October, Captain F. J. H. Pring had carried out from Gashiga a skilful and very successful minor operation with three sections of "C" Company 1st Nigeria Regiment. Making a wide detour through the mountains he completely surprised a German outpost at Gandua on the 27th September, killing eight of the enemy, including two Germans, at a cost to his own party of only two casualties. The German commander at Banyo, believing that this movement was the prelude to a strong offensive from Gashiga, at once called in his advanced posts, not only from the Gashiga direction, but also from that of Dodo and Galim. This action undoubtedly facilitated the subsequent British advance, for, though the enemy soon found out his mistake and sent advanced posts out again, they were neither as strong nor pushed out as far as they had been previously. This was especially noticeable in the case of the series of well sited trenches commanding the different stages in the steep ascent, to the south of Dodo, which led through the Genderu mountains to the central plateau. This was the only practicable pass in the vicinity, and had the Germans left only a small detachment to hold this position General Cunliffe must have found its capture both difficult and costly.

General Cunliffe advanced from Koncha with one company

of mounted infantry, three guns and four infantry companies *
on the 14th October. The enemy at and round Banyo was
reported to have recently been reinforced from Fumban and
to be 500 strong. Tibati was also said to have been reinforced.
On moving south from Dodo three days later the mounted
infantry company was detached, for reasons already mentioned,
to move by a route to the east of the Genderu pass. By the
evening of the 22nd Major Mann with two-and-a-half infantry
companies † was at Gandua, the main column at Mba and the
mounted infantry at Mbamti.

The spirit animating the Nigerian soldiery was well illustrated
at this period by an exploit of five sick men of the mounted
infantry, whom Major Porter left behind him at Dodo, when
he moved eastward, to follow with five sick horses. These
men, learning that there was a German detachment about
twenty strong near Mbamti, followed it up and surprised it,
killing two of its members and putting the remainder to headlong flight.

General Cunliffe directed the mounted infantry to move from
Mbamti and, after cutting the Banyo-Tibati road and leaving a
post there, to move round and cut the Banyo-Fumban road.
These instructions, says General Cunliffe in his despatch, were
admirably carried out by Major Porter.

The combined advance on Banyo from Gandua and Mba
commenced on the morning of the 23rd October, the converging
movement causing the enemy to evacuate his positions on the
hills covering Banyo. That evening signalling communication
was established between General Cunliffe's column to the north
of Banyo and Major Mann's column to the west; and information was received that the whole of the enemy force had retired
to a position on Banyo mountain a few miles east of the town.
Next morning Major Mann occupied the European settlement
of Banyo an hour before General Cunliffe's advanced guard
marched in.

During their advance both columns had met with only slight
opposition and the enemy parties encountered, weak in strength,
had made no attempt to make a prolonged stand in any of their
previously prepared positions. The British casualties had
only totalled thirteen, while the enemy was known to have
lost, in killed alone, at least twenty-eight, including three

---

* " B " Mounted Infantry; one section 1st Battery and one gun 2nd
Battery; " B " and " H " Companies 1st Bn., " A " 2nd Bn. and " D " 3rd
Bn. Half " B " Company 3rd Bn. remained to garrison Koncha temporarily.

† " C " 1st Bn., half " G " 2nd Bn. and " H " 3rd Bn.

Germans. The country traversed was of a difficult and mountainous nature, covered with elephant grass and intersected by numerous rivers and streams. The protective duties had consequently proved arduous and General Cunliffe had good reason to congratulate his officers and men on their fine efforts, and especially that portion of his force which had covered 445 miles in the past five weeks (including halts) between Mora and Banyo.

The advance from Tingere and Ngaundere; October 1915.

In accordance with his orders, which instructed him to act independently, Colonel Webb-Bowen advanced from Tingere on the 15th October and, on the 19th, after overcoming some slight opposition without loss, occupied Galim, where he was in a position calculated to facilitate the advance on Tibati of Colonel Brisset's force and to maintain liaison between it and General Cunliffe's headquarters.

On the 11th October, on receipt of General Cunliffe's instructions, Colonel Brisset had demurred at advancing on the 15th on the ground of the weakness of his force and also lest he should, by advancing from Tibati, be prevented from affording assistance which he had offered Colonel Morisson.* On the 19th, however, being reassured by General Cunliffe that General Aymerich had specially asked for an advance on Tibati to protect Colonel Morisson's right flank, Colonel Brisset started to advance from Ngaundere with a squadron of cavalry, two guns and two companies of infantry (all French). On the 24th October, after arrival at Banyo, General Cunliffe replaced Colonel Webb-Bowen's column at Colonel Brisset's disposal for the attack on Tibati.

Occupation of Tibati; 3rd November 1915.

The occupation of Tibati was effected successfully on the 3rd November. Colonel Webb-Bowen's column advanced directly on it from the north and, attracting the attention of the German garrison, enabled Colonel Brisset to surprise them by an advance from the south-east. A short bombardment by the French guns sufficed to cause the enemy garrison of about 150 rifles to beat a hurried retreat in the Yoko direction, without having inflicted any loss on the Allies.

Operations against Banyo Mountain.

General Cunliffe was disappointed at having failed to inflict a decisive defeat on the enemy at Banyo, and gathered that the Germans entertained hopes of holding out on the Banyo mountain and containing an Allied investing force round them

---

* Colonel Brisset had received reports that 300 troops had moved from Fumban to reinforce the German force opposite Colonel Morisson. General Cunliffe discredited this report, which proved to be either incorrect or greatly exaggerated.

till the end of the war, as Raben was doing at Mora. In fact, it appeared to be the German policy in many parts to endeavour to retain their hold on the country by occupying a number of strongly defended positions and so preventing the Allies from concentrating against the main German force round Yaunde.

General Cunliffe had by this time heard of the occupation of Kentu, but was without news of the result of the operations from Ossidinge and Bare. He decided, however, that if his own force was to advance farther, he must take the risks of attacking the position on Banyo mountain, which from all accounts was very strongly defended and amply provisioned.

Transport and supply questions were causing him considerable concern. He had insufficient carriers, and had failed to obtain the additional carriers or supplies he had hoped for from the regions his different columns had traversed, owing to the systematic German devastation and depopulation of these areas. The last year's local crops had been gathered to provision Banyo mountain and much of the new crop had been destroyed to keep it out of Allied hands. The local German political officer, it was learnt, had assured the native owners that their losses would all be made good from the big indemnity which Germany would shortly extract from Great Britain. Practically everything General Cunliffe's force required had to be brought from Yola.

Anticipating that Banyo would be his advanced base till the conclusion of operations, General Cunliffe asked the Governor-General of Nigeria to consider the question of constructing a field telegraph line from Ibi—where he was transferring his base from Yola—to as near Banyo as possible. Otherwise, when he advanced, as he hoped to do before very long, the long distances involved would much enhance his difficulties of communication.

Banyo Mountain rises as a single feature about one thousand two hundred feet above the surrounding area of broken hill country. Its slopes are very steep and covered with large boulders, many of which the enemy had incorporated in his lines of defence, linking them together by stone breastworks. Of these some three hundred altogether had been erected, while on all prominent commanding points small redoubts had been constructed. An immense amount of labour had been expended in making other arrangements for a prolonged defence. On the summit cement reservoirs had been made to hold the water from mountain springs; brick houses, with cement floors and glass windows, had been built for the Europeans and had been equipped with heavy furniture from the settlement; and some forty tons of grain, over two hundred head of cattle, hundreds of fowls and a great quantity of agricultural implements and other material had been accumulated. There was abundant evidence that the mountain was intended to afford a great rallying place for the garrisons of Banyo, Bamenda and Chang, and that there was universal and absolute confidence among the Germans in the country that it would be held till the end of the war.

For his attack on it General Cunliffe made careful and thorough preparation. By the 2nd November four-and-a-half of his Nigerian infantry companies with ten machine guns were established on underfeatures round the mountain; and in the plain behind them the mounted infantry were disposed in a wide circle to give early intimation of any attempt to break out on the part of the enemy.

On the 3rd November General Cunliffe issued orders for a general attack to commence at dawn next morning. Supported by the three mountain guns in positions to the north-east, south-west * and south, four companies were to attack in a converging advance as follows: " H " Company 1st Battalion from the north-east and " B " Company 3rd Battalion from the west, with half " G " Company 2nd Battalion on an underfeature to the north-west, forming a connecting-link between the two; " H " Company 3rd Battalion was to attack from the south-west; and " C " Company 1st Battalion from the south.

It was recognised that, as progress would probably be slow, the attack might take several days to carry through, and company commanders were made responsible for supplying their own men. They were enjoined to advance in depth, refraining from too wide extensions, and to move forward steadily and methodically, making full use of all cover, without undue hurry.

Attack commences; 4th November 1915. Daybreak on the 4th November found the mountain shrouded in thick mist, which, though it stood in the way of mutual support between the different attacking units, enabled them to make considerable progress unseen by the enemy. " H " Company 3rd Battalion in fact almost reached the summit under cover of this mist, but, coming suddenly under cross-fire

---

* Though the order said north-west the plan attached to the order shows the gun south-west.

from several directions at short range, its commander, Captain Bowyer-Smijth—one of General Cunliffe's most fearless and dashing officers—was killed and the company was forced back for a considerable distance. By midday the remaining companies had got about half-way up the mountain and had in many places attained positions within thirty yards of enemy breastworks. Here, crouching behind boulders within point blank range, they could do no more while daylight lasted than cling tenaciously to the ground they had won. As soon as it was dark the enemy began throwing dynamite bombs, a new weapon to the British troops and one which tried them so highly that, for a short period and until they realised that the noise of these bombs was worse than their effect, the situation was extremely critical. Then, extricating themselves and reorganising, the Nigerians made a further slight advance in the dark.

During the 5th progress was slow but sure, breastwork after breastwork being outflanked, till by dusk all four companies had reached positions within about one hundred yards of the summit. A violent thunderstorm intervened at 7 p.m., but at daybreak on the 6th November the summit was carried. The white flag of surrender was flying, but the enemy had fled.

Capture of Banyo Mountain; 6th November 1915.

It appears that at 5 p.m. on the 5th, the German commander, realising that the position was lost, had issued orders to his troops to break through the attacking cordon in small parties. Each party was to take with it carriers loaded with baggage and ammunition and all were eventually to rendezvous at Ngambe. The thunderstorm presented a favourable opportunity for escape and during it the enemy parties had crept cautiously down the slopes past the attacking companies. Not a great number escaped, however, as the British posts closing the routes in the plain below and pursuit parties from the mountain captured a considerable proportion of the fugitives. Out of the garrison of about 23 Germans and 200 natives, 13 Germans and 103 natives were killed, wounded or captured, including their commander, Captain Schipper, killed. An immense quantity of stores and material of all kinds was also taken.

The capture of this position, which the Germans had deemed practically impregnable, was a feat of which General Cunliffe, his officers and men have every reason to be proud. Skilful planning, resolute and gallant leadership and disciplined endurance and courage all contributed to the success. Having regard to the nature of the position and of the enemy's defences the British casualties were not excessive. They totalled sixty, including Captains C. G. Bowyer-Smijth and L. N. A. Mackinnon and Colour-Sergeant W. King killed, and Captain G. Seccombe and Lieutenant J. Chartres wounded.

Future plans; November, 1915. News of the occupation of Bamenda and Tibati reached General Cunliffe on the 9th November, followed a little later by news of the occupation of Chang; and General Cunliffe decided that his next advance would be to the line Ditam-Ngambe-Yoko.

CHAPTER X

NOVEMBER—22ND DECEMBER 1915
STEADY PROGRESS OF THE CONVERGING ADVANCE ON YAUNDE

(Maps 2, 12, 13 and 14)

It is difficult to frame anything but an approximate estimate of the effective strength and distribution of the German forces in the Cameroons at the beginning of November 1915. No authoritative German account * of the operations has apparently yet been published; the Intelligence diary maintained at General Dobell's Headquarters is missing from the records; and the estimates of the German numbers formed by the British commanders of columns in the field and the Intelligence staff appear, as a general rule, to have been too low.† On the other hand, reports received at and after the end of hostilities, including those from the Spanish authorities, all agree that the German combatant force reaching Spanish Muni totalled about 600 German and 6,000 native ranks. Of these the British estimated that not more than about 5,000 could have had rifles and that, excluding the garrison of Mora, they were organised in approximately twenty-three companies.

Enemy strength and dispositions; November 1915.

These companies evidently all varied in strength and some of them had been broken up into more or less independent groups of fifty to one hundred rifles each. Apparently six companies were being driven gradually southward towards the Sanaga river by the columns under General Cunliffe; six or seven companies were believed to be opposing the advance of

---

* The brief account in *Der Grosse Krieg*, referred to previously, hardly comes under this heading and gives no assistance in the required direction.
† It seems reasonable to attribute this tendency to under-estimate to the nature of the country, which imposed comparatively narrow fighting frontages and facilitated concealment of dispositions and numbers. Even in the case of enemy retirements it was exceptional for our men to catch more than a glimpse of the German troops.

General Dobell's troops; another six or seven companies seem to have been engaged with the Franco-Belgian force under General Aymerich; and the force in and round Ebolowa is said to have totalled about 1,000 rifles. The German European detachment (or company) had been broken up and its members distributed to replace casualties in, or to raise the strength of, the German ranks of the native companies.

Estimated effect of the capture of Yaunde. There were clear indications that the Germans were beginning to run short of ammunition, while it also seemed possible that the supply question was causing them anxiety. The capture of Yaunde, where the enemy's main depots were presumably located, was consequently calculated to hasten the end of hostilities, even if the enemy withdrew from there. His chances of doing this would gradually decrease, however, as the converging advances of the Allied columns against Yaunde and Ebolowa progressed; for, besides depriving him of other possible centres of resistance, they would ultimately form a cordon across his lines of retreat. He would, therefore, it was anticipated, be obliged to stand and fight or admit the futility of further resistance.

The Allies at Eseka and Wum Biagas; 1st–22nd November 1915. As soon as Eseka was captured General Dobell, ascertaining that the French would not have collected sufficient supplies for their further advance till the 23rd November, fixed that date provisionally for the advance from both Eseka and Wum Biagas.

This delay was in some respects beneficial. The rain had not yet ceased and—apart from the personal discomfort and danger to health from wet clothes and flooded camps—it hampered operations considerably, frequently rendered motor traffic impossible between Edea and Ngwe, and caused great delay to road construction. During November the rain grew gradually less and by the 24th, when the fifty miles of road from Edea to Wum Biagas had been completed to a motor standard, it became possible to withdraw all traffic restrictions due to weather. General Dobell, inspecting the road a few days previously, was much pleased at the regular motor service along what had only recently been a mere bush track; and he hoped to be able before long to continue the work of repairing bridges and road construction and so enable the motor vans to ply east of Wum Biagas. Here he had collected a reserve of twenty-four days' supplies (approximately 144 tons) for Colonel Gorges' column and had a body of 3,500 carriers for transport work.

The enemy, who had about a company on the Sanaga river

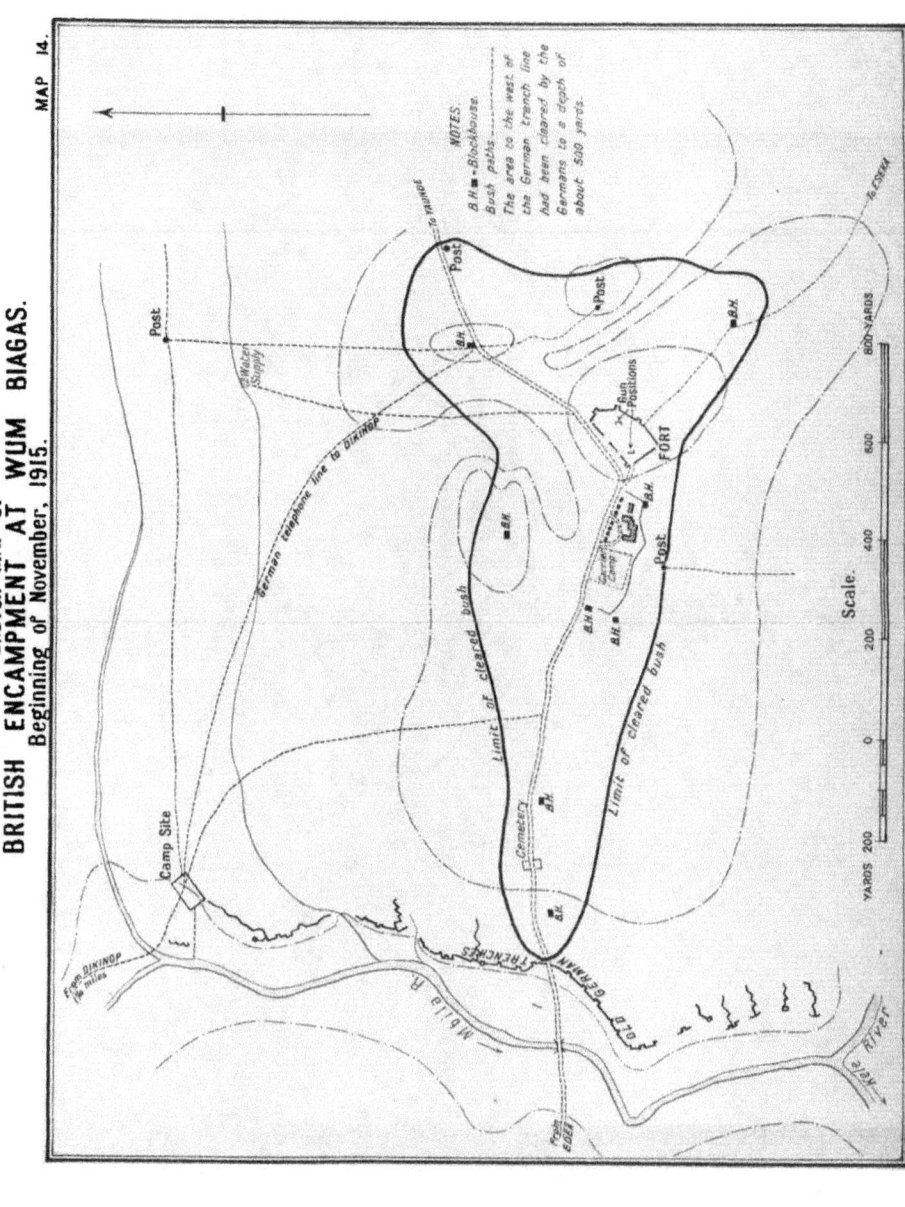

FIGHTING ROUND WUM BIAGAS

line northward of Wum Biagas, had recently been less active round Sakbajeme, and Colonel Gorges was able to reduce its garrison on the 25th October, when he established a second post at Mum to cover the northern flank of the advanced section of his line of communication. This post, garrisoned by sixty rifles Gold Coast Battalion under Captain G. A. E. Poole, was attacked by the enemy, apparently in some force with a machine gun, on the 2nd November; and Colonel Rose, at Captain Poole's request, at once dispatched to his assistance from Ndupe a detachment of fifty rifles with a machine gun.

At the same time as the attack on Mum, another enemy party made a demonstration against Wum Biagas. This enemy party (apparently about eighty strong), driving back the British standing patrol from Ntim, was encountered within about a mile of Wum Biagas by a company of the 2nd Nigerians under Major G. N. Sheffield whom Colonel Haywood had sent out that morning (2nd) to establish a new advanced post at Ngok. Major Sheffield's advance was checked by heavy fire, but, with the support of gun fire from Wum Biagas, he was able to drive the enemy back and camp for the night, with the loss of two casualties, at Ntim. Next day he only encountered slight opposition and occupied Ngok at 2 p.m.

In the meantime Colonel Haywood, learning of the attack on Mum, had dispatched, at 6.30 a.m. on the 3rd November, another company of the 2nd Nigerians under Captain J. P. D. Underwood with orders to move due north from Wum Biagas and endeavour to cut off the retreat of the enemy attacking Mum. News, however, that the Mum garrison, with the loss of one man, had beaten off the enemy attack on the 2nd before the arrival of the reinforcement from Ndupe showed Colonel Haywood that Captain Underwood would probably be too late; and this proved to be the case.

On three occasions in the next week Major Sheffield at Ngok beat off enemy attacks without much difficulty, and, with only two or three casualties in his own company, inflicted much greater losses on the enemy. Save for these attacks—which led Colonel Gorges to reinforce Ngok by fifty rifles with a machine gun—and a half-hearted demonstration against Sakbajeme, the enemy opposite the British showed little activity. On the 17th November Colonel Gorges with his headquarters arrived at Wum Biagas from Edea, and next day Major H. G. Howell joined him as senior general staff officer in place of Colonel Turner invalided.

The British had been carrying out numerous reconnaissances, but they had obtained little fresh information concerning the enemy. On the 19th November the report of a German force of about two hundred men at Kwala near the Ntol ferry over the Sanaga river led to the dispatch of Captain L. S. Biddulph with half a company to reconnoitre that area.

The French at Eseka had, meanwhile, established an advanced post at the actual railhead three miles to the east, where they were attacked on the 6th November by a strong German detachment with two machine guns. But the Germans showed little resolution and the attack was unsuccessful. On the 18th November a strong French detachment reconnoitring from Eseka came unexpectedly upon the main German camp a short distance to the eastward, but succeeded in extricating itself with the loss of only two casualties. On the 21st two German companies made a more determined attack on the French advanced post, but were again unsuccessful, though killing and wounding thirteen (including two Frenchmen) of the garrison.

After the occupation of the railhead the French had set to work to repair the seven locomotives and two hundred wagons they had captured, as well as the railway line. By the 10th November the broken bridge over the Kele river at So Dibanga was completely restored by a fine piece of work on the part of the French engineers, and so opened the way for traffic as far as the Lingen river near Sende. By the end of the month a railway service was instituted between railhead and that river; and by the 13th December the Lingen bridge was also restored.

Orders for the advance; 12th November 1915. On the 12th November General Dobell issued his instructions for the resumption, on the morning of the 23rd, of the advance from Eseka and Wum Biagas. The objective of the French, advancing from Eseka by the light railway track, would be a point near Erfa on the Kribi-Yaunde road, while the British would continue to move along the main Edea-Yaunde road. To synchronise the final advance of the two columns on Yaunde and to ensure that the enemy did not break south, Colonel Gorges was instructed not to advance east of Chang Mangas until Colonel Mayer had placed a force astride the Kribi-Yaunde road.

Both commanders were directed not to overlook the possibility of turning movements and, to this end, were enjoined to move on as broad a front as advisable by utilising parallel adjacent roads or paths. By this procedure they would also, it was pointed out, disencumber their own main lines of advance. General Dobell gave them latitude to deal with the military situation encountered on the way, but reminded them that they must keep him and one another informed of their action, that they must be prepared ultimately to co-operate with one another in the attack on Yaunde and that there was only a small Allied reserve immediately available.

Each column commander would be responsible for the safety of his own flanks and line of communication; but each should co-operate with the other against any enemy between them; and inter-communication between their columns would be by telephone through Edea or direct by runner.*

When he issued these instructions General Dobell had not yet heard of General Cunliffe's capture of Banyo and Tibati, and the only news he had of General Aymerich's recent movements was from captured German documents which showed that the Franco-Belgian eastern columns were displaying activity.

After considering these instructions Colonel Gorges wrote on the 15th November from Wum Biagas to Colonel Mayer, informing him that the enemy strength on the road opposite the British was estimated at 400 rifles and that his main position was reported to be astride the road at the Puge river (fourteen miles distant from Wum Biagas) with advanced posts at Omog, Mode, and Matem, and with patrols along the line of the Kele river to the south-east of Wum Biagas. Colonel Gorges proposed to advance in two columns on the 24th November and he asked if Colonel Mayer could co-operate by sending a detachment eastward through Bog Nso at the same time as the British moved through Matips. Colonel Mayer at first declined, as Bog Nso was so far off his line of advance, but agreed finally to send a company with a machine gun on the 23rd, though he could not promise to leave it there for more than three days.

On the 16th and 18th November General Dobell received telegrams from Lagos informing him of the capture of Banyo and Tibati and of General Cunliffe's intention to send Major Crookenden, if possible, against Fumban and to push on himself as soon as possible to Ngambe and Yoko, in which

---

* The use of the telephone, with its liability to interruption, was necessitated by the disappointing results of the experiments with the wireless sets, whose failure was attributed to atmospheric conditions or to the presence in the soil of ironstone.

direction the enemy in front of him appeared to be retiring. General Cunliffe had some hopes of cutting off the enemy's retreat on Yaunde. On the 23rd General Dobell received a telegram from Brazzaville giving General Aymerich's situation in the third week of October.

Advance of Colonel Gorges' column; 23rd November –6th December 1915.

By the 22nd November Colonel Gorges had concentrated the following troops at Wum Biagas (including the advanced post at Ngok):—

    Howitzer Detachment, R.A.
    One section each Nigerian and Gold Coast Batteries.
    Field Section 36th (Sierra Leone) Company, R.E.
    Machine gun section, West India Regiment.
    1st and 2nd Nigerians.
    Headquarters and three and a half companies Gold Coast Battalion.
    Gambia Company.
    Field Telegraph Detachment.

and along his line of communication * to Edea:—

    One and a half companies Gold Coast Battalion.
    Three companies Sierra Leone Battalion.

In order to carry out his first object, i.e., the capture of the Puge river position, Colonel Gorges decided to advance direct by the main road with his main column, detaching columns to either flank to co-operate. The right flank detachment would move through Matips, force the Kele river crossing near Lesogs and advance to Nkod Makengs, while the left flank detachment would advance via Makai and Mode.

For the advance Colonel Gorges issued certain standing orders, of some of which a copy is given in Appendix VII as likely to be of interest to military students.

23rd November 1915. On the 23rd November, Captain Biddulph's half-company (Gold Coast Battalion)—which in its reconnaissance towards Kwala had captured a German food convoy and papers showing that the enemy was drawing considerable supplies from the Sanaga valley—was ordered to move south and join the left flank detachment at Makai. On the same day, the right flank detachment under command of Colonel Cockburn—consisting of one gun Gold Coast Battery, a party of the Sierra Leone R.E., the 1st Nigerians (less one company) and medical, supply and transport details—moved southward

---

* This was organised in two sections:—No. 1 Section, under Major F. Anderson, headquarters Ngwe, Edea (exclusive) to Nkonjok; No. 2 Section, under Colonel Rose, headquarters Wum Biagas, Ndupe to Ngok.

OPPOSITION TO BRITISH ADVANCE

from Wum Biagas, crossed the Kele river and, driving back some hostile patrols, camped for the night at Log Lebog. In the meantime two companies 2nd Nigerians from the main column pushed eastward to reconnoitre the enemy position at Matem.

In this position the enemy was found next morning to be strongly entrenched with his flanks well protected by swamps. His strength appeared to be about a company, and the two Nigerian companies, suffering seven casualties during the day, failed to dislodge him. To turn the flank of his position, Colonel Gorges, who had marched that day with the main column * from Wum Biagas to Ngok, issued orders to Colonel Rose to move out from Ngok on the 25th with the left flank detachment. 24th November 1915.

On the right flank, Colonel Cockburn, moving south-eastward through dense bush, encountered continuous opposition in his advance of six miles. At first the hostile parties were in no strength, but about noon they concentrated a force of apparently some 60 rifles with a machine gun in an entrenched position, which they held till their flanks were threatened, and then withdrew along previously prepared bush paths without a man of them being seen.

Colonel Rose, with a company each of the 1st Nigerians and the Gold Coast Battalion, marched on the 25th November to Makai, where he was joined by Captain Biddulph's half-company. To give this left flank detachment time to outflank the Matem position, which the enemy was still holding, the main column remained halted at Ngok. 25th November 1915.

On the right flank, Colonel Cockburn, faced by continuous enemy opposition, managed to advance five or six miles through densely covered foothills and along a path whose appallingly bad state was accentuated by a night of rain and numbers of fallen trees. His casualties totalled seven, including Lieutenant E. R. Hills killed.

A fall of torrential rain from 3 a.m. to 6.30 a.m. on the 26th November was most unwelcome, but fortunately proved to be the last which occurred for some time. The main column, advancing from Ngok, drove the enemy—whose strength appeared to be reduced to about forty rifles with a machine gun—from the Matem position, without difficulty and at the cost of only four casualties. The British then 26th November 1915.

---

* The howitzer and two Nigerian guns, detachment R.E., machine gun section West India Regiment, 2nd Nigerians, and the pioneer company Gold Coast Battalion.

camped about two miles east of this position covered by an advanced detachment a mile in front.

Colonel Rose, moving southward from Makai in touch with hostile patrols which retired before him, found progress arduous owing to swamps—through which his men had frequently to wade waist-deep—and to his guide, terror-stricken at the idea of meeting the Germans, losing his way. Colonel Rose managed, however, to maintain the correct direction and also communication with Colonel Gorges, neither of them easy tasks.

On the right flank, Colonel Cockburn's advanced guard, moving forward at 8 a.m., at once became heavily engaged with the enemy in the hills to the west of Lesogs. The Germans had two or three machine guns in action; their well-sited trenches were so carefully concealed in the dense bush that it took some time to locate them; and their opposition was so stubborn that it was not till Colonel Cockburn had pushed into the fight his whole force, less the company on camp and baggage guard, that they were finally driven off the crest of the hill. Even then they retired only a few hundred yards along the summit to another position, from which they opened fire as soon as the British resumed their advance. By this time Colonel Cockburn's troops had suffered forty casualties, including Captains A. W. Balders and G. Walker killed, and Captain The Hon. R. Craven and Sergeant J. Hutchinson (R.A.M.C.) wounded. Most of these losses had been due to the fire of the hostile machine guns and Colonel Cockburn decided, before attacking the German second position, to make a careful reconnaissance for lines of approach which would enable him to avoid, if possible, this machine gun fire. Being 5 p.m., however, it was too late to start reconnaissance. Colonel Cockburn therefore left a detachment to hold the captured position and withdrew the bulk of his force to camp.

27th November 1915. Next morning his advanced guard moved out at 6.15 and was followed by the main body, after its units had undergone reorganisation, at 11.30 a.m.* It soon came up with the advanced guard, which had encountered opposition shortly after leaving camp; and by 3 p.m. the whole column was engaged with the enemy, who was holding positions in the amphitheatre of hills round Lesogs village. He was gradually forced back, but at 5 p.m. was still holding an extended line

---

* The wounded were also evacuated to Eseka before the main body left.

THE PUGE RIVER POSITION

from which his converging fire commanded the road. Colonel Cockburn's sections were getting scattered and he decided to break off the action for the night, successfully withdrawing all his men before dark. His casualties during the day totalled fifteen, including Sergeant W. Chadwick wounded, and he had advanced less than two miles.

On the main road the advanced guard under Colonel Haywood, consisting of a Nigerian gun and two companies 2nd Nigerians, found that morning that the enemy had evacuated his prepared position near Omog; and Colonel Haywood encountered no opposition till about 11.30 a.m., when a hostile force of about fifty rifles with two machine guns disputed a river crossing. About an hour and a half later, just before Colonel Haywood drove this force out of its position at a cost of three casualties, Colonel Gorges received Colonel Cockburn's report of his previous day's fight accompanied by an urgent request for ammunition. To keep pace with the advance of his two flanking columns, Colonel Gorges halted for the night soon after crossing the river, his camp covered by an advanced company at Mam.

On the left flank, moving eastward without opposition through a strong position at Mode, which the enemy had evacuated during the previous night, and debouching into a track cut by the enemy leading southward to the Puge river, Colonel Rose camped for the night 27th/28th a few miles northward of Mam. There, in reply to a report that he was making rapid progress, he received instructions from Colonel Gorges to endeavour to get in rear of the enemy holding the Puge river position—which Colonel Gorges hoped to force next day—and cut his line of retreat.

While awaiting the receipt from Wum Biagas of ammunition, which arrived during the day, Colonel Cockburn spent the 28th November in reconnoitring the enemy's position round Lesogs, but failed to find any paths leading towards its flanks. In this work two of his men were wounded. *28th November 1915.*

The exceptionally strong positions which the enemy had prepared at the Puge river along two successive ranges of hills were captured on the 28th by Colonel Gorges' main column practically without opposition. This was due mainly, if not entirely, to the action of Colonel Rose's left flank detachment. Moving forward at 6 a.m., with the object of getting astride the main road well to the east of the Puge river position, his column at once encountered opposition. At first the hostile parties in front of him were in weak strength but, gradually retiring from a succession of natural positions, the enemy finally concentrated, in a position at and near Ngung village on the main road, a force estimated at 150–200 rifles with three machine guns. About 2 p.m. the village was carried by a fine assault by Captain Biddulph's half-company of the Gold Coast Battalion; and the whole enemy force then retired to another position astride the road about half a mile to the east. From here they opened a heavy fire on Colonel Rose's men and maintained it till dark. At about 3 p.m. Colonel Gorges' main column arrived within communicating distance of Colonel Rose's detachment, and Colonel Rose, reinforced by a gun, was directed to camp for the night at Ngung. His casualties during the day had in the circumstances not been heavy, only totalling eight, including Captain M. E. Fell wounded.

Colonel Gorges, whose main column camped for the night at the Puge river, about two miles west of Ngung, reported that evening to General Dobell that he had received no information that day from Colonel Cockburn,* whom he proposed to reinforce with a small detachment. His own main column would move next day to Ngung, to await a supply convoy, which was due on the 1st or 2nd December, before advancing to Chang Mangas.

The hostile positions at the Puge river must have taken the enemy many weeks to construct, so numerous, intricate, and well concealed were his defences. The well sited lines of trenches were covered in one case by a stream and in the other by a river, both dammed to deepen the swamps lying between them and the thick line of abattis in front of the trenches. Fields of fire had been cleared, ranging marks erected, communication approaches prepared, and many other elaborate defensive arrangements devised. The loss of these positions was, it was subsequently ascertained, a bitter blow to the enemy, and the comparative ease with which the British had overcome the opposition so laboriously prepared was apparently one of the main contributory factors to the general demoralisation which at this time began to set in among the German troops.

<small>29th November 1915.</small> On the morning of the 29th November Colonel Cockburn discovered that the enemy had evacuated his strong position near Lesogs which, as was then found, had covered several

---

* For the next six days communication with Colonel Cockburn was much interrupted, as many of the runners carrying messages failed to get through. But whether this was owing to their own terror of the Germans or to direct enemy action is not known.

German camps, the largest of them capable of accommodating three hundred men. The position was close to the good ten-foot carrier road leading from Eseka to the main Edea-Yaunde road near Chang Mangas; it covered a good bridge over the Kele river; and it afforded the enemy an excellent centre between road and railway from which to threaten, attack, or raid the Allied flanks and communications. Unknown hitherto to the Allies, it had evidently been, for some time past, the headquarters of a force of some strength.

Leaving a strongly entrenched post of half a company with a machine gun to the west of Lesogs, Colonel Cockburn camped for the night 29th/30th with the remainder of his force in the main German camp two miles east of that village.

On the main road, on the 29th, Colonel Rose's detachment, reinforced by a company and the second gun of the Nigerian Battery, attacked the enemy who was holding strong positions about one thousand yards to the north-east and east of Ngung. These positions proved very difficult, however, to locate in the dense bush; and at nightfall the enemy was still in possession of part of them, having inflicted ten casualties on the British.

About midday, Colonel Gorges, who concentrated the bulk of his column at Ngung, received a message from Colonel Cockburn reporting his position near the bridge over the Kele river and requesting reinforcements to force the crossing. These Colonel Gorges at once dispatched in the shape of one and a half companies 2nd Nigerians under Captain J. Sargent, who was instructed to move on Kolo from Mam and endeavour to cut the line of retreat of the enemy opposing Colonel Cockburn.

The bridge over the Kele river, which Colonel Cockburn proposed to cross, was seen to be intact on the morning of the 30th November, but lay in such an exposed situation that it was necessary to reconnoitre very carefully before approaching it. As a matter of fact the enemy, possibly learning of Captain Sargent's advance, had left only a piquet to watch it and this retired after firing a few shots. After crossing the bridge Colonel Cockburn met with some further slight opposition, but reached the junction of the Omog-Kolo road without difficulty; and here, in a position to cover Captain Sargent's advance, he camped for the night. *30th November 1915.*

From the main column Colonel Haywood was sent out on the morning of the 30th to relieve Colonel Rose, who was required to resume his duties as commander of No. 2 Section of the line of communication. The enemy had already evacuated his positions to the east and north-east of Ngung and these were now occupied by the British outposts. Colonel Gorges also placed a detachment at Ssongmaal (two miles north of Ngung) to cover his left.

_{1st–6th December 1915.} To await supplies and to relieve and rest Colonel Cockburn's officers and men, Colonel Gorges remained halted at Ngung for the next six days. Captain Sargent's detachment rejoined him on the 2nd December and Colonel Cockburn's column, which occupied Nkod Makengs after some opposition, also rejoined on the 4th, having been relieved by Colonel Haywood with one gun and the 2nd Nigerians (less a company).

The brunt of the fighting during the advance from Wum Biagas had fallen on Colonel Cockburn's column, whose officers and men had displayed much fortitude in their continuous struggle, over a distance of nearly twenty miles, against constant enemy opposition, in an area of primeval forest abounding in precipitous and mountainous ground, rivers, streams, and extensive swamps; in which, even without fighting, progress would have been arduous. Colonel Cockburn reported that there had been many cases of conspicuous gallantry, and in addition to special mention of the names of Captains Balders and Walker and Lieutenant Hills, all of whom had been killed in action, he spoke with admiration of the conduct of his African stretcher bearers.

The main column and the left flank detachment had also had difficulties to cope with. The main road from Ngok to the Puge river was in a neglected state and much overgrown, all its bridges having to be repaired to bear the howitzer; while off the main road the country was of much the same nature as that traversed by Colonel Cockburn's column. As the force progressed eastward the forest had become more dense and the ground more hilly or mountainous. On the other hand, the streams and rivers had generally been fordable; and, after the rain ceased on the 26th November, the swamps and streams became shallower and the road and ground harder. Ngung itself was about 2,000 feet above sea level and its pleasant difference from Edea in temperature was some compensation for the increased exertions due to the mountainous country.

The countryside was generally deserted, though large numbers of the inhabitants must undoubtedly have been hiding in the forest; and in consequence it had been very difficult to get any one to help us, even as guides. This was

[*To face p.* 362

Nigerian Battery in Action

not surprising, as many who had assisted us in the first advance on Yaunde had been left in the lurch by our retirement in June and had suffered death or other harsh retaliatory treatment at the hands of the Germans. This state of affairs had also made it much harder to obtain information regarding the enemy. By the time Ngung was reached, however, it was estimated that the enemy under Major Haedicke opposing Colonel Gorges comprised at least five companies * of which the larger portion had been operating on the German flanks. Of the portion engaged with Colonel Cockburn some were reported to have retired in the direction of Mangeles.

The recent fighting had also shown the straits to which the enemy was reduced for ammunition. That manufactured locally by the Germans was quite ineffective and they had issued orders—which we captured—to their troops to collect all possible British and French rifles and ammunition. That they had been obtaining ammunition through Spanish Muni was also confirmed by the presence in captured trenches of cartridge cases manufactured in Germany in February 1915.† The fact that our own troops had recently been picking up larger quantities of unexpended German ammunition was, however, deemed significant of increasing demoralisation among the enemy's native troops, more especially as recently a larger number of German ranks had appeared among them and had been heard more frequently using terms of exhortation. The previous supposition that the enemy might also be short of supplies was evidently, however, devoid of foundation.

Advance of French column from Eseka; 23rd November–6th December 1915.

By the evening of the 23rd November, of the three sections of artillery, engineer detachment, and nineteen infantry companies, of which the French contingent of General Dobell's force was composed, four guns, the engineer detachment, and thirteen infantry companies were at or about Eseka, the remainder being disposed along the line of communication back to Edea and Yapoma.

That day Colonel Mayer dispatched, as arranged, a company with a machine gun to Bog Nso to assist Colonel Gorges'

---

* No. 1 (Depot), No. 4, Nos. 2 and 3 (Reserve), and No. 10 companies. The last named had, it was said, come from the east of Yaunde at the end of October.

† It was subsequently learnt from a British officer, taken prisoner by the Germans, that a German officer boasted of their use of cartridges manufactured at Spandau in February 1915.

advance. Captain Deslaurens, who commanded this detachment, reported the same day that he had found at Bog Nso some recently constructed entrenchments but no signs of the enemy, and he had received no communication from the British. There is no further mention in the records of his movements, but he appears to have soon rejoined the main French column.

On the 24th November Colonel Mayer moved out from Eseka with two guns and eight companies,* his main column of four companies with two guns advancing along the light railway towards Mangeles (twenty-three miles distant) with flanking columns, each of two companies, on either side. Immediately in front of him, astride the railway, the enemy force under Captain Priester was reported to consist of three companies (about 320 rifles) with one machine gun, while another company (200 rifles) with two machine guns under Major von Hagen from Ebolowa was said to be on the Little Malume river, a few miles to the southward.

The dense forest country was much accidented—hilly with deep ravines and numerous streams—and the light railway followed an extremely tortuous course with innumerable sharp bends.† The area was, in fact, particularly well adapted to delaying tactics, a fact of which the enemy, by careful and extensive previous preparations, made the most, offering constant and stubborn resistance to the French from the outset and contesting practically every bend in the line. The recently arrived French reinforcements were unused to bush warfare, some of them were apparently only partly trained and, as French officers told ours, the men generally were not of the same quality as those who had formed the original French contingent. On the 25th November Colonel Mayer himself returned sick to Edea, handing over command to Lieutenant-Colonel Faucon.

By the 6th December, during which period there were only two days in which it was not attacking the enemy, the French column had advanced only about half way to Mangeles. The enemy had been driven out of five or six entrenched positions and the French had incurred a total of 120 casualties, including ten French officers and non-commissioned officers.

---

* Strength about 140 French, 1,350 Senegalese, 30 levies, and 2,000 carriers.

† For some distance eastward from Eseka the easier and straighter alignment for the continuation of the Midland Railway had been cleared and partly prepared, but was in no condition for use as a road.

FRENCH OPERATIONS

In order to reach Njabesan and get into touch with Colonel Le Meillour, Captain Blum, with his Senegalese half-battalion, advanced eastward on the 5th November from Campo, the British force in the area sending parties to occupy Akak and to demonstrate towards Bipa from Moloko, in order to secure Captain Blum's line of communication and generally assist his advance. On the 11th Captain Blum attacked a party of the enemy about fifty strong at a point about five miles east of Akak, but gained no success. His men, who incurred twelve casualties, were only partly trained and they proved to be consequently of so little military value that he felt he had no option but to retire to Akak to complete their training. At this period the Governor of French West Africa had only partly trained men available, but, in answer to a request for reinforcements, he promised to send another half-battalion of Senegalese to reach Campo about the 12th December.

French operations from Campo and Bitam; November 1915. (Map 13.)

In the south, Lieutenant-Colonel Le Meillour, whose force was about Bitam, made a second attempt, on the night of the 25th/26th November, to force a crossing of the Ntem river, but was again unsuccessful.

This failure to make progress in the converging advance on Ebolowa was most disappointing and, considered in conjunction with the slow advance of the French column along the light railway from Eseka, caused General Dobell considerable apprehension lest the Germans facing Lieutenant-Colonel Faucon should break south.

General Aymerich, continuing his advance with his Eastern Cameroon columns, forced the crossing of the Ayong river after some hard fighting in the second week of November and then pushed on towards Nanga Eboko.

On the 25th November, his headquarters and a great part of his force was at Mendang (or Abanda), his dispositions being then as follows :—

Franco-Belgian operations, Eastern Cameroons; November 1915.

Right Column
- *Mendang*: Headquarters, two guns and four French companies (620 rifles).
- *Biyele*: two guns and two French companies (300 rifles).
- L. of C.: 125 rifles.

Left Column
- *Mendang*: Headquarters, two guns, two French and one Belgian companies (500 rifles).
- *Semini*: one French company (180 rifles).
- *Abong Mbang-Dume*: three guns, one French and one Belgian companies (300 rifles).
- L. of C.: one Belgian company.

General Aymerich's intention was to continue his advance by the road running westward to the Nachtigal Rapids. But a series of German attacks from the south directed against his lines of communication forced him to reconsider his plans.

On the 23rd November his outposts at Abong Mbang were violently attacked; and, as a result of other attacks on that and the next day, his outposts near Gele Menduka were driven back on to that place, which was itself then assailed. On learning of these attacks General Aymerich concluded at first that he would be able to continue his advance westward if he detached a strong force to cover his left flank. On the 28th November, therefore, while his Right Column advanced towards Tabene, his Left Column moved against Lembe (or Mugusi) where the presence of a strong enemy group was reported. On the 29th the heavy fighting which this column had to carry out before reaching Inwoghe-Tidena on the Lembe road, as well as further information which reached General Aymerich, showed him that the German offensive movement from the south was more important than he had supposed. He thereupon decided to suspend his westward movement; and he concentrated the bulk of his force to deal effectively with the enemy to the south. On the 30th November the Germans attacked Semini; but in the next four days, after further heavy fighting in which the Franco-Belgian troops incurred considerable casualties, General Aymerich occupied Lembe after driving the Germans out, a portion of their troops retiring towards Yaunde and the remainder towards Akonolinga.

It is noteworthy that news of this German counter-offensive and its defeat by General Aymerich did not reach General Dobell at Duala till over a month later. It was subsequently learnt that the Germans had confidently expected that this thrust against General Aymerich's communications would at least oblige him to retire. Its failure, therefore, coming so soon after the loss of their Puge river position in the west, disheartened them considerably.

Cunliffe's operations in the north; November–December 1915. The great moral and material effect in the north of the capture of Banyo mountain enabled General Cunliffe to commence immediately his preparations to advance and make good the line Ditam-Ngambe-Yoko, whence he anticipated that he could, if necessary, advance on Yaunde. His plan was for his own main column to move against Ngambe,

OCCUPATION OF BAGAM

while, on his right, Major Crookenden advanced on Ditam and Colonel Brisset, on his left, occupied Yoko.

Major Crookenden would first have to capture Fumban. The news of the occupation of Bamenda only reached General Cunliffe on the 9th November and next day he issued orders to Captain Parr at Kentu to join Major Crookenden at Bamenda, and to Major Crookenden to move on Fumban with as strong a force as possible as soon as he was in a position to do so.

Major Crookenden had already taken steps to this end. He did not hear of the occupation of Chang till the 10th November, but he had sent a message some days previously to be telegraphed to Duala via Lagos, intimating his readiness to move on Bagam with one gun and 250 rifles and asking General Dobell for co-operation from the Bare Column. On receiving this telegram at Duala on the 10th November, General Dobell at once sent instructions to Lieutenant-Colonel Cotton to advance from Chang with one gun and 250 rifles so as to reach Bagam on the morning of the 21st, and also directed Major Crookenden to arrange to arrive there at the same time. Direct communication between Colonel Cotton and Major Crookenden was established and the two columns met at Bagam on the 21st November. That under Colonel Cotton—consisting of one gun Sierra Leone Battery, two companies (137 rifles) 5th Light Infantry with a machine gun, one company (113 rifles) West African Regiment with a machine gun, a medical detachment and 500 carriers—had encountered only slight opposition, and Major Crookenden's column—composed of one gun 2nd Battery and 250 rifles 3rd Battalion, both of the Nigeria Regiment—no opposition at all.

Advance by the columns under Major Crookenden and Colonel Cotton; 10th November–4th December 1915.

The German troops retired from Bagam towards Fumban, and throughout the 22nd November the combined British column, advancing eastward, was engaged with their rear guard. The Nigerians, who were leading, incurred twelve casualties. Next day, continuing their advance, the British encountered little opposition till the Nun river was reached at a point about twelve miles east of Bagam. At this point the river was deep, unfordable and about three hundred yards wide, and the enemy, who had removed or burnt all the canoes and rafts, was holding a position on the further bank. Colonel Cotton, who had no authority to advance beyond Bagam and was considering whether he ought not to withdraw, now received telegraphic instructions from General

Dobell to advance with Major Crookenden on Fumban. This telegram General Dobell had sent on the 18th November, on learning that it was General Cunliffe's intention to move as soon as possible against the Fumban-Ngambe-Yoko line.

General Cunliffe also had decided on the 18th or 19th November, on receiving reports that a strong enemy force was preparing to oppose Major Crookenden's advance at the Nun river, to assist him by dispatching Major Uniacke with two companies (220 rifles of " H " Company 1st Battalion and " A " Company 2nd Battalion) and four machine guns to advance on Fumban via Gorori and threaten the rear of the enemy holding the Nun river position. Major Uniacke left Banyo on the 20th November and passed through Gorori on the 25th/26th. No news of his coming, however, reached Major Crookenden, as for some time past enemy agents and especially German missionaries at Kumbo had been stopping communications passing between General Cunliffe and Major Crookenden.

Colonel Cotton and Major Crookenden spent the 24th November in fruitless efforts to discover a way of crossing the Nun river, which in this area was bounded on both sides by extensive swamps. In the evening it was decided that Major Crookenden with his Nigerians should march northward and, crossing the river higher up, turn the enemy's position by coming in on his rear. This movement would entail a march of about 120 miles and, during the six days it would take to carry out, Colonel Cotton was to occupy the enemy's attention and get rafts made ready to cross the river. Major Crookenden started off northward at an early hour on the 25th.

Late on the 26th, however, there arrived an envoy from the Chief of Fumban, who urged Colonel Cotton to advance immediately on Fumban. The Germans were said to be evacuating the place and would, it was feared, hang the Chief before doing so, as they had already hanged some of his head men. The envoy informed Colonel Cotton that the Germans were not watching the river crossing at Bangetabe, which was about five miles upstream, and also gave assurances that ample supplies would be provided at Fumban for the British troops. Colonel Cotton thereupon agreed to cross at Bangetabe, but considered it unnecessary to attempt to recall Major Crookenden, as this change of plan, if successful, would only mean an earlier junction with him.

An advanced party left that night for Bangetabe, followed at 4 a.m. on the 27th November by the remainder of the column, less a small detachment left to occupy the enemy's attention and to receive an expected supply convoy. The march of about five miles took over seven hours to complete, the route lying entirely through marshes or along swampy forest paths, where waist-deep mud holes abounded and where, while it was dark, the dense undergrowth and low overhanging branches contributed to the difficulties of progress. To the officers and men of the 5th Light Infantry, the way in which the gun carriers from Sierra Leone managed to transport their loads through or past this continuous series of formidable obstacles was a source of astonishment and admiration. At the crossing place, which the main body reached just before midday, the one dry spot in a huge expanse of swamp was a small hill with a beach below it; and here the force was able to bivouac with some degree of comfort.

An officer and a few men of the advanced party (West African Regiment), which had arrived an hour or so previously, had already crossed on the only two available rafts, but the Fumban envoy arrived shortly with about a dozen more of these rafts. They were of most primitive construction, being formed solely of numerous layers of palm branches tied together with fibre or strips of cane,* and the best of them could only carry three armed and equipped men. The landing-place on the opposite bank was a mile and a half upstream and, on disembarking, men had to slip off the raft, selecting a practicable depth of water, and wade through a swamp to reach dry land. The passage to and fro took the best part of three hours, while the thick mist, which invariably set in at sunset, and the nature of the crossing made it impracticable to use it after dark.† It was consequently not till the evening of the 29th November that the troops, with their gun, machine guns, ammunition, and some supplies, had crossed, leaving most of the carriers to follow next day. *Crossing of the Nun river; 27th–29th November 1915.*

In the meantime, after driving back a small enemy party and repairing the damaged bridge, Major Crookenden had crossed the river at a point about sixteen miles above Bange-tabe on the 28th November and had also sent information of

---

* i.e., the local " tie-tie."
† In " From a Diary in the Cameroons " (*Cornhill Magazine*, October 1919) Major C. S. Stooks (5th L.I.) gives an interesting description of this crossing and says that a British N.C.O. of the West African Regiment, who crossed late one day, spent the night on his half-submerged raft, surrounded by bellowing hippos, owing to the failure of his boatmen to find the landing-place.

his movements to a British detachment which he learnt w
at Kumbo. On the 29th he advanced southward on the ea
side of the river and camped for the night within about a
hour's march of Jitabo, where messengers sent by the Fumba
envoy informed him that Colonel Cotton was encamped.

The two columns joined hands next day (30th) and it wa
arranged that Colonel Cotton should march direct on Fumbar
while Major Crookenden, continuing southward, attacked th
enemy guarding the main crossing before advancing on Kuti
That evening Major Crookenden, whose men had covered
125 miles in the past six days, encountered the enemy—
estimated at 200 strong with two machine guns—near Bangum
Fighting continued on that and the next day, the enemy
finally retiring during the night of the 1st/2nd December
having incurred several casualties including two men captured
The British had three men wounded. Continuing his advance
on Kuti, via Kuka, Major Crookenden encountered the enemy
again on the 3rd December and drove him back with some
loss at the cost of three British casualties. The enemy
(reported to consist of Adametz and Sommerfeld's companies,

Occupation of Kuti; 4th December 1915. of an estimated strength of 200 rifles with two or three machine guns) retired southward without further fighting from Kuti, which Major Crookenden occupied on the 4th. One of these German companies, it was said, had retired in front of the British from Kentu and Bamenda, and the other from Mbo and Chang.

Occupation of Fumban; 2nd December, 1915. Colonel Cotton, meanwhile, had occupied Fumban practically without opposition on the 2nd December, being joined there the same day by Major Uniacke's column which had also experienced very slight opposition.

The last of the enemy troops were said to have left Fumban for Kuti on the previous day, but, shortly after Colonel Cotton's arrival, the Chief received two messages in succession, announcing the arrival that day of a German, and Major Uniacke's, column respectively. Colonel Cotton at once moved out to meet the German column, which was seen from the outskirts of the town marching in from a north-westerly direction; but the attempt made to surprise it was unsuccessful and the enemy made good his escape, losing in his retirement four prisoners and some rifles, ammunition, and equipment.

Next day, news being received that there was a small German post a few miles north of Fumban, Captain H. J. Minniken was sent out with thirty rifles West Africa Regiment to attempt to surprise and capture it. This he did successfully, killing or capturing the two Germans and twelve native rifles of which it was composed, without loss to his own force.

Fumban, the capital of Bamum, was a large walled native city, whose outer ring of high mound and deep ditch enclosed several square miles of territory. Its occupation not only deprived the Germans of one of the few native centres remaining in their hands but brought us the active co-operation of its ruler, an enlightened and influential Chief.

From Banyo, General Cunliffe had sent Major Porter forward on the 8th November, with his mounted infantry company (less a section), one gun of the 2nd Battery, and one and a half infantry companies (B/1st Battalion and half G/2nd Battalion), with instructions to occupy Gorori. This place he reached without opposition on the 12th, a small hostile force on the opposite bank of the unfordable river there retiring southward a day or so later. Meanwhile another company (C/1st Battalion) had joined Major Porter at Gorori, where an advanced supply depot was formed.* In addition to reconnoitring and gaining information concerning the enemy Major Porter had also been instructed to occupy Ngambe, if possible. Having effected a crossing of the river, he accordingly advanced with the bulk of his column on the 15th November and, meeting with no opposition, occupied first Bandam and then Bamkin. Here he received a message, dispatched on the 13th by General Cunliffe from Banyo, informing him that another company (D/3rd Battalion) was being sent to reinforce him, that the bulk of the enemy's force was reported to have retired towards Ngambe and Yoko, and that Major Crookenden had been directed to advance on Fumban as soon as he was in a position to do so. The reported concentration of enemy troops to the south of Bamkin and the Mbam river, Major Porter was told, rendered it inadvisable for him to advance south of that river for the time being; but he was to endeavour to seize a crossing over it and, forming a bridgehead, collect canoes and boats and construct a bridge there.

Proceeding to carry out these instructions, Major Porter remained at Bamkin for the next week and while there received orders to detach a small party to Kumbo to bring in the German missionaries who had been stopping the British messengers. This detachment, composed of two sections of

_{Advance of General Cunliffe's main column; 8th–19th November 1915.}

---

* Within the next ten days six weeks' supplies for General Cunliffe's force were collected here.

mounted infantry and one section "D" Company 3rd Battalion, under Captain H. H. A. Cooke, reached Kumbo on the 23rd November, foiling an attempt by the missionaries * there to lead them into an ambush of German troops.

Major Porter's troops now found that the nature of the country was changing. Though still hilly or mountainous it was no longer open; the area round Bandam and Bamkin was covered with numerous groves of enormous trees; and south of the Mbam river there were large areas of dense tropical forest of the type which the troops under Generals Dobell and Aymerich knew so well.

Colonel Brisset to advance on Yoko; 17th November 1915. At a conference between General Cunliffe and Colonel Brisset, held on the 17th November near Banyo, it was arranged that Colonel Brisset should advance on Yoko from Tibati on the 23rd. He had recently been reinforced by the 95 mm. gun and Captain Popp's company from Mora, and it was agreed that the two Nigerian companies under Colonel Webb-Bowen should be withdrawn from Tibati to join General Cunliffe at Banyo.

General Cunliffe's main column; 19th November–4th December 1915. On the 19th November General Cunliffe gave Major Porter permission to use his discretion in advancing beyond the Mbam river, subject to consideration of the following points:—

(a) Ngambe was General Cunliffe's immediate objective and the earlier it was occupied the better;

(b) a bold offensive and its occupation were both calculated to affect the enemy's *moral*;

(c) its occupation would also help Major Crookenden, to assist whom two companies under Major Uniacke had been detached; but

(d) we could not afford a serious setback.

Effecting a crossing of the Mbam river on the 24th November, Major Porter, with a portion of his force, occupied the enemy position at Bumbo after slight opposition, Captain C. P. L. Marwood being unfortunately killed during the operation by a shot from an enemy sniper.

It is noteworthy that, after the capture of Banyo mountain, General Cunliffe found it increasingly difficult to gain reliable information concerning the enemy. Hitherto that gained by his Intelligence Officer, Captain E. A. Brackenbury, had been both adequate and accurate; but from now on, his agents, who seem for the most part to have been Mahomedans, were

---

* Captured documents indicated that some of the German missionaries were serving with forces in the field and that others were assisting the operations.

evidently unable to gain information in the Pagan area his columns were traversing. For instance, persistent reports from native sources imputed to the Germans, quite incorrectly as it turned out, the intention of concentrating a large force to hold a formidable position in the Ngute district about two days' march south-eastward of Ditam. This position, in which there were numerous subterranean passages and caves from which it was said to be impossible to dislodge an enemy, was famous as having formerly been the scene of two years' resistance by the Pagans in the area against all German attacks.

General Cunliffe, with his headquarters and the bulk of the troops remaining at Banyo, advanced towards Gorori from there on the 26th November. On that date the dispositions of his force, excluding the columns under Major Crookenden and Colonel Brisset, were as follows :—

Moving from Kentu to Bamenda	Two half-companies (C and E/2nd Battalion) under Captain Parr ;
Kumbo..	Two sections of mounted infantry and one section " D " Company 3rd Battalion, under Captain Cooke ;
Gorori	One section " D " Company 3rd Battalion ;
Bandam and Bamkin..	" D " Company 3rd Battalion, less two sections ;
Bumbo	Two sections of mounted infantry, two guns, and two and a half companies (B and C/1st Battalion and half G/2nd Battalion) under Major Porter ;
Between Banyo and Gorori	One gun and two and a half companies (B and H/2nd Battalion and half B/3rd Battalion), forming a reserve under General Cunliffe's personal command ;
Banyo and line of communication	" H " Company 3rd Battalion.

The movements of the various portions of his force between the 27th November and the 4th December were as follows :—

Captain Cooke at Kumbo was only waiting to give his horses the rest they required before joining Major Crookenden, with whom communication was established on the 29th November.

Major Porter, in face of continuous delaying tactics by small enemy parties in dense forest country, occupied Ngambe on the 4th December at the cost of only a few casualties.

General Cunliffe with his reserve established his headquarters on the 30th November at Gorori, whence on the

2nd December he detached Captain C. R. Hetley with a gun and half " B " Company 3rd Battalion to reinforce Major Uniacke.

<small>Colonel Brisset occupies Yoko ; 1st December 1915.</small> Colonel Brisset occupied Yoko without opposition on the 1st December and was joined there next day by the company he had detached to maintain touch with General Aymerich's force.

Thus by the 4th December General Cunliffe had made good the line Kuti-Fumban-Ngambe-Yoko.

<small>Mora ; October–November 1915.</small> Though Raben was wounded during a reconnaissance on the 30th September, the German force at Mora continued throughout October and November to show great enterprise in raids and demonstrations, undertaken, generally successfully, to obtain supplies. It appears from Raben's diary that by the 1st December they had in this way collected sufficient food to last them till the beginning of March 1916.

During the night 8th/9th October they gained a footing on the Gauala ridge, which they maintained against all the Allied efforts to dislodge them till the 6th December.

<small>General Dobell at Duala ; 7th December 1915.</small> At Duala the general situation appeared to General Dobell on the 7th December to be as follows. He had no up-to-date news of General Aymerich's advance, and he realised that the converging French movement on Ebolowa was making no progress. On the other hand, a report that the enemy had evacuated Bana and the probability that Fumban would soon fall into our hands * indicated the clearance of one of the main German concentration areas, while General Cunliffe's advance to the Ngambe-Yoko line was evidently clearing a further large area. Information of General Cunliffe's progress was still taking nearly a fortnight to reach General Dobell, but he hoped by the transfer to Nkongsamba and beyond of the wireless sets from the forest area, where they had proved of little use, to be soon receiving this information more rapidly.

For some time past there had been no signs of the enemy anywhere in the neighbourhood of Dibombe post ; and nothing but small enemy parties—and those only occasionally—had been encountered by vessels patrolling the various waterways or had been seen on the beaches by the ships of the blockading squadron.

---

* He heard next day of its capture.

It seemed evident that enemy columns from all directions were gradually withdrawing in the Yaunde direction and, as the result of fresh information received that day, General Dobell caused the following telegram to be sent on the 7th December to Colonel Gorges.

" We have received reliable information which points to the fact that the force facing you will retire on Yaunde, while that in front of the French will withdraw to Ebolowa when followed up, and one thousand may be concentrated there. Yaunde or its immediate vicinity is strongly fortified and our two guns taken at Nsanakang are there * and fire crude ammunition. It is estimated that, when all detachments are driven in, over two thousand men may be concentrated at Yaunde, but this cannot take place for some little time. The Germans have not more than three hundred Europeans fighting, but there are some two hundred non-combatants in Yaunde. We understand that the French intend to halt at Mangeles for about ten days, when they reach that place, to form a supply depot. In these circumstances and considering that the time factor is all-important, the G.O.C. has decided that the force under you should push through to Yaunde and be, for the time, independent of the French. We are prepared to place two companies Sierra Leone Battalion at your disposal practically at once and every endeavour will be made to keep your force supplied in as great detail as circumstances permit. If the country round Yaunde is as open as is reported, the maximum of artillery should be brought up and we advise your calling up section now here. Our position slightly eased as the French are sending immediately reinforcements from Dakar to Campo."

General Dobell had in fact decided on an important change in his original plan; and to make the situation clear a brief explanation of, or comment on, some of the points referred to in the above telegram seems necessary. The reader must, however, bear in mind that they are given in the light and knowledge of subsequent events. The estimate of the German numbers was undoubtedly too low, but their intention to concentrate the bulk of their force at Yaunde is believed to be correct. We know now that at this period the Germans generally had become so disheartened that they were beginning

---

* General Dobell was not then aware that the Germans had only retrieved one of our guns at Nsanakang.

to consider the question of evacuating the whole country, though information we subsequently obtained indicates that they came to no definite decision till eight days later. General Dobell, however, had reason from information received to believe that Ebermaier—a man of strong character and the soul of the German defence—had no intention of trying to leave the country but meant to stand and fight at Yaunde as long as possible. In this belief, and influenced also by the fact that the mind of the native does not understand the meaning nor necessity of delay, General Dobell considered it essential to close on Yaunde before the enemy could complete his concentration there, while his order to Colonel Gorges to advance independently of the French was in accordance with recommendations that officer had recently made, at least twice, to be allowed to do so. It was unlikely that Colonel Faucon's column would reach Mangeles for several days, and until General Dobell could see then how the situation had developed he could form no definite plan for future French action. He hoped, however, that, on reaching Mangeles, the French would be able to make use of the light railway from Eseka and so gain a wider radius of action. In directing Colonel Gorges to use the maximum of artillery in the final stages of his advance, General Dobell had in mind that hitherto on so few occasions had the country permitted of the use of guns that Colonel Gorges had left at Duala a section previously placed at his disposal.

It was noticeable at this period that all ranks of General Dobell's force were enjoying much better health.

Advance of Colonel Gorges' column. Preparatory to continuing his advance on the 7th December, Colonel Gorges' column was disposed as follows :—

Right flank detachment, under Lieut.-Colonel Haywood, about Kolo. } One gun Nigerian Battery, 2nd Nigerians (less one company).

Main column, under Colonel Gorges, at Ngung. {
Howitzer detachment.
Section Gold Coast Battery.
One gun Nigerian Battery.
Detachment 36th (S.L.) Company, R.E.
One machine gun West India Regiment.
1st Nigerians.
One company 2nd Nigerians.
Field Telephone Detachment.

Left flank detachment, under Captain J. H. Butler, at Ssongmaal. } One machine gun West India Regiment. Two companies Gold Coast Battalion.

The following movements were carried out on the 7th. **7th December 1915.** The right flank detachment advanced about 4½ miles along the carrier road to Nkod, encountering continuous and at times stubborn opposition from a small enemy party in the densely covered hills. The British casualties were six, including Sergeants F. Kennedy and C. Flanagan wounded.

The main column remained at Ngung. Its advanced detachment of two companies with one gun, after driving the enemy out of a position about a mile to the east of Ngung, was checked another mile further on where the enemy took up a second position on the eastern side of a deep and thickly wooded ravine. In this fighting the 1st Nigerians incurred two casualties.

On the left flank Captain Butler, meeting with no opposition, advanced about eight miles to the vicinity of Bongbe.

General Dobell's telegraphic instructions of the 7th December **8th December 1915.** directing Colonel Gorges to advance on Yaunde independently of the French reached that officer on the 8th.

That day Colonel Haywood's right flank detachment encountered continuous opposition, which increased in stubbornness and strength as the day went on and as the mountainous country became more difficult. Late in the afternoon Colonel Haywood arrived in front of an entrenched position, on the lower slopes of the Belok Nkonjok mountain, which the enemy appeared to be holding in some strength. This position Colonel Haywood proceeded to reconnoitre preparatory to attacking it next morning. His casualties during the day totalled three.

The advanced detachment of the main column, being reinforced, drove the enemy out of his previous day's position by a turning movement, and, advancing, took up a position for the night some four and a half miles east of Ngung, covering the camp, about one and a half miles in rear, to which the main column advanced during the day.

The left flank detachment remained in its forward situation in the vicinity of Bongbe, Captain Butler receiving instructions from Colonel Gorges to reconnoitre all pathways to the south and south-eastward with a view to selecting a position, parallel to the main road, which would both cover his own line of retirement and threaten that of the enemy.

At daybreak on the 9th December, Colonel Haywood, on **9th December 1915.** the right flank, launched his attack up the steep precipitous slopes of the Belok Nkonjok mountain. From trenches and rifle pits, constructed behind cleared fields of fire at every point of vantage, the enemy contested the British advance stubbornly. The British gun fire, directed by the battery commander (Captain R. J. R. Waller) from the infantry firing line, was, however, most effective; and though progress was slow, the summit was attained by evening, the enemy, about 100 strong with two machine guns, having been ejected from four successive positions and numerous rifle pits. The British casualties were only six, including Lieutenant D. M. Crowe wounded, their fewness being apparently largely due to the enemy's inferior ammunition and to the effect of the British gun fire.

On the main road the advanced detachment of two companies with a gun was engaged all day in unsuccessful efforts to drive the enemy out of his position covering the crossing of the Manjei river, an attempt to turn its flank having to be abandoned owing to the approach of night. In this engagement the 1st Nigerians incurred seventeen casualties, including Sergeant R. Macleod wounded.

Captain Butler moved southward from Bongbe with his left flank detachment and heard during the day that the main column was checked to the west of the Manjei river. He encountered no opposition, but the bad roads and the numerous bush paths to be reconnoitred so delayed his progress that he was quite unable to reach the vicinity of the main road before dark. The villages were all deserted and this made it impossible to obtain any local assistance or guidance.

10th December 1915. Next day (10th), in anticipation of instructions which Colonel Gorges sent him that morning but which he did not receive for some time, Captain Butler continued his southward movement so as to attack the rear of the German troops holding the Manjei river crossing. This he did most successfully. Striking the main road, he took by surprise an enemy camp at Sege, where the Germans had collected a large number of carriers and of natives whom they had driven in from the surrounding country. These scattered in all directions, adding to the enemy's confusion; and the camp was captured. Captain Butler gained possession of an enemy machine gun, about 4,000 rounds of ammunition, some rifles, stores, a quantity of food and some useful documents. Having thus interposed his detachment between the enemy's first line and his reserves, Captain Butler took up a position overlooking the main road. Here he was attacked by German troops from both east and west, but was never seriously pressed, owing, it is understood, to the demoralisation which his sudden and unexpected appearance had caused among the enemy's native soldiers. This operation, in which the British only lost four casualties, cleared the way for the advance of the main column, whose advanced detachment (two companies with a gun under Colonel Cockburn) suffered, as it was, fifteen casualties in driving the enemy out of two successive positions astride the main road.

In the meantime on the right flank Colonel Haywood had encountered strong opposition. For the first mile of his advance on the 10th he experienced little difficulty, as the enemy was in no strength. Subsequently, however, about forty German troops with a machine gun held up his advance till a British shell struck the hostile machine gun emplacement. The enemy then withdrew to a second position about a mile in rear, and here at dusk he was still maintaining a stubborn resistance. The British had incurred four casualties, including Lieutenant B. T. B. Dillon wounded.

Colonel Haywood, by a turning movement on the morning of the 11th December, forced the enemy to evacuate his position, but found himself then faced by such broken and densely wooded country that it was impossible to continue his advance immediately.

11th December 1915.

The main column advanced that day without opposition to Njuge. Here it effected a junction with Captain Butler's left flank detachment and was joined by the Gambia Company, which had been relieved on the line of communications by troops from Duala.

On the 12th December the main column, covered by an advanced detachment under Major Coles—one company 1st Nigerians, the Gambia Company, a Gold Coast gun and a detachment R.E.—reached Ndog. This advanced detachment was engaged for most of the day with a weak enemy force, which was driven from several successive positions to one to the east of Ndog where it was still holding on at nightfall. The British incurred twelve casualties—eleven, including Lieutenant A. E. Coombs, being in the Gambia Company. The country traversed was very difficult and the Royal Engineers had to rebuild or repair a number of bridges for the howitzer.

12th December 1915.

The left flank detachment under Captain Butler had kept pace with the main column, moving along pathways parallel to the main road and co-operating with the advanced detachment whenever opportunity occurred.

On the right flank, Colonel Haywood, meeting with but little opposition, advanced for a few miles.

It is worthy of note that, by this time, the casualties among the British personnel had so mounted up that most of Colonel Gorges' machine guns were now in charge of African non-commissioned officers.

13th–15th December 1915. The main column advanced about two and a half miles on each of the next three days, its progress being more hampered by difficult country and broken bridges than by enemy resistance. It had no fighting at all on the 13th December; on the 14th it encountered some opposition and incurred three casualties, including Sergeant S. F. Elliot wounded; and on the 15th, suffering four casualties, it drove the enemy back to the Kele river crossing.

Captain Butler's left flank detachment, which encountered little or no opposition, was obliged on the 14th, by the absence of paths, to join the main column on the main road.

On the right flank a succession of densely wooded ridges and valleys favoured the enemy's tactics and enabled a comparatively small force to check Colonel Haywood's advance on the 13th December at the Buba river and to inflict three casualties on the British force. Next day, by a turning movement and with effective assistance from his gun, Colonel Haywood took this position without loss and in spite of the enemy's attempts to retain it. On the 15th Colonel Haywood carried the crossing of the carrier road over the Kele river by a dash which put the enemy to flight and cost only one casualty.

16th December 1915. Pushing forward an advanced detachment under Colonel Cockburn to force the crossing of the Kele river and detaching a Gold Coast company under Captain Butler to the left to endeavour to find a parallel path which would enable him to outflank the enemy near Chang Mangas, Colonel Gorges, with the main column, remained halted on the 16th December. Colonel Cockburn, after overcoming slight opposition, carried the Kele river crossing and occupied a position about half a mile beyond.

On the right flank an enemy force of about fifty rifles with a machine gun at first offered stubborn opposition to Colonel Haywood's advance. But a succession of successful charges up the road by small groups of the British advanced guard so demoralised the enemy that his opposition almost ceased, enabling Colonel Haywood, after an advance during the day of four and a half miles, to occupy Matip Matips at a cost of

OCCUPATION OF CHANG MANGAS

only two casualties. Colonel Haywood's camp that night was at a point about 2,600 feet above sea level.

The nature of the country was now beginning to change for the better. There were considerable clearings in the forest, with more villages and cultivation and a number of banana plantations.

A letter captured at this period, which one of the German company commanders (Engelbrechten) had written from the hospital where he was sick to his subaltern, gave some useful information. It showed that the loss of their Puge river position had been a grave blow to the Germans, that their ammunition shortage was serious, and that a considerable proportion of their German ranks were sick in hospital.

At midday on the 17th December, Colonel Haywood's right flank detachment struck the main road about a mile to the east of Chang Mangas, practically without opposition, and the main column marched into that place unopposed. On the left flank, Captain Butler's detachment, cutting its way through the forest, advanced to Konalak, four and a half miles north of Chang Mangas. To the British it appeared that in the more open country during the last few days, both on the main road and on the right flank, their gun fire had been more effective and, exercising a demoralising effect on the Germans, had been largely responsible for their increasing disinclination to stand. *17th December 1915. Occupation of Chang Mangas.*

That evening a supply convoy, following Colonel Haywood along the carrier road, was attacked near Matip Matips by an enemy party of about forty rifles and lost four carriers wounded. But the escort of a half-company 2nd Nigerians drove the attackers off successfully.

Colonel Gorges now decided to halt for a few days to prepare for the final stage of his advance. Though his force, in the almost continuous fighting of the past eleven days, had sustained a total of only eighty-six battle casualties, including seven British, the country traversed had been very difficult and the calls on all ranks had been of a heavy and arduous nature. Troops and carriers all required a rest and Colonel Gorges had also to await the arrival of ammunition and supplies to form an advanced base. *Halt at Chang Mangas; 18th–22nd December 1915.*

Between the 18th and 22nd December reconnaissances were pushed out in all directions to clear the British front and flanks. Some opposition was encountered on the main road, but the enemy invariably retired as soon as his flanks were threatened, and British patrols reached a point within seventeen miles of Yaunde. At Chang Mangas itself a fort and blockhouses were constructed, in addition to stores, magazines and a clearing hospital.

The arrival of additional troops from Duala allowed of the reinforcement of the main column from the line of communication; and by the 22nd December Colonel Gorges' force was reorganised as follows :—

Main Column	Howitzer Detachment R.A. Nigerian Battery (less one gun). Section, Gold Coast Battery. Detachment 36th (Sierra Leone) Company, R.E. Machine gun section, West India Regiment. 1st Nigerians (four companies). 2nd Nigerians (four companies). Gold Coast Bn. (five companies). Gambia Company.
Line of Communication	No. 1 (Edea-Ngung) Section.—Five companies Sierra Leone Battalion. No. 2 (Sogsunge-Chang Mangas) Section.—One gun Nigerian Battery, two companies West India Regiment.

It was significant that the local natives in large numbers were now returning to their deserted villages. They appeared to welcome the British advent and many of them volunteered to act as guides and scouts, thus contributing considerably to the security of the line of communication. A certain amount of local supplies also now became obtainable.

French advance to Mangeles; 7th–21st December 1915. Lieutenant-Colonel Faucon's French column, advancing along the light railway line, crossed the Mpobe river on the 7th December and took Badog. Thenceforward it encountered stubborn opposition by an enemy force, which was apparently more determined to stop or delay the French advance than the force opposing Colonel Gorges. Whether Colonel Faucon was actually opposed by larger numbers * than Colonel Gorges is unknown, but it is easy now, in the light of subsequent events, to see that the Germans had every reason for doing their utmost to check the French advance.

---

* The reports that a considerable part of the force opposing Colonel Cockburn near Lesogs at the end of November had retired towards Mangeles were proved subsequently to be incorrect, as out of three groups involved two were afterwards encountered by the British on the Yaunde road. On the other hand, it is, of course, possible that other enemy parties reinforced the Germans fighting astride the light railway.

CAMPO–AMBAM AREA

On the 14th December Colonel Faucon forced the crossing of the Great Malume river and on the 21st he occupied Mangeles. In the continuous fighting of the past fifteen days the French had incurred a total of 175 casualties, of whom fifteen were Frenchmen. Moreover, since leaving Eseka on the 24th November 19 French and 72 Senegalese combatants, as well as 500 native carriers, had been evacuated as sick.

At Mangeles Colonel Faucon halted awhile to bring up supplies and to form an advanced base. The Midland Railway was now open for through traffic from Duala to Eseka, and on the 10th December the French captured a considerable amount of rolling stock and two engines for the light railway.

A reinforcement of two Senegalese companies (Captain Martin) from Dakar arrived at Campo on the 12th December and, proceeding to join Captain Blum, brought the total strength of the French force in the Campo area up to four companies. This increase enabled General Dobell to withdraw the company of the Sierra Leone Battalion to Duala,* thus leaving the operations in the Campo area entirely to the French, supported by the British naval posts at Campo † and Dipikar. ‡ *French advance on Ebolowa; December 1915. (Map 13.)*

The French force under Captain Martin started to advance on the 23rd December from Akak towards Njabesan, but the opposition it encountered limited its progress to an advance of two and a half miles only by the end of the month.

In the meantime, Lieutenant-Colonel Le Meillour with his South Cameroons Force had finally succeeded on the 20th December in forcing the passage of the Ntem river. He then pushed on against Ambam, which he captured on the 31st December, after overcoming obstinate enemy opposition in a series of strongly fortified positions. From Ambam, part of the enemy force retired on Ebolowa and part to the westward towards Ngoa.

After capturing Lembe General Aymerich halted there for several days, to make sure that his communications in rear were secure, before resuming his advance. On the 17th *Franco-Belgian East Cameroons Force; December 1915.*

---

* General Dobell required troops to reinforce Colonel Gorges.
† Captain Tootell, R.M.L.I., 2 seamen, 34 R.M.L.I., 15 levies, 2 machine guns.
‡ Lieutenant Thompson, R.N., 2 seamen, 16 R.M.L.I., 21 levies, one 7-pdr., one machine gun : this contingent provided a post of five men at Bongola.

December, while still at Lembe, he heard of the occupation by General Cunliffe's force of Yoko and Ngambe. General Aymerich's force was then disposed as follows :—

Captain Staup's detachment	At Mole to the north, maintaining touch with Colonel Brisset.
Right Column (Colonel Morisson)	Northern group (340 rifles) ten miles west of Tabene, southern group (600 rifles) just west of Lembe.
Left Column (Lieut.-Colonel Hutin)	Striking force (500 rifles and two guns) at Lembe. Remainder (600 rifles and three guns) L. of C., Abong Mbang and Dume.

General Aymerich decided to move the southern group of his Right Column westward so as to get into closer touch with the northern group, and to advance with his Left Column southward from Lembe to clear up the situation on the Akonolinga road. These movements started on the 18th December but did not progress according to plan. Strong enemy opposition encountered a few miles to the south-westward of Lembe called for the combined efforts of the southern group of the Right Column and of the Left Column. Neither was able to make much progress till the 28th December, and then the enemy retired so rapidly that by the next day all contact with him had been lost.

General Cunliffe's operations, Northern Cameroons; 4th–23rd December 1915.

General Cunliffe's force was disposed as follows on the 4th December :—

Kuti	Two guns and about 350 rifles, under Major Crookenden.
Bamenda	200 rifles, under Captain Parr.
L. of C. and Ossidinge	135 rifles.
Fumban	One gun and 250 rifles under Lieut.-Colonel Cotton; about 200 rifles under Major Uniacke.
En route to Fumban	Two sections of mounted infantry under Captain Cooke. One gun and half a company of infantry under Captain Hetley.
Ngambe	Two guns, half the mounted infantry company and rather under 300 rifles under Major Porter.
Yoko	Three guns (one heavy), a cavalry detachment and four companies, all French, under Colonel Brisset.

CUNLIFFE'S OPERATIONS

Gorori	General Cunliffe with his headquarters and general reserve of two companies.
L. of C. to Banyo	Two infantry companies.

Before commencing what would probably be his final advance on the Nachtigal Rapids, General Cunliffe had to make good Ditam and deal with the enemy force reported to be concentrating in the Ngute position which was close to Linte. If the enemy did not stand and fight at Ngute—as he was reported to intend doing—he would probably, it was thought, retire slowly on Yaunde.

Colonel Cotton's force had no orders from General Dobell to proceed further than Fumban and here it remained when Major Uniacke, under instructions from General Cunliffe, moved to Ngambe.

From Kuti, Major Crookenden, who had lost touch with the enemy, received false information and pursued, between the 7th and 11th December, for fifty miles in a wrong direction. It was consequently not till the 14th that he set out with his column for Ditam.

At Ngambe, Major Porter found his advance to the south blocked by the broad unfordable Kim river, the enemy, who was entrenched on the further bank, having destroyed the bridge and all the available boats and canoes. It was not till the 11th December that the new canoes, which Major Porter caused to be made, enabled him to cross the river and drive the enemy back by a skilfully executed turning movement. That day also General Cunliffe, with his general reserve, arrived at Ngambe.

On the 13th December General Cunliffe sent forward Colonel Webb-Bowen with a gun and three companies to occupy Linte and reconnoitre the reported enemy position at Ngute; and on the 15th Major C. C. West with one gun and 250 rifles was dispatched to march on Ditam.

Advancing southward from Ngambe Colonel Webb-Bowen soon entered country which was open, and on the 18th, after overcoming only slight opposition, captured Linte * and found the Ngute mountain position to be unoccupied.

On the 18th December also, Major West captured Ditam,

---

* The moral superiority attained by the British over the Germans was well illustrated during this advance by the unhesitating way in which, on one occasion, a detached party of a Nigerian corporal (" C " Company 1st Battalion) with ten rifles attacked a detachment of about forty German troops in a position, and after two hours' fighting put them to flight and pursued them for some miles.

practically without opposition, and was joined there on the 23rd by Major Crookenden, whose march had been delayed by difficulty in crossing the Mbam river.

The enemy's growing demoralisation at this period was evidenced by the increasing number of deserters among German native soldiers operating in the area south of Bamenda and Fumban, and by the greater readiness of the local inhabitants to assist the British. It was still difficult, however, to obtain reliable information of the movements of the retiring enemy.

Duala; 8th–21st December 1915. At Duala, General Dobell issued orders, on the 10th December, for a force to be despatched from Nkongsamba to Bana—which the Germans were recently reported to have evacuated—for the withdrawal of the British posts at Sanchu and Mbo and for the transference of the line of communication with Chang to the main, and shorter, road. The report of the evacuation of Bana was confirmed two days later, and a company of the West African Regiment occupied that place on the 16th December, reporting that the enemy had left it three weeks previously.

Having heard, meanwhile, of the occupation of Yoko by Colonel Brisset and of the generally favourable situation of the Allied forces in the north, General Dobell decided that there was no necessity for Colonel Cotton's column to remain any longer with General Cunliffe. Its withdrawal, now that the Northern Railway and adjacent areas were clear of the enemy, would enable General Dobell to utilise the 5th Light Infantry to garrison Fumban, Bagam, Chang, Bana * and the Northern Railway line and to concentrate the Sierra Leone Battery, R.E. detachment, and the West African Regiment for operations elsewhere. Orders were issued accordingly to Colonel Cotton, who left Fumban on the 21st December.

General Dobell's desire to concentrate a force as a reserve, or for employment elsewhere than in the Northern Railway vicinity, is easily intelligible. To reinforce Colonel Gorges he had already sent every available man from Duala, where he was left with only one company of the Sierra Leone Battalion in addition to details of other units; and he had been obliged to obtain from Captain Fuller the services of a naval detach-

---

* General Dobell hoped to obtain livestock for his force from Fumban and Bana.

[*To face p.* 386

CROSSING THE MBAM RIVER

ment to take over the Dibombe post and to detail men of the locally enlisted civil police to relieve troops in several other posts and guards.

On the 17th December General Dobell paid a visit to Eseka and was much impressed by the good work in repairing the railway, including five large bridges, that had been performed by the French engineers under Captain Chardy. The French had also made most satisfactory arrangements for protecting their line of communication, their defensive posts being constructed with admirable skill.

On the 20th December a telegram from Brazzaville was received at Duala giving General Aymerich's situation as it had been on the 23rd November; and on the same day General Dobell received a message, sent by General Cunliffe on the 16th December,* saying that General Aymerich was at Tabene on the 1st. The absence of more recent information, in view of the fact that Colonel Brisset was in touch with General Aymerich, tended to show that he was only able to make slow progress.

Meanwhile, the naval forces had continued their work of blockade, patrol and reconnaissance. On the 6th November the *Alligator* on the Nyong River engaged the enemy and was sniped near Etima when returning from a patrol to Dehane; she was hit several times but suffered no casualties. On the 1st December small hostile forces were reported to be in the vicinity of Kribi, but landing parties next day found that the enemy had disappeared. On the 5th December the *Rinaldo* and *Margaret Elizabeth* bombarded an enemy party in position at Longyi, after which an attempt was made to carry out a reconnaissance with a Royal Marine detachment. On nearing the beach, however, the boats came under heavy rifle and machine gun fire. One boat was hit, but no casualties occurred. Subsequently, the enemy's position was bombarded with satisfactory results.

On the 1st January 1916, Commander Hughes, on transfer to England, handed over the British command in the Campo district to Lieutenant-Commander Kilgour, R.N.

Naval operations; Nov.–Dec. 1915.

---

* This message was sent to Chang and thence by wireless via Nkongsamba to Duala.

CHAPTER XI

23RD DECEMBER 1915—18TH FEBRUARY 1916

THE CAPTURE OF YAUNDE, THE SUBSEQUENT ABANDONMENT OF THEIR COLONY BY THE GERMANS, AND THE SURRENDER OF MORA

(Maps 2, 12 and 13)

Resumption of Colonel Gorges' advance. For the resumption, on the 23rd December, of the advance from Chang Mangas, Colonel Gorges organised his troops in four columns : a centre column to move along the main road ; right and left flank detachments to advance parallel with it ; and a general reserve to follow the centre column within a day's march. On the arrival—planned to be simultaneous—of the centre, right and left flank columns at Mendong, Fimba and Ade, respectively, their commanders, in communication with one another, were to reconnoitre the enemy's defences, and, reporting the result, were to await Colonel Gorges' orders for the final advance.

By the evening of the 22nd December the different portions of his force were constituted and disposed as follows :—

Right Flank Detachment (Lt.-Colonel Rose)
  One gun Gold Coast Battery
  H.Q. and three companies Gold Coast Battalion
} at Gungok.

Centre Column (Lt.-Colonel Haywood)
  Howitzer detachment, R.A.
  One section Nigerian Battery
  Field Section 36th (Sierra Leone) Company, R.E.
  2nd Nigerians
} just east of Chang Mangas.

Left Flank Detachment (Major F. Anderson)
  Two companies Gold Coast Battalion
} at Konolak.

General Reserve (Colonel Gorges and his headquarters)
  One gun Nigerian Battery
  One gun Gold Coast Battery
  Machine gun section West India Regiment
  1st Nigerians
  Gambia Company
} at Chang Mangas.*

---

* A company and a half of the West India Regiment with a gun of the Nigerian Battery formed the garrison of the advanced base at Chang Mangas.

ADVANCE FROM CHANG MANGAS

Each portion of the force was accompanied by guides and partisans and by medical detachments; and each of the three leading columns took with it six days' supplies. Communication between the centre column and Colonel Gorges' headquarters would be by field telephone, but would have to be maintained with the flank detachments by patrols and partisans.

The enemy's force opposing Colonel Gorges was estimated at about seven companies* under Major Haedicke, and it was anticipated that he would hold the entrenched positions reported as prepared at the following places to the west of Yaunde:—

Opposite the British right: at Tsangmbia and Elumendan.
Opposite the British centre: at Mowonos and the Mopfu river.
Opposite the British left: at Makenge.

Advancing on the 23rd December along a good road through densely wooded hills, Colonel Rose's right flank detachment covered about five miles. His advanced guard was in constant contact with a small hostile force, which it drove slowly backwards without incurring any casualties. *23rd December 1915.*

On the main road, Colonel Haywood, with effective support from his howitzer, drove an enemy force of about a company out of two successive positions and advanced about four miles at the cost of three casualties.

On the left flank Major Anderson's column encountered a strong enemy detachment to the west of Nkoa, and failing to drive it back after several hours' fighting, withdrew in face of a hostile counter-movement. The British casualties had been fourteen, including Lieutenant H. E. Corner wounded, and, in view of the enemy strength, Major Anderson applied to Colonel Gorges for reinforcement by a gun and an infantry company.

The General Reserve made no advance.

Reinforced by a Gold Coast gun and a half-company of the West India Regiment, Major Anderson resumed his advance on the 24th December and occupied Nkoa with the loss of one man wounded. *24th December 1915.*

The centre column encountered opposition from an enemy force—estimated at about a company with three machine guns—which resisted strongly in two successive positions, and

---

* The records do not state where the additional companies were reported to have come from.

which remained in occupation of a third position when the British drew out of action at dusk. Owing to this opposition, in overcoming which his column incurred seven casualties, Colonel Haywood only advanced about two miles during the day. Enemy resistance to the advance of the right flank detachment was also more stubborn than on the 23rd, and Colonel Rose's column sustained four casualties in reaching Njame.

The General Reserve advanced and camped about two miles in rear of the centre column.*

25th December 1915. On the 25th December the right flank detachment, meeting with constant, though not serious, opposition, advanced about two and a half miles to Endugu, suffering four casualties; the centre column moved forward to Nkomenka, losing only one man wounded in spite of a large expenditure of enemy ammunition; and the left flank detachment turned the Germans out of a position, about a mile to the east of Nkoa, at a cost of one man killed.

The General Reserve moved forward to camp about two miles from Nkomenka.

26th December 1915. Considering that his column was getting too far ahead, Colonel Rose halted on the 26th December and limited his operations to reconnaissance, in which one of his patrols lost a man killed. On the main road Colonel Haywood with the centre column advanced two and a half miles to the Ngobo river, and with the effective support of his howitzer, drove the enemy out of his position there. This, thanks to his wild shooting, was effected without British loss. On the left Major Anderson advanced about two miles, also without loss.

27th December 1915. On the 27th December, the right flank detachment, advancing north-eastward and meeting with slight opposition, reached a point about a mile to the south-east of Unguot. Two of its men were wounded.

In the centre column Colonel Cockburn with the 1st Nigerians and the Gambia Company, relieving Colonel Haywood and the 2nd Nigerians, advanced about four miles to Unguot, in face of slight opposition and without loss; while the left flank detachment drove a hostile detachment out of a position on the Ngobo river with the loss of three casualties, and camped that night about four miles west-north-west of Unguot.

During the day a company of the Sierra Leone Battalion

---

* A suggestion in a German message—which was picked up on the main road in the evening—for a cessation of hostilities on Christmas Day was not accepted.

from the line of communication reinforced the General Reserve, which advanced and camped about three miles short of Unguot.

The enemy offered little opposition on the 28th December. The right flank detachment advanced to Tsangmbia, occupying the strong enemy position there without loss; the centre column advanced about a mile with one casualty; and the left flank detachment met with no opposition at all in its advance of about two miles. To this detachment the Sierra Leone company was now sent to relieve the half-company West India Regiment, required to garrison Unguot. *28th December 1915.*

During the day the armoured car—nicknamed Charlie Chaplin—joined Colonel Gorges, having succeeded with some difficulty in negotiating the road from Wum Biagas.

Colonel Rose on the right flank was opposed continuously during the 29th December, having, in his advance of about a mile, to drive the enemy out of a series of villages and natural positions. The British losses, however, were only two men wounded. On the main road Colonel Cockburn's centre column carried a strong enemy position, about four miles east of Unguot, with little difficulty and no loss; and on the left Major Anderson advanced about three miles, reaching a point on the east side of the Nga river in face of some opposition and at the cost of three casualties. *29th December 1915.*

Colonel Rose, delaying his advance on the morning of the 30th in order to gain touch with the centre column, received a message at 11.30 a.m. from Colonel Gorges saying that the centre column had crossed the Mopfu river, that the enemy appeared to be demoralised, and that all columns were to press on vigorously. Colonel Rose thereupon ordered his advanced company to push on towards Mendong. The country proved, however, to be very difficult, and combined with opposition from an enemy detachment of about 80 rifles with a machine gun to make progress slow. By nightfall Colonel Rose had only got as far as the further bank of the Mopfu river, having suffered five casualties; but he hoped to establish himself next day at Mendong. *30th December 1915.*

On the main road the enemy held that morning an extensive and strongly entrenched position on the Mopfu river near Minlo, but was driven out of it by the centre column—supported by effective howitzer fire and assisted by the armoured car—without much difficulty. The enemy's fire was so wild that Colonel Cockburn's force sustained only one casualty.

Major Anderson, on the left flank, crossed the Mopfu river without opposition; and the General Reserve moved forward to Sokwe.

31st December 1915.
On the 31st December, after a sharp engagement in which his column suffered six casualties, Colonel Rose occupied a position at Mendong astride the Yaunde-Kribi road; the centre column, with the loss of one man, occupied Fimba and engaged the enemy to the east of that place in a position which he still held at dusk; and the left flank detachment occupied Etomo without opposition. In gaining these positions the British troops traversed during the day an intricate and elaborate system of unoccupied trenches, which extended for miles, and which must have cost the enemy infinite trouble, considerable time and an immense amount of labour to construct.

Having thus reached a favourable position from which to launch a combined converging attack on Yaunde, Colonel Gorges issued orders for his right, centre and left columns to push forward vigorously next morning, co-operating with one another as far as the country and circumstances permitted.

Colonel Gorges' anticipations and intentions can be gathered from his reply to a message he received that day from Duala, which asked for information regarding the enemy's present or future intentions. General Dobell, seeing that the enemy's resistance to the British advance was lessening daily, said that any information from any source would be valuable as assisting him to formulate his future plans. The scope of his operations in the south would depend, he observed, on the Yaunde situation; and he asked if Ebermaier was in Yaunde, and if the Germans appeared to be making a last stand there.

Colonel Gorges replied that he found it impossible to say what the enemy's intentions might be. Native reports from all sides indicated that if Yaunde fell the German native troops would refuse to go to Ebolowa. Ebermaier and twenty German women were reported as having been in Yaunde four days previously, some of the women having recently, it was said, left Yaunde with a large convoy for Ebolowa so as to escape a British bombardment. This convoy, however, had since apparently halted on the way, owing to a report of a French force near Ebolowa. The above information, continued Colonel Gorges, was corroborated by a native servant, who had run away from the Germans that morning and who also said that the sound of French guns to the east had been heard at Yaunde on the previous day. Colonel Gorges con-

OCCUPATION OF YAUNDE

cluded by saying that there were indications of a final German stand at Yaunde, though it was impossible to say definitely till the inner defences were approached, which he hoped would be done next day.

As a matter of fact Yaunde was occupied without opposition. The centre column, under Colonel Haywood, his 2nd Nigerians having relieved the 1st Nigerians at an early hour, occupied Yaunde fort at 11.30 a.m. on the 1st January; and instructions were then sent to Colonel Rose's column to occupy the Catholic Mission station, which stood on a commanding ridge two miles to the south of the fort covering the roads to Kribi and Widemenge. The arrival of Major Anderson's column in the evening completed the concentration at Yaunde of the whole of Colonel Gorges' force.

Capture of Yaunde; 1st January 1916.

The situation as Colonel Gorges found it was summarised in the following telegram, which he then sent to General Dobell:—

"Enemy appears to have retired by the roads leading south and south-east towards Akonolinga, Widemenge and Ebolowa, and my outposts to-night are being heavily sniped from those roads. Ebermaier is reported to have gone to Widemenge, but reliable information most difficult to obtain. Only two Europeans found in Catholic Mission and a few natives in the hospital, but hope to gather sufficient information to-morrow to enable me to despatch columns to deal with enemy's main force. Meanwhile will patrol in all directions to keep touch with enemy and to join up with French columns reported to be near Sanaga river crossing in the north. The perimeter of Yaunde extends for some four miles, requiring considerable number of troops to garrison the place, but I have plenty of troops to spare for any further operations necessary and food supply is satisfactory. All buildings, stores, hospital, mission station, munition factory and fort found intact, but no supplies of any description. The whole place is like a dead city, with dense forest and bush outside the perimeter. Am of opinion that all non-combatants, Government and considerable number of troops left here some days ago, and that enemy force opposing us was covering the movement."

The Germans had, in fact, carried out their evacuation with complete success, and had also succeeded in keeping all news of their intention from reaching the ears of the British commander.

It appears, from information subsequently obtained, that at the beginning of December Ebermaier, having just finished a round of visits to all the fighting fronts south of the Sanaga river, would have transferred the seat of Government to Ebolowa. But he found his presence at Yaunde necessary to sustain the declining *moral* of the German force—to whom he made a strong appeal to hold out a little longer, as peace in Europe, he said, was imminent. The loss of their Puge river position, however, had greatly shaken German confidence; their shortage of ammunition precluded any idea of attempting a counter-offensive on an adequate scale; on or about the 8th December Haedicke reported his inability to stop for any length of time the British advance on Yaunde; and about the same time there occurred the failure of the *coup* against General Aymerich, from which the Germans had expected so much.

Ebermaier then convened a grand council to consider at Yaunde on the 15th December the alternatives of further resistance with inevitable surrender, or evacuation. Most of the German area commanders appear to have been present at this council, which sat throughout the night of the 15th/16th December and finally decided on the retirement of all troops to an area south of the Nyong river, and on the transfer of the Government to Ebolowa. This transfer was effected by the 25th December, though Ebermaier himself remained at Yaunde till the afternoon of the 30th, when he left with the main body of the rear guard.*

The Germans had thus, it will be seen, allowed themselves ample time, so that nothing that Colonel Gorges' column could have done would have interfered either with their evacuation or their retirement. The British advance had been well carried out, and at no stage had the enemy been able to impose any serious delay on its steady and ordered progress. When the extent and number of the positions prepared over a long period of time by the Germans to contest such an advance are considered, as well as the natural difficulties of the country, it is possible to appreciate the skilful British plans and dispositions, their fine leadership in action

---

* The account in *Der Grosse Krieg, 1914–1918*, in confirming the above information, attributes the decision to retire into neutral territory to lack of ammunition and a desire to avoid the acceptance of humiliating terms. In the severe fighting before the fall of Yaunde the Allies, it says, owed much of their success to their artillery. According to this account the German supply columns had already on the 1st January crossed the Nyong river.

and the gallantry and fortitude displayed by all ranks.* The good progress made through a very difficult country also owed much to the exertions of other portions of the force. Rapid repair or replacement of broken roads and bridges had constantly been necessary, and the work of the Field Section of the 36th (Sierra Leone) Company, R.E., under Lieutenant Banks Keast, had been of great assistance, while another noticeable feature of the march had been the very efficient way in which the administrative services had discharged their duties. The medical duties under Majors T. B. Unwin and E. B. Booth and the supply and transport work under Captain G. F. Hodgson had been admirably conducted, while the almost uninterrupted maintenance of communication throughout attested to the excellence of the work of the field telephone detachment, under Colour-Sergeant W. Linder.

On the 1st January, the main body of the French column under Lieutenant-Colonel Faucon was still at Mangeles, its advanced party having moved out eastward on the 31st December. To the east of Yaunde General Aymerich's main force was in the vicinity of Lembe. In the south of the Cameroons Lieutenant-Colonel Le Meillour was at Ambam in the neighbourhood of the Muni border; and the French column from Campo was close to Akak.† {French and Franco-Belgian columns; situation on 1st January 1916.}

To the north General Cunliffe's force was on the line Ndenge-Ngila, to which, on learning that the Ngute mountain position was unoccupied, he had ordered a general advance. This had been carried out without special incident, and by the 1st January General Cunliffe's whole striking force of about 1,600 rifles with 8 guns was distributed as follows. Colonel Webb-Bowen's column was at Ndenge, with Major West's column close in rear and Major Crookenden's column a few miles to the west; Colonel Brisset's column, in communication with the extreme right of General Aymerich's force, was at Ngila; and General Cunliffe with his reserve was at Mbwa, moving towards Ndenge. His long line of communication back to Nigeria via Gorori and Banyo was held by one mounted infantry and one infantry company. On the 26th December he had sent General Dobell information, which reached Duala {Situation in the north; 1st January 1916.}

---

* The brief account in *Der Grosse Krieg, 1914–18*, of this advance is unfortunately marred by the totally untrue statement that the Allied rank and file were induced to push their attacks by copious gifts of alcohol.

† For details of the Allied forces in the Cameroons on the 1st January, 1916, see Appendix VIII.

on the 29th, that the enemy in considerable numbers had crossed the Mbam river into the Bafia district.

Colonel Cotton, having left detachments of the 5th Light Infantry at Fumban, Bagam and Chang, had reached Nkongsamba on the 30th December, whence another detachment of the 5th Light Infantry was sent to Bana to relieve the company of the West African Regiment there. This regiment was now available for operations elsewhere.

<small>Measures to pursue the enemy; 2nd January 1916.</small> On learning of the enemy retirement from Yaunde, and in the belief that General Aymerich's columns were close at hand, General Dobell telegraphed to Colonel Gorges on the 2nd January proposing that, on General Aymerich's arrival, the British contingent should withdraw to Duala, leaving the Franco-Belgian troops to operate from Yaunde towards Ebolowa, while the British advanced in that direction from Kribi. This plan, which would bring about a converging pursuit of, or attack on, the enemy, appeared to General Dobell to have several advantages. It would avoid the administrative complications of a mixed Allied force; it would leave the supplies in the Yaunde district for General Aymerich's troops; and, besides obviating congestion on the lines of communication and advance, it would shorten the British line. Colonel Gorges, in the meantime, was to abstain from committing his troops to an extent to hinder their withdrawal. In conclusion, General Dobell said that the French, i.e., his own French contingent, would be some time before they were ready, but that the West African Regiment with the Sierra Leone Battery could be sent at once to establish a base at Kribi and to advance from there as far as their strength permitted.

A few hours later General Dobell sent Colonel Gorges another telegram, saying that Colonel Mayer had issued orders for his main column to march from Mangeles on Ebolowa, that its southward advance should commence next day, and that Colonel Gorges was to detail a small column to clear Colonel Faucon's front by moving down the Yaunde-Kribi road. General Dobell went on to inquire if the enemy's retirement on Widemenge had been confirmed, and at the same time signified his agreement with Colonel Gorges that the enemy should be pressed. This agreement, it should be noted, referred evidently to some message or report which cannot be traced in the records, but which apparently reported that, in the absence of any indication that General Aymerich's columns would arrive shortly, Colonel Gorges' troops would have to assume responsibility for commencing the pursuit from Yaunde.

As the result of reconnaissances sent out from Yaunde on the 2nd January and of information from a number of natives who came in from various directions, Colonel Gorges reported that evening to General Dobell that the enemy's retirement on Widemenge was confirmed and that Ebermaier and the British prisoners of war in German hands were reported to be at Nkolalong on the Nyong river. Colonel Gorges recommended that he should send a strong column to Widemenge and another column, after General Aymerich's arrival, by the Kribi road to co-operate with the French from Mangeles. Since the country for about ten miles round Yaunde was deserted except for natives dying of starvation, Colonel Gorges could not procure carriers locally to bring from Eseka the supplies there awaiting General Aymerich, part of whose force was reported by Hausa traders to be advancing from Akonolinga. Colonel Gorges said that he had sent letters to General Aymerich and to the French commander at Akonolinga acquainting them with the situation, and had just heard that some of General Cunliffe's troops were south of the Sanaga river. He concluded his report by saying that, pending instructions, he was pushing out strong reconnaissances to keep touch with the enemy, with whom he had established contact that day on the Widemenge and Kribi roads.*

General Dobell replied on the 3rd January, approving the despatch of a strong column to Widemenge and intimating that, pending General Aymerich's arrival, demonstrations along the Kribi road would assist Colonel Mayer. The Widemenge column might be required, said General Dobell, to co-operate towards Ebolowa, but should not overlook the possibility of an enemy retirement on Sangmelima. The strength of columns and the scope of their operations were left to Colonel Gorges' discretion.

3rd January 1916.

This telegram crossed one sent by Colonel Gorges that morning to General Dobell, saying that if both Generals Aymerich and Cunliffe concentrated their forces at Yaunde the supply situation would become serious, as existing arrangements only sufficed to maintain Colonel Gorges' troops, including a mobile column with six days' range. Should the despatch of the Widemenge column be approved, Colonel

---

* Enemy detachments had been encountered on both these roads at points about four miles south of Yaunde.

Gorges suggested that the remainder of his own force should move to Erfa—to co-operate with Colonel Mayer—changing its line of communication from the Wum Biagas to the Eseka line. For this he would require 1,500 additional carriers; but he suggested that if General Cunliffe's troops were withdrawn from Yaunde to Duala, their carriers would be available. Another alternative was that the British should carry out the operations to the south.

General Dobell replied the same day that forces were to move out at once to Widemenge and along the Kribi road, and that as soon as General Aymerich arrived he should be asked to detach a force to co-operate with Colonel Mayer in the attack on Ebolowa, this force to be supplied by the French line of communication from Eseka. General Dobell pointed out how a common line of communication for British and French troops had on previous occasions proved unworkable, and that British assistance would consequently have to be limited to an advance on Ebolowa from Widemenge. In conclusion, after directing that General Cunliffe's force was to be sent to Duala on its arrival at Yaunde, General Dobell said that he gave Colonel Gorges a free hand to make the necessary arrangements on the above lines.

In acknowledging this telegram the same day Colonel Gorges said that the Widemenge column would start on the 5th January, and that he was establishing a new post (at Atangana) as a base for operations along the Kribi road. He had no news of Generals Aymerich's or Cunliffe's columns and there was no enemy within seven miles of Yaunde, to which the natives were beginning to return in some numbers.

4th January, 1916. On the 4th January Colonel Gorges received information showing that the enemy's main force was covering the Nyong river crossings on the Widemenge and Kribi roads; and he also heard that Colonel Faucon's column had that day captured Makak. The main body of this column, which had been delayed at Mangeles by the heavy percentage of sickness among its carriers, had started eastward on the 3rd January, and had encountered considerable opposition in its advance on Makak.

Colonel Mayer received a telegram that day from the French Colonial Office, placing under his—and therefore also under General Dobell's—orders the French Campo column, which the August Allied Conference at Duala had placed under Colonel Le Meillour's control, an arrangement which in practice had proved unworkable. For the Campo column was still in the vicinity of Akak, and had heard little or nothing from Colonel Le Meillour for some time. After consultation with General Dobell, Colonel Mayer appointed Commandant Caillet—a recent arrival—to take command of the column, with fresh instructions to close to the enemy the Muni frontier from the coast to Ngoa.* To assist him in his difficult mission in the endless maze of dense forest, Colonel Mayer arranged to reinforce him with a section of mountain guns and 150 Senegalese infantry, and also obtained from General Dobell the services of a number of carriers. Neither General Dobell nor Colonel Mayer had yet heard of Colonel Le Meillour's occupation of Ambam on the 31st December.

On the 4th January also, in a telegram to General Cunliffe, General Dobell announced his intention of proceeding to Yaunde to confer with General Aymerich, and at the same time inquired if General Cunliffe proposed to advance across the Sanaga river.

Colonel Gorges' inability to despatch immediately a strong column to Widemenge was due to the time required to organise the necessary supply and transport arrangements. The column of six companies, with a detachment R.E. and two mountain guns,† marched out from Yaunde under command of Colonel Haywood on the 5th January. An enemy party was reported to be holding a position at the Mopfu river, and Colonel Haywood detached the two Gold Coast companies with a gun, under Major Anderson, to advance by the easterly of the two roads to Kribi, drive back this party and rejoin the main body at Nkolenda. Realising the necessity of rapid movement, Colonel Haywood pushed on as fast as possible, his progress being facilitated by the good road and the total absence of opposition. In fact, he found everywhere signs of a hurried enemy retreat, *e.g.*, various loads, papers and foodstuffs (including corn), etc., which had been thrown away or burnt by the retiring German force. Everywhere also the natives were returning to their villages.

5th January 1916.

On the 5th January, in repeating to Colonel Gorges information sent by General Cunliffe on the 29th December, to the effect that the enemy was undoubtedly retiring demoralised into the Bafia district, General Dobell said that he had asked General Cunliffe to co-operate in Bafia with a force which was

---
* The previous instructions to the Campo column had been to gain Njabesan so as to cover Colonel Le Meillour's left flank.

† One section Nigerian battery, field section 36th Company, R.E., 2nd Nigerians, two companies Gold Coast Battalion, and telephone section.

being sent to Yabasi from Duala. Colonel Gorges replied at once the same day saying that deserters and all native reports stated that the bulk of the enemy's forces were south of Yaunde and that only scattered bands remained to the northward. Deserters who had just come in also said that the Germans were making for Spanish Muni and that their native soldiers were deserting. Colonel Gorges consequently urged strongly that the Allies should hold the Campo-Ambam line and deprecated operations in Bafia as unnecessary. The natives, he continued, were returning to Yaunde in thousands and applying for leave to return to their homes from which the Germans had driven them. The Widemenge column had left, and he was prepared to send another column by the Kribi road within six days with rations for ten days or half-rations for twenty. The whereabouts of General Aymerich's force was unknown, but a garrison of two companies for Yaunde would be ample. For the movement of the column down the Kribi road Colonel Gorges would require 1,700 additional carriers, but hoped to obtain most of them locally.

General Dobell had, however, already issued orders for two companies West African Regiment to march from Nkongsamba to Yabasi to clear the country of stragglers and restore the confidence of the local natives; and he still hoped to cut off some of the enemy parties which had been opposing General Cunliffe. General Dobell apparently did not know that the German telephone system extended from Yaunde to Ndenge, Ngambe, Fumban and Chang, and also from Yaunde to Yoko; and neither he nor General Cunliffe were aware that the troops in those areas had probably received their orders for retirement nearly three weeks previously. On the 4th January General Dobell had ordered another company of the West African Regiment from the Northern Railway to Eseka, to escort from there to Yaunde the supply convoy for General Aymerich; and he now decided to send the rest of the regiment to Campo, arranging with Colonel Mayer that these three companies should take over from the French all the posts on the lines of communication there, thus freeing a number of troops to reinforce Commandant Caillet's striking force.

6th January 1916. There was still no news of General Aymerich, and on the 6th January, in view of persistent native reports that the French had occupied Ambam and threatened Ebolowa, and also that a French force was at Sangmelima, General Dobell issued orders for the Widemenge column to operate energetically against Ebolowa and Sangmelima. He also instructed Colonel Gorges to send a column of four companies with two guns by the Kribi road to Ebolowa, crossing the front of Colonel Mayer's force, which was about to cross the Njeke river and which would probably detach a column to move to Lolo. At the same time, General Dobell said that, as the situation required his presence at Duala, he had given up his intention of coming to Yaunde.

General Dobell now inclined to the opinion that the final enemy resistance, if any, would be made at Ebolowa, and that from that place the German members of the force might endeavour to escape into Spanish Muni.

That day Colonel Gorges received a message from the Nachtigal Rapids, despatched on the 5th January by Captain Popp, commanding the advanced portion of Colonel Brisset's column. Colonel Brisset had pushed this detachment forward —in anticipation of an order issued from Ndenge on the 3rd January by General Cunliffe—to the Nachtigal Rapids to get into close touch with General Aymerich's force. In the meantime, under General Cunliffe's orders, Major Crookenden's column was also moving south towards the junction of the Mbam and Sanaga rivers, in search of an alternative line by which to cross the Sanaga river, if this became necessary. General Cunliffe now received reports that the enemy was holding the Sanaga crossing at the Nachtigal Rapids, and on the 4th January he sent further instructions to Colonel Brisset that when Colonel Webb-Bowen—who with a gun and 350 rifles * was leaving Ndenge next day—joined the French at Ngila, the combined column under Colonel Brisset should advance, and seizing the crossing at the Nachtigal Rapids, should make all necessary arrangements for the passage of a force across the Sanaga river, in case it became necessary to send a column to Yaunde. Before these instructions reached Colonel Brisset, however, that officer, hearing of Captain Popp's unopposed arrival at the Nachtigal Rapids, had already advanced with the remainder of his column. He reached the Nachtigal Rapids on the 6th January, and learning of the capture of Yaunde, at once decided to march there himself with his whole force.

General Dobell telegraphed to Colonel Gorges on the 7th January that Colonel Mayer's force had crossed the Njeke

7th Januar. 1916.

---

* One gun 2nd Battery, " B " and " C " Companies 1st Battalion and " H " Company 2nd Battalion Nigeria Regiment.

river at three places without opposition on the previous day. Enemy opposition to the French had lessened and natives reported that one of the hostile companies opposing them had retired eastward, and that the remainder had gone southward. Colonel Mayer was issuing orders to Lieutenant-Colonel Mechet to take over command of Lieutenant-Colonel Faucon's column and press on against Ebolowa, moving first to the Yaunde-Kribi road and then turning southward to Olama.* This column should reach the Yaunde-Kribi road on the 9th January. Colonel Mayer with the remainder of his force would move to Lolo. After warning Colonel Gorges that the crossing of the Nyong river might be a difficult matter, General Dobell informed him that the reinforcements sent to Campo would disembark there on the 9th January.

Colonel Gorges replied the same day that the British column would leave Yaunde by the Kribi road on the 9th, and should be in touch with Colonel Mechet next day; that Colonel Brisset's column was expected at Yaunde on the 9th; and that General Aymerich, from whom Colonel Gorges had just heard, was also expected at Yaunde with 1,500 rifles, 6 guns and 7 machine guns on the 8th or 9th. Their arrival would make the supply situation difficult, and Colonel Gorges suggested that excess troops from these two forces should be sent to Duala.

It appears that General Aymerich's force, after losing touch on the 29th December with the enemy, remained to reorganise in the vicinity of Lembe till the 3rd January, by which time all native reports indicated a general German retirement and a British occupation of Yaunde. Next morning General Aymerich commenced a general advance westward, his right column moving towards Yaunde, in two groups, by the roads from Tabene and Lembe, and his left column by a southerly route to cover that flank. On the 5th January he received Colonel Gorges' message of the 2nd, and at once started to push on to Yaunde as fast as possible.

8th January 1916. He reached there on the 8th January and found that the situation of the Allied forces was generally as follows:—

The bulk of his own right column under Colonel Morisson was about two days' march behind him on its way to Yaunde, and his left column under Colonel Hutin was moving on Akonolinga.

---

* The French would leave the eastern and main Kribi road to the British, using themselves the western road and adjacent paths.

Colonel Brisset's column was at or approaching Yaunde, and following him was Colonel Webb-Bowen's column, which reached Ngila that day. General Cunliffe, realising that the presence of his troops at Yaunde, unless they were required to fight, would only add to the Allied supply and transport difficulties,* had never intended that either of these columns should march into Yaunde. He did not hear of its capture, however, till the 8th January, when he was too late to stop Colonel Webb-Bowen, who marched into Yaunde on the 11th. General Cunliffe in fact proposed, as he telegraphed at once to Duala, that he should withdraw his force, moving his own headquarters back to Fumban, and by relieving there, at Bagam, Bana and Chang, posts found by General Dobell's troops, release them for operations elsewhere.

Of General Dobell's force, Colonel Haywood's column, still unopposed, reached Widemenge on the 8th January, and pushed forward the same day about four miles to the Nyong river, crossing at Kolmaka. He had left a post of half a company at Nkolenda and had detached a company to reconnoitre the Mbege crossing of the Nyong a few miles west of Kolmaka. Another column under Major Coles, consisting of five companies with a gun,† was starting next day down the Kribi road, leaving two Gold Coast companies at Yaunde, where Colonel Gorges was under orders to return to Duala after handing over command to Colonel Cockburn. The detachment West India Regiment and the Sierra Leone Battalion were holding the Edea-Yaunde road, one company West African Regiment was escorting General Aymerich's supply convoy from Eseka, and the remaining companies of the same regiment were due next day at Yabasi and Campo. Colonel Faucon, who had only received on the previous day Colonel Mayer's orders to move on Olama and to hand over command to Colonel Mechet, was approaching the Yaunde-Kribi road, while the remainder of the French contingent under Colonel Mayer were on the Edea-Eseka line, the proposed movement to Lolo having been abandoned, as Colonel Mayer had insufficient troops for the purpose.‡

In the Campo area, the French column under Captain Martin had recently made very slow progress and was still only about half-way between Bitanda and Mwine.

---
* To use his own line of communication with Nigeria, which was already nearly four hundred miles long, was out of the question.
† One gun Nigerian Battery, 1st Nigerians, Gambia Company.
‡ News of this abandonment of the move on Lolo was not, however, received at Yaunde till some days later.

There was no recent news of Colonel Le Meillour. Actually he was still in the vicinity of Ambam, where he had halted to reorganise his supply and transport arrangements. On the 5th January he decided—in pursuance of his mission to advance on Ebolowa—to move forward on Nkan with the bulk of his force. He had not heard of the fall of Yaunde or of the general German retirement to the south, and as a preliminary to advancing on Nkan, was taking steps to clear the vicinity of Ambam.

As regards the enemy, a number of deserters who arrived at Yaunde on the 8th January, many of them with their arms and ammunition, reported that the German forces were all south of the Nyong river; and Lieutenant McCallum * reported that all information pointed to an enemy retirement into Muni.

On the 8th January General Dobell telegraphed the following message to Colonel Gorges for communication to General Aymerich :—

"I regret that matters here have rendered it impossible for me to be at Yaunde to meet you. I congratulate you and your force on your magnificent feat in reaching Yaunde after fifteen months' continuous marching and fighting.† Being in ignorance of your whereabouts and as the situation appeared to require that some action should be taken without delay I ordered certain moves, and these, as well as the situation generally, Colonel Gorges will give you full information of. I suggest that, as soon as your troops are ready to move, the following action will be most beneficial for them to follow. *First:* that you detail a strong force to march via Widemenge to Sangmelima and join up with the French forces already in that area. The British troops about Widemenge could then be withdrawn.‡ *Second:* that the remainder of your effectives march via Lolo to Kribi. This country requires to be traversed, as there are many small bands of the enemy in it. On arrival at Kribi, if the situation permits, the troops could be at once evacuated by steamer to French Equatorial Africa. In any case supplies will meet sick and wounded and those you wish to evacuate may be sent to Eseka, whence they can proceed to Edea or Duala to await a steamer. I shall be glad to

---

* Chief Intelligence Officer on Colonel Gorges' staff.
† Actually some of the troops had been engaged for seventeen months.
‡ Although he did not say so, General Dobell apparently had in mind the possibility of sending further British troops to Campo to assist in closing the frontier line.

know the names of places in which you place garrisons. About fifteen tons of supplies for your force should reach Yaunde on the 12th January. If you require more food to be sent up you should notify the French *sous-intendance* here, who will despatch it to Eseka, whence I must ask you to make your own arrangements to meet it, as the carriers that have gone up with the present convoy will not be available for the purpose. I hope that as soon as you have satisfactorily disposed of your force you will come to Duala to enjoy a well-earned rest. Governor-General Merlin asks that you let him know as soon as possible your food requirements. Will you let me know if the above proposals are agreeable to you. Your arrival has been reported to Brazzaville."

That evening, in camp on the north side of the Nyong river, Colonel Haywood received fuller and more definite information regarding the enemy dispositions than the Allies had obtained for some time past. At 3 p.m. a letter from Hauptmann von Stein was brought in under a flag of truce, which stated that he had orders to hand over at once 34 European and 180 African prisoners of war. Twenty-four of the Europeans were British, but only seven of them were combatants, and of the ten French, only three were combatants. All the Africans were non-combatants, the Germans having retained to accompany them into Muni all the British and French native combatants they had captured. An armistice till noon next day (9th) was thereupon arranged and the prisoners were taken over by Colonel Haywood and sent back to Yaunde.

Colonel Haywood obtained the following information from British officers thus released. The German withdrawal across the Nyong river had commenced about the 23rd December, the first troops to retire having been part of the force opposing General Aymerich. The Nyong had been crossed at Kolmaka and at two other points a few miles above and below, from all three of which the enemy had moved by roads leading to Bidegambala. By working these three crossings day and night the whole of the forces which had been opposing Generals Aymerich and Cunliffe and Colonel Gorges had passed to the south of the river by the 7th January on their way to Ngulemakong. The force opposing Colonel Mayer was said, on that day, to be missing.*

---

* Actually it appears to have been on its way to cross at Olama.

On the 8th January the main German force, some 2,500 strong, was moving towards Ebolowa via Sabade, its rear guard being about Bidegambala, and a detachment having moved towards Sangmelima. Ebermaier and Zimmermann were said to be at Sabade, where the Germans had their main hospital. The weak detachments which had been operating in the Kribi-Dehane area were about Lolo; and, south of Ebolowa, Hagen had a force of 2,000 to 2,500 rifles.* The total German combatant strength was about 500 to 600 Germans and 6,000 natives. Germans crossing the Nyong had stated openly that they were all going into Spanish Muni, if necessary recapturing Ambam, which had been in French hands since the 1st January; and they had also said that two large camps had already been prepared for them, one for the combatants in Fernando Po and the other near Bata.

The German troops passing had all appeared to be very tired, short of food and distinctly demoralised, while their supply of ammunition, especially for machine guns, was limited.

One of the British officers who gave this information further offered the opinion, from conversations he had had during his captivity with Germans, that their prolonged resistance to the Allies was mainly due to uninterrupted communication with Spanish Muni, to Ebermaier's strong personality and to the influence and example of their few regular officers.

9th–10th January 1916. During the 9th and 10th January Colonel Haywood crossed the Nyong river and established his column at Kolmaka on the south bank.

Major Coles, who left Yaunde with his column on the 9th January, had instructions to gain touch and co-operate with Colonel Faucon, who was to move across the Nyong at Olama and advance on Ebolowa. The main Kribi road was an excellent one, and Major Coles made good progress on the 9th, covering about twelve miles and being joined during the day by the armoured car, which he was instructed to use for communication purposes. On the 10th progress was slower, as damage done to the road and bridges by the retreating Germans had to be repaired. In the evening Major Coles heard from Colonel Faucon that he had that day reached Engumo, and had turned south from there along the Kribi road.

---

* It was regarding the strength of this force that the Allied Intelligence appears to have been mainly at fault.

AYMERICH'S DISPOSITIONS

After the receipt at Yaunde of the information given by the British prisoners of war, Colonel Cockburn, having taken over command from Colonel Gorges, sent on the 10th January a message to Colonel Haywood acquainting him with the instructions given to Major Coles, who might, said Colonel Cockburn, apply to Colonel Haywood for canoes to assist in crossing the Nyong river if the chain ferry at Olama was found to be destroyed. Colonel Cockburn was sending a company of the West African Regiment for Colonel Haywood's line of communication, so as to release all his six companies for his advance south of the Nyong river. General Aymerich proposed, continued Colonel Cockburn, to send a force of 800 to 1,000 of his own men under Colonel Morisson to advance in support of Colonel Haywood and to give him every assistance. They should reach Widemenge about the 15th and have crossed the Nyong by the 17th. General Aymerich would also send orders to Colonel Hutin, who was due at Akonolinga on the 16th or 17th, to send a reconnaissance to Sangmelima, thus rendering it unnecessary to send a force there from Widemenge. Colonel Brisset, who had now come under General Aymerich's orders, would remain at Yaunde in command of a reserve of 700 rifles with 3 guns ready to advance at short notice. General Aymerich advised that Colonel Haywood should maintain a steady advance towards Ebolowa till Colonel Morisson was in a position to reinforce him. It is worthy of note that both at Yaunde and Duala the estimate given of the German numbers by the British prisoners of war was considered to be very much too high.

Colonel Cockburn at the same time informed General Dobell of the arrival at Yaunde of Colonel Brisset's and Colonel Morisson's columns on the 9th and 10th January respectively, and also of General Aymerich's intentions, which had been settled in communication with Colonel Gorges and which disposed of the whole of General Aymerich's force.

Reconnaissances from Kolmaka, sent out by Colonel Haywood on the 11th and 12th January, encountered no signs of the enemy nor opposition from any direction. According to native reports, all the retiring enemy forces had crossed the Sso river; and in the expectation that supplies would reach him next day, Colonel Haywood wrote in to Yaunde proposing that he should continue his advance on the 14th. But the supplies did not arrive and on the 13th Colonel Haywood pushed forward a detachment to occupy Bidegambala. On the 14th he learnt from natives that the German

11th–14th January 1916.

rear party had evacuated its entrenched position at the Sso river, and that part of the German main force was leaving Ebolowa for Spanish Muni. His success in obtaining food locally led him to anticipate no difficulty in his further advance in supplementing the half regular rations with which he proposed to proceed.

Colonel Faucon's column when reconnoitring the Nyong crossings near Olama on the 11th January incurred two casualties; but the enemy appears to have retired immediately afterwards, for the column effected its passage of the river on the 12th and 13th without opposition. Colonel Faucon then continued his advance on Ebolowa. Major Coles' column, which camped for the night 12th/13th about eight miles north of Olama, followed the French across the Nyong on the 14th.

A column of General Aymerich's troops, consisting of five companies (850 rifles) with four guns and five machine guns under Captain Schmoll, left Yaunde on the 13th January to reinforce Colonel Haywood. General Aymerich informed Colonel Cockburn that this column would probably reach the Nyong river on the 15th, and that Colonel Haywood could continue his advance that day in the certainty of its support. Colonel Haywood, however, had already reported, before receiving this information, that he could not advance till the 16th, after a supply convoy had reached him.

Coming to the conclusion that a unified local control was necessary to co-ordinate the movements of the different Allied columns operating in the Ebolowa direction, General Aymerich—who was senior in rank to General Dobell—informed Colonel Cockburn on the morning of the 14th January that he was assuming command in the eastern area, and was appointing Colonel Morisson to command in the field the columns under Colonel Faucon (including Major Coles' column), Colonel Haywood (including Captain Schmoll's column) * and Colonel Hutin. For the time being General Aymerich himself proposed to remain with his headquarters at Yaunde, so as to keep in touch by telegraph with General Dobell, to whom he was ready to hand over command at any time that General Dobell found himself able to leave Duala for Yaunde.

On the 14th January, in accordance with orders issued by General Dobell three days previously to ease the supply

---

* Colonel Faucon's column thus totalled three guns and thirteen companies, and Colonel Haywood had a total of six guns and eleven companies.

RIVER NYONG AT OLAMA

[To face p. 408

situation at Yaunde, Colonel Webb-Bowen's column left Yaunde for Duala, whence it was sent back by sea to Lagos, arriving there on the 31st January.

Having received reports from General Cunliffe that all the country north of the Sanaga river was clear of the enemy, and from Yabasi that no enemy had been seen in that vicinity for the past three months, General Dobell issued orders on the 14th January for one of the West African Regiment companies at Yabasi to proceed at once to Campo, in which area the French appeared to be making very little progress. The first contingent of three companies West African Regiment had disembarked at Campo on the 9th, and the bulk of them had moved inland two days later, enabling Captain Martin to advance and occupy Mwine after driving back a small enemy party.

On the 14th January Colonel Le Meillour, still in ignorance of the capture of Yaunde and the German retreat, had not yet left the vicinity of Ambam.

General Aymerich issued his operation orders on the 15th January. The columns under Colonels Faucon and Haywood were to advance on Ebolowa, and Colonel Hutin's force was to move in the first instance on Sangmelima, the three columns all being placed under the command of Colonel Morisson. In his subsidiary orders, issued on the same day, Colonel Morisson * said that an advance on Ebolowa itself seemed undesirable at the moment without fresh orders, unless a favourable opportunity occurred, when it was to be immediately taken advantage of. Colonel Faucon was to move from Olama by the network of roads leading southward, keeping in touch with both Colonels Mayer and Morisson ; Colonel Haywood was to advance via Ngulemakong, detaching a strong left flank guard to gain touch with Colonel Hutin and establishing connection, on arrival at Ngulemakong, with Colonel Faucon at Elabe ; and if Colonel Hutin found before his arrival at Sangmelima that the enemy had left that place, he was to move by the shortest route to the Sangmelima-Ebolowa road and be ready to co-operate, if necessary, in the attack on Ebolowa.

15th–22nd January 1916.

After crossing the Nyong, Colonel Faucon at once continued his advance. Enemy opposition was feeble except at a river crossing on the 18th January, when a force of about two German companies offered some resistance. The French

---

* He himself left Yaunde for the front three days later.

forced the passage, however, with no great difficulty, incurring five casualties; and next day Colonel Faucon gained possession of Ebolowa, without further loss, after a short skirmish. Here he remained till relieved on the 23rd January by Colonel Mechet.

<small>Capture of Ebolowa; 19th January 1916</small>

Ebolowa, lying at a height of about 2,000 feet, was one of the principal German military, civil and trading centres and a junction of several roads. Two of these—connecting with the Kribi-Yaunde road at Lolo and a direct road to Kribi via Efulen—were found to be good motor roads, while others of the same type leading eastward, south-eastward and southward were in course of construction.

Major Coles, delayed somewhat by having to await a convoy of supplies, advanced southward from Olama by a route to the east of that followed by Colonel Faucon's column. On the 17th January, in camp near Banga, Major Coles received information of an enemy party at Elabe, and next day despatched a company of the 1st Nigerians under Captain A. H. Giles to deal with it and occupy Elabe. On the way there Captain Giles encountered an enemy force of about a company in an entrenched position and at once attacked, sending back word to Major Coles that reinforcements might be required. These arrived, however, to find that Captain Giles had already driven the enemy out after a sharp engagement, in which the Nigerians had sustained five casualties; and next day, leaving a post at Elabe, Major Coles continued his advance on Ebolowa.

Colonel Haywood at Kolmaka was joined on the 15th and 16th January by the French column under Captain Schmoll, and on the 16th Colonel Haywood commenced his advance by pushing forward Captain Gibb with two British companies and a gun to secure the passage of the Sso river. By skilful manœuvre Captain Gibb succeeded in surprising the enemy detachment holding the south bank at the crossing, and so carried out his task without loss. Colonel Haywood's main body, with detachments moving along routes on either flank, moved forward on the 17th and his reserve followed on the 18th. Though his column passed through several entrenched positions, it encountered no opposition and was able to make rapid progress, covering the forty-six miles to Ngulemakong and occupying that place by the 19th January. Next day his right flank detachment rejoined him, having established touch with Major Coles at Elabe and bringing a message from Colonel Faucon stating that on the 18th he was only seven miles from Ebolowa. Natives reported that he had since occupied Ebolowa, and Colonel Haywood decided to advance on the 21st without waiting for his left flank detachment of three French companies, whose task of wide reconnaissance eastward had prevented its more rapid progress. Colonel Haywood arrived at Ebolowa on the 22nd January, to find that Colonel Faucon's force, which was immobile for lack of supplies, had lost all touch with the enemy, who, encumbered by heavy convoys, was evidently retreating in some disorder and was reported to be making for Ngoa. No further orders from Colonel Morisson had arrived and Colonel Haywood discussed the situation with Colonel Faucon. Colonel Haywood was short of supplies and his men were somewhat exhausted after their recent efforts. But it was clearly desirable to complete the disintegration of the German forces as rapidly as possible, and Colonel Haywood decided to continue his advance next day with all his available troops.

Colonel Hutin's column, delayed by supply difficulties, had by this time not yet reached Sangmelima.

In the meantime apparently reliable reports had reached Duala on the 17th January—and were repeated to Yaunde— that Ebermaier and Hagen were at Ngoa on the 12th, and that Ebermaier had crossed into Spanish Muni. This looked as if a part of the German force had already managed to escape, and General Dobell, realising the congestion and administrative confusion that would ensue if a number of Allied columns attempted to pursue along the few roads traversing the dense forest area in the Muni direction, directed Colonel Cockburn to bear in mind the possibility of evacuating Colonel Haywood's British troops to Duala.

On the 18th General Dobell learnt from Campo that a large enemy force was reported to be at Ngoa, apparently in conflict with the Pangwe tribe, and he also heard that Colonel Faucon was near Ebolowa. Next day native reports of the occupation on the 17th of Ebolowa by Colonel Faucon reached Duala, but there was no news of Colonel Haywood.* General Dobell then sent Colonel Cockburn instructions to discuss with General Aymerich the advisability of withdrawing, after the capture of Ebolowa, the columns under Colonel Haywood and Major Coles to Kribi, and Colonel Faucon's column to Edea, leaving it to General Aymerich, with his eastern, and

* After leaving the Nyong to move south, the daily progress reports despatched by Colonel Haywood were greatly delayed in transit, and for several days no news of him was received at Yaunde or Duala.

the Campo and South Cameroons columns, to clear the country up to the Muni frontier and to garrison Yaunde and Ebolowa. Colonel Cockburn replied that he had already discussed the question with General Aymerich, who considered that the occupation of Ebolowa by no means implied a cessation of hostilities, and consequently deprecated the proposed withdrawal as prejudicing the chance of a rapid, successful and complete final decision. He was strongly of opinion that no troops should be withdrawn till the enemy had been driven into Muni and assurances received from the Spanish authorities of their internment. General Aymerich—who had, for this reason, just refused an urgent request, from Brazzaville, for the return to Chad of Colonel Brisset's force—was willing, however, to bow to General Dobell's wishes if he considered a British withdrawal imperative.

To this telegram General Dobell at once replied that he had received a written assurance from the Governor-General of Fernando Po that he would intern the German force.* In deference to General Aymerich's wishes he had issued orders, to Major Coles to withdraw and remain at Lolo, to Colonel Haywood to withdraw and remain at Kribi, and to Colonel Faucon to remain at Ebolowa. Otherwise congestion would inevitably occur, and he felt safe in relying on the French forces to clear up the Muni border. General Aymerich still considered, however, that united Allied action should continue till the enemy had surrendered or had been interned without possibility of return.

General Dobell then gave his reasons more fully. If his plan were followed, the columns under Colonels Morisson, Hutin, Le Meillour and Commandant Caillet would be immediately available to defeat the enemy and hold the frontier, Colonel Faucon's column at Ebolowa would be available as a reserve, and the British columns at Kribi and Lolo would also be no great distance off if they were required. For these last two columns it appeared to General Dobell that there would be no room to manœuvre south of Ebolowa, and also that if they remained there the supply question would become very difficult, while it would leave no troops available to deal with a possible enemy in other districts. A German force of

---

* All ships leaving Bata were, it may be noted, visited by Allied naval vessels to see that internment papers were in order and escorts provided. The Foreign Office in London also learnt at this time, through the British Ambassador at Madrid, that, in anticipation of a German retreat into Muni, the Spanish authorities had made all necessary arrangements in September 1915.

about 180 rifles had been reported as being at Lolo on the 16th January, and General Dobell wished to clear the Kribi-Lolo area of all small enemy bands. As, however, he was desirous of acting in entire accord with General Aymerich, General Dobell said that he was issuing instructions for the British troops to remain at Ebolowa till the question was settled by discussion between Colonel Cockburn and General Aymerich.

After receipt of this explanation on the 21st January, General Aymerich agreed that Major Coles' column should withdraw to Lolo, and that if the Ebolowa situation permitted, Colonel Haywood's column should withdraw to Kribi. Next day orders to that effect, to Major Coles and Colonel Haywood, were despatched from Yaunde. Naval reports now indicated that all the enemy forces had left the coast and the Dehane-Lolo-Kribi area for Muni.

The South Cameroons Force under Colonel Le Meillour had meanwhile been engaged in the vicinity of Ambam, where, on the 15th and 16th January, it carried out an indecisive attack against a strong German position at Mesele, and, on the 20th, captured Mansim. On the 21st Colonel Le Meillour received a telegram, which gave him his first intimation of the change in the general situation, and requested him to do his best to close the Ebolowa-Ngoa road to the enemy. It is to be noted that the German retirement had placed Colonel Le Meillour's force in a dangerously isolated position and that at this time he was faced on more than one side by numerically superior hostile forces. He proceeded, however, to endeavour to carry out his instructions by despatching a force of about two and a quarter companies to move westward along the south bank of the Ntem river.

General Cunliffe only received on the 14th January the intimation—despatched from Duala five or six days previously—that his troops would not be required south of the Sanaga river, and that his proposed withdrawal was concurred in. He at once sent instructions recalling Colonels Brisset and Webb-Bowen, but, as already mentioned, they were too late. Next day he began to withdraw, his own headquarters moving back to Fumban, where he arrived on the 21st January. A week later he himself left Fumban for Lagos via Duala.

General Cunliffe's departure and his past operations.

Save for the one exception of Mora, where the Germans still held out, his task of clearing the Cameroons north of the

Sanaga river of all enemy troops had been completed. Taking over command at a period when Allied inactivity in the north was causing comment and concern, his skill and energy had soon brought about a change for the better ; and his subsequent series of captures, on the central plateau, of several strongholds, which the enemy had relied on for a prolongation of his resistance pending a decision in Europe, had contributed materially to the successful plans of Generals Dobell and Aymerich.

General Cunliffe's troops had marched and fought in the past few months over several hundreds of miles, and though the mountainous area they had traversed had not been as intricate or as trying to operate in as the country further south, it had, nevertheless, presented considerable difficulties. As his reports attest, he had been well served. To the zeal, ability, tact and organising powers of Lieutenant-Colonel Wallace Wright (his senior general staff officer), General Cunliffe attributed a great measure of the success gained, and he also expressed his appreciation of the part taken by the French troops under Colonel Brisset. He brought to notice the services rendered by his different commanders, a number of individual British officers and non-commissioned officers, and of the civilians from Nigeria, official and non-official, who had so cheerfully given their services, and of whom several had lost their lives in action. He was also greatly indebted, he said, to all departments of the Nigeria Civil Service for their assistance, and especially to the residents of the frontier provinces. On the rank and file of the Nigeria Regiment, who had borne the brunt of the fighting, and the carriers, who had toiled incessantly and at times under heavy fire, he bestowed high praise. The Nigerian soldier, called upon to support a cause he but dimly understood, had for the first time in his life to face an enemy armed with modern weapons and led by highly trained officers. Yet he had not been found wanting, either in discipline, personal courage or devotion to his leaders, of whose fine personal qualities his own efficient bearing had been the best and truest test. The administrative services, manned entirely from the Nigeria Civil Services, had performed their duties admirably. To the devotion, energy and skill of the medical officers under the orders of Doctors C. E. S. Watson and R. F. Williams, of the West African Medical Staff, had been due the excellent general health which the troops had enjoyed throughout, while their supply and transport requirements had been most efficiently fulfilled by the organisation under Captain C. F. Rowe of the Nigerian Political Service.

The total casualties incurred by General Cunliffe's British force had amounted to 49 Europeans and 492 African ranks, 32 of them (including 3 Europeans) having died of disease.

Leaving a few troops at Ebolowa for convoy duties, Colonel Haywood left there on the 23rd January with three guns and about 900 rifles.* His left flank detachment under Captain Mésegué had not yet rejoined him, but he felt the urgent necessity of following up and pressing the retreating enemy to the utmost without any further delay. That day he made a long march of eighteen miles, gaining contact with the enemy in the afternoon, and obtaining ample evidence that his forces were conducting a very hurried retreat. In the evening Colonel Haywood received native information indicating that the German rear guard, of an estimated strength of about 500 rifles, was holding a position about Mafub, covering the main enemy retirement on Ngoa by a road which branched off the main Ambam road not far short of Nkan. *23rd–31st January 1916.*

Next day Colonel Haywood encountered strong opposition from a force at Mafub, which he estimated as consisting of about a company. The lack of suitable paths on either flank prevented any real turning movement, and it was only after some hours' fighting, in which the British suffered rather severely—in spite of the fact that the enemy had no machine guns in action—that the enemy was finally driven out of his position. This fighting and further strong resistance encountered beyond Mafub limited Colonel Haywood's progress during the day to four miles, and caused him a total of 22 British and 1 French casualties, including Lieutenant G. A. Anthony killed and Lieutenant K. McIver mortally wounded. The stubbornness of the enemy resistance was explained by the capture of an order sent that morning by Zimmermann to Bühler, the commander of this detachment, directing him to hold on to Mafub throughout the day at any cost. *Affair at Mafub; 24th January 1916.*

Natives reported Nkan to be strongly held by the enemy and Colonel Le Meillour's force to be south of the Mburu river on the Ambam road. Accordingly, after finding a suitable flanking path beyond Mafub, Colonel Haywood detached

---

* *Main Column (British)*: Section Nigeria Battery, Field Section 36th Company R.E., 2nd Nigerians, and one company Gold Coast Battalion (550 rifles). *Reserve Column (French)*: One gun and two companies (350 rifles) under Captain Schmoll.

Captain Schmoll's companies both to co-operate in an attack on Nkan and to endeavour to get through a letter to Colonel Le Meillour.

By leaving Ebolowa on the 23rd January Colonel Haywood had missed the order from Yaunde of the 22nd, directing him to withdraw to Kribi as soon as the situation permitted; but in the evening of the 24th he received instructions from Colonel Morisson, who had reached Ebolowa on the 23rd, to continue his movement towards Nkan and Ngoa, withdrawing to Kribi via Efulen when he judged it opportune to do so. A reinforcement of one and a half French companies from Colonel Mechet's * force at Ebolowa was being sent, said Colonel Morisson, to reinforce his column.

Sending a reply to Colonel Morisson deprecating any withdrawal, Colonel Haywood continued his advance on the 25th January and occupied Abang in face of slight opposition. Immediately south of that place, however, he encountered stubborn resistance from the hostile rear guard posted in two successive positions behind streams, from the last of which the enemy was only driven at dusk. This result was largely due to the fire of the two Nigerian guns—under Captain Waller—whose effect was so demoralising that, in spite of a very large expenditure of ammunition, the enemy only succeeded in wounding four of their British assailants. It should, however, be noted that owing to shortage of ammunition, the enemy was still without the assistance of his machine guns.

That evening Colonel Cockburn's order of the 22nd reached Colonel Haywood, and drew an immediate reply that until his troops, who were in close contact with the enemy, were replaced by an adequate French force, it was most inadvisable for him to withdraw. He hoped to have opened communication with Colonel Le Meillour and to have occupied Nkan by the 28th January, when, if French troops had arrived to replace his, it might be possible for him to withdraw.

As a matter of fact, next day his main column and Captain Schmoll's detachment arrived without opposition almost simultaneously at Nkan, whence the enemy, whose nearest forces appeared to be reduced to small covering detachments, had retired that morning towards Ngoa.

In the meantime, Colonel Hutin, who was faced by great supply and transport difficulties, had been ordered to remain at Sangmelima, and Major Coles, in accordance with orders

---

* Colonel Mechet had relieved Colonel Faucon at Ebolowa on the 23rd January.

from Yaunde, had started to move via Ebolowa to Lolo, where he arrived without opposition on the 29th January. Colonel Mayer was experiencing difficulty in organising his new line of communication and supply from Eseka to Olama, and at Yaunde General Aymerich had been obliged to obtain carriers and escorts for convoys from General Dobell.

Though he sent out a number of reconnaissances from Nkan, Colonel Haywood had to wait there for further instructions, and for a reply to his letter of the 24th January to Colonel Le Meillour. This reply, which Colonel Haywood received on the 28th, showed that Colonel Le Meillour was at Nsana, on the left bank of the Ntem river, and was preparing to launch a second attack on Owila. At this place the small column, which he had sent westward along the left bank of the Ntem river, had suffered defeat with considerable loss a few days previously at the hands of a numerically superior German force, which was evidently determined to resist stubbornly any attempt to advance on Ngoa.

Colonel Morisson meanwhile had been hoping that the columns under Colonels Haywood and Le Meillour would be able, by co-operation with one another, to bring about a decisive dispersal of the enemy's forces. Failing this, he proposed other measures, including a further advance by Colonel Haywood's column, joined by French reinforcements from Ebolowa. But the definite instructions from Yaunde—where, owing to the delay in transit of Colonel Haywood's daily progress reports, they were quite unaware of the true situation—seemed to leave him no option; and on the 29th January, on learning that no immediate effective co-operation between Colonel Haywood and Colonel Le Meillour was possible, Colonel Morisson sent Colonel Haywood orders to withdraw with his British troops to Kribi. As a matter of fact, General Dobell, learning of Colonel Haywood's fight at Mafub and his occupation of Nkan, had just sent to General Aymerich, who was on his way to Ebolowa, a message agreeing to the retention, for further operations southward, of Colonel Haywood's column. General Aymerich, however—on learning, on arrival at Ebolowa on the 30th January, that Colonel Haywood had actually commenced his withdrawal and that reliable reports from Muni (transmitted by the French gunboat *Vauban*) showed that nearly 800 German Europeans had already concentrated at, or passed over, the Spanish frontier and that all were expected to cross by the 31st January—decided not to interfere with the arrangements already made.

Subsequent events tend to show that the majority of the Germans referred to in the reports from Muni were probably non-combatants. The situation, as portrayed by Colonel Haywood and shown by subsequent information to be approximately correct, was that, though the Ebolowa-Ambam road and the country to the east of it was clear of the enemy, and though his main body had apparently made good its retreat with his convoys in the direction of Ngoa, he had not yet crossed the Ntem river, and a number of his covering detachments were holding positions at the extremities of the triangle formed by the Ntem and Mwila rivers with a line from the south of Nkan to Owila. Since the fall of Yaunde some 300 of his native troops, many of them bringing their arms and ammunition, had deserted to the Allies.

In view of the subsequent internment in Spanish territory of the whole German force, it appears doubtful, however, if any real advantage would have been gained, had misunderstanding not led to Colonel Haywood's recall. Since it had not been possible for the columns under Commandant Caillet and Colonel Le Meillour to cut off the retreat of the main enemy force, little chance remained of dealing him a blow which would compensate for the loss of life involved, while to clear the country between Nkan and Ngoa and to hold the frontier against any German return General Aymerich had as many French troops as were necessary and probably as many as he could have fed.

On Colonel Haywood himself, Colonel Morisson bestowed high praise for the skill and initiative he had displayed, while Colonel Haywood's report bears testimony to the zeal and endurance of his troops during the long and exhausting days of the pursuit, when they had frequently to march and fight on only half—and at times on quarter—rations. With his withdrawal the active participation of the British contingent came to an end. It is worthy of note, from the evidence of a British officer prisoner of war, that the Germans had a special respect for Colonel Haywood's military abilities, and that even their native troops talked of him, saying that he had war *ju-ju* and that it was no use fighting him.

The second attack by Colonel Le Meillour's troops on the German position at Owila was carried out from the 29th to the 30th January by a force of four companies with a gun under Commandant Miquelard. But the German resistance was too strong and, after suffering rather severe losses, Commandant Miquelard withdrew to await reinforcements.

AYMERICH'S FINAL OPERATIONS

In the Campo area, Commandant Caillet, who arrived at Mwine and took over command on the 15th January, had advanced with his whole battalion and had driven a strong enemy detachment out of Ngat on the 23rd January at the cost of 14 French casualties. Ngat, like all other posts on the line of communications, was then taken over by the West African Regiment, and Commandant Caillet pushed on, occupying Kok on the 29th January and Ekob on the 30th. Here he halted to reconnoitre the Ntem river passages which lay to the south-east.

By the end of January, most of the villages round Yaunde and in the Nyong river districts had been re-occupied by the inhabitants, whom the Germans had driven off in order to delay an Allied pursuit. The country was consequently assuming a more normal aspect, and considerable quantities of local food supplies were becoming procurable. The British motor transport section had reached Yaunde, and was filling up the supply depot at Olama, preparatory, if necessary, to doing the same at Ebolowa. The Allies do not appear to have previously realised the excellence of the motor roads from Kribi to Yaunde via Lolo, from Lolo to Ebolowa and from Kribi to Ebolowa via Efulen; and it seems permissible to hazard the opinion that if they had known of it they might have taken steps some time before to occupy both Lolo and Ebolowa. The results of such a course can, of course, only be surmised.

By arrangement with General Dobell the control of all operations against the enemy, who was reported to be holding tenaciously to his positions at and round Ngoa, was taken over at the end of January by General Aymerich. As he, however, found it necessary on the 2nd February to return to Yaunde, he delegated this control to Colonel Morisson.

Final operations under General Aymerich; February 1916.

On the 31st January Captain Schmoll with a gun and three companies commenced to advance on Ngoa from Nkan, and Commandant Mathieu with another three companies and a gun—from Colonel Mechet's force—started to advance in the same direction but by a more westerly route. After overcoming a good deal of opposition they both reached the right or northern bank of the Ntem river—Captain Schmoll arriving opposite Ngoa on the 8th February and Commandant Mathieu a point a little further to the north-west on the 10th. The enemy disputed the passage of the river, but Commandant Mathieu succeeded in crossing it during the night of the 10th/11th, and on the 11th drove back the enemy opposing

Captain Schmoll, enabling both columns to occupy Ngoa that day. Here on the 12th February they were joined by Colonel Morisson, with the remainder of Colonel Mechet's force from Ebolowa, and by Colonel Le Meillour, whose column had in the last stages encountered no opposition.

Captain Schmoll's men from French Equatorial Africa were much exhausted by their many months of continuous warfare, and Colonel Morisson sent them back to Ebolowa, while he himself, with Colonel Mechet's and Colonel Le Meillour's columns, pushed on towards Banyassa. On the 14th and 15th February the enemy rear parties disputed every yard of advance, but at 3 p.m. on the 15th the French reached Banyassa to find that the last of the German troops had passed into Spanish territory.

In the meantime, Commandant Caillet, after spending the early part of February in reconnoitring the passages of the Ntem to the south-east of Ekob, had crossed that river opposite Ayamintanga between the 12th and 15th February. A day or two later he received the news of the German departure; and subsequently his column and that of Colonel Le Meillour were detailed to guard the frontier.

During this final phase the French casualties, excluding those in Colonel Le Meillour's force,* totalled 48.

While these operations were in progress General Dobell visited General Aymerich, leaving Duala on the 9th February for Yaunde via Wum Biagas and returning via Kribi on the 14th.

Telegraphic report of German ex-Governor of Cameroons to his Government. On the 17th February, at the request of the Governor-General of Fernando Po, General Dobell forwarded a telegraphic message from Ebermaier to the German Government, reporting that lack of munitions had obliged him to abandon the Cameroons and take refuge in Spanish territory with the entire German force, including all his sick and wounded. The troops, he said, had begun to cross the frontier on the 4th February, and the details of their internment were in course of settlement. The German numbers which passed the frontier, according to subsequent reports from the Spanish authorities, totalled about 975 Germans, of whom some 400 were non-combatants, and 14,000 natives, of whom 6,000 were soldiers.†

---

* In this force the total casualties between the 20th December 1915 and 5th February 1916, were reported as being 205.

† The account in *Der Grosse Krieg, 1914–1918*, says that a final defensive position was taken up and fortified at the great northerly bend of the Campo (Ntem) river, till at last, lacking supplies and munitions, the troops were

"A" Company, M.I. Battalion, Nigeria Regiment

(in "review order")

German Arms collected after the surrender of Mora

The Allied naval forces continued, throughout January and February, to blockade the coast, watch the local trade routes and patrol the rivers, successful minor affairs by the *Dwarf* on the 1st January and by the *Alligator* and *Wuri* of the Nyong river flotilla on the 4th and 8th January being their last encounters with the enemy. On the 10th February and following days large numbers of native refugees arrived at Campo and had to be fed and dealt with. In all, 21,000 passed through the British naval camp. On the 1st March the coastal blockade was finally raised, the blockade of one section of the coast having already been given up on the 11th January. *[Allied Naval Forces; January-1st March 1916.]*

When General Cunliffe left Duala for Lagos on the 5th February, Captain von Raben was still holding out at Mora; and in view of the possibility of having to force its surrender General Dobell had placed at General Cunliffe's disposal the howitzer and its R.A. detachment. Before taking any further action, however, General Cunliffe, after discussion with Sir Frederick Lugard at Lagos, offered Captain von Raben terms of surrender. The message conveying these was sent for delivery to Captain Rémond, commanding the Allied investing force—in which " G " Company of the 3rd Battalion had recently been relieved by " A " Company Mounted Infantry Nigeria Regiment—and it informed Captain von Raben that all the other German forces had taken refuge in Muni, and that if he was prepared to surrender, he and his officers would be allowed to retain their swords, though with other Europeans they would be sent to England as prisoners of war, while his native troops would be set free and given safe passage to their homes. These terms were accepted, and the garrison of 11 German and 145 native ranks surrendered on the 18th February.* *[Surrender of Mora: 18th February 1916.]*

This ended the campaign, and to mark its conclusion H.M. The King sent the following telegram on the 22nd February to General Dobell :—

" I heartily congratulate you and the naval and military

---

forced, after fighting from the 5th to the 15th February, to cross the frontier in faultless order and with closed ranks. The majority of the Europeans were taken to Spain, and the faithful natives, with a number of white overseers, to Fernando Po. In referring to the large number of natives who accompanied the German force into Spanish territory, the account pays a tribute to their loyalty, which, it says, manifested their attachment to German rule. Most of them appear to have been Yaundes, the finest and most loyal soldiers recruited by the enemy, and it would be ungenerous for us to question their motives.

* Their armament consisted of 4 machine guns and 183 rifles with about 40,000 rounds of ammunition.

forces under your command on the successful termination of the operations in the Cameroons and the occupation in conjunction with our Allies of that country."

All fighting being over, the British and French Governments proceeded to discuss the question of the administration of the captured German colony. The decision eventually reached was that with the exception of certain districts on the Nigerian frontier, which, however, included the Cameroon mountain and the important districts of Buea and Victoria, the whole country, including the port of Duala and the greater part of the central plateau, should be administered by the French for the period of the war. The provisional settlement then reached formed the basis of the division of the country, which was accepted at the Peace Conference of 1919, and is embodied in the present boundaries of the Mandated Territory of the Cameroons.

On the 13th March 1916, General Dobell issued to his force the following order of the day :—

"With the departure of the troops, beginning on the 16th March, the Allied Force which I have had the honour to command during the last nineteen months commences to be broken up. I therefore take the opportunity of bidding farewell to all those who have taken part in the campaign which has terminated so successfully. I desire to express my thanks to all officers, non-commissioned officers and men of the Allied Force, both European and native, who have rendered me such loyal and unswerving assistance in achieving the arduous task which has lain before us.

" I desire also to place on record the invaluable help that has been rendered to the Allied cause by the Force commanded by General Aymerich, Brigadier-General Cunliffe, Colonel Brisset, and all under their respective commands, who have borne the brunt of much fighting and marching in difficult country.

" To all officers, petty and non-commissioned officers and men of the Allied Navies I wish to express my deepest thanks for the share which they have taken in the operations both by sea and land. Finally, I wish all those who have served under me, or have been associated with me, the best of good fortune in whatever adventure may lie before them."

CONCLUSION

To a world whose thoughts were almost entirely filled, and its attention held, by the vast and more important events in the main theatres of the war, the Allied operations in the Cameroons appeared at the time of minor interest; and few of the general public had either the inclination or opportunity to follow their progress at all closely. The successful termination of what the British Prime Minister termed " one of the most satisfactory and complete episodes, so far, in the history of the war " brought the campaign momentarily into prominence. But it is doubtful whether, even then, the public realised the conditions of service and climate under which the conquest of a territory about one and a half times the size of the German Empire had been attained.

It is true that the respective forces engaged were small, and that the number of battle casualties was in no way comparable with those incurred in most of the other theatres of war. On the other hand, the whole circumstances of the campaign were exceptional. Lack of preparedness at first necessitated rapid improvisation; information regarding the enemy country was inadequate; the difficulties due to the scattered distribution of the available forces, the wide area involved and the obstacles which the country and climate presented to movement and operations were considerable and continuous; and the dangers to health were many and constant. The responsibilities and cares of the European leaders of all ranks were numerous, while local conditions admitted of little alleviation of the continuous strain on their nerves and health. For there were in Africa no such amenities as were available for their comrades in Europe during periods of relaxation; and the depressing and enervating local conditions were consequently more than ever apt to produce intermittent attacks of despondency or disgust. More especially perhaps as there was little or no public appreciation of heroism and efforts which would in ordinary times have gained wide recognition. Enough, however, has, it is hoped, been said both here and previously to make it clear that the fine spirit which animated the European members of the Allied forces, throughout the campaign and in face of every difficulty and adversity, is worthy of our highest admiration. To this spirit and the example it set was due the fine and devoted gallantry and endurance displayed by the Africans they led, whether sailors, soldiers or carriers.

Of the several other factors which contributed to the success of the campaign one of the most notable is the complete co-operation of the Allied nationalities—civilian, sailor and soldier—which characterised every phase of the campaign. Under conditions so trying it would not have been surprising if the dissimilarities in national temperament and outlook had led to serious disagreement. But while it would be incorrect to suggest that no differences ever arose, it is most satisfactory, and a subject for mutual congratulation, to be able to record that our relations with our French Allies were always of a most cordial nature, and that all divergences were settled without delay and with sole regard to the common object. For this, thanks are mainly due to the ability and tact of Generals Aymerich, Dobell, Largeau and Cunliffe, of the British and French naval commanders and of the civil, naval and military officers serving under them.

Of this international co-operation one of the most important and admirable results was seen in the final advance on Yaunde, where, after starting some hundreds of miles apart, the Allied forces from the east and north arrived only a few days after the main column from the west, and that in spite of a total lack of adequate means of intercommunication.

Of General Aymerich's operations we possess little detailed information. But it is clear that from the outset these operations reduced materially the opposition which the enemy would otherwise have offered to Generals Dobell and Cunliffe, and that, in their continuous advance for many months through forest and swamp and in face of great difficulties and constant opposition, the Franco-Belgian troops displayed splendid qualities of courage and endurance. In these operations their casualties had been severe, totalling 118 Europeans and 1,684 Africans, of which total only 117, it is said, were due to deaths from disease.

Without the assistance of the Allied naval forces, the military forces could not, as General Dobell pointed out, have accomplished the task before them. At the outset it fell to the British under Captain Fuller to secure the passage of the Cameroon Estuary and ensure the capture of Duala ; and on them also devolved the task of exploring and patrolling the inland waterways and of co-operating with the soldiers in many advances and attacks. To the command of the sea, achieved at an early stage by the Allied navies, was due the security of the main lines of communication and the release from coast defence of important land forces to participate in the operations; while besides capturing and holding several important points on the coast and rivers, the Allied vessels (mainly British) maintained for many months a most efficient blockade. In expressing in his final despatch his indebtedness to the personnel of the Allied navies and his admiration of their unremitting and incessant toil, General Dobell brought specially to notice the valuable services rendered by the French Captain Carré—who had been Senior Naval Officer of the blockade forces for the last eight and a half months of the operations—and by Captain Fuller, the British Senior Naval Officer throughout the campaign.

Throughout the operations the Nigeria Marine bore an important and honourable part. From the outbreak of hostilities, when on them devolved the work of preparing the various harbours in Nigeria for defence against overseas attack, their work was hard and continuous. Of the invaluable assistance rendered by the officers and men of the Marine Contingent in the Cameroons there is ample evidence in the preceding narrative and in the pages of Captain Fuller's final despatch. In Nigeria itself they also performed exceptional service. Here the reduced numbers had to carry out the ordinary duties of the Marine increased by the special calls of coast defence, operations on the frontier and internal unrest, and to maintain and supply their contingent in the Cameroons. The untiring zeal and energy displayed by all ranks in Nigeria, said Commander Percival,* merited recognition of the Department as a whole, and he found it difficult to differentiate among them, limiting his "mentions" to Commander A. B. Crosse, and Messrs. G. Lumley, J. A. Houston, J. Alexander and J. B. Sancho.

In obtaining the mastery over the numerous difficulties which the country and the climate presented, and in the execution of his skilful plans to overcome enemy resistance, and of his well-conceived arrangements to maintain his force and administer occupied territory, General Dobell was always able to count on all ranks of his command for zealous and efficient support. To Colonel Mayer and to his subordinate French commanders General Dobell expressed his high and

---

* He succeeded Captain Child as Director of Marine.

grateful appreciation of the skill, energy and perseverance they had displayed, and he also paid tribute to the extreme bravery and consistent cheerfulness of the French Senegalese soldiers.

Of his own British officers and non-commissioned officers he brought to notice the distinguished and meritorious service of sixty-five, selecting the following among them for further special mention:—Lieutenant-Colonels A. J. Turner and J. Brough of the General Staff; Captain R. H. Rowe, his D.A.A. and Q.M.G., Colonel C. Pery and Major F. L. N. Giles of the Royal Engineers; and Captain D. Wallbach and Lieutenant G. E. H. Migeod, his two successive Directors of Supply and Transport. Among the officers who had led the troops in action he gave special prominence to the conduct of Lieutenant-Colonels J. B. Cockburn and A. H. W. Haywood, both of whom, as battalion or column commanders, had experienced the brunt of the hard fighting and both of whose judgment and discretion, he said, had in no case been at fault.

The work of the medical service had been of a particularly onerous nature; and to Lieutenant-Colonel J. C. B. Statham and the officers and non-commissioned officers R.A.M.C., the officers of the West African medical staff, the sisters of the nursing service and all subordinate ranks down to the native stretcher bearers, he expressed his deep gratitude for their unremitting care of the sick and wounded and for their marked contempt for life in their endeavours to save that of others.

In this connection, a study of the following total casualties among the combatants of General Dobell's force, showing the ratio of deaths from disease, affords some illustration of the excellence of the medical arrangements.*

	British		*French*	
	Europeans	*Africans*	*Europeans*	*Africans*
Killed or died of wounds..	24	192	24	249
Wounded	30	557	35	483
Died of disease	6	84	9	90
Missing, captured or drowned..	—	34	—	16

* The naval casualties are not included, and those of the French are taken from the French account by Commandant Viraud in the *Revue des Troupes Coloniales*, 1927–1929, in which the numbers differ from those given by General Dobell.

Invaliding from the combatant ranks had not been at all heavy for a tropical campaign, 151 British Europeans having been invalided out of a total of 864, and 343 French Europeans out of a total of 807 ; while of 5,927 British and 5,669 French African ranks, the numbers invalided had been 434 and 888 respectively. Among the native carriers the rate had been considerably higher. But as they could more easily be replaced than soldiers, and, unless likely to recover shortly, soon ceased to give a return for their upkeep, they were invalided much more freely. Approximately 20,000 came to Duala * from the Allied colonies and protectorates, and of these 102 were killed or wounded, 472 died of disease and 8,219 were invalided. Between 10,000 and 15,000 carriers had also been engaged locally for varying periods, but casualty figures for these are not available.

The British West African soldiers had realised General Dobell's fullest expectations. He said, " To them no day appears to be too long, no task too difficult. With a natural aptitude for soldiering, they are endowed with a constitution which inures them to hardship ; they share with their Senegalese brothers an inexhaustible fund of good humour."

The West African carrier had also done very good work. Patient and amenable, he had borne his full share in the Allies' arduous task.

General Dobell concluded his despatch by acknowledging the valuable assistance he had received from the civilians who had administered the occupied territory, and the great obligations he was under to the Governor-General of Nigeria, the Governors of the Gold Coast, Sierra Leone and the Gambia, and to Major-General J. F. Daniell, commanding the troops in Sierra Leone. Though his demands on them had been numerous, insistent and unusual, they had all been met without hesitation and in a hearty spirit of co-operation.

To render this assistance the British West African dependencies denuded themselves freely of personnel and material, straining their resources to the utmost and braving embarrassment, numerous difficulties and some risk. To these evils Nigeria's proximity to the Cameroons laid her more open, while her greater area, population and resources enabled her to give more than the other colonies and protectorates ; and

---

* There appears to be no exact record of the number of carriers (or of the casualties among them) who moved across the Nigerian frontier into the northern areas in the Cameroons.

she thus became, as Sir Charles Lucas says,* the predominant partner in the enterprise. All, however, were equally affected by the same high motives, and the aid they gave at this crisis —whether by Europeans, for whom it often spelt double work and anxiety, or by Africans, drawn by their attachment to British rule—forms a page in the history of the Empire of which present and future generations in West Africa have every reason to be proud.

---

* "The Empire at War," Volume IV.

[*To face p.* 428

BUEA

APPENDIX I

THE TERMS OF SURRENDER SUGGESTED BY MAJOR VON DOERING, AND SUBSEQUENT CORRESPONDENCE BETWEEN HIM AND LIEUT.-COLONEL BRYANT

1. Europeans to surrender with all the honours of war and to be allowed to retain their swords or side-arms.

2. One European for each firm to be allowed to remain in the colony to take care of the firm's private interests.

3. All Europeans surrendering to be sent to the same place, which should not be situated in one of the neighbouring colonies and if possible not on the West Coast of Africa.

4. Only Europeans under arms against the Allies on the 25th August, 1914, to surrender. The troops of Hauptmann von Hirschfeld, which are too far off to be reached, are not included.

5. All munitions of war, public money, as far as it is still in the hands of the Germans, and all public buildings and furniture to be surrendered.

6. Twenty-four hours to be granted for the settlement of affairs, reckoned from the time when the German representatives receive Allied approval to the terms.

7. No fighting and no movements of troops to take place in these twenty-four hours beyond what is required to concentrate German troops for the purpose of surrender.

8. Rittmeister von Roebern of the Husarenregiment Koenig to represent German interests with Unter-offizier der Reserve Kulenkampff as interpreter.

To The Acting Governor of Togoland.

AMU RIVER, 25th *August*, 1914.

With reference to the terms you ask on capitulation, I have the honour to inform Your Excellency that any surrender must be unconditional.

APPENDIX I

I have also to remind Your Excellency that private property is always respected by Englishmen, and that the *bona fide* trade of the country will be interfered with as little as possible.

(Signed) F. C. BRYANT.
Lt.-Col.
Commanding Togoland Field Force.

To The Commander
of the Anglo-French Field Force
in Togoland.

KAMINA, 25*th August*, 1914.

I have the honour to acknowledge the receipt of your letter of to-day's date.

In spite of the bravery shown by my troops, I am forced by the circumstances of the situation to accept the conditions imposed by Your Excellency. I have decided to yield to superior forces because the bearer of the flag of truce, Captain of Cavalry von Roebern, has reported from the declaration made by you a worthy treatment of the captured Europeans is to be expected. I offer you herewith my sword and await at Kamina further information concerning the surrender.

During to-day's negotiations with Captain of Cavalry von Roebern it was alleged that my troops have made use of certain bullets which do not conform with the stipulations of the Geneva Convention. I have the honour herewith to assure Your Excellency on my word of honour that I know nothing of this matter; and that, officially, only bullets covered with jackets as well as regulation solid lead bullets have been issued as equipment. If bullets which are contrary to regulations have indeed been found on individuals, then I would submit that we have never reckoned with a war in Togoland, and that those liable for service went on active service without any special plan of mobilisation, partly direct from their civil posts—thus the exchange of any irregular sporting cartridges, which they may have had, may perhaps in a few cases have been impossible.

I express my regret on account of the incident in question.

(Signed) V. DOERING.
Major and Commander of the
German Field Force in Togoland.

APPENDIX I

To The Commander
of the Anglo-French Field Force,
AMUCHU.

KAMINA, 26*th August*, 1914.

I have to acknowledge the receipt of your letter of this date. I would state in reference thereto that I have already to-day dismissed my coloured soldiers after they had handed over their arms. I referred in paragraph 4 of the offer handed to you by Captain of Cavalry von Roebern only to " all Europeans who are under arms against the English and French on the 25th August," and not to coloured troops. I was induced to effect this dismissal by the consideration that the coloured soldiers, who do not appreciate the nature of a capitulation, and the surrender of whose arms I had promised in paragraph 5, had deserted with their arms in large numbers. Inclusive of recruits, about 300 men are involved. As you had not raised any objections to my proposal, I assumed that the expression " unconditional surrender " referred to the Europeans only. As I, however, now gather from your letter of to-day that you attach importance to the surrender of the black troops, I have ordered that the black soldiers, in so far as they can still be reached, should be recalled and handed over to you to-morrow.

The outposts have been drawn in with the exception of one European, who has not yet been found, as well as of Captain von Hirschfeld, who is probably on the march to this place from Mangu and whom I am at present unable to reach.

(Signed) V. DOERING.
Major and Commander of the
Field Force in Togoland.

APPENDIX II

ORDER OF BATTLE
of the
Anglo-French Expeditionary Force against the Cameroons
23rd September, 1914

General Headquarters—

General Officer Commanding	Brig.-General C. M. Dobell, D.S.O., A.D.C. (*a*).
A.D.C.	Lieut. G. E. R. de Miremont, Royal Welsh Fusiliers (*b*).
Senior General Staff Officer	Lieut.-Colonel A. J. Turner, R.A. (*a*).
General Staff Officer	Major J. Brough, M.V.O., R.M.A. (*a*).
French Officer, attached	Captain A. Charvet (*b*).
Deputy Assistant Adjutant and Quartermaster-General	Captain R. H. Rowe, R.A. (*a*).
Director of Signals	Captain F. L. N. Giles, R.E. (*a*).
Director of Medical Services	Major J. C. B. Statham, R.A.M.C. (*b*).
Director of Supply and Transport	Captain D. A. Wallbach (*c*), (*e*).
Financial Officer	Mr. H. St. J. Sheppard (*a*).
Political Officer	Lieut. K. V. Elphinstone (*a*).
Intelligence Officer	Lieut. D. McCallum (*a*).

General Headquarters Troops—

Camp Commandant	Lieut. A. McC. Inglis, Gloucestershire Regiment (Gambia Company, W.A.F.F.).
Headquarters escort	25 rank and file, Gold Coast Regiment.
Signal Company	2 British N.C.Os., 20 native ranks (from Gambia Company and Nigeria Regiment).
Royal Engineers (*d*) (Captain P. J. Mackesy, R.E.)	Railway Section — Lieut. H. E. Kentish, R.E., 10 Europeans and 7 natives. Telegraph Section—Lieut. H. M. Woolley, 6 Europeans and 12 natives. Field Section—Lieut. C. V. S. Jackson, R.E., 1 British N.C.O. and 13 natives (from 36th Company, R.E., at Sierra Leone).

(*a*) Sailed from England in s.s. *Appam*.
(*b*) Joined *Appam* at Sierra Leone.
(*c*) From the Nigerian Service. He had fought at Tel-el-Kebir in 1882 as a Corporal.
(*d*) The Royal Engineers included ex-R.E. officers and N.C.Os. employed in Nigeria and the Gold Coast, and civilians from the Public Works, Railway and Telegraph Departments.
(*e*) Joined *Appam* at Lagos.

APPENDIX II 433

BRITISH CONTINGENT

British Contingent Headquarters—
Officer Commanding	Colonel E. H. Gorges, D.S.O.
Second-in-Command	Lieut.-Colonel F. H. G. Cunliffe.
General Staff Officer	Major W. D. Wright, V.C., Queen's Royal Regiment.
Attached General Staff	Captain H. G. Howell, R.A.
Staff Captain	Captain C. R. U. Savile, Royal Fusiliers.
Staff Captain (attached)	Captain C. H. Dinnen, King's Liverpool Regiment.
Senior Medical Officer	Major W. H. G. H. Best (R.A.M.C. Special Reserve).
Ordnance Officer	Major H. W. G. Meyer-Griffith.

Headquarters Troops—
Pioneer Company, Gold Coast Regiment (Capt. H. Goodwin, Middlesex Regiment), 5 officers, 2 British N.C.Os., 149 native ranks.

Artillery—
Sierra Leone Company, R.G.A. (Capt. N. d'A. Fitzgerald, R.A. = four 2·95-in. guns, 3 officers, 2 British N.C.Os., 46 native ranks.
No. 1 Battery, Nigeria Regiment (Capt. C. F. S. Maclaverty, R.A.) = four 2·95-in. guns, 3 officers, 2 British N.C.Os., 64 native ranks.
Section, Gold Coast Battery (Lieut. W. L. St. Clair, R.A.) = two 2·95-in. guns, 2 officers, 1 British N.C.O., 28 native ranks.

Infantry—
West African Regiment (Lieut.-Colonel E. Vaughan, Manchester Regiment) = six companies : 23 officers, 18 British N.C.Os., 643 native ranks.
No. 1 Battalion, Nigeria Regiment (Lieut.-Colonel J. B. Cockburn, Royal Welsh Fusiliers) = four companies ("A" and "F" Companies 1st Battalion and "D" and "F" Companies 2nd Battalion Nigeria Regiment): 28 officers, 12 British N.C.Os., 620 native ranks.
No. 2 Battalion, Nigeria Regiment (Lieut.-Colonel A. H. W. Haywood, R.A.) = four companies ("A," "D," "E" and "F" Companies 4th Battalion Nigeria Regiment): 21 officers, 12 British N.C.Os., 600 native ranks.
Composite Battalion (Lieut.-Colonel R. A. de B. Rose, Worcestershire Regiment) = four companies—
    Two companies ("C" and "E") Sierra Leone Battalion, W.A.F.F.: 14 officers, 6 British N.C.Os., 211 native ranks.
    Two companies ("B" and "F") Gold Coast Regiment (which did not join the force till 25th September, 1914).

Medical—
19 officers, 4 British N.C.Os., 20 natives.

Supply and Transport (Lieut. G. F. Hodgson)—
13 officers, 1 British N.C.O., 10 native superintendents and headmen, 3,553 carriers.

Total

154 officers.
81 British N.C.Os. and other European personnel.
2,460 native ranks.
3,563 carriers.
10 guns (2·95-in.).

APPENDIX II

FRENCH CONTINGENT

Headquarters—
  Officer Commanding—Colonel Mayer.
  Four staff officers, and Captain H. T. Horsford, Gloucestershire Regiment, attached as British liaison officer.

Artillery—
  One mountain battery (Captain Gerrard) = 6 guns.

Infantry—
  One company European Colonial Infantry (Captain Salvetat), 155 of all ranks.
  No. 1 Senegalese Battalion (Commandant Mechet) = four companies: 18 officers, 44 French N.C.Os., 844 native ranks.
  No. 2 Senegalese Battalion (Commandant Mathieu) = four companies: 15 officers, 51 French N.C.Os., 854 native ranks.

*Engineers—*One Section
  Captain Chardy, 9 Europeans, 20 native ranks.

Medical, ammunition and transport details.

Total

  54 officers.
  354 European N.C.Os. and men.
  1,859 native ranks.
  1,000 carriers.
  200 animals (of which 75 were battery mules and the remainder horses).

APPENDIX III

(A.) List of H.M. Ships and Vessels employed with the Cameroons Expedition

Name of Vessel	Description	Armament	From	To	Disposal of Vessel	Commanding Officer Name and Rank	From	To
"CUMBERLAND"	Cruiser	14 6-inch, 8 12-pdrs., 3 3-pdrs.	31.8.14	4.12.14	Left Cameroon waters in accordance with Admiralty orders.	Captain C. T. M. Fuller, R.N.	—	4.12.14
"CHALLENGER"	Light Cruiser	11 6-inch, 8 12-pdrs., 1 3-pdr.	23.9.14	6.5.15	do.	Captain C. P. Beaty-Pownall, R.N.	5.12.14	4.12.14
						Captain C. P. Beaty-Pownall, R.N.	—	4.12.14
						Captain C. T. M. Fuller, C.M.G., R.N.	5.12.14	30.4.15
"ASTRÆA"	do.	2 6-inch, 8 4·7-inch, 1 12-pdr., 8 6-pdrs., 1 3-pdr.	21.4.15	12.6.16	do.	Captain A. C. Sykes, R.N.	1.5.15	—
						Captain A. C. Sykes, R.N.	—	30.4.15
						Captain C. T. M. Fuller, C.M.G., R.N.	1.5.15	12.6.15
"DWARF" ..	Gunboat	2 4-inch, 4 12-pdrs.	3.9.14	—	Remained for duty on West Coast of Africa and in Cameroon waters.	Commdr. F. E. K. Strong, R.N.	—	2.6.15
"SIRIUS" ..	Light Cruiser	2 6-inch, 6 4·7-inch, 8 6-pdrs., 1 3-pdr.	6.6.15	20.4.16	Left Cameroon waters in accordance with Admiralty orders.	Commdr. W. C. G. Ruxton, R.N.	3.6.15	—
"RINALDO"	Sloop	4 4-inch, 4 3-pdrs.	,,	,,	do.	Commdr. W. H. Boys, R.N. (Ret.).	—	—
"CUMBERLAND'S" Picket Boat	—	1 3-pdr. 1 machine gun	31.8.14	15.2.16	Shipped to England per s.s. *Egba* from Bonny.	Lt.-Commdr. H. M. Garrett, R.N.	—	—
"CUMBERLAND'S" Steam Pinnace	—	2 machine guns	,,	20.5.16	Shipped to England per s.s. *Obuasi*.	—	—	—

(B.) LIST OF NIGERIA MARINE VESSELS EMPLOYED WITH THE CAMEROONS EXPEDITION

Name of Vessel	Description	Armament	From	To	Disposal of Vessel	Commanding Officer Name and Rank	From	To
"IVY"	Nigerian Govt. Steam Yacht	1 12-pdr. (12 cwt.) 1 7-pdr. M.L. 2 6-pdrs. Q.F. 2 machine guns	6.9.14	15.3.16	Returned to Lagos on completion of service with expedition.	†Commdr. R. H. W. Hughes, R.N.R.	—	8.7.15
						†Lieut. A. W. Hughes, R.N.R.	9.7.15	29.8.15
						†Lieut. C. J. Webb, R.N.R.	30.8.15	20.10.15
						†Lt.-Commdr. A. W. Hunt, R.N.R. (Rtd.)	21.10.15	—
"ALLIGATOR"	Motor-launch	1 machine gun	6.9.14	16.3.16	do.	*Sub-Lt. A. M. P. Ford, R.N.R. (Rtd.)	—	8.3.15
						Lieut. W. M. Lunt, R.N.R.	9.3.15	26.3.15
						Refitting at Duala	27.3.15	6.5.15
						*Lieut. A. P. Croxford, R.N.R.	7.5.15	31.5.15
						*Lieut. P. Gray, R.N.R.	1.6.15	31.10.15
						Lieut. W. P. Meldrum, R.N.R.	1.11.15	2.2.16
"CROCODILE"	do.	do.	6.9.14	21.5.16	Returned to Nigeria Marine officials at Bonny on completion of service with expedition.	†Mr. Campbell-Watson	—	12.9.14
						†Sub-Lt. M. D. Kennelley, R.N.R.	13.9.14	3.1.15
						† Lt.-Commdr. J. H. Fairweather, R.N.R.	4.1.15	10.5.15
						†Mr. Campbell-Watson	11.5.15	23.7.15
						†Lieut. M. Mayall, R.N.R.	24.7.15	21.11.15
						Lieut. A. J. McLeavy, R.N.R.	22.11.15	28.11.15
						Refitting at Duala	29.11.15	5.1.16
						Lieut. T. V. Roberts, R.N.R.	6.1.16	9.3.16
						Lieut. R. Thompson, R.N.	10.3.16	3.4.16

APPENDIX III (B)

"MANATEE"	do.	1 3-pdr. Q.F. 1 machine gun	24.1.15	15.3.16	Returned to Lagos on completion of service with expedition.	Employed on local work at Duala.	24.1.15	23.2.15
						Lieut. E. F. B. Law, R.N.	24.2.15	12.6.15
						Lieut. W. R. J. White, R.N.	13.6.15	3.9.15
						Refitting at Duala	4.9.15	21.11.15
						Sub-Lt. F. Bourdillon, R.N.R.	22.11.15	1.12.15
						Lieut. T. V. Roberts, R.N.R.	2.12.15	5.1.16
						Refitting at Duala	6.1.16	17.2.16
						Lieut. R. A. Clark, R.N.	18.2.16	6.3.16
"REMUS"	Steam-tug (W/T fitted)	3 12-pdrs. (12 cwt.)	15.9.14	29.1.16	do.	†Lieut. L. J. Hall, R.N.R.	—	17.9.14
						†Lieut. P. D. Henderson, R.N.R.	18.9.14	4.10.14
						†Lieut. A. E. Cripps, R.N.R.	5.10.14	30.1.15
						†Lieut. A. R. Martin, R.N.R.	31.1.15	11.2.15
						†Lt.-Commdr. J. T. Burn, R.N.R.	12.2.15	28.9.15
						Lieut. A. J. McLeavy, R.N.R.	29.9.15	25.10.15
						†Lieut. E. P. Nosworthy, R.N.R.	26.10.15	26.1.16
						†Lieut. A. R. Martin, R.N.R.	27.1.16	29.1.16

The officers marked thus † belonged to the Nigeria Marine.
The officers marked thus * were employed under Colonial Office agreement.

TABLE (B.)—continued

Name of Vessel	Description	Armament	From	To	Disposal of Vessel	Commanding Officer		
						Name and Rank	From	To
"PORPOISE"	Paddle-tug	2 12-pdrs. (12 cwt.) 1 3-pdr. Q.F.	22.9.14	26.4.16	Proceeded to Victoria on completion of operations in Cameroons, and carried out service under the direction of Nigeria Marine Officer at that place.	†Lieut. C. J. Webb, R.N.R.	—	25.9.14
						†Lieut. A. R. Martin, R.N.R.	26.9.14	30.1.15
						Refitting at Lagos	31.1.15	7.3.15
						†Lieut. A. R. Martin, R.N.R.	8.3.15	26.1.16
						†Lieut. E. P. Nosworthy, R.N.R.	27.1.16	13.3.16
						Lieut. T. V. Roberts, R.N.R.	14.3.16	18.4.16
						Sub-Lt. F. Miners, R.N.R.	19.4.16	20.4.16
						†Mr. A. T. Richmond	21.4.16	26.4.16
"VIGILANT"	Steam-launch (W/T fitted)	1 3-pdr. Q.F. 1 machine gun	6.9.14	21.2.16	Returned to Lagos on completion of service with expedition.	†Lieut P. D. Henderson, R.N.R.	—	17.9.14
						†Lieut. L. J. Hall, R.N.R.	18.9.14	22.1.15
						†Lt.-Commdr. J. H. Fairweather, R.N.R.	22.1.15	16.5.15
						Refitting at Calabar	17.5.15	19.8.15
						Despatch work at Duala.	20.8.15	2.9.15
						Lt.-Commdr. P. V. Kilgour, R.N.	3.9.15	28.1.16
						Lieut. R. A. Clark, R.N.	29.1.16	17.2.16

APPENDIX III (B)

Name	Type	Armament			Remarks				
"MOSELEY"	Steam life-boat	1 machine gun (Tempy.)	6.9.14	27.11.14	do.	—	—	—	—
"VAMPIRE"	Steam-launch	1 machine gun (Tempy.)	6.9.14	3.1.15	Returned to Lagos owing to watertubes giving out.	†Sub-Lt. M. Kennelly, R.N.R.	—	—	12.9.14
"WALRUS" (late "APAPA") (Captured at Lagos)	Steam-tug	1 machine gun (Tempy.)	6.9.14	26.3.16	Transferred on loan to French authorities at Duala on conclusion of operations in Cameroons.	Refitting at Calabar .. Midshipman L. J. Bidwell, R.N.	13.9.14 19.10.14		18.10.14 22.10.14
						†Mr. A. T. Richmond. Used for despatch work at Duala with native coxswain.	— 14.8.15		13.8.15 26.3.16
"BALBUS" ..	do.	3 37-mm. guns	6.9.14	3.11.14	Towed to Forcados by s.s. *Boulama* for refit.	†Lieut. A. R. Martin, R.N.R.	—		25.9.14
"MOLE" ..	Grab-Dredger	1 6" B.L. (W/T fitted)	2.10.14	13.11.14	Returned to Lagos on completion of service with expedition.	†Lieut. C. J. Webb .. †Mr. R. C. Jeffrey ..	26.9.14 —		3.11.14 —
"TROJAN" ..	Store supply ship for Nigeria Marine ships	—	7.9.14	22.11.14	do.	Mr. Joshua Cockburn, West Indian native.	—		—
300-ton Lighter	—	1 6" B.L.	27.9.14	1.2.16	do.	Returned to Lagos for return to Messrs. Elder Dempster & Co., Ltd., from whom it had been hired for service with the expedition.			

The officers marked thus † belonged to the Nigeria Marine.

APPENDIX IV

Captured Enemy Ships and Vessels, Armed and used by Cameroons Expeditionary Force

Name of Vessel	Description	Armament	From	To	Disposal of Vessel	Commanding Officer Name and Rank	From	To
"Hans Woermann"	Steamship	Nil Used as transport	27.9.14	10.5.15	Proceeded to England for London Prize Court proceedings.	Mr. R. McKillop, Master.	—	—
"Anna Woermann"	Steamship, used as a transport	2 3-pdrs. Q.F. for defence only	Salved 25.11.14 Trials 15.7.15	24.4.16	do.	Lieut. D. R. Mason, R.N.R.	—	—
"Lome"	Steamship, used as a transport from 17.2.16	2 12-pdrs. (12 cwt.) for defence only	Salved 13.12.14 Trials 30.12.15 (W/T Fitted)	8.3.16	do.	Lt.-Commdr. P. V. Kilgour, R.N.	17.2.16	—
"Kuka" (Renamed "Sir Hugh")	Steamship, used as a transport and on blockade duties	Armed 9.9.15 2 3-pdrs. Q.F.	Salved 13.11.14	11.5.16	Loaned temporarily to Nigerian Government on conclusion of operations, and subsequently loaned to French Administration, Duala.	Mr. J. S. Cave (Promoted Tempy. Lieut. R.N.R., 1.10.15). Lieut. M. Mayall, R.N.R. Lieut. J. S. Cave, R.N.R.	5.2.15 3.4.16 18.4.16	2.4.16 17.4.16 11.5.16
"Fullah"	do.	4 12-pdrs. (12 cwt.)	Salved 17.10.14	30.5.16	Transferred on loan to French administration at Duala on conclusion of operations.	Lieut. F. J. Lambert, R.N. Mr. F. J. Hopkins, Gunner, R.N. Mr. E. T. Sproson, Gunner, R.N.	1.12.14 21.12.14 28.10.15	20.12.14 27.10.15 30.5.16
"Hausa"	Steamship	Not armed, used for salvage work and transport	Salved 16.10.14	30.5.16	do.	Mr. F. Websdale, Master. Mr. McConechy, Master. †Mr. A. T. Richmond, Master. Mr. R. H. Mitchell, Gunner, R.N.	— 21.4.15 2.3.16 1.4.16	20.4.15 1.3.16 31.3.16 30.5.16

Name	Type	Armament	Date captured	Date commissioned	Remarks	Commanding Officer	Date of appointment	Date vacated
"HERZOGIN ELISABETH" (Renamed "MARGARET ELIZABETH")	Steam yacht	1 12-pdr. (12 cwt.) 2 6-pdrs. 1 7-pdr. 2 machine guns	Salved 30.10.14	30.5.16	do.	Commdr. R. S. Sneyd, R.N. Lieut.-Commdr. B. L. Hewitt, R.N.	13.3.15 15.10.15	14.10.15 30.5.16
"SODEN" (Renamed "SOKOTO")	Sternwheel shallow draught river gunboat	1 3-pdr. Q.F. 1 machine gun	27.9.14	31.3.16	do.	Mr. T. R. Clynick, Ch. Boatswain, R.N. Mr. F. S. Scott, Ch. Gunner (T), R.N.	28.9.14 26.4.15	25.4.16 4.4.16
"LALA"	Steam launch	1 machine gun	27.9.14	31.3.16	do.	Lieut. H. W. T. Pawsey, R.N. Lieut. W. R. J. White, R.N. Lieut. W. L. Wilson, R.N.R.	10.1.15 30.4.15 4.6.15	29.4.15 3.6.15 31.3.16
"ADRIANA" (Renamed "SIR FREDERICK")	Steam-tug	2 3-pdrs. (French guns)	27.9.14	17.4.16	Towed to Lagos for repairs to condenser, etc., prior to loan to Nigerian Government.	Lieut. F. J. Lambert, R.N. Refitting at Duala Lieut. F. J. Lambert, R.N. Lieut. E. F. B. Law, R.N. Enseigne de Vaisseau G. F. M. Prechac.	16.10.14 1.12.14 21.12.14 1.3.15 7.3.15	30.11.14 20.12.14 28.2.15 6.3.15 13.6.15
"TIKO" (Renamed "MYRTLE")	Motor-launch	1 machine gun	27.9.14	31.3.16	Placed in charge of the Prize Officer at Tiko for care and maintenance.	—	—	—
"DIKAKO"	do.	do.	27.9.14	31.3.16	On loan to Nigerian Government for use on work connected with the plantations at Victoria.	Commanded by various Midshipmen who were attached to Dibombe Post.		
"SALVATOR"	do.	do.	27.9.14	31.3.16	do.	do.		

† Nigerian Marine Officer.

APPENDIX V

Memorandum

The following memorandum is circulated for the information and guidance of all ranks of the British Contingent, and the Colonel Commanding wishes that all such portions as are applicable should be carefully explained to and impressed upon the native rank and file.

1. It would appear to be reasonable to conclude from the experience gained since the commencement of this campaign that the general policy laid down to guide the commanders of the numerons hostile columns in existence is that of an active defence. Most of the actions fought by the enemy have been in the nature of rearguard actions, the main bodies of the enemy slipping away under cover of small holding parties as soon as they became seriously threatened.

   In every case subsequent information has proved that the holding force was not as strong as was thought during the fight. The results of these actions have, therefore, been unsatisfactory, in that the enemy has been able to remove the greater part of his impedimenta and has escaped without being really shaken. A vigorous offensive on our part is the only method by which these tactics can be satisfactorily combated.

2. The German leaders have shown that they know how to turn to the best advantage the difficult nature of the forest country in the South in order to introduce into their operations that element of surprise on which our own Field Service Regulations lay so much stress. Their positions are generally so placed that a burst of fire on some portion of our columns is the first intimation of their existence, and many casualties have been caused by ambuscades laid in almost impenetrable bush which, lining both sides of the road, is a common feature in this portion of the Cameroons.

3. From paragraph 2, it is clear that time spent in scouting to the front round bends in the road, and into places likely to conceal an enemy, and in taking measures for securing the flanks will seldom be wasted.

   It has been found that in several cases the enemy, after laying an ambush, has allowed the greater portion of a unit to pass before making its attack on the rear. It is suggested that the enemy would find an increased difficulty in locating the rear of a unit if a small interval was kept between the tail of one unit and the head of another; the company for this purpose being treated as a unit. Such a formation on the line of march would enable

APPENDIX V

a following unit to take the enemy in the flank before becoming involved itself.

4. The rifle fire of the enemy's native soldiers has been found to be indifferent, while the very reverse can be said with regard to the handling and fire effect of the German machine guns. Every effort must be made to locate these guns and, when located, to report the fact that their position has been discovered, so that a commander can make arrangements to mass a superior fire against them and so put them out of action.

   On many occasions the enemy's machine guns have been placed on or close to the road by which the advance is being made, and in nearly every case attempts by the Allied forces to bring a gun into action on the road under this fire have failed.

   In spite of the difficult nature of the country every effort should be made to outflank hostile guns so placed.

5. In a country of this nature, where one's horizon is very limited, to obtain and forward information is undoubtedly a very difficult problem, but all officers of whatever rank must realise that only by obtaining accurate and early information can a commander influence the course of an action. In this respect negative information is almost as valuable as positive information.

   Nothing is more trying for a commander than to lose touch with a detachment or unit, and that nothing of interest has occurred is no excuse for failure to communicate. Where visual signalling is impossible and field telephones not available, communication by runners is only possible when commanders frequently report their positions.

6. The Colonel Commanding cannot impress too strongly upon all officers and British N.C.Os. their responsibility in seeing that the arms and ammunition of the killed and wounded are not allowed to fall into the hands of the enemy. The reasons for this are obvious.

7. The Colonel Commanding finds it necessary to address a word of caution to all officers commanding units employed in operations which necessitate the movement of troops in flotillas up the waterways which exist. Owing to the scattered nature of the enemy's forces and the excellent cover for an ambush which is generally found on the banks of these waterways, no flotilla can be considered to be safe at any place between the point of departure and that of arrival. It is, therefore, important that arrangements are made by officers in all craft for their continual protection.

   For this purpose it is essential that at all times night and day there should be told off in every craft an inlying piquet, armed and equipped, whose sole duty is to be ready for any emergency—and so enable the remainder to rest undisturbed.

APPENDIX VI

In addition to the above, steps must be taken to ensure that the men not on duty are properly controlled and that a state of discipline exists. The fact that men are very closely packed together, when being transported in the manner under discussion, is no excuse for disorganisation; the very fact that disorganisation is rendered easier by circumstances calls for stricter measures on the part of Officers and British N.C.Os.

(Signed) WALLACE WRIGHT, Major,
General Staff.

BRITISH HDQRS., DUALA.
7th November, 1914.

APPENDIX VI

Distribution and Strength of the British Contingent of General Dobell's Expeditionary Force; 30th August, 1915.

	Rifles	Guns	Machine guns	Remarks
Northern Railway—				
Bare.—Sierra Leone Company, R.G.A. (less one section)	—	2	—	
West African Regiment	192	—	2	
Gold Coast Battalion	140	—	1	
Nkongsamba.—Section Gold Coast Battery	—	2	—	
Machine gun detachment, West India Regiment	16	—	2	
5th Light Infantry (Indian Army)	155	—	—	Including 7 sick.
West African Regiment	289	—	2	
Line of Communication (including Bonaberi).—5th Light Infantry	218	—	—	Including 17 in hospital.
West African Regiment	146	—	1	
Gold Coast Battalion	134	—	3	
Dibombe Post.—Sierra Leone Battalion	98	—	1	
Victoria, Zopo and Buea.—Sierra Leone Battalion	166	—	2	
Campo Area.—Nigerian Battery	—	1	—	
One double-company, 5th Light Infantry	173	—	2	
One company, 1st Nigerians	126	—	1	
Two companies, Gold Coast Battalion	276	—	2	
One company, Sierra Leone Battalion	97	—	1	
Nyong Base.—Gold Coast Battalion	50	—	—	

APPENDIX VII

General Dobell's Expeditionary Force—*continued*

	Rifles	Guns	Machine guns	Remarks
Duala.—Sierra Leone Company, R.G.A. (less one section)	—	2	—	
Nigerian Battery (less one gun)	—	3	—	31 ranks on leave in Nigeria.
West African Regiment	40	—	—	All in hospital.
1st Nigerians	257	—	4	Includes 75 sick and excludes 292 on leave in Nigeria.
2nd Nigerians	383	—	5	Includes 51 sick and excludes 257 on leave in Nigeria.
Recruits of Nigeria Regiment	283	—	—	Includes 88 sick.
Gold Coast Battalion	100	—	—	Includes 68 sick and excludes 163 on leave in the Gold Coast.
Sierra Leone Battalion	208	—	2	Includes 32 sick.
Gambia Detachment	60	—	—	Includes 7 sick.

Notes.—The West African Regiment and Sierra Leone Battalion were each organised in six companies; the Gold Coast Battalion comprised five companies; the two Nigerian battalions each had four companies. The 5th Light Infantry was organised in three double-companies, its organisation being changed in October, 1915, to one of six companies.

APPENDIX VII

Standing Orders for the Eastern British Force

1. *Carriers.*—Before the Column leaves Wum Biagas, carriers will be allotted to O.C. Units for their ammunition, personal baggage, tools, etc. These carriers will be permanently attached to their Units and will remain with them on arrival in camp at the end of the day's march. The only carriers who will be parked *en masse* will be those of the Supply Department.
2. *Formation of Camp.*—The actual formation of the Camp must depend on the military situation, but normally the following will be the procedure:—On the order being given, camp will be formed on the second company of the advanced guard, which will extend 65 yards on either side of the road. The companies in rear will form the sides of the camp, the normal frontage being one yard per man. The leading company of the advanced guard will remain out in front and be responsible for the protective duties until camp has been formed. The company

forming the rear guard will be responsible for protection to rear until camp is complete.

3. *Ammunition.*—The amount of ammunition carried for the Infantry is 150 rounds on the man and 100 rounds per man reserve, and 6,000 rounds per machine gun.

4. *Latrines.*—On arrival in camp O.C. Units will arrange for the formation of latrines. When possible these should be constructed for day use outside the camp, either to the flanks or rear according to the wind. O.C. Units will use all possible means to prevent carriers from relieving themselves by night inside the perimeter except in the proper latrines, and any offenders in this respect must be severely dealt with.

5. *Lights Out.*—Each unit will detail an European daily who will be responsible that all lights and fires are extinguished at the appointed hour, and that the strictest silence is maintained after " lights out."

(" Lights out " will be at 8.30 p.m. unless otherwise ordered.)

6. *Halts.*—Subject to military considerations, the head of the main body will halt for ten minutes half an hour after leaving camp, and again for ten minutes after each hour. During a halt, however short the duration, every precaution must be taken against surprise, and each company or detachment must at once push out sentries on either side of the road.

C. R. SAVILE, Major,
Staff Captain, B.H.Q.

B.H.Q. WUM BIAGAS.
20/11/15.

APPENDIX VII

Plan of Camp

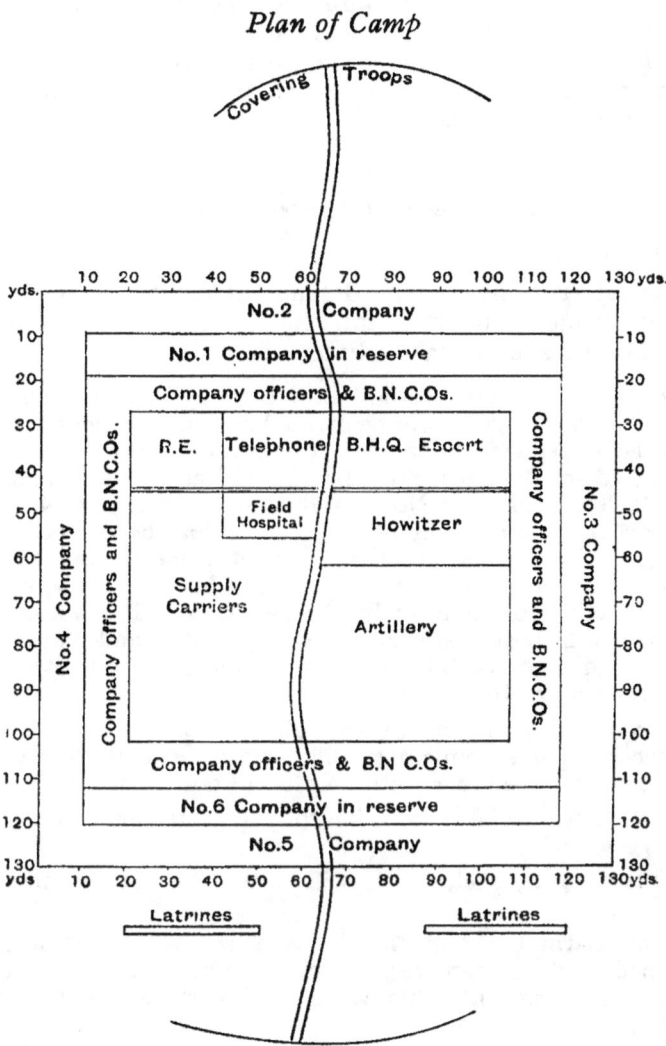

No. 1 Company is responsible for the protective duties during the formation of camp. Frequently it may be necessary to encamp one of the reserve companies some distance in front of the main camp, in order to ensure rest for the main body.

The above sketch shows the normal distribution in camp of a force consisting of six companies, with howitzer detachment and four 2·95″ guns. The actual shape of the camp will, of course, vary according to military and terrain conditions. Much time in forming camp will be saved if O.C. Units will study this plan and so have a mental picture of their positions in camp and the amount of space they are allowed to occupy under normal conditions.

Instructions for the Defence of Camps

To O.C. Units.

These instructions for the defence of camps must be read in conjunction with the Standing Orders for the Eastern British Force issued at Wum Biagas on 20/11/15.

1. To ensure the safety of the camp both by day and night the perimeter of the camp will be divided into four sections (sections will be dependent upon the strength of the column). The front face of the square will be No. 1 Section, right flank face No. 2, left flank face No. 3 and the rear face No. 4. Each section commander will be responsible for the defence of his section. He will ensure that efficient trenches and machine gun pits are dug and that every man of his section understands where he has to go and what he has to do. The section commander will post observation posts by day and piquets by night, and make certain that his section is connected up with the sections on either flank.

2. The companies in reserve will also be protected by shelter trenches. These companies will form a General Reserve and will be under the orders of the Colonel Commanding only.

3. The artillery will be responsible for the protection of their guns and personnel.

4. If time permits, shelter pits will be dug for the servants and carriers.

5. On the alarm being given, the trenches will be immediately manned and all reserves, servants, and carriers got under cover. All fires and lights will be extinguished and the utmost silence kept.

6. Transport Officers will endeavour to get the carriers quickly under cover and prevent any tendency towards panic. Any sign of panic or running wildly about the camp should be met with the most drastic measures.

7. It is equally important for the safety of the camp that fires should not be lighted within the perimeter before daylight as it is that they should be thoroughly extinguished at 8.30 p.m. All ranks should be warned that the infringement of this order will be met with by the most severe punishment. This order does

APPENDIX VIII 449

not prohibit the lighting of fires when operations commence before daylight and Europeans require food, so long as the fires are kept under cover and sheltered from view.

H. GWYNNE HOWELL, Major,
General Staff.

B.H.Q. NGOK.
25/11/15.

APPENDIX VIII

ALLIED TROOPS (COMBATANT UNITS) OPERATING IN THE CAMEROONS ON THE 1ST JANUARY 1916

(A) *Under Major-General Dobell*

Approximate rifle strength { British—4,400.
French—4,100.

Guns { British 11 (10 mountain and 1 howitzer).
French 6 (mountain).

British units {
Detachment 36th (Sierra Leone) Co., R.E.
Howitzer detachment, R.A.
Sierra Leone Company, R.G.A.
Nigerian Battery, W.A.F.F.
Section Gold Coast Battery, W.A.F.F.
Two companies and machine gun detachment, West India Regiment.
5th Light Infantry (Indian Army)=six companies.
1st Nigerians W.A.F.F.*=four companies.
2nd Nigerians W.A.F.F.†=four companies.
West African Regiment=six companies.
Gold Coast Battalion W.A.F.F.=five companies.
Sierra Leone Battalion W.A.F.F.=six companies.
Gambia Company W.A.F.F.

French units (under Col. Mayer) {
One mountain battery (three sections)=6 guns.
Engineer detachment.
Twenty-three companies of infantry.

---

* Consisted of " A " and " F " Cos. 1st Battalion and " D " and " F " Cos. 2nd Battalion, Nigeria Regiment.
† Consisted of " A," " D," " E " and " F " Cos., 4th Battalion, Nigeria Regiment.

APPENDIX VIII

(B) *Under the control of Brig.-General Cunliffe*

Approximate rifle strength { British—2,000. French—900. }

Guns—5 British and 3 French.

British units ..
{ "A," "B" and "C" Cos., Mounted Infantry Battalion, Nigeria Regiment.
Five 2·95″ guns (two of 1st and three of 2nd Battery, Nigeria Regiment).
"B," "C" and "H" Cos., 1st Battalion Nigeria Regiment.
"A," "B," ½ "C," ½ "E," ½ "G" and "H" Cos., 2nd Battalion Nigeria Regiment.
"A," "B," "C," "D," "E," "F" and "H" Cos., 3rd Battalion Nigeria Regiment. }

French units (under Col. Brisset)
{ One squadron of cavalry.
Three guns (one heavy and two mountain).
Five companies of infantry. }

(C) *Under the control of General Aymerich*

East Cameroons Force { French—10½ companies (approx. 2,000 rifles) and 6 guns.
Belgian—3 companies (approx. 500 rifles). }

South Cameroons Force (Col. Le Meillour) { French—6 companies (approx. 1,000 rifles) and 3 guns. }

INDEX

All places not followed by the name of a Colony are in The Cameroons.

Unless otherwise stated all places shown as "occupied" were taken by British forces.

All vessels are British unless otherwise described.

Abbreviations

Belg. = Belgian.
Bn. = Battalion.
Brit. = British.
Commr. = Commissioner.
Cr. = Cruiser.
Fr. = French.
G.B. = Gunboat.
Ger. = German.
Gov.-Gen. = Governor-General.

Hd.-Qrs. = Head-quarters.
I.G. = Inspector-General.
L. Cr. = Light Cruiser.
W.A.F.F. = West African Frontier Force.
W.A.M.S. = West African Medical Service.
W/T = Wireless Telegraphy.

Abang, occupied, 416
Abong Mbang, Fr. occupy, 313; loss of, 337
Accra (The Gold Coast), Executive and Legislative Council meetings, 13, 14–15
Ada (The Gold Coast), Brit. force at, 15
Adakakpe (Togoland), occupied, 33
Adametz, Capt. (Ger. Army), 99, 370
Adams, Lt. B. F., R.N., wounded, 85; 176
Adams, Capt. G. S. C., Garua, 94–7
Admiralty, 17; issues "warning" telegram, 3; to estimate force required, 60; opinion of, on Duala project, 61, 62; orders to Ad. Stoddart, 64; instructions to Capt. Fuller, 67, 74–5, 78; and recall of *Cumberland* or *Challenger*, 145, 156, 181–3; question of command, 181–3, 188; negatives blockade, 213; blockade declared, 264; *see also* Blockade; Conferences
Africa, British West, Imperial and local forces in, 1914, 42–4
Agbeluvoe (Togoland), affair of, 28–31
Aircraft, German, captured, 203
Akoafim, Ger. force at, 211; Fr. occupy, 338

Alexander, Mr. J., 425
Alligator, Motor launch, 80, 214: Dibamba river, 127–9; Tiko, 140; Yapoma bridge, 142–4; Yabasi, 147–53; Edea, 162–9; Nyong river, 308–9, 387, 421
Ambam, Fr. occupy, 383, 399
Ambas Bay, operations in, 79–80
Ammunition, captured in Togoland, 30, 39; use of softnosed, by enemy, 30, App. I., 430; scale of, for The Cameroons, 66, 69; losses of, 90; shortage of Ger., 96n, 242n, 352, 363, 395, 406, 416; affair of Nsanakang, 107, 108n; shortage of Fr., 189, 193; supply of Ger., 213n, 363; Ger., captured, 234, 283, 299, 378; destroyed, 297
Anderson, Major F., Yaunde, 356n, 388–95; 399
Andrew, 2nd Lt. F. E., killed, 238
Anglo-French Expeditionary Force, prospective strength of, 70; Brit. contingent arrives, 86, 122; organisation and strength of, 122–4, 255n; Fr. contingent arrives, 125, strength of, 255n; strength (1 Jan. 1916), 395n, App. VIII., 449–50; Order of Battle (23 Sept. 1914), App. II., 432–4; *see also* Dobell, Lt.-Gen. Sir C. M.

451

INDEX

Anthony, Lt. G. A., killed, 415
Appam, Transport, 71, 112, 113, 124, 126, 128, 154; sails for The Cameroons, 70, arrives, 122; hospital ship, 136
Appreciations, by General Staff (Aug. 1914), 75, 76–7; Nigerian Marine, 75–6; *see also* Dobell, Lt.-Gen. Sir C. M.
Archibong, occupied, 111
Armitage, Capt. C. H. (Chief Commr. Northern Territories), 32, 33
Armoured trains, German, on Northern Railway, 153, 159, 175, 200
Army Ordnance Corps, detachment in West Africa, 42
Army Service Corps, detachment in West Africa, 42
Arnett, Mr. E. J., v.
Arboussier, M., 32
Armistice, for surrender of prisoners of war, 405
Artillery, British, for The Cameroons, 65, 69–70
Artillery, British, Batteries, Gold Coast, 113, 198–202, 216–22, 226, 237, 239, 242, 290; Yaunde, 329–37; 356–64, 376–83, 388–95
—, —, —, Nigerian, 90–7, 100–2, 104–6, 110, 111, 120, 122, 138, 151–3, 158, 183, 198–202, 203, 209, 230*n*, 237, 239, 242, 250, 256–8, 277–85, 290, 318–19, 322–7, 399*n*, 401*n*, 403*n*, 415*n*, Yaunde, 329–37, 340–50, 356–64, 367–74, 376–83, 388–95
—, —, —, Sierra Leone, 126–9, 176, 184–5, 199–202, 226, 237, 239, 242, 290, 341–50, 367–74, 386, 396
—, —, —, Mountain, Gold Coast, Yabasi, 146–53
—, —, —, —, Sierra Leone, Yabasi, 146–53
—, —, Companies, Garrison, 50th, 42; Sierra Leone, 42, 70
—, French, Edea, 161–9
—, German, in The Cameroons, 65, 69
Ashanti, 6
Ashanti Mines Volunteers, *see* Volunteer Corps
Ashby, Midshipman H. J. M., 163
Aston, Major-Gen. Sir G., 2*n*
Astræa, Brit. L. Cr. (Capt. A. C. Sykes), relieves *Challenger*, 265
Aubin, Capt. A. C., killed, 95*n*
Aymerich, Gen. (Fr. Army), 117, 118, 157, 175, 189, 195, 211, 249, 282, 285, 304, 313, 316, 317, 318, 321, 346, 355, 356, 374, 383–4, 387, 394, 422, 424; strength and disposition of force under, 114–15, 320, 338, 365–6, 384; co-operation of, delayed, 274, 284, 292, 302; at Duala, 320–1; final operations, 395–420, message from Gen. Dobell, 404–5, assumes command of Eastern area, 408

Bachmann, Lt. (Ger. Army), killed, 225
Badham, Capt. J. F., Mora, 323–7
Badog, Fr. occupy, 382
Bakundi, occupied, 193
Bal, Lt. (Belg. Army), 175
Balbus, Steam tug, 80; Yabasi, 147–9; abandoned, 150, salved, 153
Balders, Capt. A. W., killed, 358, 362
Bali Bagam, affair of, 343–4
Bamenda, Ger. force at, 68, 343; occupied, 343–4
Bamkin, occupied, 371
Bana, occupied, 386
Bandam, occupied, 371
Bangum, affair near, 370
Banyo, occupied, 344–6; Ger. force at, 345
Banyo Mountain, operations against, 346–50; description of, 347–8; captured, 349, effect of, 366
Bansara, River steamer, 111
Bare, occupied, 203; enemy attacks, 218, 227; Brit. force at, 237, 239
Barker, Capt. E., carries summons to surrender Togoland, 18–19; at Lome, 20, 22, 23, 24
Basel Mission, *see* Missionaries, German
Batura, Fr. occupy, 212
Beattie, Lt. A. E., wounded, 273
Beaty-Pownall, Capt. C. P., R.N. (*Challenger*), 86; Tiko, 184; leaves in *Cumberland*, 188; 205
Beckley, Mr. A. J., 31*n*, 34, 38, 39
Bell, Chief (of Duala), Germans execute, 65*n*, 78
Bell, Mr. (Uncle of Chief Bell, *q.v.*), with Cameroons expedition, 78, 81, 84
Belok Nkonjok Mountain, captured, 377–8
Bennett, Lt. R. D., wounded, 150*n*
Bertua, Fr. occupy, 212, 313
Bettington, Capt. D. R. A., 26, 27
Bettington, Mrs., 26*n*
Biddulph, Capt. L. S., 354, 356, 357, 360
Bidwell, Midshipman L. J., wounded, 163

Bismarck, Prince, attitude of, towards colonisation, 45-6
Bitam, Fr. occupy, 310n, 313; operations from, 365
Blackburn, Lt. J. C., 104
Blockade, of The Cameroons, 63, 67, 196n, 285, 286, 288, 290, 313, 337, 374, 387, 425; Admiralty negative, 213; declared, 264; military assistance, 307-8; raised, 421
Blockhouses, 246, 265, 271, 382
Blum, Capt. (Fr. Army), 339, 340, 365, 383
Body, Lt. O. G., captured, 108
Boma, Transport, 122, 162n, 183
Bombe, occupied, 187
Bonaberi, Brit. force at, 130, 138
Bonaberi, river craft, 162n, 164
Bonga, Fr. occupy, 116
Booth, Major C. A., Gurin, 268-70
Booth, Major E. B., 395
Bouchez, Capt. (Fr. Army), 32
Bowyer-Smijth, Capt. C. G., Garua, 94-7; 307; killed, 349, 350
Boyle, Mr. A. G. (Acting Gov.-Gen. of Nigeria), 57, 59-61, 68-9, 323, 327, 341
Brackenbury, Capt. E. A., 372
Braithwaite, Com. L. W., Edea, 162-9, 197-8
Brand, Capt. E. S., Yabasi, 148-9, killed, 150n
Bridges, Munaya river, 103, 104; Bapele, partly destroyed, 138, capture of, 139; 159; repaired, 175; Yapoma, partly destroyed, 138, 139, attack on, 141-4, repaired, 207; Kake, 159; Nlohe, 199, destroyed, 200, restored, 201; native suspension, 201; Edea, repaired, 258; Kele river, 276, 334, 354, 361; Midland Railway, 287, 320; Ndupe river, 330; Mbila river, 332
Brisset, Lt.-Col. (Fr. Army), 170-3, 189-93, 195, 207, 208, 215, 228-31, 250-3, 267-8, 270; strength of force under, 171, 209, 230; Garua, 295-307; Mora, 323-7; 340-50, 267-74, 384, 386-7; final operations, 395-414; 422
Brough, Lt.-Col. J., R.M.A., 70n, 426
Brown, Lt. H. W., mortally wounded, 95n
Browne, Capt. W. S., 199-203
Bruix, Fr. Cr., 112, 121, 156, 180, 181; off Victoria, 183
Bryant, Lt.-Col. F. C., R.A., v., Act. Comdt. Gold Coast Regt., 13, 15,

22; demands surrender of Togoland, 17-19; instructions to, 19-20, 21, 24; orders concentration at Krachi, 25; at Accra, 25, 26; at Lome, 27; advances on Kamina, 28; affair of Agbeluvoe, 28-31, halts at, 33, resumes advance, 34; affair of Khra, 26-8; at Amuchu, 39; tribute to, 40
Buea, Ger. force at, 161, 175-6; capture of, 186
Bumbo, occupied, 372
Burgess, Colour-Sergt. L. J., killed, 279
Bussell, Lt. E. J. D., killed, 280n
Butler, Lt. J. F. P., awarded *V.C.*, 186; Chang, 216-22
Butler, Capt. J. H., Yaunde, 376-83

Cables, German, in English channel, cut, 3; to South America, 4n; cut at Lome, 20, 24; to The Cameroons, 52, cut, 73, repaired, 134
Caillet, Comdt. (Fr. Army), 399, 400, 412, 418-20
Callwell, Major-Gen. C. E., 2n
Cameroon Mountain, capture of, 183-8; Ger. strength on, 183, 185
Cameroon Estuary, navigability of, 61, 76-7; wreck barrage in, 63, 81, details of, 82; 83, 124, 132, description of, 73; defences in, 74, 76, 80, 86; naval operations in, 80-6, 124-30; *see also* Mines, German
Cameroon river, *see* Wuri river
Cameroons Expeditionary Force, *see* Anglo-French Expeditionary Force
Cameroons, The, preparations to invade, 42-72; description of, 45-53, 137; annexed by Germany (1884), 45; language used in, 46; frontiers of, 46, 47-50; population of, 52; administration system in, 52-3; Ger. forces in, (1914) 53-5, 65, 69, distribution, (July) 54, (18 Oct.) 160-1, (Nov. 1915) 351-2, (Jan. 1916) 406; Ger. scheme for defence of, 55n; 65, 346-7; unpopularity of Germans in, 64, 84; Fr. intentions in, 255; general situation in (7 Dec. 1915), 374-6; administration after conquest, 422
Campo, occupied, 214; operations from, 310, 317-19, 338-9, 365, 403, 409, 419; Brit. force at, 400, 409

INDEX

Campo river, operations, 213–15, 245–6, 265, 290, 309–10
Carlton, Lt. G. F., R.N.R., 80
Carnot, Fr. occupy, 157
Carré, Capt. (Fr. Navy), 339, 425
Carriers, *see under* Transport
Carter, Col. C. H. P. (Comdt. Nigeria Regt.), 59–62, arrives Lagos, 68; seeks sanction to attack Garua, 68, approved, 69; orders to Maiduguri Column, 86, 88; Yola Column, 91; instructions to Col. Cunliffe, 97; recalled, 98; instructions to Col. Mair, 100–2, 104
Cary, Lt. A. J. L., wounded, 327
Castaing, Capt. (Fr. Army), strength of force under, 33; affair of Khra, 36–8
Casualties, British, in Togoland, 29, 30, 36, 37; in The Cameroons, naval, 84, 85, 128, 142, 149n, 163, 246, 264n; Mora, 90, 172; Tepe, 92–3; Garua, 95, 297; Nsanakang, 103, 107, 108; Dibamba river, 127, 128; Maka, 140; Yapoma bridge, 142; Yabasi, 149, 150, 153; Kake, 159, 160; Edea, 163, 164; total to 26 October, 1914, 169, Jan, 1915, 228; during reconnaissances, 178, 179; Muyuka, 185; Cameroon Mountain, 185; Kosseva, 192; Ibi Column, 193, 194; Danare, 194; Northern Railway, 200, 202; Bare, 203, 227; 21 Dec. 1914, 204; Kribi, 206, 226; Chang, 216, 217, 218, 342; Ossidinge, 223; Kopongo, 225; Mbureku, 234, 237, 238; Harmann's Farm, 235, 241, 242; Beli, 250n; Ngwe, 257, 283, 284; frontier raids, 267; Gurin, 269; Wum Biagas, 272–3, 282n, 332; advance to Yaunde, 276, 277, 278, 279, 280, 281, total 284; 336, 357, 358, 359, 360, 361, 377, 378, 379, 380, 381, 389, 390, 391, 392; Gashiga, 307; Njabesan, 318; Mora, 326, 327; Moloko, 339; Bamenda, 343; Bali Bagam, 343–4; Kentu, 344; Gandua, 344; Banyo, 345; Banyo Mountain, 349, 350; advance to Fumban, 367; Bangum and Kuti, 370; Bumbo, 372; Elabe, 410; total in Gen. Cunliffe's force, 415; Mafub, 415; Abang, 416; total, 426
—, Franco-Belgian, total, 424
—, French, in Togoland, 36, 37, 39; in The Cameroons, Kuseri, 118; Mibang, 119; Yapoma bridge, 144; Yabasi, 149n; Ukoko, 156; Edea, 166, 167, 197, 225; Dzimu, 175; Mora, 190, 193, 326; Ngwe, 245, 283; Garua area, 252; So, Dibanga, 257; Sende, 273; Eseka, 274, 354; Ngok, 276; Matem, 278; So Dibanga, 282n; Monso position, 293; Ndupe river, 311; Yaunde, 337, 364, 383; Akak, 365; Ebolowa, 410; Mafub, 415; Ngat, 419; final phase, 420; total, 427
Casualties, German, in Togoland, 29, 30, 31, 38; in The Cameroons, Tepe, 92–3; Garua, 94, 95–6, 297, 298, 299; Takum, 99; Nsanakang, 108; Tiko, 140; Kuseri, 157; Kake, 160; Edea, 163, 166, 167, 197, 225; Dzimu, 175; Cameroon Mountain, 185, 186, 187; Mora, 190, 326n; Oti, 210; Bare, 218; Kribi, 224; Demsa, 229; Mbureku, 234; Gurin, 269; So Dibanga, 282n; Ngwe, 283; Koncha, 301; Tingere, 306; Kentu, 344; Gandua, 344; Banyo, 345–6; Banyo Mountain, 349
Cathie, Lt. H. W., killed, 332n
Censorship, established, 14
Chadwick, Sergt. W., wounded, 359
Challenger, L. Cr., 112, 113; for The Cameroons, 78, arrives, 86, 122; capture of Duala, 124–30; Duala, 133, 188, 205, 245n; leaves, 265
Chamba, occupied, 301
Chamley, Capt. J. W., 200
Champness, Lt. F. Q., R.N., Dibamba river, 127–9; Tiko, 140; Yapoma bridge, 141–4
Chang, preparations for advance on 204–5; capture of, and withdrawal from, 216–22, effect of, 221–2; Ger. force at, 243; re-occupied, 342–3
Chang Mangas, occupied, 381; halt at, 381–2
Chardy, Capt. (Fr. Army), 387
Chartres, Lt. J., wounded, 350
Charts, unreliable, 74
Cheron, Capt. (Fr. Navy), 181, 188
Child, Capt. H. A. (Dir. Nigeria Marine), 121; death of, 164; 425n
"Chupplies" (foot-wear), *see under* Clothing
Churcher, Major A. E., 99
Claridge, Dr. W. W., at Lome, 27
Clark, Lt. R. A., R.N., 275, 289n, 309

INDEX

Clark, Dr. W. S., 109
Clausnitzer, Herr (Dist. Commr. at Lome), 18, surrenders Lome, 20
Clifford, Sir Hugh C. (Gov. of The Gold Coast, 1914–   ), 9, 13, 40, 113, 120
Clothing, confusion caused by similar, 89–90 ; foot-wear, 96n
Cockburn, Lt.-Col. J. B. (1st Nigerians), Duala, 137 ; Yabasi, 151–3, 176–7 ; awarded Royal Humane Society Silver Medal 177n ; Nyamtan, 177 ; Chang, 220–2 ; Bare, 227 ; Mbureku, 233–4 ; Harmann's Farm, 235–6 ; Yaunde, 281–5, 256–64, 379–83, 390–5, 403, 407–8, 411–13, 416 ; tribute to, 426
Cole, Major S. J., v.
Coles, Major R. G., 204, 244, 309, 379, 403, 406–8, 410–13, 416
Collins, Lt. H. S., 28
Colonial Defence Committee, 16
Colonial Office, 300n ; issues " warning " telegram, 3, 13, 57 ; announces declaration of war, 14 ; instructions to Capt. Bryant, 19–20, 21, 24 ; and Fr. co-operation, 20, 22, 232 ; orders reinforcements from Sierra Leone and Nigeria, 31, 32, 64 ; instructions to Nigeria, 59, 62, 79, 97 ; to estimate force required, 60 ; proposal *re* Sierra Leone force, 62 ; instructions of, *re* force for The Cameroons, 67, 70–1 ; sanctions attack on Garua, 69 ; instructions to Gen. Dobell, 71, 145, 255–6 ; question of naval strength, 181–2 ; and reinforcements, 213, 215, 222, 246–8
Colonies, Crown Agents for the, supply military equipment, 9
Committee of Imperial Defence, Offensive Sub-Committee, formed, 2, decisions of, 3–4, 12, 17, 58, 60, 62, 64, 66, 69–70, 72, 145 ; 256n ; Oversea Defence Committee, 12
Communications, in Togoland, 5, 16–17 ; The Gold Coast, 6–7 ; Nigeria, 47–8 ; The Cameroons, 48–52 ; Duala, restored, 134 ; failure of (Edea), 168 ; difficulties of, 207–8, 253, 347 ; *see also* Railways ; Roads
—, British, telegraphic ; telephonic, in Nigeria, interrupted, 88, 173 ; extended, 100 ; from Buea, 187 ; cut, 218, restored, 219 ; interrupted, 266 ; success of field telephone, 395

Communications, German, telegraphic ; telephonic, The Cameroons, 52, 73 ; intercepted, 60n, 185, 209 ; across Sanaga river, cut, 155 ; coastal, destroyed, 180 ; *see also* Wireless Telegraphy
Conferences, at Admiralty, *re* attack on Duala, 63–4 ; at Lagos, 77, 122 ; Gen. Dobell and Col. Mayer, 113, 244–5 ; Anglo-German, 173 ; at Yola, 266–7 ; Allied, at Duala, 320–1, 398 ; Gen. Cunliffe and Col. Brisset, 372 ; Germans, at Yaunde, 394 ; *see also* Missions
Cooke, Capt. H. H. A., 372, 373, 384–6
Cooke, Mr. (The Gold Coast Service), 33
Coombs, Lt. A. E., wounded, 379
Corbett, Sir Julian, " Naval Operations," by, quoted, 3–4
Corner, Lt. H. E., wounded, 389
Cotton, Lt.-Col. W. L., 341–50, 367–74, 384–6, 396
Council of Defence (French), 248
Crailsheim, Capt. von (Ger. Army), Comdg. Garua, 96n, 268–70, 295–9
Craven, Capt. The Hon. R., wounded 358
Crawford, Lt.-Col. H. R. H., v.
Crocodile, Motor launch, 80, 141, 214 ; Dibamba river, 127–9 ; Yabasi, 147–53 ; Edea, 162–9, 197–9 ; Nyong river, 308–9
Crookenden, Lt.-Col. J., v., 100, 101, 103, 108, 250, 266, 340–50, 355, 367–74 ; Fumban, 368–70 ; 384–6, 395, 401 ; *see also* Infantry, British, Columns, Cross River
Crosse, Com. A. B., 425
Crowe, Lt. D. M., wounded, 378
Crown Agents for the Colonies, *see* Colonies, Crown Agents for the
Croxford, Mr., 102
Cumberland, Cr. (Capt. C. T. M. Fuller), orders to, 64 ; arrives, Sierra Leone, 67, Lagos, 68, Lome, 74, off Fernando Po, 78 ; Ambas Bay, 79, 80 ; Cameroon Estuary, 80–6 ; Edea, 161–9 ; leaves, 188 ; 205 ; *see also* Admiralty ; Fuller, Ad. Sir C. T. M.
Cumberland's picket boat, Mikanje creek, 84, Dibamba river, 126 ; Tiko, 140 ; Mungo river, 85, 144 ; Yabasi, 147, 151 ; Edea, 162 ; Mpundu, 184 ; 214 ; Nyong river, 308–9
Cumberland's steam pinnace, Cameroon Estuary, 85 ; Misselele, 14 Mpundu, 184

Cunliffe, Brig.-Gen. F. H. G., v., 96*n*, 120, 121, 122, 195, 199*n*, 209, 215, 222–3, 250, 253, 270, 313–17, 321, 355, 387, 397–400, 403, 405, 409, 421, 422, 424 ; to command in the North, 97, 146 ; instructions to, 97, 146 ; Dibamba river, 126–9 ; operations, (7–31 Oct. 1914) 169–74, (1–30 Nov.) 190–3, (March–April, 1915) 266–70, (May–July) 294–307, (Aug.–Sept.) 322–7, (Oct.–Nov.) 340–50, (Nov.–Dec.) 366–74, (Dec.) 384–6 ; at Duala, 230–1 ; concentrates at Yola, 267–8 ; Gurin, 268–70 ; strength and distribution of force under, 324, 373, 384–5, (1 Jan. 1916) 395–6 ; returns to Lagos, 413 ; tribute to, 414

Dalrymple-Hamilton, Lt. F. H. G., R.N., 138, 141
D'Amico, Dr., 186
Damiens, M., 248
Danare, affair of, 194
Daniell, Major-Gen. J. F., 427
Davidson, Capt. E., 309
Davies, Com. W. H., R.N.R., 221
Dawes, Lt. G., awarded M.C., 235*n*
Defence Schemes, The Gold Coast, 9–11, 15 ; Nigeria, 45, 55–7, 58 ; French, 115
Dehane, Allies advance from, 165, effect of, 169
Delcassé, M. (Fr. Foreign Minister), 316
de Miremont, Lt., 241
Demsa, affair of, 229
Dennis, Sergt. J., killed, 108
Desertions, of German native troops, 32, 88, 195, 386, 400, 418
Deslaurens, Capt. (Fr. Army), 278, 364
Dibamba river, 82, 124 ; attempted landing in, 126–9, effect of, 130
Dibombe Post, established, 177 ; enemy attacks on, 244
Dillon, Lt. B. T. B., wounded, 379
Dinnen, Capt. C. H., killed, 241
Ditam, occupied, 385–6
Djembe, Germans re-occupy, 157, effect of, 174–5
Dobell, Lt.-Gen. Sir C. M., v., 17, 190–6, 203–4, 206–7, 209, 216, 222–3, 225–6, 228, 233, 250, 296, 300–3, 305–6, 308–12, 323, 327, 341, 365–7, 383, 386–7, 395, 424, 425 ; I.G., W.A.F.F., 2 ; appreciations by, (3 Aug. 1914) 11–12, 57–8, (5th) 16–17, (16th) 64–6, modified, 69–70, (21 April, 1915) 258–64, 274, (23 June) 286–8, 315 ; question of attacking Duala, 62, 63 ; to command Allied force, 66–67 ; sails in *Appam*, 70, arrives, 86, 122, at Freetown, 112, Accra, 113, Lagos, 120, 121 ; Govt. instructions to, 71, 145 ; meets Col. Mayer, 113, 244–5, 258 ; capture of Duala, 124–30 ; civil and political administration under, 131–2 ; 291–2 ; consolidation of Duala, 133–69 ; Yapoma bridge, 141–4 ; Yabasi and Susa, 146–53 ; reports of, 154 ; Edea, 161–9, 196–8 ; and French operations, 174 ; Buea, 176 ; question of naval command, 181–3, 188 ; Cameroon Mountain, 183–8 ; at Buea, 187 ; Northern Railway, 199–202 ; calls for reinforcements, 213, 215, 246–8, 315 ; reinforcements sanctioned, 222 ; Chang, 218–22 ; views on command, 230–1 ; and Allied co-operation, 232 ; strength and distribution of force under, (Feb. 1915) 236, (June) 290–1, (30 Aug.) 320–1, App. VI., 444–5, (1 Jan. 1916) 395*n*, App. VIII., 449–50 ; meets French Mission, 253–5 ; War Office assume control of operations, 255–6 ; at Edea, 258, 281, 282 ; Yaunde, 271–85, 328–37, 352–64, 374–83, 292–5 ; correspondence *re* future policy, (12–23 June, 1915) 285–8, (Aug.) 314–17, 321 ; requirements for advance on Yaunde, 315 ; Allied Conference, 320–1 ; visits Eseka, 387 ; final operations, 396–420 ; message to Gen. Aymerich, 404–5 ; message from H.M. The King, 421–2 ; Order of the Day (13 March, 1916), 422 ; *see also* Anglo-French Expeditionary Force ; Conferences ; Operations, Combined
Doering, Major von (Acting Gov. of Togoland), proposal of neutrality, 15–16, refused, 17 ; receives demand to surrender, 18–19 ; concentrates at Kamina, 19–20 ; and use of soft-nosed bullets, 30, App. I., 430
Dokes, Colour-Sergt. R., wounded, 257
Dreadnought, lighter, Yabasi, 147–53 ; Edea, 162–9 ; Tiko, 184
Dresden, Ger. L. Cr., expected at Duala, 62

INDEX

Duala, W/T station at, 52, 67, destroyed, 129, 130; question of attack on, 58, 60, 61, 67, force required for, 65–6; *Dresden* expected at, 62; defences at, 63, 74–5, 76, 130; description of, 73, 130; strength of Ger. force at, 76, 80, 130; capture and consolidation of, 120–69; summoned to surrender, 125, surrenders, 129; administration at, 131–2; port facilities at, 133; strength of force at, 226; declared an open port, 264n; *see also* Cameroon Estuary; Mines, German
Duhring, Capt. von (Ger. Army), 192, 193
Dume, Fr. occupy, 313
Duranthon, M., 32
Dwarf, G.B., 42, 61, 62, 141, 183, 205, 290, 421; at Sierra Leone, 67; Lagos, 78; off Ambas Bay, 79, 80; operations in Cameroon Estuary, 80–6, rammed, 85; capture of Duala, 124–30; Edea, 161–9, 197–8, 224
Dwyer, Sergt. O., wounded, 273
Dzimu, Fr. capture, 175

Earle, Lt. J. V., 24, 284
Ebermaier, Herr K. (Gov. of The Cameroons), 52, 244, 318n, 376, 392–4, 397, 406, 411; reports surrender, 420
Ebolowa, Ger. force at, 161; supply depôt, 339n; Fr. advance on, 383, 409–10; Ger. Govt. transfer to, 394; Fr. occupy, 410.
Edea, Ger. force at, 145, 161, in area of, 195, 224; preparations to advance on, 155, 158, 161–2; importance of, 158; Allied force for, 161, capture of, 168; Ger. counter-attacks, 197, 224–7; Fr. force at, 206, 244; defences, 206–7; advance from 256–8
Eber, Ger. G.B., 55, 58, 63, 65, 80
Edington, Mr. E., 14n
Ekob, occupied, 419
Elabe, occupied, 410
Elder Dempster & Co., 70n
Elele, s.s., 22, 24, 25; arrives Lome, 26
Elephants, interfere with operations, 178, 218
Elgee, Capt. P. E. L., 25, 26; reaches Krachi, 34–5; 39
Elliot, Sergt. S. F., wounded, 380
Elmina, transport, 113

Elphinstone, Lt. K. V., v., 70n, 292; Duala, 131–2
Engelbrechten, Lt. von (Ger. Army), 202, 228, 381
Engineers, Corps of Royal, Companies, 36th (Sierra Leone), 42, 291, 386, 415n; Dibamba river, 126–9; Yapoma bridge, 141–4; Edea, 162–9; Northern Railway, 198–202; Bare, 203; Chang, 221; Edea, 257–8; Yaunde, 275–85, 328–37, 356–64, 376–83, 388–95, 399
—, French, Eda, 161–9
Eseka, Fr. capture, 273–4; terminus of Midland Railway, 274; Fr. withdraw from, 275, 276; recaptured, 336–7
Evans, Capt. C. G., v.

Fahnenfeldt, Baron Codelli von, captured, 29–30
Fane, Major J., 209–10, 222
Faucon, Lt.-Col. (Fr. Army), 364–5, 376, 382–3, 395–8, 402–3, 406, 408–12, 416n
Fell, Capt. M. E., 308, wounded, 360
Fellowes, Capt., 23n
Fernando Po, W/T station in, 52, 62; German assistance through, 179–80, 265, 310; internment arrangements in, 412
Ferrandi, Capt. (Fr. Army), 88–90, 117, 157, 253, 266–7, 298
Festing, Major A. H., 68, 93, 96, 98
Fia of the Awunas, assistance of, 15, 27, 31
Fiddes, Sir George V., 2n
Fielding, Lt. E. F., killed, 342n
Fimba, occupied, 392
Finch, Lt. H. S., wounded, 241
Fitzpatrick, Lt. J. F. J., 269
Flags, white, abuse of, 140, 220; use of, at Victoria, 144, 155, Nkongsamba, 202, Garua, 298, Banyo Mountain, 349
Flanagan, Sergt. C., wounded, 377
Fleas, *see* Jiggers
Flies, 83
Flood, Mr. J. E. W., v.
Fongdonera, Ger. force at, 243
Food, shortage of, 63, 65, 131, 136, 298; unprocurable locally, 83, 91, 134–5; *see also* Supplies
Forcados, Transport, 162n
Ford, Lt. A. M. P., R.N., wounded, 264n
Forelle, river craft, 162n, 179, 180
Fourneau, M. (Gov. of Fr. Middle Congo), 248

458 INDEX

Fowle, Capt. C. H., 301, 305–7
Fox, Major R. W., 58, 86–90, 97, 112, 170–3, 190–3, 209, 323; *see also* Infantry, British, Columns, Maiduguri
Franqueville, Capt. A. A. (Fr. Army), death of, 164, 168
Fraser, Colour-Sergt. J. H., wounded, 269
Fraser, Dr. P. T., 89, killed, 90
Freeman-Mitford, Com. The Hon. B. T. C. O., Yabasi, 147–53
French co-operation (The Cameroons), 60 61, 63, 65, 67; Mora Mountain, 88–90, 170–3; Duala area, 131; Yapoma bridge, 141–4; Edea, 161–9; Yaunde, 271–85, 328–37, 351–64, 374–83, 388–95; (May–July, 1915) 295–307; *see also* Aymerich, Gen.; Mathieu, Comdt.; Mayer, Col.; Operations, French
—— —— (Togoland), 20–2, 24, 32, 33, 34; available strength for, 22, 25–6; arrangements for, 26; affair of Khra, 36–8; *see also* Castaing, Capt.; Maroix, Major
Friant, Fr. Cr., 290, 340
Frontiers, of Togoland, 5; The Cameroons, 46, 47–50
Fuchs, Capt. (Ger. Army), 269, 270
Fullah, Transport, 162*n*, 164, 165, 214, 265, 308
Fuller, Ad. Sir C. T. M., v., orders to, 64, 67, 74–5, 78; at Lagos, 77; off Fernando Po, 78; Ambas Bay, 79–80; capture of Duala, 124–30; at Duala, 137, 205, 231, 386; Yapoma bridge, 141–4; and release of *Cumberland* or *Challenger*, 145, 156; capture of Edea, 161–9; awarded Board of Trade Bronze Medal, 164*n*; question of naval command, 181–3, 188; and blockade, 196; river flotillas, 213; coastal operations, 265; 424, 425; *see also* Blockade; Operations, Combined; Operations, Naval
Fumban, occupied, 367–71, value of, 371

Gaisser, Capt. (Ger. Army), captured, 186
Galim, occupied, 346
Gambia Company, *see under* Infantry, British, West African Frontier Force
Gambia, The, local force in, 43; instructions to, 70–1

Gandua, affair of, 344
Gardner, Capt. A., wounded, 327
Garua, Ger. force at, 61, 68, 91, 160, 191–2, 195, 230, 251, 299*n*; attack on, sanctioned, 69, 146; decision to attack, 91; first attack on, 93–7; defences of, 93, 230, 294–5; junction of Allied Columns near, 230; operations at, 252, 266–8; capture of, 294–9, 285, effect of, 286; Allied force at, 297; reasons for surrender, 299, subsequent situation, 299–300
Gashiga, advance on, 305; occupied, 307
George V, H.M. The King, message to Gen. Dobell, 421–2
Germany, annexes Togoland (1884) 4, The Cameroons (1884) 45
Gethin, Colour-Sergt., 29
Gibb, Capt. C., 200*n*, 201–2, 272, 410
Gibbs, Capt. J. T., Tepe, 92–3; Garua, 93–7
Gibson, Mr. R. E. P. (Chief Transport Officer, The Gold Coast), 25
Giles, Capt. A. H., 123, 133, 234, 410
Giles, Major F. L. N., R.E., 70*n*, 426
Glei (Togoland), occupied, 38
Glenny, Mr. H. Q., mortally wounded, 193
Glover, Capt. (afterwards Sir), John, R.N., 7
Gold Coast, The, natives of Togoland emigrate to, 5; communications in, 6–7; administration services in, 8–9; defence scheme, 9–11, 15; measures in, (29 July–5 Aug. 1914), 13–16; loyalty of natives in, 15; bears cost of Togoland expedition, 41; strength of W.A.F.F. in, 65*n*; forces for The Cameroons, 66, 67, 120; instructions to, 70–1; *see also* Defence Schemes; Police and Preventive Service; Transport, Allied, carriers, native Volunteer Corps
—— —— Mines Volunteers, *see* Volunteer Corps
—— —— Railway Volunteers, *see* Vounteer Corps
—— —— Regiment, *see under* Infantry, British, West African Frontier Force
—— —— Volunteers, *see* Volunteer Corps
Goldsmith, Capt. J., R.M.L.I., Yapoma bridge, 141–4
Goodwin, Capt. H., 128, 309

INDEX 459

Gorges, Brig.-Gen. E. H., v., 204, 223; succeeds Col. Carter, 113; Dibamba river, 126–9; Yabasi, 146–53; memo. on tactics, 179*n*, App. V., 442–4; Tiko and Mpundu, 183–5; strength of force under, 183, 184; Buea, 185–6; Northern Railway, 198–202; Bare, 203; Chang, 216–22; Nkongsamba, 236, 237, 242; Harmann's Farm, 239–42, strength of force under, 239, (March, 1915) 246; Yaunde, 328–37, 352–64, 375–83, 388–95, strength of force under, 329, 376, 382, 388; operation order, 356, App. VII., 445–9, reinforced, 386; final operations, 396–405, 407

Gorori, occupied, 371

Gosinda, occupied, 326

Gosling, Major S. B. (Dir. of Army Signals and Railways), 26, 27

Gowers, Mr. W. F., invalided, 292

Granville, Lord, 46

Grattan-Bellew, Lt. C. C., 32

Gray, Com. G. S. B., R.N.R., death of, 164

Green, Capt. H. W., 251

Greene, Lt. H. R., 138

Grieve, Dr. K. K. (W.A.M.S.), wounded, 332*n*

Grove, Lt. K. S., 160

Guillemart, Lt. (Fr. Army), 36

Guns, British, abandoned, 108, 241
— —, naval, in land operations, Yapoma bridge, 141–4, Yabasi, 147–53, Northern Railway, 198–202, Edea, 162–9, Tiko, 183, Chang, 218–22, Garua, 231, 267–8, Duala, 244, Yaunde, 275–85
— German, captured at Duala, 130

Gurin, attack on, 268–70

Haddon, Lt. R. D. B., R.N., 162–9, 199–202

Haedicke, Major (Ger. Army), 273, 278, 311*n*, 363, 389, 394

Hagen, Major von (Ger. Army), 364, 406, 411

Hall, Capt. C. L., R.M.L.I., 198, 213–15

Hall, Lt. L. J., 180

Hamilton, Lt. C., R.N.R., Edea, 165–9

Hamilton, Lt. L. H. K., R.N., 131, 141, 183, 214, 231

Hammond, Pte. A. F., wounded, 339*n*

Harmann's Farm, affairs of, 235–6, 239–42, Germans evacuate, 242

Harper, Mr. C. H. (Acting Colonial Secretary, The Gold Coast), 40*n*

Hastings, Lt.-Col. W. C. N., 319

Hausa, Transport, 162*n*, 164, 165

Haywood, Lt.-Col. A. H. W. (2nd Nigerians), 58, 101, 110–11, 255; Bonaberi, 138; Make, 139–40; Susa, 146, 153, 158–60, 175–6, 178–9; Kake, 154; Muyuka, 184–5; Bombe, 186–7; Bare, 203; Chang, 216–22; Edea, 256–8, strength of force under, 256; Yaunde, 271–85, 329–37, 353–64, 376–83, 388–95; final operations, 399–418; tribute to, 418, 426; *see also* Infantry, British, Columns, Calabar

Health, improved, 376; of Gen. Cunliffe's force, 414; *see also* Sickness

Heathcote, Capt. G. N., wounded, 344

Heathcote, Com., 27*n*

Hebblethwaite, Lt. C. J., killed, 267

Hetley, Capt. C. R., 374, 384–6

Herzogin Elisabeth, Ger. Armed Yacht (re-named *Margaret Elizabeth*), 81

Hills, Lt. E. R., killed, 357, 362

Ho (Togoland), occupied, 33

Hodgson, Capt. G. F., 395

Holme, Lt. A. C., killed, 108

Hooker, Colour-Sergt. H. R. G., killed, 234

Hopkinson, Capt. C. R. T., 100–7, killed, 107, 108; 109, 110

Hornbill, river steamer, 108, 109, 111

Hornby, Capt. C. G., 24

Houston, Mr. J. A., 425

Howell, Major H. G., 124, 125, 199–202, 353, 449

Hughes, Lt. A. W., R.N.R., 80

Hughes, Com. R. H. W., R.N.R., 144, 155, 179, 180, 309, 387; in command of Nigerian flotilla, 78, 80, 83; capture of Duala, 125–30; Edea, 161–9; Campo, 246, 317–19, 339

Hutchinson, Sergt. J., R.A.M.C., wounded, 358

Hutin, Lt.-Col. (Fr. Army), 174–5, 278, 282, 313, 321, 384, 402, 407–9, 411–12, 416; strength of force under, 211, 322, 384

Ikom, Brit. force at, 68–9, 170

Infantry, Belgian, detachment arrives, 175; *see also* Operations, Franco-Belgian

Infantry, British, Battalions—
   1st West India Regt., 42, 183n, 317, 403; Yaunde, 328-37, 356-64, 376-83, 388-95
—, —, Columns—
   Bare, operations (Oct.-Nov. 1915), 340-50
   Calabar, 58, 68; operations (3 Aug.-16 Sept. 1914), 110-11
   Cross River, strength and disposition, 173; operations (Nov. 1914) 194, (Nov.-Dec.) 209-10, (Dec.-Jan. 1915) 222-3, (Feb.-March) 250, 266, (July) 307; see also Infantry, British, Columns, Ikom
   Ibi, strength and disposition, 173, 266; operations (Nov. 1914) 193-4, 210, (Dec.-Jan. 1915) 223-4, (Feb.) 250-1, (March-April) 266, (July) 305, 307, (Aug.-Sept) 322
   Ikom, 58, 68; operations (10 Aug.-6 Sept. 1914) 99-110, (8th-16th) 111; strength and disposition, 121; see also Infantry, British, Columns, Cross River; Mair, Lt.-Col. G. T.
   Maiduguri, 58, 61, 68; operations (6-29 Aug, 1914) 86-90, (28 Aug.-13 Sept.) 111-12; strength and dispositions, 90, 121; see also Fox, Major R. W.
   Nafada, 61
   Yola, 58, 61, 207; operations (18-31 Aug. 1914) 90-7, (1-30, Nov.) 190-3; reorganised, 98; strength and disposition, 121, 191n; see also Maclear, Lt.-Col. P. R.; Webb-Bowen, Lt.-Col. W. I.
—, —, Regiments—
   West African, 42, 62, 63, 67, 70, 112, 238, 290, 291, 396, 400, 403, 407; Dibamba river, 126-9; Tiko, 140; Misselele, 141; Yabasi, 147-53, 176; Edea, 161-9; Dibombe Post, 177, 226n, 244; Northern Railway, 184, 199-202, 237, 239; Nkongsamba, 219, 236, 242, 244; Duala, 226; Yaunde, 329-37; Bare column, 341-50; operations (Nov.-Dec. 1915), 367-74, 386; Campo, 409; Ngat, 419
—, —, Indian—
   5th Light, 286; arrive, 317; Campo, 318-19; Duala, 338; Bare Column, 341-50; operations (Nov.-Dec. 1915), 367-74, 386; movements, 396
—, —, West African Frontier Force—
   2, 11, 62, 63, 64; administrative services in, 8-9, 44; composition of, 42-3; strength and dispositions of, 65n, 113-14; tribute to, 427
   Nigeria Regiment, Togoland, 32; composition and strength of, 43-4; for The Cameroons, 67; tribute to, 414
   1st Battalion, 97, 98, 230n, 266, 267n, 297-9, 305n, 322-7, 340-50, 368-70, 385n. 401n
   2nd Battalion, 86-97, 110, 193-4, 223-4, 230n, 266, 267n, 297-9, 305, 323-7, 340-50, 368-70, 401n
   3rd Battalion, 90-97, 100-2, 104-6, 108-11, 193-4, 209, 222-3, 230n, 250, 266, 267n, 268, 297-9, 301, 305n, 307, 322-7, 328, 340-50, 367-74, 421
   4th Battalion, 101, 104-5, 110-11, 209, 222-3, 250, 267n, 296-9, 322n
   1st Nigerians, 120, 122, 204, 236, 242, 244, 245, 290, 291, 403n, Dibamba river, 126-9; Duala, 131, 137; Yabasi, 147-53, 176-7; Tiko, 183-4; Northern Railway, 198-202; strength of, 205; Chang, 217-22; Mbureku, 234; Edea, 256-8; Yaunde, 271-85, 329-37, 356-64, 376-83, 388-95; Nyong river, 308-9; Campo, 310, 319; Elabe, 410
   2nd Nigerians, 120, 122, 137, 138, 244, 290, 291, 415n; Maka, 139-40; Susa, 153, 154, 158-60, 175-6, 178-9; Muyuka, 184; Northern Railway, 198-202; Bare, 203; strength of, 205; Chang, 216-22; Edea, 256-8; Yaunde, 271-85, 329-37, 353-64, 376-83, 388-95, 399n
   Composite Battalion, formation of, 120; Maka, 139; Yabasi and Susa, 151-3, 178-9; Mpundu, 184; Northern Railway, 199-202, 237; Duala, 226; broken up, 236
   Mounted Companies—
   "A," 421
   "B," 58, 61, 90-7, 98, 121, 191n, 324-7, 340-50
   "C," 58, 61, 68, 86-90, 113, 121, 322, 324-7, 328

INDEX 461

Infantry, British, West African Frontier Force—*contd.*
  Gold Coast Regiment, strength and composition of, 7–8; suggested first movements of, 12; mobilised, 13; preliminary movements, 14, 24, 25, 26; advance on Kamina, 27, 34–5; affair of Agbeluvoe, 28–31; casualties in Togoland, 29, 30; affair of Khra, 36–8; for The Cameroons, 67; Dibamba river, 138; Maka, 139–40
  —, Battalion, formation of, 236; 239, 242, 255, 258, 271, 290, 291, 309, 310, 319, 415*n*; Yaunde, 329–37, 353–64, 376–83, 388–95, 399, 403
  —, Pioneer Company, 113, 309; Dibamba river, 126–9, casualties, 128; Yapoma bridge, 141–4; Yabasi, 147–53; Tiko, 183–4; Mpundu, 184; Northern Railway, 198–202, 237; Duala, 226; Yaunde, 375–64
  Sierra Leone Battalion, 16, 31, Togoland, 32; composition and strength of, 43; 113, 120, 139–40, 222, 228, 237, 239, 242, 290, 291, 383, 403; Harmann's Farm, 235–6, 240–2; Mbureku, 238; Edea, 256–8; Campo, 318–19; Yaunde, 329–37, 356–64, 382–3, 390–5
  Gambia Company, embark, 112; 244, 256–8, 290, 291, Yaunde, 271–85, 328–37, 356–64, 379–83, 388–95, 403*n*
—, French, Battalions—
  1st Senegalese, Edea, 161–9
  2nd Senegalese, 32, 137, 138, 139; Yapoma bridge, 141–4; Edea, 162–9; Tiko, 183
  2/2nd Senegalese, 115, 116
  3/3rd Senegalese, 114
—, —, Regiments—
  1st, 115, 119
  4th, 114
  Gabon, 156
—, German, Companies—
  No. 1 (Depôt), 54, 130, 148*n*, 161*n*, 257–8, 273, 332, 363*n*
  No. 2, 54, 106*n*, 161, 194
  No. 3, 54, around Mora, 87, 160
  No. 4 (Expeditionary), 54, 140, 159*n*, 161, 185, 332, 363*n*
  No. 5, 54, 117, 157, 161, 175, 211, 293
  No. 6, 54, 117, 157, 161, 175, 211, 293
  No. 7, 54, 87, 95, 160
  No. 8, 54, 96, 160
  No. 9, 54, 161, 175, 231*n*, 293
  No. 10, 54, 161, 174, 363*n*
  No. 11, 54, 156, 161, 174, 231*n*, 293
  No. 12, 54, 117, 160, 171, 192, 207
—, —, Reserve Detachments—
  No. 1, 161, 174, 198
  No. 2, 130, 139*n*, 161, 257, 363*n*
  No. 3, 99, 161, 332, 363*n*
  No. 4, 161
Insects, *see* Fleas; Flies; Jiggers; Mosquitoes
Intelligence, British, *re* Kamina W/T station, 13; telegraphic interceptions, 14, 60*n*, 209; situation at Lome, 18; *re* defences at Duala, 63, 74–5, 76, 102; conditions Duala—Victoria, 72; Germans at Mora, 86, 87, 89; importance of Yaunde, 154–5; Edea operations, 165–6; Yabasi area, 176; *re* Ger. agents in Fernando Po, 179–80; from Ger. documents, 186, 252, 284, 333, 339*n*, 355, 381, 386; Kribi—Edea area, 205; difficulty of obtaining, 233, 372–3; from natives, 243, 334; from released prisoners of war, 405; *see also* Appreciations
—, French, *re* Togoland, 21
—, German, failure of, in Togoland, 40
Ivy, Yacht (Com. R. H. W. Hughes), 78, 80–4, 129, 144, 155, 179, 180, 265, 290, 310; Edea, 161–9; off Victoria, 183; Kribi, 206; Campo, 317–19

Jackdaw, river steamer, 108, 109, 111
Jackson, Capt. C. V. S., Yapoma bridge, 141–4, Edea, 257–8
Jackson, Ad. Sir H. B., 2
" Jiggers," a local flea, 96*n*, 236
Joly, Comdt. (Chief of Staff to Gen. Aymerich), 248
Jones, Lt. E. F. L., R.N., 84*n*, 85

Kake, occupied, 154
Kallmeyer, Lt. (Ger. Army), 87, 118, 157
Kamerun, Ger. s.s., salved, 82; 132

462 INDEX

Kamina (Togoland), German W/T station at, 4, 10, 12, 13, 16, 38, 39; advance on, 27, reached, 39
Kampe, s.s., 96
Karbati, occupied, 305
Keast, Lt. Banks, 395
Keka, Motor launch, 162–9, 177
Kennedy, Sergt. F., wounded, 377
Kentu, occupied, 344
Kete Krachi (Togoland), occupied, 25
Khra (Togoland), affair of, 35–8; strength of enemy force, 37
Kilby, Mr. R. W., 28
Kilgour, Lt.-Com. P. V., 339, 387
King, Colour-Sergt. W., killed, 350
Kitchener, Lord, 321
Kok, occupied, 419
Koncha, capture of, 301
Kopongo, enemy attacks, 221, 225; Fr. force at, 244
Kosseva, affair of, 192
Kpedome (Togoland), occupied, 35
Kribi, Ger. force at, 161; occupied, 198, enemy attacks, 206–7, 224, 226
Krooboys, deported from Duala, 63, 74
Kumasi (The Gold Coast), Brit. force at, 15
Kumbo, occupied, 372
Kuseri, Ger. force at, 61, 118; reported evacuated, 68; Germans decide to hold, 87; Fr. attack, 112, 117–18, capture, 157
Kuti, occupied, 370
Kyngdon, Lt. W. F. R., 32, 33, 35n

Lagos, Transport, 162n, 213, 214, 290
Lala, Launch, 215
Lamouroux, Capt. (Fr. Army), 323–7
Lane, Lt. C. W. T., 157
Largeau, Gen. (Fr. Army), 88, 116–17, 157, 170–1, 207, 231, 252, 270, 302–5, 424
Largeau, Fr. River steamer, 116
Law, Major J. P., 176, 199–202
Learmonth, Lt.-Com. C. J. R., 289n
Lees, Major A. C. L. D., vi., wounded, 172
Le Fanu, Dr., at Lome, 23
Lembe, Fr. occupy, 366, 383
Le Meillour, Lt.-Col. (Fr. Army), 249, 278, 313, 320–1, 338–9, 365, 383, final operations, 395–420
Leslie-Smith, Lt. J., wounded, 318n
Lesogs, affairs at, 358–60
Linder, Colour-Sergt. W., 395
Lindsay, Dr. J., 95

Linte, occupied, 385
Lobetal, Ger. force at, 161; occupied, 166
Loch, Lt. E. E., wounded, 95n; 193
Loko ja, Transport, 122
Lokundje river, operations, 213–15
Lolo, Ger. force at, 161
Lome (Togoland), port facilities at, 6; approaches to, 11–12; first objective, 16; occupation of, 19–20; situation in, 2–4; attitude of Germans in, 23; Brit. force at, 26
Lomie, Ger. force at, 231n; Fr. advance on, 249–50, 278–9; captured, 293
Lucas, Sir Charles, "The Empire at War" quoted, 46, 428
Lugard, The Rt. Hon. Lord, v., 45, 54n, 57, 79, 97, 98, 112, 120, 121, 122, 146, 174, 230, 236, 250, 256, 300, 301, 302, 305–6, 316, 323, 421; raises W.A.F.F. (1897), 42; at Buea, 187, Duala, 194
Lumley, Mr. G., 425
Lunt, Lt. W. McC., R.N.R., wounded, 246; 289n
Luxembourg, Belg. s.s., 175, 211
Luxford, Lt. C., wounded, 200

McCallum, Major D., v., 72, 124, 154, 404; at Edea, 169, 227
McCullagh, Lt.-Com. A. B., wounded, 289; 308
Macdonell, Capt. D. H., wounded, 92n
Mackesy, Capt. P. J., 35n
Machine guns, British, with Nigeria Regt., 43, captured by Germans, 90, 108
—, French, lack of, 114, 115
—, German, captured in Togoland, 30, 39; in The Cameroons, 53, 54n, at Mora, 87, 90, at Garua, 91; captured, 94, 225, 297, 299, 378; superiority of, 212; unable to be used, 415, 416
Mackinnon, Capt. L. N. A., killed, 350
McIver, Lt. K., mortally wounded, 415
Maclaverty, Lt.-Col. C. F. S., v., Harmann's Farm, 240–2; wounded, 241; Yaunde, 276–85, wounded, 276
Maclear, Lt.-Col. P. R., 58, 90–5; strength of force under, 68, 90–1; instructions to, 91; killed, 95; *see also* Infantry, British, Columns, Yola

INDEX 463

Macleod, Sergt. R., wounded, 378
Makak, Fr. capture, 398
McQuirk, Sergt. H., killed, 150*n*
Mafub, affair at, 415
Maio Kaleh, occupied, 301
Mair, Lt.-Col. G. T., 58, 99–110, 111, 121, 199, 203, 209, 210; strength and dispositions of force under, 69, 101–2, 105–6, 109, 170, 194; Ossidinge and Tinto, 222–3; invalided, 250; *see also* Infantry, British, Columns, Ikom
Maka, capture of, 139–40
Makure, Ger. Hd.-Qrs., 180
Malaria, *see* Sickness
Manatee, s.s., 310
Mangeles, Fr. occupy, 382–3
Mangrove swamps, 83, description of, 125*n*
Mann, Major G. D., 170, 173, 193–4, 210, 223–4, 251, 305, 307, 322, 340–50; *see also* Infantry, British, Columns, Ibi
Mannion, Colour-Sergt. J., captured, 108; 109
Mansim, Fr. occupy, 413
Maps, German, 141, 179
Marchand, Capt. (Fr. Army), 21
Margaret Elizabeth (ex-*Herzogin Elisabeth*), 132, 265, 387
Marina, s.s., 27*n*, 63*n*, 74; Dibamba river, 127–9
Markham-Rose, Lt. K., killed, 273
Marlow, Major J., 33
Maroix, Major (Fr. Army), 21, 26; strength of force under, 34; reaches Kamina, 39
Martin, Capt. (Fr. Army), 383, 403, 409
Marua, move towards, 190–3; Ger. force at, 190, 192, 207; evacuated, 208
Marwitz (Ger. Army), 231*n*
Marwood, Capt. C. P. L., killed, 372
Matem, affair at, 277–8
Mathieu, Comdt. (Fr. Army), 162–9, 196, 197, 206, 226, 245, 257–8, 283*n*, 311, 419; Yaunde, 333–7
Matip Matips, occupied, 380–1
May, Mr. G. C. M., 292
May, Dr. O'Hara, at Lome, 24
Mayer, Col. (Fr. Army), 112, 113, 126, 161–9, 188, 196–8, 206, 224–6, 232, 256–8, 311, 315, 317, 396–405, 409, 417, 425, at Duala, 244–5, 320–1; Yaunde, 271–85, 328–37, 363–4, strength of force under, 276, 364
Mbaiki, Fr. occupy, 117
Mbo, occupied, 219; withdrawal from, 220, reoccupied, 342

Mbureku, affairs of, 233–4, 237–8; occupied and evacuated, 242; Germans evacuate, 242
Mechet, Comdt. (Fr. Army), Yaunde, 271–85, 332–7; 402–3, 416, 419–20
Medical Services, personnel, 9; neutral zone for, agreed to, 109; organisation of, 124, 136; tribute to, 414, 426; *see also* Nsanakang
Melong, occupied, 204; concentration at, 205; withdrawal from, 221; Ger. force at, 233, 237, 239, withdraw, 243
Merlet, M., 302, 324
Merlin, M. (Gov.-Gen. Fr. Equatorial Africa), 116, 117, 327, 339, 405; at Duala, 320–1
Mésegué, Capt. (Fr. Army), 415
Meyer-Griffith, Major H. W. G., Duala, 135; killed, 277, 278
Midland Railway, 82, 125, 274, 320; open, 383; *see also* Bridges; Railways
Migeod, Lt. G. E. H., 426
Miles, Mr. L. C. C., 14*n*
Milne-Home, Lt. A., 104, 107, 108, 110
Mines, German, off Duala, 86, 125, recovered, 131
Minniken, Capt. H. J., 370
Minto, Capt. R., at Lome, 26
Miquelard, Major (Fr. Army), 156, 174, 210–12, 249, 292, 418
Misselele, attack on, 141
Missionaries, British, 45, 46
—, German, 14*n*, 167, 177, 202, 258; activities of, 368, 371–2
—, Neutral, 227
Missions, French, at Duala, 248, 249, 253–5
Mitchelmore,Leading-Seaman W.,177
Mole, Dredger, Yabasi, 147–53; Edea, 162–9
Moloko, Brit. post, 310; enemy attack, 339
Molundu, Ger. force at, 175; Fr. occupy, 211
Monde Yeraia, Pte., awarded D.C.M., 235*n*
Moorhouse, Major H. C., 121, 146
Mora, Ger. force at, 61, 68, 86, 87–8, 90, 157, 160, 195, 207; decision to attack, 86, 304–5; attack on, 170–3, 189–90; investment of, 228–30, 266–8, 322–3; considered impregnable, 267, 304, 306; (March–April, 1915) 270, (Aug.–Sept.) 322–7, (Oct.–Nov.) 374, decision to abandon attack, 327; surrender of, 421

INDEX

Mora Mountain, Ger. entrenched position on, 87, 88, 90, 171, 325; topography of, 87–8, 171
Moral, German, native, 88, 171, 202, 274, 360, 363, 375–6, 381, 385n, 386, 394
Morisson, Lt.-Col. (Fr. Army), 116–17, 157, 231–2, 249, 265, 278, 282, 293–4, 307, 313, 231–2, 337–8, 340–50, 384; strength of force under, 211–12, 266, 384; final operations, 402–20
Morrison, Capt. R. V., wounded, 342n
Moseley, s.s., 80
Mosquitoes, 82, 83, 136n
Mpundu, Ger. force at, 178; occupied, 184
Mum, Brit. post at, 353
Mungo river, navigability of, 178
Muyuka, Ger. force at, 161, 185; occupied, 185
Mwine, occupied, 409

Nachtigal, Dr., 46
Nachtigal, Ger. Armed Merchant Ship, sunk, 84–5
Nachtigal Rapids, Fr. reach, 401
Na of Yendi, 33
Natives, treatment of by Germans, 5, 34, 40, 46, 64, 84, 131, 188, 233, 250, 363, by Brit. 84; pro-British 84, 132, 204; marching ability of, 96n; risings of, 173–4; Ger. levies, 206, 207; Allied levies, 226–7, 233; Ger., mutiny, 299; return to villages, 399, 400, 419
Navy, The Royal, question of co-operation by, 58, 60; list of ships employed, App. III., 435; *see also* Operations, Combined; Operations, Naval
—, German, *see* Eber; Panther
Ndog, reached, 379
Neutrality, Germans propose, 15–16, refused, 17; of Belg. Congo, proposed, 175n
Newlands, Mr. H. S. (Political Officer), v., accompanies Capt. Barker to Lome, 18–19; at Lome, 20, 22, 23, 27; at Kamina, 39
Newstead, Lt.-Col. G. P., 222, 228; Harmann's Farm, 235–6, 240–2; mortally wounded, 241, 242; Mbureku, 238
Ngambe, occupied, 373
Ngangela, Fr. occupy, 294
Ngat, occupied, 419
Ngaundere, importance of, 224n; capture of, 300–1

Ngoa, occupied, 420
Ngok, affair at, 276–7; occupied, 353
Ngulemakong, occupied, 410
Ngung, occupied, 360, 362
Ngwe, affair of, 257–8
Niemen, Transport, 162n, 183
Niger, Transport, 122
Nigeria, strength and disposition of force in, 43–4, 65n, 121n; conditions in, 44–5, 120; measures in (30 July–8 Aug. 1914), 58–60; forces for The Cameroons, 63n, 66, 67, 120; instructions to, 70–1; situation in (Nov. 1914), 194, 195; frontier raids, 267; *see also* Defence Schemes; Nigeria Marine; Police Force; Transport, Allied, carriers, native
Nigeria Civil Service, tribute to, 414
Nigeria Marine, strength and work of, 44, 59; flotilla arrives Ambas Bay, 80; reinforced, 86; transports Fr. heavy gun, 296; tribute to, 425; list of vessels employed, App. III., 436–9
Nigeria Regiment, *see under* Infantry, British, West African Frontier Force
Njabesan, affair, 317–18
Nkan, occupied, 416
Nkoa, occupied, 389
Nkod Makengs, occupied, 362
Nkolalong, Ger. force at, 397
Nkongsamba, terminus of Northern Railway, 313; Ger. force at, 145, 154; occupied, 202–3; Brit. force at, 237, 239
Nlohe, occupied, 201
Nola, Fr. capture, 157
Norman, Leading Seaman W., 127
Northern Railway, Ger. force on, 131, 146, 153, 159, 175, 202; operations up the, 183–8, occupation of, 195–202, raids against, 227–8, 233, 237–8, 288–9, 311–12; clear of enemy, 386; *see also* Bridges; Railways
Northern Territories Constabulary (The Gold Coast), 8, 32
Nsanakang, Ger. concentration at, 102, 194; occupied, 103; strength of force at, 104; affair of, 106–9; neutral zone around, 109, 173, 194
Nsanarati, occupied, 101
Nuatya (Togoland), occupied, 34, Brit. concentrate at, 35
Nun river, crossing of the, 367–70
Nyamtam, Ger. force at, 176; occupied, 177

INDEX 465

Nyanga, Ger. force at, 176, 199
Nyong river, operations on the, 213–15, 245–6, 265, 289, 308–9, 387

O'Brien, Lt. H. D. S., wounded, 217
Obuassi, s.s., 14
O'Connell, Mr. C. W., 292
Okuri, Ger. force at, 68
Offensive Sub-Committee, *see under* Committee of Imperial Defence
Old Ossidinge, Ger. force at, 102, 104; *see also* Ossidinge
Operations, Combined, Dibamba river, 126–9; Tiko and Misselele Plantation, 140–1; Yapoma bridge, 141–4; Yabasi, 147–53; Edea area, 161–9, 196–8; Cameroon Mountain, 183–8; 424–5
—, Franco-Belgian (1–16 Nov. 1914) 188–9, (Nov.–Dec.) 210–12, (Jan. 1915) 231–2, (Feb.–March) 248–50, (March–April) 265–6, (May–June) 292–4, (July) 313, (Aug.) 321–2, (Sept.–Oct.) 337–8, (Nov.) 365–6, (Dec.) 383–4, situation (1 Jan. 1916) 395; strength of force, 293; 425
—, French, Kuseri, 112; (31 July–Sept. 1914) 114–19, (19–21 Sept.) 156–7, (Oct.) 174–5, (July 1915) 310–11, 312–13, (Nov.) 365, situation (1 Jan. 1916), 395; 424; *See also* French co-operation
—, Naval, Ambas Bay (4–7 Sept. 1914) 79–80, Cameroon Estuary (7th–23rd) 80–1, 124–6, (6–16 Oct.) 155–6, (31 Oct.–7 Nov.) 179–80, (Dec.) 205, (March–April, 1915) 264–5, (Sept.–Oct.) 337, (Nov.–Dec.) 387, (1 Jan.–March, 1916) 421, 424; river flotillas (Dec. 1914–Jan. 1915) 213–15, 227, (Feb.) 245–6, (March–April) 265, (May–June) 289–90, (July) 308–10, (Jan. 1916) 421; *see also* Blockade
—, enemy accounts of, affair of Agbeluvoe, 31; Khra, 37–8; Kamina, 40n; "Der Grosse Krieg," Vol. IV., 50n, 53n, 55n, 81, 212n, 224n, 226n, 273n, 280n, Yaunde, 312n; 351, 394, 395n; 420n; Mora, 87, 90n, 172, 190, 326, 374; Kuseri, 118
O'Shaughnessy, Major J. J. F., at Lome, 24, 26, 27
Ossidinge, Ger. force at, 68, 77, 105, 161, 195, occupied, 222; *see also* Old Ossidinge
Otu, occupied, 209; attacked, 210

Oversea Defence Committee, *see under* Committee of Imperial Defence
Oyem, Ger. force at, 174, 231; Fr. occupy, 249, 292
Ozier, Lt. (Fr. Army), 253

Panther. Ger. G.B., 55, 58, 65, 80
Parker, Lt. M. J., wounded and captured, 235
Parr, Capt. B. C., Kentu, 344, 367, 373; 384–6
Paterson, Lt. L. C., wounded, 202
Pawle, Lt. D. W., killed, 269
Pawsey, Lt. H. T. W., R.N., 215, 265
Peel, Lt. A. R., killed, 192
Percival, Com. J., R.N.R., appreciation by, 75–6, 77; Duala, 132–3; 425
Percival, Lt. M., killed 192
Pery, Col. C. C. J., R.E., 291, 426
Pfaeler, Capt. (Ger. Police Commandant), 18, killed, 31
Piggott, Lt. T. B. C., wounded, 318n
Pike, Capt. R. N., killed, 326, 327
Pitti, Ger. force at, 127, 128, withdraw, 130, 138
Police and Preventive Service, 8, casualties, 30, work of, 99
Police Force, German, strength and distribution (July 1914) 54, (18 Oct.) 161; Depôt Co., 130, 139n; Molundu, 175
Police Force, Nigeria, strength of, 44
Pollard, Dr. J. H. M., v.
Ponty, M. (Gov.-Gen. of French West Africa), 61
Poole, Capt. G. A. E., 353
Popp, Capt. (Fr. Army), 323–7, 372, 401
Porpoise, Tug, 86, 141, 143; Dibamba river, 126–9, 138; Kwa Kwa Creek, 155–6; Edea, 162–9; off Victoria, 183
Porter, Major H. A., 322, 340–50, 371–3, 384–6
Porto Seguro (Togoland), Fr. occupy, 22
Pothuau, Fr. Cr., 181, 183, 186, 205n, 206, 254n; relieved, 290n
Potter, Capt. H. B., 27; affair of Agbeluvoe, 28–31
Powell, Mr. L. A. W., v.
Poyntz, Lt. R. H., 200n
Pratt, Able Seaman A. M., wounded, 318n
Prechac, Lt. de Vaisseau (Fr. Navy), 317n
Priester, Capt. (Ger. Army), 278, 364
Pring, Capt. F. J. H., Gandua, 344

INDEX

Prisoners of War, captured by Allies, in Togoland, 29, 30, 39; in The Cameroons, Duala, 129, 130; necessity to protect, 131–2; evacuated, 132, 187; Yabasi, 153; Bibundi, 155; Cameroon Mountain, 185, 186; Buea, 187; total to 26 Nov. 1914, 187; treatment of, 187; Northern Railway, 201, 202; Bare, 203; Chang, 218, 220; Midland Railway, 274; So Dibanga, 282*n*; Monso, 293; Garua, 299; Tingere, 306; Bangum and Fumban, 370; Mora, 421
— — —, captured by Germans, Mora, 90; affair of Nsanakang, 108; Harmann's Farm, 235; released, 405
Propaganda, Ger. efforts fail, 181
Puckle, Major T. N., 94, killed, 95*n*
Puge river, Ger. position captured, 359–60, effect of, 366, 381, 394

Raben, Capt. von (Ger. Army), 87–90, 118, 193, 207, 270, 323, 347; wounded, 374; 421
Railways, in Togoland, 5, 22, 24, 27, 34; Gold Coast, 7; in The Cameroons, 48–9, 50, 51; state of, 133–4; *see also* Midland Railway; Northern Railway
—, Light, Victoria—Zopo, 187; from Eseka, 364, 376, 383
Rain, Rainfall per annum, 144*n*; *see also* Weather
Rammstedt, Capt. (Ger. Army), wounded, 108*n*
Ramsden, Lt. W. H., wounded, 336*n*
Rattray, Mr. R. S., 28
Reconnaissances, British, Military, by Maiduguri Column, 68, 88–9; Ikom Column, 100–1, 104; Calabar Column, 111; Wuri river, 137; from Susa, 154, 178–9; from Yaunde, 397; *see also* Intelligence
—, —, Naval 82, 83, 84, 124, 138; Wuri river, 141, 144; Sanaga river, 144, 155; Mungo river, 144; Nyong river, 155, 161, 246, 264*n*; Campo river, 180; Lokundje, 246
Recruiting, in The Gold Coast, 14; Nigeria, 266, 290
Redfern, Capt. A. F., 35
Reinforcements, British, for Togoland, 31, 32; Gen. Dobell calls for, 213, 215, 315; arrive, 222, 255, 317, 328, need for, 246–8, 315
—, French, 244, 258, 278, 317, 328
Rémond, Capt. (Fr. Army), 192, 209, 323–7, 421

Remus, Tug, 86, 124, 126–9, 140–4, 162–9, 184, 214, 227, 246
Rinaldo, Sloop, 290, 387
River craft, for attack on Duala, 77; manning of, 133; *see also* Operations, Naval
Roads in Togoland, 5, 11–12, 27; in The Gold Coast, 7; Nigeria, 47–8; in The Cameroons, 48–9, 50, 51; Victoria—Buea, 51;. Campo—Kribi—Longyi, 51; Edea —Yaunde, 51, 158, 329, 352; Kribi—Yaunde, 51, 419; Kribi—Ebolowa, 51, 419; Nkongsamba—Bare—Chang, 203; Bana—Yabasi, 244; from Ebolowa, 410; from Lolo, 419
Roberts, Capt. C. E., 301
Robertson, Capt. J. R., 1414
Robertson, Sir W. C. F., v., Acting-Gov., The Gold Coast, 13, 15, 17, 19, 23, 25, 26, 31, 40*n*; and French co-operation, 20, 22, 24
Roebern, Major von (Ger. Army), 39, 429–31
Rose, Lt.-Col. R. A. de B., Comdt. Gold Coast Regt., 13, 113; Gold Coast Bn., 236, 245; Yabasi, 151–3; Susa, 178–9; Mpundu, 184; Ekona, 185, 186; Harmann's Farm, 239–42, strength of force under, 239; Yaunde, 279–85, 329–37, 353–64, 388–95; Campo, 310, 317–19
Rowe, Capt. C. F., 91, 99, 415
Rowe, Lt.-Col. R. H., R.A., v., 70*n*, 123, 426
Roy, Launch, 214
Royal Army Medical Corps, detachment in West Africa, 42
Royal Marines, occupy Victoria, 183; Edea area, 197–9; in river flotillas, 213–15, 246, 308–9, 383*n*, 387
Ruxton, Com. W. C. G., 288*n*

Saich, Mr. (The Gold Coast Service), 33, 34
St. Clair, Lt. W. L., 37
Sakbajeme, occupied, 329
Salier, Lt. E. L., 104
Saligny, Comdt. Dubois de (Fr. Army), killed, 119
Salvetat, Capt. (Fr. Army), killed, 197
Sanaga river, navigability of, 158; division between Brit. and Fr. operations, 196, opinions upon, 232; *see also* Reconnaissances, Naval

INDEX

Sancho, Mr. J. B., 425
Sanchu, occupied, 342
Sandfly, river steamer, 108
Sandilands, Lt. E. A., wounded, 250n
Sanga river, navigability of, 116n
Sanitation, at Lome, 23, 24
Sargent, Capt. J., 139, 361, 362
Sava, Brit. force at, 89, 90, 170
Savile, Major C. R., 446
Saxton, Lce.-Cpl., 142n
Schipper, Capt. (Ger. Army), 269, 270 ; killed, 349
Schmoll, Capt. (Fr. Army), 408, 410, 415n, 416, 419, 420
Schneider, Lt. H. H., killed, 200
Scott-Moncrieff, Lt. R., wounded, 95n
Seccombe, Capt. G., wounded, 350
Sege, Ger. camp at, captured, 378
Sende, Fr. capture, 273, withdraw, 276, recapture, 335
Seymour, Major Lord Henry, wounded, 92
Shearing, Sergt.-Major, 234
Sheffield, Major G. N., 353
Sheppard, Mr. H. St. J., 70n
Sherlock, Lt. G. L. S., killed, 92
Shipping, captured at fall of Duala, 132 ; *see also* Spoils of War
Sickness, 83, 136, 173, 221, 275, 277, 279, 284, 285 ; deaths from, 169, 415, 424, 426, 427 ; in Fr. force, 204, 207, 245, 279, 310, 383, 398 ; Ger. 381 ; *see also* Smallpox
Sierra Leone, 12 ; Imperial garrison in (1914), 42 ; forces for The Cameroons, 62-3, 64, 67, 120 ; strength of W.A.F.F. in, 65n; instructions to, 70-1 ; *see also* Transport, carriers, native
—— —— Battalion, *see under* Infantry, British, West African Frontier Force
Simonet, Capt. (Fr. Army), 208, 209, 229
Singa, Fr. occupy, 117
Sir Frederick, Tug, 132, 214, 162-9, 184
Sirius, L.-Cr., 290
Smallpox, outbreak in Garua, 253 ; *see also* Sickness
Smyth, Capt. J. H. de Herèz, v.
Sneyd, Lt.-Com. R. S., 82, 124, 144, 214, 246, 265 ; Dibamba river, 127-9 ; Mpundu, 184 ; Nyong river, 308-9
So Dibanga, enemy attack on, 282
Sokoto, Ger. G.B. (late *Soden*), 132, 144 ; Yabasi, 147-53 ; Edea, 162-9 ; Mpundu, 184

Solf, Dr. (Ger. Colonial Minister, 1913), 53n
Sommerfeld, Capt. von (Ger. Army), 106-7, 109, 219, 380
Spanish Muni, Missionaries evacuated to, 227 ; Ger. assistance through, 265, 310, 318n, 363, 406 ; Germans reported retiring to, 400, 404, 406, 408, 417-18 ; internment arrangements, 412 ; last Ger. troops enter, 420 ; number interned in, 420
Spearber, Ger. Yacht, 65
Spee, Ad. von (Ger. Navy), Measures against, affect naval force, 181 ; 213
Spencer, Capt. E. C. (Supply and Transport), 27
Spoils of War, captured in Togoland, 30, 39 ; in The Cameroons, Duala, 130 ; Nkongsamba, 202 ; Bare, 203 ; Mbureku, 234 ; Garua, 299 ; Eseka, 337 ; Sege, 378 ; *see also* Shipping
Statham, Major J. C. B., R.A.M.C., 124, 275, 426
Staup, Capt. (Fr. Army), 338, 384
Steed, Sergt.-Major, 95
Stein, Hauptmann von, surrenders prisoners of war, 406
Steptoe, Lt. H. N., wounded, 332n
Stewart, Lt. A. H., killed, 95n
Stobart, Mr. F. St. C., 187, 292
Stoddart, R.-Ad. A. P., orders to, 64
Stoebel's Farm, occupied and evacuated, 239-40 ; Germans evacuate, 242
Stooks, Major C. S., 342, 369n
Stretton, Lt. A. L. de C., captured, 108
Strong, Com. F. E. K., 78, 80, 85, 144, 288n
Studley, Sergt., 89, 90
Sunstroke, death by, 153n
Supplies, shortage of, 17, 293, 406 ; collected at Yola, 99 ; arrangements for, 134-5, Yaunde, 275 ; loss of, 280, 281 ; difficulties of obtaining, 347 ; obtainable locally, 382
Surprise, Fr. G.B., 63, 67, 116, 119, 156, 205n, 206, 290 ; Edea, 161-9, 197-8
Susa, capture of, 146, 153 ; attempt to retake, 158-60
Swamps, *see* Mangrove swamps
Sykes, Capt. A. C., R.N. (*Astræa*), 265

Tactics, Gen. Gorges's memo., 179n, App. V., 442-4
Takum, affair of, 99

Talbot, Col. F. E. G., v.
Taylor, Capt. A. C., 140
Taylor, Lt. R. R., captured, 108 ; 109
Taylor, Lt. W. S., 227
Taylor, Sergt., 89 ; captured, 90
Tepe, affair of, 92–3
Thibault, Capt. (Fr. Army), 189
Thomas, Comdt., 338
Thompson, Lt. G. M., killed, 36
Thompson, Lt. J. P. R., R.N., Campo, 317–19 ; 383n
Thompson, Mr. (Preventive Service), 31n
Thurston, Capt. V. B., 244, 245, wounded, 276 ; 336
Tibati, occupied, 346
Tibout, Capt. (Fr. Army), 283
Tiko, attack on, 140–1 ; occupied, 184
Tingere, occupied, 305 ; enemy attack, 306–7
Tinto, occupied, 223
Togblekove (Togoland), Brit. force at, 27, 34
Togo (Togoland), Fr. occupy, 22
Togoland, annexed by Germany (1884), 4 ; Germans unpopular in, 5, 34, 40 ; topography, 5–6 ; climate, 6 ; strength of Ger. force in, 6, 11, 16, 40 ; surrender of, demanded, 17–19 ; refugees leave, 18, 19 ; events in Northern, 32–3 ; surrender of, 39, terms, App. I., 429–31 ; administration of, 41 ; *see also* Communications ; Railways ; Roads ; Wireless Telegraphy
Tootell, Capt. E., R.M.L.I., 308, 383n
Topography, of Togoland, 5–6 ; of The Cameroons, 47–52 ; Mora Mountain, 87–8, 171 ; Cross river area, 99–100 ; Dibamba river, 128 ; Nkongsamba area, 202–3 ; Chang, 217, 220 ; Edea—Yaunde, 277, 287, 362 ; Banyo Mountain, 347–8 ; Nun river, 368–9 ; Bandam and Bamkin, 372
Townsend, Mr. W. L. (Attorney-General, The Gold Coast), 40n
Transmitter, Cable ship, 134
Transport, Allied, carriers, native, for Togoland, 11, 17 ; from Sierra Leone, 64, 66, 67, 112, 123 ; from The Gold Coast, 66, 67, 113, 123 ; from Nigeria, 66, 67, 123 ; with Yola Column, 91–2 ; number employed, 123–4, 427 ; value of, 135 ; praise of, 221 ; number required, 288 ; from Middle Congo, 293

Transport, British, Animal, donkeys, with Yola Column, 92
—, —, Mechanical, Togoland, 27 ; No. 581 Co. A.S.C., Yaunde, 328–37
—, German, carriers, native, desert at Mora, 88 ; Dualese, 135
Trengrouse, Lt. R. V., wounded, 332n
Trojan, s.s., 81, 165–9
Trumper, Dr. W. A., 95
Turner, Lt.-Col. A. J., R.A., 70n, 177, 242, 330n, 426 ; Yaunde, 275–85, 333 ; invalided, 353

Underwood, Capt. J. P. D., 139–40, 353
Uniacke, Major G. L., Garua, 297–9 ; Fumban, 268–70 ; 374, 384–6
Unwin, Major T. B., 395
Uromi, s.s., 290

Vampire, Steam launch, 80 ; Edea, 162–9
Vauban, Fr. Armed trawler, 290, 417
Vaughan, Lt.-Col. E., Dibamba river, 126–9 ; Yabasi, 148–53 ; Kribi, 226 ; Mbureku, 237–8
Victoria, naval landing at, 79–80 ; *Ivy* at, 144, 155 ; Ger. Force at, 161 ; occupied, 183
Vigilant, Steam launch, 80, 86, 143, 180, 214 ; Dibamba river, 126–9 ; Tiko, 140 ; Yabasi, 151–3 ; Edea, 162–9, off Victoria, 183 ; Ebea, 198 ; Campo, 339
Viraud, Comdt. (Fr. Army), 426n
Vise, Lt. T., wounded, 332n
Vogel, German launch, 177
Volunteer Corps, Gold Coast Volunteers, Gold Coast Railway Volunteers, Gold Coast Mines Volunteers, Ashanti Mines Volunteers, 8 ; recruitment of, 14 ; Yaunde, 329–37

Wade, Sergt, F. C., killed, 150n
Walker, Capt. G., killed, 358, 362
Wallace, Mr. E., 163
Wallbach, Capt. D. A., 123, 426
Waller, Capt. R. J. R., 378, 416
Walrus, Steam tug, 80, 127–9, 141, 151–3, 162–9
Wanka, Capt. (Ger. Army), Garua, 298–9
Warne, Capt. O. H., 25

INDEX 469

War Office, 17, 300n, 312, 339n; issues "warning" telegram, 3; and employment of Gold Coast forces, 12; to estimate force required, 60; question of attacking Duala, 62; and reinforcements, 215, 222, 247–8; and Allied co-operation, 232; assume control of operations, 255–6; correspondence *re* future policy (12–23 June, 1915), 285–8 (Aug.), 314–17, 321
Warren, Lt. J. F., wounded, 273
Waters, Lt. B. E. M., R.N., 99
Water supply, 83, 173, 203, 220, 229–30, 253, 298; at Duala, 134
Watson, Dr. C. E. S. (W.A.M.S.), 414
Watt, Dr. W. G., 35n
Weapons, native, 205–6
Weather, during advance on Kamina, 38; impedes naval operations, 83n, 164; effects military operations, 89; Maka, 140; Yabasi, 149–50, 151, 177; Susa, 159; Edea, 164, 168, 169, 310; Harmann's Farm, 236; French operations, 249; Garua, 253, 298; advance on Yaunde, 279, 330, 331, 333, 334, 335, 357; Banyo Mountain, 349
Webb-Bowen, Lt.-Col. W. I., v., 170, 190–3, 195, 208, 209, 215, 229–30, 251, 252, 253, 267, 303, 305, 340–50, 372, 385–6, 395, 401, 403, 409, 413; comdg. Yola Column, 98; Gurin, 269–70; Garua, 297–9; Ngaundere, 300–1; *see also* Infantry, British, Columns, Yola
Weir, Major T. D., v.
Wesche, Lt. E. B., Kake, 159, killed, 160
West African Frontier Force, *see under* Infantry, British
West, Major C. C., 385–6, 395
Weyse, Lt. (Ger. Army), 270
Wheatley, Mr. L. H., 35n
White, Lt. W. R. J., R.N., 317n
Wickham, Capt. T. S., killed, 92
Widemenge, Ger. force at, 397; Brit. reach, 403
Williams, Dr. R. F. (W.A.M.S.), tribute to, 414
Wilson, Major-Gen. Sir S. H., 2n, 12

Wind, *see* Weather
Winter, Colour-Sergt. J.J., killed, 216
Wireless Telegraphy, Ger. station at Kamina (Togoland), importance of, 4, 13, 39; completed June, 1914, 10; destruction of, proposed, 12; interceptions from, 14, 19, 38; wrecked, 38, 39; in The Cameroons, 52, 67, 73, 129; failure of, 167–8, 355n, 374
Woolley, Lt. H. M., Duala, 134
Wright, Major W. D., Gen. Staff appreciation, 75, 76–7; 231, 250, 298, 300, 323, 444; tribute to, 414
Wum Biages, first affair of, 272, captured, 273; enemy attacks on, 282, 353; second affair of, 331, captured, 332
Wuri, launch, 162–9, 214, 421
Wuri river, navigability of, 61, 177

Yabasi, Ger. force at, 145, 161, 199, 205; capture of, 146–53; evacuated, 176–7
Yapoma, Ger. force east of, 161, retire, 164; *see also* Bridges
Yardley, Capt., 26
Yates, Lt. W. G., wounded, 107, captured, 108
Yaunde, importance of, 154–5, 263, 312, 315, estimated effect of capture of, 352; Ger. force at, 161, estimated, 287, 375, 389; first advance on, 271–85; withdrawal from, 281, 282, retrospect, 284–5; enemy force opposing, 284; Ger. Govt. reported moved from, 285, 287; advance on relinquished, 285–6, 302; lines of advance to, 287; decision to advance on, 320; second advance on, 328–37, 351–64, 374–83; capture of, 388–95, pursuit after, 396–419; situation in, 393
Yendi (Togoland), occupied, 33
Yoko, Ger. Govt. reported moved to, 285, 287; Fr. occupy, 367, 374, 386
Yola, Emir of, assistance of, 99
Yukaduma, Fr. occupy, 231

Zimmermann, Col. (Ger. Army), 130, 176, 244, 302, 318n, 333, 406, 415

www.ingramcontent.com/pod-product-compliance
Lightning Source LLC
Chambersburg PA
CBHW070754300426
44111CB00014B/2401